YOUNG'S BIBLE DICTIONARY

YOUNG'S BIBLE DICTIONARY

Dr. G. Douglas Young
GENERAL EDITOR

Dr. George Giacumakis, Jr.
ASSOCIATE EDITOR

TYNDALE HOUSE PUBLISHERS, INC. WHEATON, ILLINOIS

All Scripture, unless otherwise noted, is taken from
the New International Version of the Bible, copyright
1978 by the New York International Bible Society,
published by Zondervan Bible Publishers, Grand
Rapids, Michigan.

First printing, November 1984

Library of Congress Catalog Card Number 84-50304
ISBN 0-8423-8598-3
Copyright 1984 by Masada Press
Printed in the United States of America

This volume is dedicated to
MRS. GEORGINA S. YOUNG
the faithful wife and partner of
G. Douglas Young

NOTE Places mentioned in the dictionary are listed with their map coordinates as taken from the Survey of Israel Map. The six digit number following names enable the reader to locate the position on the map furnished in the back of the dictionary. Jerusalem, for example, is (172-131). The first three digits relate to the north-south axis of the map and the last three relate to the east-west axis.

PREFACE

The late Dr. G. Douglas Young, President Emeritus and Professor of Judaeo-Christian Studies of the Institute of Holy Land Studies in Jerusalem, saw the need for an inexpensive, one-volume dictionary of the Bible. He secured the contributions of renowned scholars to assist in this project. As general editor he completed about three-fourths of this work prior to his death in May of 1980. Since I was Dr. Young's successor, it fell to me to bring this dictionary to completion in order for students of the Bible to have it for their use.

Up-to-date one-volume dictionaries of the Bible are few in number. Those in English from a Jerusalem, Israel, milieu are almost nonexistent, and one especially prepared for the millions of evangelical laymen in particular is unique.

Likewise, the need is clear for more extensive articles in certain areas, such as those in archaeology, geography, history, and theology. These articles in this volume express the latest research in Israel and a theological viewpoint which is in conformity to the text of Scripture.

Special recognition must go to Nina Tronstein, former secretary to Dr. Young, for her tedious efforts to bring this project to light. She worked through all this material a number of times in order to produce a systematic organization of the contents. Special consideration also goes to Audrey Rosenbaum who did most of the final typing, along with assistance from Joan Hall and Marta Rios.

An expression of gratitude is in order to the twelve contributors who have been most patient until the work of their efforts has actually come into print. They faithfully met early deadlines even though the publication of this volume was delayed.

May this volume assist those who desire to study the Word of God.

George Giacumakis, Jr.
Jerusalem, Israel, 1984

CONTRIBUTORS

G.L.A. GLEASON L. ARCHER, JR., B.A., B.D., LL.B., Ph.D.
Professor of Old Testament and Semitic Studies
Trinity Evangelical Divinity School, Deerfield, IL

ISAIAH, BOOK OF; MONEY; PENTATEUCH; TABERNACLE; TEMPLE

J.C.C. J. CLEMENT CONNELL, B.A., M.A.
formerly Director of Studies and Lecturer in New
   Testament Exegesis
London Bible College, London, England

GOD, NAMES OF, GODHEAD

R.D.C. ROBERT D. CULVER, A.B., B.D., Th.M., Th.D.
formerly Professor of Theology, Trinity Evangelical
   Divinity School, Deerfield, IL
Annual Visiting Professor of Theology, Winnipeg
   Theological Seminary, Winnipeg, Manitoba, Canada

CHRIST, WORK OF; FESTIVALS; SACRIFICES AND OFFERINGS;
SALVATION, APPLICATION OF; SCRIPTURE

G.G. GEORGE GIACUMAKIS, JR., B.A., M.A., Ph.D.
Professor of History and President of the Institute
   of Holy Land Studies, Jerusalem, Israel

D.G. DONALD GUTHRIE, B.D., M.Th., Ph.D.
Vice-principal, London Bible College, London, England

CHRIST, LIFE AND TEACHINGS OF

G.W.K. GILBERT W. KIRBY, M.A.
formerly Principal and Lecturer in Practical Theology,
   London Bible College, London, England

SIN

R.N.L. RICHARD N. LONGENECKER, B.A., M.A., Ph.D.
Professor of New Testament
Wycliffe College, University of Toronto, Toronto,
    Ontario, Canada
PAUL, LIFE AND TEACHINGS OF; PAULINE EPISTLES; ROMANS,
LETTER TO THE

J.B.P. J. BARTON PAYNE, A.B., M.A., B.D., Th.M., Ph.D.
Late Professor of Old Testament
Covenant Theological Seminary, St. Louis, Missouri
ASSYRIA AND ASSHUR; BABYLON, BABYLONIA; CALENDAR;
CHRONOLOGY; EGYPT; HASMONEANS; HERODS, THE; JUDGES OF
ISRAEL; KINGS OF JUDAH AND ISRAEL; MACCABEES; PERSIA; ROME,
CITIZEN OF, ROME, ROMAN; SELEUCIDS

A.F.R. ANSON F. RAINEY, B.A., B.D., Th.M., M.A., Ph.D.
Professor of Ancient Near Eastern Cultures and
    Semitic Linguistics
Tel Aviv University, Tel Aviv, Israel
ARCHAEOLOGY

H.R.T.R. HALVOR R. T. RONNING, B.A., B.D., M.A.
Lecturer in Historical Geography
Institute of Holy Land Studies, Jerusalem, Israel
GEOGRAPHY OF THE HOLY LAND

W.B.W. WILBUR B. WALLIS, B.A., B.D., S.T.M., Ph.D.
Emeritus Professor of New Testament
Covenant Theological Seminary, St. Louis, Missouri
ACTS, BOOK OF; GOSPELS, THE FOUR; HEBREWS, BOOK OF;
REVELATION, BOOK OF

E.M.Y. EDWIN M. YAMAUCHI, B.A., M.A., Ph.D.
Professor of History
Miami University of Ohio, Oxford, Ohio
JERUSALEM

G.D.Y. G. DOUGLAS YOUNG, B.Sc., B.D., S.T.M., Ph.D.
Late President Emeritus and Regents Professor of
    Judaeo-Christian Studies
Institute of Holy Land Studies, Jerusalem, Israel

AARON When he was three years old living in Egypt with his parents and older sister, the Egyptian princess rescued his baby brother Moses in his papyrus basket at the edge of the Nile River (Ex. 2:1-10; 7:7). Aaron grew up to become the first priest and founder of the priesthood of Israel. He made his appearance in the unfolding drama of redemption at the time of God's commission to Moses to lead the sons of Israel out of Egyptian bondage into a promised land. When Moses protested that he was not a good speaker, God appointed Aaron to be his prophet (*nabi*) to speak to the people in his place (Ex. 4:10-17). He was an eloquent representative both to persuade the people of Israel that the time of their deliverance had indeed come, and to prevail upon Pharaoh to give up his bondslaves. After the Exodus, during the attack by the Amalekites, Aaron and Hur assisted Moses on the hilltop while Joshua led the fighting in the field (Ex. 17:8-13). In the incident of the golden calf, however, Aaron did not manifest the same strong character as Moses (Ex. 32:1-6). While Moses was away, on the mountain of God, Aaron allowed the people to pressure him into making the idol, bringing God's judgment on their sin.

The rich and symbolically-colored clothing for Aaron's robe as high priest is described in Exodus 39; his induction into office in Leviticus 8. Aaron alone, once a year, entered the Most Holy Place (Lev. 16). He was the Levite *par excellence.* Aaron and his sons were the sacrificing priests while the Levites, Aaron's brothers, were his assistants, ministering especially in regard to the tabernacle (Num. 3, 4, 18). Aaron's sons were ordained and anointed to minister in the priest's office. The two oldest, Nadab and Abihu, died before the Lord due to transgression (Lev. 10:1-7). The priesthood continued through Aaron's two youngest sons, Eleazar and Ithamar (Num. 3:2-4).

Neither Aaron nor Moses were allowed to enter the promised land because of their lack of trust in God (Num. 20:12). Aaron died on the top of Mount Hor at the age of 123 years, and the nation wept for him for thirty days. In the NT the priesthood of Aaron is compared and contrasted with the priesthood of Christ (Heb. 5:4; 7:11).

ABADDON *See* DEAD, ABODE OF

ABAGTHA One of seven chamberlains, a eunuch, who was sent by the Persian King Xerxes to bring Queen Vashti before him (Esth. 1:10).

ABANA *See* DAMASCUS

ABARIM The mountain range just east of the Salt Sea (Dead Sea) from which Moses viewed the land given by the Lord to the sons of Israel (Num. 27:12). This range is the last stage of the journey from Egypt, as given in Numbers 33, before the sons of Israel camped in the plains of Moab. Later it was associated with Lebanon and Bashan (Jer. 22:20). Its highest peak is Mount Nebo.

ABBA An Aramaic word meaning "father" which Jesus used in the Garden of Gethsemane (Mk. 14:36) and which Paul used in two notable passages on the children or sons of God (Rom. 8:15; Gal. 4:6). All three of its occurrences in the NT are in prayers addressed to God.

ABDA 1.   A man in charge of forced labor under King Solomon (1 Kgs. 4:6).

2.   One of the 284 Levites who lived in Jerusalem in the time of Nehemiah (Neh. 11:17); spelled Obadiah in 1 Chronicles 9:16.

ABDEEL The father of Shelemiah, a member of King Jehoiakim's court (Jer. 36:26).

ABDI One of the members of the priesthood who had married foreign women in the times of Ezra (Ezra 10:26).

ABDIEL Father of Ahi, a Gadite who lived in Bashan (1 Chron. 5:15).

ABDON Name of four OT persons and a Levitical town.

1. One of the judges of Israel.

2. The head of one of the Benjamite families living in Jerusalem in the time of David (1 Chron. 8:23).

3. A Benjamite ancestor of King Saul (1 Chron. 9:35-36).

4. A trusted official of King Josiah's court (2 Chron. 34:20).

5. A town of the tribe of Ashner given to the sons of Kohath, tentatively identified with a tell (165-272).
See also JUDGES OF ISRAEL.

ABEDNEGO *See* SHADRACH

ABEL The second son of Adam and Eve, and a shepherd by trade. Abel was murdered by his older brother Cain when Abel's offering from the firstborn of his flock was accepted while Cain's offering from the produce of the soil was not looked on with favor (Gen. 4:10, 16). He is described by the NT as a righteous man and martyr who acted by faith in the matter of the sacrifice he offered to God (Mt. 23:35; Heb. 11:4).

Abel is found as a component of place names. (See the next six entries.)

ABEL BETH MAACAH, ABEL OF BETH MAACAH A fortified town near Dan on the border with Lebanon (204-296). It was to this town that Joab pursued the rebellious Sheba after the attempted coup by David's son, Absalom (2 Sam. 20:14-22). Later it was taken by Ben-Hadad, the king of Damascus (1 Kgs. 15:20), and then by the Assyrian king, Tiglath-Pileser III (2 Kgs. 15:29).

ABEL KERAMIN A place (228-142) in Ammon, not far from modern Amman in Jordan, to which the Judge Jephthah pursued the Ammonites (Judg. 11:29-33). The place name is rendered "the plain of the vineyards" in the KJV.

ABEL MAIM A variant of, or an additional name for, Abel Beth Maacah (2 Chron. 16:4).

ABEL MEHOLAH A town (197-192) whose location has not been exactly identified, but on the boundary of King Solomon's fifth district in the Jordan Valley (1 Kgs. 4:12). Gideon pursued the Midianites this far eastward (Judg. 7:22), and it was probably the birthplace of Elisha the prophet (1 Kgs. 19:16).

ABEL MIZRAIM The Canaanites gave this name to the threshing floor of Atad. It was a meadow east of the Jordan River where the funeral cortege of the patriarch Jacob stopped for seven days of mourning. The record makes a play on the word *abel*, which can mean either "meadow" or "mourning" (Gen. 50:11).

ABEL SHITTIM *See* SHITTIM

ABI-ALBON One of David's heroes of whom nothing is known except that he was known as the Arbathite (2 Sam. 23:31).

ABIASAPH *See* EBIASAPH

ABIATHAR The only son of the priest Ahimelech who escaped the slaughter of eighty-five priests by Doeg the Edomite during the time David was fleeing from King Saul (1 Sam. 22:20-23; 23:6, 9; 30:7; 2 Sam. 15:24, 27, 29, 35-36; 20:25; 1 Kgs. 4:4). He joined King David and served with Zadok as high priest throughout his reign. When he conspired to make Adonijah, David's son, the king in Solomon's place, Solomon deprived him of his priesthood and banished him to Anathoth (1 Kgs. 1:7, 19, 25, 42; 2:22, 26, 27, 35). Jesus made reference to an Abiathar in Mark 2:25-26 who is called there a high priest and therefore perhaps is other than this son of Ahimelech.

ABIB *See* CALENDAR

ABIDA A son of Midian, and grandson of Abraham and Keturah (Gen. 25:4; 1 Chron. 1:33).

ABIDAN The representative of the tribe of Benjamin at the census in the Sinai (Num. 1:11).

ABIEL 1. The father of Kish (1 Sam. 9:1), and grandfather of King Saul (1 Sam. 14:51).

2. One of the famous thirty champions of King David (1 Chron. 11:32).

ABIEZER 1. The collective name of the descendants of Abiezer, a clan in the Gileadite branch of the tribe of Manasseh. Gideon was a member of this clan (Josh. 17:2; Judg. 6:24, 34; 8:2, 32).

2. One of David's mighty men, from Anathoth (2 Sam. 23:27).

3. A descendant of Manasseh related to Gilead (Num. 26:30; 1 Chron. 7:18).

ABIGAIL 1. The exceptionally wise and beautiful wife of the ill-mannered and wealthy Calebite, Nabal of Maon. When Nabal (whose name means "brute") dealt with David in an insulting and ill-tempered way at the shearing festival, Abigail persuaded David not to avenge himself in needless bloodshed. Later when Nabal died, David sent Abigail an offer of marriage. Abigail accepted and became David's wife, along with Ahinoam of Jezreel (1 Sam. 25).

2. One of David's two sisters, and the mother of Amasa, a commander of David's army (1 Chron. 2:16, 17).

ABIHAIL 1. A Levite of the Merarite clan (Num. 3:35).

2. The wife of Abishur (1 Chron. 2:29).

3. A Gadite who lived in the land of Bashan (1 Chron. 5:14).

4. Mother of King Rehoboam's wife Mahalath (2 Chron. 11:18).

5. Father of Queen Esther and uncle of Mordecai (Esth. 2:15; 9:29).

ABIHU One of the four sons of Aaron and Elisheba (Ex. 6:23). Abihu was included in the select number who witnessed the theophany at the ratification of the covenant received at Mount Sinai (Ex. 24:1-11). Later all four sons were admitted to the priest's office, but Abihu and his brother Nadab, in the course of their ministry, did that which was not prescribed and were struck by fire and died (Lev. 10:1-3).

ABIHUD A Benjamite, listed as the third son of Bela (1 Chron. 8:3).

ABIJAH 1. Son of Beker of the tribe of Benjamin (1 Chron. 7:8).

2. The younger son of Samuel. Abijah served as judge in Beersheba, but did not follow the ways of his godly father (1 Sam. 8:1-9).

3. A son of Jeroboam I, who died in childhood as prophesied by the prophet Ahijah (1 Kgs. 14:1-18).

4. One of the descendants of Aaron representing the eighth of the twenty-four divisions made by David for purposes of temple service (1 Chron. 24:10). The father of John the Baptist was a priest in this division of Abijah (Lk. 1:5).

5. The son and successor of Rehoboam as king of Judah. *See* KINGS OF JUDAH AND ISRAEL.

6. Mother of King Hezekiah of Judah (2 Chron. 29:1); in 2 Kings 18:2, abbreviated to Abi.

7. One of the signers of the community document at Jerusalem in the days of Ezra the scribe (Neh. 10:7).

8. One of the chiefs of the priests who returned with Zerubbabel from Babylon to Jerusalem (Neh. 12:4).

ABIJAM *See* KINGS OF JUDAH AND ISRAEL

ABILENE The district or tetrarchy ruled by Lysanias when John the Baptist began his public ministry (Lk. 3:1). This small mountainous region of the Anti-Lebanons was attached to the city of Abila on the bank of the Aban River northeast of Mount Hermon and northwest of Damascus.

ABIMAEL In the genealogies of Genesis 10 and 1 Chronicles 1, Abimael is one of the thirteen sons of Joktan, grandchildren of Eber and descendants of Shem.

ABIMELECH 1. This may be a royal title of Philistine kings, as in the use of "pharaoh" by the Egyptians and "Agag" by the Amalekites. Both Abraham (Gen. 20, 21) and later Isaac (Gen. 26) attempted to deceive an Abimelech, a Philistine king of Gerar (near Gaza) in the matter of calling their wives their sisters. Though the incidents are similar the narrative assumes that two different Abimelechs are intended, possibly the father and later his son.

2. One of Gideon's sons who had his brothers murdered and himself proclaimed king by the men of Shechem. His violent reign of three years came to an ignominious end (Judg. 9).

3. The son of Abiathar and priest during the reign of King David (1 Chron. 18:16).

4. A name designating Achish, king of Gath, in the title of Psalm 34.
See also JUDGES OF ISRAEL.

ABIANDAB 1. A man who lived on the hill of Kiriath Jearim in the days of the Judges to whom the men of the town entrusted the ark of the Lord when it was returned by the Philistines (1 Sam. 7:1).

2. The second oldest of David's seven brothers. The three oldest sons of Jesse served in Saul's army (1 Sam. 16:8; 17:13).

3. One of Saul's sons who fell with his father in the battle of Mount Gilboa (1 Sam. 31:2).

ABINOAM The father of Barak who lived in Kedesh of Naphtali (Judg. 4:6).

ABISHAG A great beauty from Shunem who served as King David's nurse and attendant during the last days of his old age

(1 Kgs. 1:1-4). After David's death, Adonijah's ambitious request for Abishag in marriage resulted in his being put to death (1 Kgs. 2:12-25) by Solomon who interpreted it as an attempt to take the throne.

ABISHAI An intrepid and loyal professional soldier in the service of David. Abishai was the oldest of the three sons of Zeruiah, David's sister. Abishai accompanied David into Saul's military camp in a daring adventure (1 Sam. 26), and was present at the battle in the "field of daggers" or "field of hostilities" near the pool of Gibeon, when his brother, Asahel, was killed by Abner, the commander of Saul's army (2 Sam. 2:16-23). In the first Ammonite campaign when Joab found it necessary to deploy David's army on the two fronts, Joab divided his forces, and those not under his command he entrusted to Abishai's leadership (2 Sam. 10:7-14). In the battle of Absalom's rebellion, the forces of David were divided between Joab, Abishai, and Ittai the Gittite (2 Sam. 18:1-8). Abishai had the honor of being the commander of the Mighty Men of David known as the "Thirty" (2 Sam. 23:18-19). It must have been one of the highlights of his career when he saved the life of the king he so faithfully served in the midst of one of David's last battles (2 Sam. 21:15-17).

ABISHALOM An alternate form of the name Absalom (1 Kgs. 15:2, 10).

ABISHUA 1. One of the sons of Bela, the firstborn of Benjamin (1 Chron. 8:4).

2. Son of Phinehas and father of Bukki in the line of Levi (1 Chron. 6:4-5).

ABISHUR Descendant of Judah, ancestor of David, Abishur was the son of Shammai the Jerahmeelite, married to Abihail (1 Chron. 2:28-29).

ABITAL The wife of David and mother of his fifth son, Shephatiah (2 Sam. 3:4).

ABITUB The son of Shaharaim and his wife Hushim, in the line of Benjamin (1 Chron. 8:8-11).

ABIUD The son of Zerubbabel and father of Eliakim; an ancestor of Jesus Christ (Mt. 1:13). Abiud is the Greek form of the Hebrew Abihud.

ABNER Saul's cousin (1 Sam. 14:51) and the commander of his army. Abner introduced David to Saul at the famous victory of David over Goliath (1 Sam. 17:55-58), and later accompanied Saul in the senseless pursuit of David in the wilderness

(1 Sam. 26). When Saul died in battle Abner supported Saul's son Ish-Bosheth as king over Israel in his father's place (2 Sam. 2:8-10). Later, as a result of censure by Ish-Bosheth, Abner negotiated with the elders of Israel for a transfer of allegiance to David. At this stage Abner met a violent death by assassination at the hand of Joab who was determined to avenge his brother's death. David grieved over Abner's tragic death, wept at his funeral, and eulogized Abner as a great prince in Israel (2 Sam. 3:22-39).

ABOMINATION That which is ritually or ethically abhorrent or repugnant to the Lord. Such practices and objects include: idolatry, as in the worship of Ashtoreth (Astarte) of the Sidonians or Milcom of the Ammonites (1 Kgs. 11:5); human sacrifice (2 Kgs. 16:3); divination and sorcery (Deut. 18:9-14); unclean beasts (Lev. 11:10); sexual perversion (Lev. 18:22, 23); lying (Prov. 12:22); unethical business practices (Prov. 20:23); and evil motivation of the heart (Prov. 6:18, 19; Lk. 16:15).

ABOMINATION THAT CAUSES DESOLATION A phrase occurring in the book of Daniel and in the teaching of Jesus (Dan. 9:27; 11:31; 12:11; Mt. 24:15; Mk. 13:14). This abomination that desolates or appalls, involving a pollution of the sanctuary of the temple in Jerusalem, apparently has reference both to the desecration by Antiochus Epiphanes in 168 B.C. and to a future desolating or appalling abomination in the end times. This teaching of Jesus has been interpreted by some as a reference to the destruction of the temple by the Roman Titus in A.D. 70 and by others as applying to the eschatological figure of the Antichrist or "man of sin" (2 Thess. 2:3), a portent of the second coming of Christ.

ABRAHAM (ABRAM) Called Abram until his name was changed by God to Abraham (Gen. 17:5). Together with Terah his father, his nephew Lot, and his wife Sarai (her name was later changed to Sarah, in Gen. 17:15), he left his birthplace in Ur of the Chaldeans in Mesopotamia for Haran on the Euphrates northwest of Ur. After the death of his father he left for Canaan and at Shechem (176-179) began his sojourn (Gen. 11:27-32; 12:1-7; 15:7; Acts 7:4). After a brief stay in Egypt because of a famine in Canaan, he returned to Canaan where Lot left him for Sodom, he himself settling near Hebron (Gen. 13:1, 8-12, 18). Lot was taken by the king of Elam but rescued in the expedition which his uncle led, as a result of which Abram met and was blessed by Melchizedek, king of Salem (Gen. 14:1-16, 18-20).

As Sarai was barren she followed the ancient custom of giving a maidservant to her husband who bore him a son, Ishmael (Gen. 16). It was at this time that God reiterated his promise to Abram that he would make him the father of a great nation and give him the land as an everlasting possession, and changed his name to Abraham (Gen. 12:2; 13:14-16; 17:5-8). Several well known stories are connected with Abraham: his intercession for Sodom and Gomorrah, the banishment of Hagar and her son Ishmael, the call to sacrifice his son, the burial of Sarah in the cave of Machpelah (Gen. 18:16ff.; 21:1-21; 22:1-19; 23:1-20).

Abraham married Keturah after Sarah's death and had a second family. He was buried in the cave of Machpelah at the age of 175 (Gen. 25:1-4, 5-10). The life of Abraham is usually dated in the beginning of the second millennium B.C.

From the NT we learn that Christ was descended from Abraham (Mt. 1:1; Lk. 3:34), and that the Christians as well as the Jews thought of him as founder of the faith and a man of great faith (Mt. 3:9; Heb. 11:8-19). Paul (Gal. 3:6-9, 14, 16-18) stated that Abraham received the promise and blessing of God by faith, that these are passed on to the Gentiles through Christ, and that those who believe in Christ are also the seed of Abraham.

ABRAHAM'S SIDE A figure of speech used by Jesus in the parable of Lazarus and the rich man signifying a place or state of rest after death (Lk. 16:19-31). In Rabbinic thought, to be in Abraham's bosom (side) was to enter Paradise.

ABRAM *See* ABRAHAM

ABRONAH A place where the Israelites camped on the way to Ezion Geber after Jotbathah (Num. 33:34, 35).

ABSALOM (twice called Abishalom in 1 Kgs. 15:2, 10). David's third son whose name means "Father is peace," was the source of intense grief to his father. Absalom, whose mother, Maacah, was daughter of Talmia, king of Geshur, was a promising son (2 Sam. 14:25), but he avenged the humiliation of his beautiful sister by having David's oldest son murdered. This initiated the fulfillment of Nathan's dire prophecy about David's future (2 Sam. 12:10, 11; 16:20-23). Absalom fled from his father and only after three years asylum at his mother's family home in Geshur and two more years in Jerusalem, but barred from the king's court, was Absalom allowed in to see David (2 Sam. 14). In the next four years Absalom plotted and executed a rebellion, driving David from Jerusalem. Absalom's death in the ensuing struggle brought forth the expression of David's deep and moving grief (2 Sam. 19:1-8).

ABYSS *See* DEAD, ABODE OF

ACACIA *See* TREES

ACBOR 1. The father of one of the kings of Edom (Gen. 36:38-40).

2. One of the King Josiah's men sent to consult the prophetess Huldah about the "Book of the Law" found in the temple (2 Kgs. 22:12-14); called Abdon in 2 Chronicles 34:20. Perhaps also an official of Jehoiakim (Jer. 26:22).

ACCAD *See* GEOGRAPHY OF THE HOLY LAND

ACCO or ACCHO From earliest times this was a key port (158-258) for the northern part of the land of Canaan. It is mentioned in the early Egyptian records, eighteenth and fourteenth centuries B.C. Assyrians conquered it in 701 and 640 B.C. In the third century B.C. its name was changed to Ptolemais, the name by which the Apostle Paul knew it (Acts 21:7). The Arabs changed the name back again but the Crusaders knew it as St. Jean d'Acre. Napoleon tried to conquer it in 1799 but failed, and it was held by the Turks until General Allenby's victory in 1918. The ancient tell is just east of the modern city. In biblical times Acco was in the land given to the tribe of Asher (Judg. 1:31). It is called Ummah in Joshua 19:30.

ACCURSED *See* CURSE and DEVOTED

ACHAIA *See* GEOGRAPHY OF THE HOLY LAND

ACHAICUS A Christian from Corinth who visited Paul at Ephesus (1 Cor. 16:17).

ACHAN A Judahite who took for himself some of the spoils from Jericho which had been dedicated to the Lord. For this the Lord punished Israel by a defeat at Ai (Jos. 7:1, 11-26) and by the stoning of Achan and all his house. He is called Achar in 1 Chronicles 2:7 and the place of the stoning "the Valley of Achor" (Josh. 7:22-26).

ACHAR *See* ACHAN

ACHISH A king of the Philistine city of Gath in the time of David. On one occasion David fled there for refuge from Saul but had to feign madness to escape from the Philistines. On another occasion he was given asylum there, however (1 Sam. 21:10-15; 27:1-12). He was the leader of the Philistine armies at Gilboa where Saul and Jonathan were killed (1 Sam. 31:1-6). *See also* ABIMELECH, 4.

ACHOR   A valley near Jericho on the boundary between the tribes of Judah and Benjamin (Josh. 7:24-26; 15:7; Isa. 65:10). Some identify it with Wadi Kelt. A curse was placed upon it which is to be lifted at Messiah's coming. *See also* ACHAN.

ACSAH   The daughter of Caleb whom he gave as wife to Othniel, the conqueror of Kiriath Sepher (later called Debir). He gave her the Negev, or south land, and upper and lower springs near to the city (Josh. 15:16-19; Judg. 1:11-15). *See* DEBIR.

ACSHAPH   (158-240) A city in the tribal territory of Asher (Josh. 19:25) which was conquered by Joshua after it had allied itself with the king of Hazor against the Israelites (Josh. 11:1; 12:20).

ACTS, BOOK OF   Acts is the logical sequence to the Gospel narratives and was written by Luke, the author of the third Gospel. In the Acts there are a series of passages narrated in the first person, the famous "we sections" (chaps. 16, 20, 21, 27, 28), which show that the author was a companion of Paul and an eyewitness of many of the events he records. Probabilities within the New Testament as well as the unanimous testimony of the church point to Luke, the beloved physician (Col. 4:14), as the writer.

Two personalities are especially prominent in Acts, Peter and Paul. Peter dominates the one major division of the book, chapters 1-12, and Paul the rest, chapters 13-28. The events of Acts cover approximately the thirty years from the resurrection of Christ to the imprisonment of Paul at Rome. The outline of the book is given in Christ's own words when he said those who believe in him would be witnesses in Jerusalem, Judea, Samaria, to the uttermost parts of the world (Acts 1:8). A series of key texts traces the major geographical frontiers the early witnesses traversed as Christianity expanded in the Roman world. Acts 6:7 summarizes the progress to that point in Jerusalem; Acts 9:31 carries us out to the next wider horizon of Judea, Galilee, and Samaria; Acts 12:24 gives us the transition from the early days in Jerusalem and Judea to the advance through Antioch into the Roman world. As Paul advanced to the Aegean shores, Luke paused (Acts 16:5) to summarize again with a note of progress, and in 19:20, after the evangelization of the Aegean shores is completed, we are told "the word of the Lord spread widely and grew in power (Acts 19:20). Finally, when Paul reached Rome, the final note of progress concludes the book (Acts 28:30-31).

Around the leading figure of Peter are grouped the main events of Acts 1-12. Peter appears as the spokesman in the choice of a successor to Judas. After the miraculous demonstration of the presence of the Holy Spirit at Pentecost

(Acts 2), Peter showed that all the evidence demonstrates that Jesus is Lord and Christ (Acts 2:36). Peter and John were instrumental in healing a lame man at the gate called Beautiful (Acts 3-4) and in explaining events as divine testimony to Jesus Christ. To Peter it fell to rebuke Ananias and Sapphira in their attempted deceit (Acts 5). Peter, when the apostles were forbidden to preach in the name of Christ (Acts 5), replied, "We must obey God rather than men!" A lengthy narrative (Acts 9-11) centering around Peter shows how God revealed his plan to include Gentiles in his church. The triumphant operation of divine power to release Peter from imprisonment (Acts 12) is the last reference to Peter in the earlier portion of Acts, though he appears again at the Jerusalem council (Acts 15).

Interwoven with the earlier narrative of the expansion of the church is the preparation for the wider mission of the church. Jesus had declared his purpose (Acts 1:8). In the implementation of that purpose, Paul, the great minister for the Gentiles, was called (Acts 9). To Peter was revealed the doctrine, in the case of Cornelius, that the Gentile was to be received into the church as a Gentile, only on condition of faith in Christ. Luke then retraced the events which led to the founding of the church at Antioch (Acts 11:19-26). Antioch became the "advance base" of mission effort in the Roman world so that the establishment of a strong church there, pastored by Paul and Barnabas, is of great significance in the unfolding of God's plan.

In chapter 13 the mission career of Paul began and can be conveniently summarized in the four main journeys of Paul. The first is narrated in Acts 13-14. Paul and Barnabas and party toured Cyprus, sailed north to the coast of Asia, preached at Pisidian Antioch, swung eastward to Iconium, Derbe, and Lystra, and returned to Attalia, whence they sailed to Antioch. Outstanding on this journey was Paul's address in the synagogue at Pisidian Antioch, featuring his proof from the resurrection and Old Testament prophecy that Jesus was the promised Messiah and the initiation of a distinctive Gentile work to which Paul had been called.

In the interval between the first and second journey, opposition to the work of Paul developed and increased. His work in Galatia was attacked, and Paul replied with the Galatian epistle. Further unrest led to the convening of the Jerusalem council with the resulting public disavowal of the doctrine and tactics of Jewish sectarians. This decision was conveyed to the Gentile churches.

At the beginning of the second journey Paul revisited the churches established on the first journey and then moved north and west through Asia Minor to Troas near ancient Homeric Troy. Thence the party sailed to Macedonia, establishing churches at Philippi and Thessalonica. After leaving Macedonia, Paul stopped briefly at Athens, delivering the famous discourse on the Areopagus. A long stay of eighteen months founded the famous but troubled church at Corinth. From there Paul wrote First and Second Thessalonians in love and encouragement to his friends at Thessalonica. Paul returned to Antioch and set out again on the third journey for Ephesus. A long ministry of over two years evangelized all Asia Minor (Acts 19:10) and established the famous churches mentioned in the seven letters of the Revelation. From Ephesus Paul wrote First Corinthians and later, from Macedonia, Second Corinthians as he journeyed toward Corinth. During a brief third visit at Corinth (2 Cor. 12:14; 13:1), Paul wrote the great epistle to Rome (Acts 20:3).

On returning to Jerusalem, Paul was accused of bringing a Gentile into the temple and was mobbed. Roman authorities intervened and kept him in custody two years at Jerusalem and Caesarea. The dilatoriness of Roman rulers compelled Paul to appeal to Caesar. No charge could be laid against Paul since he based his case wholly on the reality of the resurrection of Christ and he called on the Roman court to take judicial notice of that well-known public event (Acts 26:8, 23, 26). Acts 27 and 28 tell of the famous voyage and shipwreck of Paul's party and the final arrival at Rome. Luke was in Paul's company at this time and the book ends at this point. The most natural supposition is that the book was also written and published at this time.

In the two-year imprisonment which followed, some of Paul's most memorable work was done in the writing of Philippians, Ephesians, Colossians, and Philemon. Here Acts ends with a note of triumph and progress: Paul preaching and teaching with all boldness, none forbidding him.

Luke's historical work of Luke and Acts are the earliest and the only contemporary accounts of the beginnings of Christianity. In the fourth century, Eusebius of Caesarea wrote the first church history. In the intervening period the basic narrative of Luke and the rest of the New Testament was recognized by friend and foe as the authentic account of Christian beginnings. (W.B.W.)

ACZIB 1. An important Canaanite seaport town (159-272) in the territory of the tribe of Asher north of Acco (Josh. 19:29).

2. A Judahite town (145-116) in the western foothills (Shephelah) near Mareshah which according to the prophet would leave "deceptive to the kings of Israel" (Josh. 15:44; Mic. 1:14).

ADADAH A town in the south of Judah's territory (Josh. 15:22).

ADAH 1. The mother of Jabal and Jubal and wife of Lamech, the sixth mentioned in Adam's line (Gen. 4:19-21, 23).

2. A Hittite wife of Esau (Gen. 36:2-16).

ADAIAH 1. A descendant of Levi who ministered in song in the tabernacle (1 Chron. 6:41).

2. A son of Shimei and descendant of Benjamin (1 Chron. 8:21).

3. A priest in Jerusalem, son of Jeroham (1 Chron. 9:12).

4. Grandfather on the mother's side of King Josiah (2 Kgs. 22:1).

5. Father of Maaseiah, an army officer who helped to overthrow Queen Athaliah (2 Chron. 23:1).

6. An ancestor of a Judahite of Jerusalem (Neh. 11:5).

7. A son of Bani who married a foreigner during the exile (Ezra 10:29).

8. A son of Binnui who also married a foreigner in the exilic times (Ezra 10:39).

ADALIA One of the sons of Haman, enemy of the Jews (Esth. 9:8).

ADAM 1. A Canaanite town (201-167) on the east bank of the Jordan River near the mouth of the Jabbok River (Josh. 3:16).

2. The first man. The story of man's being formed from the dust of the ground, made in the image of God, placed in the Garden of Eden, and given dominion over the other forms of life is recorded in the first two chapters of Genesis. A major difference in the biblical account from other creation accounts is indicated in Genesis 2:7 where the record states that that which had been formed from the dust of the ground did not become animate, did not become man, a living being, until after the divine inbreathing into that which was formed from the dust. All other animal life that was made earlier was already animate, were living beings, had *nephesh hayah*, but man did not have it until this special type of creation.

Adam's mate likewise had a peculiar origin, made from a rib taken from man (Gen. 2:21, 22). Adam and Eve were instructed by God not to eat of the fruit of the tree in the middle of the garden or they would die. The serpent, however, said, "When you eat of it your eyes will be opened, and you will be like God, knowing good and evil." All mankind is physically descended from Adam and Eve (including Christ as to the flesh) and thus related. Because of this relationship, labor, pain, sin, and death passed upon all men, for, represented in their father Adam, all (Christ apart, Heb. 4:15) did sin (Lk. 3:38; Rom. 5:12; 1 Cor. 15:22).

ADAMAH A city in the tribal area of Naphtali, vicinity of Sea of Galilee, but its exact location is not known (Josh. 19:36).

ADAMI NEKEB (193-239) A city in the tribal area of Naphtali (Josh. 19:33).

ADAR *See* CALENDAR

ADBEEL One of the twelve sons of Ishmael who were princes of tribes. In the first millenium B.C. a tribe of that name was located between Canaan and Egypt (Gen. 25:13).

ADDAN *See* ADDON

ADDAR *See* ARD

ADDI One in the genealogy of Jesus (Lk. 3:28).

ADDON or ADDAN An unidentified place in Babylonia from which some returned with Zerubbabel after the exile (Ezra 2:59; Neh. 7:61).

ADIEL 1. A man of the tribe of Simeon (1 Chron. 4:36).

2. The father of a priest who returned from the exile in Babylon (1 Chron. 9:12).

3. The father of the keeper of the treasuries of David (1 Chron. 27:25).

ADIN The head of a large family which returned from the Babylonian exile and one of the signers of Nehemiah's covenant (Ezra 2:15; Neh. 10:16).

ADINA A leader in David's army from the tribe of Reuben (1 Chron. 11:42).

ADITHAIM An unidentified town listed with others in the northern end of the western foothills (Josh. 15:36).

ADLAI The father of one of David's herdsmen (1 Chron. 27:29).

ADMAH An unidentified city in the Jordan Valley which revolted against the king of Elam and was later destroyed along with Sodom and Gomorrah (Gen. 10:19; 14:2, 8; Deut. 29:23).

ADMATHA One of the seven princes of Media and Persia in the days of King Xerxes (Esth. 1:14).

ADNA 1. An Israelite whom Ezra induced to divorce his foreign wife after the exile (Ezra 10:30).

2. A priest in the days of Nehemiah (Neh. 12:15).

ADNAH 1. An officer of King Saul who deserted to David when he was at Ziklag (1 Chron. 12:20).

2. An officer in the army of King Jehoshaphat (2 Chron. 17:14).

ADONI-BEZEK A Canaanite king who had his thumbs and big toes cut off after his capture by the men of Judah, just as he had done to seventy others. He died in captivity in Jerusalem (Judg. 1:5-7).

ADONIJAH 1. A son and heir to David's throne. However, one of David's other wives, Bathsheba, with the help of the priest Zadok and the prophet Nathan, secured the succession for her son Solomon (2 Sam. 3:4; 1 Kgs. 1). After the death of David, Solomon had him put to death (1 Kgs. 2:25).

2. One of the Levites whom King Jehoshaphat sent out to teach the Law in Judah during his reforms (2 Chron. 17:7-9).

3. The head of one of the families that returned from the Babylonian captivity with Ezra and Nehemiah (Neh. 10:16). He is called Adonikam in Ezra 2:13; 8:13, and Nehemiah 7:18.

ADONIKAM *See* ADONIJAH, 3

ADONIRAM Served kings David, Solomon, and Rehoboam as superintendent of the corvee of forced labor (2 Sam. 20:24; 1 Kgs. 4:6; 2 Chron. 10:18). Rehoboam sent him to collect tribute from the ten northern tribes that had revolted but they stoned him to death (1 Kgs. 12:18). In some places the Hebrew text reads ADURAM.

ADONI-ZEDEK A king of Jerusalem who made an alliance with four other kings against Joshua and the Israelites. After Joshua defeated them at Gibeon they hid in a cave at Makkedah, were discovered, killed, and buried in the cave (Josh. 10:1-28).

ADOPTION Two clear cases of adoption, taking another's child into one's own family, are noted in the OT. Moses was adopted by Pharaoh's daughter, and Esther by Mordecai (Ex. 2:10; Esth. 2:7, 15). There is no clear evidence to show that the Israelites, in Israel, practiced adoption. In the NT adoption is a figure of speech which expresses the relation of either the Israelites to God or individuals who have a certain type of faith to God. These are spiritual relations of sonship and not physical or creation relationships. God adopted Israel as sons (Ex. 4:22; Deut. 14:1; Rom. 9:4). He also adopts as sons all who come unto him through faith in Jesus Christ (Eph. 1:4-12; Rom. 8:14-21; Gal. 4:5). These are subject to

God's control, have his Spirit dwelling within them, receive
his corrective chastisement in this life, and his inheritance in
the world to come (Gal. 4:6; Heb. 12:5-11; Rom. 8:23). God
redeemed Israel from the bondage of Egypt and made them
his sons. So God redeems from the bondage of sin all those
who have faith in Christ as Savior and Lord, and ultimately
by resurrection he redeems them from death itself. *See*
"Redemption" in article CHRIST, WORK OF.

ADORAIM A city (152-101) in the tribal area of Judah and one of those
fortified by King Rehoboam. Dura, an Arab village, marks the
site today (2 Chron. 11:9).

ADRAMMELECH A son of the Assyrian King Sennacherib who was involved in
the murder of his father at Nineveh (2 Kgs. 19:37). *See
also* DEITIES.

ADRAMYTTIUM A seaport city in Mysia in Asia Minor. Paul sailed from
Caesarea to Sidon, passed near to Cyprus, and landed at
Myra in Asia Minor on a ship registered at Adramyttium
(Acts 27:2-5).

ADRIATIC SEA On Paul's shipwreck journey to Rome the ship was badly
tossed on the Adriatic Sea (Adria) between Crete and Malta
where it was finally wrecked (Acts 27:27).

ADRIEL The man to whom King Saul gave his daughter Merab as
wife in spite of the fact that she had been earlier promised to
David (1 Sam. 18:17, 19; 2 Sam. 21:8).

ADULLAM A city (150-117) in the western foothills conquered by Joshua
and assigned to the tribe of Judah (Josh. 12:15; 15:35).
Before the captivity in Egypt Judah had married a girl of
Adullam (Gen. 38:1-2). It was one of Rehoboam's fortified
towns which continued down to the Babylonian captivity and
was repopulated after the return from that exile (2 Chron.
11:5-12; Neh. 11:30). The place is perhaps best known in the
phrase "cave of Adullam" from the incidents in David's life
when he made it his headquarters during his flight from Saul
(1 Sam. 22).

ADULTERY In the OT, adultery took place only when the woman in the
case was either betrothed or married. A married man,
apparently, could have intercourse with a woman other than
his wife, provided of course that she was not married, without
committing adultery (Gen. 38:12-16). Adultery was strictly
forbidden and was punishable by death by stoning (Lev.
18:20; 20:10; Deut. 22:22, 24). In common with local practices
in other middle eastern countries in antiquity, a wife suspected

by her husband could be obliged to undergo a test by "the bitter water that brings a curse" (Num. 5:13-31).

In the NT Jesus condemned not only the act itself but also one who has adulterous thoughts. It is also adultery to divorce a wife and marry another. Christians are repeatedly warned against adultery and fornication. In the NT the husband is bound by as strict a morality as is the wife (Mt. 5:21-27; Mk. 10:11, 12; 1 Cor. 6:9).

ADUMMIM An ascent or pass which went up through a wadi (steep valley) through which in antiquity passed the road from Jericho to Jerusalem. It was a part of the border between the tribes of Judah and Benjamin (Josh. 15:7; 18:17).

ADVERSARY *See* DEVIL

ADVOCATE A person who is a representative of one or more individuals before another or others. Christ speaks to the Father in man's defense (1 John 2:1). The Greek word *parakletos* used here is elsewhere rendered "Counselor" and is applied by Christ to the Holy Spirit (John 14:16, 26).

AENEAS A paralytic inhabitant of Lydda whom Peter healed, a miracle which caused all who lived in Lydda and Sharon to turn to the Lord (Acts 9:32-35).

AENON An unidentified place, probably in the Jordan Valley, where John baptized (John 3:23).

AGABUS A NT prophet who at Antioch predicted a famine would spread over the entire Roman world. It came in the time of Claudius. At Caesarea he predicted the imprisonment of Paul in Jerusalem (Acts 11:27, 28; 21:10, 11).

AGAG, AGAGITE 1. In Balaam's oracle it is said that Israel's king will be "greater than Agag." No other information is given (Num. 24:7).

2. An Amalekite king captured by King Saul. Saul saved his life and this was considered an act of disobedience to the Lord worse than divining. For this Saul lost his kingship (1 Sam. 15:8, 20-23).

3. Haman, who sought to destroy all the Jews at the Persian court, was an Agagite (Esth. 3:1).

AGATE *See* PRECIOUS STONES AND METALS

AGEE Father of one of David's mighty men (2 Sam. 23:8, 11).

AGRIPPA *See* HEROD

AGUR The author of the thirtieth chapter of Proverbs.

AHAB A false prophet, condemned by the true prophet Jeremiah and executed by King Nebuchadnezzar of Babylon by roasting in a fire (Jer. 29:20-23). *See also* KINGS OF JUDAH AND ISRAEL.

AHARAH The third son of Benjamin (1 Chron. 8:1).

AHARHEL A Judahite, son of Harum (1 Chron. 4:8).

AHASBAI The father of one of David's heroes (2 Sam. 23:34).

AHASUERUS *See* XERXES

AHAVA A place in Babylonia where Ezra gathered the Jews who came back with him from the captivity in Babylon (Ezra 8:15, 21, 31).

AHAZ One of Saul's descendants through his son Jonathan (1 Chron. 8:35; 9:42). *See also* KINGS OF JUDAH AND ISRAEL.

AHAZIAH *See* KINGS OF JUDAH AND ISRAEL

AHBAN A Judahite of the house of Jerahmeel (1 Chron. 2:29).

AHER A man of the tribe of Benjamin (1 Chron. 7:12).

AHI A Gadite (1 Chron. 5:15).

AHIAM One of David's mighty men (2 Sam. 23:33).

AHIAN A man of the tribe of Manasseh (1 Chron. 7:19).

AHIEZER 1. A leader of the tribe of Dan during the desert wanderings (Num. 1:12; 2:25).
2. One of David's mighty men, a Benjamite, an archer and slingshot expert (1 Chron. 12:1-3).

AHIHUD 1. A leader of the tribe of Benjamin who helped Moses in the division of the land of Israel (Num. 34:27).
2. The head of a house in Benjamin (1 Chron. 8:7).

AHIJAH 1. A descendant of Judah (1 Chron. 2:25).
2. One of the mighty men of David's army (1 Chron. 11:36).
3. A man who had the charge of the treasuries of the temple in David's time (1 Chron. 26:20).
4. A prophet who told Jeroboam that God was going to take the kingdom from Rehoboam and give ten tribes to him

(1 Kgs. 11:29-32). He also predicted the end of the line of Jeroboam (1 Kgs. 14:1-11).

5. The father of one of the kings of Israel, Baasha (1 Kgs. 15:27).

AHIKAM King Josiah sent him to ask the prophetess Huldah about the Book of the Law discovered in the temple (2 Kgs. 22:11-20). He was also one who helped Jeremiah when his life was threatened (Jer. 26:24). After the kingdom of Judah had been taken into captivity his son Gedaliah was made the ruler over the people left behind and thus was the last ruler in Jerusalem at the time of the end of the kingdom (2 Kgs. 25:22).

AHILUD 1. The father of one of the recorders in the reigns of David and Solomon (2 Sam. 8:16; 1 Kgs. 4:3).

2. The father of one of the men who had to provide food for King Solomon one month in each year (1 Kgs. 4:12).

AHIMAAZ 1. The father of one of the wives of King Saul (1 Sam. 14:50).

2. During the revolt of Absalom against his father David, Ahimaaz was one of the two who stayed at the court to keep David posted on developments there (2 Sam. 15:27, 36).

3. A son-in-law of King Solomon and one of the men responsible for providing the king's food for a month each year (1 Kgs. 4:15).

AHIMAN 1. One of the three giants, sons of Anak, whom Caleb expelled from Hebron and was later defeated by Judahites (Josh. 15:14; Judg. 1:10). He and his two brothers were noted by the twelve Israelites who came up to spy out the land earlier (Num. 13:22-33).

2. A gatekeeper of the camp of the Levites in the days of King Saul (1 Chron. 9:17).

AHIMELECH 1. A priest at Nob who gave holy bread and the sword of Goliath to David when he was fleeing from King Saul (1 Sam. 21:1-10). When Saul heard of this he had all the priests at Nob, plus the other residents, killed for their aiding David. Only one escaped, the son of Ahimelech, Abiathar (1 Sam. 22:17-21).

2. A Hittite soldier who followed David in the years he was fleeing from Saul (1 Sam. 26:6).

3. The son of the Abiathar and grandson of Ahimelech, noted above; a priest in David's reign (2 Sam. 8:17; 1 Chron. 18:16).

AHIMOTH A descendant of Levi in the line of Kohath (1 Chron. 6:25).

AHIANDAB King Solomon's officer in charge of his food services at Mahanaim, one of twelve such officers (1 Kgs. 4:14).

AHINOAM 1. One of Saul's wives (1 Sam. 14:50).

2. A wife of David and the mother of his first child, Amnon (1 Sam. 25:43; 2 Sam. 3:2).

AHIO 1. One of the two sons of Abinadab who drove the cart that carried the Ark from Kiriath Jearim to Jerusalem (2 Sam. 6:3, 4).

2. A Benjamite and uncle of King Saul (1 Chron. 8:29-31).

3. Another Benjamite (1 Chron 8:14).

AHIRA A prince of the tribe of Naphtali during the exodus from Egypt (Num. 2:29; 10:27).

AHIRAM A son of Benjamin (Num. 26:38); perhaps the Aharah of 1 Chronicles 8:1.

AHISAMACH A Danite and father of one of those selected to work on the building of the tabernacle (Ex. 31:6; 38:23).

AHISHAHAR A descendant of Benjamin (1 Chron. 7:10).

AHISHAR One of King Solomon's officials in charge of his palace (1 Kgs. 4:6).

AHITHOPHEL A valued counselor of David and father of one of his mighty men (2 Sam. 16:23). However, when David's son Absalom revolted against his father, Ahithophel joined him, and later after the rebellion had been crushed, fearing the outcome, he hanged himself (2 Sam. 15:31; 17:23).

AHITUB 1. The father of one of Saul's priests (1 Sam. 14:2, 3).

2. The father of Zadok, David's priest (2 Sam. 8:17).

3. The grandfather of Zadok, the priest of David (1 Chron. 9:11). The identification and separation of the several men by this name is not clear.

AHLAB A Canaanite city (172-303) in the tribal area of Asher (Judg. 1:31).

AHLAI 1. One of the descendants of Judah (1 Chron. 2:31).

2. Father of one of David's mighty men (1 Chron. 11:41).

AHOAH A grandson of Benjamin (1 Chron. 8:4).

AHONI The grandfather of one of David's three mighty men (2 Sam. 23:9).

AHUMAI A descendant of Judah (1 Chron. 4:2).

AHUZZAM A descendant of Judah (1 Chron. 4:6).

AHUZZATH An advisor of Abimelech of Gerar who visited Isaac (Gen. 26:26).

AHZAI A priest (Neh. 11:13).

AI 1. Abraham encamped between Bethel and Ai and built an altar to the Lord there. The place is called Ha'ai in the Hebrew text, which literally means "the ruin" (Gen. 12:8; 13:3; Josh. 8). After Abraham's trip to Egypt he returned first to Ai. Later at the start of the conquest under Joshua, the Israelites were first defeated there because of the disobedience of Achan but, after his punishment by the Lord, their second attempt to take it was successful. It is called Aiath and Aija also (Isa. 10:28; Neh. 11:31). Modern scholars have been identifying Bethel with Beitin (172-148) and Ai with et-Tell nearby. There are many problems with this identification, however. Some suggest that the two places should be nearer to Jerusalem and that their identity is not yet established.

2. A place that seems to be near Heshbon, east of the Jordan (Jer. 49:3).

AIAH 1. A grandson of Seir the Horite (Gen. 36:24; 1 Chron. 1:40).

2. A parent of one of King Saul's concubines (2 Sam. 3:7; 21:10, 11).

AIATH Some consider Aiath as another name for Ai. Aharoni gives it a possible second location at (175-145). *See also* AIAI.

AIJA *See* AI

AIJALON 1. A valley west and slightly north of Jerusalem that was under the control of Egypt before the Israelite conquest under Joshua. Here Joshua won an important victory when the sun stood still at Gibeon and the moon in the valley of Aijalon (Josh. 10).

2. A town (152-138) within the valley by the same name. It was given to the tribe of Dan as one of the Levitical cities. They failed to conquer it and only in David's days did this take place. Solomon gave it to the tribal area of Benjamin (Josh. 19:42; Judg. 1:35). King Rehoboam made it one of his

defense cities but the Philistines took it later (2 Chron. 11:10; 28:18).

3. An unidentified town in the tribal area of Zebulun (Judg. 12:12).

AIN 1. A town (212-235) on the eastern border of Israel's territory (Num. 34:10-12).

2. A town in the tribal area of Judah and thought by some to be near Beersheba (Josh. 15:32).

AKAN A descendant of Esau and Seir the Horite (Gen. 36:27; 1 Chron. 1:42).

AKELDAMA In Acts 1:19 it is called "Field of Blood" where Judas fell and "burst open" after his remorse over his betrayal of Jesus. Matthew records that the chief priests took the betrayal money from Judas, thirty pieces of silver, and bought the field for a place of burial for strangers. Matthew calls it "Field of Blood" but does not use the term Akeldama (Mt. 27:3-10). While its exact location is not known, an ancient tradition places it on the south slope of the eastern end of the Hinnom Valley, south of Jerusalem's walled city.

AKIM One in the genealogy of Christ (Mt. 1:14).

AKKUB 1. A descendant of David and Solomon who lived after the Babylonian captivity (1 Chron. 3:24).

2. One of the temple gatekeepers in the time of Nehemiah (Neh. 7:45).

3. A temple servant mentioned in Ezra 2:45.

4. One of those who helped the people understand the Law in the days of Ezra (Neh. 8:6-8).

AKRABBIM *See* SCORPION PASS

ALABASTER A stone, carbonate of lime, used in ancient times for making flasks and boxes for holding perfumes and ointments. A jar of alabaster contained the ointment with which a woman anointed the head of Jesus (Mt. 26:7).

ALAMOTH *See* PSALMS, TITLES OF

ALEMETH 1. A descendant of Benjamin (1 Chron. 7:8).

2. A descendant of Saul and Jonathan, and also a Benjamite (1 Chron. 8:36).

3. A village (176-136) in the tribal areas of Benjamin (1 Chron. 6:60). It is also called Almon (Josh. 21:18).

ALEXANDER 1. Alexander the Great, King of Greece, conqueror of the east at the end of the fourth century B.C. He was not mentioned by name in the Bible.

2. The son of Simon of Cyrene, who was compelled to carry the cross of Jesus (Mk. 15:21).

3. A member of the high priestly family before whom Peter and John were tried (Acts 4:6).

4. One who made "shipwreck" of his faith and was handed over to Satan for it by Paul, perhaps the coppersmith who did Paul much harm (1 Tim. 1:19, 20; 2 Tim. 4:14, 15).

5. One who tried to speak for the Jews during the riot in Ephesus over their god Artemis (Acts 19:33, 34).

ALEXANDRIA A city in Egypt founded by Alexander the Great in the end of the fourth century B.C. and the home of a large Jewish community. Apparently those of this community also maintained a synagogue at Jerusalem for some of them opposed Stephen and thus contributed to his death by stoning (Acts 6:9, 10; 7:57, 58). Apollos of Alexandria helped Paul at Ephesus and Corinth (Acts 18:24; 19:1).

ALGUM *See* TREES

ALLAMMELECH An unidentified town in the tribal area of Asher (Josh. 19:26).

ALLEGORY A figurative treatment of one subject under the guise of another. An allegory is a symbolical narrative. A prime illustration is found in Galatians 4:24ff. rendered "figuratively" (allegory in Greek text of the NT). It is used in OT times only rarely (Ezek. 17:2; 24:3; 20:49), but a number of cases in addition to the above are found in the NT (Mk. 4:10-20; 1 Cor. 5:6-8; 10:1-11; Rev. 11:18). After NT times, extensive use was made of allegory in both Jewish and Christian circles.

ALLON A descendant of Simeon (1 Chron. 4:37).

ALLON BACUTH An unidentified place perhaps near Bethel where the nurse of Rebekah, wife of Isaac, was buried (Gen. 35:8).

ALMIGHTY *See* GOD, NAMES OF

ALMODAD One of the descendants of Shem, son of Noah (Gen. 10:26; 1 Chron. 1:20).

ALMON *See* ALEMETH, 3 and BETH DIBLATHAIM

ALMOND *See* TREES

ALMON DIBLATHAIM One of the stops of the Israelites in their exodus from Egypt (Num. 33:46), somewhere in Moab.

ALMS The giving of alms is the voluntary giving of contributions to or for the poor. In OT times it was required and practiced even though the word is not found in the text (Deut. 15:7-11). This act came later to have very great significance, even that one could himself be forgiven by practicing it (Dan. 4:27). In later Judaism and in the NT it takes on even greater importance for the observant (Acts 3:1-3; 10:2; 24:17). It was prominent in the teaching of Jesus (Mt. 6:2-4; 25:31-40; Mk. 9:41).

ALMUG *See* TREES

ALOES *See* PLANTS, PERFUMES AND SPICES

ALPHA AND OMEGA *See* GOD, NAMES OF

ALPHAEUS The husband of one of the Marys of the NT and the father of James and Joseph (Joses) (Mt. 10:3; 27:56; Mk. 15:40).

ALTAR A place for making sacrifices to God or to pagan deities. An altar for the God of Israel had to be built from earth or from unhewn stone and could not be so high that it required steps to reach its top (Ex. 20:24-26). In early biblical times some were to commemorate the appearance of deity or to mark an important event (Gen. 12:7; Deut. 27:1-8). The horned altar puts in its appearance in the time of King Solomon. It was a square pillar with hornlike protrusions at each of its upper four corners. On the horns of these special altars a part of the blood of the sacrifice was to be placed, and fugitives could claim asylum by taking hold of them (Ex. 29:12; 1 Kgs. 2:28). Gradually over a period of time the altar of the temple in Jerusalem became the legal place of sacrificing.

ALUSH One of the stopping places on the Israelite exodus from Egypt, somewhere in the Sinai peninsula (Num. 33:13, 14).

ALVAH A chief of Edom, descended from Esau (Gen. 36:40; 1 Chron. 1:51).

ALVAN Ancestor of a subclan in Edom (Gen. 36:23; 1 Chron. 1:40).

AMAD An unidentified town in the tribal area of Asher (Josh. 19:26).

AMAL One of the descendants of Asher (1 Chron. 7:35).

AMALEK, AMALEKITES A people descended from Esau, the son of Abraham, who lived south of Judah in the desert area (Gen. 36:9, 12; Num. 13:29). Their wars with Israel began during the exodus where their first defeat took place at Rephidim (Ex. 17:8-16). Wars between Amalekites and Israel continued sporadically until the times of King Hezekiah (Num. 14:45; Judg. 3:13; 1 Sam. 14:47, 48; 15:7; 30:1, 17, 18; 1 Chron. 4:43). Moses at the command of God declared their ultimate overthrow (Ex. 17:14; Deut. 25:17-19).

AMAM An unidentified town of southern Judah (Josh. 15:26).

AMANA A place associated with Lebanon and Hermon in Song 4:8.

AMARIAH 1. A descendant of Levi, Kohath, and Aaron (1 Chron. 6:7; 23:19).

2. A chief priest in the days of King Jehoshaphat (2 Chron. 19:11).

3. One of the Levites in charge of the free will offerings in the days of King Hezekiah (2 Chron. 31:15).

4. An ancestor of the prophet Zephaniah who was probably in the royal line of Judah (Zeph. 1:1).

5. One of those who had married foreign women in the time of the Babylonian captivity (Ezra 10:42).

6. A leading Judahite who lived in Jerusalem in the days of Nehemiah (Neh. 11:4).

7. One of the signers of the covenant in the days of Nehemiah, perhaps also one who came up from Babylon with Zerubbabel (Neh. 10:3; 12:2).

AMASA 1. A relative of King David who sided with Absalom when he revolted against his father (2 Sam. 17:25), but whom David forgave and later set as the head of his armies in the place of Joab (2 Sam. 19:13). Joab suspected him of treachery and later killed him (2 Sam. 20:9-13).

2. A chief of the northern tribal confederacy who stood up against King Pekah when he tried to take Judean prisoners (2 Chron. 28:12).

AMASAI 1. A Levite descended from Kohath and Levi (1 Chron. 6:35) who assisted King Hezekiah in his reforms (2 Chron. 29:12).

2. Chief of David's Thirty, one who came to him at Ziklag (1 Chron. 12:1, 18).

3. One who blew trumpets before the Ark of God in Jerusalem in the days of David (1 Chron. 15:24).

AMASHSAI A priest in the days of Nehemiah who volunteered to live in Jerusalem (Neh. 11:13).

AMASIAH One of the builders for King Jehoshaphat in Judah (2 Chron. 17:16).

AMAZIAH 1. A king of Judah. *See* KINGS OF JUDAH AND ISRAEL.

2. A descendant of Simeon (1 Chron. 4:34).

3. A Levite descended from Merari (1 Chron. 6:45).

4. A priest at Bethel in the days of King Jeroboam who opposed the prophet Amos (Amos 7:10-17).

AMEN Transliteration of a Hebrew word expressing agreement, similar to the English "so be it" (Num. 5:19-22); used also in prayers and in liturgies (Deut. 27:15-26; Ps. 106:48; Jer. 28:6). In the NT it is most frequently used in the conclusion of either an ascription of praise to God or a prayer (Rom. 11:36; 15:33; Phil. 4:20). Jesus used it in the beginning of many of his statements (John 5:24) where it appears as, "I tell you the truth." It appears as a name for Jesus himself (Rev. 3:14).

AMETHYST *See* PRECIOUS STONES AND METALS

AMI A son of one of Solomon's servants (Ezra 2:57).

AMITTAI The father of the prophet Jonah (Jonah 1:1).

AMMAH An unidentified hill where Joab and Abner confronted one another (2 Sam. 2:24).

AMMIEL 1. The Danite representative in the twelve spies who went to spy out the land for the Israelites (Num. 13:12).

2. The father of Bath-shua (Bathsheba), one of David's wives and mother of Solomon (1 Chron. 3:5).

3. The father of Machir who was the protector of the last son of King Saul (2 Sam. 9:4-6).

4. A son of Obed-Edom, one of the gatekeepers (1 Chron. 26:5).

AMMIHUD 1. The name of four men, one in each of four tribes: Ephraim, Simeon, Naphthali, and Judah (Num. 1:10; 34:20, 28; 1 Chron. 9:4).

2. The father of Talmai, the king of Geshur, with whom Absalom hid out from David for three years (2 Sam. 13:37).

AMMIANDAB 1. The father-in-law of Aaron (Ex. 6:23), and an ancestor of David and Jesus Christ (Ruth 4:19; Mt. 1:4).

2. A Levite, the son of Kohath and father of Korah (1 Chron. 6:22).

3. A Levite head of a family in the time of King David (1 Chron. 15:10, 11).

AMMISHADDAI A member of the tribe of Dan, father of the leader of the camp of Dan following the host in the wilderness wanderings (Num. 10:25).

AMMIZABAD Son of one of David's mighty thirty men (1 Chron. 27:6).

AMMONG *See* GEOGRAPHY OF THE HOLY LAND

AMNON 1. David's first son. Amnon dishonored his half-sister and was murdered for his actions by his half-brother Absalom (2 Sam. 3:2; 13:1-22).

2. A descendant of Judah (1 Chron. 4:20).

AMOK A chief of the priests who came with Zerubbabel from Babylon after the captivity (Neh. 12:7).

AMON 1. The governor of Samaria in the reign of King Ahab (1 Kgs. 22:26).

2. A descendant of one of Solomon's servants who returned from the Babylonian captivity (Neh. 7:59). *See* KINGS OF JUDAH AND ISRAEL and DEITIES.

AMORITES A people who lived in the land of Amurru, west of Mesopotamia, probably in Syria and at least a part of Palestine. Some also lived in the Judean hill country, others east of the Jordan in Heshbon and Bashan (Josh. 9:10; 10:5). According to 1 Chronicles 1:13, 14, they descended from Canaan. In the middle of the third millennium B.C. the Akkadian records of Sargon the First, and again the records of the Sumerian Gudea at about 2000 B.C., refer to campaigns against the Amorites to secure building materials. One of their important centers was the city of Mari on the Euphrates River east of Byblos and Tadmor. After the beginning of the second millennium B.C., they spread widely but their empire ended with the conquest by King Hammurabi of Babylon who took Mari and scattered the people. They intermarried with Indo-Europeans, and others existed for many centuries scattered in smaller states as we have already noted. There are many references to them in the Amarna Letters from Egypt of the fourteenth century B.C.

Their language was a dialect of northwest Semitic. The early kings had Semitic names even though later Horite and Hittite names were more prominent. As a buffer state, its precarious existence in this area came to an end in 1297, with the Battle of Orontes after which it came under Hittite control until that empire too came to its end a hundred years later. References are found to them in the Bible from the patriarchal times to the time of King Solomon, at which time we find them as slaves (Gen. 15:18-21; Josh. 24:8; 2 Chron. 8:7).

AMOS, BOOK OF *See* PROPHETS, MINOR

AMOZ The father of the prophet Isaiah (Isa. 1:1).

AMPHIPOLIS An important trading center in Greece through which Paul passed on one of his missionary journeys (Acts 17:1).

AMPLIATUS A Christian at Rome, beloved of Paul, to whom he sent greetings (Rom. 16:8).

AMRAM 1. A grandson of Levi who married Jochebed, his father's sister, and became the father of Miriam, Moses, and Aaron (Ex. 6:16, 18, 20).

2. Father of some men who had married foreign women during the Babylonian captivity but who later put them away (Ezra 10:34, 44).

AMRAPHEL The king of Shinar who, among others, invaded patriarchal Palestine and took the goods of Sodom and Gomorrah and along with them the nephew of Abram (Abraham), Lot (Gen. 14:1, 8, 9, 12). The identification with Hammurabi, king of Babylon, is not accepted by most scholars of Babylonian history.

AMZI 1. A descendant of Levi (1 Chron. 6:46).

2. A priest who served in the second temple (Neh. 11:12).

ANAB A town (143-089) in the hill country of Judah near Hebron and Debir (Josh. 11:21).

ANAH A son of Zibeon, the Hivite. His daughter was one of Esau's wives (Gen. 36:2, 14, 24, 29).

ANAHARATH A town (194-228) of the tribe of Issachar SE of Mt. Tabor (Josh. 19:19).

ANAIAH One who signed the covenant after the return from the Babylonian captivity and stood with Ezra when he read the Book of the Law to the people (Neh. 8:4; 10:22).

ANAK,
ANAKITES A people found in Palestine in the days of Joshua's conquest among whom were apparently many large people, even giants. They were also known as Rephaites and called Emites by the Moabites (Deut. 2:10, 11, 21). After Joshua their remnants lived in the Philistine cities (Josh. 11:21, 22).

ANAMITES A tribe or group descended from Mizraim (Egypt) (Gen. 10:13).

ANAMMELECH *See* DEITIES

ANAN One of the men who signed the covenant in the days of Nehemiah (Neh. 10:26).

ANANI A son of Elionai, a descendant of King Solomon (1 Chron. 3:24).

ANANIAH 1. Grandfather of one who repaired on the walls of Jerusalem after the return from the Babylonian captivity (Neh. 3:23).

2. A town (174-131) settled by Benjamites after the return noted above (Neh. 11:32).

ANANIAS 1. One who, together with his wife Sapphira, was involved in a lie in the days of the early church, was rebuked by Peter, and struck down by death for the lie (Acts 5:1-11).

2. One who was used to restore sight to the Apostle Paul after his conversion, and to baptize him (Acts 9:10-19).

3. A pro-Roman high priest before whom Paul was tried (Acts 23:1-5).

ANATH Father of one of Israel's judges, Shamgar (Judg. 3:31).

ANATHOTH 1. A town (174-135) of Benjamin just north of Jerusalem given to the priests, also the home of Jeremiah the prophet (Josh. 21:13, 17-19). It was resettled after the Babylonian captivity (Ezra 2:23).

2. A grandson of Benjamin (1 Chron. 7:8).

3. One of those who signed the covenant with Nehemiah (Neh. 10:19).

ANCIENT OF DAYS A title for God found only in Daniel (Dan. 7:9, 13, 22).

ANDREW *See* APOSTLES

ANDRONICUS One whom Paul refers to as a "relative" who had been in prison with him, a man outstanding among the apostles (Rom. 16:7).

ANEM A city of refuge from the tribe of Issachar somewhere in the vicinity of Mt. Tabor (1 Chron. 6:73).

ANER 1. An Amorite chief who was allied with Abraham against the eastern kings (Gen. 14:13).

2. An unidentified town in Manasseh which was given to the Kohathites (1 Chron. 6:70).

ANGEL A translation given to the Hebrew word which basically means "messenger" as we know from such usages as found in Judges 6:35. The Greek word used to render this Hebrew word was *angelos* which ultimately came into English as "angel." These messengers could be human or they could be superhuman agents of God. Two appeared in human form to Abraham with "the Lord" (Gen. 18: 1, 2, 22). See also CHERUBIM and SERAPHS. They ate, were able to fight, and could be charged by God with error (Gen. 18:8; 32:1; Job 4:18). When God sent prophets to his people, angels were often intermediaries bringing messages in visions (Ezek. 8:1-8). After the return from Babylon the picture of angels in the Bible becomes much more complex; also in the Dead Sea Scrolls. Some are found with individual names such as Gabriel (Dan. 8:16; Lk. 1:19) and Michael (Dan. 12:1; Rev. 12:7). In the NT Christ refers to their existence, but they no longer are intermediaries to bring God's messages since that role is now put into the hands of Christ or the Holy Spirit (Acts 9:5; Gal. 1:12). Because of abuses it was necessary for Paul to warn the churches against the worship of angels (Col. 2:18). There are two references to an archangel (1 Thess. 4:16; Jude 9).

One is called the Angel of the Lord who seems to have been a special messenger of God, and in some passages even God himself (Gen. 31:11-13). The term "angels of the churches" in Rev. 1:20; 2:1—3:22 refers to the leaders of the individual churches.

ANGER *See* WRATH

ANIAM A descendant of Manasseh (1 Chron. 7:19).

ANIM A town (156-084) in the hill country of Judah (Josh. 15:50).

ANNA A prophetess descended from the tribe of Asher, a widow of many years, who spent her time worshiping, fasting, and praying at the temple. When she saw the child Jesus she spoke of him to all who were looking for redemption in Israel, accepting him as Messiah (Lk. 2:36-38).

ANNAS For nine years a high priest in Jerusalem; the father-in-law of Caiaphas who was the high priest at the time of Jesus' arrest (Lk. 3:2; Jn. 18:13, 14). Deposed by the Romans, he was still considered high priest by the Jews (Acts 4:6).

ANOINT, ANOINTED The application of oil to a person or thing for healing or as a sacred rite (Jas. 5:14; Mk. 6:13; Ex. 30:22-33; Ps. 23:5). Kings, priests, and sometimes even prophets were consecrated to their offices by having oil poured on their heads (2 Kgs. 9:1-3). In the NT the prophet, priest, and king *par excellence* was Christ who is called the "Anointed One" (Acts 4:24-28). The Hebrew word for anoint was transliterated into Greek as *messias* and then later into English as "messiah." The usual Greek word for anointed, *christos*, came into English as "Christ." Both are applied to Jesus as titles in the NT.

ANT *See* BEASTS, 6

ANTELOPE *See* BEASTS, 2

ANTHOTHIJAH A descendant of Benjamin (1 Chron. 8:24).

ANTICHRIST In the eschatological war, of the end of days, the last hour, the great opponent of Christ who will finally be vanquished. John noted that there are also many antichrists, those who deny that Jesus is the Christ (1 Jn. 2:18, 22).

ANTIMONY *See* PRECIOUS STONES AND METALS

ANTIOCH The name of many cities which were named after the father of the founder of the Seleucid dynasty, whose dynasty was centered in Antioch of Syria. Two of these cities are noted in the NT.

1. Antioch of Syria on the Orontes River about fourteen miles east of the Mediterranean Sea and one of the most important centers of commerce in the Middle East. In post NT times the Romans conquered it and made it the capital of their province of Syria, 69 B.C. Under persecution in Jerusalem, many early Christians fled to Antioch and there established a thriving church to whose assistance Barnabas and Paul were sent. Here it was that the followers of Jesus were first called Christians (Acts 11:19-26). This church at Antioch became the center of the early missionary outreach. Paul's first two missionary journeys began here (Acts 13:1, 2; 15:35, 36). It was a center of the attempt to mix law and grace so vigorously opposed by Paul, which led to the council at Jerusalem of the leaders of the church (Gal. 2:11; Acts 15). The results of this council were delivered to Antioch in a letter.

2. Antioch of Pisidia, a city which bordered on the province of Pisidia, but which was actually in the province of Galatia. Paul visited it in his missionary journeys (Acts 13:14; 2 Tim. 3:11).

ANTIOCHUS In intertestament times a number of the Seleucid kings of Syria bore this name. Perhaps the best known is Antiochus IV Epiphanes (175-163 B.C.) who tried to Hellenize the Jews, an attempt which failed, resulting in the Maccabean revolt that set Judea free from Syrian rule. He was not mentioned in the Bible although some scholars see Epiphanes predicted in the Book of Daniel (Dan. 11:36).

ANTIPAS 1. One of the names of Herod the Tetrarch. *See* HEROD.

2. An early Christian martyr in Pergamum (Rev. 2:12, 13).

ANTIPATRIS A town (143-168) founded by Herod the Great at the foot of the central mountain range in Palestine between Jerusalem and the coast. Paul stayed there overnight when he was being taken as a prisoner from Jerusalem to Caesarea (Acts 23:31). *See also* APHEK.

ANUB A descendant of Judah (1 Chron. 4:8).

ANVIL A common tool of the metal worker (Isa. 41:7).

APE *See* BEASTS, 3

APELLES A Christian of Rome greeted by Paul (Rom. 16:10).

APHEK 1. A Canaanite town (143-168) on the edge of the Plain of Sharon which later became a Philistine base used against Israel. Josephus states that Herod built the town of Antipatris on its ruins. Today it is known as Rosh ha-Ayin (Josh. 12:18; 1 Sam. 4:1; 29:1). *See also* ANTIPATRIS.

2. A town located in the Plain of Acco (160-250) in the tribal area of Asher (Josh. 19:30).

3. A town (210-243) near the Sea of Galilee where King Ahab defeated the Syrians under Ben-Hadad (1 Kgs. 20:26-34).

APHEKAH An unidentified town in the hill country of Judah (Josh. 15:53).

APHIAH A Benjamite ancestor of King Saul (1 Sam. 9:1).

APOCALYPSE A word commonly used as a name for the Book of Revelation.

APOCRYPHA *See* SCRIPTURES

APOLLONIA An unidentified town in Greece through which Paul and Silas passed en route to Thessalonica (Acts 17:1).

APOLLOS An Alexandrian Jew who came to Ephesus and was there instructed by Aquila and Priscilla. He preached in Achaia and later acquired a following in Corinth (Acts 18:24-28; 1 Cor. 3:4; 16:12; Tit. 3:13). Paul encouraged him to revisit Corinth (1 Cor. 16:12) and had asked Titus to help him (Tit. 3:13).

APOLLYON *See* DEAD, ABODE OF

APOSTASY A turning away from the tenets of one's religion. It is rendered "rebellion," something which is to take place in the church before the second coming of Christ (2 Thess. 2:12).

APOSTLES A term applied generally, but not exclusively, in the NT to the twelve men chosen by Christ to learn of him and then to bear witness of him to the world. They were: Simon, also called Peter, and his brother Andrew; the sons of Zebedee, James and John; Philip; Bartholomew, also called Nathanael; Matthew, also called Levi; Thomas; James, son of Alphaeus; Judas, son of James, also called Thaddaeus; Simon the Zealot; and Judas Iscariot (Mt. 10:2-4; Mk. 3:16-19; Lk. 6:14-16; Acts 1:13). Most of them were Galileans. Three were especially close to Jesus—Peter, James, and John—who were with Jesus on several key occasions including the transfiguration and in the Garden of Gethsemane (Mt. 17:1; Mk. 14:33). Judas Iscariot, after his betrayal of the Lord and his suicide, was replaced by Matthias (Acts 1:26). Paul, Barnabas, and others are also called apostles (Acts 14:14; Gal. 1:19; Rom. 16:7).

APPAIM A descendant of Judah (1 Chron. 2:30).

APPHIA A Christian woman to whom Paul sent greetings (Philem. 2).

APPIUS, FORUM OF A town through which Paul passed en route to his trial in Rome, some forty miles south of Rome (Acts 28:15).

APPLE *See* TREES

AQUEDUCT A channel for conveying liquids, in this case water (2 Kgs. 18:17; Isa. 7:3; 36:2). King Hezekiah's famous conduit is known in Jerusalem to this day. In his case it was an underground tunnel carved out of solid rock. The Romans built upon channels supported where necessary by arches, as at Caesarea and elsewhere.

AQUILA A Jew of Pontus who with his wife Priscilla, had moved from Rome to Corinth because of the expulsion of the Jews from

Rome by the emperor in A.D. 52. Paul lived with them during his ministry in Corinth and they moved with him to Ephesus later where their house was the center of activity for the church there (Acts 18:19; Rom. 16:3-5; 1 Cor. 16:19). They instructed Apollos in the things of Christ (Acts 18:24-26).

AR A town of Moab, or on its border, near the Arnon River (Num. 21:15; Deut. 2:18).

ARA A descendant of Asher (1 Chron. 7:38).

ARAB (153-093). A hill country town in the tribal area of Judah (Josh. 15:52).

ARABAH *See* GEOGRAPHY OF THE HOLY LAND

ARABIA *See* GEOGRAPHY OF THE HOLY LAND

ARABS Originally the inhabitants of the Arabian peninsula south of Syria, particularly the inhabitants of the northern part of this area, consisting of many different tribes; Ishmaelites, Midianites, Sabeans, Hagarenes, Amalekites. They descended from Abraham by Keturah and from Ishmael. With their camels they traveled lucrative trade routes from Egypt to Babylon and all areas between (Isa. 60:6; Ezek. 27:21, 22). Perhaps one of the best known stories of interconnections with Israel is that of the visit of the Queen of Sheba to Solomon (1 Kgs. 10:1-13). During the period of the kings of Israel and Judah there were times of harassment by these tribes and a time when they were under tribute to Judah (2 Chron. 17:11; 21:16, 17; 22:1; 26:1-7). At least one Arab was among those who opposed the work of Nehemiah, Geshem by name (Neh. 2:19). In the NT Paul referred to Arabia (in the Sinai) (Gal. 4:25) and noted his time spent in Arabia after his conversion. Men from Arabia were among the multitude on the day of Pentecost (Acts 2:11). Exactly when and from where the ancestors of the modern Arabs came to Palestine is not known with certainty. It could not have been before the end of NT times and probably not until after Roman times which ended in the fourth century.

ARAD 1. A descendant of Benjamin (1 Chron. 8:15).

2. A Canaanite city (152-069). An Israelite city (162-076). The excavations at Tell Arad have shown that the latter was unoccupied between Early Bronze and Israelite times, a gap of 2000 years. Thus archaeologists place the Canaanite city at Tell Malhata nearby, which was occupied in Middle Bronze and Late Bronze times. The army of the king of Arad (Malhata) defeated the Israelites during their exodus from

Egypt (Num. 21:1-3). In Joshua's conquest, however, the
victory went the other way (Josh. 12:14). The relatives
of Moses' in-laws then lived in the area (Judg. 1:16).
Archaeological excavations at Tell Arad conducted by Dr.
Yohanan Aharoni of Tel Aviv University have uncovered the
Israelite Arad, a city occupied from Solomonic times down to
the end of the Kingdom of Judah. One of the most fascinating
parts of the excavation was the discovery of an Israelite
temple founded in the earliest period and used through the
times of Josiah. This temple was smaller but of the same
proportions as the Solomonic temple in Jerusalem.

ARAH A descendant of Asher and the collective name of his
descendants who came with Zerubbabel from the Babylonian
captivity (1 Chron. 7:39; Ezra 2:5).

ARAM 1. A descendant of Asher (1 Chron. 7:34).

2. One of the ancestors of Jesus, called Ram in Ruth 4:19;
Mt. 1:3; Lk. 3:33.

ARAM EANS A country and a people. *See* GEOGRAPHY OF THE HOLY LAND.

ARAMAIC
LANGUAGE A north Semitic language which was introduced to Syria and
Mesopotamia by the Arameans and which became the *lingua
franca* of the entire area until it was superseded by Greek
after the conquest of Alexander the Great in the end of the
fourth century B.C.. As the Arameans were successful traders
their language as well as their trade went with them. The
earliest extant inscriptions in this language go back to the
ninth century B.C. It existed in a number of dialects and was
written in a number of differing scripts, for example, the
dialect and script of the brief passages of Aramaic in the Bible
(Ezra 4:8—6:18; 7:12-26; Jer. 10:11; Dan 2:4—7:28). In
the NT a number of Aramaic words are also found (Mk.
5:41; 7:34; 15:34; etc.) It is probable that Jesus usually
spoke this language, and sometimes also both Greek and
Hebrew. There is a debate as to whether the NT was
written originally in Greek, Hebrew, or Aramaic. The last is
the least likely.

ARAM MAACAH An Aramean kingdom in the area of Bashan and Mount
Hermon, sometimes called Maacah.

ARAM NAHARAIM *See* EBER

ARAN A descendant of Esau (Gen. 36:28).

ARARAT A kingdom near Lake Van called Urartu in Assyrian. The
sons of the Assyrian king Sennacherib fled there after they

had murdered their father (2 Kgs. 19:37). Noah's ark rested on "the mountains of Ararat" after the flood had receded (Gen. 8:4). There are a number of traditions relative to the particular location.

ARAUNAH The Jebusite owner of a threshing floor on Mount Moriah which was bought by David, where he brought the Ark of the Covenant and built an altar (2 Sam. 24:16-24; 1 Chron. 21:15) and where Solomon later built the temple (2 Chron. 3:1). In the Hebrew text he is also called Ornan. (See footnote 1 Chron. 21:15.)

ARBA The father of Anak and founder of the city of Kiriath Arba, later called Hebron (Josh. 15:13; 21:11).

ARBATHITE Identifies the place of origin of Abi-Albon, one of David's thirty mighty men. He was from Beth Arabab or from the Arbah itself (2 Sam. 23:31).

ARBITE A native of the town Arba (2 Sam. 23:35).

ARCHAEOLOGY or ARCHEOLOGY Materials, history, methods, and philosophy of. The scholarly investigation of past human life, especially as it is revealed through relics, i.e., material objects that have survived from ancient times. The word is derived from the Greek *archaio* and *logos*, i.e., the orderly arrangement of facts regarding ancient things. During the Hellenistic age, the term was used in the sense of "antiquarian lore," "ancient legends," "history." For example, Josephus' famous history of the Jews called the *Antiquities* in English, was called *Ioudaikes archaiologias*. The term came to be used by scholars in the eighteenth century to mean all study of antiquity. In that broadest sense, it was applied to areas that today might be limited to physical anthropology on the one hand or to art history and linguistics on the other.

The emphasis on everyday life as the legitimate study of archaeology can be seen in nineteenth century works on biblical and Jewish antiquities based on the written documents. The biblical and Talmudic references to buildings, utensils, rituals, food stuffs, and agriculture were collected systematically and studied philologically like any other cultural or historical subject.

Today "archaeology of the Near East" is a specialty in its own right. Within this field there is what many call "biblical archaeology." One cannot divide them very easily because some parts of the Bible deal with adjacent countries such as Egypt, Mesopotamia, Iran, and others. From a logical point of view, the archaeology of Palestine (Eretz-Israel) is a special area of study which greatly overlaps but is not necessarily the equivalent of biblical archaeology. The legitimacy of the latter term has recently been brought into question. It is best to admit that the Bible, the most extensive written document to survive from the ancient Near Eastern World, deals a great deal with the life of Israel and its neighbors. Therefore, it is reasonable and desirable that the material side of Israelite and contemporary cultures be elucidated by archaeological research. Such investigations will be seen to have a legitimacy of their own, however, apart from their connection with biblical tradition.

More complex today is the question of where archaeology belongs in the range of academic disciplines. It will often be found associated with anthropology in the framework of the social sciences. This is especially true of prehistoric archaeology, particularly in the New World, in the Western Hemisphere, and also the islands of the Pacific. On the other hand, archaeology that began with an interest in the Old World, mainly classical Greece and Rome and the Near East, was closely associated with the literary and linguistic research in those fields. Thus, archaeology became a branch of classical studies, such as Greek and Latin, and subsequently of biblical and ancient Near Eastern studies. This placed archaeology within the humanities. The same overlapping occurs, therefore, as in the field of history, which partakes of both the social sciences and the humanities. Furthermore, new applications of the natural sciences are being utilized every year in the analysis of archaeological materials. Fortunately, modern archaeology now benefits from the current ecological concern. The total environment of ancient man is studied in all its facets. He is seen as not only a military and political but also as a social being who was influenced by and who influenced his physical surroundings. As will be seen below in the discussion of the philosophy of the discipline, archaeology is a combination of all three fields, though the final interpretation of any given mass of materials must be conducted in terms of the human value judgments of the investigators. In that sense, it is more a part of the humanities, even though statistical studies and scientific analyses may be utilized.

Materials. During the Renaissance the classical authors received new attention along with the objects of Graeco-Roman art. With the campaign by Napoleon to the Middle East, the western world became aware of the vast monumental culture of Egypt. The savants who accompanied the French army in 1799 recorded surface remains, such as pyramids, temples, and tombs. Other explorers began to bring back to Europe their reports, drawings, and tracings of buildings, ruins, inscriptions, and other objects. In addition, the study of life in the Moslem countries of the nineteenth century became

a special object of interest and many parallels to aspects of
biblical culture were discerned. The materials that attracted
the interest of scholars varied greatly.

Inscriptions, especially the hieroglyphs and cuneiform,
became a focus of research for many specialists. The texts in
these scripts were usually found on "archaeological" objects,
such as stelae, statues, temple walls, bas reliefs, and their
decipherment can legitimately be called archaeological research.
The Phoenician script, first discovered in statues from Malta,
was also decoded in the early nineteenth century, thus
providing the key to later finds of Hebrew inscriptions from
Palestine.

Architecture naturally has become a major field of archaeological research because in some countries, such as Greece
and Egypt, there were major buildings, mainly temples,
which survived the ravages of time. They can be excavated
and at least partially reconstructed. Monumental tombs also
provide details of an architectural nature, the abodes of the
dead being built in a manner analogous to those of the living.
With the advance of excavation technique (see below), interest
has been attracted to the badly ravaged remains of architecture
found buried beneath the ruins of subsequent cities. Fortifications, including the earthen ramparts used to create city
mounds, gate complexes, postern gates, and other innovations
have come to light. Public and private buildings are often
preserved only in their stone foundations, the brick superstructure having been obliterated by the action of nature and
of man. Even the flimsy dwelling of primitive man can
sometimes be retrieved by careful excavation of the traces in
the soil, postholes, and other perishable details leaving traces
in the ground.

Decorative aspects of architecture such as wall paintings
and sculptured columns belong, in one sense, to the study of
ancient art. Their connections with minor glyptic and miniature
painting are often the subject of special study.

Small objects cover a wide range of human activity. The
most ubiquitous of all is pottery. From the time of ceramic
utensils (Neolithic pottery, see below), man has used and
broken vast amounts of pottery. It has been demonstrated
that techniques of manufacture and styles of design and
decoration underwent a development throughout the ages.
The classification of these details according to their chronological
appearance was made possible by comparisons with similar
finds in Egypt where the vessels came from datable tombs.
Thus, there are certain features such as styles of burnishing
and painting, shapes of rims and bases, and others, which
are now identifiable as belonging to particular periods in the
country's history. Even sherds bearing such recognizable
characteristics can be used as a rough indication for dating.

Nevertheless, the pottery chronology holds good only for major periods in most cases. Refinements for shorter phases of time, such as the centuries of the Judean monarchy, are far from satisfactory.

Weapons are another class of artifacts requiring special study. The objects found in excavations can be compared to representations in Assyrian and Egyptian art. When metals are involved, modern technology is helping to analyze the alloys used, and geologists are searching for the sources of the original ore. Metal objects of agricultural and other domestic use receive similar treatment. For the later periods, coins comprise a valuable category of metal finds often with datable inscriptions.

Personal ornaments often appear in tombs and, on occasion, in stratified excavations. Since a large percentage of such items were imports from neighboring cultures, they are of special value for chronological and cultural relationships. Ivory plaques carved as furniture decorations have also been found. Their study is an important aspect of ancient art in Eretz-Israel and its cultural ties with Phoenicia and Egypt.

Only in the dry climate of the desert was it possible for items of clothing to be preserved. Finds of that nature have occurred in caves of the Judean Desert and Northern Sinai. In Egypt, however, an abundance of cloth samples from various periods has been recovered along with whole plants and other organic materials.

Special skills have been developed, mostly by trial and error, for the recovery and preservation of small finds. Care must be taken in removing them from the ground (after exact recording of the find spot), sometimes by using wax, plaster, or other preservatives. Then comes the stage of cleaning, particularly the metal objects, and repair when possible. The objects must be drawn and photographed after which the real scientific study begins. Comparisons with similar finds from other excavations must be made and conclusions drawn. The richest source for details of everyday life from which to deduce parallels for finds in Eretz-Israel is Egypt where most phases of everyday life are amply illustrated by pictures, captions and even the objects themselves, marvelously preserved.

Periods. Archaeology deals only with the remains of human life while geology, of course, treats the whole history of the earth's crust. Prehistorians refer to the ages of most ancient man as the Paleolithic (Old Stone), Mesolithic (Middle Stone), and Neolithic (New Stone) Ages. They date the Old Stone Age in the Pleistocene (or Glacial) period, that is, the last million years of the earth's existence. During that time, prehistoric man was a hunter and food-gatherer. In the New Stone Age, belonging to the Holocene (or Recent)

Epoch, since about 9,000 B.C., man became a food producer, cultivating cereals and domesticated animals. He begins to use pottery about 6,000 B.C.

For Eretz-Israel, one may say that the Proto-historic period begins with the Chalcolithic Age, about 5000-3200 B.C., when copper tools were used alongside stone. The Early Bronze Age (3200 to 2200) corresponds to the Old Kingdom of Egypt and the Sumerian and Akkadian periods of Mesopotamia. Written texts are absent in the Levant except for the rich archive recently discovered at Elba in Northern Syria. When the last of the Early Bronze city states were destroyed, the country was largely given over to a seminomadic culture in which only temporary settlements of a flimsy nature were established (Middle Bronze I, really an Intermediate period). By about 2000 B.C. the city-state regime of the Levant was reestablished and the predominant ethnic elements seem to have been Amurrite (Amorite). This was the Middle Bronze Age proper (Middle Bronze IIA). By about 1800 B.C. the life of the area is illuminated by the archives from Mari on the Euphrates. The Late Bronze Age, when some historical texts finally shed light on the land of Canaan (the central and southern Levant), extends from about 1550 to 1200 B.C. With the introduction of iron tools, we enter the Iron Age when historical/ethnic names can be used with more facility. The Israelite period from 1200 to 586 B.C., is followed by Babylonian rule until 539 when the Persian period begins. The Hellenistic Age is inaugurated by Alexander's conquests in 331 and the Roman period can be counted from Pompey's arrival in 63 B.C. The latter extends to A.D. 323.

The calculations for dating the above-mentioned periods are based on various lines of evidence. The earliest periods, especially those of prehistory, are derived from geological evidence and also from Carbon 14 tests on organic materials preserved in excavations. The earlier historic periods are defined in terms of relationships with the chronology of Egypt which is at least partly anchored in astronomical observations. There are some similar tie-ins with the chronology of Mesopotamia. The relative absence of datable inscriptions in the Levant make the establishment of solid historical/cultural contacts with Egypt most imperative.

Legally, the remains of medieval and early and modern times also fall within the scope of the antiquities laws in most Middle Eastern countries, including Israel. Thus, one finds archaeologists active in the study of those later periods as well. At many sites, one must first deal properly with the later remains, for otherwise the earlier remains and their degree of preservation (or disturbance) cannot be adequately understood.

Biblical archaeology covers such a wide range of these interests that one may find scholars in that field working on everything from prehistoric to medieval materials and sites.

History of Research. Modern archaeological research developed out of western man's curiosity about himself and his world. During the Renaissance, attention was drawn to the artistic works of classical Greece and Rome but with the Age of Enlightenment, scholars took an active interest in the physical world. Throughout the centuries there had been pilgrims visiting the Holy Land and its sacred sites but the solid scholarship in geographical study like that of the Church Fathers (Eusebius and Jerome) was not renewed until the eighteenth century.

The first excavations in ancient ruins were conducted at the two Roman cities destroyed by Vesuvius, in A.D. 79, beginning at the seaport of Herculaneum (in 1738) and later in the main city of Pompeii (1748). However, it was the campaign of Napoleon in 1799 that opened up the Near East to western scholars. The staff of savants that accompanied him brought back an abundance of information about the antiquities and the natural history of Egypt and the Levant. The first modern map (1:100,000) of the Palestinian coastal plain was produced.

Thus, the nineteenth century was ushered in for the land of the Bible. During the first thirty years, there were some pioneer explorers such as Seetzen and Burckhardt. They copied Greek inscriptions, noted archaeological remains on the surface, and recorded many Arabic names of places and geographical features. It was clear from their reports that names from the Bible and other ancient sources were still preserved.

After the conquest of the land by Mohammed Ali in 1831, the more stable social conditions that ensued encouraged further serious exploration by westerners. In 1838 Robinson and Smith made their landmark trip across the Sinai and around southern Palestine recording the locations and names of dozens of places. Their memories provided the first scientific philological and geographical description of the land and their compass readings were the basis for Kieppert's map which held the field for many years. Robinson and Smith made a second trip fifteen years later to complete their survey. Meanwhile, other travelers, such as Porter and Thompson, continued to explore other parts of the country and to furnish the western world with information about the life and customs of the land. The increase of influence by the colonial powers within the Ottoman Empire and the use of steamships contributed to an increase in tourism and travel by clergymen and scholars.

More intensive scientific exploration began in earnest after the Crimean war. The Palestine Exploration Fund was established in 1865 and fielded teams to explore Sinai and to excavate in Jerusalem. During the 1870s their team made the first complete map of Western Palestine using modern methods of surveying and cartography. They and other scholars associated with the Palestine Exploration Fund, Clermont-Ganneau, Warren, Wilson, and others, recorded antiquities all over the country and contributed studies on special biblical and historical topics.

In Mesopotamia, explorers such as Botta and Layard had proved in the 1830s and 1840s that the large mounds (*tells* in Arabic) contained the remains of ancient cities. They were recovering impressive monuments in stone for their respective national museums. In Egypt, teams of scholars made epigraphic surveys of inscriptions and wall reliefs, and individual excavators, such as Mariette, brought to light the remains of ritual installations as well as statuary and other funerary remains. But in Palestine, not all scholars had learned the lessons of Mesopotamia. Conder, head of the Palestine Exploration Fund Survey, denied that the tells were the sites of ancient towns. In general, archaeology was concerned with surface remains: temples, churches, burial caves, pillars, and other architectural pieces. Warren and the American Selah Merill, among others, were already contending that the tells were the real deposits of ancient remains from the Old Testament period. The controversy raged until it was finally settled by the excavations of Flinders-Petrie at Tell el-Hesi in 1890 (see below).

During the nineteenth century books on archaeology were also written by philologists. The details of everyday life as described in the Bible and the Talmud were assembled in a systematic manner. The various terms were treated linguistically and the texts were analyzed. Very little was as yet available from the material finds of field research to illustrate the points raised by such philological studies.

The great turning point was with Flinder-Petrie's work at Tell el-Hesi in 1890. He worked for six months and demonstrated that the mounds of Palestine were built of layers of debris deposits during the various building and destruction phases in the life of the settlement.

He showed that the artifacts within the respective layers changed in style with the progress of the ages, from the more primitive to the more advanced. This was especially true of the pottery both in terms of manufacture and decoration. Henceforth, excavations were conducted at other sites, such as Macalister at Gezer (1902-09) and Sellin and Watzinger at Jericho (1908-09). Attention was paid to the ceramic evidence, the sherds within the debris. There was yet no agreement as to the proper dating of many pottery styles. On the other hand, careful attention to the architectural remains and their associated soils was initiated by Reisner and Fisher during three years at Samaria (1908-10).

Only after World War II was there any agreement achieved in pottery chronology. This was done especially by the great University of Chicago effort at Megiddo from 1925 to 1936, the reports of which are still basic to all architectural and ceramic interpretation in Palestinian archaeology. Though the expedition suffered somewhat by changes in its leadership, its massive achievements, removing several strata of that most important site and publishing them handsomely, have hardly been surpassed to this day. At the same time, Albright conducted a parallel endeavor on a much smaller scale at Tell Beit Mirsim from 1926 to 1932. He was first in print with his pottery chronology and thus earned the credit as the man who brought order out of chaos in ceramic chronology. His site was also dug with fairly careful stratigraphic and architectural control and his publications are lucid and trustworthy. In spite of certain excusable errors in interpretation, the Tell Beit Mirsim excavation is still basic to understanding the discipline.

During the 1930s there were several major expeditions. Beth-Sahn was excavated by the University of Pennsylvania from 1921 to 1933 but its publication was only partial. Starkey began work in a very systematic fashion at Tell ed-Duweir in 1932 but was murdered by Arab villagers in 1938 on the eve of the uprising against the mandate authorities. A new joint expedition was launched at Samaria and Garstang renewed work at Jericho. In pre- and Proto-history, there were expeditions to the Carmel caves and to Teleilat el-Ghassul, respectively.

Surface exploration was begun east of the Jordan by Glueck during the 1930s. In the previous century there were partial efforts made but the region in its entirety had not been thoroughly covered or even mapped properly. Glueck sought, with only relative success, to apply the method of pottery dating to surface surveys. His work pointed the way to more sophisticated work in the post World War II period.

After the Israel War of Independence in 1948, work was renewed mainly by Israeli expeditions in Israel and by American, French, and British teams in Jordan and the West Bank. A leading figure in these efforts was K. Kenyon, whose work at Jericho helped to solve some of the questions left unanswered by Garstang, particularly with regard to its destruction in the middle of the millennium. Other expeditions, led by less experienced personnel, began to adopt her stratigraphic methods (see below). In a way this was healthy but unfortunately, the Kenyonist doctrinaire attitude to certain

dogmas of interpretation became even more extreme among
her followers. Her work at Jerusalem in the 1960s only
served to muddle most of the major problems troubling the
students of that city's history.

Meanwhile, a more practical application of stratigraphic
excavation was developing among the Israeli excavators. The
great expedition to Hazor, actually a group of excavations
directed by experienced scholars each in a separate area,
coordinated by Y. Yadin, provided them an opportunity to
establish methods of recording that utilized the lessons learned
by Teisner and Fisher with the pottery analysis of Albright
and the Megiddo publications. Henceforth, the archaeologists
of the Hazor team branched out to major excavations in
various parts of the country: Aharoni to Ramat Rahel and
Arad, Amiran to Arad and Tell en-Najila, Dothan to Ashdod,
and Yadin to Masada. The nationwide and even municipal
archaeological departments were busy rescuing antiquity sites
from the threat of modern land development. Government
departments of antiquities in all Levantine countries continued
the work of the former mandated authorities of Britain and
France.

Survey was also continued, especially by a nationwide
effort in Israel. Foreign teams are now working intensively in
Jordan. Hundreds of sites are being recorded, placed under
the protection of the antiquities law, and settlement patterns
from various historic and prehistoric periods are being studied.
Modern cartographic methods are also making it easier to do
archaeological and ecological studies.

Methods. Various techniques have been developed over the
years for the uncovering and recording of ancient deposits.
Considerable controversy has arisen with regard to methods
of excavation although the opposing schools are doing basically
the same kind of work. After the major developments of the
late nineteenth and twentieth centuries, that is, recognition of
the architectural and cultural layers and the analysis of
ceramics and other artifacts by chronological periods, further
refinements were made in the post World War I period.
M. Wheeler had developed the study of the debris deposit,
his "geology of the site," with emphasis on vertical sections
cut through the soil and recorded in drawings. He was thus
able to define more clearly such features as foundation
trenches for walls, associated floors, intrusive pits, and others.
His chief disciple, K. Kenyon, brought his method to the
Near East. However, this approach was also accompanied by
certain tenets of interpretation which diverge from reality,
for example, that a floor should be dated by the sherds under
it and in its makeup rather than by the pottery vessels found
in situ on it. The recording produced by holders of this
view are somewhat clumsy in that each layer of soil is treated

as a locus even when it may represent only a passing phase, for example, a wind deposit during a period of abandonment. The vertical sections between excavation areas are often left in place through a sequence of several strata thus hampering the illucidation of whole structural complexes such as rooms and buildings. Pottery restoration is also hindered when part of a room is not excavated since parts of various vessels may remain in the balks. Defenders of the Wheeler-Kenyon method may thus fall into a trap. They may become servants of a system instead of making the system serve them.

Stratigraphy is, in fact, a three-dimensional feature of the antiquity site. The occupation levels are built on the ruins of the predecessors and pits, foundation trenches cut through the deposits below. Stubs of older walls are often incorporated into later structures and soil containing earlier artifacts was used to fill in constructing floors and other features in the latest stratum. Potsherds from earlier periods thus work their way up in a mound and later sherds work their way downward. For that reason, dating should be based on whole vessels *in situ* wherever possible.

Recording must also be designed to cope with the three-dimensional situation. Vertical sections in the five-meter squares preserve only one dimension of the deposits. The photographs, taken constantly during the excavation process, give a realistic dimension to the structures and other features, especially when a person is included as a human measuring stick. But the most accurate record is that on the horizontal plane, the draftsmen's accurate scale plan of the area, with recorded levels for floors, walls, and other features. Artifacts must be recorded in their exact position both by depth and area. The finds are related to their feature (pit, floor, etc.), the feature to its structure or structures, and these later are then associated with all other such features that were contemporary on the site. Prose descriptions of each locus and of each occupational level (consisting of all the loci that originally came into existence during the same period) serve to fill in the picture.

Philosophy. Methods of excavation and other research will naturally be shaped to suit the goals of the project. The attitude of the investigator to archaeological research determines his goals and thus his methods. First and foremost, archaeology should devote itself to the material way of life of ancient man. Only when actual epigraphic finds are made can it be said that the excavation is producing *historical* information. Too often the archaeologist has assumed that his goal was to excavate the history of the site. The method chosen is that of excavating a narrowly restricted area "to get the sequence" of occupation levels. Though sometimes necessary, such a method is destructive of the real occupation features that played a role in the life of the inhabitants. It is better to uncover larger areas, logical assemblages of loci that together will illustrate the character of the occupation in its respective phases. The sequence will also be obtained but not at the expense of spatial stratigraphy.

Interpretation of archaeological information, even when it includes many laboratory reports and even the most careful and objective recording, is still a subjective affair. Though the objects found have an objective reality, their meaning as witnesses to life on the site can only be grasped by the exercise of human judgment. For example, two major activities in the past, public building works in times of prosperity and brutal destruction in times of war, usually leave their traces in the ruins of an ancient site. However, the dating of such features as structures and destruction levels, depends upon some precise link with known historical events. In even the best of cases, that essential link between material finds and historical or even ethnic factors is tenuous in Palestinian archaeology. This is due to the paucity of written materials discovered in stratified contexts. Recently there has been some criticism of the "biblical" archaeologist for being too bound up with his philological and historical studies to do objective work in the field. If anything, the "biblical" archaeologist has given too much credence to the "objectivity" of his material finds at the expense of sound historical analysis apart from mere archaeological evidence. One must work in the two disciplines separately and then exercise the utmost caution when trying to link them up. Most archaeologists' historical syntheses are highly tentative at best.

For the time being, it is better to concentrate on illucidating the material culture reflected at a particular site along with its chronological development. Every modern excavation should be coordinated with a level regional survey as well as geological and other investigations aimed at archaeometric evaluations. The cultural analysis of artifacts and the social organization reflected in the layout of the site play a dominant role in this interpretation. All these factors together may then be placed in the framework of the known historical details and an attempt at synthesis be made. (A.F.R.)

ARCHANGEL *See* ANGEL

ARCHELAUS *See* HEROD

ARCHER *See* ARMS AND ARMOR

ARCHIPPUS A Christian of Colossae to whom Paul refers as "our fellow soldier" (Col. 4:17; Philem. 2).

ARD, ARDITES A grandson of Benjamin who is also called Addar. His descendants were known as Ardites (Num. 26:40; 1 Chron. 8:3).

ARDON A descendant of Judah and Caleb (1 Chron. 2:18).

ARELI A son of Gad and founder of the family of the Arelites (Num. 26:17).

AREOPAGUS The name of a group of learned people in Athens who on one occasion met to hear Paul. In these meetings of the Areopagus the judges of Athens conducted court, examined candidates and appointed lecturers. Paul was taken before them to explain his message (Acts 17:16ff.).

ARETAS The dynastic name of the kings of Nabatea. One is mentioned in the NT, probably Aretas IV, the father-in-law of Herod the Tetrarch, whose governor at Damascus tried to seize Paul (2 Cor. 11:32).

ARGOB A region which included sixty fortified cities in Bashan which was conquered by and became the tribal area of one-half of Manasseh (Deut. 3:4; Josh. 13:29, 30; 1 Kgs. 4:13).

ARIDAI One of Haman's sons (Esth. 9:9).

ARIDATHA One of Haman's sons (Esth. 9:8).

ARIEL 1. A man of Israel with Ezra in Babylon (Ezra. 8:16).
2. A symbolic name given to the city of Jerusalem by Isaiah in which he compares Jerusalem with the area of the altar in the temple (Isa. 29:1, 2, 7).

ARIMATHEA The unidentified hometown of one Joseph who took possession of the body of Jesus after the crucifixion and buried it in a tomb which he had prepared for himself (Mt. 27:57).

ARIOCH 1. One of the kings in the confederacy which plundered Sodom and Gomorrah (Gen. 14:1).
2. The executioner of King Nebuchadnezzar of Babylon (Dan. 2:14-16).

ARISAI One of Haman's sons (Esth. 9:9).

ARISTARCHUS A Macedonian traveling companion of Paul who was later also one of his fellow prisoners (Acts 19:29; 27:2; Col. 4:10).

ARISTOBULUS A Christian at Rome to whom Paul sent greetings (Rom. 16:10).

ARK   1. Noah's ark. A ship of wood built by Noah about the size
of a light cruiser which had three stories and a door on
one of its sides. It housed Noah and his family, seven pairs of
every kind of clean animal and one pair of every unclean
(Gen. 6:11—8:22).

2. Ark of the Covenant of the Lord, also called Ark of the
Testimony, Ark of the Lord, and Ark of God (Deut. 10:8;
Ex. 25:22; 1 Sam. 3:3; Josh. 3:13). It is described in Exodus
25:10-22 in the cloud over which the Lord appeared (Ex.
25:17). It was covered by a gold lid called an atonement
cover. Bezalel was the master craftsman who worked under
the direction laid down by Moses (Ex. 37:1-9). In it were
kept the two tablets of stone on which were inscribed the
Ten Commandments, a gold jar of manna, and beside it a
copy of the Book of the Law (Heb. 9:4; Deut. 31:26). The
whole was housed in the Most Holy Place of the tabernacle
(Ex. 26:34). The Ark, under the charge of the Kohathites,
went with the Israelites during the years of wandering in the
exodus. It was at the head of the people as they crossed
the Jordan and was put in a sanctuary at Shiloh (Num. 3:29-
32; Deut. 31:9; Josh. 3:11, 17; 1 Sam. 1:3; 3:3). It was
taken by the Philistines to Ashdod, moved to Gath and Ekron,
and later returned by them to Beth Shemesh from which
place it came eventually to Jerusalem in the days of David by
way of Kiriath Jearim, finally to be placed in the Most Holy
Place in the temple built by Solomon (1 Sam. 5:1, 8, 10; 7:1;
2 Sam. 6:2, 3, 17; 1 Kgs. 8:1, 6). Since the destruction of
the first temple the Ark has been lost.

ARKITE   An inhabitant of a village on the border between Ephraim and
Benjamin. David's friend Hushai was one (Josh. 16:2;
2 Sam. 16:16; 17:5). See also ARKITES.

ARKITES   A group of people descended from Canaan who originated in
the area of Sidon (Gen. 10:17).

ARMAGEDDON   The location of the "battle on the great day of God Almighty"
(Rev. 16:14, 16). The word translated means "Mount
Megiddo." In the great valley below the ancient city of
Megiddo many famous battles of antiquity were fought and
hence many consider the word Armageddon to refer to
an eschatological battle that will be fought in that valley, the
Valley of Jezreel. *See also* GEOGRAPHY OF THE HOLY LAND.

ARMLET   A band worn on the upper arm as distinct from a bracelet
which was worn on the lower arm. They were considered
items of luxury (Num. 31:50).

ARMONI A son of Saul who with his brother and five of the grandchildren of Saul were given to the Gibeonites by David. They were hanged by the Gibeonites (2 Sam. 21:8).

ARMOR-BEARER The leaders were accompanied into the battle by young men who bore their implements, whether shield, spears, or arrows, and who gave the *coup de grace* to fallen enemies (1 Sam. 17:7; 2 Sam. 18:14, 15; Judg. 9:54).

ARMS AND ARMOR In defense the body was covered with a helmet, a coat of mail or breastplate, and greaves of bronze. A shield or buckler was carried. Offensive weapons consisted of the sword, spear or javelin, sling, bows and arrows, battering rams.

Helmets were often nationally distinctive but no description of an Israelite one exists. Some were made of bronze (1 Sam. 17:5, 38). The word is also used in both testaments, figuratively, of salvation (Isa. 59:17; Eph. 6:14). Greaves were of leather or metal and protected the legs both front and back from ankle to knee. Goliath wore greaves of bronze (1 Sam. 17:6).

Shields or bucklers were probably leather strips fastened over a wooden frame. They were either round or oval in shape. Those covered with bronze, and even gold, were known (Ps. 35:2; Jer. 46:3; 1 Kgs. 14:26, 27). The shield too was used symbolically, for divine protection, salvation, and faith (Ps. 3:3; 18:2; Eph. 6:16).

Swords were of at least three types. One was of a short two-edged variety carried by all the foot soldiers (Judg. 3:16; 1 Sam. 25:13). A second was long handled and sickle-shaped. The third type was a long straight-edged sword of iron. In the Bible the sword is also used symbolically, of war and destruction. In the NT it symbolizes the penetrating power of the word of God (Mic. 4:3; Eph. 6:17).

The spear, lance, or javelin was a weapon of offense (Josh. 8:18; Job 41:29). The same were heavy, long, and tipped with flint or metal, while others were lighter and designed rather for throwing than jabbing (1 Kgs. 18:28; 1 Sam. 18:11).

The bow and arrow were used in longer range offensive actions by the archers. Bows were made of a strong elastic wood or were of the composite type made of alternating layers of wood and horn glued and bound together. The strings were of gut from one of several animals. The arrows were made of reeds or light wood, and feathers, and were usually tipped with flint or metal. Some were either incendiary or the figure at least is of fire (Ps. 7:13; Eph. 6:16). Arrows were kept in quivers usually carried by the armorbearer.

The sling was of two thongs of leather braided cords with a pocket between them for the smooth, rounded stone. The stone was fired by whirling the apparatus round and round the head and then suddenly releasing one of the thongs (1 Sam. 17:40, 49; 2 Chron. 26:14). Each army had special corps of slingers and the Benjamites seemed to have been specialists (1 Chron. 12:2). "Machines" were also used. These consisted of catapults and battering rams. The former slung arrows or large stones (2 Chron. 26:15). The latter were either simple beams of great length, sometimes metal-tipped, and housed in a protective tower mounted on wheels. They are noted in Ezekiel 4:2 and were possibly used in 2 Samuel 20:15.

The axe, war club, hammer, and deadly weapons were also used by the warrior for close-range fighting (Prov. 25:18; Jer. 46:22; 51:20; Ezek. 9:2).

ARMY In earliest times able-bodied men were expected to bear arms and support their chief. The men were called to arms by a messenger or the ram's horn (Judg. 6:35; 1 Sam. 13:3). Conscription seems to have started with the monarchy under the first king, Saul (1 Sam. 14:52). By David's time the army was arranged in twelve parts of 24,000 each with each part serving one month each year (1 Chron. 27:1). Males twenty years old and over were liable for service (Num. 1:3). Something of the organization is reflected in 2 Chron. 25:5; Num. 2:33; Deut. 20:5-9; 24:5. The men received no pay but all did share in the booty (1 Sam. 30:24, 25). The first mechanized units appear in the Israel of King Solomon with his chariots (1 Kgs. 4:26). The army units consisted of families, thousands, hundreds, fifties, and tens. Commanders are mentioned and officers, without further detail (1 Chron. 27:1).

ARNAN A descendant of David (1 Chron. 3:21).

ARNI *See* ARAM, 2

ARNON A river which flows into the Sea of the Arabah (the Salt or Dead Sea) near its middle on the east, separating Moab and Ammon (the Amorites) and later the tribes of Reuben and Gad (Num. 21:13; Deut. 3:16).

ARODI A son of Gad, whose descendants were known as Arodites (Gen. 46:16; Num 26:17).

AROER 1. A city (228-097) on the northern bank of the Arnon gorge on the southern border of the kingdom of Sihon king of the Amorites (Num. 32:33) and later in the tribal area of Reuben.

Later it was fought over by the Moabites and the Syrians (Josh. 12:2; Deut. 3:12; 2 Kgs. 10:33 and the Moabite Inscription).

2. A town (148-062) in the territory of Judah near Beersheba (1 Sam. 30:28).

AROMA That which affects the sense of smell favorably, otherwise an odor, or mere smoke. This is true in both the literal and figurative senses (Num. 15:3; Jn. 11:39; Isa. 65:5).

ARPAD A city of Syria which fell to the Assyrians in the middle of the eighth century B.C. and used as a warning to Israel by the Assyrians (2 Kgs. 18:34; Isa. 10:9).

ARPHAXAD A son of Shem and ancestor of Abraham; probably also a tribal group (Gen. 10:22, 24; Lk. 3:36).

ARROW *See* ARMS AND ARMOR

ARTAXERXES A Persian king, son of Xerxes, who reigned from 465 to 424 B.C. He permitted both Ezra and Nehemiah to return with groups to rebuild the temple and the walls of Jerusalem (Ezra 7:1-7; Neh. 2:1, 5, 6).

ARTEMAS A companion of Paul (Tit. 3:12).

ARTEMIS *See* DEITIES

ARUBBOTH An unidentified site perhaps in the Plain of Sharon near Socoh (1 Kgs. 4:10).

ARUMAH A city (180-172) near Shechem (Nablus) where Abimelech lived for a time (Judg. 9:41).

ARVAD A leading Phoenician city (229-473) north of Byblos and an important maritime center (Gen. 10:18; Ezek. 27:8, 11).

ARZA When King Baasha of Israel was drinking in Araz's house he was murdered by Zimri who took Israel's throne (1 Kgs. 16:9, 10).

ASA 1. A Levite son of Elkanah (1 Chron. 9:16).

2. *See* KINGS OF JUDAH AND ISRAEL.

ASAHEL 1. A nephew of David and brother to Joab (1 Sam. 2:18). He was one of David's mighty men (2 Sam. 23:24) but was killed by Abner.

2. A Levite instructor in the Law in the time of Jehoshaphat (2 Chron. 17:8).

3. A temple overseer in the time of Hezekiah (2 Chron. 31:13).

4. A contemporary of Ezra (Ezra 10:15).

ASAIAH 1. A descendant of Simeon (1 Chron. 4:36).

2. A descendant of Levi who helped David bring the Ark to Jerusalem (1 Chron. 6:30; 15:11-15).

3. A returnee from the captivity in Babylon (1 Chron. 9:5).

4. A servant of King Josiah in the group that went to inquire of the prophetess Huldah about the Book of the Law discovered by Hilkiah (2 Kgs. 22:12-14).

ASAPH 1. One of David's musicians, a descendant of Levi, who with his family after him played and sang in the service of music before the Ark (1 Chron. 15:17; 16:4, 5). One hundred and twenty eight of these singers came back from Babylon with Zerubbabel and resumed their duties in the second temple (Ezra 2:41; 3:10). Twelve Psalms are entitled "A Psalm of Asaph" (Ps. 50, 73-83).

2. The father of a recorder in the days of King Hezekiah (2 Kgs. 18:18).

3. A keeper of the king's forest who was instructed to help Nehemiah to secure lumber (Neh. 2:8).

4. One whose descendants were gatekeepers in the days of David (1 Chron. 26:1).

ASAREL A descendant of Judah (1 Chron. 4:16).

ASARELAH One of David's temple musicians, also called Jesharelah (1 Chron. 25:2).

ASCENSION While the word is not used, the conception of the ascension of Christ is clear from the several passages which note that he "ascended" to the Father (Jn. 20:17; Eph. 4:8).

ASCENTS, SONG OF *See* SONG OF ASCENTS

ASENATH A daughter of Potiphera, priest of On, and the wife of Joseph (Gen. 41:45).

ASHAN An unidentified town in the tribal area of Judah and Simeon which became a Levite city (Josh. 15:42; 19:7; 1 Chron. 6:59).

ASHBEL A son of Benjamin (Gen. 46:21).

ASHDOD *See* PHILISTINE CITIES

ASHER A son of Jacob (Gen. 30:13) and founder of the tribe by that name which located on the seacoast north of the Carmel range and west of the Jezreel Valley.

ASHERAH, ASHERIM, ASHEROTH *See* DEITIES

ASHHUR A son of Caleb (1 Chron. 2:24).

ASHIMA *See* DEITIES

ASHKELON *See* PHILISTINE CITIES

ASHKENAZ A people and country on the upper Euphrates near Armenia (Gen. 10:3; Jer. 51:27).

ASHNAH Two towns in the western hills of Judah between Eshtaol and Hebron (Josh. 15:33, 43).

ASHPENAZ Chief of court officials at Babylon in the time of Nebuchadnezzar (Dan. 1:3).

ASHTAROTH 1. Plural of Ashtoreth; *see* DEITIES.

2. The capital of Og, king of Bashan, a city (243-244) inhabited by giants (Rephaites) (Deut. 1:4; Josh. 12:4). After the Israelite conquest, this city was in the tribal area of Manasseh, (Josh. 13:31) one of the Levitical cities (1 Chron. 6:71).

ASHTEROTH KARNAIM Where Kedorlaomer and the kings with him defeated the Rephaites (Gen. 14:5).

ASHTORETH *See* DEITIES

ASHURITES A group over which Abner made Ish-Bosheth, Saul's son, the king (2 Sam. 2:9).

ASHVATH A descendant of Asher (1 Chron. 7:33).

ASIA *See* GEOGRAPHY OF THE HOLY LAND

ASIEL A descendant of Simeon (1 Chron. 4:35).

ASLEEP A word sometimes used to denote death (1 Thess. 4:13).

ASNAH His sons were a special class of temple servants who returned from Babylon with Zerubbabel (Ezra 2:50).

ASPATHA One of the sons of Haman (Esth. 9:7).

ASRIEL A descendant of Manasseh (Num. 26:31).

ASSHUR A son of Shem who gave his name to a country, Assyria. (Gen. 10:22). *See* ASSYRIA AND ASSHUR.

ASSHURITES A group descended from Delan who was a grandson of Abraham by Keturah (Gen. 25:3).

ASSIR Two persons descended from Kohath (1 Chron. 6:22, 23).

ASSOS A seaport town to which Paul walked from Troas (Acts 20:13, 14).

ASSYRIA AND ASSHUR Among the five sons of Shem was Asshur (Gen. 10:22), from whom came the Assyrian people. In their highland territory in northern Mesopotamia (*see* GEOGRAPHY OF THE HOLY LAND), they developed as rugged shepherds (Nah. 3:18). But their culture began under the Hamite Nimrod (Gen. 10:11) from the south; Sumerians settled in Assyria in about 2900 B.C. and Sargon of Accad included it in his Semitic empire of 2400. Language and religion, except for the national god Asshur, were thus borrowed from others; but the Assyrians proved to be good organizers, disciplined and warlike, similar to the Romans in later history. Puzur-Ashur I (2100) first assumed the kingship; but while Assyria developed commercial colonies as far as Cappadocia, it remained generally under the control of Babylon.

Assyrian independence came under Ashur-uballit I in 1375. The greatest of the early Assyrians, however, was Tiglath-Pileser I, who brought order and empire to the Near East from his capital city of Asshur, 1115 on. He twice captured Babylon, conquered to the Black Sea, and took as far south as Arvad on the Mediterranean. He rehearsed, indeed, the Sargonid conquests of the eighth and seventh centuries. Of his immediate successors, only Ashur-rabi III showed strength: in 1000 B.C. he conquered to the northeast corner of the Mediterranean but just missed contact with his contemporary David, who had advanced to the Euphrates.

Assyria experienced a century of power under four monarchs from 884 to 782 B.C. Ashur-nasir-pal II (884-859) was one of the most hideous figures of all history, cruel, but a powerful soldier directing his Assyrian bowmen. He took Carchemish and as far as Lebanon; and it is possible that Omri of Israel may have paid him tribute, 876 B.C. Shalmaneser III (859-824), after various campaigns, reached Qarqar, north of Hamath on the Orontes in 853 B.C. Syria, Israel under Ahab, and others held him off in a great battle. But in 841 (*see* CHRONOLOGY) he ravaged the Syrian country; and Jehu of Israel paid him tribute, as depicted on the "black obelisk." Shamshi-Adad V (824-811) was not in the west but did break Babylon. Adad-nirari III (811-782) overran Syria in 803; and, because of the Assyrian intervention, Jehoahaz of Israel was able to defeat Damascus in three battles (2 Kgs. 13:5). Weak kings followed in Assyrian Nineveh from 782 to 745, under one of whom Jonah the prophet, an advisor to Jeroboam II of Israel (793-753), won an audience as he could not have before or after, perhaps in connection with the solar eclipse of 763 (Jonah 3:5).

In 745 a general Pulu (biblical "Pul," 2 Kgs. 15:19) revolted and put an end to the dynasty of Tiglath-Pileser I. Significantly, he assumed the title Tiglath-Pileser III (1 Chron. 5:26); and under him and his successors, the Sargonids, Assyria rose to even greater heights than it had known under his namesake. Azariah of Judah headed a western confederacy to oppose him but was defeated in 743. Menahem of Israel and Rezin of Damascus, though not Azariah himself, who escaped, were forced to pay heavy tribute to Assyria (2 Kgs. 15:19). In seeming retaliation Rezin and Pekah of Israel attacked Azariah's grandson Ahaz of Judah, who foolishly appealed to Nineveh for help (16:7). Tiglath-Pileser marched to Gaza in 734, took three-and-a-half Israelite tribes of Gilead and Galilee captive in 733 (15:29), and destroyed Damascus in 732. He died in 727, to be succeeded by Shalmaneser V, who took Samaria just before his death in 722 (17:3-6); and Sargon II deported the remaining six-and-a-half Israelite tribes (v. 18), replacing them with the foreign "Samaritans" (vv. 24-41; cf. Ezra 4:2, 10; Isa. 7:8).

Hezekiah of Judah was left to face Assyria. He twice submitted before the attacks of Sargon in 720 and 711, only to revolt upon the accession of his rash son Sennacherib (705-681), in defiance of Isaiah's warnings (Isa. 22:8-14; 30:1-7). Sennacherib advanced, and in 701 lost much of Judah and Hezekiah was forced to pay a heavy indemnity (2 Kgs. 18:13-16). Yet when the Assyrian broke his truce, demanded further surrender, and went on to blaspheme the God of Israel (36:15, 20), God sent his angel, who struck down 185,000 of the Assyrian army in one night (by plague?) and accomplished a deliverance for his people that ranks second only to their crossing of the Red Sea 750 years before (37:36).

Hezekiah's son Manasseh gave up the independence that had been so dearly won by submitting to Esarhaddon (681-669) in 675 as the latter prepared to attack Egypt. He was later taken captive by Ashurbanipal (669-626), perhaps after the eastern revolts of 652-648 (2 Chron. 33:11). But this was Israel's last contact with Assyria. The later Sargonids had overextended themselves. After 628 Scythian barbarians flooded over the once great Assyrian empire; and Nineveh itself fell to the combined forces of Media and Babylon in 612, just as the prophets Balaam and Nahum once predicted (Num. 24:24; Nah. 3:1, 19). (J.B.P.)

ATARAH The wife of one of the descendants of Judah (1 Chron. 2:26).

ATAROTH 1. A town (213-109) given to and built by the tribe of Gad in the former area of Sihon, king of the Amorites (Num. 32:33, 34).

2. A town in the territory of the descendants of Joseph (Josh. 16:2, 7).

3. *See* ATAROTH ADDAR.

ATAROTH ADDAR A city on the border between Benjamin and Ephraim (Josh. 16:5; 18:13).

ATER One or more persons who came back from the Babylonian exile with Zerubbabel. One seems to have been the head of the clan, another a gatekeeper, another a signer of the covenant with Nehemiah (Neh. 7:21, 45; 10:17).

ATHACH An unidentified town in southern Judah where David sent some of the plunder from Ziklag (1 Sam. 30:30).

ATHAIAH A descendant of Judah who lived in Jerusalem (Neh. 11:4).

ATHALIAH 1. *See* KINGS OF JUDAH AND ISRAEL.

2. A descendant of Benjamin (1 Chron. 8:26).

3. One who came up with Ezra from Babylon (Ezra 8:7).

ATHARIM A trade route in the Negev (Num. 21:1).

ATHENS The capital of the Greek state of Attica with a long and illustrious history. Here Paul presented his case to the Areopagus (Acts 17:15—18:1). *See* AREOPAGUS.

ATHLAI A Jew who divorced his foreign wife in the time of Ezra (Ezra 10:28).

ATONEMENT *See* CHRIST, WORK OF

ATONEMENT, DAY OF *See* CALENDAR and FESTIVALS

ATROTH BETH JOAB A descendant of Judah (1 Chron. 2:54).

ATROTH-SHOPHAN An unidentified town in the region of Moab east of the Jordan (Num. 32:35).

ATTAI 1. A descendant of Judah. His father was an Egyptian slave (1 Chron. 2:35, 36).

2. A descendant of Gad who joined David at Ziklag (1 Chron. 12:11).

3. A son of King Rehoboam of Judah (2 Chron. 11:20).

ATTALIA A seaport town in the Roman province of Pamphylia from which Paul sailed to Antioch at the end of his first missionary journey (Acts 14:25).

AUGURY *See* DIVINATION

AUGUSTUS The name conferred by the Roman senate on the emperor of Rome at the time of the birth of Jesus (Lk. 2:1). Herod built Caesarea and Caesarea Philippi in his honor.

AVEN 1. A place in the kingdom of Damascus referred to as "Valley of Aven" in Amos 1:5.

2. See also BETH AVEN.

AVENGER OF BLOOD Often in primitive societies, in the Mosaic Law as well, a murderer was to be killed by the avenger of blood who was the nearest relative of the murdered. The OT makes a clear distinction between manslaughter and willful murder, however. One accused of the former could flee to a city of refuge and be safe until the judges heard his case. The entire procedure is carefully prescribed (Num. 35:9-34).

AVITH An unidentified Moabite town, residence of the king (1 Chron. 1:46).

AVVA A city from which the Assyrian king brought people to Samaria after he removed captives from the latter. These were among those who intermarried and the Samaritans were the result (2 Kgs. 17:24).

AVVIM A town of Benjamin (Josh. 18:23).

AVVITES 1. The inhabitants of the area near Gaza who were destroyed and replaced by the Philistines (Deut. 2:23).

2. A people in Samaria after the prisoner exchange policy of the Assyrian king at the time of the captivity of the ten tribes; their gods were Nibhaz and Tartak (2 Kgs. 17:31).

AWL A small tool for boring mentioned in connection with the practice of permanently enslaving an individual (Ex. 21:6).

AXE *See* ARMS AND ARMOR

AYYAH A town of Ephraim (1 Chron. 7:28).

AZALIAH A scribe in the days of King Josiah (2 Kgs. 22:3).

AZANIAH A descendant of Levi who signed the covenant with Nehemiah (Neh. 10:9).

AZAREL 1. A Benjamite who joined David at Ziklag (1 Chron. 12:6).

2. A musician at the temple (1 Chron. 25:18).

3. A leader in the tribe of Dan in David's day (1 Chron. 27:22).

4. A man who married a foreign woman during the Babylonian captivity (Ezra 10:41).

5. A priest in Nehemiah's day (Neh. 11:13).

6. A musician in Nehemiah's day (Neh. 12:36).

AZARIAH 1. *See* KINGS OF JUDAH AND ISRAEL.

2 and 3. Two descendants of Judah (1 Chron. 2:8, 38).

4. A priest, a high official in Solomon's time (1 Kgs. 4:2).

5. One over the officers in Solomon's time (1 Kgs. 4:5).

6, 7, and 8. Three Levites in the time of David (1 Chron. 6:9, 10, 36).

9. A prophet in the days of King Asa who urged reforms (2 Chron. 15:1-7).

10. A son of King Jehoshaphat (2 Chron. 21:2).

11 and 12. Two commanders of hundreds who helped the priest Jehoiada to overthrow Queen Athaliah and put Josiah on the throne. The second may be the same as 3 above (2 Chron. 23:1).

13. The high priest in King Uzziah's day who rebuked the king for assuming a priestly prerogative (2 Chron. 26:16-20).

14. A chief of Ephraim who supported the prophet Oded in not allowing the Israelites to keep captives of Judah taken in a battle (2 Chron. 28:8-14).

15. Father of a Levite who helped in the cleansing of the temple in the days of King Hezekiah (2 Chron. 29:12).

16. A Levite who was involved in the cleansing of the temple as in 16 above (2 Chron. 29:12).

17. A high priest in the days of King Hezekiah (2 Chron. 31:10).

18. One of the builders of the wall in the time of Nehemiah (Neh. 3:23).

19. One who came up from the Babylonian captivity with Zerubbabel (Neh. 7:7). He is called Seraiah in Ezra 2:2.

20. One who helped the people understand the Law in the time of Ezra (Neh. 8:7).

21. One who signed the covenant with Nehemiah (Neh. 10:2).

22. One who was in the dedication procession at the completion of the building of the walls by Nehemiah (Neh. 12:33).

23. A leader who called Jeremiah the Prophet a liar because of the message he brought (Jer. 43:2).

24. The Hebrew name of Abednego one of Daniel's three friends in Babylon (Dan. 1:6).

AZAZ A descendant of Reuben (1 Chron. 5:8).

AZAZEL On the Day of Atonement two goats were selected. Aaron as the high priest was instructed to cast lots on them to see which one was to be sacrificed and which one was to be driven out into the wilderness bearing the sins of the people. The latter was the goat for Azazel (Lev. 16:7-26). There are a number of surmises as to the interpretation of this word, but that it was intended as an object lesson for the people to remind them of the removal of their sin is clear.

AZAZIAH 1. A descendant of Ephraim (1 Chron. 27:20).

2. A Levite temple musician (1 Chron. 15:21).

3. An officer in charge of the contributions and tithes in the days of King Hezekiah (2 Chron. 31:13).

AZBUK Father of a Nehemiah (not the leader and author of the book) who worked on the restoration of the walls in Nehemiah's days (Neh. 3:16).

AZEKAH A city (144-123) in the western foothills (shephelah) taken by Joshua and allocated to the tribe of Judah, in the buffer area between Judah and the Philistines (Josh. 10:10; 15:35; 1 Sam. 17:1). Just east of Azekah David vanquished the giant Goliath. It was one of the last cities to hold out against the Babylonian invaders as is also interestingly confirmed by the Lachish Letters of archaeological fame (Jer. 34:7). Judeans still lived there after the Babylonian captivity (Neh. 11:30).

AZEL A descendant of Saul and Jonathan (1 Chron. 8:37, 38).

AZGAD The head of family that came back from the Babylonian captivity with Zerubbabel and signed the covenant with Nehemiah (Ezra 2:12; Neh. 10:15).

AZIEL *See* JAAZIEL

AZIZA One who put away his foreign wife in Ezra's day (Ezra 10:27).

AZMAVETH 1. One of David's mighty men (2 Sam. 23:31).

2. A Benjamite whose son joined David at Ziklag, perhaps the same as 1 above (1 Chron. 12:3).

3. A descendant of Saul who came back from the Babylonian captivity (1 Chron. 8:36).

4. An official in charge of the treasury in David's day, perhaps the same as 1 above (1 Chron. 27:25).

5. A village (175-138) resettled after the Babylonian captivity (Neh. 12:29). Also called Beth Azmaveth (Neh. 7:28).

AZMON A town (085-010) on Judah's southern border not far from the "Wadi of Egypt" (Josh 15:4).

AZNOTH TABOR A city (186-237) in the tribal area of Naphtali (Josh. 19:32).

AZOR A descendant of Zerubbabel in the ancestry of Jesus (Mt. 1:13, 14).

AZOTUS *See* PHILISTINE CITIES

AZRIEL 1. A leader of that part of the tribe of Manasseh which stayed east of the Jordan (1 Chron. 5:24).

2. A descendant of Naphtali (1 Chron. 27:19).

3. The father of one whom King Jehoiakim commanded to burn the scroll which Baruch wrote at Jeremiah's dictation (Jer. 36:24-27).

AZRIKAM 1. A descendant of David through Solomon (1 Chron. 3:23).

2. A descendant of Saul through Jonathan (1 Chron. 8:38).

3. A Levite who returned from the Babylonian captivity (1 Chron. 9:14).

4. The commander of King Ahaz's palace (2 Chron. 28:7).

AZUBAH 1. A wife of Caleb (1 Chron. 2:18).

2. The mother of King Jehoshaphat of Judah (2 Chron. 20:31).

AZZAN A descendant of Issachar (Num. 34:26).

AZZUR 1. A signer of the covenant with Nehemiah (Neh. 10:17).

2. Father of the false prophet Hananiah in the days of King Zedekiah and the prophet Jeremiah (Jer. 28:1).

3. Father of one of the leaders of the people in the days of the prophet Ezekiel (Ezek. 11:1).

B

BAAL The word Baal means "lord" or "husband." It is also the name of a deity. Hence names compounded with Baal mean the owner, the lord of, or the particular Baal-deity worshiped in that place after which the place gets its name.

1. An unidentified city in Simeon, perhaps the Baaleth Beer (Ramah in the Negev) of Joshua 19:8 (1 Chron. 4:33).

2. A descendant of Reuben (1 Chron. 5:5).

3. A descendant of Benjamin (1 Chron. 8:30).

4. *See also* DEITIES.

BAALAH 1. An alternate name for the town of Kiriath Jearim (159-135) on the border between Judah and Benjamin (Josh. 15:9). The Ark of the Covenant, lost to the Philistines in battle in the days of the priest, Eli, eventually was returned by way of Beth Shemesh to Kiriath Jearim (1 Sam. 6:21; 7:1) from which place, also called Baalah of Jud, King David brought it to Jerusalem (2 Sam. 6:2). It is also called Kiriath Baal (Josh. 15:60).

2. A location on the border of the tribe of Judah near Jabneel called Mount Baalah (Josh. 15:11).

3. One of the most southerly towns on the border of the tribe of Judah, in the Negev (Josh. 15:10) also belonging to the tribe of Simeon called Balah and Bilhah (Josh. 19:3; 1 Chron. 4:29).

BAALATH A town (129-138) in the original tribal area of Dan later rebuilt by Solomon for grain storage (Josh. 19:44; 1 Kgs. 9:18). *See also* BAAL, 2.

BAALATH BEER *See* BAAL, 2

BAAL-BERITH *See* DEITIES

BAAL OF JUDAH *See* BAALAH, 1

BAAL GAD An unidentified town at the foot of Mount Hermon taken in the conquest by Joshua (Josh. 11:17).

BAAL HAMON The unidentified site of one of Solomon's vineyards (Song 8:11).

BAAL-HANAN 1. A king of Edom (Gen. 36:38).
2. The tender of David's olive and sycamore trees (1 Chron. 27:28).

BAAL HAZOR The place near Ephraim (177-153) where Absalom's servants killed Amnon (2 Sam. 13:23ff.).

BAAL HERMON A site in the area of the half of the tribe of Manasseh whose allotment was east of the Jordan (Judg. 3:3).

BAALIS A late king of Ammon (Jer. 40:14).

BAAL MEON A city in Moab that was rebuilt by the Reubenites after the conquest by Joshua, but retaken by the Moabites in the ninth century and its destruction prophesied. It is also called Beon, Beth Baal Meon, and Beth Meon (Num. 32:3, 38; Josh. 13:17; 1 Chron. 5:8; Jer. 48:23; Ezek. 25:9).

BAAL PEOR *See* DEITIES

BAAL PERAZIM A place whose exact location is unknown but where David defeated the Philistines. Perhaps the Mount Perazim of Isaiah 28:21 (2 Sam. 5:18-20).

BAAL SHALISHAH An unidentified place from which food was brought to Elisha and his school of prophets, where it was multiplied to feed a large number (2 Kgs. 4:42-44).

BAAL TAMAR A place from which the attack of Gibeah was launched in the battle between Israel and the men of Benjamin (Judg. 20:33).

BAALZEBUB *See* DEITIES

BAAL ZEPHON 1. An unidentified place in Egypt near where the Israelites camped just before crossing the Red (Reed) Sea (Ex. 14:2).

2. *See also* DEITIES.

BAANA 1 and 2. Two of Solomon's officers who provided food for the king, one from the Megiddo area and the other from Asher (1 Kgs. 4:12, 16).

3. Father of a Zadok who worked on the walls with Nehemiah (Neh. 3:4).

BAANAH 1. One who with his brother murdered Saul's son Ish-Bosheth and was on that account executed by David (2 Sam. 4:5ff.).

2. Father of one of David's mighty men (1 Chron. 11:30).

3. One of the important returnees with Zerubbabel from the Babylonian captivity (Ezra 2:2).

BAARA One of the divorced wives of a descendant of Benjamin (1 Chron. 8:8).

BAASEIAH An ancestor of the temple singer Asaph (1 Chron. 6:40).

BAASHA *See* KINGS OF JUDAH AND ISRAEL

BABEL 1. Part of the kingdom of Nimrod, son of Cush, son of Ham, son of Noah, a mighty hunter (Gen. 10:10). In some versions it is called Babylon.

2. The word has two interpretations: *bab ili* (gate of God) or *balal* (confusion), the name of the city where men tried to build a tower with its top in the heavens, where God confused the existing single language of man into many and then scattered mankind over the face of the earth (Gen. 11:1-9).

BABOON *See* BEASTS

BABYLON, BABYLONIA The history of Babylon in Mesopotamia commences with the kingdom of the Hamite Nimrod, three generations after the Flood (Gen. 10:10). Soon thereafter it became the site of the "ziggurat," or temple-tower of Babel, mankind's attempt at self-glorification which God frustrated by the introduction of differing languages (Gen. 11:7, 8). The very name comes from *balal* "to confound" (verse 9), though the Babylonians preferred to derive it from the Akkadian, *bab ili*, meaning "gate of God." During the third millennium B.C., the center of

Mesopotamian power shifted southward, first to various Sumerian city-states (biblical Shinar) for the two centuries following 2400 to the Semitic empire of Sargon I of Akkad, and then again from 2100-2000 to Sumer. In its renaissance under the third dynasty of Ur on the Persian Gulf, it was the home of Abraham before his call to Canaan (verses 28-31). *See also* CHRONOLOGY.

Sumu-abu founded the first, or Amorite, Dynasty of Babylon, 1850-1550 B.C. Hammurabi (1728-1686), the sixth king, took Sumer and held to the north. He made Babylonian, in the Sumerian character, an international language and is best known for his law code, certain elements of which find parallels in the Pentateuchal codes that God revealed to Moses some two and a half centuries later. The modern, lower dating for Hammurabi makes it impossible to equate him, as was once done, with the Amraphel of Shinar (Gen. 14), whose hostile contact with Abraham preceded the year 2000 (*see* CHRONOLOGY). About 1550 a Hittite raid destroyed Babylon. Barbarian Kassites invaded and held power until about 1180 B.C. Dynasty II of Isin then produced Nebuchadnezzar I (in Hebrew text also spelled Nebuchadrezzar), who showed great power but finally lost out before 1100.

Assyrian intervention characterized Babylon for centuries, until the rise of Naponassar (747-735 B.C.) marked the beginning of a new era, with struggles for independence. Marduk-pal-iddina II of Chaldea (biblical Merodach-Baladan) held the throne in Babylon from 721 to 710 and conspired with Hezekiah of Judah against Assyria (Isa. 39:1, 2), so that the prophet Isaiah announced a future exile of the Jews to this same Babylon (39:6, 7; 48:20). Sargon II of Assyria, however, proceeded to drive out Marduk-pal-iddina and personally took the throne of Babylon in 709.

Following the decline of Assyrian strength, Nabopolassar (626-605 B.C.), a native Babylonian, rose to power in Chaldea. Pushing northward he held all Babylonia by 616. He allied himself with Kyaxares the Mede and advanced to the final attack on Nineveh in 612, thus founding the Neo-Babylonian empire. At Carchemish in 605, Neco II of Egypt (see 2 Chron 35:20-24) was routed by the armies of Nabopolassar under his son Nebuchadnezzar (Jer. 46:2). (Nebuchadrezzar is rendered as Nebuchadnezzar consistently in the NIV. Some occurrences are footnoted as "Hebrew Nebuchadrezzar.") Nebuchadnezzar proceeded to occupy Judah and all the west (2 Kgs. 24:7). The prophet Jeremiah then spoke of seventy years of Babylonian domination of the Near East (Jer. 25:11; 29:10); and Daniel described Babylon as "the head of gold," the first of the four great empires that would climax in the Rome of New Testament times (Dan 2:37, 38, compare 7:4).

Succeeding to his father's throne, Nebuchadnezzar II (605-562) was faced by continuous unrest and revolt in Judah, which led to the four deportations of the divinely ordained Babylonian exile: In 605, only Daniel and a few other noble hostages (Dan. 1:1-3; 2 Chron. 36:6, 7); in 597, King Jehoiachin, Ezekiel, and 10,000 of the leaders of the people (2 Kgs. 24:12-14); in 586, King Zedekiah and the main body of the people, after the final destruction of Jerusalem (25:8-11); and in 582, some 745 others who were left after the murder of Gedaliah, the governor for the remnant (2 Kgs. 25:25; Jer. 52:30). Israel grieved by the waters of Babylon (Ps. 137), but God promised recompense for the empire's wanton cruelties (Jer. 50-51). Meanwhile Nebuchadnezzar built huge fortifications and the "hanging gardens of Babylon," which were one of the seven wonders of the ancient world. His power led to a form of insanity, "lycanthropy," described in Daniel 4.

Amil-Marduk (biblical Evil-Merodach), 562-560 B.C., granted certain honors to the captive Jewish king, Jehoiachin (2 Kgs. 25:27-30), and was succeeded by Nergal-shar-usur (biblical Nergal-Sharezer), 560-556, who had been an officer of Nebuchadnezzar at the destruction of Jerusalem (Jer. 39:3, 13). Soon thereafter the religious and commercial powers in Babylon diverted the throne to a wealthy scholar, Nabunaid, who was faced by increasing unpopularity. After 552 these powers appointed Nabunaid's son Belshazzar as regent. In October of 539 the armies of Cyrus the Persian attacked the Babylonians under Belshazzar at Opis, defeated them, and received the submission of the city of Babylon without further fighting. Daniel interpreted the handwriting on the wall against Belshazzar, and that night the citadel was taken and he was slain (Dan. 5).

Babylon continued on as one of the Persian capitals (Ezra 6:1) but gradually decreased in importance. When Peter fled from Herod Agrippa I in A.D. 44 (Acts 12:17) he may have removed to Babylon (1 Pet. 5:13), unless this last is merely a symbolic name for Rome as the corresponding harlot-city of that day (compare Rev. 17:3-6, 18). (J.B.P.)

BACA A valley noted in Psalm 84:6.

BAHURIM, BAHARUMITE Bahurim is an unidentified town between Jerusalem and Jericho, probably nearer Jerusalem. Both Shimei (who cursed David) and Azmaneth (one of David's mighty men who is called a Baharumite and a Barhumite) came from there (2 Sam. 16:5; 23:31; 1 Chron. 11:33). Jonathan hid from Absalom in Bahurim (2 Sam. 17:18ff.).

BAKBAKKAR A Levite who returned from the Babylonian captivity (1 Chron. 9:15).

BAKBUK The father of some of the men who returned from the Babylonian captivity (Ezra 2:51).

BAKBUKIAH 1. A leading Levite among the returnees from the Babylonian captivity (Neh. 11:17).

2. A temple officer after the return (Neh. 12:25).

BALAAM A man from Mesopotamia summoned by Balak, king of Moab, to come and curse the Israelites as they were entering Palestine from Egypt. An angel met him on his journey to Palestine and ordered him to bless, not curse, which he did (Num. 22-24). The incident of Balaam's ass seeing the angel before his master did is found in Num. 22:21ff. Later the Israelites killed Balaam after he had tried to involve them in idolatry (Num. 31:8; cf. also Jude 11; Rev. 2:14).

BALADAN The father of one of the kings of Babylon (2 Kgs. 20:12). *See* BABYLON, BABYLONIA.

BALAH *See* BAALAH, 3

BALAK The king of Moab who tried to get Balaam to curse the Israelites (Num. 22-24; Rev. 2:14; Jude 11).

BALANCE *See* WEIGHTS AND MEASURES

BALM *See* PLANTS, PERFUMES, AND SPICES

BALSAM *See* TREES

BAMAH The word is transliterated only in Ezekiel 20:29 where the prophet is making a play on words; elsewhere it is translated "high place" (Jer. 32:35).

BAMOTH One of the stops of the Israelites east of the Jordan during their exodus wanderings (Num. 21:19).

BAMOTH BAAL An unidentified site east of the Jordan where Balak took Balaam to try to get him to curse Israel. Later it was in the tribal area of Reuben (Num. 22:41; Josh. 13:17). It is called simply Bamoth in Numbers 21:19.

BANI 1. One of David's thirty mighty men (2 Sam. 23:36, KJV).

2. A man of Judah who returned from the exile in Babylon (1 Chron. 9:4).

3. An ancestor of one of David's temple singers and a descendant of Levi (1 Chron. 6:46).

4. One or several Levites in Jerusalem in the days of Nehemiah (Neh. 3:17; 8:7; 10:13, 14).

5. An ancestor of men who married foreign women during the Babylonian captivity (Ezra 10:29).

BANK, BANKER *See* MONEY

BANQUET *See* FEAST

BAPTISM A word transliterated from the Greek word *baptisma* with various meanings during different periods of time and with a variety of groups: baptisms in the OT, that of John, that of Jesus, and finally that of the church. The word itself appears in the NT but not in the OT. The Greek translators of the OT use it three times. The one clear context is 2 Kgs. 5:14 where Naaman the leper "dipped" himself in the Jordan River and was made clean. While this word, being Greek, is not used in the OT, the concept of washing with water for cleansing is clear (Lev. 15:8; 17:15, 16). Both sprinkling of the water and washing were used, or perhaps they were used together (Num. 19:17-19). In OT times proselytes were baptized, washed, as a part of the initiatory rites into the community. This practice was found also at the Dead Sea Scroll community.

John's baptism added something new, an emphasis on personal repentance from sin. It may also have been an initiatory rite to community, but it now involves personal activity in repentance and dedication to a new life (Lk. 3:3, 10-13).

The baptism of Jesus was by John but there was a difference. It was not for repentance from sin: It was to "fulfill all righteousness" (Mt. 3:13-15). Jesus was approaching the age of thirty and ready to begin his ministry (Lk. 3:21, 23). At the beginning of his ministry, the high priest and his sons were washed. Later priests began their service the same way at the age of thirty (Ex. 29:4; Num. 4:3). Christ came as the High Priest and his ministry was inaugurated in the traditional manner by washing with water.

The church's baptism was linked with repentance and with admission to the community of the church. A mature individual, recognizing the fact that he or she is a sinner, believing in Jesus Christ as Savior and Lord, and having confessed this before men, was given the rite of baptism as a sign of spiritual cleansing and purification and admission to the Church visible. Circumcision was given to sons of the faithful in OT times and baptism was given to all infant children of the faithful from earliest NT times. Those who hold this latter position base it in measure on Col. 2:11, 12. Many hold to adult baptism only. It is not a rite that regenerates the one to whom applied but is merely an outward sign that one has professed his faith in Christ and obedience to him and thus is ingrafted into Christ and partakes of all his benefits, or in the case of the infant it signifies an act of faith and obedience on the part of the parents (1 Cor. 12:12, 13; Rom. 6:1-5).

In many contexts, the word "baptize" clearly implies immersion, but that is not always the meaning as is clear from Luke 11:38, where it is rendered in English by "wash" and Mark 7:4 where the washing is also of utensils and even dining couches (reading with the footnote).

BARABBAS An insurrectionist against the Romans caught in the act. During the trial of Jesus before the Roman procurator, Pilate asked the assembled crowd whether they wanted him to give amnesty to Barabbas or to Jesus, and the crowd elected that Barabbas should go free (Mt. 27:17, 21).

BARAKEL, BARACHEL The father of one of Job's friends (Job. 32:2).

BARACHIAH BARAKIAH The father of the martyred OT personage Zechariah (Mt. 23:35).

BARAK *See* JUDGES OF ISRAEL

BARHUMITE *See* BAHURIM

BARIAH A descendant of David (1 Chron. 3:22).

BAR-JESUS A magician and false prophet on the island of Cyprus whom Paul struck with temporary blindness. Also called Elymas (Acts 13:5-12).

BARKOS Father of some who returned from the Babylonian captivity (Ezra 2:53).

BARLEY *See* PLANTS, PERFUMES AND SPICES

BARNABAS A native of Cyprus who sold his property and gave the proceeds to the apostles in Jerusalem (Acts 4:36, 37), and later encouraged the Christians in Jerusalem to receive Paul as one of them (Acts 9:17-19, 26-29). It was Barnabas who brought Paul to the work at Antioch and later accompanied him on his missionary journeys (Acts 11:25, 26; 13:1-3). Together they were at the Jerusalem Council where policy concerning Gentile converts was established (Acts 15:1-

2, 12). He parted company with Paul over John Mark, but both continued on missionary journeys. Paul speaks well of him later although nothing more is known of his activities (Acts 15:36-40; 1 Cor. 9:6; Col. 4:10).

BARSABBAS 1. The defeated candidate in the casting of the lot to Judas among the twelve apostles; also known as Justus and Joseph (Acts 1:23).

2. One chosen by the Jerusalem Council to go with Paul to the brethren in Antioch, Syria, and Cilicia with the message of the Council; also called Judas (Acts 15:22).

BARTHOLOMEW *See* APOSTLES

BARTIMAEUS A blind beggar of Jericho who was healed by Jesus (Mk. 10:46-52).

BARUCH 1. The secretary of the prophet Jeremiah who wrote at his dictation (Jer. 36:26, 32). This writing so angered the king that he ordered it burnt but Jeremiah redictated it and it is apparently an unidentified part of the Book of Jeremiah (Jer. 36). He accompanied Jeremiah on his exile to Egypt after the start of the Babylonian captivity of Judah (Jer. 43:6-7).

2. One of the builders of the walls of Jerusalem in the days of Nehemiah (Neh. 3:20), and perhaps one of the signers of the covenant with him (Neh. 10:6).

3. Father of one of the dwellers in Jerusalem after the return from the Babylonian captivity (Neh. 11:5).

BARZILLAI 1. A Gileadite from east of the Jordan who befriended King David when he was fleeing from Absalom. David on his deathbed instructed his son Solomon to show loyalty to his descendants (2 Sam. 17:27-29; 1 Kgs. 2:7). His descendants also came back from the Babylonian captivity (Ezra 2:61).

2. The father of one of King Saul's sons-in-law (2 Sam. 21:8).

BASEMATH 1 and 2. Two of the wives of Esau (Gen. 26:34; 36:3).

3. A daughter of King Solomon (1 Kgs. 4:15).

BASHAN *See* GEOGRAPHY OF THE HOLY LAND

BAT *See* BEASTS, 7

BATH *See* WEIGHTS AND MEASURES

BATH, BATHING Apart from the cases of the daughter of Pharaoh bathing in the river, and Bathsheba the wife of Uriah the Hittite bathing on the rooftop and witnessed by David, bathing as we know it in the twentieth century is not discussed in the Bible (Ex. 2:5; 2 Sam. 11:2). It was a common practice to wash the dusty feet of guests (Gen. 18:4; Song 5:3, Lk. 7:44). In NT times washing hands before eating was a ritual act (Mt. 15:2, 20). See PURIFICATION on the subject of ritual bathing.

BATH RABBIM The name of a city, east of the Jordan (Song 7:4).

BATHSHEBA The wife of Uriah the Hittite whom David saw bathing on her roof top. David coveted her and had her husband killed so that later he could marry her. Nathan the prophet was sent by God to rebuke David for this murder and adultery. Their first child died, but the future King Solomon was the second (2 Sam. 11-12; 1 Chron. 3:5).

BATHSHUA A Canaanitess who bore three sons to Judah (1 Chron. 2:3).

BATTERING RAMS *See* ARMS AND ARMOR

BAZLUTH A temple servant in the days after the return from the Babylonian captivity (Neh. 7:54; Ezra 2:52).

BEALIAH A Benjamite who joined David when he was fleeing from Saul (1 Chron. 12:5).

BEALOTH An unidentified town in Judah (Josh. 15:24).

BEAM A large piece of timber used to support the roof of a building (1 Kgs. 6:9, 10). In the parable traditionally associated with the "mote and beam in the eye" the NIV renders these words by speck and plank (Mt. 7:3-5). In the case of the weaver's rod (beam) it is the bar on which the warp was bound in the loom (1 Sam. 17:7).

BEANS *See* PLANTS, PERFUMES, AND SPICES

BEAR *See* BEASTS, 8

BEARD Carefully groomed hair on the face was a sign of manly vitality. Its neglect was a sign of mental derangement (1 Sam. 21:13; 2 Sam. 19:24). While in mourning the beard was either cut off or plucked out (Jer. 41:5). To cut off a man's beard was to humiliate him (2 Sam. 10:4, 5). The Israelites were forbidden to cut the hair at the sides of their heads (Lev. 19:27), and later the hair around their temples was grown long as with the "orthodox" of today.

BEASTS 1. *Cobra, Serpent, Snake, Viper.* Reptiles seem to be the broadest term. They breathe air, are vertebrate, and crawl

on the belly or creep on short legs (1 Kgs. 4:33; Rom. 1:23).
The serpent is an elongated, limbless reptile with scales
(Gen. 3:14; Prov. 30:19). Synonymous with the word serpent
or snake are the viper and the cobra, all poisonous (Gen.
49:17; Deut. 32:33; Ps. 140:3; Prov. 23:32; Isa. 11:8).

2. *Antelope, Deer, Doe, Gazelle, Ibex, Mountain Sheep, Roe
Deer.* These are among the clean animals (Deut. 14:4, 5).
The doe is parallel to gazelle in Song 2:7 and is probably a
synonym. The doe is mentioned in Proverbs 5:19 where it is
a synonym for deer. While there are many varieties and
species known today, and while many doubtless existed in
biblical times, the clearest analogy for the modern reader is
to forms of deer and wild sheep.

3. *Ape, Baboon.* Monkeys probably from India, probably not
the large animals known by those terms today (1 Kgs.
10:22).

4. *Bull, Camel, Cattle, Cow, Donkey, Goat, Heifer, Herds,
Horse, Ox, Sheep.* The domesticated clean animals were cattle
or herds and flocks. Cattle and herds refer to the larger
animals, cow, ox, bull, and their heifers. The word flock
covers the smaller animals, the sheep and goats. The donkey
and the horse were unclean: the former was the work animal
while the latter was used in war. The camel too was among
the unclean animals but was very useful in the Palestinian
country as a beast of burden whose hair was used for making
cloth. Certain types could cover 150 miles in a day or carry
a load of 400 pounds.

5. *Coney* (Rock Badger), *Rabbit, Rat, Sea Cow.* All are
unclean animals. The coney is a small hoofed animal much
like the rabbit in size. It lives in rocky areas and is totally
unlike the animal called "badger" in modern times (Deut.
14:7; Ps. 104:18; Lev. 11:29). From the sea cow came the
skin for the cover of the Ark.

6. *Ant, Bee, Chameleon, Cricket, Flea, Fly, Frog, Gecko,
Gnat, Grasshopper, Hornet, Katydid, Lizard, Locust, Maggots,
Scorpion, Skink, Slug, Spider, Worm.* While the group covers
different phyla there is one characteristic they have in
common. They are small. On reptiles, see below and also
number 1 above. The others in this group are arachnids,
insects, or reptiles. The *frog* is a tailless, leaping amphibian
and is noted mostly in the incidents of the ten plagues in
Egypt (Ex. 8:2-15). The *spider* and the *scorpion* are arachnids.
The former have in common that they spin webs. This in
the Bible is a symbol of frailty (Job. 8:14). There are many
species of both the spiders and the scorpions. Scorpions are
characterized by the curved stinging tail (Deut. 8:15). Among
the insects are the clean ones, the *katydid* (a type of

grasshopper), *locust, grasshopper,* and *cricket* (Lev. 11:22; Ps. 78:46). These have wormlike larvae which are unclean and are called *maggots* or *worms* (Job 25:6). The *flea* is a jumping, wingless insect, referred to in 1 Sam. 24:14. References to the *fly* are mostly in connection with the account of the ten plagues (Ex. 8:21-31). The word *gnat* may refer to the gnat as we know it, or to the mosquito or sand fly. It, too, is used mostly in connection with the ten plague account (Ex. 8:16-18). With one exception the *bee* and *hornet* are noted for their stinging feature (Deut. 1:44; 7:20). The exception is in the case of Judges 14:8 where honey is mentioned in connection with the insect that produces it. Reptiles not discussed in number 1 above include the *chameleon, gecko, skink* and several kinds of *lizards* (the great lizard, the wall lizard, the monitor lizard). They are all unclean. In the first the feature is the changing of color. The second is an animal of rather uncertain character, perhaps a reptile. The *skink* is a harmless smooth-scaled lizard, has a long tail and usually short legs (Lev. 11:29, 30). They are all unclean animals. The *slug* is mentioned in Psalm 58:8.

7. *Bat.* A nocturnal flying mammal which because it flies is listed with birds (unclean birds) (Lev. 11:19).

8. *Bear, Dog, Fox, Hyena, Jackal, Leopard, Lion, Wolf, Weasel.* All are carnivorous mammals (Isa. 11:7; Judg. 15:4; Mt. 8:20; Isa. 34:14; Ps. 63:10; Isa. 11:6; Jer. 13:23; Hab. 1:8; Judg. 14:5; Ps. 7:2; Jn. 10:12; Jer. 5:6; Lev. 11:29). The *dog* is a domesticated carnivorous mammal (Ex. 11:7). It is also used as a term of contempt for a man, especially an enemy, in the form "dead dog." A temple male prostitute or sodomite could be called a dog (1 Sam. 17:43; 24:14; Ps. 22:16, 20; Deut. 23:18; Phil. 3:2).

9. *Behemoth, Dragon, Leviathan, Rahab, Monster of the Deep* (seas or water), *Sea Cow.* The *behemoth* mentioned in Job 40:15 is thought by some to be the hippopotamus or the elephant. In early extrabiblical literature it is a name for one of the mythical monsters. *Leviathan, rahab, and the monster of the deep* (seas or water) are all sea monsters, undefined (Job. 7:12; Ps. 74:13, 14; Job 3:8; Isa. 27:1; Job 26:12; Ps. 89:10). In some they seem to be mythological only, while in others some of them would seem to have been real also. For *dragon, see* DEITIES and DEMONS. *Sea cows* are called *badgers* in the KJV. Their skin was used to cover the tabernacle.

10. *Boar, Pig.* The former, a wild swine or pig, is noted in Ps. 80:13. There are many references to the latter in both Testaments (Lev. 11:7; Mt. 8:30; Isa. 66:3).

BEATITUDES A word which is used to refer to the teaching of Jesus which begins with "Blessed are" in Matthew 5:3-12 and Luke 6:20-23.

BEBAI The father of some who returned from the Babylonian captivity (Ezra 2:11; Neh. 10:15).

BECORATH A descendant of Benjamin and ancestor of King Saul (1 Sam. 9:1).

BED The common man in biblical times could not afford a bed in the modern sense of that word. He slept on the ground wrapped in his outer cloak or on some sort of mat on the floor (Ex. 22:26, 27; Acts 5:15). Simple beds were known and are probably reflected in 2 Samuel 17:28 and 1 Samuel 19:15. Beds as luxury items are referred to frequently, decked with tapestries, perfumed with spices, inlaid with ivory, and with headboards (Amos 6:4; Prov. 7:16, 17; Gen. 47:31). Guests at a banquet, at least by Roman times, reclined on beds or couches arranged around the banqueting table and this was probably what took place at the last passover, the first Lord's Supper (Jn. 13:23).

BEDAD Father of one of the kings of Moab (Gen. 36:35).

BEDAN A descendant of Manasseh (1 Chron. 7:17).

BEDEIAH One who married a foreign woman during the captivity in Babylon (Ezra 10:35).

BEE *See* BEASTS, 6

BEELIADA A son born to David in Jerusalem, also known as Eliada (1 Chron. 14:7; 2 Sam. 5:16).

BEELZEBUB *See* DEITIES and DEVIL

BEER 1. A stopping place for the Israelites during their exodus from Egypt, on the border of Moab (Num. 21:16).
2. The place to which Jotham fled from Abimelech (Judg. 9:21).

BEERA A descendant of Asher (1 Chron. 7:37).

BEERAH A descendant of Reuben captured by the Assyrian king Tiglath-Pileser (1 Chron. 5:6).

BEER ELIM An unidentified town in Moab (Isa. 15:8).

BEERI 1. The Hittite father of one of Esau's wives (Gen. 26:34).

2. The father of the prophet Hosea (Hos. 1:1).

BEER LAHAI ROI An unidentified site in the Negev where the angel appeared to Hagar when she was fleeing from Sarah (Gen. 16:14). Isaac and Rebecca met and later settled there (Gen. 24:62; 25:11).

BEEROTH A city (167-137) of Gibeon and later Benjamin. Saul's murderers and Joab's armor-bearer came from there (Josh. 9:17; 18:25; 2 Sam. 4:2; 23:37). Some of its inhabitants came back from the Babylonian captivity (Ezra 2:25).

BEERSHEBA A town (134-072) originally in the tribal area of Judah and later assigned to Simeon, called "the well of the oath" or "the well of the seven" (Josh. 15:28; 19:2; Gen. 21:22-32). Many ruins from the end of the fourth millennium B.C. exist in the region of modern Beersheba, but the tell (Sheva) of antiquity was not yet occupied in the days of the patriarchs. The Beersheba of those days had no king. The patriarchs sacrificed to God somewhere in the area in a place they called Beersheba (Gen. 21:33; 46:1). The phrase "from Dan to Beersheba" was the standard for describing the limits of Palestine (Judg. 20:1). It was the site of a religious sanctuary in the days of the kings of Judah (Amos 5:5). The largest horned altar yet discovered indicates the existence of a temple altar, but nothing remains of the temple itself. It was still occupied even after the return from the Babylonian captivity (Neh. 11:27). Persian and Roman remains have been excavated on the site.

BE ESHTERAH A city in the tribal area of Manasseh east of the Jordan given to the Levites (Josh. 21:27).

BEGGAR To beg or to ask alms was an accepted practice in biblical times. Cases appear in both Testaments (Ps. 109:10; Lam. 4:4; Mk. 10:46; Lk. 18:35; Acts 3:2).

BEHEMOTH *See* BEASTS

BEKA *See* WEIGHTS AND MEASURES

BEKER 1. A son of Benjamin (Gen. 46:21).

2. A descendant of Ephraim, also called Bered (Num. 26:35; 1 Chron. 7:20.)

BEL *See* DEITIES

BELA 1. A king of Edom (Gen. 36:32).

2. Benjamin's first son (Gen. 46:21).

3. A descendant of Reuben who lived east of the Jordan (1 Chron. 5:8).

4. Another name for the city of Zoar. Its king was involved in the battle at Sodom and Gomorrah (Gen. 14:2, 8).

BELIAL An archenemy of Christ so called in 2 Corinthians 6:15. In the OT the word is translated: wicked men, troublemakers, or scoundrels (Deut. 13:13; 1 Sam. 2:12; 10:27; 1 Kgs. 21:10).

BELIEVE A synonym for "to have faith." In OT times when a man believed God it was accounted to him for righteousness (Rom. 4:3). In NT times righteousness and eternal life are given to those who believe in Jesus as Son of God, Savior and Lord (John 3:15, 16, 18, 36; 1 John 4:5-12; 2 Pet. 3:18).

BELL Small bells of gold alternated with other ornaments on the lower part of the high priest's robe (Ex. 28:33-35). There is a reference to "bells of the horses" which is even less revealing as to the nature of these bells (Zech. 14:20).

BELLOWS An important part of the blacksmith's workshop and that of the refiner. The word is found in Jeremiah 6:29 but the concept is also clear in Isaiah 54:16. These were leather bags fastened to wooden or ceramic nozzles which were operated either by hand or by treading with the feet.

BELLY *See* EMOTIONS

BELSHAZZAR The last Chaldean king to reign over Babylon. He reigned as co-regent with his father Nabonidus who is sometimes called the last king. He is called son of Nebuchadnezzar in the Bible, but in that context the word "son" is used in one of its normal semitic usages of "descendant" (Dan. 5:2, 30, 31). *See also* BABYLON, BABYLONIA.

BELT *See* DRESS

BELTESHAZZAR *See* DANIEL, 4

BEN-ABINADAB A son-in-law of King Solomon who was in charge of collecting his food in the area of Naphoth Dor (1 Kgs. 4:11).

BENAIAH 1. One of David's mighty men, who also supported Solomon for the throne and killed Joab (2 Sam. 23:20; 1 Kgs. 1:38; 2:28-31).

2. Another of David's mighty men who later was one of King Solomon's officers (2 Sam. 23:30; 1 Chron. 27:14).

3. A descendant of Simeon (1 Chron. 4:36).

4. One of David's musicians, a Levite (1 Chron. 15:18).

5. One who was to blow the trumpet before the Ark in David's day (1 Chron. 15:24).

6. The grandfather of Jahaziel through whom God spoke of victory over Moab to King Jehoshaphat (2 Chron. 20:14).

7. An overseer in the reign of King Hezekiah (2 Chron. 31:13).

8, 9, 10, and 11. Men who married foreign wives during the Babylonian captivity (Ezra 10:25, 30, 35, 43).

12. Father of one of the princes who gave evil counsel to the men of Jerusalem, and died for it (Ezek. 11:1, 2, 13).

BEN-AMMI Grandson of Lot and founder of the Ammonites (Gen. 19:38).

BEN-DEKER An officer of King Solomon (1 Kgs. 4:9).

BENE-BERAK A town (133-160) in the original tribal area of Dan (Josh. 19:45).

BENE-JAAKAN A stop in the wilderness wanderings of the Israelites during the exodus from Egypt (Num. 33:31).

BEN-GEBER One of King Solomon's twelve food collectors, in the area of Ramoth-Gilead (1 Kgs. 4:13).

BEN-HADAD The name of three kings of ancient Syria at Damascus.

1. Ben-Hadad I captured parts of Israel from its King Baasha at a time when Baasha was at war with King Asa of Judah (1 Kgs. 15:18-21).

2. Ben-Hadad II, son of Ben-Hadad I, who was defeated by Ahab of Israel, forced to give back the territory his father had seized from Israel, and to give certain commercial rights (1 Kgs. 20). Later they were allies against the Assyrians at Karkar but soon fought again with one another (1 Kgs. 22:1-36).

3. Ben-Hadad III was the son of the servant Hazael of Ben-Hadad II who had usurped his master's throne (2 Kgs. 8:7-15; 13:3). Jehoash, king of Israel, defeated him and forced him to return all the territories captured from Israel (2 Kgs. 13:25).

BEN-HAIL A prince sent by King Jehoshaphat to teach in Judah (2 Chron. 17:7).

BEN-HANAN A descendant of Judah (1 Chron. 4:20).

BEN-HESED One of King Solomon's food collecting officers in Judah (1 Kgs. 4:10).

BEN-HINNOM A man whose name was given to a valley immediately west of the ridge on which the city of Jerusalem was built (Jer. 19:2, 6). It is from this name that the term Gehenna eventually arose.

BEN-HUR King Solomon's food collector in the area of the hill country of Ephraim (1 Kgs. 4:8).

BENINU One of the Levites who signed the covenant with Nehemiah (Neh. 10:13).

BENJAMIN, BEN-ONI 1. The last son of Jacob and second by Rachel. Born in sorrow and pain just before Rachel died, she called him Ben-Oni, but Jacob later named him Benjamin (Gen. 35:16-18). Founder of one of the twelve tribes. The relationship in Egypt with his older and full brother Joseph is beautifully narrated (Gen. 42-45).

2. A descendant of Benjamin (1 Chron. 7:10).

3. One who married a foreign wife during the Babylonian captivity (Ezra 10:32).

4. A builder of the walls with Nehemiah (Neh. 3:23).

BENO A descendant of Aaron who served in the priesthood (1 Chron. 24:26).

BEN-ONI *See* BENJAMIN, 1

BEN-ZOHETH A descendant of Judah (1 Chron. 4:20).

BEON A place east of the Jordan where the tribes of Gad and Reuben resided (Num. 32:1-5).

BEOR 1. The father of Balaam who failed to curse Israel as he was requested (Num. 22:5-6).

2. Father of a king of Edom (Gen. 36:32).

BERA The king of Sodom defeated in the battle of the kings (Gen. 14:2).

BERACAH 1. A descendant of Benjamin who joined David at Ziklag (1 Chron. 12:3).

2. A valley near Bethlehem which got its name from King Jehoshaphat's blessing the Lord there (2 Chron. 20:26).

BERAIAH A descendant of Benjamin (1 Chron. 8:21).

BEREA A city in Macedonia not far from Thessalonica where Paul's message met with success (Acts 17:10, 13; 20:4).

BERED 1. An unidentified site in the wilderness of Shur (Gen. 16:14).

2. A descendant of Ephraim (1 Chron. 7:20).

BEREKIAH 1. A son of Zerubbabel (1 Chron. 3:29).

2. The father of Asaph the singer (1 Chron. 6:39).

3. A Levite who returned from Babylon (1 Chron. 9:16).

4. A Levite doorkeeper for the Ark (1 Chron. 15:23).

5. A prince in Ephraim at the time of King Pekah (2 Chron. 28:12).

6. A builder of the walls with Nehemiah (Neh. 3:4).

7. Father of the prophet Zechariah (Zech. 1:1).

BERI A descendant of Asher (1 Chron. 7:36).

BERIAH 1. A son of Asher (Gen. 46:17). His descendants are called Beriites (Num. 26:44).

2. Son of Ephraim (1 Chron. 7:23).

3. A descendant of Benjamin who lived in Aijalon (1 Chron. 8:13).

4. A descendant of Levi (1 Chron. 23:10).

BERIITES *See* BERIAH, 1

BERNICE The oldest daughter of Herod Agrippa I and sister of Herod Agrippa II. Married to her uncle she was intimate with her brother after her husband's death. She was with this brother and Governor Festus in Caesarea when Paul's case was heard there (Acts 25:23; 26:30).

BEROTHAH A city on the boundary of the land in the prophetic account by Ezekiel (Ezek. 47:16).

BEROTHAI A Syrian city (257-372) captured by David; also called Cunqu (2 Sam. 8:8).

BERYL *See* PRECIOUS STONES AND METALS

BESAI One who returned with Zerubbabel from the Babylonian captivity (Ezra 2:49).

BESODEIAH The father of one who worked with Nehemiah to repair the Old Gate of Jerusalem (Neh. 3:6).

BESOR A brook, wadi, or ravine that runs from near Beersheba to the sea near Gaza (1 Sam. 30:9, 10, 21).

BETEN A town (160-241) in the lot of the tribe of Asher (Josh. 19:25).

BETH ANATH A town (190-289) in the tribal area of Naphtali (Josh. 19:38).

BETH ANOTH A town (162-107) in the tribal area of Judah (Josh. 15:59).

BETHANY A town just east of Jerusalem where the home of Mary, Martha, and Lazarus was located. Jesus spent much time there and it was there that he raised Lazarus from the dead (Mt. 26:6; Mk. 11:1; Jn. 12:1).

BETH ARABAH A town (197-139) near Jericho on the border between Judah and Benjamin (Josh. 15:6).

BETH ARBEL A town (229-218) destroyed by Shalman (Hos. 10:14).

BETH ASHBEA An unidentified town where a family of linen workers lived (1 Chron. 4:21).

BETH AVEN A town (175-141) near Ai and Michmash on Benjamin's border, on the edge of the Judean wilderness (Josh 7:2; 18:12; 1 Sam. 13:5). Translated this means "house of wickedness," a symbolic name for Bethel which means "house of God" (Hos. 10:5).

BETH AZMAVETH Men from this town came up from the Babylonian captivity, perhaps identical with Azmaveth (175-138) (Neh. 7:28).

BETH BAAL MEON A city (219-120) east of the Jordan allocated to the Reubenites (Josh. 13:17).

BETH BARAH An unidentified site near the Jordan River, a staging area in Gideon's fight against the Midianites (Judg. 7:24).

BETH BIRI *See* BETH LEBAOTH

BETH CAR An unidentified site to which the Israelites pursued the Philistines after one of their battles (1 Sam. 7:11).

BETH DAGON 1. A town (134-156) in the tribal area of Asher (Josh. 19:27).

2. An unidentified town in the lowlands of Judah (Josh. 15:41).

BETH DIBLATHAIM A city (228-116) in Moab (Jer. 48:22; Num. 33:46), perhaps also Almon Dibliathaim.

BETH EDEN Probably the Bit-adini of the Assyrian records. The "people of Eden" came from there. A city-state near the Euphrates (2 Kgs. 19:12; Amos 1:5).

BETH EKED An unidentified place between Samaria and Jezreel (2 Kgs. 10:12, 14).

BETHEL 1. A town (172-148) generally thought to be at Beitin. Questions have been raised since Bethel is said to be twelve miles north of Jerusalem according to the *Onomasticon* of Eusebius while Beitin is farther. Ai is located near the biblical Bethel. Abraham built an altar between these two towns (Gen. 12:8). Jacob's dream happened there (Gen. 28:10ff.). In the Israelite invasion Joshua captured its king (Josh. 12:9), and it was assigned to the tribal area of Benjamin (Josh. 18:22). The Ark of God was there for some time in the days prior to the monarchy (Judg. 20:26-27). Because it was the site of a strategic road intersection it had great importance in the days of the kings of Judah and Israel. When the ten tribes split off from the two, Jeroboam set up a statue of a golden calf in the temple he built there (1 Kgs. 12:28-31). The prophets cried against this idolatry (1 Kgs. 13:1, 2; 2 Kgs. 10:29), and only after the fall of Samaria was the temple destroyed (2 Kgs. 23:15-20). It was reoccupied after the return from Babylon (Ezra 2:28).

2. A town in the tribal area of Simeon also known as Bethul and Bethuel (Josh. 19:4; 1 Chron. 4:30).

BETH EMEK A city (164-263) in the tribal area of Asher (Josh. 19:27).

BETHESDA A pool in Jerusalem where invalids came for healing (Jn. 5:2, 3).

BETH EZEL A town probably in Judah (Mic. 1:11).

BETH GADER A town in the tribal area of Judah (1 Chron. 2:51).

BETH GAMUL A city (235-099) of Moab (Jer. 48:23).

BETH GILGAL One of the towns from which the singers came at the time of the dedication of Nehemiah's rebuilt wall (Neh. 12:29).

BETH HAGGAN King Ahaziah fled in this direction (178-207) from Jehu (2 Kgs. 9:27).

BETH HAKKEREM A town (170-127) of Judah perhaps at the site of modern Ramat Rachel south of Jerusalem (Neh. 3:14; Jer. 6:1).

BETH HARAM, A town (214-136) and a valley in which the town was located
BETH HARAN east of the Jordan in the tribal area of Gad (Num. 32:36;
Josh. 13:27).

BETH HOGLAH A Benjamite city (197-136) in the Jordan Valley
(Josh. 18:19-21).

BETH HORON Reference is made (Josh. 10:10; 16:3, 5) to "going up to
Beth Horon," to "Lower Beth Horon" (158-144), and to
"Upper Beth Horon" (160-143). The road of the ascent
of Beth Horon was from the earliest times the main road up
into the hill country from the coast at Jaffa. The road passed
between two Beth Horons and thus it and the two cities
were of extreme importance militarily. After the battle at
Gibeon, Joshua pursued the kings down this road as did King
Saul the Philistines later (Josh. 10:10, 11; 1 Sam. 13:18). It
was still important in Hellenistic, Roman, and Crusader times.
The two towns were in the tribal area of Ephraim on the
southern border (Josh. 16:3; 18:13). King Solomon fortified
these cities, but in the time of the divided monarchy they
were in Israel (2 Chron. 8:5; 25:13).

BETH JESHIMOTH A town (208-132) in Moab taken by the Israelites and assigned
to the tribal area of Reuben (Num. 33:49; Josh. 12:3; 13:20).
It had been retaken by the time of the prophet Ezekiel
(Ezek. 25:9).

BETH LEBAOTH An unidentified town in the tribal area of Judah-Simeon called
Beth Biri in 1 Chronicles 4:31, and Lebaoth in Joshua 15:32
(Josh. 19:6).

BETHLEHEM 1. A city (169-123) in the tribal area of Judah near which the
patriarch Jacob's wife Rachel was buried and from which
King David came (Gen. 35:19; 1 Sam. 16:1, 18). It was a
Philistine stronghold through the days of King Saul and into
David's days also (2 Sam. 23:16). King Rehoboam of Judah
built up towers of defense there (2 Chron. 11:6). It was
still inhabited by Jews after the return from the Babylonian
captivity (Ezra 2:21), and was the birthplace of Jesus Christ,
prophesied by Micah and recorded in the Gospels (Mic.
5:2; Mt. 2:5; Lk. 2:4).

2. Bethlehem (168-283) in the tribal area of Zebulun in the
north (Josh. 19:15).

BETH MAACAH The same as Abel Beth Maacha (2 Sam. 20:14, 15).

BETH MARCABOTH A city in the tribal area of Simeon, not identified (Josh. 19:5).

A city east of the Jordan that came under judgment (Jer. 48:23).

BETH MILLO 1. An unidentified site near the ancient city of Shechem (Judg. 9:6, 20).

2. King Joash's officials assassinated him at "Beth Millo, on the road down to Silla" (2 Kgs. 12:20).

BETH NIMRAH A town (210-146) in the tribal area of Sihon, king of Heshbon, on the east side of the Jordan (Josh. 13:27).

BETH OPHRAH The people of Samaria and Jerusalem are told to mourn in this city by the prophet Micah (Mic. 1:10).

BETH PAZZEZ A town in the tribal area of Issachar (Josh. 19:21).

BETH PELET A town in the tribal area of Judah near the border with Edom (Josh. 15:27). After the return from the Babylonian captivity it was again occupied (Neh. 11:26).

BETH PEOR A city in the tribal area of Reuben east of the Jordan. The Israelites during their exodus from Egypt camped near there and Moses is buried nearby (Josh. 13:20; Deut. 3:29; 4:46; 34:6).

BETHPHAGE A village near Bethany and Jerusalem known in the Bible only from the references to it connected with the triumphal entry of Jesus to Jerusalem (Mt. 21:1).

BETH RAPHA An unidentified site in the tribal area of Judah (1 Chron. 4:12).

BETH REHOB An unidentified town in the upper Jordan Valley where inhabitants fought against David and were defeated (Judg. 18:28; 2 Sam. 10:6).

BETHSAIDA The town of Philip, Andrew, and Peter on the northern shore of the Sea of Galilee. Jesus healed a blind man there (Mk. 8:22) and later denounced the city for its unbelief (Mt. 11:21).

BETH SHAN A city (197-212) long inhabited by man because of the warmth of its climate and the abundance of water. From the fourth millennium to about 1500 B.C. it was settled first by nomads and then by Canaanites. It was an important Egyptian fortress city for a time and was followed by Canaanite and then Philistine occupancy. The Philistines placed the body of Saul on the city wall after they defeated Israel and killed the king. David finally captured it and it became important during Israelite times (Josh. 17:16; Judg. 1:27; 1 Sam. 31:10;

1 Kgs. 4:12). In NT times it was a Roman city called Scythopolis, one of the cities of the Decapolis.

BETH SHEMESH 1. A city (147-128) located at the northern end of the western foothills (Shephelah) with a history going back to the fourth millennium B.C. It was in the area allocated to the tribe of Dan but they were unable to drive its inhabitants out. This was the Ark's first stop when it was making its journey back from its Philistine captivity (Josh. 15:10; 1 Sam. 6:9ff.). It is called Ir Shemesh or sun city in Josh. 19:41. Solomon made it an administrative center but later King Ahaz lost it to the Philistines who held it until the Babylonians destroyed it in the sixth century.

2. A city (181-271) in the tribal area of Naphtali from which the Israelites were not able to drive out the natives but upon whom they put forced labor (Josh. 19:38; Judg. 1:33).

3. A town (199-232) in the tribal area of Issachar (Josh. 19:22).

BETH SHITTAH An unidentified town in the Valley of Jezreel to which Gideon chased the defeated Midianites (Judg. 7:22).

BETH TAPPUAH A city (154-105) in the tribal area of Judah also called Tappuah (Josh. 15:53; 1 Chron. 2:43).

BETH TOGARMAH *See* TOGARMAH

BETHUEL 1. *See also* BETHEL, 2.

2. The father of Rebekah and nephew of Abraham (Gen. 22:23).

BETHUL *See* BETHEL, 2

BETH ZUR A city (159-110) in the tribal area of Judah. Rehoboam fortified it and it was still inhabited after the return from the Babylonian captivity (Josh. 15:58; 2 Chron. 11:7; Neh. 3:16).

BETONIM A town (217-154) in the tribal area of Gad (Josh. 13:26).

BETROTH To promise in marriage. *See* MARRIAGE.

BEZAI 1. Head of a family that returned from the Babylonian captivity with Zerubbabel (Ezra 2:17).

2. One who signed the covenant with Nehemiah (Neh. 10:18).

BEZALEL 1. The chief architect of the tabernacle, a worker in wood, metal and precious stones (Ex. 31:1ff.).

2. An Israelite who married a foreign woman during the days of the Babylonian captivity (Ezra 10:30).

BEZEK After the death of Joshua it was here (187-197) that the men of Judah and Simeon defeated the Canaanites and Perizzites, and here Saul mustered the men for the battle to deliver Jabeth Gilead (Judg. 1:4-5; 1 Sam. 11:8-11).

BEZER 1. A descendant of Asher (1 Chron. 7:37).
2. A city (235-132) in the tribal area of Reuben east of the Jordan which became a city of refuge (Josh. 20:2, 8).

BICRI The father of Sheba who mounted an unsuccessful revolt against King David (2 Sam. 20:1).

BIDKAR The military aide of Jehu before the latter became king (2 Kgs. 9:25).

BIER A portable framework for the transport of the dead before burial (2 Sam. 3:31), translated "coffin" in Luke 7:14.

BIGTHA A eunuch of King Xerxes in Susa (Esth. 1:10).

BIGTHAN, BIGTHANA One of the officers of the Persian King Xerxes who plotted against his monarch but was killed for it (Esth. 2:21-23).

BIGVAI 1. One who returned with Zerubbabel from the Babylonian captivity (Ezra 2:2).
2. One who signed the covenant with Nehemiah (Neh. 10:16).

BILDAD One of Job's friends (Job. 2:11).

BILEAM A city of refuge in the tribal area of Manasseh (1 Chron. 6:70).

BILGAH, BILGAI 1. A priest in David's time (1 Chron. 24:14).
2. A priest who returned from the Babylonian captivity with Zerubbabel (Neh. 12:5, 18); also called Bilgai (Neh. 10:8).

BILHAH 1. See BAALAH, 3.
2. Rachel's maidservant who became a concubine of her husband Jacob and bore Dan and Naphtali. Later her stepson Reuben also had relations with her (Gen. 29:29; 30:5-8; 35:22).

BILHAN 1. A Horite chief (Gen. 36:27).
2. A descendant of Benjamin (1 Chron. 7:10).

BILSHAN A leader who returned with Zerubbabel from the Babylonian captivity (Ezra 2:2).

BIMHAL A descendant of Asher (1 Chron. 7:33).

BINEA A descendant of Saul and Jonathan (1 Chron. 8:37).

BINNUI 1. Father of a priest in Ezra's temple (Ezra 8:33).

2. One who worked on the city wall after the return from the Babylonian captivity (Neh. 3:18, 24), also called Bavvai in some Hebrew manuscripts.

3. Ancestor of some who returned from the captivity with Zerubbabel, also called Bani (Neh. 7:15; Ezra 2:10).

4 and 5. One who married a foreign wife during the Babylonian captivity and the ancestor of such a one (Ezra 10:30, 38).

6. A Levite who came back from the captivity with Zerubbabel (Neh. 12:8).

BIRDS 1. *Bat.* A mammal that flies, and for that reason listed with birds.

2. *Cock, Hen, Rooster* (Mt. 26:34; Prov. 30:31; Mt. 23:37). Their eggs were used for food (Lk. 11:12; Job 6:6). The crowing of a cock is mentioned in one significant incident, Peter's denial of Jesus (Mt. 26:34, 74, 75).

3. *Cormorant.* One of a family of large sea birds that feed on fish; mentioned in the passages where the unclean birds are listed—the birds that observant Jews could not eat (Lev. 11:13-19; Deut. 14:12-18).

4. *Dove, Partridge, Pigeon, Quail, Swift, Thrush, Turtledove.* Birds not found in the list of unclean animals. The *Dove, Turtledove,* and *Pigeon* were used in making sacrifices. The word translated "dove" is loosely applied to a number of smaller species of pigeon. It is used to symbolize innocence and purity (Lev. 1:14; 14:22). The *Partridge* was hunted in the mountains (1 Sam. 26:20), and the *Quail,* which seems to be a small type of *Partridge,* appears in the account of the feeding of the Israelites in the wilderness wanderings (Gen. 15:9; Ex. 16:13; Num. 11:31). The *Swift* and *Thrush* are noted in Isaiah 38:14.

5. *Eagle, Falcon, Gull, Hawk, Heron, Hoopoe, Black and Red Kites, Osprey, Owl, Stork, Vulture, Black Vulture.* All of these are unclean birds. It was forbidden to eat them. They are all listed as such in Leviticus 11:13-19 and Deuteronomy 14:12-18. The precise identification of some of these birds in modern terminology is uncertain. There are six varieties of *Owls* listed: *Little, Horned, Screech, Great, White, Desert.* One of these is quite likely the ostrich. Some were tall wading

birds with long bills, necks, legs, and wings. What we may know of most of them (not those with varieties) may be learned from any standard dictionary or encyclopedia on birds. Some are water birds, of course, and others are birds of prey on land. Special note on the *Eagle* and *Falcon* may be seen in Deuteronomy 28:40; 32:11; Job 28:7; 39:26; Ezekiel 17:3; and Proverbs 30:17. The *Hoopoe* has a head crest of erectile plumes and a long, curved bill.

6. *Ostrich.* A large desert bird that inhabits waste places. It is described as a swift runner, faster than a horse, and lays its eggs in the open; an unclean bird (Job. 39:13-18).

7. *Peacock.* In the NIV translated twice "baboons" and once as "ostrich" (1 Kgs. 10:22; Job 39:13).

8. *Raven.* An unclean bird (Lev. 11:15). In the OT some of its features are used for illustrations: the black locks of hair, its nesting in lonely places, its being fed by God (Song of Sol. 5:11; Isa. 34:11, Ps. 147:9). Jesus used the ravens to illustrate God's provision (Lk. 12:24). It was a raven that was sent out first from Noah's ark (Gen. 8:7). Elijah was fed by them (1 Kgs. 17:4-6).

9. *Sparrow.* The Hebrew word rendered "sparrow" (Ps. 84:3) is often translated "bird" or "fowl" in the Bible. A bird commonly sold in the market (Lk. 12:6, 7).

10. *Swallow.* A bird noted for its swift flight (Prov. 26:2), often used in parallel with the sparrow (Ps. 84:3). The meaning of the Hebrew word in contemporary terminology is not certain.

BIRSHA The king of Gomorrah (Gen. 14:2).

BIRTHDAY Specific celebrations of birthdays are mentioned for the Pharaoh of Egypt and King Herod Antipas, but not in general (Gen. 40:20; Mt. 14:6; Mk. 6:21).

BIRTHRIGHT The portion of the inheritance of the firstborn son, even if the wife was unloved (Deut. 21:17). The inheritance was divided into portions, with the firstborn receiving two portions, or a double portion. Esau sold his birthright to Jacob (Gen. 25:29-33); it could be lost by misconduct (1 Chron. 5:1).

BIRTHSTOOL *See* STOOL

BIRZAITH A descendant of Asher (1 Chron. 7:31).

BISHLAM An officer of the Persian king who was opposed to the rebuilding of Jerusalem (Ezra 4:7).

BISHOP *See* OVERSEER

BIT *See* BRIDLE

BITHIAH A daughter of Pharaoh who married a Jew (1 Chron. 4:18).

BITHYNIA A region in NW Asia Minor where Paul and Timothy wished to go but were forbidden by the Spirit (Acts 16:7).

BITTER HERBS *See* PLANTS, PERFUMES, AND SPICES

BIZIOTHIAH A town in the tribal area of Judah in the south (Josh. 15:28).

BIZTHA One of the eunuchs of the Persian King Xerxes (Esth. 1:10).

BLASPHEMY Dishonoring and reviling the name, work, or being of God by word or deed. It is sometimes translated "cursed" or "profaned" (1 Kgs. 21:10, 13; Isa. 52:5; Ezek. 20:27; 36:20). Death by stoning was the penalty (Lev. 24:16).

BLASTUS A trusted personal servant of Herod Agrippa who acted as an intermediary for the people of Tyre and Sidon (Acts 12:20).

BLEMISH *See* SICK, SICKNESS

BLESS, BLESSING The word "bless" and its derivatives in both Testaments are synonyms for the word "happy" (Gen. 30:13). In the Beatitudes it has this meaning in Matthew 5:3-12. It also denotes thanks to God (Mt. 26:26). To bless someone is to ask divine favor on that one (Ps. 129:8). Blessings are gifts from God, or man. In Joshua 15:19 the Hebrew word is translated "special favor."

BLOOD In the OT the picture presented is of life in the blood and the blood itself was life. It could not be eaten and it is the blood that makes atonement (Gen. 9:4-6; Lev. 17:11, 14; Deut. 12:23). "Whosoever sheds the blood of man, by man shall his blood be shed." The offering of blood was part of the ritual of atonement so that when the sacrifice was killed its blood had to be poured out on the altar (Ex. 24:8; 29:12, 16, 20; Lev. 16:15, 16, 27). In the NT it is the blood of Jesus Christ that makes the atonement, which means that his death was considered a sacrifice and the blood was poured out to make the atonement. Life is in the blood and there can be no remission of sin without its being shed. Therefore, it required the death of a lamb without blemish or defect to make the sacrifice in OT times. That is why Christ is called both sinless and the Lamb of God (Heb. 9:11-14, 22; 10:19; 1 Pet. 1:19; 1 Jn. 1:7).

BLOOD, AVENGER OF *See* AVENGER OF BLOOD

BLOODGUILT *See* AVENGER OF BLOOD

BOAR *See* BEASTS

BOAT *See* SHIP

BOAZ 1. A Bethlehemite who married Ruth the Moabitess after the death of her husband. From the descendants of this union came King David and Jesus (Ruth 4:1-10, 18-21; Mt. 1:5-6).
2. The name of one of the two bronze pillars that stood in the vestibule of Solomon's temple (1 Kgs. 7:15-22).

BOHAN A son of Reuben; his stone (landmark) was on the border between Judah and Benjamin (Josh. 15:6).

BOIL *See* SICK, SICKNESS

BOKERU A descendant of Jonathan (1 Chron. 8:38).

BOKIM An unidentified site near Gilgal where men wept (*bokim*) because of Israel's disobedience to God (Judg. 2:1-5).

BONDAGE, *See* SLAVE, SLAVERY
BONDMAN

BONES In the OT often a synonym for "body" (Ps. 42:10). The dry bones of Ezekiel's vision represent the scattered Israelites in exile and their coming together represents the regathering and coming to life again of Israel (Ezek. 37). It was required that no bone of a sacrificial animal could be broken, and in the NT the fact that no bone of Jesus was broken in his death was considered the fulfillment of prophecy as he was the sacrifice (Ex. 12:46; Ps. 34:20; Jn. 19:36).

BOOK *See* SCROLL

BOOK OF LIFE, *See* SCROLL
BOOK OF
REMEMBRANCE

BOOTHS, *See* CALENDAR and FESTIVALS
FEAST OF

BOR ASHAN An unidentified site to which David sent part of the spoil after his return to Ziklag from fighting the Philistines (1 Sam. 30:30).

BOUNDARY Stones could be markers of boundaries (Josh. 15:6; 18:17),
STONES but landmarks of an unspecified nature also are noted as

being important. It was forbidden to remove them (Deut. 19:14; Prov. 22:28).

BOW *See* ARMS AND ARMOR

BOWELS *See* EMOTIONS

BOWL These vessels could be made of gold or other metal but the vast majority would have been made of baked clay. Some would have been glazed and some painted. It is by the glazing and painting on bowls and sherds (broken pieces of these vessels) that archaeologists date some of the strata in their excavations.

BOX The Hebrew word is also translated chest, horn, and flask (1 Sam. 6:8; 2 Kgs. 9:1; 1 Kgs. 1:39). The woman who anointed Jesus had an ointment filled alabaster jar (box) (Mt. 26:7).

BOZEZ One of the two steep cliffs which were landmarks near Michmash (1 Sam. 14:4, 5).

BOZKATH An unidentified site in Judah (Josh. 15:39; 2 Kgs. 22:1).

BOZRAH 1. A city (289-214) in Moab east of the Jordan (Jer. 48:24).
2. An important Edomite city (208-016) at the junction of the Kings Highway and the Way of Shur (Isa. 63:1). Its destruction was foretold (Jer. 49:13).

BRACELET A common adornment worn on the lower arm by both men and women, made of gold in the case of luxury but usually of iron, silver, or glass (Gen. 24:47; Ezek. 16:11).

BRAMBLE *See* PLANTS, PERFUMES, AND SPICES

BRANCH A number of different Hebrew words are translated into English as branch (Gen. 40:10; Ex. 25:33; Jer. 11:16). Some are used figuratively in the sense of "offspring" or even "head" and some designate the Messianic King who is to come (Job 15:32; Isa. 9:14; 11:1; Jer. 33:15). In the NT it is frequently used to refer to believers. Christ is the vine and the believers are the branches (Jn. 15:5).

BREAD A basic staple in the diet of ancient Israel usually made from wheat or barley ground in a mill and rubbed between two stones or by being beaten in a mortar with a pestle and then kneaded in a kneading-trough. Unleavened bread was baked immediately after grinding without the use of yeast and it was this bread that was used at Passover and during the Feast of Unleavened Bread. It could be baked as small cakes (like modern pancakes) on a griddle placed over a fire (Lev. 2:5), on hot coals (1 Kgs. 19:6), or in an oven (Lev. 2:4). Archaeologists have discovered numerous ovens, circular in shape. The fire was built inside the circular clay oven and when the clay walls were hot the wet dough would be stuck on the hot clay sides until it dropped off when cooked. Bread was baked by both women and men (Gen. 40:16; Jer. 37:21). In the NT Christ is presented as "the bread of life" (Jn. 6:35). He who believes in Christ is said to partake of this "heavenly bread" and will live forever (Jn. 6:50, 51).

BREASTPIECE Its exact nature is not clear but it was a part of the high priest's garment, made of the best of fabrics (Ex. 28:15), and was attached to the ephod by four golden rings (*see* EPHOD). On it were two jewels, each one bearing on it the name of six of the tribes of Israel. The Urim and the Thummim were in it and the high priest would bear these and the names of the tribes before the Lord when he entered the Holy Place (Ex. 28:29-30). *See* URIM AND THUMMIM.

BREASTPLATE *See* ARMS AND ARMOR

BREECHES *See* DRESS

BRETHREN OF THE LORD Brothers of Jesus: James, Joseph, Simon, and Judas (Mt. 13:55). It is significant that "his brothers" did not believe in him until after his resurrection (Jn. 7:1, 3-5; Acts 1:14), and that they are distinguished from the apostles (1 Cor. 9:5). These two facts indicate that these were real brothers of Jesus, children of Joseph and Mary.

BRIBE The giving of a gift of something of value intended to influence the recipient in his exercise of a legal duty (1 Sam. 8:3). Bribery was prohibited in Israel (Ex. 23:8).

BRIDE, BRIDEGROOM *See* MARRIAGE

BRIDLE, BIT As we know them today, these were also used in biblical times. The words are used both in a literal and figurative sense (Ps. 32:9; Isa. 30:28).

BRIER *See* PLANTS, PERFUMES, AND SPICES

BRIMSTONE The word rendered "brimstones" in some versions is translated in the NIV as "sulphur," usually found in volcanic areas. The destruction of Sodom and Gomorrah was by fire and sulphur (Gen. 19:24, 28), which could have resulted from a volcanic eruption or even an earthquake that released sulphuric gases that killed the people. "Fire and brimstone" (burning sulphur) as a method of divine punishment is also found in Revelation (Rev. 14:10; 19:20).

BRONZE An alloy or mixture of copper and tin. Brass is a mixture of copper and zinc, which was not used in biblical times. Bronze has also a reference to hardness (Lev. 26:19) or obstinancy in sin (Isa. 48:4-5).

BROOK Several Hebrew words are so translated into English. One is a perennial stream, brook, or river as we know it (Ps. 42:1). The others are what are called in the Middle East *wadis* which are stream beds, dry except immediately after a rain (Deut. 2:13; 2 Sam. 15:23).

BROOM Broom is mentioned in Isa. 14:34. It is implied in a few other passages (Mt. 12:44).

BROTHER-IN-LAW, DUTY OF (Levirate Marriage) *See* MARRIAGE

BUCKLER *See* ARMS AND ARMOR

BUKKI 1. The representative of the tribe of Dan in the dividing of the land of Canaan (Num. 34:22).

2. A descendant of Aaron (Ezra 7:4).

BUKKIAH A Levite leader of the temple musicians (1 Chron. 25:4).

BUL *See* CALENDAR

BULL *See* BEASTS, 4

BUNAH A descendant of Judah (1 Chron. 2:25).

BUNNI 1. A Levite who was with Ezra when the law was read (Neh. 9:4).

2. One who sealed the covenant with Nehemiah (Neh. 10:15).

BURIAL To the Israelite burial was very important. Not to be buried was a curse (Ps. 79:3; Isa. 14:18-20). After death the eyes were closed by a relative or friend, and the body was washed, anointed, wrapped in linen with a special cloth over the head, and placed in a room of the house until the time of interment which usually took place on the same day (Gen. 46:4; Mk. 16:1; Mt. 27:59; Jn. 11:44; Acts 9:37). Friends followed the bier to the grave or tomb (2 Sam. 3:31; Judg. 8:32).

BURNT OFFERING *See* SACRIFICE AND OFFERING

BURNT SACRIFICE *See* SACRIFICE AND OFFERING

BUSHEL *See* WEIGHTS AND MEASURES

BUZ 1. A nephew of Abraham (Gen. 22:21).
2. A descendant of Dan (1 Chron. 5:14).

BUZI The father of the prophet Ezekiel (Ezek. 1:3).

CAB *See* WEIGHTS AND MEASURES

CABBON An unidentified site in Judah in the western foothills (Josh. 15:40).

CABUL 1. A town in the tribal area of Asher (Josh. 19:27).

2. A part of the tribal area of Naphtali which Solomon gave to Hiram king of Tyre but which he refused to accept (1 Kgs. 9:13).

CAESAR The family name of a series of Roman emperors: Octavius (Augustus), Tiberius, Caligula, Claudius, and Nero. They were all related in some way to Julius Caesar and bore his name. Later the term became a title by which the emperor of Rome was designated. *See also* ROME.

CAESAREA A coastal city NW of Jerusalem built by Herod the Great on the site of an earlier Phoenician port also of major importance in NT times. After Herod it became the capital of the Roman province of Palestine. Here Herod Agrippa I was struck with blindness (Acts 12:19-23). An inscription bearing the name of Pontius Pilate was discovered there by archaeologists. An early Christian, Philip, lived there (Acts 8:40; 21:8). It was the home of the centurion Cornelius who sent for Peter (Acts 10:1ff.). Paul was in prison there for two years before being sent on to Rome (Acts 24:27; 27:1-2).

CAESAREA PHILIPPI One of the main sources of the water of the River Jordan comes out of the rocks at the foot of Mt. Hermon which in antiquity had the name Paneas after the Roman god Pan. Herod the Great built a temple there and his son Philip enlarged the city, naming it after the Roman emperor Tiberius Caesar. Jesus visited the city with his disciples (Mt. 16:13).

CAIAPHAS A son-in-law of the high priest Annas, who was appointed to his post by the Romans (Jn. 18:13). He made the statement, "It is better for you that one man die for the people than that the whole nation perish" (Jn. 11:49, 50). After Jesus' arrest and appearance before Annas, he was taken to Caiaphas, who sent him on to Pilate (Jn. 18:28, 29). He also sat on the trial of Peter (Acts 4:6).

CAIN The first son of Adam and Eve, a tiller of the soil, who killed his brother Abel, being jealous because God received Abel's offering but not his own (Gen. 4:1-8). *See also* KAIN.

CAINAN An ancestor of Jesus (Lk. 3:36, 37). *See also* KENAN.

CALAH A city of Mesopotamia founded by the hunter Nimrod (Gen. 10:11, 12).

CALAMUS *See* PLANTS, PERFUMES, AND SPICES

CALCOL One of the wise men of whom it is said that Solomon was wiser (1 Kgs. 4:31).

CALDRON The English translation of several words used for cooking pots (1 Sam. 2:14).

CALEB One of the twelve spies sent by Moses to spy out the land of Canaan, one of the two of them who brought back a good report. For this he was promised entrance into the Land of Canaan while all the others of his age died in the wilderness. Joshua gave him Hebron, and in turn Caleb gave Debir to his daughter and son-in-law (Num. 13:2ff.; 14:24; Josh. 14:13ff.; 15:15ff.). A variant Hebrew spelling is Kelubai (1 Chron. 2:9).

CALENDAR A calendar is a system of reckoning time, with special references to the limits and subdivisions of the year. Throughout its history, biblical Israel based its calendar upon solar years with their changing seasons. Thus the very name for year in Hebrew, *shana*, means "change," in contrast with Egypt's system of a slowly shifting date for New Year's.

Originally "the end of the year" seems to have occurred after the fall harvest in September or October (Ex. 23:16; 34:22); but from the exodus onward Passover (spring) marked "the first month of the year" (Ex. 12:2). Israel later returned to the fall (as in the modern "Jewish New Year's"), yet the Mosaic month numbering was retained, so that, paradoxically, the regnal years of the Judean kings began in their seventh month. In 2 Kings 22:3, for example, an event in Josiah's eighteenth year is followed (2 Kgs. 23:23) several months later by a Passover (first month) in the same eighteenth year.

Month	Modern Equivalent	Canaanite	Babylonian	Reference	Sacred Feasts
1	April (or late March)	Abib	Nisan	Ex. 13:4 Neh. 2:1	14th day, Passover; 15-21, Unleavened Bread
2	May	Ziv	Iyyar	1 Kgs. 6:1	
3	June		Sivan	Esth. 8:9	6, Pentecost (Weeks, or Harvest)
4	July		Tammuz		
5	August		Ab		
6	September		Elul		
7	October	Ethanim	Tishri	1 Kgs. 8:2	1, Trumpets (Rosh Hashanah—New Year's Day); 15-21, Tabernacles (Booths, Ingathering)
8	November	Bul	Marcheshvan	1 Kgs. 6:38	
9	December		Kislev	Neh. 1:1	25, Dedication-Hanukkah (Lights)
10	January		Tebeth	Esth. 2:16	
11	February		Shebat	Zech. 1:7	
12	March		Adar	Ezra 6:15	14-15, Purim

The year was divided into months, with designations that indicated the seasons: Abib, "new grain" (Lev. 2:14), for instance, refers to the initial month of spring, when the barley ripened (Ex. 23:15; Deut. 16:1). Similarly the "Gezer Calendar," found in 1908, preserves in the scratched writing of a tenth century B.C. schoolboy the agricultural operations throughout the twelve months, starting in the fall. The Hebrew names for month are *hodesh yerah*, which mean "new moon" and suggest lunar months that began with the first appearance of the new moon (Gen. 1:14; Ps. 104:19). Yet the true lunar month consists, approximately, of an awkward 29½ days, so that in its earliest records (Moses' writings in Genesis), perhaps due to Egyptian influence, each month has thirty days (Gen. 8:3, 4 compared with 7:11; see also Num. 20:29 and Deut. 34:8 compared with Deut. 21:13). Then, by adding either five or six days at the end of a year, or a thirteenth intercalated month every several years, Israel's calendar continued to reflect the true solar year. But Israel soon shifted back into lunar months of either twenty-nine or thirty days, so that the first of every month was a new moon feast and Passover's fourteenth day fell at full moon (Ps. 81:3).

The Bible reflects three different ways of naming the months. From early times, descriptive Canaanite names were used, though only four are mentioned in the Bible; from the time of Moses onward, the months were simply numbered, starting in the spring; and after the exile Syro-Babylonian names were adopted. These are as follows, with Israel's feasts:

Each month was divided into weeks of seven numbered days, which ran consecutively, irrespective of the months. The shabbath, or seventh day, might thus fall on any day of the month, though at Christ's crucifixion it seems to have coincided with Passover on the fourteenth of Nisan (Jn. 19:31), which was indeed the case on April 7, A.D. 30; *see also* CHRONOLOGY. (J.B.P.)

CALF, GOLDEN Three golden calves are noted. One was made by Aaron and the other two by Jeroboam I of Israel. These were all idolatrous and condemned (Ex. 32; 1 Kgs. 12:28, 29).

CALNEH, CALNO 1. An unidentified city in Mesopotamia founded by Nimrod (Gen. 10:10).

2. An unidentified Syrian city (Amos 6:2; Isa. 10:9).

CAMEL *See* BEASTS, 4

CAMP It appears that, in nomadic days men pitched their tents in a circle around their cattle and sheep for protection and this was their encampment. Out of this grew other types of protective encampments such as that around the tabernacle during the wilderness wanderings of the Israelites in their exodus from Egypt. Three tribes pitched their tents on each of the four sides of the central rectangular area in which the tabernacle was pitched. In an inner circle about the tabernacle were the four major groups of the Levites, as in Numbers 2-3.

CANA A NT town usually identified with a village on the edge of Nazareth but more probably with a ruin approximately 8 miles farther north called Khirbet Kana. Here Jesus performed his first miracle, changing water into wine, and from here he healed a nobleman's son living in Capernaum (Jn. 2:1ff.; 4:46). This was Nathanael's village (Jn. 21:2).

CANAAN, CANAANITES *See* CONQUEST OF CANAAN and GEOGRAPHY OF THE HOLY LAND

CANDACE A queen of Ethiopia whose treasurer was baptized by Philip (Acts 8:26ff.).

CANE *See* PLANTS, PERFUMES, AND SPICES

CANNEH An unidentified town named with Haran and Ashur (Ezek. 27:23).

CAPERNAUM A town on the northern shore of the Sea of Galilee where Jesus spent much time. It is even called his own town on one occasion (Mt. 9:1). Here Jesus healed the servant of a Roman centurion (Mt. 8:5ff.); it was the home of Matthew, a tax collector who became an apostle (Mt. 9:9); here he healed Peter's mother-in-law and performed many other miracles of healing (Mt. 8:14, 15; 9:1ff.; Jn. 4:46ff.). Here too he gave his address to the multitude on the day after the feeding of the 5,000 (Jn. 6:24ff.). For their unbelief he predicted the ruin of the city (Mt. 11:23, 24).

CAPHTOR The country or area from which the Philistines came (Jer. 47:4; Amos 9:7). Because of the close connections between Egypt and Crete (called Keftiu) that go back into the third millennium B.C., it is thought by some that the Philistines come from Crete (the Kerethites of Ezekiel 25:16) and that this is Caphtor. Others feel that the term Caphtor covers a wider coastal area in Asia Minor from which the Philistines came in the general movement of the Sea Peoples towards the end of the second millennium B.C. At least it is clear from the different kinds of headgear of the Philistine soldiers that they were not all from one group.

CAPITAL An ornamental decorative item on the tops of pillars usually of massive size—Doric, Corinthian, Ionian, Proto-Ionic, depending on style and place of origin of the design.

CAPPADOCIA *See* GEOGRAPHY OF THE HOLY LAND

CAPSTONE *See* CORNERSTONE

CAPTAIN An officer of some kind whose exact identity is not clear, attested by the fact that it is used to translate a large number of Hebrew and Greek words. This is the case since we know very little about army ranks in biblical times. Reference is made to "the captain of the temple guard" who was second only to the high priest; called "chief officer" in the OT (Acts 4:1; 5:24; Jer. 20:1).

CAPTIVITY The Bible recognizes three dispersions, exiles, or captivities of Jews. One was the 400 years in Egypt from which they were led back by Moses and Joshua (Gen. 15:13, 14). The second was seventy years in Babylon. From this they came back under Zerubbabel, Ezra, and Nehemiah (Jer. 25:11). The third is pictured as a worldwide diaspora. No specific time for return is associated with this diaspora but it is clearly stated to be a regathering from all the countries of the world (Deut. 30:1-5; Ezek. 36:24). As the word "captivity" is used, the usual thought is of the Assyrian and Babylonian one. The ten northern tribes were taken captive by the Assyrians in 722/721 B.C. while the two southern tribes, Judah and Benjamin, were taken by the Babylonians in a series of deportations spread over a number of years ending with the final one in 586 B.C. (2 Kgs. 25:1-4, 8-10). *See also* DIASPORA.

CARBUNCLE *See* PRECIOUS STONES AND METALS

CARCAS A eunuch of the Persian King Xerxes (Esth. 1:10).

CARCHEMISH A strategic site located on the Euphrates River at the place of an important ford. It was the capital of the Hittite empire in the east and guardian of the crossroads between Asia Minor and Mesopotamia and between the province of Palestine and Mesopotamia. In the days of Josiah, king of Judah, Pharaoh Neco of Egypt fought the Babylonians at Carchemish (2 Chron. 35:20). However, a few years later the Babylonians under Nebuchadnezzar defeated the Egyptians there (Jer. 46:2).

CARITES Thought by some to be the same as the Kerethites (2 Kgs. 11:4, 19).

CARMEL 1. A mountain range in Palestine. *See* GEOGRAPHY OF THE HOLY LAND.

2. A town (162-092) in the hill country of Judah (Josh. 15:55; 1 Sam. 15:12; 2 Sam. 23:35).

CARMI 1. A son of Reuben (Gen. 46:9).

2. Father of the Achan who sinned at Ai (Josh. 7:1).

CARNELIAN *See* PRECIOUS STONES AND METALS

CARPENTER A worker in wood and timber. The best description of the art of the carpenter is found in Isaiah 44:13-17. The Phoenicians seem to have been good carpenters (2 Sam. 5:11). Jesus worked with his father, Joseph, as a carpenter (Mt. 13:55; Mk. 6:3).

CARPUS Paul's host at Troas where he left a cloak (2 Tim. 4:13).

CARSHENA A prince at the court of King Xerxes in Persia (Esth. 1:14).

CART Used for carrying persons or goods in civilian rather than military use (Gen. 45:19; 1 Sam. 6:7, 8). These were of wood with wooden wheels and drawn by a pair of oxen or cows (Num. 7:3; 1 Sam. 6:7).

CASIPHIA An unidentified site in Babylonia (Ezra 8:17).

CASLUHITES An unidentified group of people (Gen. 10:14).

CASSIA *See* PLANTS, PERFUMES, AND SPICES

CASTANET *See* MUSICAL INSTRUMENTS

CATAPULT *See* ARMS AND ARMOR

CATTLE *See* BEASTS, 4

CAUDA A small island south of Crete (Acts 27:16).

CAVE From earliest times the caves in the soft limestone of Palestine served as homes (Gen. 19:30), temporary refuges (Josh. 10:16), and tombs (Gen. 23:9ff.).

CEDAR *See* TREES

CEDRON *See* KIDRON

CENCHREA A seaport near Corinth visited by Paul and the home of a Christian he commends to the church at Rome (Acts 18:18; Rom. 16:1).

CENSER A vessel usually of bronze but sometimes of gold for burning incense (Lev. 10:1; Ex. 27:3; 1 Kgs. 7:50). There is no biblical description but archaeologists have found samples of small bowls with long handles.

CENSUS At Mount Sinai two years after the start of the exodus from Egypt the first counting of the Israelites was made. The census was made of men twenty years old and over (Num. 1:1-3) excluding Levites (1:47), the total of which was 603,550 (Num. 1:45, 46). The Levites were numbered separately, every male a month old or more, and totaled 22,000 (Num. 3:39). The second census took place forty years later just before the start of the conquest of Palestine when those who were punished for their failure to believe God forty years earlier had died in the wilderness. There were 23,000 Levites and 601,730 other males (Num. 14:20-24; 26:1, 2; 51-62). King David took an unauthorized census during his reign for which he and the people were punished. It showed 800,000 men of fighting age in Israel and 500,000 in Judah (2 Sam. 24:2, 9, 15). One census is noted in the NT, that of Caesar Augustus in the days when Quirinius was governor of Syria. It was at this time that Jesus was born in Bethlehem (Lk. 2:1-5).

CENTURION 1. *See also* CORNELIUS and IMPERIAL REGIMENT.

2. A Roman officer in command of 100 foot soldiers. Those referred to in the Bible are mentioned in a good light (Mt. 8:8; Mk. 15:39; Acts 10:1; 22:26; 27:43).

CEPHAS One of the names of the Apostle Peter (Jn. 1:42).

CEREAL OFFERING *See* SACRIFICES AND OFFERINGS

CHALDEA, CHALDEANS A region in and/or the inhabitants of southern Babylonia. They were a tribal people (warriors, Ezek. 23:15) and not a part of the city-dwelling Babylonians. Their living together was upset when the Assyrians invaded the south. Out of this struggle the Chaldeans came to be masters in the area. What is sometimes called the neo-Babylonian period was in actuality Chaldean, from Nabopolassar to Nabonidus when the Persians conquered the area in 538 B.C. The wise men of this group then went into other parts of the world as magicians and astrologers (Dan. 2:10). Abraham left Ur of the Chaldeans to emigrate to Canaan (Gen. 11:28). Chaldeans are called Babylonians in Jeremiah 37. *See also* DIVINATION.

CHAMELEON *See* BEASTS, 6

CHANT *See* MUSIC

CHARIOT A two-wheeled vehicle like the cart but used in battle rather than for carrying burdens. They were introduced to the Middle East, at some time before the eighteenth century, from the east, and introduced to the Egyptians by the Canaanites later. They were made of iron or wood covered with metal plates. They carried two or three persons: the driver of the horse, an archer or spearman, and a shield bearer (2 Chron. 18:33; 1 Kgs. 22:34; Josh. 17:16). King

Solomon was the first Israelite to make extensive use of the military chariot (1 Kgs, 10:26). An Assyrian record indicates that King Ahab of Israel had a great army of chariots. There is a debate among archaeologists as to whether the great stables at Megiddo were Solomonic or from the time of Ahab.

CHARMER *See* DIVINATION

CHARMS Small objects, amulets, usually pierced and worn around the neck, which were intended to give protection or ward off evil spirits.

CHEBAR *See* KEBAR

CHEDORLAOMER *See* KEDORLAOMER

CHEESE In the ancient Middle East cheese was made from the milk of goats, sheep, cows, and camels. Because of lack of refrigeration and the abundance of milk at the same time, the cheese of milk was a staple part of the diet (2 Sam. 17:29; Job 10:10).

CHELAL *See* KELAL

CHELLUH *See* KELUHI

CHELUB *See* KELUB

CHEMOSH *See* DEITIES

CHENAANAH *See* KENAANAH

CHENANI *See* KENANI

CHENANIAH *See* KENANIAH

CHEPHAR-HAMMONAI *See* KEPHAR AMMONI

CHEPHIRAH *See* KEPHIRAH

CHERAN *See* KERAN

CHERETHITES *See* KERETHITES

CHERITH *See* KERITH

CHERUB They are represented in art and statuary as winged human-animal forms with various types of animal, or even human faces (Ezek. 1:5-12; 10:8, 14). They guarded the entrance to Eden after Adam and Eve were expelled. A likeness in pure gold of two of them was on either side of the mercy seat on top of the Ark of Testimony. They were embroidered on the curtains of the tabernacle and on the veil of the temple (Gen. 3:24; Ex. 25:22; 26:1; 2 Chron. 3:14). King Solomon had gold covered wooden ones placed in the temple (1 Kgs. 6:23-28). *See also* KERUB.

CHESALON *See* KESALON

CHESED *See* KESED

CHESIL *See* KESIL

CHEZIB *See* KEZIB

CHIDON *See* KIDON

CHIEF The leader of a family, clan, or tribe (Gen. 36:15; Zech. 12:5).

CHILEAB *See* KILEAB

CHILION *See* KILION

CHILMAD *See* KILMAD

CHIMHAM *See* KIMHAM

CHINNERETH *See* KINNERETH

CHIOS An island in the Aegean Sea opposite which Paul's ship anchored for a night on his final trip to Jerusalem (1 Cor. 1:11).

CHISLON *See* KISLON

CHLOE A woman from whose household some reported to Paul on the quarelling among the members of the church at Corinth (1 Cor. 1:11).

CHOIR *See* MUSIC, MUSICAL INSTRUMENTS

CHOIRMASTER *See* PSALMS, TITLES OF

CHORAZIN *See* KORAZIN

CHOSEN PEOPLE God has an "eternal purpose, according to the counsel of His will, whereby, for His own glory, He hath foreordained whatsoever comes to pass" (Westminster Shorter Catechism). In implementing this eternal purpose God chooses individuals or groups out of the masses in order to achieve his goals. *(See* ELECTION for a discussion of his choice of individuals.) The concept in the OT is that Israel was God's chosen people. He chose Abraham while he was in Ur and brought him to Canaan and there made an everlasting covenant with him and for his descendants after him. This covenant included two parts: God's promise to bless the world through Abraham's seed; and to give the land of Canaan as an everlasting possession to him and his seed after him, the land from the River of Egypt to the great river, the Euphrates (Gen. 12:3; 15:18; 17:19; 18:10; Gal. 3:16). God chose the seed of Abraham when he brought them out of the bondage in Egypt and gave them their way of life in the law. This he did at Sinai. The victory over the peoples of Palestine was his gift so that they would have their national home as promised to Abraham (Ex. 3:6-10; Deut. 6:21-25; Isa. 43:1; 51:2; Acts 13:17). God's spiritual purpose in this choice or election of a people was that he would have a people to be holy to himself, to be his witnesses in the world, and to bring his blessings of salvation to all peoples through the Messiah who was to be descended from them (Deut. 7:6; Isa. 43:10-12; 42:1-7; Mt. 12:15-21; Rom. 11:17-24; Eph. 2:11-13; Isa. 49:6).

CHRIST, LIFE AND TEACHINGS OF Jesus Christ is the central figure in Christianity. His importance cannot be exaggerated either in the religious or secular sense. The calendar of the western world revolves around his birth. Many secular institutions have been influenced by his teaching. The importance of Christ can be best understood by considering a number of questions about him.

To answer the question, *"Who is he?"* we cannot do better than note some of the names used of him, or used by him. In a Hebrew setting the name represented the nature, and the meaning of names was more important than in Western culture. The name by which he is most generally known is Jesus Christ. The first of these means "Savior," which shows him to be one who came in some sense to deliver his people from bondage. The other name, Christ, is really a title meaning the Anointed One (Messiah), and came to be used in the Jewish world for the coming leader who would introduce a new era. The main idea current at the time was that Messiah would rid his people of the Roman overlords, but this was far from the purpose of Jesus. When the title was applied to him it was used in a spiritual sense of a deliverer from moral bondage. The name Jesus Christ therefore puts in a nutshell what Jesus came to do.

Jesus avoided the use of the title Messiah since it would
have been misunderstood. He was no revolutionary in a
political sense, although his teaching contained many revolutionary ideas. He chose to speak of himself as the Son of
Man. There has been much discussion over what he meant
by it, but it seems most likely that he used it to represent all
that the Jewish prophets and other teachers had predicted
about the hoped-for deliverer, without implicating himself in
current political ideas about the Messiah. It also focused
attention upon Jesus as a true man. Another title used of him
and by him was Son of God. He spoke in such a way that it
is clear that he had a special relationship with God as Father.
This colored his whole ministry.

Jesus used many metaphors to describe himself. He
referred to himself as the Shepherd of the sheep, as the
Door to the sheepfold, as the Light of the world, as the Life
of men. These claims are astounding but he made them
without any apology. He stated them as facts. These are the
terms on which his life and importance must be considered.

When considering the biography of any person, one's
first concern is for reliable sources. In the case of the life of
Jesus Christ, we have only the four accounts in our Gospels.
Outside these books there is very little mention of Jesus by
the secular historians of the time. Tacitus says that Christ
was executed in the reign of Tiberius by the procurator
Pontius Pilate. Suetonius refers to uprisings in Rome over
one Chrestus, who may be identified as Christ, but says no
more about him. The fact is the pagan world passed him
by with no more than the scantiest references. Even the
Jewish historian Josephus makes only slight passing reference
to him. Our sources therefore are almost wholly written by
Christians.

The four Gospels are not biographies. They are Gospels,
which means simply Good News. What they tell us about
Jesus Christ is with a definite purpose in view. One of them,
John, said quite specifically that he wrote to encourage people
to believe that Jesus was the Messiah and Son of God. If
we want a bare record of facts, we shall not find it in any of
these Gospels. But this does not mean that we can know
no facts about the life of Jesus. Although the writers were
men who had come to believe in Jesus in a certain way, they
were nevertheless concerned to present a true account of
him.

The question naturally arises, Where did they obtain their
information? It seems certain that our Gospels were either
written by eyewitnesses or else by those in close touch with
eyewitnesses. This is important since otherwise we could
have no confidence in the Gospels as sources of historical
information. Some of the writers may have used other sources

which were themselves based on eyewitnesses, but if so this would not affect the reliability of the Gospels. It is widely believed, for instance, that Matthew and Luke were based on Mark and that both of them drew from another source which has not been preserved. Any attempt to find out at this stage exactly how the Gospel writers collected their information must in the nature of the case be largely speculative. Some scholars have tried to maintain that much of the material used gives rather what the Christians thought happened than what actually did happen. But the early Christians would not have been prepared to suffer and even die for the creations of their own imaginations. We may proceed to outline main events in the life of Jesus with confidence.

There were six main stages in the story of Jesus as far as it can be reconstructed. From his birth to the beginning of his public work occupied about thirty years. The Gospels were not interested in this period, except for some details of his birth and one incident of his childhood. Something will be said about his birth or incarnation in the next section dealing with the question of why he came. The second stage was the period of preparation, which is more particularly concerned with the way in which the coming of Jesus was announced by John the Baptist who appeared in the garb of an ancient prophet and proclaimed judgment and the need for repentance. He used the rite of baptism as a symbol of repentance. He preached the coming of the Kingdom. He in fact set the stage for the public ministry of Jesus.

The second stage is composed of two events. First, Christ's baptism by John in the River Jordan. This was not because Jesus needed to repent, but because he wished to identify himself with the needy people around him. One special feature of the baptism of Jesus which marked it out from all others was the descent of the Spirit of God upon him. The writers speak of the Spirit in the shape of a dove in order to make clear that something visible descended. Moreover, a voice was heard, at least by John the Baptist, which gave God's approval to the ministry of Jesus. John himself seemed to have had special insight into the coming mission of Jesus for he pointed him out as the Lamb of God who was to take away the world's sin. The other important happening of a preparatory character was the temptation of Jesus. Matthew and Luke both record the same sample of temptations which Jesus faced at the beginning of his ministry and which must have recurred at times throughout. He was tempted to use supernatural power or spectacular methods to achieve his ends rather than following the path of God's will.

The third stage of the story was set in Judea. This is reported briefly by John, who concentrated on certain important

features. The first disciples were called to follow Jesus,
although it was not until later that they left their normal
occupations to assist in his ministry. Among other features
were two remarkable conversations which Jesus had, one
with a Jewish teacher and the other with a Samaritan woman.
In both cases Jesus made a deep impression on the minds of
his hearers. Of special note is the fact that Jesus was not
prepared to allow Jewish nationalist prejudice to prevent him
from conversation with a Samaritan. The most notable aspect
of his early Judean ministry was the spiritual emphasis in
the teaching of Jesus. It may be said to set the tone for the
whole ministry.

The fourth stage may be called the Galilean ministry. A
wide variety of events are related which took place mainly in
the vicinity of the Sea of Galilee, particularly in and around
Capernaum. The whole of this period may be conveniently
divided into three. The earliest period is marked by the
gathering together of the twelve disciples whom Jesus specially
called to share his mission with him. These were the men
drawn from various walks of life, many of them fishermen,
but at least one a professional man, a tax collector. They
were sent out on a preaching tour and given specific instructions
as to their behavior and message. Jesus was training these
men to carry on his work later. His own preaching was being
warmly acclaimed, but there were already rumblings of
opposition from the Pharisees, who soon detected that Jesus
was unorthodox.

The next period of the Galilean ministry was at the time
when Jesus withdrew from northern Galilee. As in the first
period, there were miracles of healing and controversies,
notably about the Sabbath. With regard to the many healings
which Jesus performed, in most cases there was some act
of faith on the part of the person to be healed, which shows
that Jesus did not perform miracles for their own sake. He
was not a wonder-worker in the common sense of the term.
The Pharisees developed their opposition. They even accused
Jesus of casting out demons by the prince of the demons.
He reserved until later a scathing denunciation of their abuses.
But it was not only the Pharisees who rejected him. The
people of Nazareth where he had been brought up refused to
believe in him. Yet the common people were still favorable
to him, particularly as a result of a miracle of mass feeding.
Some of them even tried to make him king, but this was
no part of his mission.

In the third period, which ended with the departure of
Jesus from Galilee, the most significant event was Peter's
confession at Caesarea Philippi. Jesus drew out of the disciples
their own idea of who he was, which led Peter to declare
him to be the Messiah, the Son of God. This was a turning

point in the ministry, after which Jesus turned his attention more specifically to the twelve. Although he accepted the testimony of his disciples, he did not want them to publish it, no doubt because he knew it would be misunderstood. It was at this stage that he told Peter and the others about his church. Immediately after this, three of the disciples had an extraordinary experience of seeing Jesus transformed before their very eyes on a mountain. This experience shows the supernatural side of the nature of Jesus. Yet it was linked with the first of a threefold prediction that Jesus was to die a violent death, a fact which none of the disciples could grasp.

The fifth stage of the ministry of Jesus may be loosely described as the movement from the activity in the north towards the final events in Jerusalem. It was a period of further activity and teaching, the latter mainly in the form of parables. Such well-known parables as the Good Samaritan and the Prodigal Son are set in this period. Once again that religious hostility, which was to reach its climax in the crucifixion of Jesus, was much in evidence. During the same period must be set some incidents and teaching in Jerusalem recorded by John but not by the other Gospel writers. Jesus drew spiritual lessons from common things as, for instance, the shepherd and his sheep and through this means taught men the things of God. All the time he was preparing his own disciples for the time when he would no longer be with them. At length he drew near to Jerusalem for the last time, spending a brief period east of the Jordan in a district known as Perea. The real climax of this period was reached when he raised Lazarus from the dead in the village of Bethany just outside of Jerusalem. This not only caused amazement but hardened the determination of the religious leaders to do away with Jesus, because they feared he might undermine their position.

The sixth stage—the last week of Jesus' life are told by all four writers in considerable detail, which shows the importance that each attached to them. It is almost as if they were more interested in his death than in his life. The entry of Jesus into Jerusalem on a donkey while being acclaimed by a large crowd of people must have appeared to some like the inauguration of his Kingdom, but events were to show that his Kingdom was not of this world. One side of the story which is illuminating is the weeping of Jesus over the city, for its coming doom was more evident to him than to his contemporaries. His action in clearing the money changers out of the temple in a commanding gesture of religious indignation was too much for the authorities, who after several vain attempts to trap him in his teaching hatched up false charges against him.

With the assistance of Judas Iscariot, one of the twelve, they arranged to arrest him at night away from the popular clamor. That same evening Jesus instituted in the presence of his disciples the Supper which was to remind them of him and to explain the meaning of his death as a sacrificial offering. Having arrested him, his enemies proceeded to put him on trial, if such it could be called. The Jewish Council condemned him but needed the ratification of their sentence by the Roman governor. The latter repeatedly declared that he found no fault in Jesus but the priestly party stirred the crowds to demand crucifixion, the cruelest method of execution used widely by the Romans in their dealings with the Jews. The disciples of Jesus had all forsaken Jesus by this time and one of them, Peter, had denied that he even knew him.

It seemed that the mission of Jesus had ended in disaster, but all this was changed when he rose from the dead on the third day as he said he would. The tragedy became a triumph. The fearful disciples became bold men with a message of hope. It was not until the day of Pentecost that they began preaching the message, because Jesus had told them to wait until they were filled with the Spirit of God. But henceforth men were to find a deeper meaning in Jesus than his own disciples had ever suspected during his lifetime.

Why did he come? It is only when we stand back and look at the life of Jesus that we realize some of the deep questions it poses. It is clear that he was no ordinary man. His own claims and the confessions of others show him to be the Son of God in a special sense. When writing his Gospel, John made the profound statement that he (under the title of the Word) was with God and was God (Jn. 1:1), and that he became flesh (Jn. 1:14). This sums up what is meant by the incarnation. Although possessing the nature of God he became man. Moreover John clearly gave one of the answers to the question why he came. It was to give authority to all who believed in him to become children of God. He came therefore to make possible a new relationship, with God as Father in a new way. He came moreover to fulfill the Jewish Messianic hopes in a new way, in a spiritual rather than a materialistic sense. He came to be a perfect man in order to be a perfect representative for man before God. (For a fuller discussion of why he came, *see also* CHRIST, WORK OF.)

What did he teach? As much importance must be attached to the teaching of Jesus as to his actions. A considerable proportion of the Gospels is concerned with what he said. As a teacher he was distinguished from the Jewish teachers of his day by the authority with which he spoke. He even claimed superiority over Moses in the content of his teaching.

The teaching may be summarized in two parts, one

doctrinal, the other ethical, yet closely related to each other. He taught new truths about God, especially in the realm of Fatherhood, which while not unknown to Jewish minds was never the intimate family relationship of which Jesus spoke. The teaching of Jesus about himself has already been referred to when mentioning his names in the first section. There is no doubt that he intended men to regard him as unique and to recognize that their own destiny was affected by their relation to him. When speaking of the Kingdom, Jesus sometimes spoke of it as present in the hearts of believers and sometimes as an event which belongs to the end of the present age. It is therefore a present reality and a future hope. Another aspect of the teaching of Jesus was his promises about the coming Spirit of Truth or Counselor, who was to make Jesus real to all who came to believe in him. He drew a clear distinction between believers and unbelievers. Faith alone entitled men to entry into the Kingdom.

The ethical demands of Jesus were exacting. In the Sermon on the Mount, the fullest account of his ethical teaching, he frequently exhorted to actions which went beyond what might normally be expected, such as turning the other cheek to the one who strikes you and even loving your enemies. For this reason some have considered the ethics of Jesus to be too idealistic to be practical, but it is because he came to establish a new and higher order of living that his demands are so high. He never expected anyone to adhere to a higher or a lower moral standard than he adopted himself, and he knew that only through him could they achieve it.

What did others think about him? Two main sources enable us to reconstruct what the earliest Christians thought about Jesus Christ. The Book of Acts gives samples of speeches made by apostles, which set out the central message. It is evident that the most important theme is the death and resurrection of Jesus. These men had come to see how the Easter event had completely transformed things. They saw Jesus as the one predicted in the OT and were constantly stressing the idea of promise and fulfillment. It was the risen Christ who was preached. Moreover, he was proclaimed as Savior and Lord.

The other source of information on men's view of Christ is the collection of Epistles. The Apostle Paul had an exalted view of him. He described him as the "image of the invisible God" (Col. 1:15). He was the firstborn of all creation. Not only were all things created by him, but for him all things exist. Moreover, Paul's whole theology revolved around what Jesus Christ had done for men. Christians could now be said to be "in Christ." The other NT writers had no less an exalted view of him. In Hebrews he was presented as the great High Priest; in 1 Peter he was Lord, Shepherd, and

Guardian; in the Johannine Epistles Jesus Christ the Righteous, the advocate with the Father and Son of God; in the Revelation the slain Lamb of God now exalted on the throne.

These Christians were more interested in relating what Jesus had become to them than what he did and said while living among men. Yet the very fact that four records of his doings and sayings were written and treasured in the early church shows that they were not without deep interest in the historical Jesus.

Jesus Christ has never lost his relevance. In the vastly changed world of the twentieth century, his message and importance remain unchanged because he met the fundamental needs of mankind and not merely those of his own age. There is a sense, therefore, in which the life of Christ still continues in the life of the people of God. (D.G.)

CHRIST, WORK OF An expression frequently encountered in Christian theology is "the person and work of Christ." It designates the subject matter of Christology, which might be stated as, Jesus Christ, who he was and what he came to do. No understanding of the work of Jesus Christ is possible apart from an understanding of both who he was and is.

The centrality of Jesus Christ's person and work in Christian belief is indicated in the "Apostles' Creed," the earliest of the "ecumenical" creeds, in continuous use in the church now for over 1700 years. It is still today used in public worship, baptismal confession, and instruction of the young in most of the branches of Christendom in all parts of the world. In English translation it reads:

"I believe in God the Father almighty, maker of heaven and earth; and in Jesus Christ His only Son, our Lord; who was ,conceived by the Holy Ghost; born of the virgin Mary; suffered under Pontius Pilate; was crucified, dead and buried; *He descended into hell* [a later addition]; the third day He rose again from the dead, He ascended into heaven, and sitteth on the right hand of God the Father almighty; from thence He shall come to judge the quick and the dead. I believe in the Holy Ghost, the holy catholic church, the communion of saints, the forgiveness of sins, the resurrection of the body, and the life everlasting. Amen."

There are 109 words in this creed; 69 of them relate to Jesus Christ directly, and of these, 21 relate to his person while 48 relate to his work. This proportion is an accurate representation of the emphases given in true Christianity.

The work of the Lord may not be separated from the God-man who performed it. Noteworthy also is the fact that not one word suggests that the significance of Jesus was that of the teacher of a new religion (or even the best teacher of an old one), nor example of ethical rectitude, nor revelation of the highest humanity, as modern religionists frequently misrepresent his significance. Christians will readily acknowledge many of these compliments to their Lord, but will still insist that they miss the point, for "the Father has sent his Son to be the Savior of the world" (1 John 4:14). Thus the *doing* was part of *being;* his work was not to tell us what to do but to do something for us.

The ancient creed cited is little more than a brief selection from and summary of the NT Scriptures. In these Scriptures there is constant focus on the fact that Jesus was destined, indeed, predestined, to accomplish his work by dying for the sins of men. Jesus did not say much about it, for he did not come to talk about dying, but rather to die. Yet he did make himself plain; " . . . the Son of Man did not come to be served, but to serve, and to give his life as a ransom for many" (Mt. 20:28). Immediately after his announcement of purpose to build "my church" (Mt. 16:13-18), it is reported, "From that time on Jesus began to explain to his disciples that he must go to Jerusalem and suffer many things at the hands of the elders, chief priests and teachers of the law, and that he must be killed, and on the third day be raised to life" (Mt. 16:21). To Peter his crucifixion was by "God's set purpose and foreknowledge" (Acts 2:23), and his sacrifice was "precious blood . . . of a lamb . . . chosen before the foundation of the world" (1 Pet. 1:19, 20), and to John the Revelator he is "the Lamb that was slain from the creation of the world" (Rev. 13:8). So central is a proper understanding of the death of Christ to biblical Christianity that the Apostle Paul could write to the churches where he preached, "I resolved to know nothing while I was with you except Jesus Christ and him crucified" (1 Cor. 2:2). In keeping with this emphasis the cross has been almost the only universal symbol of their faith employed by Christians.

Explanation of the emphasis on the death of Christ in apostolic ministry is found, in part, in the leading place it has in the Christian gospel. Christianity is a missionary faith; it has a message to proclaim. Any program of human betterment is secondary. That message (gospel, preachment, Gr. *kerygma*) is what, when received of men, saves them: "God was pleased through the foolishness of what was preached to save those who believe" (1 Cor. 1:21). That gospel was of Christ, and that is of his person and work, who he was and his career, especially his atoning death (1 Cor. 15:1-4; Acts 10:36-43).

The distinctively Christian value of the OT is found in the predictions therein of the Savior, especially of his redeeming death. It also furnishes the categories for interpretation of the Savior's career. At several junctures in the Gospel narratives of the Lord's last days before Calvary, the ruling force of OT prophecies in shaping those events of passion and death is introduced. When, at the time of his seizure by Jewish authorities, Peter thought to defend Jesus with a sword, Matthew 26:53 records that Jesus said, "Do you think I cannot call on my Father, and he will at once put at my disposal more than twelve legions of angels? But how then would the Scriptures be fulfilled that say it must happen in this way?" (See also Matthew 27:9; Mark 14:27; Luke 22:37; John 12:37-41; 15:25; 17:12; 19:24, 28, 36, 37.) During the forty days before the ascension of Jesus he frequently interpreted the events just past as fulfillment of Scripture, even upbraiding his disciples for failing to see this (Lk. 24:25-27, 44-46). After the ascension, during the early period when the apostolic church remained near Jerusalem, Peter preached several sermons in which he connected the betrayal, passion, death, and resurrection with specific OT prophecies (Acts 2:23-36), and even went so far as to say that "all the prophets," the whole OT, was foretelling of the death of Christ (Acts 3:17, 18, 24). Many years later, addressing a synagogue, Paul startled his audience by declaring, "The people of Jerusalem and their rulers did not recognize Jesus, yet in condemning him they fulfilled the words of the prophets that are read every Sabbath" (Acts 13:27; see also 28-41). In fact, the invariable argument used by the apostles in appealing to Jews was based on the OT prophecies of the passion, death, and resurrection of Jesus.

Furthermore, as indicated above, the Lord himself and his apostles held that the OT prophecy, ritual, and history interpreted the meaning of the crucifixion and related events. Isaiah 52:13—53:12, a comprehensive prophecy of the Lord's suffering and dying servant, lies in the background of interpretation of Jesus throughout the NT, from the words of the Father at the beginning of Jesus' ministry (Mt. 3:17; cf. Isa. 52:13), the comments of Matthew on his preaching and healing ministry (Mt. 8:14-17; cf. Isa. 53:4; Mt. 12:15-21; cf. Isa. 52:13; 42:1ff.) to his suffering and death (1 Pet. 2:22; cf. Isa. 53:9 and 2 Cor. 5:21; 1 Pet. 2:23; cf. Isa. 53:7; Heb. 12:3; 1 Pet. 2:24; cf. Isa. 53:4, 11; 1 Cor. 15:3; Heb. 9:28; 1 Pet. 2:24; cf. Isa. 53:5; 1 Pet. 2:25; cf. Isa. 53:6). Millions of Bible-reading Christians have read the Gospels and then later read Isaiah 53 only to say, Isaiah has drawn a picture of our Savior's death in our place.

The OT figures in another very important fashion in interpreting the "work" of Christ. We refer to his threefold office of *prophet, priest,* and *king.* It will help to understand this triplex office to observe several things. First, the comprehensive nature of his work as the God-man is indicated

by the name "mediator" given by Scripture to his "office" —
"For there is one God and one mediator between God and
men, the man Christ Jesus, who gave himself as a ransom
for all men" (1 Tim. 2:5, 6).

Notice his mediatorial work is traced especially to his death
as a "ransom." Second, though Christ came later to be used
as a name for Jesus, it first appears as his title as the predicted
Messiah of the OT. The nation of Israel observed the custom
of inducting official persons connected with their commonwealth
into office by the ceremony of anointing with oil. This first is
mentioned in Scripture in connection with Aaronic priests
(Ex. 28:41). It is mentioned also in connection with induction
into office of Israel's first king (1 Sam. 9:15; 10:1). Though
the practice is seldom mentioned in that connection, prophets
were also sometimes so inducted into office (1 Kgs. 19:16,
cf. Gen. 20:7; Ps. 105:15). The Hebrew word "to anoint
with oil" is *masah*; the derived adjective *masiah*, anointed,
becomes in the Greek translation of the OT, *Messias*, whence
the English word "Messiah." A step further, the Greek
translation of this word is *Christos* (derived from *Chrio*, to
pour oil). This is transferred to Latin as *Christus* and from
Latin to English as Christ. Hence the title Christ points
directly to his threefold office: prophet, priest, and king.

The function of a prophet is to convey a written or spoken
message from God to men, that is, he was to teach with
divine authority. Jesus did just that. In his person, words, and
deeds he revealed the Father (Jn. 8:26; 14:9; 17:8), and he
taught the people (Mt. 5-7). He was declared to be a prophet
and was said to have done a prophet's work (Deut. 18:15;
cf. Acts 3:22; Mt. 13:57; Lk. 13:33; Jn. 6:14). In keeping
with the requirements for a prophet (Deut. 18:14ff.), he
produced the signs of a prophet, miracles and fulfilled
predictions. There can be no doubt that Jesus' work as
Messiah, the Christ of God, included that belonging to his
office of prophet.

Jesus also fulfilled the office of anointed priest. The biblical
function of a priest was to mediate religiously between God
and man in two ways: the offering of sacrifices (especially
blood sacrifices at the brazen altar) and to make intercession.
Of these two, in the Mosaic ritual system, offering sacrifices
was exclusively the priest's duty and right. The priest was
mediator in a sense the prophet and king were not, it being
his role to represent God to the people in the functions at
the altar and likewise to represent them to God in prayer.

That Jesus fulfilled both these functions and did so as
divinely appointed priest is explicitly stated in Hebrews 7:24-
28. In connection with a "priesthood" which he holds
"permanently" he "always lives to intercede for them" and

"once for all when he offered himself." Jesus was both victim
and sacrificing priest. This is the work of redemption to
which, in a sense, all other is ancillary and supplemental.

The third aspect of his office work is that of king. So
Nathanael could confess, "You are the King of Israel" (Jn.
1:49); Jesus could speak of his kingship (Jn. 18:36) and when
Pilate declared "You are a King, then!" (Jn. 18:37), Jesus
could answer, "You are right in saying I am a king" (Jn. 18:37),
or as Luke put his affirmative answer, "Yes, it is as you say"
(Lk. 23:3). In the great prophecy of Psalm 2:6, the Lord
God says of him, "I have installed my king on Zion, my holy
hill." Likewise, in Psalm 110, a prophecy Jesus appropriated
for himself as Messiah, God proclaims, "Rule in the midst
of your enemies" (v. 2). This messianic rule, though it began
before his ascension among the disciples, was formally
inaugurated at the session at God's right hand (Phil. 1:19-23).
That reign focuses, in the present age, on the church, a
kingdom of grace and spiritual power. It will expand to a
visible kingdom, when at his second coming, he will assume
the throne of David over Israel (Ps. 72) and from that throne
rule all the nations as King of kings and Lord of lords
(1 Tim. 6:15; Rev. 19).

This OT background of the title of office "Christ" explains
the confession of Peter (Mt. 16:16) and of Mary in John
11:27. The former "You are the Christ, the Son of the living
God" and the latter, "You are the Christ, the Son of God,
who was to come into the world" were by pious Jews steeped
in the OT religious outlook. They could hardly have understood
the title in any other way than that of designating one or all
aspects of the threefold office. The NT clearly indicated
that Jesus fulfilled all three designations of the title.

Having seen something of the full scope of his work, let
the field of inquiry now focus on the stages of his work
rather than the aspects of his work. These, as related to our
subject are Jesus' sinless life, his suffering (passion), death
for sinners, burial, resurrection and post-resurrection ministry
(the forty days), his ascension, session at the Father's right
hand, present ministry in heaven, and his Second Advent.

1. *Jesus' Sinless Life.* More than once during his life with
his disciples, Jesus called attention to his perfect rectitude. It
is a striking thing that men so intimately acquainted with a
man, as Jesus' disciples were, would guilelessly and without
refutation, irony or embarrassment pass on reports of such a
claim. John 8, for example, reports a bitter controversy
with the Jews over purity and fatherhood—possibly with
overtones of his own mother's claim to a virginal conception
of her son (Jn. 8:25, 33, 39, 41, 48). Jesus, on the other
hand, most pointedly accused all his hearers of various sins

and challenged his audience with these words, "Can any of you prove me guilty of sin? If I am telling the truth, why don't you believe me?" (Jn. 8:46).

Others, not among his own supporters, gave striking testimony to his innocence. Judas in remorseful terror cried out that he had betrayed "innocent blood" (Mt. 27:4), and we read how Pilate's wife intervened in the trial proceedings with the warning, "Don't have anything to do with that innocent man" (Mt. 27:19). Pilate could find nothing deserving punishment in him and three times pronounced him innocent (Lk. 23:14, 15, 22), even citing Herod in confirmation (v. 15). The overwhelmed centurion pronounced him a "righteous man" (Lk. 23:47), while one of the thieves, admitting his own guilt, testified that Jesus had "done nothing wrong" (Lk. 23:41).

One of his apostles was so impressed by Jesus' holy life that over thirty years later he wrote that his life was "an example, that you should follow in his steps. He committed no sin, and no deceit was found in his mouth" (1 Pet. 2:21, 22).

The sinlessness of Jesus is introduced in the NT record, not just to show that his condemnation was unjust, but to show that he who was slain by "wicked hands" was God's authentic sacrifice for sin—in the language of sin offering and Passover sacrifice employed by John the Baptist, "Look, the Lamb of God, who takes away the sin of the world!" (Jn. 1:29). The Lamb of the Passover had to be without blemish. The same was true of the sin offering (Ex. 12:5; Lev. 22:18-20; cf. 1 Pet. 1:19; Heb. 9:14). This, his active obedience (as the theologians have called it) to the law of God, qualified him to be the perfect and sufficient sacrifice for all human sin. He being an infinite person thus qualified himself later. To use Paul's striking language in 1 Corinthians 5:21, "God made him who knew no sin to be sin for us, so that in him we might become the righteousness of God."

2. *Jesus' Passion.* Question 37 of the Heidelberg Catechism (1563): "What does thou understand by the word suffered (in the Apostles' Creed)? Answer: That all the time He lived on earth, but especially at the end of His life, He bore in body and soul, the wrath of God against sin of the whole human race, in order that by His passion, as the only atoning sacrifice, He might redeem our body and soul from everlasting damnation and obtain for us the grace of God, righteousness, and eternal life."

This venerable affirmation testifies that the passion of Christ has no importance to Christians apart from its culmination in his death. Christians witness to this by their frequent use of the expression, "the suffering and death" of Jesus.

This suffering had its beginning in the treatment he received from his own household and neighbors. Long before the "passion week" his own brothers rejected him (Jn. 7:5). At a point very early in his ministry the men of his home village, when they heard him speaking in the local synagogue, "got up, and drove him out of the town" and, except that he escaped them, would have killed him by throwing him over a nearby cliff (Lk. 4:28-30).

For a while he gained a sympathetic hearing, but for various reasons he lost support. Early in his ministry "he began to teach them that the Son of Man must suffer many things and be rejected by the elders, chief priests and teachers of the law, and that he must be killed" (Mk. 8:31). Though all the elements of the martyrdom-seeker were absent from him, he always understood that it was "written that the Son of Man must suffer much things and be rejected" (Mk. 9:12). He explained to his disciples: "The Son of Man is going to be betrayed into the hands of men. They will kill him" (Mk. 9:31). While walking toward Jerusalem for the last time, "He took the Twelve aside and told them what was going to happen to him. We are going up to Jerusalem . . . and the Son of Man will be betrayed to the chief priests and teachers of the law. They will condemn him to death and will hand him over to the Gentiles, who will mock him and spit on him, flog him and kill him" (Mk. 10:32-34).

Finally, even his disciples "all forsook him and fled." Of his immediate circle only a few women supporters and a boy (the youngest apostle) showed up for the crucifixion, even while "a large number of others followed him" to the cross (Lk. 23:27).

Three things made the suffering most acute: it was inflicted by those whom he loved and whom he had come to save; it was endured alone; the final blow was dealt by his Father: "It was the Lord's will to crush him and cause him to suffer" (Isa. 53:10).

All Christians accept a great deal of unfathomable mystery in this. The mystery is simply the mystery of the government of God over all in an intensified form. They glory in it. They know that existence would hold no mystery, only very obvious hopelessness, without it. They see the power of God ruling and overruling, making the wrath of man to praise him. They see Christ as "the stone that builders rejected"; nevertheless, by God's providence, it "has become the capstone" (1 Pet. 2:7). And though not excusing wicked men for their violent deed, Christians nevertheless proclaim, "The Lord has done this, and it is marvelous in our eyes" (Ps. 118:22, 23).

3. *The Death of Jesus.* As indicated above, though the Gospels justify us in finding some distinction between the

Lord's suffering and death, they lead us as they did the authors of the Confession cited, to discern the consummation of our Lord's suffering in his atoning death. In fact, though all life long he was "a man of sorrows, and familiar with suffering" (Isa. 53:3), when his cross was less than eighteen hours away he spoke of his suffering as still ahead: "I have eagerly desired to eat this Passover with you before I suffer" (Lk. 22:15). The suffering consummated in and found its meaning and purpose in his death.

The nature of the death Jesus experienced is no problem. Once a fully biblical view is taken of his person—incarnate God, fully God, fully man, as the ecumenical creeds also state—it can be understood. Death is three things: physical death, spiritual death, and—yet ahead for lost humanity, that even utterly horrible to contemplate—"second death" (Rev. 20:14), involving eternal exclusion from the presence of God. That physical death took place in Jesus' case has never been doubted except by a few ancient heretics. He bowed his head and commended his spirit to God (Lk. 23:46). Shortly thereafter a spear was thrust into his side, and blood and water gushed out, evidence that a separation of vital fluids in the heart region had taken place. The centurion testified to Pilate early in the evening that Jesus had already died (Mk. 15:42-45). Shortly thereafter, Joseph and Nicodemus buried him (Mk. 15:46; Jn. 19:38-42).

Spiritual death, that alienation from God which is the invariable effect of sin also took place. This alone, as has always been generally understood, accounts for Jesus' agony in the garden and his many remarks about revulsion from his "cup." The pitiful efforts of certain recent commentators to show that Jesus' agony arose simply out of fear of nonexistence (contrast with Socrates' last hours is noted) is shortsighted, unbiblical, and disrespectful of what the Bible says about the nature of man. The idea that the agony in the garden was caused by resistance to efforts of Satan to kill him prematurely is bizarre.

Spiritual death was the immediate consequence of sin in the first pair. It is the state into which all men are now naturally born (Eph. 2:1-3; 4:17-19). This alienation which took place in those moments when he took upon himself our guilt and penalty, described in prophecy as making "his life a guilt offering" (Isa. 53:10), and God's making him "sin for us" (2 Cor. 5:21), is expressed in the Savior's heartbroken cry, "My God, my God, why have you forsaken me?" (Mt. 27:46). No other godly man has ever been forsaken by God at the time of death (Ps. 23:4).

The Heidelberg Catechism, in question 39, reads: "Is there something more in His having been crucified than if He had died some other death? Yes, for by this I am assured that He took upon Himself the curse which lay upon me, because the death of the cross was cursed by God (Gal. 3:13). Christ redeemed us from the curse of the law, having become a curse for us—for it is written, Cursed is everyone who hangs on a tree" (cf. Deut. 21:23).

Did Jesus experience the "second death" also? Was it "eternal"? If it was a substitutionary death (and it was), and if that is the destiny of unrepentant men (and according to the Bible it is), then his death was in some sense "eternal," or as might better be said, of infinite value in the remission of sin. As Anselm (*Cur Deus Home*) argued and as orthodox interpreters usually agree, since he was an infinite being as second person of the Godhead he could suffer that eternal punishment in moments. Many have interpreted the "He descended into hell" clause of the creed in this manner, excluding any reference to a spatial journey.

Many different expressions are used in the Bible to interpret the Lord's death "for us," "for all," "for many," "for the whole world," etc. Most of the expressions are drawn from the OT sacrificial ritual (*see* SACRIFICES AND OFFERINGS). The Book of Hebrews explains that these sacrifices were insufficient in themselves to "take away sin" and had a typical value as foreshadowing God's own sufficient sacrifice at Calvary. The death of Christ is interpreted as:

a. *A sacrifice (or offering) for sins* (Heb. 10:10-12). This text and context (10:1-9) show that Jesus' death did what no other sacrifice had ever done. It removed completely and forever all guilt for the sin of those for whom it was offered. It leaves the conscience of the offerers free.

b. *A ransom* (Mt. 20:28; 1 Tim. 2:5). The idea is not a payment to the devil, or even to God, but a price paid to release or deliver. The figure is the release of captives. The NT Greek word *lutron* gets its meaning from the Greek OT which uses it at such places as Leviticus 19:20.

c. *Redemption* (Phil. 1:7). This word in the original is closely related in form and meaning to ransom. It refers to the deliverance secured by the price paid. The Greek OT uses the same word at Exodus 21:8.

d. *A fragrant offering* (Eph. 5:2; Lev. 1:9). The pleasing of God by voluntary, uncoerced sacrifice is the emphasis.

e. *A sin offering* (Isa. 53:10; Lev. 5:17-19; 2 Cor. 5:21; Rom. 8:3). In the Mosaic ritual this was a required sacrifice and had special reference to the removal of guilt for sins.

f. *Atoning sacrifice (propitiation or expiation in other versions).* This word is the usual translation of the Greek words involved in ancient Greek literature and has reference to a satisfaction rendered to the persons and laws. Though it never appears in the KJV, *expiate* and *expiation* appear in the RSV NT wherever the KJV has *propitiate* and *propitiation*. It is a word relating to the offended party. It related to offense and offender. It is generally acknowledged that in Greek literature outside the NT *propitiate* and *propitiation* are the correct rendering. The texts involved are 1 John 2:2; 4:10; and Romans 3:25.

g. *Reconciliation* (Rom. 5:10, 11; 11:15; Eph. 2:16; Col. 1:20; 2 Cor. 5:19). This indicates that the death of Christ effected a reconciliation between man the sinner and his offended Creator. Since this is represented as a finished work, those interpreters who relate it to propitiation and removal of wrath through the execution of divine penalties on the sinners' substitute are correct. We live in a world that has been potentially reconciled. God has done all he as God can do. As Paul points out in 2 Corinthians 5:19, it remains for sinners to accept it. Scripture teaches that those who die in rejection of God's reconciling sacrifice have no further expectation except renewal of God's fiery wrath (Heb. 10:26-31). This is a stern doctrine yet it is the NT teaching.

Readers of the KJV are accustomed to find *atonement* in the sense of at-one-ment = reconciliation at Romans 5:11. The NIV and RSV have *reconciliation*. Elsewhere, in the OT, *atone* and *atonement* appear dozens of times in connection with the sacrifices, which are said to *atone* or *make atonement*. In most cases the words so translated mean "to pacify," "to cover over," "appease," all relating to positive correction of the problem of sin as offense toward God. It seems likely that these numerous OT occurrences have brought about wide usage of "the atonement" as the comprehensive name for the work of Christ, for the OT sacrificial atonements were as we have seen, typical of Christ's final work of atonement—reconciliation.

h. *A substitutionary sacrifice.* It is not possible merely to cite a few texts connected with this aspect of interpretation of Jesus' death. It is involved in all of the above. The idea of substitution of the life of the sacrificial victim for the life of the offerer was implicit in the act of laying the offerer's hand on the beast about to be slain in the several blood sacrifices (*see* SACRIFICES AND OFFERINGS), and it was nearly explicit in the action of the priest in confessing the people's sins over the beast in the case of the sin offerings on the Great Day of Atonement (Lev. 16:20-22; 4:22-26). These sacrifices were typical of Christ's (Heb. 10:1ff.). The typical significance of OT sacrifices points directly to a vicarious atonement for human sin in Jesus' sacrifice.

It is taught directly in many texts. No one who believes that Jesus' work of atonement is the subject of Isaiah 53:4-6 can doubt this. More than one famous commentator has written to the effect that if these verses do not describe vicarious (substitutionary) sacrifice, then it is impossible for human language to convey the idea. Elsewhere it is written: "For Christ died for sins once for all, the righteous for the unrighteous, to bring you to God" (1 Pet. 3:18); he became "a curse for us" (Gal. 3:13); "He himself bore our sins in his body on the tree, so that we might die to sins and live for righteousness; by his wounds you have been healed" (1 Pet. 2:24).

The Bible is inexplicable without this feature and they do injustice to that book who seek to expunge that meaning from it. How, for example, can one explain why "it was the Lord's will to crush him" (Isa. 53:10) or why the Father abandoned the Son (Mt. 27:46) on any other grounds? On what other grounds can the conscience of men be "set free"? This doctrine moves not through Scripture like a thread but like an irresistible avalanche sweeping all before it.

4. *The Burial of Christ.* The Apostles' Creed makes special mention of it. Paul's recital of the main elements of the gospel includes, "that he was buried" (1 Cor. 15:4). This event is important for a number of reasons. In the first place it was the beginning of a new epoch in his work. Association with guilt, being abused by the ungodly came to an end with the thrust of the soldier's spear. After that the hands of wicked men never touched him again. He was buried by righteous men in a rich man's tomb (Mt. 27:57-60; Jn. 19:38-42), because "he had done no violence, nor was any deceit in his mouth" (Isa. 53:9). In this perspective, death on the cross must be viewed as the end of humiliation and his burial the beginning of the change to exaltation. Yet from the fact that his death and burial are so frequently associated in Scripture it has association with his humiliation too. Many have observed that Jesus' burial proved that he was truly dead. The Roman watch was in part to ensure that public impression. Furthermore, Scripture speaks of union with him in his death as being "buried with him," of which baptism is a figure. One must not neglect to note that he made his burial in earth for a short period of time and his emerging alive a proof of his Messianic mission (Mt. 12:40; Jn. 2:18ff.).

5. *The Resurrection of Christ.* Five chapters in the four Gospels as well as part of the first chapter of Acts are devoted to narrative of Jesus' resurrection. No one can even explain Jesus' resurrection. It is a miracle which if explicable

would not be a miracle. Miracles are by definition inexplicable by natural causes. To discuss its significance fully is not possible. Eight propositions summarizing the NT's own interpretation of it will summarize its significance.

a. The resurrection of Christ was *a fulfillment of prophecy*. Though less is made of this than in the case of Jesus' death there is considerable attention to it. Jesus, of course, prophesied it to his disciples several times (Mt. 16:21; 17:23), and obliquely hinted at it to his enemies (Mt. 12:40; Jn. 2:19). After this event he declared that it was a matter of OT prophecy (Lk. 24:44, 45). The apostles insisted it occurred "according to the scriptures" (1 Cor. 15:4) and they preached many sermons on this subject. They cited Psalm 16 (Acts 2:25-28; 13:35), and Psalm 2 (Acts 13:33), among other passages. This is a recurring theme in apostolic preaching. They never sought to prove the resurrection took place. They knew Jesus had not compelled faith by such a flourish as reappearing to Caiaphas or Pilate, but they knew that they had seen him in the same body in which he suffered and died. They knew his appearances were not subjective visions or even spiritual experiences (Lk. 24:35-43). They claimed that their own witness, buttressed by prophetic Scripture, was sufficient to establish the fact.

b. The resurrection *declared his deity*: "who through the Spirit of holiness was declared with power to be the Son of God by his resurrection from the dead: Jesus Christ our Lord" (Rom. 1:4). This is the declaration that rang clear to doubting Thomas and led him to exclaim, "My Lord and my God."

c. The resurrection *certified his Messiahship*. Men should have acknowledged him as the Christ by the many credentials he presented, but nevertheless this was to crown the divine certification (Mt. 12:38-40; Jn. 2:13-22).

d. The resurrection *completed his victory over sin* and its penalty. "God raised him from the dead, freeing him from the agony of death, because it was impossible for death to keep its hold on him" (Acts 2:24; 1 Cor. 15:1-11).

e. The resurrection *enabled him to share his own righteousness* (by justification) with us: "God will credit righteousness—for us who believe in him who raised Jesus our Lord from the dead. He was delivered over to death for our sins and was raised to life for our justification" (Rom. 4:22-25).

f. The resurrection also *enables him to share with us his own eternal life*, thus providing basis for the many biblical promises of eternal life *now* to those who believe in Christ (Jn. 5:24; Rom. 6:3, 4).

g. The resurrection of Christ *assures believers of their own future glorious resurrection* (see all of 1 Cor. 15, esp. vv. 12-20).

h. Of inestimable value to Christians of all generations is the resurrection of Jesus as the *ground of Christian evidences,* proof that our faith is founded on the rock of factuality. So Peter argued before Jews (Acts 2:22-36; 3:12-26). So Paul argued before Gentiles (Acts 17:16-34). So faithful apologists and evangelists declare to the present day.

6. *The Ascension of Christ.* This event, though described only in Luke 24:50, 51 and Acts 1:11 is referred to many times in the NT (Jn. 13:3; 14:2, 28; 16:7-10; Lk. 9:51; Mk. 16:19; 1 Tim. 3:16). It marked the end of his earthly ministry. Jesus put it in that perspective (Jn. 16:28). It prepared for the coming of the Holy Spirit and the inauguration of the Church (Jn. 16:7; 1 Cor. 12:13). The present age, between the ascension and second coming of Christ is sometimes designated "the dispensation of the Holy Spirit." The giving of the Church's gifts of leadership and ministry are likewise connected with this event (Eph. 4:7-16). Christians see in this consummation of the Son of God's career by an ascension to heaven a strong assurance of a similar destiny for themselves. This assurance becomes for them an "anchor of the soul" (Heb. 6:18-20), cast into heaven wherein their "forerunner" has entered before them.

7. *Christ's Session at God's Right Hand.* The nature of this event prevents any "this-worldly" eyewitness report. Yet the NT provides by revelation both the fact itself and the meaning of it.

With reference to the fact, Jesus predicted it (Mt. 26:64) during his trials before Caiaphas. Peter in the first Christian sermon announced that Jesus had been exalted to the right hand of God (Acts 2:24). Stephen in his dying moments saw Jesus at the "right hand of God" (risen from his throne to receive to glory the first Christian martyr (Acts 7:56). Through the NT the event is related to Christian doctrine, comfort, and admonition.

From the viewpoint of redemption, the session at the Father's right was a signal that redemption was a finished work. By one sacrifice—once and for all—he had finished his work (Heb. 10:11-14). Thus the seated Savior is a ground of assurance of full forgiveness for the Christian. It completes the matter of setting the conscience free (Heb. 1:3; 12:2).

As in the case of other aspects of Messiah's work the session is regarded as predicted in prophecy, prophecy which shaped the very language by which the whole subject is treated in the NT. That prophecy, to which this essay has before given attention, is Psalm 110: "The Lord says to my Lord: 'Sit at my right hand until I make your enemies a footstool for your feet.' . . . rule in the midst of your enemies. . . . The Lord is at your right hand; he will crush kings on the day of his wrath." This phraseology is clearly recognizable in NT references to the session. Here at the fountain are the elements of Christ's kingly reign, a beginning in which he is declared king and a reign which takes place at first "in the midst of . . . enemies" but which will later triumph openly over all other sovereignties.

The appropriation by Christ of his kingly power, won by death and resurrection, took place at his session at the right hand of the Father, and it is this which gives it great significance. It marks the beginning of the reign of Christ. This is the meaning assigned: "Jesus Christ . . . who has gone into heaven and is at God's right hand—with angels, authorities and powers in submission to him" (1 Pet. 3:21, 22). This reign, as Psalm 110 says, is "in the midst" of enemies and will progress until all of them are "under his feet" (Ps. 110:1, 2, 5; Ps. 8:4-6; Heb. 2:6-9). That reign, presently invisible and acknowledged on earth only by Christians, will become visible at his second coming as King of kings and Lord of lords (Rev. 5:6-14; 11:15; 19:11-21). At that time will occur the resurrection of the righteous dead (Rev. 20:1-5), to be followed by Christ's millennial reign (Rev. 20:4-6). Then ensue the resurrection and judgment of "the rest of the dead" and their final judgment (Rev. 20:7-15), including presumably also all wicked angels, demons, and Satan. This will be succeeded (who knows how long?) by a merging of the reign of Christ with that of his Father, "for he must reign until he has put all his enemies under his feet" (1 Cor. 15:23-25; Phil. 2:9-11).

The Church's present share in and relation to the reign of Christ from the Father's right hand is mentioned at Ephesians 1:20-23; 4:15; 5:23, and Colossians 1:18-20. It has been observed that the Christian confession, "Jesus Christ is Lord," is an acknowledgement of this reign and that this doctrine brings about inevitable collision whenever "Caesar" seeks to replace Christ as the object of ultimate allegiance.

8. *Christ's Present Ministry in Heaven.* There is other work than redemption for the Son of God in heaven. He there intercedes for believers in the presence of the Father as their great high priest (Heb. 7:23—8:7). He also is the believers' "advocate" with the Father in heaven (1 Jn. 2:1). This is connected with the development of personal holiness, growth in grace, of all Christians on earth.

9. *Christ's Second Advent.* This will complete the span of the church age, or "age of the Holy Spirit." Jesus announced

in the "upper room" discourses of John 14—16 that it was necessary for him to go in order for the Spirit to come. But he prefaced the announcement by saying: "In my Father's house are many rooms. . . . I am going there to prepare a place for you. And if I go and prepare a place for you, I will come back and take you to be with me that you also may be where I am" (Jn. 14:2, 3). At the ascension, the apostles were visited by divine messengers who said, "This same Jesus, who has been taken from you into heaven, will come back in the same way you have seen him go into heaven" (Acts 1:11).

His work will then be to complete the Christian's salvation by complete sanctification (1 Thess. 3:13; 5:23), the resurrection of dead believers (Phil. 3:20, 21) and the transformation of all believers' bodies according to the pattern of Christ's own resurrection body (1 Thess. 4:13-18; 1 Cor. 15:51-58). (R.D.C.)

CHRISTIAN The term was first used at Antioch in Syria to refer to the NT disciples in the earliest days of the church (Acts 11:26). Peter referred to "suffering as a Christian" (1 Pet. 4:16). It was used by King Agrippa who asked Paul, "Do you think in such a short time you can persuade me to be a Christian?" (Acts 26:28). Paul described the basis of the Christian gospel, the basis of the faith of the Christian, in these words: "Christ died for our sins according to the Scriptures, that he was buried, that he was raised on the third day according to the Scriptures" (1 Cor. 15:3, 4). The faith that makes a Christian is personal trust, apart from any deeds or works, in Jesus as Lord and as the one who "was delivered over to death for our sins and was raised to life for our justification" (Rom. 4:24, 25).

CHRONICLES, THE BOOKS OF *See* KINGS, BOOKS OF

CHRONOLOGY *See also* KINGS OF JUDAH AND ISRAEL, ASSYRIA, BABYLON, BABYLONIA, EGYPT, HASMONEANS, HERODS, ISRAEL, JUDGES, MACCABEES, PERSIA, ROMANS, SELUCIDS. The study that measures historical time is called chronology. It divides the total lapse of time into units, primarily of numbered years; and it assigns events to their proper points in this sequence. Like all real history, the biblical events have a chronology in time, just as they have a geography in space. Such a chronology serves to clarify the record, by indicating the sequence and relative position of the incidents of Scripture, both with respect to each other and to the happenings of the ancient empires that surrounded God's people Israel. It also serves to authenticate the record by emphasizing how the biblical events fit in with known history and are not just "stories" (see Acts 26:26 or 2 Pet. 1:16). God has, moreover, providentially preserved within the Bible enough information so that most of its major events may be dated with considerable accuracy (*see* CALENDAR).

Yet except for the wilderness period (Exodus through Deuteronomy) and a few times later (as Josh. 4:19; 5:6 or 1 Kgs. 6:1), when events were dated in terms of Israel's exodus from Egypt (Ex. 40:17; Num. 10:11; Deut. 1:3), the Bible used no one fixed point of reference for its dates. It used instead only a "relative" chronology, for example, in the first, second, third, etc. year of the life of a certain patriarch or reign of a king. Recourse must therefore be had to the nearby, but non-Israelite, pagan cultures that do furnish the information necessary for building up a system of absolute, B.C. and A.D. dates.

The years of Babylonia's rulers from 747 B.C. down to the second Christian century were accurately recorded in The Canon of Ptolemy, a Greek geographer and astronomer of Egypt who died about A.D. 161. Ptolemy also recorded and dated by reign over eighty verifiable astronomical phenomena, such as the eclipses of the moon on March 17, 721, and July 16, 523 B.C.. Similarly, the neighboring Assyrians maintained "eponym" lists, in which each year was assigned the name of an important official. Since the "eponym" lists also include an eclipse of the sun on June 15, 763, the whole can be dated from 892 to 648 B.C.. Prior to 892, Assyrian king lists carry us back to about 2000 (*see* ASSYRIA AND ASSHUR) and became fairly reliable from about 1700 B.C. onward, with a margin of error of less than ten years after 1400. Other king lists from Egypt, which can be cross-checked with the Assyrian and with other astronomical observations, produce dates of about 2133-1990 for Dynasty XI, when Abram entered Egypt (Gen. 12:10-20), of 1990-1786 for Dynasty XII (Middle Kingdom) with only a negligible margin of error, when Joseph and then his whole family entered Egypt (Gen. 37-50), and of 1570-1095 for XVIII-XX (New Empire; *see* EGYPT), from the final century of Israel's Egyptian oppression to near the end of Israel's judges.

Biblical events may then be assigned absolute dates whenever they are mentioned in these other datable records. Thus the Babylonian Nebuchadnezzar's capture of Jerusalem in his eighth year (2 Kgs. 24:12) can be dated precisely to March 16, 597. Again, the Assyrian Shalmaneser III's contacts with Kings Ahab and Jehu can be dated 853 and 841 respectively; and, while neither contact is discussed in the Bible, the fact that between Ahab and Jehu appear two other kings that occupy exactly twelve years proves that 853 must have been the last year of Ahab and 841 the first of

Jehu. Counting backward from these dates, one establishes Solomon's death and the division of the kingdom in 930 B.C. and the exodus in 1446 (1 Kgs. 6:1). Among the more significant of the Old Testament's absolute dates are these:

Event	Reference Point	Biblical Basis	Date
Nehemiah's wall	Twentieth yr. of Artaxerxes I of Persia	Neh. 2:1	444 B.C.
Return decreed	First yr. of Cyrus II of Persia over Babylon	Ezra 1:1	538
Fall of Jerusalem	Nineteenth yr. of Nebuchadnez-zar II of Babylon	2 Kgs. 25:8	586
Fall of Samaria	Last yr. of Shalmaneser V of Assyria	2 Kgs. 17:3	722
Division of Kingdom	Seventy-seven yrs. before sixth yr. of Shalmaneser III	(see para. above)	930
Temple founded	Fourth yr. of Solomon	1 Kgs. 11:42; 6:1	966
Exodus from Egypt	480th yr. before temple's founding	1 Kgs. 6:1	1446
Descent into Egypt	Inaugurating a 430 yr. sojourn there (but 397 there, plus 33 in Canaan, for "the sons of Israel," according to the Gk.	Ex. 12:40	(Hebrew text, 1876)
			Gk/Heb Text
Jacob born	130 yrs. before	Gen. 47:9	1973 (2006)
Isaac born	60 yrs. before	Gen. 25:26	2033 (2066)
Abraham born	100 yrs. before	Gen. 26:5	2133 (2166)

Prior to Abraham, biblical chronology becomes indefinite. Usher's famous date of 4004 B.C. for the creation of Adam assumed that the twenty pre-Abrahamic patriarchs (Gen. 5 and 11:10-26) overlapped, without gap. But the ancients often counted long periods by successive lifetimes, not by overlapping generations. Thus in Genesis 15, Israel's four centuries in Egypt (v. 13), which actually covered some ten generations (1 Chron. 7:25-27), is said to entail only four such lifetime generations (v. 16). Applied to Genesis 5, this counting by "successive" patriarchs would mean, for example, that while Adam begat (an ancestor of) Seth when he was 130 (v. 3), the Seth of verses 6-8 actually arose as Scripture's next prominent figure only after Adam's full life of 930 years (v. 4). Adam would then date about 15,000 B.C., or a millennium before the famous Lascaux cave paintings. Further, the two sets of ten patriarchs before and after the Flood may compare with the three sets, each of fourteen ancestors, in the genealogy of Christ (Mt. 1:1-17); and, just as the latter could omit three generations in verse 8 ("Joram begat [an ancestor of] Uzziah"), so Genesis may have omitted a number of links as well.

New Testament chronology covers but a single century: from the birth of Christ in about 5 B.C. (shortly before the death of Herod the Great in 4 B.C.), through his ministry covering four Passovers (Jn. 2:13; 5:1; 6:4; 12:1) from A.D. 26 to 30, to Jerusalem's fall to Rome in 70 and John's last Epistles some 25 years later. (J.B.P.)

CHRYSOLITE *See* PRECIOUS STONES AND METALS

CHRYSOPRASE *See* PRECIOUS STONES AND METALS

CHURCH A word that is used to translate the Greek *ekklesia* which has the root meaning of an assembly and is thus translated in Acts 19:32, 41. The Hebrew equivalent was *qahal* which in a religious sense referred to Israel as a religious body. The early church carried this religious sense over to *ekklesia* and considered itself to be a part of the true Israel of God, those from any background who had the faith of Abraham (Rom. 4:16-18; 9:6-8; Gal. 3:14, 29). The early believers began to organize themselves in groups or churches with various officers. Thus it is clear that the early church thought of itself as a visible organization as well as an "invisible" one, namely, a body of all those in space and time who had a specific faith content (1 Cor. 12:13; Col. 1:24).

CILICIA *See* GEOGRAPHY OF THE HOLY LAND

CINNAMON *See* PLANTS, PERFUMES, AND SPICES

CIRCUMCISION The ceremonial cutting off of the foreskin of male children on the eighth day after birth. It was practiced by Israel's neighbors with the exception of the Philistines. For the Israelites it was a sign of the covenant between God and Israel (Gen. 17:9-14). Israelite slaves and any stranger who wished to keep the Passover also were required to be circumcised (Gen. 17:13; Ex. 12:48-49). Presumably all the early Christians, being Jews, were circumcised. The practice continued in the early church for converts from Judaism. Paul had Timothy circumcised for he had a Jewish mother (Acts 16:3). Before the practice was dropped for converts from among the Gentiles there was a vigorous controversy among the early Christians. Paul refused to let Titus be circumcised (Gal. 2:3). A council of the church was called for in Jerusalem to discuss whether it was necessary to be circumcised according to the custom taught by Moses in order to be saved. The decision was negative; and the practice gradually died out in the church (Acts 15:1-31).

CISTERN A natural or man-made reservoir for storing water. In Palestine, with its abundance of limestone hills, there were many. Those made in other ways had their walls lined with waterproof lime plaster. These were both communally owned and each man could have his own (2 Kgs. 18:31). The winter rains were collected in them for later use but springs for "living" water, fresh water, were vitally necessary as well as for the maintenance of a population.

CITADEL Translation of a Hebrew word that is frequently rendered "fort." In archaeological parlance it is sometimes referred to as "tower," a part of a fortification (2 Chron. 17:12; Neh. 7:2; Prov. 18:19).

CITY, TOWN The normal pattern of settlement in the biblical world was that of a cluster of unwalled villages around a central fortified town or city (Josh. 17:11). Prime requisites for the establishment of such a complex were availability of water, farmland, proximity to trade routes, and considerations of defense. The gate or gates of a city were of great importance as they would be the weakest part in the circumvallation wall. Here too the elders and judges sat to hear cases and give advice. Here important proclamations were made (Ruth 4:1-11; 1 Kgs. 22:10; Neh. 8:1). The cities had their own markets within and merchants or manufacturers tended to live together in the same area of the city with others of the same trade. Apart from these natural groupings there is little evidence of city planning. In most cases the population of each city or town is not given. Thus it is not possible always to distinguish between the two and the English words are used interchangeably in the text of this dictionary.

CITY OF REFUGE Among the forty-eight cities assigned to the Levites scattered throughout all of Israel, six were chosen to be places of refuge for the person who killed another. The avenger of blood could not touch the manslayer while he remained in the city of refuge. A trial for the manslayer was required and only if found guilty could he be turned over to the avenger of blood and executed. If the killing was found to be accidental, the manslayer could stay in the city and be safe from this form of reprisal. Only after the death of the current high priest could he return to his home and be safe. Three of these cities were on each side of the Jordan. Later three more were added west of the Jordan (Num. 35:6-32; Josh. 20:2; 3; 21:13-38).

CITY OF SALT An unidentified town in the desert near En Gedi (Josh. 15:62).

CLASPS Fastenings made of gold or bronze which held together the linen curtains or other hangings of the tabernacle (Ex. 35:11; 36:13, 18).

CLAUDIA A Christian lady in Rome who sent greetings to Timothy (2 Tim. 4:21).

CLAUDIUS 1. The fourth Roman emperor A.D. 41 to 54 in whose days there was a severe famine (Acts 11:28). He expelled the Jews from Rome (Acts 18:2).

2. One whose original name was Lysias, an officer in charge of the Roman garrison in Jerusalem in the days of Paul, who had purchased his Roman citizenship with great price (Acts 22:28; 23:26). On two occasions he rescued Paul and on the second started him on his long journey to Rome (Acts 21:31-40; 22:24-29; 23:10-33).

CLEAN AND UNCLEAN These terms referred to ritual and not physical cleanliness, ritual purity or defilement. Certain things were declared "clean" by the law. Some things were never clean, such as the unclean animals. Other things had to be purified or cleansed ritually when they became unclean (Deut. 14:3-20; Lev. 7:21; Num. 19:11, 13). The ritual for cleansing is spelled out in a number of cases, for example, that for the "leper" is recorded in Leviticus 14:1-9. Paul stated that the law was put in charge to lead men to Christ, to bring men to see their need for purity and deliverance and that once a man by faith had his sins forgiven he no longer needed this function of the law. The law had its place but that place was not for salvation (Gal. 3:23-29). Legislation is very easily capable of legalism. Men can follow the letter of the law and sidestep the spirit of it. This accounts for the controversies between Jesus and the Pharisees (Mt. 9:10-13; Lk. 11:37-52). While Jesus did not himself abandon the ritual purity laws (Mt. 8:2-4), his emphasis on inward (spiritual) cleanliness rather than outward (physical) cleanliness (Mt. 15:18) soon caused the Christians to abandon the OT laws of purity.

CLEMENT A co-laborer with Paul at Philippi (Phil. 4:3).

CLEOPAS One of the two disciples with whom Jesus walked and conversed on the way to Emmaus on the day of the resurrection (Lk. 24:18).

CLOAK *See* DRESS

CLOPAS The husband of one of the Marys who stood at the foot of the cross (Jn. 19:25).

CLOTH, CLOTHES, CLOTHING *See* DRESS

CLOUD These were the source of life-giving rain. They veiled the presence of God from human sight (Judg. 5:4; Ex. 19:9). God is described as one who rides in the heavens or rides on the clouds. Daniel's "one like a son of man" comes riding on the clouds of heaven, as does the Son of Man, and the Christians are at the end of days to be caught up into heaven in the clouds to meet the Lord in the air (Ps. 68:4, 33; Dan. 7:13; Mt. 26:64; 1 Thess. 4:17).

CLOUD, BRIGHT *See* GLORY OF THE LORD

CNIDUS A city of Asia Minor past which Paul's ship sailed on its way to Rome (Acts 27:7).

COAL As used in the Bible this does not refer to mineral coal but rather to charcoal which is made by burning wood (Ps. 120:4; Isa. 54:16).

COAST *See* GEOGRAPHY OF THE HOLY LAND

COAT *See* DRESS

COAT OF MAIL *See* ARMS AND ARMOR

COBRA *See* BEASTS, 1

COCK *See* BIRDS, 2

COFFIN These were not in general use among the Israelites. One only is mentioned in the Bible, that of Joseph in which his body was transported from Egypt to Canaan (Gen. 50:26). *See also* BIER.

COIN *See* MONEY

COL-HOZEH A descendant of Judah whose son repaired the Fountain Gate after the return from the Babylonian captivity (Neh. 3:15).

COLONY A settlement of Romans somewhere within that empire, usually for soldiers and their families (Acts 16:12).

COLORS The basic natural colors noted in the Bible include: white and black, red and green. They were seen in nature in the snow, milk, and wool, in the hair and ravens, in blood and wine, in plants and grasses (Ex. 4:6; Gen. 49:12; Rev. 1:14; Lev. 13:31; Song 5:11; 2 Kgs. 3:22; Ex. 10:15). Gray was the color of old men's hair (Ps. 71:18). The striped, speckled, spotted, and mottled were of course mixtures of various colors (Gen. 30:32; 31:10). Some colors or dyes were extracted from mollusks, insects, copper, or iron ore. These were variously rendered as blue, red, purple, or scarlet (Ex. 26:1, 31; Ezek. 23:14).

COLOSSE A city in Asia Minor mentioned only once in the Bible, but about which we may learn from Paul's letter to the church there (Col. 1:2). Along with Laodicea and Hierapolis the area was visited by early evangelists, but not Paul. A church was started there (Col. 2:1; 4:13).

COLOSSIANS, BOOK OF *See* PAULINE EPISTLES

COMMANDMENTS *See* LAW

COMMUNITY In the OT two Hebrew words are used to convey the idea of community, assembly, or Lord's people, and are thus translated (Ex. 12:3; Josh. 8:35; Num. 31:16). In the NT the concept is sometimes rendered by its word congregation, *ekklesia*, the church, or assembly (Acts 13:43).

COMPASSION Synonym of mercy and pity in Scripture, abounding in love and faithfulness, gracious (Ps. 86:15). Since this was the characteristic of God, he expected his people to show the same to their brethren and even to strangers in their midst (Zech. 7:9, 10; Isa. 1:17; Mt. 18:33). This was a very prominent characteristic in the life, ministry, and teaching of Jesus (Mt. 9:36; 15:32).

CONANIAH 1. A Levite who was the chief officer in charge of the contributions, tithes, and offerings under King Hezekiah (2 Chron. 31:12, 13).

2. A chief among the Levites who in the reign of Josiah gave lambs for the Passover to the other Levites (2 Chron. 35:9).

CONCUBINE A secondary wife usually taken from servants, slaves, or as booty in war, often because the principal wife was barren, as in the case of Abraham, with Sarah and Hagar (Gen. 16:1, 2). This practice was regulated by law in the world of the time outside the Bible area (Code of Hammurabi, Nuzu Laws, for example), and it appears so also in the Bible (Deut. 21:15-17). Polygamy was practiced in OT times: Esau and Jacob, Gideon, David, and Solomon (Gen. 26:34; 28:9; 29:28;

1 Kgs. 11:3) but to what extent among the common people is not clear.

CONEY *See* BEASTS, 5

CONFESSION In both Testaments the basic idea is acknowledgement, whether of sin, of Jesus as Lord unto salvation, as a witness, or in praise (Lev. 5:5; 1 Kgs. 8:33; Mt. 3:6; Rom. 10:9; 14:11, 12; 1 Jn. 1:9; 1 Tim. 6:13; Heb. 13:15).

CONGREGATION *See* COMMUNITY

CONIAH Son and successor of King Jehoiakim in Judah, usually called Jehoiachin and sometimes Jeconiah (2 Kgs. 24:6; 1 Chron. 3:16; Jer. 22:24). See the footnotes in the NIV. *See also* JEHOIACHIN and KINGS OF JUDAH AND ISRAEL.

CONQUEST OF CANAAN Led by Joshua the Israelites conquered Canaan at the end of their years of wandering in the wilderness after their exodus from Egypt. Many archaeologists have concluded that it took place late in the thirteenth century B.C. on what they say is the evidence from the excavated sites. First Kings 6:1, on the other hand, as the text stands, would put it in the fifteenth century. Lines are sharply drawn on this point between "liberal" and "conservative" scholars and the arguments of each may be found in many volumes.

CONSECRATION Dedicating or setting a person or thing apart for the service of God. Animals, tithes and offerings, persons, or groups of persons, could be and were consecrated to God, the animals for sacrificial purposes (2 Chron. 29:33; 31:6; 29:5, 31). In the NT the word "sanctifying" carries the same meaning (2 Thess. 2:13; 1 Pet. 1:2). The Greek word also is rendered holiness or holy (1 Cor. 1:30; 1 Thess. 4:3).

CONVERSION *See* CHRIST, WORK OF and SALVATION, APPLICATION OF

COPPER *See* BRONZE

COR *See* WEIGHTS AND MEASURES

CORAL *See* PRECIOUS STONES AND METALS

CORBAN *See* SACRIFICES AND OFFERINGS

CORIANDER *See* PLANTS, PERFUMES, AND SPICES

CORINTH A city, great commercial and port center of Greece on the isthmus between the mainland and the Peloponnese on one of the most important east-west trade routes. Paul spent eighteen months there working as a tentmaker and established a church (Acts 18:3, 11). Here Paul was tried and released by the Romans (Acts 18:12-16). Troubles developed in the church after Paul left and this accounts for his epistles to them. *See also* PAULINE EPISTLES and PAUL, LIFE AND TEACHINGS OF.

CORINTHIANS, BOOKS OF *See* PAULINE EPISTLES

CORMORANT *See* BIRDS, 3

CORNELIUS A Roman centurion commanding the Italian Regiment who was converted to Christianity and baptized by Peter (Acts 10:1, 3, 17-48).

CORNERSTONE A large stone at the corner of a wall to bind the two walls together. In the OT it usually means a foundation stone and is a symbol of stability (Job 38:6; Ps. 118:22; Isa. 28:16). In the NT Christ is the foundation and cornerstone. The NT references are quotations or reflections of the reference in Psalm 118:22 where the NIV renders "capstone" (Eph. 2:20; 1 Pet. 2:6).

COS An island off the coast of Asia Minor. Paul's ship passed it on the way to Rhodes on his final recorded voyage to Rome (Acts 21:1).

COSAM An ancestor of Jesus in Luke's genealogy (Lk. 3:28).

COUNCIL *See* SANHEDRIN

COUNSELOR One who gives counsel or advice such as a parent, an elder, a prophet or wise man, and God himself (Prov. 1:8; Ezek. 7:26; Jer. 18:18; Ps. 16:7). The revelation of God, the Bible, is itself a counselor, and God gave his Holy Spirit to be a counselor (Ps. 119:24; Jn. 14:16). In the OT there is an additional usage. This seems to have been a title for a very close adviser to kings (2 Chron. 25:16; Dan. 3:24).

COURSES *See* LEVITES

COVENANT A pact, agreement or treaty between persons or nations or in the Bible also between God and man (Gen. 21:27; 1 Sam. 18:3; 1 Kgs. 20:34; Gen. 9:9-11; 17:1-14). It was customary to seal the covenant by a sacrifice in one of several ways and the blood of the sacrificial animal might even be applied to the covenantors (Ps. 50:5; Jer. 34:18; Ex. 24:8). Several covenants of major significance between God and man are noted in the Bible: (1) With Noah after the flood (Gen. 9:9ff.); (2) with Abraham when the sign of circumcision was given (Gen. 17:7-10); (3) with Abraham in connection with the land of Palestine and blessing to the world (Gen. 17:7, 8); (4) with the Israelites at Sinai when they were leaving the captivity in Egypt (Ex. 6:4-8); (5) and (6) with Adam and with Christ the second Adam. (While the word "covenant" is not used in the case of God and Adam, all the concomitants of a covenant are there: parties, agreements or conditions, and rewards. In this case God on the one hand and Adam and those who descend from him on the other were the parties. The rewards and conditions were life if Adam proved faithful and sin and death on all mankind if he did not. The Adamic and the covenant between God and the Second Adam, Christ, (sometimes called by theologians the covenant of grace or redemption), are brought together in Paul's discussion (Mt. 26-28; Rom. 5:12, 18, 19).

The covenant with Noah promised that God would never again destroy all mankind by a flood (see 1 above). God promised to make a great nation out of Abraham and to be his God. Circumcision was its sign (see 2 above). God promised the land of Palestine to Abraham and his seed forever and that in him and his progeny all the families of the earth would be blessed (see 3 above). God promised to deliver his people to Canaan and to be their God. This was the national covenant of Israel and the Law given at Sinai was its charter and basis of operation. The covenant with Adam, when broken, brought sin into the world (see 5 above). Christ, the second or last Adam (1 Cor. 15:45ff.), fulfilled all righteousness and then offered himself in his death as the sacrifice that redeems all who "come unto God by him," (Heb. 9:11-26). Those who appropriate the condition of this covenant (see 6 above), who exercise faith in Christ and obedience to him, receive the blessing promised, eternal life.

Other covenants should also be noted: (1) the covenant of peace or perpetual priesthood (Num. 25:12, 13); (2) that made with David and reaffirmed with Solomon that there would always be one to sit on his throne (2 Sam. 23:5; 7:12-16); and (3) another covenant of peace that will bring utopia to earth prior to eternity (Ezek. 34:25-31; Isa. 11:1-9).

COVENANT, BOOK OF THE The phrase comes from Exodus 24:7 where Moses took this book and read it to all the people at Mount Sinai. This was at least the Ten Commandments, but may have been more. Some refer the title to the portion in Exodus 20:22—23:33. In 2 Kings 23:2, 21 it refers to the entire Deuteronomic law, or perhaps even to the entire legal system of the Pentateuch.

COVET To express avarice, greed, envy; desiring what another has. It is considered sinful and is legislated against in the Ten Commandments (Ex. 20:17). In the NT the noun form is "greed" and the picture is that he who loves "things" is in danger of not loving God fully and may even carry it to the extent that it can be called idolatry (Mk. 7:21-23; Rom. 1:29; Eph. 5:3; Col. 3:5).

COW *See* BEASTS, 4

COZBI A Midianite woman with whom an Israelite played the harlot and brought a plague on Israel (Num. 25:5-9, 18).

COZEBA A descendant of Judah (1 Chron. 4:22).

CREATION, CREATURE The Bible presents the story of creation in the first two chapters of Genesis and clearly states it as a fact in other places (Heb. 11:3; Jn. 1:3, 10). In summary, the picture that the Bible presents is one of all matter having a beginning, coming into existence only through the will and word of the eternal God. While there are many problems connected with the interpretation of the creation account, it is clear that the writers of Scripture accepted an *ex nihilo* beginning for matter. The idea of natural development by natural causes from one simple beginning is not supported by the author of Genesis. This is most especially true in the account of the creation of man since the account of that states that man was not animate before the creative act that made him man (Gen. 2:7). He became what the animals were, living only after the divine inbreathing into the inanimate thing formed from the dust.

Some hold that there are two accounts of creation in the first two chapters of the Bible. In the first chapter, however, we have a presentation of the creation of the universe as a whole while in the second chapter we find a detailed account of man's creation. What some call the second account has nothing to say about many of the items found in the first chapter, the creation of matter, the heavenly bodies, light itself, plants, or animals except for the simple notice that the creation of animals took place before the creation of man. Some allege that these two chapters contain different orders of the creation of things, but chapter two is primarily concerned with the creation of man and woman. Thus the second chapter supplements and complements the information found in the first.

The Greek word *ktisis* in the NT means that which has been created whether that be matter or a living thing, creation or creature (Rom. 1:25; 8:39; Heb. 4:13). The new creation of 2 Corinthians 5:17 refers to a man who has had a spiritual experience with God in Christ that has made him new in his thinking and in his relationship to God. Paul taught that the creation will be delivered from its bondage to corruption at the time that the creature will receive his adoption, his resurrection (Rom. 8:18-23).

CRESCENS A Christian friend of Paul's in Rome who later went to Galatia (2 Tim. 4:10).

CRETE *See* GEOGRAPHY OF THE HOLY LAND

CRICKET *See* BEASTS, 6

CRIME Used in the Bible in the same sense as it is used in normal speech, "wrongdoing." In addition, however, the Greek word so translated is also used in the sense of "accusation" or "charge" (Lk. 23:4; Jn. 19:6).

CRISPUS A ruler of the synagogue at Corinth converted and baptized by Paul (Acts 18:8).

CROSS History records that from as early as the times of the Assyrians men were impaled on upright posts as a means of execution. By the time of the crucifixion of Christ by the Romans, men were affixed by nailing or by tying or both to crossed beams of wood. These were of four forms: the shape usually associated with the event where the upright beam extends above the crossbar; one that was T-shaped; one where the four extensions were of equal length and the upright was perpendicular to the ground with the vertical at right angles to it; and, a similar one except that the form was like the modern letter "X." Crucifixion was a painful death, which ended in heart failure accompanied by suffocation. The word is used in three senses in the Bible: its literal sense, a wooden form; crucifixion; and, as a symbol for redemption (Lk. 23:26; Heb. 12:2; Phil. 3:18).

The cross is an integral part of Christian theology for it was on the cross, that particular form of death, by which atonement was made to God for man the sinner, and reconciliation was achieved. In Christian theology there is no divine remission of sin without the shedding of blood in the death of a savior and that redemption was achieved through Christ's cross. This is sometimes misunderstood as being an innocent victim who is made to die for the salvation of others. This must be understood to be true and not true at the same time if the theology of the cross, of crucifixion, is to be understood. Christ was an innocent sinless victim, and he was made to die for others. However, Christ was also God the Son who had taken to himself a human form (Phil.

2:5-8), and therefore his death was within the Godhead itself rather than God picking some third party to make this atoning sacrifice (Eph. 2:13-17; Col. 1:19, 20; 2:13, 14). The Apostle Paul, a Jew and a Roman citizen, for whom the death on a cross was considered a curse and something to be scorned, could only be "not ashamed" because of his conviction that the One who died there was the Son of God, dying for man's redemption (Rom. 1:16; Gal. 2:20).

CROWN The word has several symbolic uses in addition to its reference to a part of the body (the top of the head), and to something that literally encircles the head, whether of the victor, the priest, or the king (Deut. 28:35; Prov. 4:9; 2 Sam. 12:30). References are made to crowns of glory, righteousness, and life and crowns symbolic of triumph in the Christian life (2 Tim. 4:8; James 1:12; 1 Pet. 5:4). A good wife is declared to be the crown of her husband and the hoary or white head is a crown of glory also (Prov. 12:4; 16:31). Before his crucifixion Christ was mockingly crowned with a crown of thorns by the Roman soldiers (Mt. 27:29).

CRUCIFIXION *See* CROSS

CUBIT *See* WEIGHTS AND MEASURES

CUCUMBER *See* PLANTS, PERFUMES, AND SPICES

CUMI *See* KOOM

CUMMIN *See* PLANTS, PERFUMES, AND SPICES

CUN Sometimes called Berothai, a Syrian town from which David took much bronze (1 Chron. 18:8). *See* BEROTHAI.

CUP A vessel with many sizes and shapes usually made of baked clay but also of metal, even gold. In addition to its use for drinking it was also used for divining (Gen. 40:11; Mk. 9:41; Gen. 44:5). In the Scriptures it is a figure of the wrath of God (Isa. 51:17, 22; Rev. 16:10). It is synonymous with "lot" or "fate" (Mt. 26:39). It has several symbolic usages: cup of consolation, sending food and drink to the bereaved; cup of salvation; cup of blessing, or cup of the Lord, which refers to the ritual communion cup (Ps. 116:13; 1 Cor. 10:16, 21). The cup is used in connection with drunkenness (Prov. 23:31), and we read of the cup of staggering, the cup of horror and desolation, and the cup of fury or anger (Ezek. 23:33; Rev. 14:10; 16:19).

CUPBEARER An officer of very great importance at a royal court (1 Kgs. 10:5). Nehemiah was cupbearer to the King of Persia and a lengthy account of the cupbearer of the Pharaoh in Egypt is recorded in the Joseph accounts (Neh. 1:4; Gen. 40:2).

CURDS An important part of the diet of the poor or common man in the Middle East where milk was plentiful but refrigeration was not available. Milk was placed in a goatskin and churned together with sour curds left over from the last churning (Gen. 18:8; Prov. 30:33).

CURSE An interdict by God against man for sin, or an asking the deity to bring evil or harm to the object of the curse; an imprecation (Deut. 28:20; 27:15-26; Ps. 109:17; 35:4-8). It was forbidden to curse the king, a deaf man, one's parents (Ex. 21:17), or God. Death was the penalty (Lev. 24:14-16). In Scripture it is considered a virtue, is even commanded, to bless those who curse you (Ps. 109:28; Lk. 6:28).

CURTAIN The fabric from which tents were made; in the Bible particularly associated with the tabernacle and the temple (Ex. 26:2; Mt. 27:51). The rent curtain in the NT is a symbol of the rending of Christ's flesh as the curtain that separates man from God (Heb. 10:20).

CUSH 1. An unidentified country through which the River Gihon flowed as found in the creation account (Gen. 2:13). Some equate one of the references to Cush with Ethiopia, others with an area in Asia.

2. The son of Ham, grandson of Noah, and also of Nimrod (Gen. 10:6-8; 1 Chron. 1:8-10).

3. A Benjamite mentioned in the title of Psalm 7.

CUSHAN A land or people mentioned in connection with Midian. Perhaps the words are synonyms (Hab. 3:7).

CUSHAN-RISHATHAIM A king of Mesopotamia in the days of the Judges of Israel whom they served for a time (Judg. 3:8-10).

CUSHI, CUSHITE 1. The father of the prophet Zephaniah (Zeph. 1:1).

2. An ancestor of a member of King Jehoiakim's court (Jer. 36:14).

3. A member of the Cushite people. One of the notables was the wife of Moses (Num. 12:1; 2 Sam. 18:21).

CUTH, CUTHAH A Babylonian city from which were settlers brought by the Babylonian king who settled them in Israel. They intermarried in Israel and the Samaritans were the result (2 Kgs. 17:24, 30).

CUZA A steward of King Herod whose wife helped to provide the needs of Jesus, his disciples, and those with them (Lk. 8:3).

CYMBAL *See* MUSIC

CYPRESS *See* TREES

CYPRUS *See* GEOGRAPHY OF THE HOLY LAND

CYRENE, CYRENIANS The capital of Libya and a Greek colony where Jews also lived. These had a synagogue in Jerusalem in NT times (Lk. 23:26; Acts 2:10; 11:20; 6:9).

CYRUS The founder of the Persian Empire, who under Darius the Mede, his vice regent, took the city of Babylon and brought that empire to an end (Dan. 5). He encouraged the Jews to return to their ancestral home and to rebuild their temple (2 Chron. 36:22; Ezra 1:1; Isa. 44:27, 28). His tomb has been found at Pasargadae and his clay cylinder noting his decree given after his capture of Babylon encouraging all peoples to take their gods and go home.

D

DABBESHETH A border town (165-230) in Zebulun, exact location unknown; perhaps Tell esh-Shamman (Josh. 19:11).

DABERATH Modern Daburiyeh (186-234). A Levitical town in Issachar on the border with Zebulun (Josh. 19:12; 21:28; 1 Chron. 6:72).

DAGON *See* DEITIES

DALMANUTHA Neither this place (Mk. 8:10) nor the location Magadan, with which it is associated in Matthew 15:39, are identifiable. Perhaps they are to be found on the western shore of the Sea of Galilee.

DALMATIA The southern part of the Roman province of Illyricum (Rom. 15:19) east of the Adriatic (2 Tim. 4:10).

DALPHON One of Haman's ten sons (Esth. 9:7).

DAMARIS A lady convert of Paul at Athens (Acts 17:34).

DAMASCUS An oasis located on a plateau some 2200 feet above sea level, between the Anti-Lebanon Mountains and the desert, northeast of Mount Hermon. Throughout history it has been

famous for its gardens and orchards produced in the rich
soil with abundant water from the rivers Barada and el-A'waj
(biblical Abana and Pharpar, 2 Kgs. 5:12). From earliest
times it has been an important center of commerce and
religion, located where most important military and trade
routes met, and the capital of both modern and ancient Syria
(Aramea). It is mentioned in the Abraham narratives (Gen.
14:15). David captured and garrisoned in it (2 Sam. 8:5, 6).
Rebels took control of it in David's time (1 Kgs. 11:23-25),
and throughout Israel's history it was one of her chief sources
of opposition (1 Kgs. 15:18; 20:34; 2 Kgs. 8:7ff.). Captured
by the Assyrians (733-732 B.C.) it never again became
prominent in biblical times. The Romans made it a Nabatean
kingdom. In Paul's day its population included many Jews
and Christians (Acts 9:2; 22:5, 6, 11, 12; 26:12).

DAN, DANITES The fifth son of Jacob, full brother to Naphtali, born of Rachel's
maid Bilhah (Gen. 30:1-6). Dan was the name of one of the
twelve tribes of Israel and of one of her cities. One of the
most famous members of the tribe was Samson (Judg. 13:2,
24). The Danite tribe settled in the low country west of
Jerusalem but later most of the tribe moved north, making
their seat at Laish (called Lesham in Joshua 19:47), giving it
the name Dan, modern Tell el-Qadi (211-295). This is the
northern town in the reference "Dan to Beersheba" (Josh.
19:40-47; Judg. 1:34; 18:1ff.; 18:29; 20:1).

DANCE In the OT dancing most frequently had a religious character.
Except where pagan influence was present, the sexes danced
separately with rhythmic, harmonious body movements
expressing spiritual joy or devotion before God. Women
engaged in it on occasions of national liberation, after military
victories, and at religious festivals (Ex. 15:20; Judg. 21:19-
21; 1 Sam. 18:6). It was accompanied by instrumental and
vocal music (Judg. 11:34). David danced before the Ark,
and on other occasions so did men in groups in their praising
the Lord (2 Sam. 6:16; Ps. 149:3). In the NT there is a
reference to children calling out to others and saying, "You
did not dance when we played the flute for you" (Mt. 11:17).
It was done on the occasion of the prodigal's homecoming,
and when Salome danced before Herod (Lk. 15:25; Mk.
6:21, 22).

DANIEL 1. Second son of King David, also called Keleab (1 Chron.
3:1; 2 Sam. 3:3).

2. A priest who came up with Ezra from Babylon and sealed
the covenant with Nehemiah (Ezra 8:2; Neh. 10:6).

3. A man noted for his righteousness and wisdom and
mentioned together with Noah and Job. Tradition identifies

him with the prophet (4 below), some with the Ugaritic mythological "Daniel" (Ezek. 14:14, 20; 28:3).

4. A man of royal or noble family, of the tribe of Judah, carried into captivity in Babylon in 605 B.C. and there trained for royal service (Dan. 1:1-6). The book of the Bible bears his name. (The reliability of this date 605 and, in fact, many of the historical items noted in the book that bears his name stand even though consistently attacked since the second century. See the parenthetical note in the article DARIUS.) He was given the name Belteshazzar in Babylon, where, because of his divinely given wisdom and good judgment, he held important posts under several Babylonian and Persian kings. He acquired especial fame as an interpreter of dreams. Only traditions remain relative to his end. Jesus refers to a portion of his book in a manner that regards both the portion and the man as historical (Mt. 24:15).

DANIEL, BOOK OF Traditionally, and to this day by evangelicals, considered a sixth century B.C. document written by Daniel the Prophet. It is assigned by critics, however, to 165 B.C. and to an unknown author. They say: (1) it contains historical inaccuracies; (2) if written in the sixth century much of it would have to be considered predictive and forecasting the future is impossible; and (3) it would have no real purpose in the sixth century, while in the second it would serve to encourage the Jews in their revolt against the Seleucids. (On these and other critical matters see DARIUS.) Of the twelve chapters seven are historical.

DANITES *See* DAN

DANNAH A Judean town (area of 152-095) in the hill-country district of Debir (Josh. 15:49).

DARDA, DARA Descendant of Judah, a skilled musician, and second only to Solomon in his wisdom (1 Kgs. 4:31; 1 Chron. 2:6). The footnote in the Chronicles passage reads: "most Hebrew manuscripts read 'Dara.'"

DARIUS The name of several rulers of the Persian period after 538 B.C.

1. Darius the Mede, son of Xerxes (Hebrew Ahasuerus), ruled after Belshazzar, the last of the neo-Babylonian kings (Dan. 5:30-31), being made king of the realm of the Babylonians (*see* CHALDEANS) at the age of sixty-two (Dan. 9:1; 5:31; 6:6, 9, 25, 28). He set up 120 governors (satraps) under three presidents of whom Daniel was one (Dan. 6:1-3) and ruled only very briefly contemporaneously with Cyrus, the

founder of the Persian Empire (Dan. 6:28). Thus the data as presented in the Book of Daniel. (Some consider the OT account of this reign a conflation of confused traditions and that this Darius never existed.) The historicity of the Book of Daniel, including the account of Darius has long been a watershed between "conservative" and "liberal" scholars. The negative arguments may be found in numerous encyclopedias and commentaries. The following brief bibliography may be found helpful, however. It presents not only the arguments against historicity but in addition attempts both to evaluate those negative arguments and to support positively the presentation of the text of Daniel. *Darius the Mede*, J.C. Whitcomb, 1959; *Exposition of Daniel*, H.C. Leupold, 1949; *The Prophecy of Daniel*, E.J. Young, 1949; *Studies in the Book of Daniel*, Series I, 1917, Series II.

2. Darius the Great, called Hystaspos (522-486 B.C.), in secular history was the most famous of this name, defeated by the Greeks at Marathon, and in biblical history noted for his enabling the returned Jews to rebuild the temple at Jerusalem (Ezra 4:5ff.; Hag. 1:1; Zech. 1:1).

3. Darius, known as Nothus, son of Artaxerxes I (423-404 B.C.; Neh. 12:22).

4. Darius Codomanus (336-330 B.C.) the last king of Persia, defeated by the Greeks.

DARKNESS *See* LIGHT

DARKON One of Solomon's servants whose sons returned with Zerubbabel from the exile (Ezra 2:56; Neh. 7:58).

DATHAN *See* KORAH

DAVID The youngest son of Jesse, of the tribe of Judah, born in Bethlehem, second king of Israel (c. 1040-970 B.C.). The account of his life is found in 1 Samuel 16—1 Kings 2, and 1 Chronicles 11-29. The Book of Ruth traces his Israelite and Moabite ancestry. Items from the more than seventy Psalms ascribed to David as well as his other poems (2 Sam. 23:1; 1:17; 3:33) give valuable insights into his character, personality, and religious feelings and beliefs. In the Bible this name is reserved for this one individual alone (some 800 times in the OT and fifty-eight in the NT) indicating something of the place he held in both Jewish and Christian tradition. To the Jews he became a religious symbol and their messianic hope was attached to his descendants. They looked for a Messiah who should sit on the throne of David forever (Jer. 33:17). To the Christians, Jesus the Messiah came of the seed of David, according to the flesh, and was the King to sit on the throne of David forever (Rom. 1:3; Rev. 22:16; Mt. 22:42-45; Acts 2:25-36). In addition to king, warrior, and writer of poetry he was also a skilled musician (1 Sam. 16:23; 2 Sam. 6:5; Neh. 12:36, 45, 46; Amos 6:5). His history is one of the most colorful in all Scripture.

Reared a shepherd, at an early age he became musician and armorbearer to King Saul who soon became jealous of his prowess and popularity. When Saul tried on several occasions to kill him he fled the court and became a fugitive and wanderer until the death of the king. After Saul's death, David became a great king, laid the foundation for the nation, planned and made preparation for the building of the temple, and set up the organization of the temple staff (1 Chron. 23-26). Many of the stories from his life are exceedingly colorful: his victory over the giant Goliath (1 Sam. 17); the mutual love of David and Jonathan (1 Sam. 18-20); his famous lament over the deaths of Saul and Jonathan (2 Sam. 1); and, even the story of his sin with Bathsheba and the murder of her husband Uriah (2 Sam. 11). His reign was turbulent. Four times the ten tribes were split away from the two by palace or external rebellions. After some of them the king had to become a fugitive. Through all of these God was preparing the man, the musician, the poet, and the prophet. *See also* KINGS OF JUDAH AND ISRAEL.

DAVID, TOWN OF 1. *See* JERUSALEM.

2. In Luke 2:11, Bethlehem, the birthplace and early home of David, is called "the town of David."

DAWN Hebrew *shahar*, the start of day and a poetic name for the place where the sun rises (Job. 38:12; 3:9; 41:18). The phrase "O morning star, son of the dawn" of Isaiah 14:12 is applied to the king of Babylon. In the KJV the "day star" is rendered "Lucifer" (literally "light bearer," day star) and because of the similarity with Luke 10:18 and Revelation 9:1 the reference is made by some to Satan instead of the king of Babylon.

DAY 1. Denotes time from sunrise to sunset, the time of daylight (Gen. 1:5).

2. A space of time from sunrise to sunset or vice versa, twenty-four hours (Gen. 1:5; Neh. 13:19).

3. Time in general (Ps. 37:3).

4. It is also used figuratively in reference to the day of the Lord (Ezek. 13:5; Joel 1:15).

DAY OF ATONEMENT *See* CALENDAR and FESTIVALS

DAY OF THE LORD Any time when God intervenes to punish sin (Amos 5:16-20; Isa. 13:6, 9). The climax comes when God intervenes personally to show his anger on foes and to deliver his people (Zeph. 1:7ff.; 14ff.; 2:2, 3). In the NT this day is the second coming of Christ (1 Cor. 1:8; 2 Thess. 2:2) and is accompanied with physical cataclysms on the earth (Lk. 21:7-33; 2 Pet. 3:12ff.) and great social changes. It includes both the judgments preceding the millennium and the millennial utopia itself which follows (Rev. 4-19, 20; Isa. 11:1-9; 65:17-25). This day will culminate in the new heaven and earth (Rev. 21:1ff.).

DAY STAR *See* DAWN

DEACON, DEACONESS The basic meaning of the Greek word *diakonos* and its derivatives is "minister" or "servant." Out of some 100 occurrences in the NT the Greek word is translated three times as deacon or deacons. The lady Phoebe is called a servant of the church, but the footnote says "deaconess" (Rom. 16:1; Phil. 1:1; 1 Tim. 3:8, 12). It usually conveys the idea of servant, even table-service, and is rendered in the great miracle of Cana. Jesus and Paul are called deacon-servants (Rom. 15:8; 1 Cor. 3:5). As a church office the concept comes from Acts 6:1-7. Opinions differ as to whether women held such an office as a deaconess as a regular matter in the early church. The weight of evidence seems in its favor.

DEAD, ABODE OF This place is designated in the Scriptures by a number of words. One that refers to the abode of both good and bad in the OT is *Sheol*. It is rendered by "the grave," whether it refers to its final abode of the wicked or of the good (Ps. 9:17; Gen. 37:35). It is found over sixty times in the OT and is usually translated simply as "grave" but is also rendered "Destruction" (Job 31:12; 28:22). It was inside the earth (Num. 16:30-33). In some cases it was considered a place of severe punishment (Ps. 9:17; 116:3); in another this concept is missing (compare Ps. 16:10; Acts 2:27, which refer to the body of Jesus). The translation there is "grave." In the NT the most frequent word for the abode of the wicked is hell (Gehenna in the Greek) (Mt. 10:28; 18:9; Mk. 9:43; Jude 7). Fire, "eternal," or "fiery lake of burning sulfur" (Rev. 21:8) or "fiery furnace" (Mt. 13:42, 50) are usually associated with retributive punishment. In the NIV, it is also sometimes translated "depths" (Lk. 10:15; Mt. 11:23, with Hades in the footnote). The Greek *hades* is rendered in English for the words hell, the grave, and Hades itself (Lk. 16:23; Acts 2:27, 31; Rev. 1:18; 6:8; 20:13, 14). Along with death, Hades is a temporary state for both are eventually to be cast into "the lake of fire which is the second death" (Rev. 20:13, 14). The place of fire is also called the "Abyss" (Rev. 9:1, 2; 20:1-3). The "angel" of the Abyss is called *Abaddon* in the Hebrew and *Apollyon* in the Greek (Rev. 9:11). Abaddon is also found in the Hebrew text of Job 31:12, 26:6, and 28:22. The NIV translates it as "Destruction" but places Abaddon in the footnotes in each case. The demons feared the Abyss (Lk. 8:31).

The NT abode of the righteous is called heaven. The word paradise is used three times (as in Lk. 23:43). It is the abode of God and angels, where the redeemed will exist and be rewarded some day, where Christ has gone and from where he will return for his own (Ps. 102:19; Rev. 5:11; Mt. 5:12; 1 Thess. 4:16).

In summary, the words of the OT generally carry both meanings, the abode of good and of the wicked. The separation of the concepts of punishment and blessedness are developed in the NT.

DEADLY WEAPON *See* ARMS AND ARMOR

DEAD SEA *See* SALT SEA and GEOGRAPHY OF THE HOLY LAND

DEAD SEA SCROLLS *See* SCROLLS, DEAD SEA

DEATH It is the opposite of life, the normal end of life which comes with the departure of the spirit from the body (Deut. 34:5, 7; Eccl. 12:7). It is the result of sin (Gen. 2:7, 17; Rom. 5:12; 6:23) which causes the disintegration of the physical body and leaves the spirit in an intermediate state until it returns to the resurrected body in the end of days. (On the intermediate state see DEAD, ABODE OF. *See also* RESURRECTION.) In the concept of both Testaments some are resurrected to everlasting life, some to everlasting contempt (Dan. 12:2; 2 Thess. 1:8-10; Jn. 3:36). A "second death" is noted (Rev. 2:11; 20:6), which is eternal separation from God in a lake of fire for the wicked but from which the righteous are delivered (Rev. 20:6, 14).

DEBIAH An ancestor of some who came back from the captivity with Zerubbabel but were not able to prove their families were descendants from Israel (Ezra 2:59, 60). Also called Delaiah in Neh. 7:62.

DEBIR 1. A king of Eglon, SW of Jerusalem (Josh. 10:3).

2. A town on the border between Judah and Benjamin, between Jerusalem and the Salt Sea (Josh. 15:7).

3. A town in the tribal area of Gilead east of the Jordan River (Josh. 13:26).

4. A Canaanite city in the hill country (Josh. 15:48, 49) and not in the western hills as some formerly thought. It is located south of Hebron at modern Khirbet Rabud, and was also called Kiriath Sannah and Kiriath Sepher (Josh. 15:49, 50).

Conquered by Joshua (Josh. 10:38, 39) the area was given by him to Caleb (Josh. 15:13). Caleb's nephew, Othniel, was given Debir as a reward for having captured it (Josh. 15:13-19). It became a possession of the priestly family of Aaron (Josh. 21:15). It was formerly thought to be located at Tell Beit Mirsim farther to the west. The presence of Late Bronze Age pottery together with the upper and lower springs support the Rabud site (Josh. 15:18, 19).

DEBORAH 1. Rebekah's nurse who came with her from Mesopotamia (Gen. 35:8; 24:59).

2. A prophetess in Israel, also listed with the judges who roused the tribes of Israel under Barak to revolt against the Canaanites. Her story and her beautiful victory song are recorded in Judges 4 and 5. *See also* JUDGES OF ISRAEL.

DEBT, DEBTOR In the Mosaic Law special provisions were provided to protect the Jewish debtor from his fellow. On matters of interest and pledges for loans see LOAN. The law was ignored later and debtors were often cruelly treated (2 Kgs. 4:1ff.). In NT times these laws were not adhered to and debtors were thrown into prison (Mt. 18:25-30, 34).

DECALOGUE *See also* LAW. Commonly called the Ten Commandments, the basic laws given by God to Moses at Sinai (Ex. 20; Deut. 5) which were intended to be the blueprint for the moral conduct of Israel. It, together with the rest of the laws of the OT, was given by God to Israel to be their way of life when they came into the land he had promised them in contradistinction to the way the Egyptians lived, from where he had delivered them and to the way the Canaanites lived, who occupied the area to which he was taking them (Lev. 18:4-5). Its goal was to be a way of life, holy to the Lord, and a righteous life. One had to keep it totally to achieve righteousness. Its content and the NT support (Mt. 19:17-19) indicate its permanent and binding character.

The NT teaches that since man could not keep the law fully and thus could not acquire righteousness something had to be done in addition. This was to be done through Jesus, the Messiah, who kept it fully during his earthly life. The law was "put in charge to lead us to Christ that we might be justified by faith" (Gal. 3:24). Therefore Christ is the goal of the law for righteousness and not "the end of the law" (Rom. 10:4). *See also* LAW. The law was to show man his inability and to make him look to God for help and righteousness.

DECAPOLIS Ten cities south and east of the Sea of Galilee, occupied by Greeks after the conquest of Alexander in the fourth century B.C. which formed a league after the Roman occupation of Palestine in the first century B.C. (Mt. 4:25; Mk. 5:20; 7:31). The footnote in each reference reads "That is, the Ten Cities."

DECAY The decomposition of organic matter. In Scripture it has a special or theological meaning as well, the change and decay naturally associated with death. Christ did not suffer "corruption" decay (Ps. 16:10; Acts 2:27; 13:34, 37). Man's body will decay and perish, but at its resurrection it will be made imperishable (1 Cor. 15:42ff.).

DECISION, VALLEY OF The place of God's judgment on the nations in the end of days, sometimes called the Valley of Jehoshaphat (Joel 3:2, 12, 14). Tradition identifies it with the Kidron Valley, but this is not certain.

DEDAN, DEDANITES 1. Dedan was a descendant of Noah through Ham and Cush (Gen. 10:1, 6, 7).

2. A grandson of Abraham by his concubine Keturah (Gen. 25:3).

3. A place in NW Arabia south of Edom, the home of the Dedanites, an important trading people as is known from extrabiblical sources (Isa. 21:13).

DEDICATION, FEAST OF An annual feast of eight days duration commencing on the twenty-fifth of Kislev commemorating the rededication of the temple in December 165 B.C. after it had been desecrated by Antiochus Epiphanes three years earlier. It has been known as the Feast of Lights, and currently as Hanukkah (Jn. 10:22, 23). *See also* CALENDAR and FESTIVALS.

DEEP A translation of various Hebrew and Greek words which refer to the primeval chaos (Gen. 1:2), the flood (Gen. 7:11), the waters of the Red Sea (Ex. 15:5), the ocean (Job 41:31), underground water (Deut. 33:13), and which sometimes carry a figurative meaning (Ps. 88:6). In the NT the reference is to the depth of the Sea of Galilee (Lk. 5:4).

DEER *See* BEASTS, 2

DEFILE, DEFILEMENT *See* CLEAN AND UNCLEAN

DEITIES I. Foreign gods, some of which were introduced in Israel.
Ammonite and Moabite deities *Chemosh, Milcom/Molech/
Moloch. Chemosh* was the god of the Moabites (Num. 21:29)
and in a passage which Jephtha addressed to the Ammonites
(Judg. 11:12, 23, 24, 28) *Molech, Milcom,* and *Moloch* would
appear to be three variants of the same Ammonite deity
(1 Kgs. 11:5; Lev. 18:21; Acts 7:43). *Milcom* is noted in the
footnotes to *Molech*. There is some evidence that all of
these names are but titles for the god *Athtar*, an astral deity,
and not the actual name of deities themselves. As a part of
their rites the sacrifice of children was included (2 Kgs. 3:27;
23:10) in spite of the death penalty commanded by Moses
for anyone offering his child to Molech (Lev. 20:2-5). Solomon
built a high place for Chemosh and Molech which Josiah later
destroyed (1 Kgs. 11:5, 7; 2 Kgs. 23:13). The cult seems
to have continued, however (Ezek. 16:20, 21).

Assyrian and Babylonian deities *Nisroch, Bel, Marduk
(Merodach), Nebo, Nergal, Succoth-Benoth. Nisroch* (2 Kgs.
19:35-37; Isa. 37:36-38), a name not found elsewhere but in
the Bible, is the Assyrian deity in whose temple Sennacherib
was killed by his sons after his return from Judah and
Jerusalem. *Bel* was one of the three primary gods of ancient
Sumer and is mentioned in the Bible along with *Marduk*
the chief god of Babylon. The Hebrew text is vocalized
Merodach (Jer. 50:2). *Nebo* (Babylonian Nabu) was a god of
all science, who had a temple in all major cities of both
Assyria and Babylonia (Isa. 46:1). *Nergal* was associated with
wars and disaster and was worshiped throughout Assyria
and Babylonia with his chief temple being at Cuthah. Exiles
from Cuthah brought his cult to Samaria after the fall of
the northern kingdom (2 Kgs. 17:30). The men of Babylon
who were brought to Samaria after 722 B.C. made *Succoth-
Benoth* their god (2 Kgs. 17:30).

The one deity of Egypt noted in the Bible is *Amon* of the
city of Thebes (Nah. 3:8), called *No Amon* in the footnote.
The doom of this city, once the most magnificent of Egypt's
capitals was foretold by Jeremiah (Jer. 46:25) as he describes
God's punishment of its deity.

The gods of Greece are represented by four, *Artemis,
Hermes, Zeus,* and the twin gods *Castor* and *Pollux. Artemis*,
the Greek goddess of hunting, corresponds to the Roman
Diana whose temple at Ephesus was one of the seven
wonders of the ancient world (Acts 19:23—20:1). *Hermes*
was the deity of literature, commerce, and youth and is noted
in the Bible at Acts 14:12, as is also *Zeus*, the Roman *Jupiter*.
Castor and *Pollux* were protectors of sailors. They were
especially worshiped at Sparta in Greece (Acts 28:11).

In Philistia the god was *Dagon* (Judg. 16:23; 1 Sam. 5:2-7;
1 Chron. 10:10), a Semitic deity from at least 2500 B.C.

onward but in biblical times known in connection with the
Philistines at Gaza, Beth-shean, and Ashdod where, we read,
the Maccabees destroyed his temple. By such names as
Beth-Dagon in the tribal areas of Judah and Asher we know
that he had shrines outside the Philistine area as well (Josh.
15:41; 19:27). A temple was built to him at Ras Shamra-
Ugarit, north of the Bible world, that was the rival of Baal's.
Current scholarship rules out his origin as a fish deity and
suggests a grain deity. Ekron, one of the major Philistine
cities, had its own deity, *Baal-Zebub* (2 Kgs. 1:2, 3, 6, 16).

After the fall of the Israelite Kingdom in 722 B.C. foreigners
were brought to Samaria by the conquering king of Assyria.
These peoples brought some of their gods with them already
noted with respect to the gods *Nergal* and *Succoth-Benoth*.
Other gods similarly brought to Samaria at that time were:
Ashima, known only from this reference in the OT, who was
brought from Hamath (2 Kgs. 17:30; Amos 8:14ff.), *Nibhaz*
and *Tartak* who were brought by the Avvites from their
homeland (2 Kgs. 17:31) and *Anammelech* and *Adramellech*
brought to Samaria by the Sepharvites (2 Kgs. 17:31). The
Sepharvites burned their children in the fire to these two
gods, suggesting some relation to the gods of Moab and
Ammon noted above.

II. Pagan gods, more commonly known in Israel.
Asherah, Asherim (masculine plural) and *Asheroth* (feminine
plural), words that refer both to the west Semitic goddess
and to the cult object that represented her (translated
incorrectly "groves" in the earlier versions). The RSV does
not distinguish in its translation between the goddess and the
object, transliterating in both cases by "Asherah." In Ras
Shamra-Ugarit *Athirat* is the mother-goddess and consort of
El, but in the OT she is associated with *Baal* (Judg. 3:7).
She was widely worshiped throughout the ancient eastern
world. Four hundred of her prophets ate at Jezebel's table in
the time of Elijah (1 Kgs. 18:19). King Manasseh put her
image in the temple at Jerusalem (2 Kgs. 21:7). Josiah
endeavoured to stamp out her cult practices during his revival
(2 Kgs. 23:4-7). The Israelites were forbidden to put her
cult objects in the tabernacle and were told to cut them down
and burn them (Deut. 12:3; 16:21; Ex. 34:13).

Ashtoreth (Ashtaroth, the plural form) goddess of the
Sidonians also worshiped by Solomon (1 Kgs. 11:5). Her
center in Jerusalem was later destroyed by Josiah (2 Kgs.
23:13). She was the *Ishtar* of the Babylonians and the *Astarte*
of the Greeks, closely associated with the idea of life giver.

The Semitic word *Baal,* means "lord" or "possessor." The
lord or possessor of a given piece of property or area was
its *Baal* and as such was worshiped. The *Baals* of individual
localities were identified by the names of the localities as was

the case with *Baal of Peor* or *Baal Zephon,* for examples
(Num. 25:3; 33:7). Later *Baal* came to be recognized as one
god. His cult received a serious setback in the days of
Elijah when 450 of his prophets were destroyed (1 Kgs.
18:19, 40). The cult was obliterated in the time of Jehu
(1 Kgs. 18:17-40; 2 Kgs. 10:18-28; 11:18) but was revived
and again partially destroyed in the reforms of Josiah. Even
after these two destructions it still had strength to revive
itself, however (2 Kgs. 23:4, 5). *Baal-Berith* was a god with
a shrine at Shechem mentioned in Judges 8:33 and 9:4.

Beelzebub is found only in the NT. (For Baal-Zebub see
above under Philistine gods. In Matthew 12:24, 27 the
footnote reads "Greek Beezeboul or Beelzeboul".) Both Jesus
and his opposition apply this term to the prince of demons,
to Satan (Mt. 12:24, 27; Lk. 11:18, 19).

Kaiwan, Sakkuth, Star-gods are found only in the footnote
to Amos 5:26. *Rephan* is the only one from Amos 5 found
in the quote of that passage in Acts 7:43. Scholars are
divided as to whether the first two were deities.

III. Teraphim Images and Serpent.
The "household gods" is a translation given to the Hebrew
word *teraphim* (Gen. 31:19). In Genesis 31:30 Laban called
them his *elohim,* gods. They were small enough to go in a
camel saddle and for Rachel to hide them by sitting on them.
Yet in 1 Sam. 19:13-16 where the translators used the
word "idol" they would seem to be the size of a man. They
are mentioned in every period of Israel's history from the
time of the patriarchs to the fall of Israel and Judah (Gen.
31:19; Judg. 18:14; 2 Kgs. 23:24; Ezek. 21:21; Zech. 10:2).
They would seem to have been used especially in divination
and from the archaeology of the Nuzu period, it is known
that heirs considered them important. Whoever held them
received estate rights upon the death of the parent. This
explains Rachel's interest in taking them when she left her
father Laban.

Idols, Images, Carved Images were representations in
various forms, some animal, some human, which were used
in pagan worship and by the Israelites in idolatrous worship.
They were carved from wood or stone, or cast in copper,
silver, or gold (Isa. 44:14-17; 1 Kgs. 14:9). They were
condemned in the Ten Commandments (Ex. 20:4) and
throughout all of Israelite history (Jer. 8:19; Mic. 5:13; Isa.
30:22).

Serpent. In the entire ancient world serpent deities were
known. In the Bible it is sometimes the symbol of Satan
(Rev. 12:9).

DELAIAH 1. A priest of the twenty-third order of those to minister in the sanctuary as set up by David (1 Chron. 24:18).

2. A descendant of the royal line of David after and through Zerubbabel (1 Chron. 3:24).

3. An officer of King Jehoiakim (Jer. 36:12, 25).

4. Father of one of Nehemiah's close friends (Neh. 6:10).

DELILAH The Philistine woman from the Sorek Valley near Beth Shemesh (147-130) who by seduction delivered Samson to bondage (Judg. 13-16).

DELIVER,   *See* CHRIST, WORK OF
DELIVERANCE

DELIVERER The references are to human deliverers or to God's deliverers (Judg. 3:9, 15; 2 Sam. 22:2; Ps. 70:5). Moses is called deliverer (Acts 7:35). Also to be noted is the prophetic item: "The deliverer will come from Zion" (Rom. 11:26) cited by Paul from Isaiah where the word is "Redeemer." The reference according to Paul is to a future coming of the Messiah, Christ.

The main theme of the Bible is the work of God in delivering man from the power of sin and death through Christ his Redeemer and Deliverer. *See* CHRIST, WORK OF.

DELUGE *See* FLOOD

DEMAS A fellow laborer with Paul who later deserted him "because he loved this world" (Col. 4:14; Philem. 24; 2 Tim. 4:10).

DEMETRIUS 1. A well-spoken-of Christian, commended by John (3 Jn. 12).

2. An Ephesian silversmith who stirred up a riot against Paul (Acts 19:23-27).

DEMON,   In the OT the demon is considered a nondivine but supernatural
DEMONIAC being, an evil spirit, one who can exercise power and influence, mostly destructive. Demons are also called gods to whom their sons and daughters were sacrificed (Deut. 32:17; Ps. 106:37). In the NT the demon is a spiritual being hostile to God and man, and the demoniac a demon-possessed individual. Demons are agents of Beelzebub (Mk. 3:22). When possessed, a man may be dumb, live in tombs, refuse to wear clothes, act like an epileptic, have abnormal strength, or a combination of these (Mt. 12:22-24, 43-45; Mk. 9:17-20; Lk. 8:27; 11:14). In Matthew 4:24 it is noted that possession by a demon is something different from sickness. In the NT most of the occurrences are associated with opposition to the

ministry of Jesus. Exorcising of these evil spirits was not easy.

DENARIUS *See* MONEY

DEPUTY A vice-regent (1 Kgs. 22:47).

DERBE A city in the southern part of Asia Minor, NW of Tarsus, which was visited by Paul on his missionary journeys and from which came his traveling companion Gaius (Acts 14:6, 20; 16:1; 20:4).

DESERT, DESERTS The translation of a number of Hebrew and Greek words which refer to wilderness, waste, and arid regions (Gen. 16:7; Isa. 48:21). Unlike the concept of a desert as a completely barren area, the biblical desert was usable for grazing flocks, contained many rich oases, and had soil that only needed water to make it fertile (Gen. 16:7; 1 Sam. 17:28). One of these words (Arabah) when found with the article refers to the Jordan Valley from north of the Salt Sea to the Gulf of Aqaba. In the NT the translation "solitary place" is also found (Mt. 14:13; Mk. 1:35).

Several major deserts are mentioned in the Bible. The Desert of Zin was just south of the Negev (Num. 13:21). Kadesh Barnea (Ex. 32:8) was located in the Desert of Zin. The Desert of Shur is at the extreme west of the Sinai and opposite the Desert of Zin (Ex. 15:22). The location of the Desert of Zin is not certain but the Israelites were there between their time in the Desert of Shur and the Desert of Sinai. Probably it is on the eastern sea coast of the Red Sea between Shur and Sinai (Ex. 15:27; 16:1). The great central part of the Sinai, from east until the Desert of Sin, is called the Desert of Paran (Num. 10:12); and the Desert of Sinai is at the southern tip of the Sinai (Num. 3:4, 14).

DESOLATION, SACRILEGE *See* ABOMINATION OF DESOLATION

DESTROY, DO NOT *See* PSALMS, TITLES OF

DEUEL The father of a leader of the tribe of Gad while they were in the wilderness during the Exodus from Egypt (Num. 1:14). In some manuscripts he is called Reuel (see footnote at Num. 2:14).

DEUTERONOMY, BOOK OF The last of the five Books of Moses, the Torah, the Pentateuch, the Law. Its first four chapters contain Moses' review of the events from Sinai to the time of his expected

death. His review of the laws given by God at Sinai for
the conduct of the life of the people (Deut. 30:19, 20; Lev.
18:5), together with his emphasis on their spirituality and his
urgent plea that they be observed, follow in chapters 5
through 26. This section includes a repetition of the Decalogue
in chapter 5. Moses' final blessings, instructions, exhortations,
and farewell song are recorded in chapters 27-33 and his
death in 34. Especially since the nineteenth century no portion
of the Bible, unless it be the Book of Daniel, has caused
more difference of opinion among scholars than the Pentateuch
in its entirety or in each of its five parts. Some consider it a
late compilation from other sources and Moses not its author.
Most recent views tend to a more conservative position on
its unity and are assigning its writing to earlier periods. It
is stated in the book that Moses wrote this Law (Deut. 31:9,
22, 24-27). The implications of the rest of the OT and the
NT support this view. Jesus affirmed the Mosaic authorship
of the Law in his teaching (Mk. 10:5; 12:26; Jn. 5:46, 47;
7:19, 23). According to biblical chronology he lived at the end
of the fifteenth century B.C. *See also* PENTATEUCH.

DEVIL In the OT demons and evil spirits are mentioned more
commonly than devils (*see* DEMON). In the OT the chief of the
evil spirits is called "the Satan" (1 Chron. 21:1; Job. 1:6-9;
2:1-7; Zech. 3:1, 2). In the NT the archenemy of God and
man is the devil called Satan, ancient serpent, great dragon,
Beelzebub and tempter (Rev. 12:9; Mt. 4:1-11; Lk. 8:12;
Jn. 8:44; 13:2; Mk. 3:22; Lk. 11:18, 19; 1 Pet. 5:8). He, or
through his angels or spirits, is able to possess men. Jesus
healed such demon-possessed people (Acts 10:38). The devil
has many characterizations in the NT: "god of this age"
(2 Cor. 4:4), "ruler of the kingdom of the air" (Eph. 2:2),
"the accuser of our brethren" (Rev. 12:10), "the one who
leads the world astray" (Rev. 12:9) and "the deceiver of
men" (Rev. 20:7, 8). The concept of adversary or accuser at
court well describes one of his chief roles (Zech. 3:1; Rev.
12:10). His end is to be cast into eternal fire together with
his angels (Mt. 25:41; Rev. 20:10).

DEVOTE,
DEVOTED
THING
Denotes things forbidden forever to common use. No person
or thing devoted could be spared or ransomed (Lev. 27:28).
A person devoted to destruction could not be ransomed
but must be put to death (Lev. 27:29; 1 Sam. 15:3). This is
the "curse" that is to be removed from the heavenly Jerusalem
(Rev. 22:3). Material things devoted to the Lord could
become the property of the priests (Lev. 27:21). These differ
from things to be sacrificed which could be recalled at any
time before the sacrifice was to be made. The devoted thing
could never be taken back by its offerer. *See also* CURSE.

DEW In Palestine where there was no rain during the six months
of summer, dew, the condensation of the moisture in the
air at night time, was vital to prevent a complete drought and
consequent famine. It is very important to agriculture and is
often linked with rain in Scripture (1 Kgs. 17:1; 2 Sam. 1:21)
and like rain is used as a symbol of blessing (Ps. 133:3;
Deut. 33:13).

DIADEM Represents four Hebrew words and one Greek word; it is
sometimes translated "turban" or "crown"; something wound
around the head and worn by priests and kings as a symbol
of the right to rule (Zech. 3:5; Isa. 62:3; Rev. 12:3; 19:12).
It differs from the *stephanos*, also translated "crown" but a
symbol of the victor. The distinction is not always exactly
maintained. *See also* CROWN.

DIAMOND *See* PRECIOUS STONES AND METALS

DIASPORA A word which may refer in Scripture to the Jews when not in
their own land, or to the foreign places in which they are
living (Jn. 7:35; Jas. 1:1). In the NIV it is usually translated as
"scattered." While there were small colonies of Jews living
outside Palestine earlier, the first major dispersion began with
the deportations to Assyria and Babylon in the eighth and
sixth centuries B.C.. Some of the Jews returned under Ezra
and Nehemiah but some remained in Babylon and became
a large and influential community. Between the first century
before and the first century after Christ, the Jewish colonies
in Egypt became the most influential outside of Palestine
itself. By the end of the first century A.D. Jews were widely
settled in many settlements outside of Palestine (Acts 2:9-
11). Relations between the Jews and their neighbors in these
places were not always good and persecution and riots
frequently erupted, even as early as NT times (Acts 18:1, 2).
From Palestine, Babylon, Egypt, and other centers the
Jews were driven from country to country about the world,
with continuous persecution; after the first and second
centuries A.D. this was very frequent but not only by Christians
and in "Christian" lands. This culminated in the Nazi holocaust.
In NT times Paul started his ministries in foreign cities in
their synagogues (Acts 17:1-2, 10). The Jews abroad maintained
close connections with those at home, frequently making at
least one of the three annual pilgrimages. The communication
was two way as we note from Jas. 1:1 and 1 Pet. 1:1,
where letters were addressed to the Jewish Christians who
lived abroad and perhaps others too. It is interesting to
note that the early Christians who had converted from Judaism
considered themselves also to be in the *diaspora* when not
in Palestine. The Scriptures indicate a worldwide regathering

from this diaspora to "their own land." Some feel that the modern State of Israel is at least the forerunner of this (Ezek. 11:17; 28:25; 36:24; and many others). *See also* CAPTIVITY.

DIBLAIM Father-in-law of the prophet Hosea (Hos. 1:3).

DIBON, DIBON-GAD 1. A town in the tribal area of Judah settled by Jews after the exile (Neh. 11:25).

2. A town (224-101) in Moab east of the Jordan. The Israelites took it during their exodus wanderings and the tribe of Gad settled there (Num. 32:34). Mesha, King of Moab, rebelled about 900 B.C. but was beaten by the Israelites (2 Kgs. 3:4-27). He left a valuable contemporary record on stone, the Moabite Stone, found in the modern excavations of Dhiban.

DIGNITARIES *See* ELDERS

DIKLAH A son of Joktan thought to have lived in Arabia (Gen. 10:27; 1 Chron. 1:21).

DILEAN An unidentified town in the western foothills of Judah (Josh. 15:38).

DILL A kind of seed used for seasoning. *See* PLANTS, PERFUMES, AND SPICES.

DIMNAH One of four Levitical towns in the allotment of Zebulun (Josh. 21:35).

DIMONAH A town in the south of Judah thought by some to be the same as Dibon (Josh. 15:22). *See* DIBON.

DINAH A daughter of Jacob by Leah (Gen. 30:21) over whose honor her brothers destroyed Shechem (Gen. 34:24-30).

DINHABAH An unidentified city of Bela, king of Edom (Gen. 36:32).

DIONYSIUS A member of the Areopagus group, converted through the ministry of Paul (Acts 17:34).

DIOTREPHES An early Christian unfavorably described as one who puts himself first (3 Jn. 9).

DIRBI A Danite who was stoned for blasphemy, the son of a mixed marriage, Israelite and Egyptian (Lev. 24:10-16).

DISCIPLE A pupil, one who follows some doctrine or teacher. In the OT the Hebrew word is rendered thus only once (Isa. 8:16).

In the NT this is not a specific designation of the Twelve.
In the Gospels and Acts it is used over 250 times and in at
least 90 percent of the time it refers to followers of Christ in
general, later called Christians (Acts 6:1; 9:38; Mt. 22:16).
Sometimes it means followers of others, John the Baptist or
Moses for example (Mt. 9:14; Jn. 9:28). Occasionally it
refers to the twelve apostles (Mt. 10:1).

DISEASE For the most part the diseases of the Bible are those that
still prevail; diseases seen in the skin such as leprosy; internal
diseases such as dysentery, plague, malaria, tuberculosis;
diseases caused by intestinal and other worms; eye diseases;
mental disorders, and the like (see under separate names).
From the limited descriptions given in the Bible some are
difficult, if not impossible, to identify in modern terms. *See
also* SICK, SICKNESS.

DISHAN A clan chief of the Horites in Edom (Gen. 36:30; 1 Chron.
1:38).

DISHON 1. Son of the Horite clan chief Anah (Gen. 36:25, 30;
1 Chron. 1:38, 41).

2. Son of the Horite clan chief Seir (Gen. 36:21). (A possibility
exists linguistically that Dishon may be the place name of
the clan and we should read in 36:30 the chief of Dishon.)

DIVINATION, Predicting the future by inspiration or efforts to discern the
DIVINE future by a special means known to certain classes of persons
through the use of readings or the interpretation of omens.
The practice was almost entirely limited to the OT. OT
prophecy was a form of inspirational divination, when God
revealed certain future events to his prophets, or seers
(1 Sam. 9:9). One NT illustration is a case of fortune-telling
as well. Paul considered this possession by an evil spirit
and exorcised it (Acts 16:16-18). *See also* the word magician
below for a NT incident. In the Bible the following terms
are used:

1. *astrologers*, who received information from the stars (Isa.
47:13; Dan. 2:5, 10).

2. *enchanters, magicians, sorcerers*, those who use spells,
charms, omens, or magic to achieve their magical effects
(Deut. 18:11; Dan. 2:27; 5:7; Acts 13:8; 19:19; Dan. 2:2).

3. *medium, witchcraft*, those acquainted with the secrets
of the unseen world and/or in touch with the dead (Deut.
18:11; 1 Sam. 28:7; 2 Chron. 23:6; Deut. 18:10, 14).

4. *seer*, one who sees above (Deut. 18:10; Ezek. 21:21).
Divination, except for illumination to a prophet, was
prohibited by God as a sin as evil as idolatry (Lev. 19:31; 20:6;

1 Sam. 15:23). In spite of this, however, Israel was full of diviners in the days of the prophets. They used many different means: dreams or trances, visions, wood or arrows, teraphim, livers, necromancy or the consultation of the dead through a medium, and astrology (Ezek. 21:21; Zech. 10:2; 1 Sam. 28:7, 11). Wise men, diviners, those who practice sorcery or cast spells, spiritists, those who consult the dead are all condemned (Deut. 18:10, 11, 14; Dan. 5:7; 2 Chron. 33:6).

DIVORCE The dissolution of the marriage bond between husband and wife. In the OT this was largely at the instigation of the husband and on the ground of the fact that he found in his wife "something indecent about her." It was consummated by his writing a bill of divorce, putting it in her hand, and sending her from his house with the formula "She is not my wife, and I am not her husband" (Deut. 24:1; Hos. 2:2). The "indecency" was usually interpreted as unchastity. They could not be remarried unless the wife had in the meantime married another who had later died or divorced her (Deut. 24:2-4).

In NT times a wife could under certain circumstances initiate a divorce. To divorce a wife except on the ground of marital unfaithfulness was to make her commit adultery, and anyone who married a woman so divorced, committed adultery. A man who divorces his wife except for marital unfaithfulness and marries another commits adultery. If a woman divorces her husband, which was permitted, and marries another man, she commits adultery except as noted below (Mt. 5:32; 19:9; Mk. 10:11, 12; Lk. 16:18). In the NT an unbelieving partner who wishes to separate may do so but the separation is not encouraged. Regulations concerning a husband or wife who separate for such a reason are carefully spelled out in 1 Corinthians 7:10-16.

A married woman is released from the law of marriage after her husband dies and may then remarry without being guilty of adultery (Rom. 7:2-3; 1 Cor. 7:39). Heated debates are frequently conducted among clergymen over the question of the right of the "innocent party" in a divorce to remarry without committing adultery. Some argue that the one who committed the adultery that led to the divorce and then married another, is considered dead, the bond is broken and the "innocent party" then may remarry. There is no specific Scripture on the point.

DIZAHAB One of the places, east of Jordan, unidentified where Moses gave his farewell addresses to Israel (Deut. 1:1).

DODAI One of David's captains or mighty men (1 Chron. 27:4; 2 Sam. 23:9).

DODAVAHU Father of the prophet who prophesied against King Jehoshaphat (2 Chron. 20:37).

DODO 1. Grandfather of one of Israel's minor judges (Judg. 10:1).

2. Some equate with Dodai, but in any case the father of one of David's mighty men (2 Sam. 23:9).

3. A Bethlehemite, father of another of David's mighty men (2 Sam. 23:24).

DOE *See* BEASTS, 2

DOE OF THE MORNING *See* PSALMS, TITLES OF

DOEG An Edomite in Saul's employment who executed eighty-five priests of Nob and slew all that lived there (except Ahimelech's son who escaped and David), men, women, and cattle because Ahimelech of Nob had helped David (1 Sam. 21:1-9; 22:19-23).

DOG *See also* BEASTS, 8. Occasionally in the ancient middle east this word was applied to sodomites, male homosexuals (Deut. 23:18 footnote; Phil. 3:2).

DOMINION To be master of, to rule, to have power over, to have authority. Ultimate and eternal rule belongs to God. He permits men to rule over nature and nations. In the end of days dominion will be given to the saints, the people of the Most High (Ps. 22:28; Gen. 1:26; Dan. 7:27). In the NT this dominion ascribed to God is a number of times ascribed to Christ, thus equating Father and Son as God (Rev. 1:5; Mt. 28:18).

DONKEY *See* BEASTS, 4

DO NOT DESTROY *See* PSALMS, TITLES OF

DOPHKAH One of the stopping places of the Israelites during their exodus from Egypt, the first after leaving the Desert of Sin; in other versions called the Wilderness of Zin (Num. 33:12).

DOR An ancient coastal town on the Mediterranean north of Caesarea (142-224). Founded after 1500 B.C., its king defeated by Joshua, visited by the Egyptian Wen-Amon in the eleventh century, located in the tribal area of Manasseh, it was still an important town in Roman days (Judg. 1:27). Naphoth Dor probably refers to the same town (Josh. 11:2; 12:23; 1 Kgs. 4:11).

DORCAS The Greek name of a charitable Christian woman of Joppa whose Semitic name was Tabitha, whom Peter raised from the dead (Acts 9:36-40). Dorcas societies are named after this charitable woman.

DOTHAN A city (175-205) where Joseph found his brothers and from which he was sold into slavery in Egypt (Gen. 37:17ff.). Here too God protected Elisha from the armies of Syria nearly 1000 years later (2 Kgs. 6:13ff.). The Joseph P. Free excavations indicate continuous occupancy of the site from 3000 to 700 B.C. with a small Hellenistic occupation later.

DOUBLE SHARE *See* FIRSTBORN

DOVE *See* BIRDS, 4

DOVE ON FAR-OFF TEREBINTHS *See* PSALMS, TITLES OF, 5

DOWRY *See* MARRIAGE

DRACHMA A Persian gold coin of 8.424 grams, used in Palestine after the return from Babylon (Ezra 2:69; Neh. 7:70 ff.).

DRAGON *See* DEVIL and BEASTS, 9

DREAM A vision received usually at night while the recipient slept. In the OT God was the source and often a special interpreter was necessary to determine its meaning. Joseph and Daniel were renowned for their interpretative powers. Dreams are not too frequently mentioned and play no significant part in the OT. The NT gives even less importance to them (Gen. 20:6; 37:5ff.; 41:1ff.; Dan. 2:3; 4:5; 1 Kgs. 3:5; Mt. 1:20). Dreamers who tried to lure people from following God were to be killed (Deut. 13:1-5). *See also* DIVINATION, DIVINE.

DRESS Knowledge of the dress of the Bible times comes chiefly from ancient monuments and paintings in Egypt, Mesopotamia, and the land of the Hittites. Some Bible statements are relevant, and the traditions and usages of modern Bedouin, who through the centuries resisted change in this area, are important. Apart from ornaments, belt, foot and head wear, the dress consisted of an outer garment (cloak, mantle, or robe), an undergarment (robe, coat, tunic, or similar garment), and a loincloth or waistcloth. The last was usually of linen and worn next to the body (Judg. 14:12; Jer. 13:1; Mk. 14:51, 52). Elijah wore one made of hair and a leather belt around it. John the Baptist wore one of camel's hair and also a leather belt (2 Kgs. 1:8; Mt. 3:4). See also Ex.

28:42; Lev. 6:10. The terms used for the outer and inner garments are general terms for clothing and in the translations they are interchangeable in many cases. Worn next to the skin, made of linen or wool, draped over one shoulder and extending to the knees or ankles, with or without sleeves, was the *kuttonet* (Hebrew) or *chtion* (Greek). These words are translated as cloak, robe, tunic, garment (Gen. 37:3; 2 Sam. 13:18, 19; Ex. 28:4, 39; Job. 30:18; Mt. 5:40; Lk. 6:29; Jn. 19:24). As a sign of mourning the robe was torn (Job. 1:20). The *kuttonet* or *chtion* was also worn as the outer garment. When something was worn over it, it would be the *simlah* (Hebrew) and probably the Greek *imatia*, also translated coat, cloak, clothing, tunic, garment, mantle, or robe. This was a square or rectangular piece of cloth, thrown over one or both shoulders, with openings for the arms at the sides. It was not worn while working, and it was the garment used for a covering at night, thus it was not to be kept in pledge overnight by a creditor (Mt. 24:18; Ex. 22:26, 27; Deut. 22:3). The "hem" is part of the outer garment (Ex. 39:24). These flowing robes were held in by a sash, girdle, or belt made of wool, leather, or linen and worn by both men and women (2 Sam. 20:8; Isa. 3:24).

Headgear is not particularly mentioned in connection with men, except in connection with mourning or despair (2 Sam. 15:30; Esth. 6:12; Jer. 14:3). Turbans were worn by the three cast into the fiery furnace (Dan. 3:21). Women wore "headdresses" or turbans and veils with which they also covered the upper part of the body. Priests wore a head covering. In the NT while praying or prophesying men were not permitted to wear a head covering and women were required to wear one (1 Cor. 11:4, 6).

Many of the special items worn by women are mentioned in Isaiah 3:18-24. The poor usually went barefooted but others wore sandals made of leather or wood and held on with thongs, removed on entering a house (Amos 2:6; 8:6; Mk. 1:7). There is evidence of considerable variety in the quality of wearing apparel, even though not in style, and the disparity between the rich and the poor is particularly notable.

DRINK Water, beer, milk, wine, and vinegar were the chief liquids drunk in biblical times. The first came from cisterns or wells and milk was usually goat's milk (Prov. 27:27). Wine could be sweet (the juice of the grape), sour (vinegar of wine), or fermented (Num. 6:3; Gen. 9:21; 14:18). It was considered a food (Isa. 55:1). Beer is noted in Proverbs 20:1. "Fermented drink," frequently in the Scriptures coupled with wine, was prepared by a formula from either wine or grain. It was forbidden to priests (Aaron and his sons) and Nazirites, and while not forbidden to others it was accompanied with

warnings that it might pervert the judgment of its users
(Deut. 14:26; Prov. 20:1; Lev. 10:9; Num. 6:3, 4; Prov.
31:4, 5). Wine was not banned in Israel, nor even fermented
drink, but drunkenness is always considered a disgrace and
condemned (Jer. 13:13, 14; Gen. 19:31-36; Prov. 20:1).

DROPSY A symptom rather than a disease. It manifests itself by an
unnatural effusion of watery fluid in the tissues or some
cavity of the body (Lk. 14:2). *See also* SICK, SICKNESS.

DRUNKENNESS *See* DRINK

DRUSILLA The youngest daughter of Herod Agrippa I, who lived between
the time of the death of Christ and that of Paul. She became
the wife of the Judean procurator Felix after leaving her
first husband. Paul made a defense before the couple (Acts
24:24, 25).

DUMAH 1. A son of Ishmael and ancestor of one of the Arabian tribes
(Gen. 25:14).

2. A Judean town (148-93) in the hill country near Hebron
(Josh. 15:52).

3. An unidentified place in Edom (Isa. 21:11; *see* footnote).

DUNGEON *See* PRISON

DURA A plain near Babylon where Nebuchadnezzar's image was set
up to be worshiped (Dan. 3:1).

DYED, Known and practiced from antiquity it was used by the
DYEING Israelites in the preparing of the skins for the covering of the
tabernacle and in the temple (Ex. 26:1, 31; 2 Chron. 3:14).
The wealthy and the nobility used highly colored materials for
their clothing (Prov. 31:22; Lk. 16:19). The Phoenicians had
a near monopoly on this art but at Solomon's request taught
it to his workmen (2 Chron. 2:7). Dyeing vats have been
discovered in a number of excavations.

DYSENTERY A disease of the lower bowel characterized by ulceration and
hemorrhaging from which Paul healed the father of Publius
on the island of Malta (Acts 28:7-8). *See also* SICK, SICKNESS.

EAGLE *See* BIRDS, 5

EAR *See* EMOTIONS

EARRING *See* ORNAMENTS

EARTH In the OT two words commonly rendered "earth" and "ground" have a wide range of meanings, some of which they have in common. A material substance (Gen. 2:7), a territory or land (Gen. 28:15), the physical world in which man lives as opposed to the heavens (Gen. 1:1; Deut. 31:28; Ps. 68:8; Dan. 6:27).

EARTHQUAKE Since Palestine lies within the active earthquake zone which records 20 percent of the earth's tremors, it is natural that the biblical writers should record such phenomena. While such trembling of the earth is caused sometimes by volcanic activity, the geological formation of the Jordan Valley and the fault lines which run into it from both E. and W. provide the necessary conditions for movements of the earth's surface, which more frequently than volcanic action produce earthquakes. Severe waves of vibration produce spectacular secondary effects which accompany the quakes, such as fissures in the earth (Num. 16:32), thunder, rumblings, and flashes of lightning (Rev. 8:5). Earthquakes are recorded during the days of Moses (Ex. 19:18); Saul (1 Sam. 14:15); Elijah (1 Kgs. 19:11); Uzziah (Amos 1:1; Zech. 14:5); and Paul and Silas (Acts 16:26). In the excavations of Hazor evidence of the one in Uzziah's day was found. Josephus described a severe earthquake during the reign of Herod (Antiq. 15:2), of which archaeological evidence was found in the buildings of the Qumran community.

It is described as a feature of the Lord's presence for revelation (Ex. 19:18), and for destructive judgment (Isa. 29:6). The earthquake is prophetically listed among the catastrophic elements of the last days (Mt. 24:7; Mk. 13:8; Lk. 21:11; Rev. 6:12; 8:5; 11:13, 19; 16:18).

EAST (or EASTERN) SEA *See* SALT SEA

EASTER Since the Council of Nicea in A.D. 325, the church celebrates the resurrection of Jesus Christ on this day. There was no celebration of the resurrection in the New Testament. Later the Gentile Christians observed the day on Sunday while the Jewish believers connected it with Passover and celebrated it on the fourteenth of Nisan. Following the Nicean Council, Easter has been observed on the first Sunday following the full moon after the vernal equinox, varying between March 22 and April 25.

EBAL 1. The son of Joktan (1 Chron. 1:22, footnote).

2. The third son of Shoban, a Horite clan chief in Edom (Gen. 36:23; 1 Chron. 1:40).

3. A mountain just N. of Nablus (Shechem), 3077 feet high, *Jebel Eslamiyeh*, commands an extensive view over most of Galilee and Samaria. It is separated from Mount Gerizim, directly to the S. by a very important east-west pass. Following their entry into the land of Canaan, the Israelites gathered here to confirm their covenant with the Lord and to recite the blessing and cursing (Deut. 27:4-26). Joshua built an altar on Mount Ebal in accordance with Moses' earlier command (Josh. 8:30-35).

EBED 1. Father of Gaal who unsuccessfully rebelled against Abimelech in Shechem (Judg. 9:26-45).

2. Son of a Jonathan, one of the fifty men of the family of Adin who returned from Babylon under Ezra (Ezra 8:6).

EBED-MELECH A Cushite (Ethiopian) whom the Lord promised safety and protection during the destruction of Jerusalem (Jer. 39:15-

18), for his role in requesting the king's permission to have Jeremiah the prophet drawn from a dungeon (Jer. 38:7-13).

EBENEZER A town near Aphek where the Israelites camped before being defeated and losing the Ark of God to the Philistines (1 Sam. 4:1-22). Following a subsequent victory over the Philistines, Samuel set up a memorial stone, calling it Ebenezer, "the stone of help" (1 Sam. 7:12).

EBER Meaning "the other side," "across," from which according to some the Gentile form "Hebrew" is derived and is explained as denoting those coming from the "other side of the river" (the Euphrates), that is, from Haran (Gen. 11:31), in Aram Naharaim, the home of Abraham and Nahor (Gen. 24:4, 7, 10). The name appears frequently:

1. A descendant of Shem. He was the son of Shelah, and the father of Peleg (in whose time the earth was divided) and Joktan (Gen. 10:21-25; 11:14-16; 1 Chron. 1:19-25).

2. Head of a Gadite family (1 Chron. 5:13).

3. Two Benjamite families (1 Chron. 8:12, 22).

4. The head of a priestly family in the days of Joiakim (Neh. 12:20).

5. Eber is also mentioned in Luke 3:35 in the genealogy of Jesus as an ancestor of Abraham.

EBEZ A town in Issachar whose location is unknown (Josh. 19:20).

EBONY The highly prized, black core wood of the tree *Diospyros ebenum* imported into Palestine and Syria from S. India, Ceylon, and perhaps Ethiopia for use in the manufacture of fine furniture, valuable turned vessels, scepters, and idols. It was highly prized by the Egyptians, Phoenicians, Babylonians, Greeks, and Romans, and is mentioned along with ivory tusks as a part of Tyre's trade with the men of Rhodes (Ezek. 27:15).

EBRONAH *See* ABRONAH

ECBATANA Founded by the Median king, Deioces (Herodotus 1:96), and located at the foot of the Elvend Mountain, Ecbatana became the capital of Media. Following its capture by Cyrus the Great, it became a favorite summer residence of the Achaemenian kings. Ecbatana was where a copy of Cyrus' decree authorizing the rebuilding of the Jerusalem temple was found (Ezra 6:2). The city remained famous for its luxury after its capture by Alexander the Great from the Persians in 330 B.C. and became a summer capital of the Parthian rulers. Though suffering a minor decline during Sassanian rule, the town was rebuilt following the Islamic conquest, and continues to be one of the principal cities of Iran to the present time, known as Hamadan. Esther and Mordecai are said to be in Hamadan.

ECCLESIASTES, BOOK OF The title, which comes to us through Jerome from the Septuagint, is a translation of the Hebrew word *Koheleth*, a word which means teacher or preacher (Eccles. 1:12), and which possibly means "one who participates in a popular assembly" or "one who assembles wise sayings for the purpose of teaching." Like Job, it is a fine example of OT wisdom literature.

EDEN 1. The environment in which God created an enclosed idyllic arbor which was Adam and Eve's residence until their expulsion because of sin. The location of this "garden" is said to be watered by four rivers (Gen. 2:11-14), two of which are identified as the Tigris and Euphrates. The most commonly held theory places the garden somewhere in southern Mesopotamia where the Pishon and Gihon were either canals or tributaries connecting the other two rivers. It has been suggested that the Hebrew word translated "streams" in Genesis 2:6 may correspond to an Akkadian loan-word from the Sumerian word for "river," indicating that the river overflowed the ground and provided natural irrigation. The delightful nature of the "paradise" of Eden became illustrative material for later Scripture writers (Isa. 51:3; Ezek. 28:13; 31:9, 16, 18; 36:35; Joel 2:3). Though the idea of a primeval paradise seems well developed in many ethnic religions (Persian, Indian), only indirect parallels to the Garden of Eden are found in the Sumerian "land of Dilmun" and the Babylonian "cedar forest of Irini" and "garden of Siduri."

2. A Gershonite who served under Kore in distributing the holy oblations during the time of Hezekiah (2 Chron. 29:12; 31:15).

EDEN, PEOPLE OF An Aramaic city-state between the Euphrates and the Balikh River, identified with Bit-adini in the Assyrian records, which blocked Assyrian expansion to N. Syria. Its main city, Til Barsip, modern Tell Ahmar, on the east bank of the Euphrates, was taken by Shalmaneser III and became an Assyrian province in 855 B.C. The Bible mentions "the people of Eden who live in Tel Assar" taken together with Gozan, Haran, and Rezeph (2 Kgs. 19:12; Isa. 37:12), and predicts that its population of Beth Eden would be exiled to Kir (Amos 1:5). It was one of the places trading with Tyre (Ezek. 27:23).

EDER 1. A sheepfold "tower" where Jacob camped following the death of Rachel, between Bethlehem and Hebron (Gen. 35:21).

2. A son of Mushi, the son of Merari. A Levite of David's time (1 Chron. 23:23; 24:30).

3. A Benjamite family (1 Chron. 8:15).

EDOM, DESERT OF *See* GEOGRAPHY OF THE HOLY LAND

EDOM, EDOMITES *See* GEOGRAPHY OF THE HOLY LAND

EDREI 1. The royal city (253-224) of Og, King of Bashan (Deut. 1:4; Josh. 12:4), located at the extreme southern boundary of Bashan near the southern source of the Yarmuk River, about ten miles NE of Ramoth-Gilead, and about thirty miles E-SE of the Sea of Galilee. Og was defeated by the Israelites at Edrei (Num. 21:33-35; Deut. 3:1-3); and the city was assigned to the half-tribe of Manasseh (Josh. 13:12, 31). In the temple of Ammon in Karnak, Edrei is listed among the cities which Thutmose III (1490-1436 B.C.) claimed to have conquered or dominated in Upper Retenu (Syria-Palestine).

2. A fortified city of Naphtali, near Kedesh (Josh. 19:37).

EDUTH, SHUSHAN *See* PSALMS, TITLES OF

EGLAH The wife of David who was the mother of his sixth son, Ithream (2 Sam. 3:5; 1 Chron. 3:3).

EGLAIM A town on the border of Moab (Isa. 15:8). Its location is unknown.

EGLATH SHELISHIYAH A place mentioned in the oracles against Moab, location unknown (Isa. 15:5; Jer. 48:34). The KJV translates as "an heifer of three years old."

EGRON 1. A Canaanite royal city (124-106), probably to be identified with Tell el-Hesi, seven miles SW of Lachish at the edge of the foothills extending into the coastal plain of Philistia. One of the five-city Amorite coalition led by the King of Jerusalem against the Gibeonite confederacy, which was defeated by the Israelites under Joshua (Josh. 10:3ff.). Joshua captured the city, and it was later assigned to Judah (Josh. 15:39).

2. A King of Moab who invaded Israelite territory in the region of Jericho with the help of the Ammonites and Amalekites (Judg. 3:12, 13). The payment of annual tribute, required of Israel for eighteen years, provided the opportunity for Ehud's assassination of the obese monarch (Judg. 3:20-25).

EGYPT The Egyptians are a Hamitic people descended through Mizraim (Gen. 10:6), Hebrew for "Egypt" (*see* GEOGRAPHY

OF HOLY THE LAND). A native priest named Manetho, writing in about 300 B.C. divided the history of his nation into thirty dynasties, a system that is still employed. There is also a predynastic period, extending from 4500 to 3000 B.C. with the dual kingdoms of Upper Egypt (south) and Lower Egypt, the Nile delta to the north. They reunited under Menes, traditionally the first pharaoh, who inaugurated the protodynastic period of Dyn. I-II, 3000-2600. While the Old Kingdom, Dyn. III-VI, with its capital at Memphis at the apex of the delta, was the age of the pyramid builders, the absolute power of the pharaoh suffered a decline in it. The First Intermediate Period, Dyn. VII-XI, was one of feudalism. This may account for the remarkable reception that the Hebrew patriarch Abraham received near its close (Gen. 12:10-20).

Dyn. XII constitutes the Middle Kingdom, about 2000-1780 B.C.. Wars created a standing army that broke the power of the feudal nobility, who were replaced by a bureaucracy. Under such conditions Joseph, who came to Egypt before 1850, was able to rise to power (Gen. 39-41; 45:8). This probably occurred under Senusert III, who conquered from Syria to the second cataract of the Nile. Joseph's brothers and their families then emigrated to Egypt (Gen. 46), where they multiplied (Ex. 1:7). During the succeeding centuries of the Second Intermediate Period, Dyn. XIII-XVII, 1780-1580, the Israelites suffered oppression (Gen. 15:13), especially under the foreign Hyksos dynasties XV-XVI. A native dynasty, XVII, then arose at Thebes in the south and slowly drove back the hated Asiatics.

Egypt's New Empire, Dyn. XVIII-XX, 1580-1100 B.C. began with the expulsion of the Hyksos. The early XVIIIth Dyn. rulers, in fervent nationalism, intensified Israel's oppression (Ex. 1:13-22) and carried the antiforeign attack on into Syria. Thothmes III (1504-1450), the greatest of the pharaohs, fought seventeen campaigns, had fleets in the Aegean, and held from the fourth cataract to the Euphrates. He was probably the king from whom Moses fled but who died just prior to Israel's exodus in 1445 B.C. (Ex. 4:19; see CHRONOLOGY). His son Amenhotep II thus becomes the ill-fated monarch of the ten plagues and the Red Sea (Ex. 5-15). His grandson Amenhotep III abandoned Egypt's northeastern empire, opening the way for Joshua's conquest of Canaan, 1406-1400. Egypt recovered parts of Syria under Rameses II (1304-1237), in the chaotic days of Israel's judges; but only the victory stele of his son Merneptah mentions defeating Israel.

Egypt's Dyn. XXI-XXX, 1100-332 B.C., constitutes the Period of Decline. It was nevertheless, an honor when Solomon (970-930 B.C.) married a daughter of one of the last pharaohs of the XXIst Dyn. (1 Kgs. 3:1). Sheshonk I (biblical

Shishak), founder of Dyn. XXII, raided both Judah and Israel, exacting tribute from Solomon's son Rehoboam in 926 (1 Kgs. 14:25, 26); but Zerah the Cushite, who may be associated with his son Osorkon I, was routed during a similar attempt in 895 by Asa of Judah (2 Chron. 14:9-13). Later Hebrew intrigues with "So king of Egypt" (2 Kgs. 17:4), perhaps Osorkon IV, and with Tirhakah of the XXVth or Cushite Dyn. (2 Kgs. 19:9), led respectively to the Assyrian destruction of Samaria and Israel in 722 and to the partial capture but miraculous deliverance of Judah and Jerusalem in 701. As the Assyrians said, Egypt was a "splintered reed of a staff, which pierces a man's hand and wounds him if he leans on it" (2 Kgs. 18:21; compare Isa. 20; 30:1-7).

Egypt revived briefly under Neco II of the XXVIth Dyn., who slew Josiah at Megiddo in 609 (2 Kgs. 23:29) and controlled Judah (vv. 32-35) until its loss to the Babylonians, following his defeat at Carchemish in 605 (2 Kgs. 24:7). It was again Egyptian intrigue, with Pharaoh Hophra (Ezek. 17:15-17; Jer. 37:5; 44:30), that led to the Babylonian destruction of Jerusalem in 586. A number of Jews then fled to Egypt, despite Jeremiah, whom they took with them (Jer. 42-44). Years later, after Egypt's last XXXth Dyn. had been succeeded by the Macedonians and then the Romans, the baby Jesus and his family found refuge from Herod in this ancient land (Mt. 2:14, 19-21). (J.B.P.)

EGYPT, WADI OF The southern boundary of the land promised to Abram's descendants in Genesis 15:18, usually considered to be Wadi el-Arish, a streambed marking the SE boundary of the Egyptian province of Canaan with the boundary of the tribe of Judah (Num. 34:5; 1 Kgs. 8:65; 2 Kgs. 24:7; 2 Chron. 7:8; Isa. 27:12; Ezek. 47:19; 48:28; Josh. 15:4, 47). With the northern boundary is the "entrance of Hamath," except in Isaiah 27:12 where the Euphrates is mentioned. In other references to the S boundary of the territory yet to be taken in the days of Joshua, the Shihor (Josh. 13:3; 1 Chron. 13:5) and the Brook of the Arabah (Amos 6:14) are named. These may all refer to Wadi el-Arish, originating in the middle of the Sinai Peninsula and flowing into the Mediterranean midway between Gaza and Pelusium.

EGYPTIAN, THE An unnamed leader who started a revolt and led terrorists, whom the Roman (Acts 23:26) commander of the fortress of Antonia, Claudius Lysias, mistook for Paul when he was mobbed in the temple precincts (Acts 21:38). Josephus mentions that this Egyptian with a band of rebels came to Jerusalem in A.D. 84 and persuaded a multitude of common people to follow him to the Mount of Olives where he would demonstrate his powers as prophet in commanding the walls of Jerusalem to fall down. Roman soldiers took the initiative to disperse his followers, but the Egyptian escaped.

EHI A son of Benjamin (Gen. 46:21).

EHUD *See* JUDGES OF ISRAEL

EKER A grandson of Jerahmeel and son of Ham (1 Chron. 2:27).

EKRON *See* PHILISTINE CITIES

ELA The father of Shimei, Solomon's commissary officer for the tribe of Benjamin (1 Kgs. 4:18).

ELAH 1. A tribal chief in Edom descended from Esau, possibly of the district Elah (Elath?) (Gen. 36:41; 1 Chron. 1:52).

2. The father of Hoshea, the last king of Israel (2 Kgs. 15:30; 17:1; 18:1, 9).

3. A son of Caleb (1 Chron. 4:15).

4. A Benjamite residing in postexilic Jerusalem (1 Chron. 9:8).

See also KINGS OF JUDAH AND ISRAEL.

ELAH, VALLEY OF The valley of confrontation between the Israelites and the Philistines when David killed the Philistine champion, Goliath (1 Sam. 17:2, 19; 21:9). It is identified with the fertile Wadi es-Sunt ("Valley of the Acacia"), about fifteen miles W-SW of Bethlehem, the entrance of which was protected by the fortress of Azekah (Tell ez-Zakariyeh (144-123)).

ELAM, ELAMITES 1. A son of Shem (Gen. 10:22; 1 Chron. 1:17).

2. A son of Shashak, a descendant of Benjamin (1 Chron. 8:24).

3. A Korahite son of one of the gatekeepers in the time of David (1 Chron. 26:3).

4. The head of a family of 1254 which returned with Zerubbabel (Ezra 2:7; Neh 7:12). Another "Elam" family is mentioned with the same number of members, called "the other Elam" (Ezra 2:31; Neh. 7:34).

5. The father of two sons who returned from exile with Ezra (Ezra 8:7).

6. A descendant of Elam who urged Ezra to take action against mixed marriages (Ezra 10:2). Six of the same family put away their foreign wives (Ezra 10:26).

7. A chief who sealed the covenant with Nehemiah (Neh. 10:14).

8. A priest who took part in the dedication of the rebuilt wall of Jerusalem (Neh. 12:42).

9. An area covering the territory of the Zagros Mountain range and of modern Luristan and Khuszistan with its capital at Susa. The language of the various tribes that made up its population, largely written in cuneiform, may well have continued centuries after Elam ceased to exist as an independent nation. Different from Sumerian, Semitic, and Indo-European, the script is largely undeciphered. The long history of the people, known through Mesopotamian documents and what is known from the Elamite tablets recovered mostly at Susa, beginning with urban communities and settlements as early as the end of the fourth millennium, was marked by alternating periods of ascendancy and suppression. Control of the trade routes to the Iranian plateau, and to the SE, prompted regular attacks against Elam from the plains of Mesopotamia.

ELASAH 1. One whom King Zedekiah sent to Nebuchadnezzar carrying Jeremiah's letter of advice to the exiles in Babylon (Jer. 29:3).

2. One of the sons of Pashur who was guilty of marrying foreign wives (Ezra 10:22).

ELATH A seaport town (150-882) located near biblical Ezion Geber in the area where modern Elat and Aqaba are situated at the head of the Red Sea. A stop in the Israelites' exodus from Egypt (Deut. 2:8). King Solomon later built ships and a fort there, the latter to guard his trade route (1 Kgs. 9:26). King Azariah (Uzziah) rebuilt and restored it to Judah taking it back from the Edomites (2 Kgs. 14:22; 2 Chron. 26:2). Azariah is called by that name in the king's record and Uzziah in that of the Chronicles. Elam (the Syrians) took Elath later only to be driven out, together with the Israelites, by the king of Edom (2 Kgs. 16:5, 6). It served the Romans in NT times as a military post.

EL-BERITH A god worshiped at Shechem (Judg. 9:46).

EL BETHEL The name which Jacob gave to the place of his vision on his way back from Paddan Aram (Gen. 35:7, 9). *See also* GOD, NAMES OF.

ELDAAH The last of the five sons of Midian, from the Abraham-Keturah line (Gen. 25:4).

ELDAD One of the seventy elders appointed by Moses to assist him in the government of the Israelites during the wilderness sojourn, who together with Medad were not present at the door of the tabernacle to receive God's message and the gift of prophecy. In spite of their absence at the appointed place, Eldad and Medad shared equally in the endowment where they were in the camp. When Joshua objected to the seemingly irregular display of divine power, Moses responded with the wish that all God's people were prophets (Num. 11:24-29).

ELDER Since in most civilizations authority has been committed to those best qualified to rule by reason of age or experience, it is natural that leaders in many ancient communities have had this title which comes from a root meaning "old age." Thus references are made to dignitaries ("elders" in the Hebrew text) among the Egyptians (Gen. 50:7), the elders of the Moabites and Midianites (Num. 22:7) and the Israelite elders (Ex. 3:16). The seventy elders of Moses' appointment (Ex. 24:1; Num. 11:16) continued to function until after the wilderness period when according to Deuteronomic legislation every city seems to have had a ruling body of elders who also acted as judges. A constant feature of Israel's life from the days of Moses to those of Ezra, this national body exercised considerable influence, especially in civil matters under the monarchy.

In New Testament times each Jewish community had its council of elders, the most important of which was the Sanhedrin of Jerusalem, which served as a kind of "supreme court" for all Jewry. While they maintained the general administrative control over the Jewish communities and represented the Jews before Roman authorities, their main duty was their interpretation and maintenance of the law. Similarly, the Qumran community also recognized elders and a supreme council. The church quite naturally adopted the institution which functioned in ways comparable to the Jewish Sanhedrin (Acts 11:30; 15:2, 4, 6, 22, 23; 16:4; 21:18). These Christian elders exercised spiritual oversight in the congregations (Jas. 5:14; 1 Pet. 5:1-4; Rom. 12:8; 1 Thess. 5:12, 13).

ELEADAH A descendant of the tribe of Ephraim killed by the men of the city of Gath (1 Chron. 7:20).

ELEALEH A city west of the Jordan which was rebuilt by Reuben and later became a Moabite possession (Num. 32:3, 37; Isa. 15:4; 16:9; Jer. 48:34), identified with El-al (228-136), about two miles N-NE of Heshbon.

ELEASAH 1. A member or family of the Jerahmeelites of the tribe of Judah (1 Chron. 2:39, 40).

2. A Benjamite, descended from Saul (1 Chron. 8:37; 9:43).

ELEAZAR 1. The third son of Aaron and Elisheba (Ex. 6:23; Num. 3:2). Following the death of his older brothers, Nadab and Abihu (Lev. 10:1, 2), Eleazar was designated (Num. 3:32) and later invested by Moses as Aaron's successor (Num. 20:25-28). As the chief priest, he assisted Moses in the numbering of the people (Num. 26:1, 2) and was responsible for dividing the spoils following a battle with the Midianites (Num. 31:25-54). He was appointed to help in the dividing of the promised land among the tribes (Num. 34:17; Josh. 14:1; 19:51).

2. A son of Abinadab who was consecrated to care for the Ark after it was brought to his father's house at Kiriath Jearim from Beth Shemesh (1 Sam. 7:1; 6:19).

3. A son of Dodai, one of David's thirty mighty men who gained special recognition in his battles with the Philistines (2 Sam. 23:9, 10; 1 Chron. 11:12-14).

4. A Levite, in the time of David, a son of Mahli. Eleazar had only daughters who then married their cousins (1 Chron. 23:21, 22; 24:28).

5. One of the Levite custodians of the temple treasures which were returned to Jerusalem by Ezra (Ezra 8:33).

6. A descendant of Parosh, mentioned in a list of laymen who had married foreign women while in exile (Ezra 10:25).

7. A Levite musician who participated in the dedication of the walls of Jerusalem (Neh. 12:42).

8. An ancestor of Joseph, the husband of Mary of whom was born Jesus (Mt. 1:15).

ELECTION Since the Fall of man (Gen. 2:15-17; 3:1-20) all men descended by natural generation from Adam are born in a state of sin and grow to rebel against the Creator. The redeeming grace of God is needed to deliver one thus shackled by sin. The concept of election is that God, "out of his mere good pleasure, from all eternity, elected some to everlasting life, and did enter into a covenant of grace, to deliver them out of the estate of sin and misery, and to bring them into an estate of salvation by a Redeemer" (Westminster Shorter Catechism). This is the most restricted usage of the Greek word *ekloge* rendered in English by several words: elect, choose, and select (2 Tim. 2:10; 1 Pet. 1:1, 2; Eph. 1:3-5, 11). There is no obligation upon God to bring into his presence any of those who are in sin or rebellion against him, and thus uninterested in any particular relationship with him. In his grace, however, through election, he sees that some, a vast multitude, will come to him. In the NT the concept is almost always in relation to individuals. In the OT one of its chief usages is of the choosing of Israel as a people because he loved them and had to keep the oath he swore to their fathers when he brought them out of Egypt.

EL ELOHE ISRAEL The name of Jacob's altar erected near Shechem (Gen. 33:20).

ELHANAN 1. A son of Jair, who killed Lahmi, Goliath's brother (1 Chron. 20:5). (Jair is called Jaare-Oregim in 2 Sam. 21:19, but see the footnote.)

2. One of David's thirty mighty men, a son of Dodo the Bethlehemite (2 Sam. 23:24; 1 Chron. 11:26).

ELI A descendant of Ithamar, the fourth son of Aaron, high priest at Shiloh who judged Israel for forty years (1 Sam. 1-3; 14:3; 1 Kgs. 2:27). The sinful conduct of Eli's sons, Phinehas and Hophni, and the failure of Eli's influence over them, culminated in the prophecy of the fall of the house of Eli (1 Sam. 2:27-36) and its fulfillment in the Philistine capture of the Ark, the death of Phinehas and Hophni, the destruction of Shiloh, and finally the demise of Eli upon hearing of Israel's defeat (1 Sam. 4:11-18). Eli was already old when Hannah brought the baby Samuel to give him to serve the Lord for his entire life (1 Sam. 1:24-28).

ELIAB 1. A son of Helon, Zebulun tribal representative appointed to help Moses (Num. 1:9; 2:7; 7:24, 29; 10:16).

2. A Reubenite whose sons Dathan and Abiram were involved in the rebellion of Korah against the leadership of Moses and Aaron (Num. 16:1, 12; 26:8-10; Deut. 11:6).

3. An ancestor of Samuel the prophet (1 Chron. 6:27), also called Elihu (1 Sam. 1:1), and Eliel (1 Chron. 6:34).

4. David's oldest brother (1 Sam. 16:6; 17:13, 28) whom Samuel thought might be the Lord's appointed for kingship (1 Sam. 16:6). While serving in Saul's army against the Philistines he was incensed at the suggestion that David, his youngest brother, would confront Goliath (1 Sam. 17:28).

5. A Levitical musician of David's time (1 Chron. 15:18, 20; 16:5).

6. A Gadite warrior who became an officer in David's army (1 Chron. 12:8, 9).

ELIADA 1. One of David's sons born to him in Jerusalem (2 Sam. 5:16; 1 Chron. 3:8).

2. Father of Rezon, leader of a guerilla band against Solomon (1 Kgs. 11:23).

3. Commander of a Benjamite military corps stationed at Jerusalem during Jehoshaphat's reign (2 Chron. 17:17).

ELIAHBA A Shaalbonite, one of David's Thirty or mighty men (2 Sam. 23:32; 1 Chron. 11:33).

ELIAKIM 1. A son of Hilkiah, and successor of Shebna as King Hezekiah's palace administrator (2 Kgs. 18:18, 26, 37). He attempted to negotiate for Hezekiah with the representatives of Sennacherib (2 Kgs. 18:17-37; Isa. 36:1-22), and later headed a company directed to appeal for Isaiah's help (2 Kgs. 19:2; Isa. 37:2).

2. Pharaoh changed one by this name to Jehoiakim and Neco made him the puppet king of Judah (2 Kgs. 23:34).

3. A priest at the dedication of the rebuilt wall of Jerusalem in Nehemiah's time (Neh. 12:41).

4. A grandson of Zerubbabel named in the genealogy of Jesus (Mt. 1:13).

5. A son of Melea in Jesus' genealogy (Lk. 3:30).

ELIAM 1. The father of Bathsheba, the wife of Uriah the Hittite whom David had killed so that he could have his wife (2 Sam. 11:3); called Ammiel in 1 Chronicles 3:5.

2. A son of Ahithophel and one of David's Thirty (2 Sam. 23:34).

ELIASAPH 1. Son of Deuel. The tribal leader of Gad who assisted Moses in the census of Israel and with other duties in the Desert of Sinai (Num. 1:14; 2:14; 7:42, 47; 10:20).

2. Son of Lael, and tribal leader of the Gershonites who cared for the tabernacle in the Desert of Sinai (Num. 3:24).

ELIASHIB 1. A priest in the time of David (1 Chron. 24:12).

2. A descendant of King David and of Zerubbabel (1 Chron. 3:24).

3. A high priest in the time of Nehemiah, who directed the rebuilding of the Sheep Gate in the city wall (Ezra 10:6; Neh. 3:1, 20, 21).

4. A postexilic singer who had married a foreign wife (Ezra 10:24).

5. Son of Zattu who had a foreign wife (Ezra 10:27).

6. Son of Bani who also had a foreign wife (Ezra 10:36).

7. Father of Johanan who assisted Ezra (Ezra 10:6; Neh. 12:23).

ELIATHAH A son of Heman the king's seer and grandson of Asaph involved in the ministry of music in the temple in David's reign (1 Chron. 25:4, 27).

ELIDAD A Benjamite, one of those assigned the oversight of the division of Canaan to the nine and one half tribes to be settled west of the Jordan (Num. 34:16-18, 21).

ELIEHOENAI 1. The eighth son of a gatekeeper from the family of Korah (1 Chron. 26:3).

2. Head of a family who returned to Jerusalem with Ezra (Ezra 8:4).

ELIEL 1. A chief or family head of the half of the tribe of Manasseh E of Jordan (1 Chron. 5:24).

2. A Levitical musician in the temple (1 Chron. 6:34).

3. Two chiefs or family heads of Benjamin (1 Chron. 8:20, 22).

4. Three of David's mighty men (1 Chron. 11:46, 47; 12:11).

5. A Levite connected with bringing the Ark to Jerusalem (1 Chron. 15:9, 11).

6. A Levite of the time of Hezekiah (2 Chron. 31:13).

ELIENAI A son of Shimhi and descendant of Benjamin (1 Chron. 8:20).

ELIEZER 1. Abraham's servant, and heir until Ishmael was born (Gen. 15:2). He may have been the unnamed servant sent to secure a bride for Isaac (Gen. 24).

2. The second son of Moses and Zipporah (Ex. 18:4; 1 Chron. 23:15, 17; 26:25).

3. A grandson of Benjamin (1 Chron. 7:8).

4. A priest who blew a trumpet before the Ark as it was being returned to Jerusalem (1 Chron. 15:24).

5. A Reubenite chief in David's time (1 Chron. 27:16).

6. A prophet who rebuked Jehoshaphat for his military alliance with Ahaziah (2 Chron. 20:37).

7. A leader sent to encourage Israelites to return with Ezra (Ezra 8:16, 17).

8. A priest, a Levite, and a descendant of Harim who had married wives while in the exile (Ezra 10:18, 23, 31).

9. Mentioned in the genealogy of Jesus (Lk. 3:29).

ELIHOREPH A son of Shisha, a secretary and chief official in Solomon's court (1 Kgs. 4:3).

ELIHU 1. The father of Jeroham and great-grandfather of Samuel (1 Sam. 1:1). Also called Eliel (1 Chron. 6:34).

2. A Manassite, who deserted Saul to join David in Ziklag (1 Chron. 12:20).

3. A Korahite gatekeeper in David's time (1 Chron. 26:7).

4. David's brother who became the officer over Judah (1 Chron. 27:18).

5. The youngest of Job's friends (Job 32:2-6; 34:1; 35:1; 36:1).

ELIJAH A ninth-century prophet from Tishbe of Gilead in the northern kingdom (1 Kgs. 17:1) who led in the struggle against the encroachment of Tyrian Baal worship (1 Kgs. 17). The struggle of the Lord against Baalism which was fostered by the marriage of Ahab to Jezebel centered in Elijah's denunciation of Ahab's compromise, false tolerance, and syncretism which were incompatible with the exclusive allegiance God required of Israel (1 Kgs. 18). King Ahaziah also was denounced for inquiring of the Baal oracle of Ekron (1 Kgs. 18:17-19; 2 Kgs. 1:1-8). Elijah sent a letter to King Jehoram promising punishment for his apostasy (2 Chron. 21:12-15). The impact of his words and acts ultimately claimed for him the role of harbinger of the eschatological age (Mal. 4:5, 6). An expectation of Elijah's return is stated frequently in the NT (Mt. 11:14; 17:10-13; Mk. 9:13; Lk. 1:17; Jn. 1:21, 25; Mt. 16:13, 14; Mk. 9:4, 5; Lk. 9:30-33).

ELIKA A Harodite who belonged to David's Thirty (2 Sam. 23:25).

ELIM An oasis marked by twelve fresh water springs and seventy palm trees, the fourth stop of the Israelites after crossing the Red Sea (Ex. 15:27; 16:1; Num. 33:9, 10). It has been identified with a site about sixty miles from Suez called Wadi Gharandel, where vegetation, palms, and water are plentiful even today.

ELIMELECH An Ephrathite from Bethlehem, who with his wife Naomi and two sons, Mahlon and Chilion, migrated to Moab in the time of the Judges to escape a famine in Judah. He is remembered mainly because of the faithfulness of his daughter-in-law, Ruth, to Naomi following his death and the death of his sons (Ruth 1:2).

ELIOENAL 1. A postexilic descendant of David (1 Chron. 3:23, 24).

2. A Simeonite clan head (1 Chron. 4:36, 38).

3. A grandson of Benjamin (1 Chron. 7:8).

4. A son of Pashur who had married a foreign wife in the exile (Ezra 10:22).

5. A son of Zattu who had married a foreign wife while in the exile (Ezra 10:27).

6. A postexilic priest involved in one of two choirs at the dedication of the rebuilt wall of Jerusalem (Neh. 12:41).

ELIPHAL A member of David's mighty men (1 Chron. 11:35).

ELIPHAZ 1. The eldest son of Esau and his Hittite wife, Adah, who married a Horite concubine, Timna, and became the ancestor of a number of Edomite tribes (Gen. 36:4, 10, 11, 15; 1 Chron. 1:35, 36).

2. The first speaker in the dialogue against Job. He was known for his wisdom (Jer. 49:7). Eliphaz reasoned that Job's suffering was the natural outcome of his sin and that conversion was the only escape from God's continued retribution (Job 4, 5, 15, 22).

ELIPHELEHU A Levite harp player appointed by David to the musical ministry during the recovery of the Ark (1 Chron. 15:18, 21).

ELIPHELET 1. A son of David born in Jerusalem (1 Chron. 3:6, 8; 14:5).

2. One of David's Thirty (2 Sam. 23:34).

3. A Benjamite and descendant of Saul (1 Chron. 8:39).

4. An exile who returned with Ezra (Ezra 8:13).

5. A son of Hashum who had married a foreign wife while in exile (Ezra 10:33).

ELISABETH *See* ELIZABETH

ELISHA The disciple and successor of Elijah who was a prophet during the reigns of Jehoram, Jehu, Jehoahaz, and Joash, kings of Israel (2 Kgs. 1-13). Continuing Elijah's battle against Baal worship, Elisha's ministry is marked by many miracles related to both relieving of private needs and affairs of state. As the recognized head of the prophetic schools, he enjoyed access to the royal courts because of his gifts of knowledge and foresight and capacity for miracle working. He endeavored to mold the nation's future by the prophetic proclamation of the Lord's will.

ELISHAH One of the descendants of Japheth in the "Table of Nations" (Gen. 10:4; 1 Chron. 1:7), whose name was later applied to a maritime region and its inhabitants who exported purple and blue dyed products to Tyre (Ezek. 27:7). It has been identified with Alashia, a part of Cyprus from which copper and other raw materials were exported. It is mentioned in cuneiform tablets from Mari, Alalakh, Ugarit, Tell el-Amarna and Khattushash, from the eighteenth to the thirteenth centuries B.C., and has been identified by C.F.A. Schaeffer with Enkomi on the east coast of Cyprus, where an important Late Bronze Age trading center has been excavated.

ELISHAMA 1. An Ephraimite at the census in the Desert of Sinai, the grandfather of Joshua (Num. 1:10; 2:18; 7:48, 53; 10:22; 1 Chron. 7:26).

2. One of David's sons born in Jerusalem (2 Sam. 5:16; 1 Chron. 3:6, 8; 14:7).

3. The grandfather of Ishmael, a member of Judean royalty who killed Gedaliah at the time of the Exile (2 Kgs. 25:25; Jer. 41:1).

4. A descendant of Judah (1 Chron. 2:41).

5. A priest sent to teach Judeans the law (2 Chron. 17:7, 8).

6. A secretary at Jehoiakim's court (Jer. 36:12, 20, 21).

ELISHAPHAT A Judean commander of a unit of 100 who assisted Jehoiada the priest in the revolt that brought Joash to the throne (2 Chron. 23:1-11).

ELISHEBA The wife of Aaron (Ex. 6:23).

ELISHUA A son of David born in Jerusalem (2 Sam. 5:15; 1 Chron. 14:5).

ELIUD The father of Eleazar and ancestor of Jesus (Mt. 1:14-16).

ELIZABETH The wife of the priest Zachariah and mother of John the Baptist (Lk. 1:5-66). She was a woman of piety, faith, and spiritual gifts of the lineage of Aaron. Her barrenness was overcome in old age by the birth of the herald of the Messiah's coming.

ELIZAPHAN 1. The head of the Kohathites in the Desert of Sinai (Num. 3:30).

2. The Zebulun representative among the tribal leaders responsible for dividing the land of Canaan (Num. 34:25).

ELIZUR The leader of the Reubenites who assisted Moses in taking a census of Israel in the Desert of Sinai (Num. 1:5; 2:10; 7:30, 35; 10:18).

ELKANAH 1. A son of Korah, and leader of a Levite clan (Ex. 6:24; 1 Chron. 6:24).

2. The father of Samuel the prophet (1 Sam. 1:1, 4, 8, 19, 21, 23; 2:11, 20; 1 Chron. 6:34).

3. An ambidextrous Benjamite warrior who left Saul to join David at Ziklag (1 Chron. 12:2, 6).

4. An official of the court of Ahaz who was killed by Pekah when he invaded Judah (2 Chron. 28:6, 7).

5. A name frequently used among the Levites, especially by the Kohathites; some were temple musicians (1 Chron. 6:23, 25, 26, 35, 36; 9:16; 15:23).

ELKOSH The home of Nahum the prophet (Nah. 1:1). Of a number of suggested locations, the chronological and circumstantial setting of the prophet's ministry is most in keeping with a S Judean town.

ELLASAR One of the city states allied with Kedorlaomer, which invaded Palestine and fought against the cities of the plain in Abraham's time (Gen. 14:1). It has been identified by some with the S. Babylonian kingdom of Larsa.

ELMADAM An ancestor of Jesus (Lk. 3:28).

ELNAAM The father of Jeribai and Joshaviah, two of David's men (1 Chron. 11:46).

ELNATHAN 1. Father of Nehushta, Jehoiachin's mother (2 Kgs. 24:8), who possibly was the one who led a party sent by King Jehoiakim to bring back the fugitive prophet Uriah from Egypt (Jer. 26:22, 23). A reference from Lachish Ostracon III, which comes from this period, may record this action: "The commander of the host, Coniah son of Elnathan, hath come down in order to go into Egypt."

2. The name appears three times among those returning to Jerusalem from the exile (Ezra 8:16).

ELOHIM *See* GOD, NAMES OF, GODHEAD

ELOI, ELOI, LAMA SABACHTHANI A transliteration of the Hebrew-Aramaic expression recorded in Matthew 27:46 and Mark 15:34; from Psalm 22:1 as the central of Jesus' seven utterances from the cross. The translation which the Gospels then give for the readers unfamiliar with either Hebrew or Aramaic, "My God, my God, why have you forsaken me?" had earlier been explained by Jesus in his discussion of the meaning of his death (Lk. 24:45, 46). The footnote to Matthew 27:46 in the NIV reads "Some manuscripts Eli, Eli."

ELON *See* JUDGES OF ISRAEL

ELON, ELONITES 1. A son of Zebulun (Gen. 46:14; Num. 26:26).

2. The Hittite father of one of Esau's wives, Basemath (Gen. 26:34; 36:2).

3. A minor judge from Zebulun (Judg. 12:11, 12).

4. A village in the territory allotted to the tribe of Dan near Timnah (Josh. 19:43). Later the Danites moved north. Elon may possibly be identified with 'Alein, W of Beit Mahsir, or Khirbet Wadi 'Alin between Deir Aban and 'Ain Shems (Beth Shemesh).

ELON BETHHANAN A Danite village in Solomon's second administrative district (1 Kgs. 4:9).

ELPAAL A Benjamite family (1 Chron. 8:11, 12, 18).

ELPARAN The most southerly extent of Kedorlaomer's raid into Palestine (Gen. 14:6).

ELPELET One of David's sons born to him in Jerusalem (1 Chron. 14:5; 2 Sam. 5:16).

ELTEKEH A Danite town assigned to the Levites which later fell into Philistine hands together with Timnah (Josh. 19:44; 21:23). A decisive victory by Sennacherib over the Egyptians at Eltekeh led to the capture of the city and Timnah and the ultimate invasion of Judah in 701 B.C. Eltekeh was N of Ekron (Khirbet el-Muqanna) and has been identified with Tell Shalaf (128-144).

ELTEKON A village of Judah in the district of Beth-zur, possibly to be identified with Khirbet ed-Deir, about four miles W of Bethlehem (Josh. 15:59).

ELTOLAD An unidentified city of Simeon in the S of Judah, near Ezem and Hormah (Jos. 15:30; 19:4), called Tolad in 1 Chronicles 4:29.

ELUL *See* CALENDAR

ELUZAI A Benjamite warrior who defected to David at Ziklag (1 Chron. 12:5).

ELYMAS *See* BAR-JESUS

ELZABAD 1. A warrior from the tribe of Gad who defected to David at Ziklag (1 Chron. 12:12).

2. A Korahite doorkeeper (1 Chron. 26:7).

ELZAPHAN A Kohathite Levite (Ex. 6:22; Lev. 10:4; Num. 3:30; 1 Chron. 15:8; 2 Chron. 29:13).

EMBALMING *See* BURIAL

EMBROIDER Found chiefly in connection with the embroidery for the tabernacle (Ex. 26:36; 27:16; 28:39).

EMERALD *See* PRECIOUS STONES AND METALS

EMITES Tall, powerful, inhabitants of Moab, associated with the area of Shaveh Kiriathaim (Gen. 14:5) who were later dispossessed by the Moabites (Deut. 2:10, 11). A tribe similar to the Rephaim and Anakim. *See* REPHAIM.

EMMANUEL *See* IMMANUEL

EMMAUS A village, about seven miles from Jerusalem, to which two disciples were going when Jesus joined them in a post-resurrection appearance (Lk. 24:13-35). At least four modern sites, Qaloniyeh (near modern Motza Ellit), El-Qubeibeh, Abu Ghosh, and Amwas, ranging from four to twenty miles from Jerusalem, have been proposed for NT Emmaus. The first, between the tribal areas of Judah and Benjamin, seems most probable.

EMOTIONS In the Bible the emotions are frequently referred to by a term which literally translated would mean a particular part of the body. There are also, of course, specific abstract terms. The most common parts of the body referred to as seats of emotions include: belly, stomach, ear, eye, heart, and liver. All have several translations and without checking in the Hebrew or Greek texts it is impossible to distinguish in most cases.

1. *Belly, stomach* and *inmost being* refer to the innermost part or soul of man, to the seat of his intellectual powers, to the seat of avarice and passion (Job. 20:15, 23; Prov. 20:27, 30; Job 32:17, 18).

2. *Ear*, almost the equivalent of the mind, expresses the entire faculty of understanding (Job 13:1, 17).

3. *Eye*, in addition to seeing and expressing sorrow and gladness, can speak of desire, lust, and understanding (Job 17:7; 1 Sam. 14:27; Eccl. 4:8; 2 Pet. 2:14; Jer. 5:21; 7:11).

4. *Heart*. Almost all the emotions are somewhere in the Bible attributed to the heart (Ps. 64:6), seat of the intellect or understanding, volition, moral life, actions, psychic life, and compassion. It is even rendered "mind" in Job 12:3.

5. *Liver* in the Bible is usually mentioned in connection with the sacrifices. In other literature it is connected also with divination. It is also thought of as the seat of sorrow, exultation, glory, and honor. It is even rendered in Lamentations 2:11 and Psalm 16:9 as "heart." In Job 19:9 it is rendered "honor."

EMPEROR, EMPIRE The title, derived from the Latin *imperator*, was originally used to honor a general temporarily after a victory, but following the example of Julius Caesar who used the title permanently it came to refer to the supreme military authority, or the ruler of the Roman empire. Augustus and his successors continued to use it in this way, while in theory the emperor ruled as princeps, "chief of state," rather than imperator.

Following both oriental and Hellenistic precedents, reverence was often paid the Roman emperor, whether living or dead, as a divine being. Though unofficial enthusiasm recognized a degree of deity in some of the emperors while living (such as Julius Caesar and Augustus), officially Rome recognized the difference between the gods and the living emperor. Deity could only be recognized after the ruler's death by vote of the senate. It was felt that the approval of the Roman people, through the senate's vote, would recognize a divinity partially inherent in the emperor during his lifetime.

In the outlying areas of the Roman empire, worship of a living emperor was encouraged by local authorities as an important symbol of solidarity during times of crisis. Thus in Pontus and Bithynia Christians for a time were required to offer incense and wine before statues of the gods and the emperor Trajan. Those who rejected worship of the emperor were suspected of disloyalty. The word is used only in Acts 25:21, 25.

ENAIM, ENAM One of the fourteen cities in the lowland of Judah and on the road to Timnah. It was in the area of Jarmuth, Azekah, Beth Shemesh, and Socoh (Gen. 38:14, 21; Josh. 15:34), but there called Enam.

ENAN The father of Ahira, the leader of the tribe of Naphtali in the Desert of Sinai (Num. 1:15; 2:29; 7:78, 83; 10:27).

ENCHANTERS *See* DIVINATION, DIVINE

END *See* ESCHATOLOGY

ENDOR A village of Manasseh (Josh. 17:11, 12) from which the Israelites were unable to drive out the Canaanites. Saul visited the local medium before his last battle with the Philistines (1 Sam. 28:7). Possibly located at En-dur, four miles S of Mount Tabor.

EN EGLAIM Mentioned together with En Gedi on the shores of the Dead Sea (Ezek. 47:10). The probable location is Ain Feshka, about one and one-half miles S of Khirbet Qumran.

EN GANNIM 1. A town (196-235) in the tribal area of Issachar, assigned to the Levites (Josh. 19:21; 21:29).

2. A town of Judah in the western foothills, site unidentified (Josh. 15:34).

EN GEDI An ancient oasis (187-097) in the tribal area of Judah in the desert near the Salt Sea (Dead Sea). It was occupied throughout biblical history. David hid there from Saul who sought his life (Josh. 15:62; 1 Sam. 23:29). In the mid-ninth century B.C., King Jehoshaphat won an important battle there. It is also called Hazezon Taman (2 Chron. 20:2; Gen. 14:7). It is prophesied that men will catch fish from En Gedi to En Eglaim in the end of days (Ezek. 47:10).

ENGINE *See* ARMS AND ARMOR

EN HADDAH A town (196-232) in the tribal area of Issachar (Josh. 19:21).

EN HAKKORE A spring from which Samson drank after a battle with Philistines (Judg. 15:19).

EN HAZOR An unidentified town in the tribal area of Naphtali (Josh. 19:37).

EN MISHPAT An earlier name for a Kadesh in the Salt Sea area (Gen. 14:7).

ENOCH 1 and 2. Cain's oldest son and a city built for the son by Cain (Gen. 4:17).

3. A descendant of Seth and the father of Methuselah. The record notes that he did not die but that "he was no more, because God took him away" (Gen. 5:18, 21, 24; Heb. 11:5).

ENOS, ENOSH Grandson of Adam, son of Seth (Gen. 4:26; 1 Chron. 1:1).

EN RIMMON A city in the tribal area of Judah-Simeon occupied after the return from the exile in Babylon (Neh. 11:29).

EN ROGEL A spring in the Kidron Valley on the border between Benjamin and Judah south of Jerusalem, not to be confused with the spring of the Gihon (Josh. 15:7; 18:16; 2 Sam. 17:17; 1 Kgs. 1:9).

EN SHEMESH A town (175-131) on the border between Benjamin and Judah just east of Bethany (Josh. 15:7).

EPAPHRAS Called fellow servant and fellow prisoner by Paul. He was a native of Colosse and the founder of the church there (Col. 1:7; 4:10, 12).

EPAPHRODITUS A fellow soldier and fellow worker of Paul's who brought Paul gifts from Philippi when he was in prison and carried back to his town the thanks of Paul (Phil. 2:25, 30; 4:18).

EPENETUS A Christian at Rome greeted by Paul (Rom. 16:5).

EPHAH 1. *See* WEIGHTS AND MEASURES.

2. A son of Abraham and Keturah (Gen. 25:4).

3. A concubine of Caleb (1 Chron. 2:46).

4. A descendant of Judah (1 Chron. 2:47).

EPHAI His sons were among the leaders in Judah after the Babylonian captivity had begun and before the total exodus of 586 B.C. (Jer. 40:8).

EPHER 1. A grandson of Abraham by Keturah (Gen. 25:4).

2. A descendant of Judah (1 Chron. 4:17).

3. Head of a house in the part of the tribe of Manasseh that lived east of the Jordan (1 Chron. 5:24).

EPHES DAMMIM Called Pas Dammim in 1 Chronicles 11:13; a place between Azekah and Socoh where the Philistines and the Israelites fought (1 Sam. 17:1).

EPHESIANS, BOOK OF *See* PAULINE EPISTLES

EPHESUS A seaport city of fame in Roman times where Paul lived and taught for nearly three years (Acts 19:1, 8-10; 20:31). In Paul's day Artemis (the Diana of the Romans) was the goddess of the city (Acts 19:25ff.). Massive results of archaeological work and remains are to be seen there and in the museum in East Berlin.

EPHLAL A descendant of Judah (1 Chron. 2:37).

EPHOD 1. A leader of the tribe of Manasseh, the son of Joseph (Num. 34:23).

2. A garment originally worn by the priests but later by others as well, Samuel and David at least (Ex. 28:4; 2 Sam. 6:14). The details of its construction are found in Exodus 28:4ff. and 39:2ff. While its full function is not clear it was used in part at least for seeking divine direction (1 Sam. 23:12). Gideon and Micah misused an ephod (Judg. 8:27; 18:18-20).

EPHPHATHA A word uttered by Jesus as he was healing a deaf man (Mk. 7:34). It means "Be opened."

EPHRAIM 1. *See* GEOGRAPHY OF THE HOLY LAND.

2. A son of Joseph and the head of one of the twelve tribes, born of Asenath the daughter of an Egyptian priest (Gen. 41:52). The word came later to designate Israel, the ten northern tribes (Hos. 4:16, 17). The central hill country of Palestine was their tribal area (Josh. 16:5-10).

3. An unidentified village near the desert (Jn. 11:54).

EPHRAIM, FOREST OF The place in Gilead, east of the Jordan, where the forces of David crushed the rebellion of Absalom (2 Sam. 17:26; 18:6).

EPHRAIM, MOUNT *See* GEOGRAPHY OF THE HOLY LAND

EPHRATH, EPHRATHAH 1. Rachel began to give birth to Benjamin at a place called "some distance from Ephrath." She was buried on the way to Ephrath, that is Bethlehem (Gen. 35:16-19).

2. A wife of Caleb (1 Chron. 2:19).

3. A former name of Bethlehem (Mic. 5:2). *See also* 1 above.

EPHRON 1. A Hittite from whom Abraham bought the cave of Machpelah for a burial place (Gen. 23:7-10).

2. A mountain ridge on the border between Judah and Benjamin (Josh. 15:9).

3. A city taken by Judah from Israel in the days of King Jeroboam (2 Chron. 13:19).

EPICUREANS *See* SECTS

EPILEPSY *See* SICK, SICKNESS

ER 1. A son of Judah and husband of Tamar. The Lord put him to death because of his wickedness (Gen. 38:1-3, 6, 7).

2. A descendant of Judah (1 Chron. 4:21).

3. One mentioned in the genealogy of Jesus (Lk. 3:28).

ERAN A son of Ephraim (Num. 26:36).

ERASTUS Friends of Paul having the same name (Acts 19:22; Rom. 16:23; 2 Tim. 4:20).

ERECH An early Babylonian city, called by them Uruk and today Warks, north of Ur and south of Baghdad. After the Assyrian captivity of Israel men from there were settled in Samaria. Their descendants were the Samaritans (Gen. 10:10; Ezra 4:9, 10).

ERI A descendant of Gad (Gen. 46:16).

ERR, ERROR *See* SIN

ESARHADDON A son of Sennacherib who succeeded him on the Assyrian throne. He brought additional deportees to Samaria (2 Kgs. 19:37; Ezra 4:2; Isa. 37:38).

ESAU Grandson of Abraham and twin brother of Jacob (Gen. 25:24-26). Although he was the older he sold his birthright to the younger when he was hungry (Gen. 25:29-34). He married two Hittite wives and settled in the area of Mt. Seir (Gen. 26:34; 33:16). Paul used incidents from his life to show God's sovereign rights (Rom. 9:10-13).

ESCHATOLOGY The theology of last things such as *death, resurrection, the after life, divine judgment, the end of the age* and *the second coming of Christ.* (The last two items only are discussed here. For the after life, heaven and hell *see* DEAD, ABODE OF. *See also* RESURRECTION, JUDGMENT, KINGDOM OF HEAVEN, KINGDOM OF GOD.)

Historically four major points of view have been held relative to the manner of the end of the age. One of these is the wide range of views, but basically one, held by followers of the schools of "Old Liberalism," "consistent eschatology," "realized eschatology," and "form criticism." Some of these views are almost mutually exclusive. In most of these views Jesus is human only, not God manifest in the flesh, and a source material from a Scripture which is also of human origin and not "divinely inspired revelation." The church is the Kingdom of God, Christ through the Spirit is now reigning having given his Kingdom powers to his followers who are carrying on his work in the Kingdom. These are the "last times," Christ is present by his Spirit in the church at all times and at the same time his "coming again" is "drawing nigh." The two are, to all intents and purposes, one: his presence in the church and his coming in the church. These views attempt to interpret the teachings of a human Jesus and Scripture which is the result of human authors only.

Clearly over against all these views are three, differing the one from the other, yet, having in common a regard for the Scriptures themselves, and they present a physical, literal second coming of the same Jesus who was earlier here on earth to found the church and to make provision for its salvation through his own life, death, and resurrection. "This same Jesus, who has been taken from you into heaven, will come back in the same way you saw him go into heaven," that is, physically (Acts 1:11). The three do not differ as to the fact or manner of Christ's second coming, but they do differ as to the time of it in relation to his Kingdom and as to the nature of the Kingdom itself. The three agree that the same Jesus will return to earth in his divine glory at a literal point in time somewhere between this present age and the beginning of eternity. This event will mark the "end of the age."

The chiliasts or millennarians expect this age to end with the physical coming of Christ to be followed by 1000 years of his rule in his Kingdom prior to the beginning of the eternal state which will begin immediately thereafter. Another group, the amillennialists, do not believe in a literal millennium, or 1000-year reign of Christ on earth after his coming. In the early eighteenth century the third view, postmillennialism, arose, believing that the last 1000 years of this present age will be the utopia in which all the promises and prophecies of universal peace and righteousness on earth will be fulfilled, the Kingdom, after which Christ will return and the eternal state begin.

ESEK The name given to a well dug by Isaac's men but contended for and taken by the men of Gerar (Gen. 26:20).

ESHAN, ESHEAN An unidentified town in the Judean hill country (Josh. 15:52).

ESHBAAL A son of King Saul (1 Chron. 8:33; 9:39). Because of objection to Baal names he is also called Ish-Bosheth (2 Sam. 2-4). Abner tried to make him king of Israel after Saul's death but he was murdered (2 Sam. 2:8-10; 4:5-7).

ESHBAN A descendant of Esau who lived in Edom (Gen. 36:26).

ESHCOL 1. An ally of Abram in his battle against the invading kings (Gen. 14:13, 24).

2. A valley in the Judean hill country from which the twelve spies brought back the large cluster of grapes to Israel (Num. 13:23, 24).

ESHEK A descendant of King Saul, a Benjamite (1 Chron. 8:39).

ESHTAOL A town (151-132) in the western foothills, first assigned to the tribe of Dan but which later came into Judean hands. Samson was born, lived and was buried in the Eshtaol-Aprah area (Josh. 15:33; 19:41; Judg. 13:25; 16:31; 18:2, 8, 11).

ESHTEMOA, ESHTEMOH 1. A town (156-089) of Judah assigned to the Levites and a city of refuge (Josh. 21:9, 13, 14). Eshtemoh in Joshua 15:50.

2 and 3. Two descendants of Judah (1 Chron. 4:17, 19).

ESHTON A descendant of Judah (1 Chron. 4:11).

ESLI An ancestor of Christ (Lk. 3:25).

ESSENES *See* SECTS

ESTHER A Jewish orphan who became Queen of Persia. Her Hebrew name was Hadassah (Esth. 2:7-9, 16, 17). One of the famous lines of history comes from this story: "And who knows but that you have come to royal position [the kingdom] for such a time as this?" (4:14). She was instrumental in getting the Jews delivered from the evil scheme of Haman who wanted to kill them (8:5-8). This deliverance is still celebrated by Jews in the Feast of Purim.

ESTHER, BOOK OF Written in the last part of the fifth century B.C. by an unknown author who never uses the name of God in his writing. Yet it is a book of the Hebrew Bible, the OT. From very early times apocryphal additions to the book existed and this may account for the debates about its canonicity at times in its history. It deals with an aspect of the history of the Jews remaining from the captivity in the Persian capital of Susa, how Haman desired their liquidation, and how through the Jewish orphan, become Queen of Persia, they were delivered.

ETAM 1. A cave where Samson hid out from the Philistines (Judg. 15:8).

2. A village of the sons of Simeon after the exile, unidentified (1 Chron. 4:32).

3. A city (166-121) in the hill country of Judah fortified by King Rehoboam (2 Chron. 11:6).

ETERNITY Refers to an endless span of time whether before the creation or after the end of the present age. Called "forever" it is inhabited by God himself (Isa. 57:15). Several Hebrew words are used for perpetuity, *ever, everlasting,* and *forever. Eternal life* is mentioned many times in the NT referring to the future life of man. Other things called eternal include: God (Deut. 33:27; Rom. 16:26); purpose of God (Eph. 3:11); dominion of God (1 Tim. 6:16); the gospel (Rev. 14:6); God's covenant, salvation, redemption, judgment (Heb. 13:20; 5:9; 9:12; 6:2); God's inheritance for the believer (Heb. 9:15); eternal fire and punishment (Mt. 25:41, 46; Jude 6, 7).

ETHAM An unidentified place on the desert route of the Israelites after they left Egypt and Succoth (Ex. 13:20; Num. 33:5-8).

ETHAN 1. A wise man, possibly a contemporary of Solomon, called the Ezrahite (1 Kgs. 4:31).

2. A descendant of Judah (1 Chron. 2:6).

3 and 4. Two temple musicians listed in 1 Chron. 6:42, 44.

ETHANIM *See* CALENDAR

ETHBAAL A king of Sidon whose daughter Jezebel married King Ahab of Israel and brought pagan priests with her who corrupted Israel (1 Kgs. 16:31).

ETHER 1. A village (138-113) in the western foothills of Judah (Josh. 15:42).

2. An unidentified village in the tribal area of Simeon (Josh. 19:7).

ETHIOPIA *See* CUSH

ETHIOPIAN EUNUCH The treasurer of the Queen of Ethiopia who was reading the Book of Isaiah, to whom the Lord sent Philip to explain it. Upon declaring his faith he was baptized (Acts 8:26ff.).

ETH KAZIN, ITTAKAZIM An unidentified town in Zebulun (Josh. 19:13).

ETHNAN A descendant of Judah (1 Chron. 4:7).

ETHNI An ancestor of Asaph, David's head of the service of music in the Tent of Meeting (tabernacle) and later in Solomon's temple (1 Chron. 6:41).

EUBULUS A Christian who sent greetings to Timothy (2 Tim. 4:21).

EUNICE Timothy's mother, a Jewess married to a Greek, who was careful to bring up her son in the knowledge of the Scriptures (Acts 16:1; 2 Tim. 1:5; 3:15).

EUNUCH A castrated male (2 Kgs. 9:32). Sometimes the word simply means an officer (Gen. 39:1; 2 Kgs. 23:11; Esth. 3:21). Translated "director" and "trusted arsenal servant" (Rom. 16:23; Acts 12:20). Eunuchs could not be full members of the Jewish community (Lev. 21:16, 20; Deut. 23:1). "Eunuchs made eunuchs by men" (Mt. 19:12) are those who have given up reproduction in order to devote themselves to the service of God.

EUODIA A Christian woman in the church at Philippi with whom Paul pleaded that she live peaceably with Syntyche (Phil. 4:2).

EUPHRATES The largest river in western Asia. It rises in the mountains of Armenia, flows west until it is turned south by the mountains of Lebanon and then runs 1000 miles to the Persian Gulf. In ancient times it divided between the Empire of Assyria and the Hittite Empire. One of the great cities of antiquity, Carchemish, was on its bank. Here many important battles took place, some noted in the Bible (2 Kgs. 24:7; Jer. 46:2). Ultimately Israel's territory is to extend, by Divine promise, to this river (Gen. 15:18) as it did in its great days under David and Solomon.

EUTYCHUS A youth of Troas who having fallen asleep fell to the ground from a third-story window and died while Paul was preaching there. Paul restored him to life (Acts 20:9-12).

EVANGELIST The word that describes one who conducts the activity of preaching the gospel, especially in areas where it had not been preached before; the founder of groups later cared for by the pastor. The use of the word to refer to the writer of a canonical book, and to the reader of the lections in the liturgy is postbiblical. It is used only three times in the NT (Acts 21:8; Eph. 4:11; 2 Tim. 4:5). Currently the difference between a missionary and an evangelist would seem to be that the former opens up new territory where the gospel is not or is only little known, while the latter ministers in Christian areas and groups to stir them up to greater dedication to Christ and his service.

EVE The first woman, the wife of Adam, created by divine action from a rib taken from Adam (Gen. 2:18-22). Through disobedience to God on the part of Eve, followed by Adam, sin passed upon all mankind (Rom. 5:12). Her name is found twice in the NT (2 Cor. 11:3; 1 Tim. 2:13).

EVERLASTING *See* ETERNITY

EVI A king of Midian killed by the Israelites in the time of Moses (Num. 31:8).

EVIL *See* SIN

EVIL-MERODACH A king of Babylon, the son of Nebuchadnezzar, who was murdered by his brother-in-law. He released King Jehoiachin of Judah from prison in Babylon and cared for him there (2 Kgs. 25:27-30). *See also* BABYLON, BABYLONIA.

EVIL SPIRITS *See* DEMON, DEMONIAC

EXILE *See* CAPTIVITY

EXODUS, BOOK OF *See* PENTATEUCH

EXORCISM, EXORCIST The expelling of evil spirits from persons or places by incantations or magic charms (Acts 19:13). While the words are never used in the NT, the work of exorcism and the persons who do them, exorcists, are mentioned. Jesus cast out demons by the Spirit of God or in his own name and passed this power on to his disciples who did it in his name (Mt. 12:28; Mk. 9:25; 6:7; Acts 16:18).

EXPIATE, EXPIATION 1. *See* CHRIST, WORK OF.

2. Sin is both a failure to conform to the law of God and actual transgression against it and two things are necessary to get rid of it. One is expiation and the other propitiation. The first requires satisfaction, the covering or blotting out of sin by a sacrifice. The second views this satisfaction as appeasing the wrath of God because of his anger against sin. Man's sin is expiated by the sacrifice of Christ on the Cross, and God's wrath against sin is propitiated. Some consider the idea of satisfaction, sacrifice, expiation, and propitiation as barbaric and out of keeping with a loving God. Such a God should not require the suffering of an innocent one for the guilty. What these fail to notice, however, is that it is God himself, God the Son, who does the suffering on the behalf of some third party (Rom. 3:25; Heb. 2:17, 18; 1 John 2:2; 4:10). Similarly it is God propitiating himself when Christ is sacrificed.

EYE *See* EMOTIONS

EZBAI The father of one of David's mighty men (1 Chron. 11:37).

EZBON 1. A descendant of Gad (Gen. 46:16).

2. A grandson of Benjamin (1 Chron. 7:7).

EZEKIEL A Hebrew writing prophet and a priest (Ezek. 1:3). He was taken from Jerusalem into captivity to Babylon in the deportation of 598/597 B.C. In Babylon he lived with the other Jewish exiles in a place called Tel Aviv by the river Kebar (Ezek. 3:15; 1:3). He was married (24:18), began prophesying in the fifth year of his captivity (1:2), and was still prophesying in the twenty-seventh year (29:17). Otherwise we know very little about his personal life.

EZEKIEL, BOOK OF Two periods of history are reflected in this book. Up to chapter 24 the prophet spoke of the sin of Jerusalem and her coming punishment. After an eight-chapter interlude of judgments against foreign nations he directs his attention to the coming Kingdom of God with a message of comfort for the people (chaps. 33-48). In the last section he notes that God will end the captivity, restore them to their land from all nations wherever they have been scattered (36:24) and give them a new heart to serve him (chaps. 34 and 36). The Gentile powers are to be defeated (chaps. 38 and 39) and a great new temple is to be built with all its holy services restored (chaps. 40-46).

EZEM An unidentified city in the tribal area of Simeon within the area of Judah (Josh. 15:29; 19:3; 1 Chron. 4:29).

EZER 1. A descendant of Esau and Seir (Gen. 36:21).

2. A descendant of Judah (1 Chron. 4:4).

3. A descendant of Ephraim (1 Chron. 7:21).

4. A descendant of Gad who joined David at Ziklag (1 Chron. 12:9).

5. One of those who worked on the wall with Nehemiah (Neh. 3:19).

6. A Levitical musician in the days of Nehemiah (Neh. 12:42).

EZION GEBER A city (147-884) on the Gulf of Aqaba near Elath where the children of Israel stopped just before going up to Kadesh for the second time (Num. 33:35, 36). It was a fortress of Solomon's guarding his sea trade route with Ophir. Solomon built ships there (1 Kgs. 9:26-28). Until recently it was thought that this city was an industrial one where copper was smelted in Solomon's day. Archaeologists, have now abandoned this idea. Some years later in the days of King Jehoshaphat and King Ahaziah, trading ships were built there, but they were destroyed before leaving the port (1 Kgs. 22:48, 49).

EZRA 1. A priest who came back from the Babylonian captivity with Zerubbabel; also called Azariah (Neh. 12:1; 10:2).

2. A Jewish scribe and priest, descended from the priestly line of Aaron, author and chief character in the book that bears his name, co-worker of Nehemiah, leader in the return from the Babylonian captivity, and builder of the second temple. On his return he found many Jews married to foreign, heathen women and encouraged the annullment of those marriages. He kept a record of those who were thus married (chap. 10), reinstituted the reading of the Law and its observation, the keeping of the festivals, and directed the building of the second temple (5:2; 6:15). The book that bears his name is almost an autobiography.

EZRA, BOOK OF Covers the history of the Jews from 536 to 432 B.C. from the return from the Babylonian captivity to the return of Ezra himself in 458 and then the rebuilding of the temple and institution of service there. If the book was not written by Ezra it bears that name because he is the principal character in it. Modern critics cast doubt on the historicity of Ezra himself and feel that this book, together with Nehemiah and 1 and 2 Chronicles, was one book written by a "Chronicler" some time in the fourth century B.C. Its right to a place in the canon and its own trustworthiness, however, are not related to the question of its authorship. The author apparently made extensive use of existing written sources, as a good historian, and some think this accounts for the use of the two languages (Hebrew and Aramaic) in its writing, and for the differences of style that appear in the book.

The earlier historical books of the Bible (Kings and Chronicles) tell the history of Israel to the time of the destruction of Jerusalem by the Babylonians and the beginning of that captivity in 586 B.C. This book picks up that history fifty years later. Together with Nehemiah, Haggai, and Zechariah we are given the history of the fifth century. Chapters 1-6 of Ezra give the account of the return of the Jews under Zerubbabel to the rebuilding of the temple. The last part of the book contains the history of the return of a second group with Ezra as its leader and of the religious reforms he instituted.

EZRI King David's minister of agriculture (1 Chron. 27:26).

FACE Used literally of the human or an animal face, and also figuratively in several senses. "To hide the face" is an idiom that expresses displeasure, "to set the face against" means opposition, "to make the face shine upon" means blessing and is found in the well-known Aaronic blessing "the Lord make his face shine upon you" (Num. 6:25).

FAIR HAVENS A harbor on the S side of Crete where Paul stopped on his prison voyage to Rome (Acts 27:8).

FAITH, FAITHFULNESS These have the two senses of trust and trustworthiness. They may refer to the reliability of God (Rom. 3:3) but in the great majority of cases they refer to man's religious trust in something: in God; in his commandments; in the fact that Jesus is the Messiah; in Jesus himself. In Paul's teaching, faith is trust in the person of Jesus as God, in the truth of his teaching, that his death accomplished redemption from sin. In short it is a total submissive trust in Christ, his work, and his message (Gen. 15:6; Ps. 119:66; Jn. 11:27; 1 Cor. 15:1-3). To become a Christian one must believe, have faith, trust. To live as a practicing and active Christian one must show faithfulness. It is a part of that complex of attributes known as "the fruit of the Spirit" (Gal. 5:22). *See also* CHRIST,

LIFE AND TEACHINGS OF; SALVATION, APPLICATION OF; and
PAUL, HIS LIFE AND TEACHING.

FALCON *See* BIRDS, 5

FALL, THE The term given to the incident in the life of Adam and Eve in
which they disobeyed God and thus not only sinned but
brought sin on all the race descended from them by natural
generation. The account is in Genesis 3, and its implications
in Romans 5:12, 17, 18.

FAMILY *See* MARRIAGE

FAMINE Many are mentioned in the Bible (Gen. 41:56; Ruth 1:1;
2 Sam. 21:1; 1 Kgs. 18:2; 2 Kgs. 6:25; Acts 11:28). In
Palestine they could be caused by lack of rain, rain at the
wrong time, or hail, locusts and their caterpillars, or by
military siege. They were sometimes caused by God as a
judgment on his people. The word is also used in a figurative
sense, a time when the words of God were not being heard
(Amos 8:11).

FARMING When Joshua had completed the conquest of Canaan the land
was divided among the tribes of Israel and carefully marked
out with landmarks. It was forbidden in Israel to remove
these "boundary stones" (Deut. 19:14). The land inheritance
was not to pass from one to another. If for any reason a
person lost his land, it had to be returned in the Year of
Jubilee, which recurred every fifty years (Lev. 25:28).
Irrigation or means of fertilizing were limited. The inhabitants
depended on rainfall and dew, allowing the land to remain
fallow every seventh year for a substitute for water and
fertilizers as well as for the foraging of animals (Ex. 23:10,
11). The early rains came in December-February and the
latter rains in March. Thus sowing time was around February
and reaping time was between Passover and Pentecost.
First came the barley harvest, then the wheat. The grain
was placed on a hard flat area some twenty feet or more in
diameter. Animals dragged something like sledges over it,
and men turned it periodically until the kernels would be
separated from the stalks. The floor was always placed where
there would be a good wind so that the grain could be
winnowed, a process of tossing the grain into the air and
allowing the wind to blow the chaff away and the kernels to
fall to the floor. This was sieved to remove impurities and
then stored. The dangers to the crop could come from failure
of the former rain's coming at the proper time to soften the
soil for the primitive plowing, the failure of the latter rain
to fill out the ears of grain, hot desert winds coming too near

harvesttime, locusts, hail, or other natural causes coming while the grain was growing.

FAST, FASTING Abstinence from eating and drinking was for humbling oneself (Ps. 35:13). The fast on the Day of Atonement was the only one required in the Mosaic legislation, but individuals did fast for special reasons or special fasts were sometimes called by the leaders for particular reasons (1 Sam. 7:6; 2 Sam. 12:16). Because of national calamities regular fast days were set to commemorate them. Four in particular are noted. It is stated that they will ultimately be turned from days of sorrow to days of joy (Zech. 7:3-5; 8:19). Fasting was apparently quite common in the days of Jesus. He himself did it on occasion (Lk. 2:37; 18:12; Mt. 4:2). Jesus discussed fasting on two occasions, stressing the voluntary character required and that purity of heart and motives are integral to an acceptable fast (Mt. 6:16, 17; 9:14, 15). The NT perspective is that fasting is not condemned but neither is it required. Fasting for personal or corporate reasons is voluntary and acceptable. *See also* FESTIVALS.

FAT The internal fat of the sacrificial animals was burned as a pleasing aroma to the Lord. It was forbidden to the Israelites to eat it (Lev. 4:31; Lev. 3:3-5; 7:23-25).

FATHER, FATHERS Commonly the word refers to the immediate male or female progenitor (Gen. 2:24; 28:13). It is also used, however, in the sense of "ancestor." When parallel genealogies are compared and some names are not in one or the other, this meaning of "father" helps to explain the discrepancy.

FATHERHOOD OF GOD *See* GOD, NAMES OF, GODHEAD

FATHERLESS A very great emphasis is placed throughout the OT on the need for the care of the orphan, the fatherless (Deut. 10:18; Jer. 7:5-7). It is even mandatory for the people of God.

FATHOM *See* WEIGHTS AND MEASURES

FEAR The word has two senses in Scripture, in both Testaments: fear in the sense of being afraid, and fear in the sense of reverence. As used in the OT it is almost the equivalent of NT faith which is reverential belief in and committal to (Eccles. 12:13; Mal. 3:16; Prov. 9:10).

FEAST Banqueting was a favorite form of eating and entertainment in antiquity (Eccles. 7:2; Jer. 16:8; Job 1:5; Esth. 9:17). These were festive occasions at which the guests were robed, had their feet washed, and their heads anointed. There was often entertainment as well. Guests were seated or reclined at the banqueting benches, in assigned order of age or importance. It was not uncommon that food would be sent to others not able to attend (Gen. 43:34; Lk. 14:10; Neh. 8:10). On the religious feasts see FESTIVALS and CALENDAR.

FELIX The Roman governor at Caesarea to whom Paul was sent from Jerusalem, and before whom Paul was tried. He left Paul in prison for two years (Acts 23:24-26; 24:2ff.; 25:14).

FESTIVALS The festival-holy day calendar of biblical religion is summarized neatly in Exodus 23:10-17. It consisted of three annual festivals, one in late spring, another in early summer, a third in autumn harvest. The system is elaborated in Leviticus 23, presenting a calendar of seven feasts and fasts grouped in relation to these three main feasts.

Some information on Jewish reckoning of time is necessary in order to understand this calendar. The *day* was counted as beginning at sunset (Lev. 23:32) possibly from the circumstance that the first day of the month could not be determined until the appearance of the new moon, after sunset. The *week* was a seven-day period loosely connected with the phases of the moon. The seven days were not named, but rather numbered from the first to the seventh though the seventh was also called the sabbath (rest); hence weeks were sometimes called sabbaths (Lev. 23:15; Deut. 16:9). The *month* was approximately four weeks. The Jews early learned to calculate the day of new moon (1 Sam. 20:5). The year was of twelve lunar months—354 days, 8 hours, 48 minutes, 38 seconds. An extra month was added to the year periodically to keep in fair conformity with the solar year. If no adjustment had been made the feast would have made a complete cycle of the seasons every thirty-four years, impossible in a system geared to the agricultural cycle. Since the beginning of the year was counted from about the time of the spring equinox, four times every eleven years an "intercalary" or thirteenth month was added.

It is assumed by some that there came to be two calendars in use: a ritual-religious calendar beginning with Nisan (or Abib) our March-April. This was ordained by God to be the first month at the time of the Exodus (Ex. 12:2; cf. Josephus, *Antiquities*, I, III, 3). There appears to have been a civil year also in vogue. In Exodus 23:16 and 34:22 a seventh month is mentioned as the end of the year. Leviticus 25:8-10 shows that the Year of Jubilee began in the seventh month of the ritual year. The months were named in later times (*see* CALENDAR for names).

In this calendar there were six feasts, listed below in chronological order (Ex. 23:14-17; Lev. 23:1-44; Num. 28:1—29:40; Deut. 16:1-17). At three of these times in the year all the men were required to appear before the Lord (in Jerusalem), at the Feast of Unleavened Bread, Feast of Harvest, and Feast of Ingathering or Tabernacles (Ex. 23:14-17; 34:23).

1. *The Passover.* The institution of Passover on the night of the exodus from Egypt is set forth in Exodus 12. It was the forepart of the Feast of Unleavened Bread, the first of the three when every male was to "appear before the Sovereign Lord," hence called one of the pilgrimage feasts (Ex. 23:14-17; Lev. 23:4, 5). It was held at the end (evening) of the fourteenth day of the first month. It celebrated deliverance from condemnation and bondage in Egypt and beginning of new life.

2. *The Feast of Unleavened Bread.* Although the institution is found at Exodus 12:15-20, its place in the ritual year is at Leviticus 23:6-8. It began on the fifteenth day (on sunset the previous day) and continued seven days, through the twenty-first day. The Passover lamb, killed late afternoon of the fourteenth and eaten at "supper," really opened this festival. The chief feature was the eating of unleavened bread through the week, during which time every house was cleansed of leaven.

3. *The Feast of Weeks, Harvest, or Firstfruits.* The first is called *Shavuot* in Hebrew and occurs fifty days (seven weeks plus one day) after Passover (Greek Pentecost). On this day ancient Israel presented the firstfruits "of all that you produce" (Deut. 26:2). While this day was "firstfruits" (the occasion of the wheat-harvest), the presentation of firstfruits could take place at any time between the Feast of Weeks and the Feast of Tabernacles (Num. 28:26; Ex. 23:9ff.; 34:22; Lev. 23:10-22; Deut. 16:9, 10; 26:1-11). The festival falls in the third month of the Hebrew calendar, Sivan, May or June in the non-Hebrew calendar. In the NT the name of this festival for the Christians was Pentecost (Acts 2:6; 20:16; 1 Cor. 16:8).

4. *The Feast of Trumpets.* The Bible does not furnish much information about it. What little we know is drawn mainly from Leviticus 23:23-25. It occurred the first day of the seventh month (first of September of the modern calendar). It was followed on the tenth day of the same month by the great Day of Atonement (Lev. 23:26). The first day was announced by the blowing of trumpets and it was a special rest day. It was the beginning day of the civil year as Passover was the religious one. This is Rosh Hashanah, the beginning of the year of present day Judaism.

5. *The Day of Atonement (Yom Kippur or Yom Hakippurim).*
The institution, in detail, is to be found at Leviticus 16, its
place in the calendar at Leviticus 23:26-32. The elaborate
ritual, the symbolism of which underlies much of the NT
discussion of the atonement of Christ, is too complex to
discuss here. It was on this day only (the tenth day of
the seventh month) that the high priest entered the holy of
holies of the tabernacle (or temple) to sprinkle sacrificial
blood on and before the atonement cover of the Ark (called
"mercy seat" in many versions) (Lev. 16:14). A part of
the ritual was the ceremony of the "scape-goat." It differed
from the others in having certain aspects of a fast day, it
being required that the people had to "deny" themselves
(Lev. 23:27). It was the high point of the ritual year, religiously
speaking.

6. *The Feast of Tabernacles* (or booths). This was held at
the end of the fall harvest—somewhat earlier in Palestine
than in Northern, Western, Central Europe and most of North
America. It began on the fifteenth day of the seventh month
and thus just after the Day of Atonement, and continued for a
full week (Ex. 23:16; Lev. 23:33-43). The people spent the
week camping out, as we would call it today. The weather is
invariably good there in late September and early October.
The heat of summer is over and the "early rains" are still
several weeks away. The crops have been in process of
harvest since the barley harvest in May, wheat some weeks
later, then figs, olives, and grapes (wine). This was a week
of family vacation, rest, recreation, and national rejoicing
(Deut. 16:13-15). It was the end of the calendar of festivals
associated with OT biblical religion.

During their history before the opening of NT times, the
Jewish people added the feast of Purim and the feast of
Dedication. The origin of the feast of Purim is found in Esther
9 and 10. It was not a pilgrim feast and, as observed, was
more nationalistic than religious. Its observance (the fourteenth
and fifteenth of Adar, the twelfth month, March) has attained
great popularity in the new state of Israel. There is no
mention of it in Scripture outside the book of Esther.

The Feast of Dedication (also of Lights) celebrates the
time when in 164 B.C. the temple, desecrated by Antiochus
Epiphanes, was purified, restored to use, and rededicated to
Jehovah. It began on the twenty-fifth of Kislev (December),
the ninth month, and lasted eight days. Its origin is described
in the Apocrypha (1 Maccabees 4:56-59 and 2 Maccabees
10:6ff.). Josephus (*Antiquities* XII, vii, 7) said it was called
"Lights" from the first and described it as a joyful festival. It
was, and still is, a time of illuminating homes and at first of
the temple area also with candles, lamps, and lanterns. Since
it falls at the same season of the year as Christmas, scholars

have supposed the Christian festival's date and many of its features were derived from it. It is mentioned only once in Scripture (Jn. 10:22). *See also* CALENDAR. (R.D.C.)

FESTUS The successor of Felix as Roman governor at Caesarea who also tried Paul. Paul appealed from this trial to Caesar at Rome (Acts 24:27; 25:10, 14).

FETTERS Chains or shackles (any of various fastening devices) usually for the feet (Judg. 16:21; 2 Sam. 3:34; Mk. 5:4).

FEVER *See* SICK, SICKNESS

FIFTIES A military unit as well as an administrative one in ancient Israel (Ex. 18:21, 25; 2 Kgs. 1:13).

FIG, FIG TREE *See* TREES

FILIGREE Ornamental work with fine gold wire, usually as a setting for jewels. In the Bible it is mentioned in connection with the work of the priest's ephod and breastpiece (Ex. 28:11; 39:6, 13, 16, 18).

FINGER *See* WEIGHTS AND MEASURES

FIR *See* TREES

FIRE Besides the normal uses of fire it is pictured in the Bible with two special functions—punishment and purification. God uses it in both senses (Lev. 10:2; 1 Cor. 3:12-15). *See also* "lake of fire," "eternal fire," "fiery furnace" in DEAD, ABODE OF.

FIREPAN A vessel used for carrying live coals especially in connection with the burning of incense. The Hebrew word is also rendered "censers" and "trap" (Num. 4:14; Lev. 10:1, Ex. 25:38).

FIRSTBORN The word refers to the firstborn of man and animals (Ex. 11:5). These had to be consecrated to God, the humans being redeemed and the animals sacrificed (Ex. 34:19, 20; Num. 3:41, 46, 47). The firstborn was the heir who received a double portion of the inheritance. This was determined by the number of sons plus one. For example, if there were six sons there were to be seven shares or portions in the inheritance. The firstborn was to receive two of these portions or shares, called a double share or portion. In a special usage Christ was the firstborn among many brethren (Rom. 8:29; Col. 1:15).

FIRST FRUITS *See* SACRIFICES AND OFFERINGS, CALENDAR, and FESTIVALS

FIRSTLING *See* SACRIFICES AND OFFERINGS

FISH, FISHING In the many biblical references to fish, no clues are found to assist in their identification by species. They were important for food, caught by net or hook and line. Only fish with fins and scales were clean and could be eaten. Even the proverbial whale that swallowed Jonah is called by the simple words "great fish" (Hebrew *dag gadol*) (Lev. 11:9-12; Mt. 17:27; Jn. 21:6).

FLAGON *See* WEIGHTS AND MEASURES

FLASK Several different kinds of juglets or jars (2 Kgs. 9:1; Mt. 25:4; Lk. 7:37).

FLAX *See* PLANTS, PERFUMES AND SPICES

FLEA *See* BEASTS, 6

FLEECE The shorn wool of sheep, the first of which was a part of the tithe, the pay of the priests (Deut. 18:4). Gideon used a fleece to check on the revelation that God had given him (Judg. 6:37-40).

FLESH The meaty part of the bodies of man and animals and by metonymy mankind (translation of Hebrew word for "flesh" [Num. 16:22] or "all living creatures" from the Hebrew of Genesis 6:19 which says: "from all living, from all flesh"). It also refers to the human as distinct from the spirit part of man, "the spirit is willing but the body (literally flesh) is weak" (Mt. 26:41). A modification of the latter is human nature under the control of sin and not dominated by God's Spirit, translated in NIV by "worldly" and in other versions by "carnal" (1 Cor. 3:1-3). A further example is the NIV translation of "flesh" as sinful nature (Gal. 5:16-21) in contrast to the "fruit of the Spirit."

FLINT A very hard variety of the mineral quartz. When it is fractured it tends to leave sharp edges. Early man used flint for knives, axes, sickle blades, razors, and arrow heads. From it the knife used in circumcision was made (Ex. 4:25; Josh. 5:2). It was used as a symbol of hardness or determination (Isa. 50:7).

FLOOD The Flood in the days of Noah has been much discussed and debated in both "liberal" and "conservative" Christian circles, especially its date and its pictured universality. Its story is told in Genesis 6-8. Jesus and Peter also spoke of it, implying its great scope (Mt. 24:38, 39; 2 Pet. 2:5). Its reality cannot be questioned, then, even if its scope and area covered are debated. The biblical account is of a flood that covered "all the earth" and mountains to a depth of twenty feet, that lasted for about a year (Gen. 7:6; 8:13). The waters flooded the earth 150 days (Gen. 7:24) and killed all that breathes through its nostrils except for Noah and his immediate family, two of all kinds of animals and seven pairs of the clean ones. The meaning of the word "all" is the point of debate and some hold to a flood of limited scope, limited to the then inhabited area. Others hold a universal flood (Gen. 7:19).

FLOWERS *See* PLANTS, PERFUMES AND SPICES

FLUTE *See* MUSIC

FLY *See* BEASTS, 6

FOOD Little is known about the food consumed prior to the time of the Flood in the days of Noah. By that time man was eating meat as well as fruits and vegetables that grew wild. Clean and unclean animals went into the ark, those that could be eaten and those forbidden (Gen. 7:2, 3). Blood could not be eaten as the concept was that it was life blood (other versions render "because its life is in the blood"). Cooking was very primitive, in an earthenware pot over a small fire of thorns or brush. Wheat and barley were ground from which bread was baked. Milk and leben or curdled milk was abundant. Earlier men were food gatherers. Later people began to cultivate foods. *See also* FISH, PLANTS, PERFUMES, AND SPICES, and BEASTS.

FOOL The word is translated in the NIV as "fools," "lawless," "simple," "mockers," and "blind fools" (Ps. 14:1; Prov. 1:22; 19:29; 2 Sam. 13:13; Mt. 23:17). A dozen Hebrew words are commonly used to convey the idea of scorners, scoffers, impious, and other like terms, some of which are also translated in the NIV as "fools."

FORD A shallow place in a river or other body of water where men and animals could cross on foot. These included the ford at the Jabbok River, the fords across the Jordan River that led to Moab, those of the Annon River, and the fords in the desert, a reference to crossings of the Jordan (Gen. 32:22; Judg. 3:28; Isa. 16:2; 2 Sam. 17:16, 21).

FOREIGNER *See* STRANGER

FOREST Land covered with trees, shrubs, or thickets. Various forests are mentioned in the Bible, including the forest of Lebanon from which came the cedars for the temple (1 Kgs. 10:17, 21). There was a forest of Hereth in the land of Judah, a forest of Ephraim, and even forest land in the Negeb or semi-desert area in the south (1 Sam. 22:5; 2 Sam. 18:6; Ezek. 20:46, 47).

FORGIVENESS Pardon or remission usually based on one's repenting and being willing to make restitution or reparation. It results in the parties involved being returned to their former relationship. To restore God's favor to man after the Fall required his forgiving man. This in turn required the atonement provided in the death of Christ (Col. 1:14; 2:13, 14). Man must repent of his sin, turn from it with desire to make restitution by living a new life. Considerable emphasis is laid on the need of men forgiving one another just as God forgives men (Mt. 6:14, 15; Lk. 6:37). There is only one sin for which there is no forgiveness—blaspheming the Holy Spirit (Mk. 3:28, 29). Scholars are not agreed as to just what is involved in this sin.

FORNICATION Often understood to mean sexual intercourse outside of marriage. It is a symbol for idolatry, harlotry against God (Mt. 15:19; Rev. 17:4; 21:8). A distinction is made by some that fornication is sexual intercourse between unmarried people while adultery involves married people. Adultery and fornication are listed together in lists of sin but the distinction does not stand up in Scripture. See Matthew 5:32 where "marital unfaithfulness" is a translation of the Greek word often rendered "fornication." *See also* ADULTERY.

FORT, FORTRESS, FORTIFICATION These consisted of a wall (often double or of the casemate variety) which surrounded all or part of a city and included the citadel. Their construction differed at various times in history. For example, there were the Early Bronze Age massive mud walls, the Hyksos glacis, and the casemate wall of Solomon's time. At the turns of the wall it was customary to have towers which sometimes protruded for visibility for the defenders. The building material was usually stone where that was available and sun-dried mud bricks where it was not.

FORTUNATUS A Christian from Corinth who was with Paul at Ephesus (1 Cor. 16:8, 17).

FORTY While it has no religious or cabalistic value significance, the number forty is widely used in Scripture as a round number expressing considerable duration. It is commonly considered to be the length of a separation. A man reached his prime at forty, double that was old age and triple was a life span (Ex. 2:11; Acts 7:23; 2 Sam. 19:34, 35; Gen. 6:3; Deut. 34:7). Certain significant events took forty days and forty nights: it rained forty days and nights in the case of Noah's Flood; Moses was on the mount forty days and nights; Moses' spies were spying out the land of Canaan forty days; Elijah went forty days and nights in his flight to Horeb; Jesus fasted forty days and nights (Gen. 7:4; Ex. 24:18; Num. 13:25; 1 Kgs. 19:8; Mt. 4:2). The Israelites were forty years in the desert, long enough for an entire generation to die; Eli led the people forty years, and many of the kings reigned a generation or forty years (Ex. 16:35; Num. 32:13; 1 Sam. 4:18; 2 Sam. 5:4; 1 Kgs. 11:42; Judg. 3:11).

FORUM OF APPIUS *See* APPIUS

FOUNDATION Usually refers to the base upon which a building stands, but has also many figurative uses, such as the foundation of the world, and "creation" (Mt. 13:35). Jesus Christ is the foundation of the Christian faith (1 Cor. 3:11); Paul laid the foundation of a number of churches (1 Cor. 3:10), and the church is founded on the prophets and the apostles as well as on Christ (Eph. 2:20).

FOUNTAIN A place where water springs forth from the ground or from the rocks. In a climate without rain for seven or eight months each year these springs become strategically important both in times of peace and in times of siege. Towns and villages are built around such a source of water: En Gedi, En Eglaim, En Gannim, and En Rogel (Song 1:14; Ezek. 47:10; Josh. 21:29; 15:7). The word is also used figuratively of both good and evil sources (good sources: Ps. 36:9; Prov. 14:27; 16:22; evil source is rendered in the NIV as "polluted well," Prov. 25:26).

FOWLER A hunter and catcher of birds; figuratively used of those who trap or snare persons (Jer. 5:26; Ps. 124:7).

FOX *See* BEASTS, 8

FRANKINCENSE *See* PLANTS, PERFUMES AND SPICES

FREE MAN, FREEDMAN The opposite of a slave, one who is free or who has been freed. Figuratively it refers to those who have been freed from the shackles of sin by the redemption in Christ (1 Cor. 7:22, 23; Rev. 6:15; Jn. 8:34-36; Rom. 6:16-18, 22, 23).

FRINGES In the NIV the word is translated as "tassel" (Deut. 22:12; Num. 15:38, 39). A twisted cord ending in a sort of tassel sown at the four corners of the outer garment to remind the Israelite of his obligation to the commandments of God. They are worn by the "religious" Jew to this day.

FROG *See* BEASTS, 6

FRUIT *See* TREES

FRUIT, FIRST *See* SACRIFICES AND OFFERINGS and CALENDAR

FUEL Fuel consisted of a number of varieties of dried vegetable matter used for making fires (Isa. 44:14-16; Ezek. 15:1-6). Wood and its derivative charcoal, thorn bushes, dried grasses, and the dung of animals are used even today by the bedouin.

FULFILLED Completion or fulfillment are the basic meanings (2 Chron. 36:21). The best definition of the word occurs in John 19:28: "Later, knowing that all was now completed, and so that the Scriptures would be fulfilled. . . ." When love is said to be the fulfilling of the Law the reference is probably not to the concept that to love God and one's fellow man fully is to keep the Law (Rom. 13:10).

FULLER One who washed, cleaned, and bleached cloth. Because of the odor involved, this work was usually done outside the city. Where the fuller's field, called Washerman's Field in the NIV, of Kings and Isaiah was located is not known with certainty (2 Kgs. 18:17; Isa. 7:3; 36:2). The representative of the King of Assyria stood there and was able to be heard on the walls of old Jerusalem. Soap in the modern sense was unknown so that the "soap" mentioned in Malachi 3:2 refers to some alkali from the ashes of certain plants. The Hebrew word is translated also "bleach" (Mk. 9:3; Mal. 3:2).

FULLNESS or Literally that which fills (Deut. 33:16). Christ is the incarnation
FULNESS of God (Col. 1:19; 2:9). When Paul spoke of "attaining to the whole measure of the fullness of Christ" he was speaking of full maturity of Christian character in Christ (Eph. 4:13).

FURLONG *See* WEIGHTS AND MEASURES

FURNACE *See also* "fiery furnace" under DEAD, ABODE OF and OVEN. The furnace must be distinguished from the oven. Furnaces were made of brick reinforced with stone, varied greatly in size, had a place for the fire, a chimney to assist with the draft, and a container where the bricks and other ceramics, including vessels, were to be fired. Ore was smelted in such furnaces and the smelted ore could be heated for forging or melted for casting. Archaeologists have found many examples (Prov. 17:3; Ezek. 22:18; Rev. 1:15). The word is also used figuratively in the phrase "furnace of affliction" (Isa. 48:10).

G

GAAL One who led and lost the revolt against Abimelech at Shechem (Judg. 9:39, 40).

GAASH A hill in the mountains of Ephraim with ravines by the same name. Joshua was buried near there (Judg. 2:9; 2 Sam. 23:30).

GABBAI A descendant of Benjamin (Neh. 11:8).

GABBATHA The Aramaic word for "pavement" (Jn. 19:13) where Pilate placed his judgment chair for the trial and judging of Jesus. There is very good reason to believe that this pavement may be seen today in the basement of the Ecce Homo Church in the Convent of Our Lady of Zion within the walled part of the city of Jerusalem.

GABRIEL *See* ANGEL

GAD 1. The seventh son of Jacob and the father of one of the tribes of Israel (Gen. 30:9-11). At the time of the conquest the clan numbered 40,500 and since they were sheep and cattle raisers they settled east of the Jordan (Num. 26:18; Josh. 18:7). Ultimately Assyria under her King Pul (Tiglath-

Pileser) took them captive (1 Chron. 5:26).

2. A prophet to King David (1 Sam. 22:5). God sent him with a message to David when David sinned in numbering the people (1 Chron. 21:9, 10). He kept a written chronicle of the affairs of King David, also Samuel and Nathan (1 Chron. 29:29). He was involved in arranging the musical service for David (2 Chron. 29:25).

3. A pagan deity. His name is seen in some of the compound names of the Bible such as Migdal Gad (Josh. 15:37).

GADARENES Gadara was one of the cities of the Decapolis in NT times. In the Hebrew text there are variant readings: Gerasenes and Gergesenes (see the footnote to Matthew 8:28 and Luke 8:26). The city of Gadara is identified with modern Um Qeis some five miles SE of the Sea of Galilee. Its total area, the area of the Gadarenes apparently reached to the Yarmuk river and to the Sea of Galilee itself.

GADDI The spy who represented the tribe of Manasseh among those who went from Kadesh Barnea to spy out the land (Num. 13:11).

GADDIEL The Zebulunite spy, one of the twelve whom Moses sent to spy out the land (Num. 13:10).

GADI The father of one Menahem who usurped the throne of Israel from his predecessor (2 Kgs. 15:14, 17).

GAHAM One of the sons of Abraham's brother Nahor by a concubine (Gen. 22:20-24).

GAHAR Some of his descendants were temple servants who came back from the captivity in Babylon with Zerubbabel (Ezra 2:47).

GAIUS 1. Paul's host at Corinth whom he also baptized (Rom. 16:23; 1 Cor. 1:14).

2. A companion of Paul seized in the riot in Ephesus (Acts 19:29).

3. A Christian of Derbe who accompanied Paul (Acts 20:4).

4. The addressee of the book 3 John.

Some of these may be the same person. The information is scant.

GALAL Two Levites of postexilic times (1 Chron. 9:15, 16).

GALATIA *See* GEOGRAPHY OF THE HOLY LAND

GALATIANS, BOOK OF *See* PAULINE EPISTLES

GALBANUM *See* PLANTS, PERFUMES, AND SPICES

GALEED Jacob's name for the pile of stones raised by him and Laban his father-in-law as a sign of their covenant (Gen. 31:46-48).

GALILEE *See* GEOGRAPHY OF THE HOLY LAND

GALILEE, SEA OF *See* GEOGRAPHY OF THE HOLY LAND

GALL A bitter and poisonous herb. It was mixed with wine and given to criminals before crucifixion to deaden pain. Jesus refused it (Mt. 27:34). It has a symbolic meaning also, bitterness (Acts 8:23). *See also* POISON.

GALLIM An unidentified site in Benjamin (1 Sam. 25:44).

GALLIO The Roman proconsul of Achaia before whom Paul was tried and acquitted (Acts 18:12-17).

GALLOWS *See* HANGING

GAMAD An unidentified place in Syria. Men from there were in the army of Tyre (Ezek. 27:11).

GAMALIEL 1. A head of the tribe of Manasseh who was to help Moses (Num. 1:10; 10:23).

2. A Pharisee, a highly honored teacher of the law, who was also Paul's teacher (Acts 5:34; 22:3). He is the author of the widely known judgment: "Leave these men alone! Let them go! For if their purpose or activity is of human origin, it will fail. But if it is from God, you will not be able to stop these men; you will only find yourselves fighting against God" (Acts 5:38, 39).

GAMUL The head of one of the lots in the division of the priests after the return from the exile (1 Chron. 24:17).

GARDEN An area planted with trees, shrubs, and flowers and usually surrounded by a stone wall or a wall of thorny shrubs. When guarding would be needed, a watchman would man a tower (Prov. 24:30, 31; Isa. 5:5, 6; 1:8; Mk. 12:1). Several gardens are noted in Scripture, among them: the garden by the cave purchased by Abraham for a burial place (Gen. 23:17); the garden of Gethsemane noted for the incident in the life of Jesus on the eve of the crucifixion (Mt. 26:36ff.); the first one, Eden (Gen. 2:8). The word is also used in an allegorical sense expressing spiritual prosperity if it is well watered and spiritual barrenness if it is not (Isa. 58:11; 1:30).

GAREB 1. One of David's thirty mighty men (2 Sam. 23:38).

2. An unidentified place near Jerusalem to which the Lord told Jeremiah the city would expand (Jer. 31:39).

GARLIC *See* PLANTS, PERFUMES, AND SPICES

GARMENT *See* DRESS

GARMITE An unclear designation of the place Garm, the place of Keilah (1 Chron. 4:19).

GATAM A grandson of Esau (Gen. 36:11; 1 Chron. 1:36).

GATE An opening in a wall, usually a city wall. As these were the weakest parts of the walls of a city they were usually protected by flanking towers. The approach road was sometimes perpendicular to the line of the gate thus forcing the attackers to approach the gate with their sides exposed to the soldiers on the wall. A good city gate was made up of a series of gates or barriers one inside the other through which the enemy would have to fight. This was where the elders and judges sat to hear cases and supply witnesses. The market was usually located there. The area inside a particular gate would be called by the name of its gate (Deut. 21:18, 19; Ruth 4:1; 2 Kgs. 7:1).

GATH 1. For the Philistine Gath *see* PHILISTINE CITIES.

2. As there is a location in the Asher area and one in the Sharon area called in Arabic "Jett" (Hebrew "Gat") it is assumed that there were additional towns by the name of Gath (172-264 and 154-200). It means simply "winepress" and there were many such presses, for example, Gath Hepher, and Gath Rimmon.

GATH HEPHER A bordertown (180-238) in Zebulun and the home of the prophet Jonah (Josh. 19:13; 2 Kgs. 14:25).

GATH RIMMON 1. A city (132-166) in the tribal area of Dan (Josh. 19:45).

2. The suggestion has been made Tell Jerisheh beside the Yarkon River in Tel Aviv is the Danite Gath Rimmon (Josh. 21:24).

3. An unidentified city in Manasseh (Josh. 21:25).

GAZA *See* PHILISTINE CITIES

GAZELLE *See* BEASTS, 2

GAZEZ A son and a grandson of Caleb (1 Chron. 2:46).

GAZZAM Ancestor of some temple servants who returned from the exile in Babylon (Ezra 2:48).

GEBA Means "hill" in Hebrew and there are very many in Palestine-Israel. Thus, it should not be unexpected that many towns and villages were called by that name.

1. Geba in Benjamin (175-140), is the one most frequently mentioned in the Bible. It was between Jerusalem and Bethel near the border with Judah (1 Sam. 13:3; 14:5), east of Gibeon and just south of Michmash. It was a Levitical town (Josh. 21:17; 1 Kgs. 15:22).

2. Geba in north Benjamin (174-158) where Josiah in his return broke down the shrines and gates and desecrated the pagan high place (2 Kgs. 23:8).

3. Geba in Samaria (171-192), located just four miles north of the city of Samaria, is mentioned in the Samaria ostraca. The name is in the ancient records but not in the Bible.

4. Geba-shemen (159-237), was northwest of Megiddo about halfway to modern Akko. Pharaoh Amen-hotep's records list the name. The site is not mentioned in the Bible.

5. Geba-carmel is likewise in ancient records but not found in the Bible, nor is its location known today.

GEBAL 1. A city (210-391) between Tripoli and Beirut, ancient Byblos (1 Kgs. 5:18).

2. An area in Edom in the mountains south of the Salt Sea (Ps. 83:7).

GEBER One of King Solomon's chief administrators (1 Kgs. 4:19).

GEBIM An unidentified city in Benjamin on the predicted route to be taken by the invading Assyrian army (Isa. 10:31).

GECKO *See* BEASTS, 6

GEDALIAH 1. The last ruler of Judah, made a governor by Nebuchadnezzar after the fall of the southern kingdom (2 Kgs. 25:22ff.).

2. A temple musician in the time of David (1 Chron. 25:3, 9).

3. A priest who had married a foreign wife during the time of the Babylonian captivity but put her away and for his guilt made a sacrifice (Ezra 10:18, 19).

4. One who urged the king to execute Jeremiah (Jer. 38:1-4).

5. Grandfather of the prophet Zephaniah (Zeph. 1:1).

GEDER An unidentified Canaanite city near Debir taken by Joshua (Josh. 12:13).

GEDERAH An unidentified town in the western foothills of Judah (Josh. 15:36).

GEDEROTH An unidentified city in Judah in the Lachish region (Josh. 15:41).

GEDEROTHAIM An unidentified village in Judah, distinct from Gederah and Gederoth (Josh. 15:36, RSV).

GEDOR 1. A city (158-115) in the hill country of Judah near Hebron (Josh. 15:58).

2. An unidentified town in Benjamin from which men came to David at Ziklag (1 Chron. 12:7).

3. A descendant of Benjamin who lived at Gibeon (1 Chron. 8:31).

GE HARASHIM 1. Translated this word means "valley of the craftsman" and so it appears in Neh. 11:35.

2. Joab of Judah is "father," which here means "founder" of the city. Note the sentence which immediately follows it in 1 Chronicles 4:14. It was located somewhere on the southern border of the Plain of Sharon.

GEHAZI The servant of the prophet Elisha. He is involved in the incidents of the raising of the Shunammite's son, in the restoration of the Shunammite's land, and also in the account of the healing of the leprosy of the Syrian captain Naaman (2 Kgs. 4:12ff.; 5:20ff.; 8:4ff.).

GEHENNA *See* HINNOM, VALLEY OF

GELILOTH The name of an unidentified place on the border between Judah and Benjamin. Some also equate it with the Gilgal in Josh. 15:7, not the one near Jericho (Josh. 18:17).

GEMALLI Father of the representative of the tribe of Dan among the twelve whom Moses sent to spy out the land (Num. 13:14).

GEMARIAH 1. A messenger sent by King Zedekiah to the court of Nebuchadnezzar in Babylon with a letter written by Jeremiah for the exiles from Jerusalem (Jer. 29:3).

2. A prince who opposed the burning of Jeremiah's scroll (Jer. 36:25).

GENEALOGY A list of descendants or ancestors. These lists have their special functions. To make a list of every possible member is not one of them. Frequently names are omitted. Major genealogical lists are found in Genesis 4 and 5, Numbers 1-3, 1 Chronicles 1-9, Ezra 2 and 8, Nehemiah 7, and those of Jesus in Matthew 1 and Luke 3.

Some of the major genealogical listings, including lists of place names and others, are found in the following books and chapters. The order of presentation is the order they are found in the Bible.

Table of nations (Gen. 10).

Adam to Abraham (1 Chron. 1).

Esau's descendants, the Edomites (Gen. 36; 1 Chron. 1).

Jacob's descendants, who went to Egypt (Gen. 40).

Family of Moses and Aaron (Ex. 6).

Census 1 and 2 taken by Moses (Num. 1, 26).

Arrangement of the tribal camps around the Tent of Meeting (Num. 2).

Israel's exodus wanderings (Num. 33).

Kings defeated by Joshua (Josh. 12).

Allotment of the two and one-half tribes east of the Jordan (Josh. 13).

Allotment of the rest of the tribes west of the Jordan (Josh. 14-19).

Descendants of the tribes (1 Chron. 2-5, 7-9).

Cities of refuge, Levitical towns, Levite descendants and David's singers, and treasury officials (Josh. 20, 21; 1 Chron. 6, 23-26).

David's thirty mighty men and other officials (2 Sam. 23; 1 Chron. 11, 12, 27).

Solomon's officials (1 Kgs. 4).

Exiles who returned from Babylon (Ezra 2, 8; Neh. 3, 11, 12).

Returnees guilty of marrying foreign women (Ezra 10).

Builders of Nehemiah's walls of Jerusalem (Neh. 3).

Those who sealed the covenant with Nehemiah (Neh. 10).

Jesus' genealogy, Abraham to Mary (Mt. 1).

Jesus' genealogy, Adam and Joseph, the father, so it was thought, of Jesus (Lk. 3).

Friends Paul greeted from Rome (Rom. 16).

GENERATION In the OT a generation may refer to a period of time or to the people living in a given period of time and perhaps also to a place (Ps. 102:24; Gen. 7:1; Isa. 58:12 where the NIV translates it "age-old"). Its plural in the OT refers to genealogies. In the NT it has the meanings noted above as in the OT and also "race" or "nation" (Mt. 1:17; 11:16; Acts 13:36; Mt. 24:34; 1 Pet. 2:9).

GENESIS, BOOK OF *See* PENTATEUCH

GENNESARET, LAKE OF *See* GEOGRAPHY OF THE HOLY LAND

GENNESARET, LAND OF *See* GEOGRAPHY OF THE HOLY LAND

GENTILES A translation of the Hebrew word *goy*, plural *goyim*. Basically the word means nation and is so consistently translated in the NIV. It usually means a non-Israelite people but on occasion even Israel is called a *goy*, a nation (Gen. 12:2; Josh. 3:17; 4:1; Zeph. 2:9). In many places the sense is that of heathen nations and so the word is translated "heathen," in some versions. Jesus worked almost exclusively with the people, the Jews, not the nations or Gentiles. His work of atonement in life and death was for all peoples. Paul taught that Jesus broke down the barrier between Jew and Gentile (Gal. 3:28). This was theologically the case. Practically differences and even enmity existed. Paul became the apostle to the Gentiles (Acts 9:15).

GENUBATH A son of the Edomite Hadad by the sister of the Queen of Egypt (1 Kgs. 11:19, 20).

GEOGRAPHY OF THE HOLY LAND
I. PREFACE Palestine of today is ruled by the State of Israel, inhabited mainly by Jews, who speak Hebrew, and Arabs who speak Arabic. The capital is Jerusalem, which has also been known as Salem, Jebus, City of David, Zion, Yerushaliyim, Ariel, Aelia Capitolina, and El Kuds. Often places have numerous names in the Holy Land. Complexity in the naming of a country desired and controlled through the centuries by so many different peoples can be expected.

A few basic names can be briefly explained. The land Canaan may take its name from the expensive "royal purple" dye made from murex shells along the Mediterranean. (The name *Phoenicia* is not Semitic, but is apparently derived from the Greek word for "purple.") The term *Hebrew* was first applied to Abraham who "crossed over" the Tigris River from *Mesopotami* to a land known there as "Across the River." His grandson Jacob was renamed Israel after a confrontation with God. Jacob's son Judah was the father of a tribe who lived in Judah (*Judea* in Greek) and were known as "Jews."

"Palestine" comes from *Philistine*, invaders from the sea, from *Crete* or *Cyprus*.

The lay of the land and the conditions it provides for human settlement are also extremely complex if one goes into detail.

II. INTRODUCTION   Geography is the study of the earth's surface as divided up into areas. This means, theoretically, that there are as many divisions to geography as there are kinds of forces acting to make distinctions between different parts of the earth.

III. TOPOGRAPHY   The setting of Israel is water and rock. To the sunset is
  SETTING   ocean; to the sunrise is desert. In other words, to the west is the Mediterranean (the Great Sea, the West Sea); to the east is Arabia (the wilderness, the desert). East is "before" and west is "behind" in the ancient world, because one takes directions from the rising sun. So the "West Sea" is our way of translating what the Bible literally calls the "Sea Behind." So the "East Country" (or East Sea, East Wind, or East Gate,) is literally the "Country Before." Between the "before" and the "behind," the sunrise and the evening, is a long, narrow country of land largely fertile and arable, though often demanding arduous toil to terrace the hills or irrigate the oasis areas within it.

To the north and the south were the great powers of old. From the far north, out of the peninsulas of the Mediterranean, came the Greeks of Macedonia and the Romans of Italy. From the high mountain plateau around the Halys River of Asia Minor came the Hittites. From the great plains of the Tigris and Euphrates rivers of Mesopotamia came the Assyrians and Babylonians. From the mountains to the east of those rivers came the Persians. Small wonder then that north is "the hidden, the dark," the quarter from which all these invaders came, the quarter from which one does not know what to expect. These peoples all came down from the north—though spread from Italy to India—because the sea and the desert gave no other choice.

To the south, at least, there was always only Egypt, but the pharaohs came too, and often, in both second and first millenia B.C. They came out of an even more narrow land, because the Egyptians are confined almost entirely to the banks of one mighty river, the Nile. So it could be promised as regarding the Hebrew slaves in Egypt, I will "bring them up . . . into a good and spacious land" (Ex. 3:8). The Promised Land was broad symbolically too, a land where the people would be freed from the oppression, the troubles ("narrows" in Hebrew) of oppression in a foreign land (Zech. 10:11; Ps. 107:6ff.).

To reach Egypt to the southwest one must first cross the Sinai peninsula, which is mostly desert. But between it and the fields of Canaan, the Promised Land, is the southernmost part of Canaan, a wide border area of pasturage and, in wet years, considerable grain. This border area is called the *Negev*, the "dry place" (Gen. 12:9; 20:1), but since it is to the south, it also very often refers to that direction, "the south" or "southwards" (Gen. 13:14; 28:14). The Negev is where the patriarchs Abraham, Isaac, and Jacob lived. Their descendants became numerous during the years they were slaves in Egypt. Their descendants, the Israelites, returned eventually to occupy the entire Promised Land.

FORMATIVE FORCES   *Geology.* Forces from within the earth have, it seems, raised and lowered the land many times throughout the centuries. What are now the hills of Israel were once plains submerged and raised, submerged and raised, again and again from the Great Sea to the west. This movement is evidenced by the many layers of sedimentary limestone and chalk rocks of which these hills are made. High up in the hills are found beautiful fossils of sea shells.

The Arabian plateau, or tableland to the east, was less affected. Its basis is a mighty platform of hard igneous granite rock from the depths of the earth. Above it is the red sandstone sometimes exposed by erosion. This sandstone is also sedimentary, but is formed above water in contrast to the limestones and chalks formed underwater. The sea did at times cover this plateau too, but the platform was high and hard and resisted change.

This resistance was important at the time when the hills of Israel were formed.

Regardless of whether it really happened just this way there is a helpful way to picture the process. Imagine a great force under the Western Sea which pushed a vast area of land eastward. But the land could not proceed because it came up against the hard granite platform, so it buckled. For the most part the buckling took place in one long wave, a long ridge running from north to south the entire length of Canaan. However, in the Negev area in the southern part of Canaan, it rippled into five waves, each one a bit higher than the next, as it approached the platform. The final highest waves were more or less the continuation of the long wave to the north.

So then, the hills of Israel can be schematically represented as a long ridge running from north to south and fanning out, to the south and southwest, into a number of smaller ridges which extend into the plains of the upper Sinai peninsula. Down at the tip of the peninsula, wild rugged mountains again appear. Among them is Mount Sinai where Moses received the Torah. But the land not only buckled and rippled—in some places it cracked and broke. One great break, some

places a double break, runs all the way from Asia Minor to
the long slender lakes of Tanzania and Nyasaland of Western
Africa. Along these breaks the earth's crust sank. The surface
of the Salt Sea, lying in this rift valley, is 1,295 feet below
sea level, the lowest spot on the face of the earth. Joshua
and the Israelites came down off the platform and entered
the Promised Land near Jericho (192-142) just north of
the Salt Sea. Moses who had brought them up out of Egypt
was buried high up on the platform at Mount Nebo (220-
131). Moses was left behind, even though he had been
transmitter of God's Torah to God's people (Deut. 34; Josh.
4). Many lesser cracks or faults in the earth's crust were
exploited by runoff rainwaters. Rushing down the sides of the
central ridge, they eroded out the innumerable gullies and
creek beds and often magnificent gorges of the hill country.

Climate. Forces of climate acting above on the surface of
the land worked further on the crude topography formed
from below. Water did the main work of carving out the
valleys and creating alluvial plains with the earth it carried
away. But its action is controlled by sun and wind.

The sun is hot at 31°45′ latitude (Jerusalem), so temperatures
rarely fall below freezing even in January. Average temperatures in January in the *eastern plateau* are in the mid-40s
F.; in the *central hills*, the upper 40s; at the *coast*, the mid-
50s; and in the *rift valley*, warmest of all, the upper 50s.
In August temperatures are: hills, mid-70s; coast and plateau,
upper 70s; and the *rift valley*, around 90°F. These averages
can be misleading till one takes note of the range of temperature,
generally most extreme in the desert areas. A clue to range
is the all-time low, recorded in *Galilee*, +8.6°F., and the
all-time high, recorded in the rift valley, +129.2°F. But it is
more helpful to note that in the winter there are occasional
frosts even down in the valley (in the north) and snowfalls
in the hills, and rather often in the summer temperatures are
over 100°F.

The prevailing winds of the winter bear rain from the
west. In summer local conditions take over. Since hot air
rises from the eastern desert during the day, the cooler air
over the Mediterranean Sea flows in toward the east. Since
warm air rises above the sea at night, breezes from the
more quickly cooling desert flow out to sea during the night
and early morning, till the sun warms up the desert again and
the flow reverses directions once more.

Scattered periods of oppressive heat last several days at a
time during the summer, especially during the turning of
the seasons. The first is at the beginning of the nearly
absolutely dry summer in April-May, and the second is at the
beginning of the rainy winter after September-October. At

these times, for a day to several days, an east wind comes
off the desert, blowing its dry heat all day, scarcely letting up
at night. Young plants cannot stand its withering, shriveling
force which aggravates people as well.

Rain is carried in from the sea by the winter westerlies.
As the winds push eastward, they force the warm moist air
up over the mountain ranges, where the air cools and dumps
its rain. The dry air then pushes eastward into the rift,
quickly warms up again, and by the time it reaches sea-level
altitudes again, it is all rained out, a system that has over
many years produced the Arabian desert.

There is an east-to-west pattern of rainfall: Total rainfall on
the west coast near Tel Aviv (126-162) is about twenty
inches annually. This figure drops somewhat as the wind
proceeds inland. But soon the land rises, cooling the air and
forcing out water, so Jerusalem (172-131) gets even a bit
more—twenty-two inches at her elevation of 2,600 feet at
the top of the ridge. Further east, down below sea level
in the rain shadow, lies Jericho (192-143) getting only four
inches. Jericho exists as a luxuriant spring-water oasis in the
small but awesome, wild, rugged desert which lies along
these back eastern slopes ("the slopes") of the central hills.
The nearby *Salt Sea* and the ruins of *Qumran* (194-128)
(source of the Dead Sea Scrolls) get only about two inches.
Climbing 4,300 feet to *Es-Salt* (218-161), 3,000 feet above
sea level, the wind drops its last rain there—thirty inches
annually.

The general rule as one crosses Palestine is that the
weather gets hotter and drier the further east or south or
downhill one goes. Even though the progression described
was eastward (and one would expect the climate to be drier),
the height of Es-Salt was so great that it overcompensated
this eastward progression. As one approaches the equator,
the west winds come across the Sahara Desert and not
the Mediterranean Sea. To the east the wind loses both its
cooling power and moisture as it leaves behind the Mediterranean, source of these two factors. And down in the *rift
valley*, the air is the densest on earth (most capable of holding
heat) as well as being in the rain shadow of the hills. There
is also a north-to-south pattern of rainfall: From north to
south, *Mt. Hermon* (225-305), 9,200 feet, on the edge of the
plateau and towering above it, gets sixty inches; *Mt. Meron*
(189-267) in the central hills gets forty-four inches; *Jerusalem*
(172-131), twenty-two inches; *Beersheba* (134-072) in the
Negev, ten inches; and *Elath* (145-884) on the Red Sea, one
inch or less. Here, of course, the effect is exaggerated
because of the downward as well as the southward trend.

A final important point on climate is the irregularity of
rainfall in the whole country, but especially in the great rift

valley and the Negev. In these latter areas, rainfall can be as little as one-third of the annual average, or as much as twice the average amount. Rain also tends to come in concentrated doses, sudden, short-lived storms. Radical examples are 2.6 inches in *Beersheba* in twenty-four hours (1934), and 5.75 inches in a day in Sinai (1925). In general Jerusalem (172-131) and London get roughly the same amount of rain, only the former in fifty days and the other in three hundred. The irregularity hurts most in the *Negev*. Here it is not just a matter of getting a poorer crop, if the early (fall) rains or the late (spring) rains do not come, but of getting any crop at all. The "aridity border" runs through this area. This is the line beyond which with less than ten inches of rain-fall annually crops will surely fail. In fact, one has to consider a safe margin at fourteen inches, because there are many below-average years. In this area wells are of life and death importance for the flocks. Numerous Bible stories tell of contests over water, especially in the area formerly inhabited by the patriarchs (Gen. 21:25-31; Ex. 2; Jn. 4).

Dew provides some moisture even during the dry summer. More common in coastal areas than elsewhere, it is most heavy on Mt. Carmel, which rises out of the sea at *Haifa* (149-249). Here dew can appear 250 nights a year. About thirty miles to the east may be the setting of the story of Gideon's fleece (Judg. 6).

THE RESULTS OF THE FORMATIVE FORCES   *North-South Strips.* Four parallel strips run in a north-south direction. They are (a) the Mediterranean coastal plain; (b) inland to the east the central hill ridge of Galilee, Samaria and Judea; (c) the Jordan valley with the Sea of Galilee and the Salt Sea; and (d) the *plateau* east of the Jordan.

East-West Interruptions and Resulting Divisions of the Strips. These parallel north-south strips are interrupted in a few places by east-west features. The coastal plains of Galilee to the north (Asher, Zebulun, Acre, Haifa Bay—some other names for this area) are separated from the plains of Carmel by Mt. Carmel, a spur of land branching off from the central ridge out into the Mediterranean Sea. This ridge forms the bulge in the coastline at Haifa (149-249). The narrow Carmel coast is separated from the Sharon plains by the Crocodile River. Sharon and Philistia are separated by the Yarkon River which empties just north of Joppa (126-162).

The main interruption of the central hill ridge is a generally flat valley which extends all the way from Haifa (149-249) on the Mediterranean Sea, past Megiddo (167-221) to Jezreel (181-218), where it slopes downwards to Beth Shean (197-212) below sea level in the Jordan Valley. Throughout the centuries this has been the major east-west pass. The Kishon River drains it to the sea, and the Harod drains the eastern

section to the Jordan. This valley separates Galilee to the
north from Samaria to the south. It is called Armageddon (or
Jezreel, or Esdraelon).

The *Beersheba basin*, another major interruption of the
hills, is just south of Judea. It is almost a complete interruption
from the coast to the Jordan Valley. It begins up at *Arad*
(162-076), perched up just west of the southern basin of the
Salt Sea, and extends all along the southern end of the hills
of Judea, past Beersheba (134-072). It then flows into the
Besor Brook, which empties into the sea south of Gaza (099-
101) near the southern edge of the *Philistine plain*. It is the
heart of the Negev. It too has been a pass since ancient
times. In NT times the area was called "Idumea" because
the Edomites were forced to come here from their homeland
east of the Jordan.

No other equivalent east-west interruption exists. Judea
(Judah) especially is well isolated as a unified hilly plateau
area. Only near its northern border does the deep narrow
Sorek Valley cut way back inland from the coastal plain. The
Rephaim branch of the Sorek reaches to Jerusalem (172-131)
itself, which perches on the water divide between the
Mediterranean Sea and the Jordan Valley.

From Jerusalem, at a low point on the water divide, one
proceeds northward up into the hills of *Samaria*. Samaria
is not so well isolated because it is deeply penetrated by
deep narrow branches of the Yarkon which drains just north
of Joppa (126-162). Such branches are the Ajalon, the Shiloh
and the Kanah. Just to the north of the latter and contrasting
with these narrow winding valleys or wadis is the straight
and wider Shechem (176-179) valley. This valley comes up
from the Sharon plain and actually cleaves a low pass through
the heart of the hills. Above this pass are Mt. Gerizim to
the south and Mt. Ebal to the north of the town of Shechem
(176-179) (Gen. 12) located at the top of the pass (modern
Nablus). The pass continues down a magnificent narrow
gorge to the northeast into the neighborhood of present-day
Tubas (182-188), called earlier Tirzah (1 Kgs. 15:33). There
the route continues down to the southeast through the wider
straight Wadi Fari'ah to the Jordan Valley. The turbulence and
early downfall of the northern kingdom of Israel might have
been considerably influenced by the geographical openness of
its home in these hills of Samaria, that is, by the lack of
easily defendable borders such as Judea had.

Southern or Lower Galilee is yet more open and was
rarely if ever a major power center. Here we cannot even
properly speak of a central hill ridge, because actually there
are four small east-west hill ridges. Nestled up in the middle
of the southernmost of them is Nazareth (178-234), mentioned
in the NT (Mt. 2; Lk. 2). Nazareth overlooks the wide flat

plains of Megiddo (167-221) (Armageddon, Kishon basin, Esdraelon plain, or Jezreel valley—the latter referring in Scriptures to the eastern part drained by the Harod), which separate it from Samaria to the south. Rising separately above the plain to the southeast of Nazareth (178-234) are Mt. Tabor (188-232) like a great inverted bowl, and the volcanic Hill of Moreh with Nain (182-223) on its southern slopes.

Beautiful, picturesque, flat little east-west valleys lie between these ridges of Lower Galilee. But the last valley to the north is bounded by the great scarp of Upper Galilee which thrusts up into the wildest, most isolated area of the country. This area of rich vegetation is drained by several magnificent gorges. It is bounded on the north by the Litani (Leontes) River, which comes from the great rift valley north of the sources of the Jordan and cuts straight across out westward to the sea just north of Tyre (168-297).

The great rift valley continues practically uninterrupted from Mt. Hermon (225-305) (see Ps. 29:6; 89:12) in the north to Elath (145-884) on the Red Sea in the south. Mt. Hermon (Deut. 3:9) towers over 9,000 feet to the northeast just above the Huleh Valley, the northern section of the rift valley where the Jordan sources are located. In fact, its height allows it to catch sixty inches of rain annually, which it feeds out into the rich springs of Snir (or Hasban), Dan, and Hermon (Banias). These join in the Huleh Valley into the new Jordan River channels which have now replaced the Huleh lake and swamps.

The swamps are a result of a lava outflow related to the volcanic cones of the Golan Heights to the east. The outflow dammed the Jordan River and lake, but this degenerated into swamps.

From the Sea of Galilee (nearly 700 feet below sea level) the Jordan river meanders more than seventy-five miles along a nearly flat slope to the Salt Sea (Sea of the Arabah) or Dead Sea about 1,300 feet below sea level. The river bed of these meanderings is dwarfed by the immense floor of the rift valley down whose middle the river makes its way. This great valley floor, the Ghor, was not eroded out by the Jordan, but resulted from the sinking of the earth's crust along great north-south rifts. Near Jericho the floor is called the Plains of Jericho and just across the river to the east, the Plains of Moab (Num. 36:13). The end of the Jordan is a deep sea with no outlet, the Salt Sea. Solid materials in its slimy solution measure between 25 and 30 percent of its total content.

South of the Salt Sea, the land rises in the Arabah section of the rift valley. It rises gradually to over 650 feet above sea level and then subsides gradually to the Red Sea at Elath

(145-884). In this great valley far to the north, across from the island of Cyprus, is its northern gate, the city of Hamath, which corresponds to Elath (145-884) in the south. Coming south up the Orontes River on which Hamath is located, are high mountains on both sides, the Lebanon, ancient Phoenicia, to the west along the Mediterranean, and the Ante-Lebanon to the east on the fringe of the Arabian desert plateau, which ends at Mt. Hermon (225-305). Its foothills extend out into the rift valley just north of the Huleh basin and somewhat choke up the valley (the region of Ituraea). The valley route is difficult here. However, just north of Mt. Hermon (or Mt. Sirion; see Ps. 29:6), there is a pass across the Ante-Lebanon. This pass became important, especially since an oasis at its east end right on the desert fringe permitted the building of a great city, Damascus. This city was the home of the Aramean and later Syrian kingdoms, who gathered wealth from their position on the trade routes.

South of Damascus, and up east of the Huleh Valley begins the plateau east of the Jordan (the Transjordanian plateau), the last of the four north-south strips. The first east-west interruption of this strip is the canyon of the Yarmuk River, which empties into the Jordan just south of the Sea of Galilee. The territory between it and Mt. Hermon is Bashan, (or Golan Heights). It gets sufficient rainfall for crops and rich pasturage for two reasons. Rainbearing winds off the Mediterranean get through the east-west valleys of Lower Galilee without being forced to lose much moisture, and the gradual slope of the Bashan plateau upward toward Mt. Hauran in the east forces the moisture out. Only beyond Hauran does the desert begin in earnest, but the rocky "torn" area (*Trachonitis*) just to the northwest of Mt. Hauran is scarcely habitable either, except as a refuge.

South of the Yarmuk is the region of Gilead. Here and to the south the desert approaches ever closer to the edge of the plateau near the rift valley, both because the plateau tilts down toward the east, and because it gets higher and higher as one goes south. What water is left in the clouds after already being tossed over the Samarian and Judean hills gets forced out mostly at the steep rise of the edge, leaving none for the plateau slanting eastward. Through the middle of Gilead runs the Jabbok River in whose upper reaches dwelt the *Ammonites* at Rabbath Ammon (238-151) (see Gen. 19:38).

Along the east side of the Salt Sea was Moab (Num. 21-24), home of the Moabites. Through it runs the fantastic Arnon gorge with cliffs 1,600 feet high over a canyon scarcely 100 feet wide.

At the south end of the Salt Sea, the Zered flows out of its canyon. South of the Zered, along the rugged plateau edge called Mt. Seir, dwelt the *Edomites* (Num. 20:14) with

their center at Sela (Petra?) (192-971). In Christ's day, the
Nabateans lived here. The Edomites had been forced out
across the rift into the Negev south of Judea. The Negev
then became known as Idumea.

Distribution of Water. Even though the lay of the land is
largely formed as a result of climatic forces, the topography
in return affects the climate by increasing rainfall. For example
Mt. Carmel (155-238) gets thirty-six inches of rain, though
only 1,500 feet high because its steep slopes up above
the sea. Mt. Meron (189-267) nearly 4,000 feet, in Upper
Galilee, is the highest west of the Jordan and gets the most
rain, over forty inches. Across the Jordan, Mt. Hermon, over
9,000 feet, gets sixty inches. Bashan, because it is tilted up
to the east, is watered far inland, whereas Edom, higher
up, gets about the same amount of rain, twenty inches, even
though it is much further south. Only a small area at the
edge of the plateau is watered because it is tilted down toward
the east.

Topography has also produced deserts. Eastward lie the
Deserts of Edom and Moab and the vast Arabian desert. No
moisture is left after the winds have been twice tossed
high and cooled. To the south of Judea there is desert because
there is little moisture in winds that have come across the
Sahara Desert of Africa. The wild, rugged, barren little
Desert of Judea (Jeshimmon), is on the eastern slopes and
cliffs of the Judean Hills as they drop down steeply below sea
level to the Salt Sea ($-1,300$ feet). Only two inches of rain
fall in this amazing "rainshadow." Here lay En Gedi (187-
097), David's refuge from King Saul (1 Sam. 24). Also here
was the refuge of the Essenes who wrote the Dead Sea
Scrolls at their Qumran (194-128) settlement. And here at
Masada (184-081) was the tragic refuge of the last Jewish
survivors of the Great Revolt against Rome A.D. 66-73,
where over 900 committed suicide rather than become Roman
slaves.

Basically the general location of Israel makes it the meeting
place of two major world climatic zones; seacoast
(Mediterranean) and desert (Saharo-Sindian of Africa across
to India). On examining the vegetational zone, it is evident
that yet three more major climatic zones are represented;
the sparsely watered mountain plateaus of Persia and Turkey
are represented on the desert fringes; the tropics of Africa
and India on tropical oases in the rift valley, and even the
often snowbound areas of Europe and Siberia on the cool
heights of Upper Galilee. Especially in the case of the latter
two zones, it is obvious that topography is responsible for the
cool heights and the sultry depths. But even in the case of
the desert fringe it has provided an unusually expansive
fringe in the Negev, the Beersheba basin. Plants adapted to

suffer lack of water both from summer drought and also from winter cold are able to manage with the scanty rainfall here. This pattern provides a very great variety of plant species— up to 2,250 kinds, as over against 1,700 in wet England, or 1,500 in dry Egypt.

Topography is related not only to rainfall as mentioned, but also to the ground water supply. Springs are frequent in Israel along the edges of the central hills and especially along the edges of the rift valley. Along such edges deep watertight strata are exposed which give back rain that fell years earlier up in the hills. Gradually it seeps down to gather in underground streams that in some places come literally gushing to the surface. So deep are some of the strata that in a number of places the water comes back as hot springs—the most famous since antiquity being those already then developed as resorts near the Sea of Galilee and the Salt Sea. There are even towns called Hamath (201-241) which are named after these "hot" springs (Josh. 19:35).

Often a stream erodes a valley till it cuts into a water-bearing layer; then the stream is reinforced by spring water as well. This is important in Israel because otherwise all of the wadis or streambeds would dry up in the summer—as so many of them do. Ancient Jerusalem, Jebus (172-131), owed its existence to such exposure of the Gihon spring. Thus some springs are found up in the hills as well, although they are not so mighty as those down at the edges.

The Yarkon, located inland from the old seaport of Joppa (126-162), is such a stream arising at Aphek (143-168) where the hills meet the plain; today it supplies not only the modern city of Tel Aviv and Jaffa, but its water is pumped up to Jerusalem as well.

The most impressive springs are the Dan (211-294) and the Banias (215-294) in the Huleh Valley at the foot of Mt. Hermon (225-305); together with the Iyon and the Snir (Hasbani) they form the headwaters of the Jordan. Such drama in nature inspired primitive man as well. Semitic deities as well as the Greek god, Pan, were worshiped at the spring of "Banias" (earlier, Paneas, from Pan). In Jesus' day the town of Caesarea Philippi (215-294) was located here. Against this pagan cultic setting Jesus asked, "Who do people say the Son of Man is?" and "Who do you say that I am?" Peter answered, "You are the Messiah, the Son of the living God!" (Mt. 16).

Near the Salt Sea it is only this precious spring water which makes possible such oasis towns as Jericho (192-142) and En Gedi (187-097).

Sometimes erosion has not lowered a valley floor or creek bed far enough to expose the underground streams, but has gotten close enough so man can dig a well to reach the water. Such is Jacob's Well at Sychar near Shechem (176-179). There Jesus revealed himself to the Samaritan woman as the Living Water, the Messiah who can be worshiped any place in the world in spirit and in truth, and not at any specific cultic place alone (Jn. 4).

Such underground streams near the surface are extremely important in the Negev. Witness the frequent struggles over wells here in the period of the patriarchs and the very story of the name of Beersheba (134-072) itself (Gen. 21). Still further southwest out in the desert, in the Desert of Paron, lay Kadesh Barnea (096-006) (Num. 13:26; 20:22), the oasis whose springs and wells supported the Israelites for most of their forty years in the wilderness after the Exodus from slavery in Egypt.

IV. SETTLEMENT ON THE LAND

DETERMINING FACTORS

Chief essential factors of any settlement, in order of priority, are: water, land, safety, and trade. The significance of topography is immediately apparent. Abundant water and usable agricultural land are generally located low, in valley bottoms or out on plains. But safety in ancient times demanded a position that could be well fortified and easily defended. Usually this meant choosing some place high up on a hilltop, preferably with cliffs all around, such as Masada (184-081) or Petra (192-971) so no enemy could storm its walls. Fear drove people to such places, a burden on the everyday life of the farmer. How valuable water was, and how carefully it was used.

It is clear that fear and the need for safety hindered not only easy access to food and water, but trade connections as well. Trade routes naturally follow the shortest and easiest lines, and pass large towns where provisions can be obtained. Only when enemies controlled the better routes would the trade caravans be forced into mountains and along desert fringes to secondary markets or provision centers. For example, in periods of strong foreign control over the whole land the most important administrative centers were often down on the Sharon seacoast plain. Egyptian centers were at Gaza (099-101) and Gezer (142-140) in the Canaanite period, a Roman center was at Caesarea (140-212) in the time of Jesus, and an Arab center was at Ramle (138-148) throughout the early Middle Ages—in preference over Jerusalem (172-131), tucked way up on the water divide of the central hill range. Defensive needs also clarify passages which speak of a city with its villages (Josh. 19); in time of peace the villages were the farmers' homes, but the city was the fortified point where provisions could be stored and people could flee in times of attack and siege.

ANCIENT
ROUTES AND
MAJOR TOWNS

Relationships. Factors determining the location of the routes are: profit, safety, and ease of travel. The last factor requires routes that are comfortable, the shortest possible, well supplied with water, food, and resting inns. For example, those few valleys in the Carmel range which have chalky soil became the natural passes—at Jokneam (160-230), Megiddo (167-221), and Dothan (172-202)—both because such soil beats down into a smooth hard-surfaced roadbed and also because erosion has made the general terrain in such areas much more gradual and rounded than the surrounding rugged limestone areas. In fact caravans proceeding northwards out of Shechem (176-179) in the hills of Samaria did not take the shortest line straight north but swung around to either the east past Tirzah (182-188) or to the west past Shomron (Samaria) (168-187) in order to follow the chalk valleys which allow the traveler to avoid the hard rock of Mt. Ebal.

Fear could easily keep caravans off the easiest routes. For example the most gradual route from the coast to Jerusalem (172-131), the modern railroad route, is past Beth Shemesh (147-128) and on up the Sorek Valley and its Rephaim tributary. This may be the way the strong Philistines came up to attack David (2 Sam. 5). But this valley is narrow and winding, and therefore very dangerous if suddenly a defender appears above on the steep sides around the next bend. Because of this, attacking armies have throughout history often preferred the Beth Horon (160-143) (Josh. 10:10) route which climbs up a ridge just north of the neighboring Ajalon Valley. Caravans, often armed for protection, were frequently forced to make such deliberations, to choose a less convenient route for safety's sake.

Routes play a large part in the location of many towns. After availability of water and land have established the location of major populated areas and connections have sprung up between distant areas, then the connecting routes in turn influence the location of supply centers, especially the junctions of importance. The towns of the Carmel passes are good examples, Jokneam (160-230), Megiddo (167-221), Taanach (171-214), Dothan (172-202), and also rift valley towns like Jericho (192-142), Beth Shean (197-212), and Hazor (203-269). Extreme examples are desert towns like Avdat (128-023) and Shivtah (115-033), which lived only for trade, and whose inhabitants had to make clever, strenuous schemes to maintain some agriculture in the vicinity. David moved his capital from Hebron (160-103) to Jerusalem (172-131) into a more dangerous area in order to get near a better route as well as into a more central position for consolidating the tribes.

Once grown, a junction town not only supplied traffic but drew traffic to its own markets—or drew jealous armies.

When Jerusalem was strong it could impose customs even on caravans passing along the coast. The Egyptian Pharaoh himself with all his army could not pass safely down there (2 Kgs. 23). Even when Jerusalem was not strong enough to stop the coastal traffic, it was still feared; the Greek Seleucid generals of Syria on their way to Egypt secured the safety of their passing armies by first conquering Jerusalem before pushing on south.

Major North-South Routes. Of all ancient routes the most loaded with dramatic history is the "Way of the Sea." This was the main trail from Mesopotamia to Egypt. Century after century commercial and military expeditions were conducted between these two old power centers, and usually on this trail.

Angling southwest from Mesopotamia toward the Mediterranean, the trail passed the Tadmor (Palmyra) and Damascus oases on the fringe of the desert and crossed Bashan down into the rift valley at Hazor (203-269) in the Huleh region. Going straight south it reached the Sea of Galilee near Tiberias (203-243) and then started angling southwest again up past the base of Mount Tabor (188-232) across the valley plains of the Kishon Brook to the strategic city of Megiddo (167-221) at the opening of the chief pass across the Carmel range. This area is likely the most famous battleground of history, all the way from the contests of the ancient giant powers to the battles of this twentieth century. Known by several names, Megiddo, Jezreel, Esdraelon, Armageddon, the area reveals its importance in the last name, where it has come to stand for the climactic battle of the Judgment Day (Rev. 16:16).

Passing through the Carmel hills, the trail again heads more directly south along the coastal plains of Sharon. Nearby, Herod the Great built Caesarea (140-212), destined to be the administrative capital and leading seaport of the country (Acts 10:23ff.). Further south the route branched at Aphek (143-168), also known as Antipatris, near the Yarkon spring (1 Sam. 4). One branch continues directly south past Gezer (142-140) and along the edges of the western foothills of Judea (Shephelah—"lowlands" when viewed from the higher range itself), until it swings out across the Philistine plain toward the sea south of Gaza (099-101) (Judg. 16). The other branch goes immediately out to the sea at Joppa (126-162) and continues south just inside the beach dunes through Ashdod (117-129), Ashkelon (107-118), and Gaza (142-140), leading Philistine cities. Then it crosses the desert, passing the wadi of Egypt, and finally through the Desert of Shur into the Nile delta of Egypt itself.

Another route south from Mount Tabor (188-232) continues straight south across the Kishon into the Samarian hills and

after passing Dothan (172-202) and Shechem (176-179) follows
the water divide of the central hills past such venerable sites
as Shiloh (177-162) (1 Sam. 1), Bethel (142-148) (Gen.
28), Jerusalem (172-131), Bethlehem (169-123), Hebron (160-
103), and then runs southwest down to Beersheba (134-
072) and on into the desert in the region of Kadesh Barnea
(096-006). Finally it crosses westward from there into Egypt.
The water divide section of this route has later been called
the "Way of the Patriarchs," because its towns are the
settings for most of the stories about them.

There are two other notable north-south routes, both of
which run from Damascus down the whole length of the area
east of its Jordan. The King's Highway (Num. 20:17; 21:22)
goes along the water divide at the edge of the plateau above
the rift valley. "The Way of the Desert" of Moab (Deut.
2:8) or of Edom (2 Kgs. 3:8) skirts around the upper reaches
of the canyons which cut back from the rift valley eastwards
into the desert fringe. This way avoids having to climb in and
out of each of these canyons as the King's Highway must
do, but the disadvantage is the lack of food and water, since
there is scarcely a village so far out in the desert. The King's
Highway in contrast went right through the heart of the
populated areas. It passed through or near such towns as
Karnaim (247-249) and Ashteroth (243-244) in Bashan,
Ramoth Gilead (244-210) and Rabbath Ammon (238-151) in
Gilead, Heshbon (226-134) and Kir Hareseth (217-066) in
Moab, and Bozrah (208-016) in Edom.

Major East-West Routes. There are several routes eastward
out of Egypt across Sinai. It is not clear which one was used
by the Israelites following the Exodus from oppression in
Egypt. It is clear that they did not follow the Way of the
Philistines, the line of forts along the shortest route across
the northern Sinai peninsula. This is part of the famous
Way of the Sea.

Further south, the Way of Shur crossed the Desert of Shur
(Ex. 15:22), just outside of Egypt and continued east to the
area of the oasis of Kadesh Barnea (096-006). Its extension
eastward was the way to the Arabah, the rift valley south
of the Salt Sea.

Right across the middle of the Sinai a vast area then called
Mount Paran in its Desert of Paran (Deut. 33:2), ran the
Way to Seir (Edom). It crossed at the head of the Red Sea
near Elath (145-884) and Ezion Geber (147-884). The
southernmost route from Egypt dropped south along the Red
Sea Coast through the Desert of Sin (?) to the Desert of
Sinai and Mt. Sinai (Ex. 19), traditionally located near the
southern tip of the peninsula. Then it went up along the
eastern branch of the Red Sea toward Seir (Edom).

The coastal Way of the Sea (Via Maris) and the King's Highway east of the Jordan finally met at Damascus, but from the Negev northwards are a number of east-west trails connecting them. These routes are most easily named and identified by the junction towns, many right on the water divide of the central hills, which was a north-south route. Such junction towns are Beersheba (134-072) in the Negev, Hebron (160-103) near the high point of the Judean hills, and the Jerusalem (172-131) area where the routes passed from Joppa (126-162) (Acts 10; Jonah 1:3; 2 Chron. 2:16) seaport to tropical Jericho (192-142). From Joppa came the Way of Beth Shemesh (147-128) up to the Sorek Valley, and the way of Beth Horon (160-143) came up a steep ridge north of the Ajalon Valley. The former crossed the divide at Jebus or Jerusalem (172-131), which is located on a small ridge below Mt. Moriah. The trail then dropped down the slopes of the Mount of Olives by way of the Pass of Adummim to Jericho (192-142) (Josh. 2; 15:7; 18:17). The latter crossed just north of Jerusalem and could descend to Jericho down the way of the Arabah past Ai on the slopes.

Further junction towns are Shiloh (177-162)—located in the hills of *Ephraim, Shechem* (176-179) on the comfortable pass cutting between Mt. Gerizim and Mt. Ebal and on down the Wadi Fari'a eastward to Adam (201-167) on the Jordan: and most famous of all, Megiddo (167-221)—not only controlling the most strategic Carmel pass just southwest of it, but also on a second coast-to-valley route, the one proceeding southeast down to the rift valley at Beth Shean (197-212) nestled just below Mount Gilboa.

Located at this junction between the Sharon Plain and the Huleh Valley, and also between the Galilean coastal plains and the Beth Shean Valley, Megiddo has been destroyed and rebuilt over twenty times. Today this one-time grand chariot city of King Solomon (1 Kgs. 9:15) and of King Ahab lies in ruins and by its name, Armageddon (Rev. 16:16), testifies to a final reckoning by God with the mighty of this world.

Acre (158-258), known also as Akko and Ptolemais (Acts 21:7), must be mentioned as the strongest seaport of the country. From it routes crossed Lower Galilee and the rift valley to the King's Highway. One branch descended to the Plain of Gennesaret on the western shores of the Lake of Galilee and continued past Capernaum (203-255), Jesus' second home after Nazareth (178-234), and Bethsaida (209-257) up onto the Bashan plateau (Mt. 4:13; 11:23).

"NOT ONLY FULLNESS OF TIME," BUT "PRECISION OF PLACE"

This land is the Promised Land. It, or major parts of it, have been known by many names representing different languages and periods of history: Canaan, Land of the Habiru, Land of the Israelites, Israel and Judah, Palestine, Cis-Jordan and

Transjordan, and the Holy Land, for example.

It was promised by God to Abraham, the father of faith, whose family was to be God's people through whom he would bring the Messiah to the world (Gen. 12:7).

Parts of God's revelation are more precisely understood in the light of certain climate and terrain in the Holy Land. For example, unless one works diligently, the stormy winter cloudbursts wash away the powdery soil pulverized by months of searing summer heat, and the land quickly turns to rocky wastes. But if worked, the fertile land gives abundant fruit. One does not learn only diligence and self-help from these conditions. The great irregularity of the winter rains in much of the country also keeps one amply aware of dependence on superior forces for the success of one's crops. Topographical, climatic, and vegetational variety are immense. Snow-capped mountains and tropical valley, ocean coasts, and desert expanses exist almost side by side. A traveler from any part of the world can find something familiar, something easy and natural to understand. Since three continents meet here at this crossroad for the contact of their civilizations, it is no wonder that the caravans and the armies that have passed here are innumerable.

Just because these innumerable influences all converge on this land, one could suppose that its people would be overwhelmed by various and conflicting opinions, ideologies, philosophies, and religions. In fact, they often were over-whelmed.

But God had other plans. He chose and prepared this central location as "precisely the place" where his gospel message could be focused in explosive intensity. Here people would become so overwhelmed and emboldened by his love that they would reverse the incoming tides of influence and become themselves an influence aimed at reaching the ends of the earth.

God's style is hereby revealed. He chooses the *particular* (a man—Abraham, a nation—the Jews, his Son—Jesus . . . all in a specific location) in order to demonstrate and prove his love and faithfulness in a concrete, specific, believable way, but then the universal invitation goes out to join the particular family he chose and is yet gathering to himself. (H.R.T.R.)

GERA 1 and 2. A son and a grandson of Benjamin (Gen. 46:21; 1 Chron. 8:3).

3 and 4. Father of an Ehud, a Benjamite, and a descendant of Ehud, also a Benjamite (Judg. 3:15; 1 Chron. 8:7).

5. Father of the Shimei who cursed David (2 Sam. 16:5).

GERAH *See* WEIGHTS AND MEASURES

GERAR A town (112-087) on an important caravan route near Gaza. Abraham and later Isaac sojourned there with King Abimelech. Here King Asa of Judah later defeated the Cushites (Ethiopians?). The modern name of the site is Tell Abu Hureirah (Gen. 20:1-2; 26:1ff.; 2 Chron. 14:13, 14).

GERASENES *See* GADARENES

GERIZIM, MOUNT *See* GEOGRAPHY OF THE HOLY LAND

GERSHOM One who returned from the Babylonian captivity with Ezra (Ezra 8:2).

GERSHON, GERSHONITES 1. The first son of Moses, born in Midian (Ex. 2:22; 6:16).
2. The first son of Levi (1 Chron. 6:1; Gen. 46:11). The Gershonite Levites were in charge of the tabernacle, the tent of meeting (Num. 3:25-26). The family continued in the services of the temple in Solomon's time and later (1 Chron. 26:21; 2 Chron. 29:12).

GERUTH KIMHAM An unidentified place near Bethlehem (Jer. 41:17).

GESHAN A descendant of Caleb (1 Chron. 2:47).

GESHEM An Arab who tried to oppose the building of the walls by Nehemiah (Neh. 2:19; 6:1-6).

GESHUR, GESHURITES 1. A part of the area of Syria-Aram (2 Sam. 15:8; Deut. 3:14). David married the daughter of one of their kings (2 Sam. 3:3).
2. A people who lived in the south, the Negeb, near the Philistines (Josh. 13:2).

GETHER A grandson of Shem (Gen. 10:23).

GETHSEMANE The place in the Kidron Valley on the lower slopes of the Mount of Olives where Jesus prayed the evening when Judas betrayed him. The word means "oil vat" (Mt. 26:36).

GEUEL The representative of the tribe of Gad among the twelve sent by Moses to spy out the land of Canaan (Num. 13:15).

GEZER An important site (142-140) on the rise between the Aijalon and Sorek valleys guarding the most important road (the Beth Horon Road) up into the hill country of Judah. The Egyptians held it in the middle of the second millennium B.C. and the pharaoh gave it as a wedding gift to Solomon when he married a daughter of the pharaoh (Josh. 16:3; 1 Kgs. 9:15-17). David drove back the Philistines from Gibeon to Gezer (2 Sam. 5:25). Solomon later rebuilt it.

GHOST A departed spirit (Isa. 29:4; Mk. 6:49).

GIAH An unidentified place near Gibeon where Joab pursued Abner (2 Sam. 2:24).

GIBBAR Father of ninety-five persons who came back from the Babylonian captivity in Ezra's time. He is called Gibeon in the parallel account (Ezra 2:20; Neh. 7:25).

GIBBETHON A Levitical city (137-140) in the tribal area of Dan which the Philistines took and held for many years in spite of Israelite attempts to conquer it (Josh. 19:44; 21:23; 1 Kgs. 15:27; 16:17).

GIBEA A grandson of Caleb (1 Chron. 2:49).

GIBEAH 1. A city of Benjamin (172-136) sometimes called also Gibeah of Saul, the king (Judg. 19:12; 1 Sam. 11:4). Here the concubine of the Levite was abused and murdered by the Benjamite inhabitants, leading to her dismemberment and the decimation of the men of Benjamin by the rest of Israel (Judg. 19 and 20). Many important incidents in the lives of Saul and Jonathan took place here (1 Sam. 10-15).

2. An unidentified town in the hill country of Judah (Josh. 15:57).

3. An unidentified town in the hill country of Ephraim where Eleazar, one of Aaron's sons, was buried (Josh. 24:33).

GIBEAH OF GOD An unidentified site where there were Philistines. Here Saul met a band of prophets and himself joined them (1 Sam. 10:5).

GIBEATH HAARALOTH A hill where Joshua circumcised the Israelites after their entry into the land of Canaan from the forty years of wandering in the desert (Josh. 5:3).

GIBEON A city (167-139) in the tribal area of Benjamin. Its original inhabitants were Hivites (Josh. 9:3, 7). Here took place the incident of the sun and moon standing still for the pursuit after the battle of Gibeon (Josh. 10). Here too took place the hand to hand fight between twelve men of Benjamin and twelve men of Judah under Abner and Joab. Since all of them died in the fight, it was a no-decision contest. A battle therefore followed (2 Sam. 2:12-28). Joab slew Amasa at Gibeon and David gave the Philistines a severe defeat there

(2 Sam. 20:8; 1 Chron. 14:16). After the Babylonian captivity men returned to Gibeon from Babylon and worked on the repair of Jerusalem's city wall (Neh. 3:7).

GIDDALTI A temple musician in the time of David (1 Chron. 25:4, 29).

GIDDEL 1 and 2. Ancestors of two groups who returned from the Babylonian captivity (Ezra 2:47, 56).

GIDEON *See* JUDGES OF ISRAEL

GIDEONI The father of Abidan the leader of the people of Benjamin (Num. 7:60; 10:24).

GIDOM An unidentified site east of Gibeah to which the Israelites pursued the men of Benjamin in the affair of the Levite concubine (Judg. 20:45).

GIFT, GIFTS These may be natural gifts, men to men; or sacrifices, men to God; or spiritual endowments, God to men. The first may be gifts as we consider them or as it is sometimes translated as "present" or "tribute" or may even be a bribe (Gen. 33:11; 2 Sam. 8:2; Prov. 18:16). The second type is the most frequently noted in the Bible, for example Leviticus 1:10 and 17:4. People could even be referred to in this sense. The Levites were a gift to Aaron to help him (Num. 8:19). In the third sense, God to men, the most basic gift was that of righteousness and eternal life through the life and death of Jesus Christ, his Son, given to men to be appropriated by faith (Rom. 5:15-17; 6:22, 23). Beyond this God has endowed all those in Christ with the indwelling presence of his Holy Spirit to lead, guide, and sanctify them (Acts 2:38; 10:45). He also gives various spiritual gifts for special tasks to individuals of his choice (1 Cor. 12:1), such as the ability to speak in an unknown tongue, the ability to drive out unclean spirits, the ability to heal the sick, to prophesy, to preach, to have discernment and special knowledge (1 Cor. 12:8-11; Rom. 12:6; 1 Cor. 2:4). The presence and work of the Holy Spirit in a life is intended to produce a life that exemplifies love, joy, peace, patience, kindness, goodness, faithfulness, gentleness, and self-control (Gal. 5:22, 23).

GIHON 1. One of the four rivers in Eden, possibly in SE Mesopotamia (Gen. 2:13).

2. A spring in the Kidron Valley in Jerusalem. Solomon was anointed to be king here. King Hezekiah built his famous conduit here in order to get the water from the spring through the rock ridge into the city especially in time of siege (1 Kgs. 1:33-45; 2 Chron. 32:30).

GILALAI A Levite musician in the time of Nehemiah (Neh. 12:36).

GILBOA, MOUNT *See* GEOGRAPHY OF THE HOLY LAND

GILEAD 1. *See also* GEOGRAPHY OF THE HOLY LAND.

2. A descendant of Manasseh whose name passed over to the tribal area (Num. 26:29, 30).

3. The father of the judge Jephthah. *See* JUDGES OF ISRAEL.

4. A family of the territory of Gad (1 Chron. 5:11, 14).

GILGAL The first camp (193-143) of the Israelites in Canaan after their exodus from Egypt (Josh. 4:19, 20). Here Saul was made the king over Israel (1 Sam. 11:15), and later angered God by acting as a priest and making a sacrifice (1 Sam. 13:9).

2. An unidentified site in the story of Elijah and Elisha (2 Kgs. 2:1; 4:38).

3. An unidentified site whose king was defeated by Joshua (Josh. 12:23).

4. An unidentified site noted in Deuteronomy 11:30, in the Arabah.

5. An unidentified site noted in Joshua 15:7 but in the tribal area of Judah.

GILOH, GILONITE An unidentified village in the hill country of Judah (Josh. 15:51; 2 Sam. 15:12; 23:34).

GIMZO A city (145-148) of Judah in the western foothills near Beth Shemesh (2 Chron. 28:18).

GINATH The father of the Tibni who tried to seize the Israelite throne (1 Kgs. 16:21, 22).

GINNETHOI A priest who came back from the Babylonian captivity with Zerubbabel, called Ginnethon in the NIV text (Neh. 12:4, footnote).

GINNETHON 1. One who signed the covenant with Nehemiah (Neh. 10:6).

2. A priest in the days of a Joiakim (Neh. 12:16).

GIRDLE *See* DRESS

GIRGASHITES A Canaanite tribe whom God said the Israelites would drive out (Gen. 10:16; Josh. 3:10).

GIRZITES An unknown people among those raided by David when he was living in Philistine territory (1 Sam. 27:8).

GISHPA An officer over the temple servants who lived on the hill of Ophel in the time of Nehemiah (Neh. 11:21).

GITTAIM A town (140-145) in Benjamin to which the Beerothites fled from Saul (2 Sam. 4:3). Returnees from the Babylonian captivity settled there (Neh. 11:33).

GITTITE A name for an inhabitant of Gath (Josh. 13:3). *See* PHILISTINE CITIES.

GITTITH *See* PSALMS, TITLES OF

GIZONITE A man from the unknown town of Gizon who was one of David's mighty men (1 Chron. 11:34).

GLASS A substance well known as early as the third millennium B.C. in Egypt and a specialty of the Phoenicians later. It is not mentioned in the OT of the NIV. The NIV notes "mirrors" but in antiquity these were made of a polished reflecting metal (Job 37:18). In the NT only in Revelation 4:6 (sea of glass, clear as crystal), Revelation 15:2 (sea of glass), Revelation 21:18 (glass), Revelation 21:21 (transparent glass). Glass begins to appear commonly in the archaeological records only in Roman times.

GLAZE "Like a coating of glaze over earthenware" (Prov. 26:23). In antiquity paints were sometimes rubbed on earthen vessels, hand polished to brightness, and then baked a second time to give a shiny glaze. The footnote to the Proverbs text reads "of silver dross."

GLEANING About half of the appearances of this word in the OT are in the Book of Ruth. The poor were allowed to follow the reapers and gather the gleanings, or what was left, a practice established by Mosaic Law (Lev. 19:9, 10; 23:22). The practice is noted throughout Israelite history (Ruth 2:2; Isa. 24:13; Mic. 7:1). The word is also used figuratively to describe the total destruction of Israel (Jer. 6:9).

GLOOM In both Testaments reference is made to the gloom of darkness. In the OT it frequently refers to the Day of the Lord as a day of gloom and punishment. The NT refers to the nether region of gloom where the fallen angels and others are reserved until the final day of judgment (Joel 2:2; Zeph. 1:15; 2 Pet. 2:4, 17; Jude 6).

GLORY OF THE LORD (SHEKINAH) God came among his people on earth in various ways. He was in the pillar of cloud and fire that led the Israelites through the wilderness in the exodus from Egypt. The word "Shekinah" from the Hebrew word "to dwell" is not found in the Bible, but it was used by the early rabbinic writers to refer to the appearing of God to his people as in the pillar of cloud and fire. For an example, God spoke to Moses through the "Shekinah" out of the burning bush. Allusions to this are found in the NT in such passages as John 1:4 and Romans 9:4. Glory is both literal and spiritual in the NT, seen both physically and spiritually (Lk. 2:9; Jn. 17:22). A bright cloud overshadowed Jesus and the three disciples on a high mountain when Jesus was transfigured. The face of Jesus shone like the sun and his garments became white like light, which was another incident of the same (Mt. 17:1-8).

GLOSSOLALIA *See* TONGUES, GIFT OF

GNAT *See* BEASTS, 6

GNOSTICISM *See* SECTS

GOAD A long wooden stick tipped with a sharp point sometimes of metal used to clean the plow tip and also to prod the plow animals if they slowed down. A judge of Israel killed 600 Philistines with one. The word is also used to illustrate the futility of kicking against a superior power. The words of the wise can be a prod, or goad (1 Sam. 13:21; Eccl. 12:11; Acts 26:14).

GOAT *See* BEASTS, 4

GOB An unidentified place where David fought twice with the Philistines (2 Sam. 21:18, 19).

GOD, NAMES OF, GODHEAD Throughout the Bible the existence of one true God is never questioned. The inspired writers had no need to argue proofs of God's existence. They did not describe his nature in abstract theological definitions, because God is known by what he does and what he says. Yet the many names of God reveal the many aspects of his nature and of his relationship to mankind and to all creation. God is the eternal Person, the only and supreme Creator of the universe, perfect in wisdom, righteousness, power, and love. God is to be worshiped, obeyed, and loved by all people.

1. *El, Elohim.* Elohim is the plural of El, the form most often used in the OT, translated "God" in English. This, the oldest word for God, is used without specifying any particular aspect of God. It usually refers to the God of Israel, but it

can be used of other gods, and heathen nations also described
their gods by this word. In the OT the plural word "Elohim"
is nearly always used with a singular verb when it means
the true God, but when the writer means the gods of the
nations it has a plural verb. Many explanations of this plural
form have been given, that it indicates the greatness of God,
or even the three Persons of the Trinity. But since this
plural is found even in heathen writings it probably points to
the concentration in one person of the several divine powers
or beings that men had in mind of the sum total of deity.
"Elohim" is also used to describe lesser beings. In Psalm 8:5
the LXX and KJV render it "angels." The NIV renders it
"heavenly beings." It can even mean human leaders (Ps.
82:6), such as judges (Judg. 21:6).

The singular El is more often joined to a further descriptive
title, such as *El Roi*, "God of seeing" (Gen. 16:13); *El-
Shaddai*, "God almighty" (Gen. 17:1; Ex. 6:3). El is also
used in names of people, such as *El-eazar*, "God is helper"
(Ex. 6:25), *El-hanan*, "God is gracious" (1 Chron. 20:5), and
many others.

2. *Yahweh.* The KJV uses Jehovah, the RSV and NIV use *Lord.*
The Hebrew gives only the four consonants JHVH. The
vowels in Jehovah are taken from the Hebrew *Adonai* (Lord)
and those in Yahweh are a probable guess. In the KJV and
RSV Yahweh is usually rendered as LORD in capital letters
(see below under LORD). Yahweh is the distinctive title
for God among the people of Israel. It is the name by which
God revealed himself to them as being the God of the
Covenant, the God who chose them to be his own special
people. When God made the covenant with their first parent
Abraham, he revealed himself by the name *El-Shaddai* (God
Almighty in the NIV footnote; see also below) (Gen. 17:1, 2,
footnote), so also to Isaac and Jacob (Gen. 28:3, footnote;
35:11, footnote). But when the time came to establish the
covenant relationship with the developed nation, he used the
name Yahweh, "LORD" (Ex. 6:2-9). This does not mean
that the name Yahweh was unknown to Abraham or even to
his predecessors (Gen. 15:7), but to Abraham in his weakness
God came as the God of power, and to the nation of Israel
as the God of love, the eternal God who would be faithful to
the covenant by which he bound himself to them. The exact
significance of JHVH cannot be decided, but the idea of
"being" is certainly at the root of the name. The same root
word is found in Exodus 3:14 "I AM" but here it is EHYEH
in Hebrew, perhaps "I will be," indicating something of the
content of the name Yahweh which is used in verse 15. This
was the name by which God was to be remembered by
every generation of Israelites, and it was in this name that

God always called them back to true faith and obedience.
Exodus 36:22-38, in the combination "Sovereign LORD" (see
below under LORD).

3. *Almighty.* The name *El-Shaddai,* "God Almighty," seems
to be one of the oldest names for God. Shaddai probably
means sovereign power. It is used some fifty-five times in
the OT (see above), thirty-one of them in Job where it
is always in the simple form "the Almighty." The LXX
translates Shaddai as *pantokrator,* the all powerful, and it is
this word which is used in the NT, once by Paul (2 Cor.
6:18) and eight times in Revelation.

4. *Lord.* The English "Lord" represents two different Hebrew
words, Adonai and Yahweh. Adon is commonly used of men
as a term of respect, sir or master. The plural Adonai
describes God as the supreme Master, and is written "Lord"
in English Bibles. The capital letters LORD are used to
translate the Hebrew JHVH. Later generations of Jews
developed a rather artificial respect for the divine name
Yahweh and would not say it aloud, but always read out
Adonai instead, so the LXX translated it as *Kurios,* "Lord,"
making it no different from their translation of Adonai. The
English "LORD" represents Yahweh, and "Lord" Adonai.
Sovereign LORD, found many times in the NIV is the translation
of Adonai JHVH or Lord LORD (Ezek. 36:22ff.). In the NT
Jesus is called Lord, at first as a term of respect (Mk. 7:28),
but when his divine glory was realized the title Lord made
him equal to Yahweh. Words spoken of Yahweh in the OT are
even applied to Christ in the NT (Heb. 1:10-12).

Lord Almighty, Yahweh Tsebaoth (translated Lord of Hosts
in some other versions). In its earlier use "Hosts/Almighty"
may mean the armies of Israel or the spiritual forces used
by God (1 Sam. 17:45). But the full sense of the title as used
by the prophets (282 times) reveals God as sovereign over
all the powers of the universe (Isa. 6:5; Mal. 1:14).

5. *Father, Fatherhood of God.* God's fatherly care for his
people is revealed throughout the OT, but the idea of God
being father is used only to describe their dependence on
God as their Creator and therefore their obligation to him and
to one another, and God's covenant relation to his chosen
people (Ex. 4:22-23; Hos. 11:1; Mal. 1:6). God is clearly the
Creator and Lord of all the nations, but these passages in
the OT give no ground for regarding God as the father of all
men in the sense of a special personal relationship. Each is
written primarily concerning Israel. It is through Jesus that
the fatherhood of God comes fully in the light. He frequently
calls God "My Father" (Mt. 7:21), and to his disciples says,
"your Father" (Mt. 6:6; Mk. 11:25; Jn. 20:17), but never
"our Father" because his own relationship to the Father is

unique (Mt. 11:27). Jesus' prayer was that of a son talking to
his father (Lk. 10:21, 22; Mk. 14:36; Lk. 23:46), and ours
is to be the same (Mt. 6:6-9). The nature of God's fatherhood
is seen in the Sermon on the Mount (Mt. 5:43—7:11),
summed up in 6:32, "your heavenly Father knows that you
need them." It involves a believing and obedient response
from his children (Mt. 7:21-23), and also discipline from the
Father (Heb. 12:5-11). People prove that they are true
children of the Father by behaving as he does (Mt. 5:43-48).
The fact that God is kind to the unjust as well as to the
just does not imply, nor does the Bible indicate, that God is
the Father of all men. This relationship is made only by being
born anew into God's family through faith in his only Son
Jesus Christ (Jn. 1:12, 13; 3:6-8; 1 Pet. 1:22, 23; Phil. 2:15).

6. *Holy Spirit, Spirit of God.* The word "spirit" speaks of
living breath. The Spirit of God is the living energy of God
active in the world and among men. The Spirit of God brought
order out of chaos at the first creation (Gen. 1:2); gave
intelligence and skill (Ex. 31:3); strength (Judg. 13:25; 14:6);
ecstatic utterance (1 Sam. 10:10; 16:13, 14); prophetic
ministry (Mic. 3:8). The outpouring of this Spirit was promised
in the future for all God's people, no longer for specialized
individuals (Joel 2:28, 29), as fulfilled on the Day of Pentecost.
The name *Holy* Spirit is found in Isa. 63:10, 11, because
God is the Holy One and this is the Spirit of God. God's
holiness is the totality of his unique divine attributes. Thus
the title Holy Spirit indicates that the Spirit also is divine.
Since God is the supreme Person the activity of God's Spirit
must also be personal, but the OT does not clearly show that
the Holy Spirit is a distinct Person within the Godhead,
although there are some indications of this (Isa. 48:16; 63:14).
In the NT the activity of the Spirit comes into prominence.
At first the Spirit of prophecy is seen as in the OT. John the
Baptist, the last of the prophets, is filled with the Holy
Spirit from birth (Lk. 1:15). By the Spirit Zacharias prophesied
(Lk. 1:67). Jesus was conceived by the Holy Spirit (Lk.
1:35), and also equipped for his ministry (Lk. 3:22; 4:1, 18).
Jesus was to baptize in the Holy Spirit (Mk. 1:8), and so
he promised the Spirit to his disciples (Lk. 11:13; Acts 1:4,
5). In John's Gospel the function of the Holy Spirit was amply
described, creating new life (Jn. 3:5-8; 7:38, 39), and
especially in taking the place of Jesus after his return to the
Father (Jn. 14:16-18, 26; 15:26; 16:7-15). From these
passages it is clear that the Holy Spirit is divine and personal.
He is "another Counselor" ("comforter" in the KJV), Jesus
being the *first* Comforter (Jn. 14:16). The Spirit will do
for them what Jesus has already been doing, but further he
will now work within them (Jn. 14:17), revealing the truth

concerning Jesus Christ and bringing conviction to the world. By the Holy Spirit the disciples became effective witnesses of Jesus Christ (Acts 1:8; 5:32; 1 Cor. 2:4, 5), and in many ways demonstrated the power of God in their lives. That the Holy Spirit is a distinct Person within the one Godhead is confirmed by Acts 5:3-5, where Ananias lies to the Holy Spirit, that is, to God. The personal action of the Holy Spirit appears in his sending out Saul and Barnabas (Acts 13:2-4) and directing their work (16:6); also in his giving special powers to some people as he chooses to bestow them (1 Cor. 12:4-11). It was by giving the Holy Spirit to the Gentiles that God proved that he accepted them into salvation (Acts 10:44-47). Divine qualities of character are produced in people by the Holy Spirit (Gal. 5:22, 23).

7. *Alpha and Omega.* These are the first and last letters of the Greek alphabet. The name indicates that God is eternal: nothing comes before or after him; therefore all is under his control. He is the Almighty. Both God the Father and Jesus claim this same title (Rev. 1:8; 21:6; 22:13, 16).

8. *Messiah.* The word "Messiah" in the English text occurs only in John 1:41; 4:25, in the NIV. The Hebrew word is translated in the NIV in Daniel 9:25-26 as the "Anointed One." The Hebrew word means "anointed." By anointing with oil men were consecrated to a special ministry, high priests (Lev. 21:12), kings (1 Sam. 24:6, 10), prophets (Ps. 105:15). In later times the title was applied to the great deliverer whom for centuries God had been promising for the restoration and salvation of his people. These promises were fulfilled in Jesus, who was therefore called "the Christ" (Greek for Messiah, Jn. 1:41). The OT gives indications that this person has divine powers (Ps. 110; 72:5-7). Jesus, being God made man, perfectly accomplished the service of the anointed priest, prophet, and king. The apostles declared that this Jesus was the expected Christ, but also the Lord (the divine name) (Acts 2:36; 17:3).

9. *Son of God.* Israel is called the firstborn son (Ex. 4:22-23; Hos. 11:1; 1:10). Angelic beings were also called sons of God (Job 38:7, footnote), and later in writings outside the OT it was a title for the expected Messiah. A special relationship to God is therefore indicated by this name, but when Peter said, "You are the Christ, the Son of the living God," he expressed a truth so high that God alone could reveal it to him (Mt. 16:16, 17). This title signified more than it did in the OT. This was the eternal Son standing in a unique relationship to God, being himself divine. The union of the divine and human had been ensured by his unique birth, so the angel told Mary, "So the holy one to be born will be called the Son of God" (Lk. 1:35). The devil recognized

Jesus' divine nature when he said, "If you are the Son of
God, tell these stones to become bread" (Mt. 4:3; *see* 8:29).
The awed disciples used this title when they saw in Jesus
the power of the Creator commanding wind and wave (Mt.
14:33). The purpose of John's Gospel was to create faith that
"Jesus is the Christ, the Son of God" (Jn. 20:31). Therefore,
in this Gospel the deity of Jesus is most completely revealed.
The title "one and only son" ("only begotten Son" in the
KJV, "only Son" in the RSV) assures us that as the Son of
God Jesus is truly divine (Jn. 1:14, 18; 3:16). The original
word does not mean that the Son was produced by the
Father, but that his sonship is uniquely close, divine. Jesus
rarely used the title Son of God himself, but accepted it from
others (Mt. 16:16; 26:63, 64). For the apostles it signified
the one who was the object of their highest faith and worship
and the source of eternal salvation (Rom. 1:3, 4; Gal. 2:20).

10. *Son of Man.* This is the name by which Jesus most
frequently referred to himself. It may come from Daniel
7:13-41 where "one like a son of man" is given universal and
eternal sovereignty. Jesus did not call himself Messiah
because the people expected the Messiah to be a conquering
warrior king. The name Son of Man possibly conveyed
Messianic ideas (as in Daniel) but was not associated with the
false expectations of the people. In Jesus' use of it the name
was linked with his coming suffering and resurrection (Mk.
8:31) and with his divine glory. The Son of Man has authority
to forgive sins, which only God can do (Mk. 2:7-10); he is
lord of the Sabbath (Mk. 2:28); and he will return enthroned
in glory (Mt. 16:27; 24:30; 25:31). The name combines
the reality of his human life with the highest authority of his
divine status.

11. *The Word.* The Greek word *logos*, translated "Word" in
John 1:1-14, signifies not only speech, but the content of
speech, the reason and wisdom which are expressed in the
uttered word. A man's words tell what is in his mind. His
very personality is made known by his words and by them
his purposes are put into effect. When the Son of God came
into the world in the person of Jesus, the personality of
the unseen God was visibly made known and his saving
purposes were put into effect. Jesus is therefore rightly
called "The Word." He is not a being halfway between God
and man. He is God yet not the same person as God the
Father, for "The Word was God," and yet at the same time
"the Word was with God" (Jn. 1:1). By the word God created
the universe, for "by the word of the Lord were the heavens
made, their starry host by the breath of his mouth" (Ps.
33:6, 9). Likewise, of the Word, John wrote, "through him all
things were made" (Jn. 1:3). Although Greek and Jewish

philosophers also used this title *logos*, it was not from them
that John gathered it. The origins of this title for the Son
of God are rather to be seen in the OT as in Psalm 33 and
Proverbs 8 where wisdom is regarded almost as a person
equal with God in his creative power. "In the past God spoke
to our forefathers through the prophets at many times and
in various ways, but in these last days he has spoken to
us by his Son . . . through whom he made the universe"
(Heb. 1:1, 2). (J.C.C.)

GOG 1. A descendant of Reuben (1 Chron. 5:4).

2. The chief prince of Meshech and Tubal of the land of
Magog. Gog is the leader of the hosts of evil against God and
his people in the end of days, the nations which Satan will
lead (Ezek. 38; Rev. 20:7-10).

GOIIM A people whose king was Tidal who were involved in the
battle at Sodom in Abraham's day (Gen. 14:1, 9).

GOLAN A city (238-243) in Bashan in the tribal area of Manasseh
east of the Jordan in the north. It was a Levitical city of
refuge (Deut. 4:43; Josh. 20:8; 1 Chron. 6:71).

GOLD *See* PRECIOUS STONES AND METALS

GOLGOTHA The place of Christ's crucifixion, the anglicized version of an
Aramaic and Greek word meaning "skull." The Latin word
for the same is *calvarius* from which comes our word Calvary.
All refer to the same place outside the city wall of Jerusalem
(Mt. 27:33; Mk. 15:22; Jn. 19:17).

GOLIATH A giant in the army of the Philistines who defied Israel to
send out a single champion for a duel. David killed him by
felling him with a sling shot and then cutting off his head
(1 Sam. 17:4, 23; 21:9; 22:10).

GOMER 1. Eldest son of Japheth, grandson of Noah, whose name
was passed on to a people, perhaps the Cimmerians (Gen.
10:2, 3; Ezek. 38:6).

2. The wife of the prophet Hosea (Hos. 1:3).

GOMORRAH One of the five cities of the plain at the southern end of the
Salt Sea. Its site is not identified. God destroyed it because
of the wickedness of its people and it is held up as an example
of depravity and subsequent judgment and destruction (Gen.
10:19; 13:10; Deut. 29:23; Isa. 13:19; Mt. 10:15; Jude 7).

GONG *See* MUSIC, MUSICAL INSTRUMENTS

GOPHER WOOD *See* TREES

GOSHEN 1. A city (137-087) of Judah located in the hill country near Debir (Josh. 15:51).

2. A geographical area occupied by Joshua, somewhere in the southern part of Palestine, the Negev (Josh. 10:41; 11:16).

3. The "Land of Goshen" in Egypt, probably in the northeast part of the delta, where the Israelites spent their 400 years in Egypt (Gen. 45:10; Ex. 9:26).

GOSPEL A word used in the NT, derived from an Anglo-Saxon word which means "good news." In current usage reference is either to the essence of Christianity or to the books in which are found the story of Christ's life and teaching. The good news was that Christ died according to the Scriptures and rose again the third day according to the Scriptures and that the purpose of this was atonement, man's redemption from sin (Mk. 1:1; Rom. 1:2; 1 Cor. 15:1-4). *See also* GOSPELS, THE FOUR.

GOSPELS, THE FOUR The four Gospels form one pillar of the historical testimony concerning the origin of Christianity, the other pillar being the testimony of Paul linked to the Book of Acts.

There is good reason for advocating the traditional authorship of the Gospels, two by apostles, Matthew and John, two by men closely associated with apostles, Mark with Peter and Luke with Paul. We are thus assured of the highest degree of historic truth from eyewitness sources. If the apostolic link with Christ and the beginnings of Christianity be broken by denying the truthfulness of the Gospels, the church's own testimony to her origins is destroyed and nothing has been or can be devised to fill up the gap. It is good history and good sense to face the issue of the deity of Christ and the truth of his claims, for thus a reasonable explanation of the origin of the church is provided and we can have a reasonable hope of the success of the church's mission in the world. If the church has grossly erred in its account of its own origin, what confidence can we have in the rest of its message?

The Gospels are not complete biographies of Jesus Christ. Rather, the emphasis falls on those parts of his life which are of decisive importance for human redemption. Hence it is that all four Gospels unequivocally regard Jesus as the Son of God, basing this conviction on his own revealed self-consciousness of who he was and is, and his purpose in coming into the world. Proceeding from this unanimous perspective, each of the Gospels emphasizes certain features of Jesus' work and person which are relevant to basic human needs.

From a combined report of the four Gospels we learn of Jesus' birth at Bethlehem in the time of Herod the Great, 5 or 6 B.C., when Augustus was Caesar. The early church, in calculating the year from the founding of Rome which they proposed to designate as the year 1, erred. When the error was discovered, so many dates had been fixed on this erroneous basis that the date of the birth of Christ was expressed as B.C. and is recognized as an anachronism. One scene from the Lord's youth is given in Luke 2 as he stands in the temple in the midst of the teachers, amazing them with his understanding and answers. The years intervening up to the time of the beginning of Jesus' ministry are passed over in silence by the Gospels, leaving us to infer that he must have been reared as a carpenter's son in Nazareth.

Highly significant events mark the beginning of Christ's work. His baptism, associated with the descent of the Spirit as a dove, explains his name and title as the Anointed One (Messiah, Christ). He, marked by the presence of the Holy Spirit as the eternal Son of God, has grace and power to bring many sons into glory by his redeeming work.

His temptation followed his baptism. In the biblical scheme of redemption it is clear that Christ as Second Adam vindicated himself by successfully overcoming the Tempter and temptations before which Adam fell. He thus proceeded to accomplish the redemptive work laid out for him. It was fitting and proper that he, through whom and for whom all things are, in bringing many sons into glory, himself be made perfect through sufferings. Jesus established a residence in Capernaum and returned to Judea for a preliminary ministry. He and John the Baptist ministered concurrently until John was imprisoned. Jesus then moved to Galilee for the ministry which lasted about a year and a half. The Synoptic Gospels (Matthew, Mark, and Luke) have a very similar outline which gives much detail about this Galilean ministry. The whole narrative shows the plan and will of Christ leading toward a clearly defined goal.

Jesus' work in Galilee began with his appearance at Nazareth (Lk. 4) and his claim, in the words of Isaiah, that the Spirit of God was enabling him to preach and minister. He was rejected, and proceeded to present himself in the synagogue at Capernaum, showing his power to heal, challenging the evil power of Satan. Part of Christ's plan was to establish a community in the world, and to that end he chose men whom he appointed as apostles and trained for that great and momentous task. The Synoptic Gospels list their names. The twelve are divided into three groups of four. The first name of each group is always the same; the order of others within the group may vary. Peter is always first; Philip always fifth; James of Alphaeus always ninth. The first group is the two pairs of brothers: Peter and Andrew, James and John. Philip and Bartholomew (Nathanael), Matthew and Thomas compose the second group. James of Alphaeus, Simon the Cananaean, Judas of James, and Judas Iscariot complete the list.

The work of teaching, training, and healing progressed in the face of increasing opposition. After the twelve were chosen, it was logical and necessary to lay before them the challenging outline of teaching which Jesus had in mind. This we find in the famous Sermon on the Mount, delivered in the spring or early summer at the Horns of Hattin, overlooking the Sea of Galilee. The sermon began with the Beatitudes, which analyzed the law which underlies them. It called men to seek the grace of God, assuring them that if they, being evil, knew how to give good gifts to their children, in infinitely greater degree would their heavenly Father give good gifts to those who seek him. Jesus' own claim to Lordship dominated the discourse, and he presented himself as Final Judge of the eternal destinies of man. The message concluded with the vivid pictures of the foolish and wise men building respectively on the sand or the rock of Jesus' teachings.

The work in Galilee continued. The servant of the centurion in Capernaum was healed; demons were cast out, occasioning the bitter taunt that he cast out demons by complicity with Beelzebub.

The increase of suspicion and opposition led to a new form of teaching, the parables spoken by the sea. Because of the simplicity and naivete and charm of the parable, even the hostile and dull heard him and got the main point that men must choose for or against the grace of God. The best-known parable, under the figure of the sower, shows four relations of men to the message of God. The seed has no effect on the hard-trodden path where the birds can take the seed away immediately. Shallow, stony soil induces a quick generation, but gives no depth for rootage and growth. Thorns and weeds in another can prevent fruitful maturity of the seed. Few hearers would miss the lesson of the good ground where the seed produces a crop. The notable miracle of stilling the storm on Galilee falls in this period of Jesus' ministry.

As the Galilean work neared completion, Jesus sent out the twelve in pairs to minister. They returned, exulting in the power and results, even the devils were subject to the name of Jesus. Their return from this period of labor culminated in retirement to the east of the Jordan in the territory of Bethsaida. The eager multitude followed and was miraculously fed. John 6 shows that Passover was near. This Passover was just a year from the crucifixion.

The remainder of the time in Galilee was especially devoted to training the twelve for their future work. A lengthy journey to Tyre and Sidon gave relief from the busy public ministry. The return journey followed a wide circuit through the Decapolis beyond the Jordan, ending in the miraculous feeding of four thousand on the southeastern shore of the lake. Who would fail to see the parallel between One who could create food for the hungry and One who gave manna in the wilderness? Jesus' journeys of retirement and instruction next led to Caesarea Philippi (Banias). Peter, speaking for all, confessed Jesus as Messiah, and on that fact was based Jesus' subsequent teaching and action. Thenceforward, Jesus walked purposefully to the cross, and the fact and meaning of his death was made ever clearer.

The months between late summer of the year A.D. 29 and the Passover of the year 30 were devoted to Jesus' concluding ministry in all parts of the land. The fall and winter brought the notable visit to Jerusalem at Tabernacles (Jn. 7-10), a period of travel and teaching (Lk. 9-18), a visit to Jerusalem at Dedication (Hanukkah) (Jn. 10), and a brief visit from retirement beyond Jordan to the raising of Lazarus from death (Jn. 11). This miracle crystallized the opposition to Jesus and led to his retirement to Ephraim until time to make his final journey to Jerusalem.

The events of the Passover week are told in detail, occupying nearly half of the Gospel narratives. This literary fact corresponds to the emphasis the church later gave to the proclamation of Jesus' death and resurrection, in accordance with Jesus' own emphasis.

Jesus arrived in Bethany Sabbath eve, March 31 (8 Nisan), A.D. 30. At supper Sabbath evening came Mary's beautiful act of devotion in anointing Jesus. Judas was present and Jesus' rebuke (Jn. 12) helped explain Judas' treachery. On Sunday Jesus crossed the Mount of Olives at Bethphage, securing a donkey to ride to the city, thus clearly presenting himself in the manner of the ancient kings in what is traditionally known as the Triumphal Entry.

On Monday began a series of incidents which led to the cross. Jesus asserted his authority, casting out of the temple the money changers and tradesmen. When challenged, he answered with the question, "John's baptism, was it from heaven, or from men?" (Mt. 21:25).

Tuesday brought the lesson in prayer taught by the withered fig tree, and a series of conversations with opponents who sought to catch Jesus in some utterance. With majestic wisdom and confidence Jesus turned the questions about payment of taxes and resurrection, finally propounding his own question, "What do you think about the Christ? Whose son is he?" (Mt. 22:42). The day closed as Jesus and his apostles gathered on the Mount of Olives for the conference at which Jesus presented the view of the last things known as the Olivet Discourse. The central point of the discourse is its parallel to the Book of Daniel. Jesus predicted in the last days the appearance of the abomination mentioned by Daniel (Dan. 9) and said that event will be the sign of his return on the clouds of heaven.

Wednesday was spent in retirement. On Thursday, April 6, 14 Nisan, Jesus sent Peter and John to prepare the Passover, and that evening Jesus and the twelve celebrated it. In connection with the Passover meal, Jesus instituted the symbolic and memorial supper observed ever since in the church.

After the supper, with the help of Judas, Jesus' enemies arrested him in Gethsemane, and after early morning ecclesiastical trials, sent Jesus to Pontius Pilate. Jesus died claiming he was the Messiah. Pilate, though admitting Jesus' innocence of any capital crime, delivered him over to be crucified. It is well that Jesus taught in advance of the event the true meaning of his death so that what seems so senseless and tragic is seen to be a triumphant act of Divine grace: the Lamb of God bears the sin of the world. Jesus was crucified on Friday, 15 Nisan, April 7 A.D. 30 outside the city. The ancient rubric for the sin offering directed that the body of the Asham (sin offering) be deposited outside the city. Because the darkness was coming late on Preparation (Friday), Jesus was laid in a tomb nearby. His friends rested on the Sabbath, and early on the first day of the week, when they came with spices to prepare his body for proper burial, found the tomb empty. An angel announced that he had risen, and later that day on five occasions, Jesus appeared to his friends.

On these simple facts rest the church and its testimony. The courage and conviction arising in the hearts of those who believed in Jesus led to the establishment of the church. The presence of a risen Savior with his church ever since is the only adequate explanation of its existence and persistence through history. (W.B.W.)

GOURD *See* PLANTS, PERFUMES, AND SPICES

GOVERNOR One who rules an area, territory, or province on behalf of a supreme ruler to whom he is responsible. The Bible mentions both Jewish and non-Jewish governors: Joseph in Egypt, Daniel in Babylon, Gedaliah in Jerusalem appointed by a foreign ruler, Tattenai, and Nehemiah (Gen. 42:6; Dan. 2:48; Jer. 40:5; Ezra 5:3; Neh. 5:14).

GOYIM 1. An unidentified place in Gilgal (Josh. 12:23).

2. *See also* HAROSHETH HAGOGIM.

GOZAN One of the cities in northeast Mesopotamia through which the Habor river flowed and in which some of the Israelites were placed into captivity there by the Assyrian king (2 Kgs. 17:6).

GRACE The words grace, gracious, graciously are not found many times in the Bible. The word "grace" is found very frequently in the NT, but only infrequently in the OT and there the reference is almost always to God's grace. (In the OT the word that is rendered "grace" in the KJV is frequently rendered in the NIV as "find favor.") This indicates that the words gracious and graciously have a general, ordinary usage while the word grace in the NT has a specialized or technical meaning. Grace in the NT has a Christian theological meaning: God's free and unmerited love and favor for sinful man shown when he "did enter into a covenant of grace, to deliver them out of the estate of sin and misery, and to bring them into an estate of salvation by a Redeemer." The Redeemer is "the Lord Jesus Christ, who, being the eternal Son of God, became man, and so was, and continueth to be God and man in two distinct natures and one person forever." The redemption was achieved by Christ's "once offering up himself a sacrifice to divine justice, and reconciling us to God, and in making continual intercession for us." (The three quotations are from the Westminster Shorter Catechism.) This is the grace of the NT where God himself in the person of the Son sacrificed himself in the crucifixion and thereby reconciled the sinner to God and made himself propitious to that sinner. This is free grace, not earned or earnable by man. The classical reference in the NT is found in Ephesians 2:1-22 and 3:1-7, passages which should rejoice the heart of the Gentiles who were outside the pale of God's dealings with man prior to that time, when his dealings were with Israel.

GRAPE *See* PLANTS, PERFUMES, AND SPICES

GRASS *See* PLANTS, PERFUMES, AND SPICES

GRASSHOPPER *See* BEASTS, 6

GRAVE *See* DEAD, ABODE OF

GRAVEN IMAGE *See* DEITIES

GREAVES *See* ARMS AND ARMOR

GREECE *See* GEOGRAPHY OF THE HOLY LAND

GREEK In the RSV the word is used in three senses, Greek nationality, Greek language, and in the sense of non-Greek (sometimes Jew). The NT was written in the Greek language and the OT was very early translated into Greek in a version known as the Septuagint. This latter version was begun in Egypt early in the third century B.C. The word is used only once in the OT where God was rebuking the Phoenicians and Philistines for selling the people of Judah and Jerusalem to the Greeks (Joel 3:6; Jn. 19:20).

GUARANTEE A pledge or assurance that something will be done as specified. Used only in the NT and there in the sense that God has given his Holy Spirit to all believers as a guarantee of their ultimate resurrection and salvation (2 Cor. 1:22; 5:5; Eph. 1:14). In the OT the word "pledge" is in the Judah-Tamar account (Gen. 38:18).

GUDGODAH A stop on the Israelite exodus from Egypt, in the deep south of the Negev (Deut. 10:7).

GUILT The words guilty, guilt, and guiltless are found many times in the Bible, most of them in the OT. This is to be expected since the OT makes so much more of law than does the NT. To be guilty is to be deserving of punishment for the breaking of a law or the failure to conform to it. As ignorance of the law is no excuse in modern society so it was in the OT (Lev. 5:17). God set up that society so that there was collective guilt for law breaking (Josh. 22:20). In the NT Jesus placed a great emphasis on the importance of the attitude of the heart in law keeping as over against mere outward conformity to law (Mt. 5:21, 22, 27, 28, 31, 32, 43, 44). Paul in Romans 5:12-21 taught that the guilt of Adam in his first sin was imputed to all his progeny. It is stated (v. 12) that all men sinned together with him in that sin, even though they were not yet born. This is the statement but just how it took place is one of the mysteries that have concerned theologians.

GUILT OFFERING *See* SACRIFICES AND OFFERINGS

GULL *See* BIRDS, 5

GUNI 1. A son of Naphtali (Gen. 46:24).

2. A man of Gad (1 Chron. 5:15).

GUR An elevated area north of Samaria where Jehu's men mortally wounded Ahaziah the king of Judah (2 Kgs. 9:27).

GURBAAL A city or town where some Arabs lived against whom King Uzziah of Judah fought. Location is thought to be somewhere in Edom or in the southern Negev (2 Chron. 26:7).

H

HAAHASHTARI A descendant of Judah (1 Chron. 4:6).

HABAIAH *See* HOBAIAH

HABAKKUK, BOOK OF *See* PROPHETS, MINOR

HABAZINIAH One of the family of the Recabites (Jer. 35:3).

HABOR *See* GOZAN

HACALIAH The father of Nehemiah (Neh. 1:1).

HACMONI One from Hachmon who was one of David's mighty men (1 Chron. 11:11). Father of one of the men who attended David's sons (1 Chron. 27:32).

HADAD 1. *See* HADAD RIMMON.

2. A son of Ishmael (Gen. 25:15).

3 and 4. Two kings of Edom (1 Chron. 1:46, 50).

5. A prince of Edom who fled to Egypt in David's days and returned when Solomon became king (1 Kgs. 11:14-19; 21, 22).

HADADEZER King of Zobah who ruled an area NE of Damascus and conquered all the way to the Upper Euphrates. David fought several battles with him and after defeating him put a garrison in Damascus and took tribute from him (2 Sam. 8:3-8; 10:6-14, 15-18; 1 Chron. 18:3-10).

HADAD RIMMON A combination of two names, Hadad and Rimmon. The first is the Amorite storm god, perhaps the god of thunder. The second is either another similar deity or a title for Hadad. A great mourning was made for this deity in the Valley of Megiddo (Zech. 12:11; cf. 2 Kgs. 5:18).

HADAR Variant of Hadad, 3, a king of Edom (Gen. 36:39).

HADASHAH A village in the tribal area of Judah in the western foothills (Josh. 15:37).

HADASSAH A Jewish girl who became the queen of the Persian king Xerxes (Esth. 2:7), who was instrumental in saving her people from their destruction planned by Haman.

HADES *See* DEAD, ABODE OF

HADID A village (145-152) in the tribal area of Benjamin at the NW corner of the western hill country together with Lydda and Ono and others that were at the mouth of the Valley of Aijalon (Ezra 2:33; Neh. 7:37), to which several hundred returned from the captivity in Babylon.

HADLAI Father of one of the chiefs of the Ephraimites (2 Chron. 28:12).

HADORAM 1. A descendant of Shem (Gen. 10:27; 1 Chron. 1:21).

2. Son of Tou the king of Hamath who was sent to congratulate David on his victory over the king of Zobah. Also called Joram (1 Chron. 18:10; 2 Sam. 8:9).

3. King Rehoboam's taskmaster over his labor force (2 Chron. 10:18, footnote).

HADRACH A town in the NW part of Lebanon (Zech. 9:1).

HAELEPH A word whose meaning is not certain, found only in Joshua 18:28. Some suggest that it is to be joined with the preceding word as a proper noun, name of an unidentified place.

HAGAB The ancestor of a family that returned from the Babylonian captivity (Ezra 2:46).

HAGABA,
HAGABAH Ancestor or ancestors of some who returned from the Babylonian captivity with Zerubbabel (Neh. 7:48; Ezra 2:45).

HAGAR The Egyptian slave girl of Sarah, Abraham's wife, who was given to Abraham as a concubine. The son of this union was Ishmael who at Sarah's instigation was driven away. Ishmael became an ancestor of Arabs. His wife was an Egyptian. Paul uses Sarah and Hagar figuratively of the difference between law and grace (Gen. 16:1, 4, 15; 21:14; Gal. 4:24, 25).

HAGGAI,
BOOK OF *See* PROPHETS, MINOR

HAGGEDOLIM Father of one of the overseers in the time of Nehemiah after the return from the Babylonian captivity (Neh. 11:14).

HAGGI A son of Gad (Gen. 46:16; Num. 26:15).

HAGGIAH A descendant of Levi (1 Chron. 6:30).

HAGGITH A wife of David and mother of Adonijah who tried to take the throne in place of Solomon to whom David had promised it (2 Sam. 3:4; 1 Kgs. 1:5, 11; 2:13).

HAGRI Father of one of David's mighty men (1 Chron. 11:38).

HAGRITE A nomadic tribe living east of the Jordan in Moab, descendants of Hagar, and enemies of Israel. The Reubenites conquered them (1 Chron. 5:10, 19, 20; Ps. 83:6). One of them was overseer of David's flocks (1 Chron. 27:30).

HAHIROTH The same as Pi Hahiroth (Num. 33:8, footnote).

HAIL 1. A greeting used only in the Gospels (Jn. 19:3).

2. Hailstorms are recorded in the Bible as doing much damage to crops and to life of men and animals. They are often accompanied with violent wind, rain, or snow (Ex. 9:18-34; Josh. 10:11; Ezek. 38:22; Isa. 30:30; Ps. 148:8). This was a phenomenon of nature God often used to punish the people.

HAIR Nazirites, Samson, and others were never allowed to cut their hair. It may be that long hair was preferred by Israelite men (Num. 6:1, 5; Judg. 13:5; 2 Sam. 14:25, 26). It was forbidden to the men of Israel to cut the corners of the beard, the hair above and to the face side of the ear (Lev. 19:27). Today the *pe'ot* or "prayer-locks" reflect this commandment. In the NT, however, long hair on men was considered a disgrace (1 Cor. 11:14). Hair turning white quickly on the body could be a sign of leprosy, but if there was no raw flesh then the leprosy was considered healed. Thin yellow hair was symptom of another disease, not leprosy but related to it (Lev. 13:9-17, 29-37; 14:9).

HAKILAH A hill somewhere in the region of Hebron where David hid from King Saul (1 Sam. 23:19; 26:1-3).

HAKKATAN A man that came up from the Babylonian captivity with Ezra (Ezra 8:12).

HAKKOZ 1. One of the priests mentioned in the divisions of the "sons of Aaron" (1 Chron. 24:10).

2. One of the priests coming back after the exile in Babylon with Zerubbabel who could not find his family record (Ezra 2:61).

HAKUPHA Ancestor of some temple servants who returned with Zerubbabel from the Babylonian captivity (Ezra 2:51).

HALAH A town in Assyria on the Habor River where the Assyrian king exiled some of the Israelite captives (2 Kgs. 17:6; 18:11).

HALAK, MOUNT OF The southern limit of the conquest of Joshua, a mountain ridge (Josh. 11:16, 17).

HALHUL A town (160-109) in the hill country of Judah near Hebron (Josh. 15:58).

HALI A town (162-241) on the southern border of the tribe of Asher (Josh. 19:25).

HALL A room hall or pillared porch (colonnade) for living or eating or an audience room for judgment (1 Kgs. 7:6, 7; Dan. 5:10; Acts 25:23).

HALLELUJAH A word used widely in the Bible and transliterated in basically this form into many languages; a Hebrew word consisting of two parts, *hallelu* meaning "praise ye (plural)" and *ya*, a shortened form for the word for Lord or God.

HALLOHESH Father of one who worked on Nehemiah's wall and perhaps the same as one who signed the covenant with Nehemiah (Neh. 3:12; 10:24).

HALLOW *See* HOLINESS

HAM 1. A son of Noah and father of Cush, Egypt, Put, and

Canaan. See further on each of these four. While they may
have all been dark skinned they were not the progenitors of
the negroid races, but rather of peoples associated with
Egypt in the north of the continent of Africa. The Egyptians
thought of Canaan as one of their provinces even into very
late times (Gen. 5:32; 10:6; Ps. 105:23, 27).

2. Another name for Egypt as in Ps. 105:23.

3. A city (226-213) of the Zuzim, situated on the King's
Highway. Not related to the son of Noah (Gen. 14:5).

HAMAN The enemy of the Jews in the days of Esther who endeavored
to have them all destroyed. He himself was hanged on the
gallows he prepared for Mordecai, the uncle of Queen Esther
(Esth. 3:1—7:10).

HAMATH 1. *See* GEOGRAPHY OF THE HOLY LAND.

2. A very ancient and important town situated on the Orontes
River in northern Syria. Its start was in neolithic times
according to its excavators. The Israelite spies went that far
north (Num. 13:21), but the Israelites did not control it
until the time of Jeroboam II of Israel who "recovered" it for
Israel (2 Kgs. 14:28).

HAMATH ZOBAH An unidentified town known by this name, by the name
Zobah, or even by the name of Hamath, belonging to the
kingdom of Zobah. Mentioned only once (2 Chron. 8:3).

HAMMATH 1. A city (201-241) in the tribal area of Naphtali located on
the western shore of the Sea of Galilee (Josh. 19:35).

2. Archaeologists know a Hammath in the Jordan valley
south of Beth-Shan (197-197).

3. A town or area from which came the Kenites who were
descended from Caleb (1 Chron. 2:55).

HAMMEDATHA Father of the villain of the Book of Esther, Haman (Esth.
3:1).

HAMMER These were of two types, the hammer proper or the mallet
for driving tent pegs, both are called hammers in the NIV.
Figuratively the hammer is the instrument God on occasion
uses in punishment (Jer. 23:29; Judg. 4:21) called "war club"
in Jer. 51:20.

HAMMOLEKETH Sister of Gilead and ancestress of several groups in the tribe
of Manasseh (1 Chron. 7:18).

HAMMON 1. A place (164-281) in the tribal area of Asher south of Tyre
(Josh. 19:28).

2. A Levitical city in Naphtali of unidentified location (1 Chron. 6:76).

HAMMOTH DOR An unidentified city of Naphtali (Josh. 21:32).

HAMMUEL A descendant of Simeon (1 Chron. 4:26).

HAMONAH An unidentified city where the hosts of Gog are to be destroyed after an unsuccessful attack on Israel (Ezek. 39:16).

HAMON GOG A valley which is to be set aside for the burial of the dead after the battle of Gog against Israel (Ezek. 39:11, 15).

HAMOR The father of the Shechem who violated Dinah, Jacob's daughter. Abraham bought there a burial plot from his sons (Gen. 33:19; Acts 7:16).

HAMRAN *See* HEMDAN

HAMUL A descendant of Judah through Perez (Gen. 46:12).

HAMUTAL The mother of King Jehoahaz of Judah (2 Kgs. 23:31).

HANAMEL A cousin of the prophet Jeremiah (Jer. 32:7-9).

HANAN 1. A descendant of Benjamin (1 Chron. 8:23).

2. A later descendant of Benjamin through Saul (1 Chron. 8:38).

3. One of David's mighty men (1 Chron. 11:43).

4. A man of God who lived in the temple (Jer. 35:4).

5. An ancestor of some temple servants who came back from the Babylonian captivity (Ezra 2:46).

6. A Levite who helped others to understand the law (Neh. 8:7).

7, 8, and 9. Levites who signed the covenant with Nehemiah (Neh. 10:10, 22, 26).

10. An assistant to one of Nehemiah's treasurers (Neh. 13:13).

HANANEL, TOWER OF A tower on the north wall of Jerusalem. Both Jeremiah and Zechariah predicted it would be rebuilt (Jer. 31:38; Neh. 3:1; Zech. 14:10).

HANANI 1. Father of the prophet Jehu who rebuked both Baasha and Asa king of Judah. Asa put him in prison for it (1 Kgs. 16:1, 7; 2 Chron. 16:7, 10).

2. A Levite musician in David's day (1 Chron. 25:4).

3. A musician in Nehemiah's day (Neh. 12:36).

4. A brother of Nehemiah who brought him news to Babylon and was later made a ruler in Jerusalem (Neh. 1:2; 7:2).

HANANIAH 1. A priest denounced by Jeremiah for falsely prophesying and whose death he predicted (Jer. 28:1-17).

2. Father of an official by the name of Zedekiah in Jeremiah's day (Jer. 36:12).

3. Grandfather of the captain of the guard Irijah who seized the prophet Jeremiah (Jer. 37:13).

4. One of Daniel's three friends to whom the Babylonians gave the name Shadrach (Dan. 1:6, 7).

5. A descendant of Benjamin (1 Chron. 8:24).

6. A Levite musician in David's day (1 Chron. 25:4).

7. One of King Uzziah's royal officials (2 Chron. 26:11).

8. A son of Zerubbabel who was in the royal line (1 Chron. 3:19).

9. One who returned from the captivity (Ezra 10:28).

10 and 11. Two who helped Nehemiah build the wall of Jerusalem (Neh. 3:30; 7:2, see footnote).

12. A leader who signed the covenant with Nehemiah (Neh. 10:23).

13. Head of a priestly family in the days of Joiakim (Neh. 12:12).

14. A priest who was present at Nehemiah's dedication of the walls of Jerusalem (Neh. 12:41).

HANDBREADTH *See* WEIGHTS AND MEASURES

HANES A city of Egypt mentioned in the Bible only in Isaiah 30:4.

HANGING Capital punishment, death by strangulation, is not taught in the Scriptures. The custom in those times was to give additional degradation to a criminal by hanging the corpse, after death, over specially erected posts or from a tree. Pharaoh's servant was killed and then hanged (Gen. 40:19). The same is reflected in the Deuteronomic law (Deut. 21:22, 23). Ahithophel and Judas Iscariot committed suicide by hanging themselves (2 Sam. 17:23; Mt. 27.5).

HANNAH The mother of the prophet Samuel (2 Sam. 1, 2).

HANNATHON A city (174-243) on the northern border of Zebulun (Josh. 19:14).

HANNIEL 1. A descendant of Asher, Jacob's son (1 Chron. 7:39).

2. The representative from the tribe of Manasseh involved in the dividing of the land among the tribes (Num. 34:23).

HANOCH 1. A grandson of Abraham by Keturah (Gen. 25:4).

2. A son of Reuben, Jacob's first son (Gen. 46:9).

HANUKKAH *See* DEDICATION, FEAST OF

HANUN 1. An Ammonite king who insulted King David's messengers and so brought war on himself (2 Sam. 10:1-17).

2 and 3. Two who repaired the wall of Jerusalem with Nehemiah (Neh. 3:13, 30).

HAPHARAIM A city (192-223) in Issachar (Josh. 19:19).

HAPPIZZEZ A descendant of Aaron and the name of one responsible for duties as a temple priest (1 Chron. 24:15).

HARA An unidentified place to which some of the Israelite captives were taken by the Assyrians (1 Chron. 5:26).

HARADAH An unidentified stop on the Israelite exodus route from Egypt (Num. 33:24, 25).

HARAN 1. Abraham's brother and father of Lot (Gen. 11:26-32).

2. A son of Caleb (1 Chron. 2:46).

3. A Levite who lived in the days of David and Solomon (1 Chron. 23:9).

4. A city in N Mesopotamia to which Abraham's family moved and from which Abraham himself emigrated to Palestine after his father's death. Both Isaac and Jacob got their wives from a family that remained in Haran (Gen. 11:31; 24:4; 27:43; 29:4, 5; Acts 7:2-4).

HARARITE Three of the mighty men of David had fathers who were Hararites. This was either the name of a tribe or an area (2 Sam. 23:11; 1 Chron. 11:34, 35).

HARBONA A eunuch of the Persian king Xerxes who suggested the hanging of Haman (Esth. 1:10; 7:9).

HAREM A word used only in Esther referring to the abode of the women at the court of the Persian king (Esth. 2:3-14).

HAREPH A descendant of Caleb and Hur (1 Chron. 2:51).

HARHAIAH The father of a goldsmith who worked with

Nehemiah to rebuild the walls of Jerusalem (Neh. 3:8).

HARHAS Grandfather of the husband of the prophetess Huldah, also called Hasrah (2 Kgs. 22:14; 2 Chron. 34:22).

HARHUR Ancestor of some of the temple servants who returned from the Babylonian captivity with Zerubbabel (Ezra 2:51).

HARIM 1. Head of a priestly division in David's time (1 Chron. 24:8).

2. Some men who returned with Zerubbabel from the Babylonian captivity came from this town. They had foreign women (Ezra 2:32; 10:31).

3. Ancestor of some priests in the same condition as the men of 2 above (Ezra 2:39; 10:21). A descendant was a head of a priestly family in the days of Joiakim (Neh. 12:15).

4 and 5. Two who signed the covenant with Nehemiah (Neh. 10:5, 27).

HARIPH 1. His descendants came back from the Babylonian captivity with Zerubbabel, also called Jorah (Neh. 7:24; Ezra 2:18).

2. One who signed the covenant with Nehemiah (Neh. 10:19).

HARMON An unidentified place noted only in Amos 4:3 (*see* NIV footnote).

HARNEPHER A descendant of Asher (1 Chron. 7:36).

HAROD, HARODITE 1. A spring at the foot of Mount Gilboa where God selected 300 from Gideon's fighting men (Judg. 7:1-7).

2. Either the clan of, or more probably the place from which came, two of David's mighty men (2 Sam. 23:25; 1 Chron. 11:27). In the Chronicles passage he is called the Harorite.

HAROEH A descendant of Judah (1 Chron. 2:52).

HARORITE *See* HAROD

HAROSHETH HAGOIM An unidentified site from which came Sisera, Jabin's army captain (Judg. 4:2, 13, 16).

HARP *See* MUSIC

HARROW A farming practice in the ancient world the nature of which is not exactly known but it is connected with breaking up the soil (Isa. 28:24).

HARSHA Ancestor of some temple servants who returned from the Babylonian captivity with Zerubbabel (Ezra 2:52).

HART *See* BEASTS

HARUM Father of a clan leader in Judah (1 Chron. 4:8).

HARUMAPH The father of one who helped Nehemiah rebuild the wall of Jerusalem (Neh. 3:10).

HARUPHITE The designation of one of the men who joined David at Ziklag (1 Chron. 12:5). He came either from the clan or place Haruph.

HARUZ The grandfather of King Amon of Judah (2 Kgs. 21:19).

HARVEST, FEAST OF *See* FESTIVALS and CALENDAR

HASADIAH A son of Zerubbabel in the royal line (1 Chron. 3:20).

HASHABIAH A common name particularly for priests and Levites; so much is this so that it is possible that there is some duplication below.

1. The ancestor of Ethan whom David made a temple singer (1 Chron. 25:3).

2. Another musician, son of Jeduthan in David's time (1 Chron. 25:3).

3. One of the officers in charge of the temple treasure in David's time. He was from Hebron (1 Chron. 26:30).

4. One of David's officers over the tribe of Levi (1 Chron. 27:17).

5. A Levite official in the time of King Josiah (2 Chron. 35:9).

6. A Levite who returned with Ezra from the Babylonian captivity (Ezra 8:19).

7. The ancestor of a Levite who came back from the Babylonian captivity (1 Chron. 9:14).

8. One worked on the wall of Jerusalem with Nehemiah next to some Levites (Neh. 3:17).

9. A Levite who signed the covenant with Nehemiah (Neh. 10:11).

10. The grandfather of a gatekeeper among the new servants of Jerusalem in the days of Nehemiah (Neh. 11:22).

11. A head of a priestly family in the days of Joiakim (Neh. 12:21).

12. A leader of the Levites in Nehemiah's day (Neh. 12:24).

HASHABNAH One who signed the covenant with Nehemiah (Neh. 10:25).

HASHABNEIAH 1. The father of one who repaired the walls of Jerusalem with Nehemiah (Neh. 3:10).

2. A Levite who commanded the people to praise God (Neh. 9:5).

HASHBADDANA One who stood with Ezra when the law was read to the people (Neh. 8:4).

HASHEM The father of some of David's mighty men; also called Jashan (1 Chron. 11:34; 2 Sam. 23:32).

HASHMONAH An unidentified stop of the Israelites in their exodus from Egypt (Num. 33:29, 30).

HASHUBAH A son of Zerubbabel (1 Chron. 3:20).

HASHUM 1. Ancestor of some who returned from the Babylonian captivity with Zerubbabel who had married a foreign wife (Ezra 2:19; 10:33).

2. One who stood with Ezra when the law was read (Neh. 8:4).

3. One who signed the covenant with Nehemiah (Neh. 10:18).

HASMONEANS *See also* CHRONOLOGY, MACCABEES and SELEUCIDS

In 168 B.C., when Antiochus IV of Syria outlawed Jewish religious practices and attempted to substitute a Hellenistic culture in Israel (*see* SELEUCIDS), an elderly priest named Mattathias, of the Hasmonean family, revolted in the Jewish village of Modin (1 Macc. 2:1). He refused pagan sacrifice and slew a Jew who yielded. The death of the officiating Syrian followed, and Mattathias issued his ringing declaration of war, "Whosoever is zealous for the law, and maintaineth the covenant, let him come forth after me" (v. 27). He roused the pious in Israel to guerilla attack against both Syrians and apostate Jews. Mattathias died in 167, but he appointed his son Judas as leader who succeeded, at the end of two years, in driving back the pagans and cleansing the temple in Jerusalem from its abominations (*see* MACCABEES). After Judas had fallen in battle in 161, the remaining Hasmonean brothers fought on to achieve a corresponding political independence.

Jonathan (161-143 B.C., 1 Macc. 9:23—12:53) followed Judas as the guerilla leader and began to regain power. Three years later, in 158, the Greek general Bacchides, who had crushed Judas, answered the appeal of the Jewish Hellenizers and returned to Israel. But he could not break Jonathan, who was able to gain a truce. Thus, left alone, Jonathan proceeded to destroy the Greek sympathizers from among the Jews (1 Macc. 9:58-73). In 153, Alexander Balas, who was a contender for the Syrian throne, sought to gain the support of Jonathan by appointing him to be high priest of Israel (10:1-66). Later, another contender, Tryphon, treacherously captured Jonathan and put him to death. But the struggle was continued by Simon, the last of the sons of Mattathias. In 143 B.C., Tryphon's rival Demetrius II granted to Simon the national sovereignty that was the goal of the Hasmoneans (13:36-43).

As an independent high priest, Simon in 142 struck coins, starved out the Syrian garrison that still remained in the citadel at Jerusalem, and built up Judea (13:51). He was confirmed in his position by the Romans (14:16-24). In 135 both Simon and his sons Judas and Mattathias were murdered by his son-in-law Ptolemy.

John Hyrcanus I (135-105 B.C.), the surviving son of Simon, drove out Ptolemy but was temporarily subdued by Antiochus VII of Syria (for the political relationships of this period, see SELEUCIDS). Having recovered his position, Hyrcanus I established it by a treaty with Rome, on the strength of which he conquered the east of the Jordan, Idumea, and Samaria. He destroyed the Samaritan temple on Mt. Gerizim in 128.

Aristobulus I (105-104), son of Hyrcanus I, shared the rule with his brother, Antigonus I, but soon murdered him. Though Hyrcanus I may have sought the title of king, it is Aristobulus I who is first known to have assumed it. Despite cruelties and Hellenistic sympathy he ruled well and added Galilee, which he compelled to Judaize. Strict Jews opposed his kingship as non-Davidic.

Alexander Jannaeus (104-78 B.C.), another brother of Aristobulus I, was designated king by the latter's widow, Alexandra, whom he proceeded to marry. By constant warfare he enlarged the kingdom even further, but he was personally unfit to be a high priest and faced wide opposition.

In 95 B.C. the rising nation of the Nabatean Arabs under Aretas III extended their power to Damascus and defeated Alexander, who had to make concessions. The geographical expansion of the Hasmoneans was at an end. Seven years later Alexandra (78-69), his widow, succeeded as regent, though their son Hyrcanus II acted as high priest. The party of the Pharisees through their domination of the Sanhedrin held the actual rule.

Upon the death of Alexandra, Aristobulus II (69-63) displaced the rightful succession of his brother Hyrcanus II. But Antipater, a governor in Idumea, stirred up Hyrcanus II to make an alliance with Aretas and attack Aristobulus II. When the Roman general Pompey intervened, Aristobulus II resisted. The Romans took the citadel in Jerusalem after a three-month siege, and in 63 B.C. Hasmonean independence came to an end. Judea was reduced in size, Hyrcanus II was retained only as high priest and "ethnarch" under the province of Syria, and many Jews were taken captive to Rome. Antipater continued as the power behind the mild Hyrcanus II.

But then Antigonus II, a son of Aristobulus II, took Jerusalem with Parthian (Persian) help and deposed Hyrcanus II. Antipater's son Herod, who had married a granddaughter of Hyrcanus, fled to Rome to promote the cause of his young brother-in-law Aristobulus III but was himself appointed king. Backed by Roman troops, Herod recaptured Jerusalem in 37 and Antigonus II was executed. Aristobulus III served briefly as high priest, but with his murder at the hands of the suspicious Herod the Hasmonean dynasty came to an end.

HASMONEAN PRIEST-KINGS

Mattathias
(167-166)

John	Simon	Judas	Eleazar	Jonathan
	(143-135)	(167-161)		(161-144)

Judas	John Hyrcanus I	Mattathias	Daughter married
	(135-105)		Ptolemy

Aristobulus I	Antigonus I	Alexander Jannaeus
(105-104)	(105)	(104-78)
		married Alexandra
		(78-69)

Hyrcanus II	Aristobulus II
(63-40)	(69-63)
Alexandra married Alexander	Antigonus II
(daughter of Hyrcanus II) (son of Aristobulus II)	(40-37)
	Mariamne, married	Aristobulus III
	Herod the Great	(36-35)

End of Hasmonean Dynasty

(J.B.P.)

HASRAH *See* HARHAS

HASSENAAH Father of those who built the Fish Gate in the days of Nehemiah (Neh. 3:3).

HASSENUAH An ancestor of the Benjamites who returned from the Babylonian captivity (1 Chron. 9:7).

HASSHUB 1 and 2. Two who helped Nehemiah in the repair of the wall of Jerusalem (Neh. 3:11, 23).

3. One who signed the covenant with Nehemiah (Neh. 10:23).

4. Father of a Levite who lived in Jerusalem after the return from the captivity (Neh. 11:15).

HASSOPHERETH Descendant of some of Solomon's servants who returned from the Babylonian captivity with Zerubbabel, called Sophereth also (Ezra 2:55; Neh. 7:57).

HASUPHA Ancestor of some temple servants who returned from the Babylonian captivity with Zerubbabel (Ezra 2:43).

HATHACH A eunuch who waited on the Persian Queen Esther (Esth. 4:5).

HATHATH A descendant of Judah and David (1 Chron. 4:13).

HATIPHA Ancestor of a temple servant who returned with Zerubbabel from Babylon (Ezra 2:54).

HATITA Ancestor of a gatekeeper who returned from the Babylonian captivity with Zerubbabel (Ezra 2:42).

HATTIL Ancestor of one of Solomon's servants who returned from the Babylonian captivity with Zerubbabel (Ezra 2:57).

HATTUSH 1. A descendant of David who came back from the Babylonian captivity with Ezra (Ezra 8:2).

2. One who helped Nehemiah repair the wall of Jerusalem (Neh. 3:10).

3. One who signed the covenant with Nehemiah (Neh. 10:4).

4. A priest who returned with Zerubbabel from the captivity (Neh. 12:2).

HAURAN *See* GEOGRAPHY OF THE HOLY LAND

HAVENS *See* FAIR HAVENS

HAVILAH 1. A descendant of Noah, Ham, and Cush (Gen. 10:7).

2. A descendant of Shem (Gen. 10:29).

3. An unidentified land where there was gold and around which the unidentified river Pishon flowed (Gen. 2:11).

4. The Ishmaelites lived in a land by this name located "from Havilah to Shur, near the border of Egypt or toward Asshur" (Gen. 25:18).

HAVVOTH JAIR A cluster of villages that were taken by Jair the son of Manasseh in Gilead (Num. 32:41).

HAWK *See* BIRDS, 5

HAZAEL When Ben-Hadad the king of Syria was sick he sent his servant Hazael to the prophet Elisha who told Hazael that Ben-Hadad would die and that he would be the next king of Syria (2 Kgs. 8:7, 8, 13). After ascending the throne Hazael attacked the two and a half tribes of Israel east of the Jordan, and then Judah itself (2 Kgs. 10:32; 12:17, 18).

HAZAIAH A descendant of Judah who lived in Jerusalem after the return from the Babylonian captivity (Neh. 11:5).

HAZAR ADDAR A city (100-999) on the southern border of the tribal area of Judah (Num. 34:4); also called Addar (Josh. 15:3).

HAZAR ENAN 1. A village on the northern border of Israel (Num. 34:9, 10).

2. A place on the northern boundary of Damascus with the border of Hamath to the north (Ezek. 47:17; 48:1).

HAZAR GADDAH An unidentified southern town in the tribal area of Judah (Josh. 15:27).

HAZARMAVETH A descendant of Shem (Gen. 10:26).

HAZAR SHUAL An unidentified town in the tribal area of Judah (Josh. 15:28).

HAZAR SUSAH, An unidentified town in the tribal area of Judah which was
HAZAR SUSIM given later to Simeon (Josh. 19:5), also called Hazar Susim (1 Chron. 4:31).

HAZER Mentioned only in Ezekiel; a place on the border in his vision
HATTICON of the future Israel (Ezek. 47:16).

HAZEROTH A stopping place of the Israelites on their exodus from Egypt. Aaron and Miriam rebelled against Moses here (Num. 11:35; 12:1-16).

HAZEZON A city (173-024) in the Wadi Arabah south of the Salt Sea,
TAMAR, formerly thought to be on the western shore of the Sea itself
HAZAZON (Gen. 14:7; 2 Chron. 20:2).
TAMAR

HAZIEL A Levite who served David in his latter years (1 Chron. 23:1, 9).

HAZO An uncle of Rebekah (Gen. 22:22).

HAZOR 1. A Canaanite royal city (203-269) and the head of all the kingdoms of that area in the time of Joshua, conquered and sacked by the Israelites (Josh. 11:10-13; 12:19). Later King Jabin who reigned in Hazor was defeated by Deborah and Barak (Judg. 4:3, 17). King Solomon rebuilt it as a grain storage center and it remained in Israelite hands until taken by the Assyrians in 732 B.C. (1 Kgs. 9:15; 2 Kgs. 15:29). Archaeologists have discovered twenty-one strata going back to Chalcolithic times, a fine example of a Solomonic gate, and several temples of importance, together with a massive and unusual water system within the acropolis area itself.

2. A town in the Negev in the tribal area of Judah also called Kirioth Hezron (Josh. 15:23, 25). *See* KIRIOTH HEZRON.

3. An unidentified town N of Jerusalem occupied by Benjamites after the return from the Babylonian captivity (Neh. 11:33).

4. An unidentified place attacked by Nebuchadnezzar, King of Babylon (Jer. 49:28-33).

HAZOR HADATTAH An unidentified site in the southernmost part of the tribal area of Judah (Josh. 15:25).

HAZZELELPONI, HAZELELPONI A woman descended from Judah (1 Chron. 4:3).

HEALING, HEALTH Some six or more Hebrew and Greek words are used in the Bible to refer to health with the basic idea of being whole or complete or of well-being, safety, and peace. One of the words in each testament is translated in some cases as "salvation." That word in the OT is the same root as the proper names "Joshua" and "Jesus." It is frequently rendered "deliver," "deliverance" or "rescue" (Ps. 3:8; Phil. 1:19; Acts 7:25). Its uses to refer to physical salvation and deliverance, which would include deliverance to health, are many (Isa. 33:2; Jonah 2:9; 1 Sam. 2:1; Isa. 25:9). Words or concepts rendered "health" are also used figuratively or in the sense of spiritual health and healing (Jer. 30:17; 1 Pet. 2:24; Mt. 13:15). For a description of the diseases noted in the Bible *see* SICK, SICKNESS. These are in the body, including demon possession or mental problems.

Healing may be the restoration to normalcy of these organic or psychological disorders. Probably in the great majority of cases this healing was by natural means, because of the lack of scientific knowledge of the causes of disease, and of medicine or therapy. There are, however, very many cases in both Testaments of miraculous healings, where the healing is attributed to the direct intervention of God or through one of his servants (Num. 12:9-16; 2 Kgs. 4:32-37; Lk. 4:40; 7:11-15; Acts 3:1-8, 16; 9:36-40; 28:8). These were not just cases of healing for the sake of healing. They were for the purpose of attestation of the healer, of his relationship to God, and of the power of God. With the close of the period during which God thus spoke to the world through prophets, and with the close of the period of the writing of Scripture, this phenomenon was much less frequent even though it has not ceased to this day.

One part of the health question that should not be overlooked is the matter of hygiene and sanitation. The first five books of the Bible show a wealth of information about selection and inspection of foods, clean and unclean foods, methods of slaughter, control of certain infectious diseases, disposal of sewage and even corpses, water supply, bathing, personal and public hygiene. One may even find suggestions which, if followed, would lead to good mental health and the prevention of bad mental health by such means as thoughtful care of the more needy and intra-family attitudes.

HEART *See also* EMOTIONS. The word occurs hundreds of times in the Bible but almost exclusively in a figurative sense (Ps. 119:2; Prov. 6:18; Judg. 5:16; Ps. 4:4; Mt. 15:19; Lk. 2:19). The heart is the seat of almost all of the human emotions: sadness and gladness, fearfulness and confidence, loving and hating, good and bad desires (Neh. 2:2; Isa. 35:4; 2 Chron. 17:6; Ps. 105:25; Acts 14:17; Rom. 1:24; 10:1). It is translated in the NIV also as "mind" and "idea" (Isa. 46:8; Num. 16:28) as well as literally (Neh. 4:6).

HEAVEN *See* DEAD, ABODE OF

HEBER 1. Grandson of Asher (Gen. 46:17).

2. The husband of the Jael who killed Sisera (Judg. 4:11).

3. A descendant of Judah and Caleb (1 Chron. 4:18).

4. A descendant of Benjamin (1 Chron. 8:17).

HEBREW A term used by Israelites and foreigners alike in reference to the descendants of Abraham (Gen. 14:13; 39:17; Jer. 34:9). Whether they originate with Eber (Gen. 10:21) or with Abraham is debated. Their language is that of the OT, a dialect of NW Semitic and particularly of Canaanite. Their religion is, of course, that presented in the OT.

**HEBREWS,
BOOK OF** Hebrews does not tell us the name of the author nor the location of the recipients. However, the identity of the writer seems well known to his reader (13:19, 22, 23). The ancient tradition of Pauline authorship is early and not to be ignored, though it has been widely rejected in modern times. Pauline influence and material are recognized in the book, and recent critical estimates of its date (about A.D. 63) bring it within the range of Paul's life.

The letter must have been written before the fall of the temple in A.D. 70. The language of 8:4, 9:6, and 10:1 seems to contemplate the temple ritual as going on.

The epistle is written to a group of people who know their OT and who seem to have had intimate knowledge of Christian beginnings but whose faith was wavering and who needed encouragement to faith and patience. The exact situation they faced is not revealed in detail, but the argument of Hebrews seems to be directed against the doctrine of salvation by Levitical priesthood and sacrifice. The categorical statement of 10:4 and 10:11 that the blood of bulls and goats cannot take away sins would imply that the idea was in the minds of the readers. 7:11 and 7:12, by the phrasing as a contrary-to-fact condition, sharply negates the idea that there was "perfection" (salvation) by the Levitical priesthood.

Assuming this basic problem in the mind of the readers leads to a helpful analysis of the contents of the book. There is apparently an eager interest in pointing out the gospel in the OT, and it is assumed that the readers would accept the identification of Jesus as the Son of God, "the same yesterday and today and forever" (13:8). The key argument of Hebrews is that if Jesus and the gospel were known to OT believers, then it is a misinterpretation of the OT to expect "perfection" or salvation by Levitical priesthood and sacrifice.

The main argument of Hebrews runs from 1:1 through 10:18 and the remainder is a powerful exhortation. The argument alternates with a series of warnings and pleas. The series of argumentative portions are: 1:1-14; 2:5—3:6; 4:14—5:10; 7:1—10:18. Christ, the eternal Son of God, is the true and proper High Priest of his people, who took flesh and blood that he might bring many sons into glory through sufferings. He is the Son of God's house, whose house we are, the word "we" including believers of all ages.

He is qualified as High Priest by divine appointment based on sonship. Though the language of chapter 7 is subtle and allusive, the divine attribute of eternal being seems to be Melchizedek, and hence he must be regarded as the Son of God in a preincarnation theophany. If this eternal priest received tithes from Abraham and gave blessing to Abraham, then Abraham's descendants, the Levitical priests, must themselves be dependent on Melchizedek for salvation and cannot by their offerings bring eternal salvation to others. Christ then is the minister and surety of the everlasting covenant, serving in the greater and more perfect heavenly tabernacle, and offering the better sacrifice, even the sacrifice of himself. Having willingly offered this one sacrifice for sins forever, he has resumed his place at the right hand of God and "waits for his enemies to be made his footstool" (10:13).

There follows the moving exhortation to accept the salvation of this great High Priest, drawing near to God in the way opened by the death of Christ, and living a life of faith. So great is the work of our High Priest and so great the reward before us, "So do not throw away your confidence: it will be richly rewarded. You need to persevere so that when you have done the will of God, you will receive what he promised" (10:35, 36). The citation of the great text from Habakkuk, "The righteous will live by his faith" (Hab. 2:4), leads to the uniquely great display of men of faith (Heb. 11), with the ensuing application: "Therefore, since we are surrounded by such a great cloud of witnesses let us throw off everything that hinders and the sin which so easily entangles, and let us run with perseverance the race worked out for us . . ." (12:1, 2). Christ's example is presented for endurance and encouragement in discipline and trials. These great principles lead to the detailed ethical applications of chapter 13 in life and worship. The epistle concludes with the picture of Christ, the Great Shepherd of the sheep, brought again from the dead in the blood of the eternal covenant, equipping his people to do the will of God. (W.B.W.)

HEBRON 1. A city (160-103) SW of Jerusalem favored by nature with a good altitude, plenty of arable acreage, and an abundance of water. With such an endowment it doubtless has a very much older occupation than the written sources give it. Its earliest known name was Kiriath Arba, named for Arba who was the greatest man among the Anakites (Josh. 14:15). Its earlier archaeological record is unknown but the biblical account refers to its "founding" seven years before Zoan in Egypt thus giving the founding date of about 1700 B.C. (Gen. 23:2; Num. 13:22). Abraham tented in the vicinity and bought a burial place for Sarah his wife from a Hittite who lived there (Gen. 13:18; 23:2-20). The tradition of the burial of the patriarchs here is preserved to the present in the great mosque built over a cove in the city called by the Arabs today *el-Khalil*, the friend. The reference is to Abraham as the friend of the merciful one, the friend of God, a tradition well preserved in the Bible itself (Isa. 41:8; 2 Chron. 20:7; Jas. 2:23). At the time of the conquest under Joshua the city was taken by the Israelites and given to Caleb (Josh. 15:13, 14). Here too David was anointed to be king of Judah and

Israel (2 Sam. 2:4; 5:3). It became one of the important fortified cities of Judah in the days following King Solomon and was still occupied by the men of Judah after their return from the captivity in Babylon (2 Chron. 11:10; Neh. 11:25). In postbiblical times it became the fourthmost sacred place of the Muslim, was taken by the Crusaders, and later retaken by the Muslim.

2. A son of Kohath and an uncle of Moses and Aaron. He had the oversight of Israel for God and king west of the Jordan River in the days of King David (Ex. 6:18; 1 Chron. 26:30).

3. A descendant of Judah and of Caleb, but not the Caleb who was one of the twelve spies and the inheritor of Hebron above (1 Chron. 2:42, 43).

HEDGEHOG *See* BEASTS

HEGAI The king of Persia's eunuch in charge of all the women (Esth. 2:3).

HEIFER *See* BEASTS, 4 and RED HEIFER

HEIR The son of an owner of property. According to the NT picture presented in Galatians, sons were treated like slaves, under guardians until set at liberty by the father. Paul uses this to illustrate the relationship of men prior to their spiritual salvation, under bondage to law until set free by adoption as sons (Gal. 4:1-7). *See also* FIRSTBORN.

HELAH A wife of Ashhur of a clan of Judah (1 Chron. 4:5-7).

HELAM An unidentified site in Syria where David defeated their king Hadadezer (2 Sam. 10:15-19).

HELBAH An unidentified town in Asher (Judg. 1:31).

HELBON An unidentified site in the Damascus area mentioned for its wine (Ezek. 27:18).

HELDAI 1. David's military commander of the twelfth month (1 Chron. 27:15).

2. One who brought silver and gold to the prophet Zechariah to make a crown for the high priest Joshua (Zech. 6:10-14).

HELEB Some think him the same as Heldai in 1 above (2 Sam. 23:29ff.).

HELECH Thought by some to be the name of an area in SE Asia Minor. Noted only once in the NIV (Ezek. 27:11).

HELED Heldai (1 Chron. 27:15), a Netophathite. Heled is one of David's mighty men (2 Sam. 23:29).

HELEK A descendant of Manasseh (Num. 26:30).

HELEPH A town (189-236) on the border of Naphtali (Josh. 19:33).

HELEZ One of David's Thirty (2 Sam. 23:26; 1 Chron. 11:27; 27:10).

HELI The father of Joseph, the husband of Mary, of whom Jesus was born (Lk. 3:23).

HELIOPOLIS, ON The capital of an Egyptian province located near the place where Cairo is located today. As it was called *iwnw* by the Egyptians it came over into Hebrew as *on*. Called "the temple of the sun" in the text of the NIV, but see also the footnote to Jeremiah 43:13.

HELKAI A priest in the days of Joiakim (Neh. 12:15).

HELKATH A Levitical town (160-232) on the border of the tribal area of Asher (Josh. 19:25; 21:31) also called Hukok (1 Chron. 6:75).

HELKATH HAZZURIM A place in Gibeon where twelve of the young men of Abner met in a hand to hand fight with twelve of those of Joab. All were killed (2 Sam. 2:16).

HELL *See* DEAD, ABODE OF

HELMET *See* ARMS AND ARMOR

HELON The father of the head of the census for the tribe of Zebulun which was taken after leaving Egypt (Num. 1:9; 7:24-29).

HEMAN 1. A man whose wisdom was exceeded by that of Solomon (1 Kgs. 4:31).

2. A son of Zerah descended from Judah (1 Chron 2:6).

3. A descendant of Levi also called "the Ezrahite" in the title of Psalm 88, who was assigned to the ministry of music (1 Chron. 6:33; 15:17; 2 Chron. 5:12).

HEMDAN A descendant of Abraham through Ishmael's life (Gen. 36:26), also called Hamran in the footnote at 1 Chronicles 1:41.

HEN *See* BIRDS, 2

HENA A city on the Euphrates north of Babylon (2 Kgs. 18:34).

HENADAD Father of some Levites who came back from the Babylonian captivity and helped in the rebuilding of the temple and walls of Jerusalem. They were also signatories of the covenant with Nehemiah (Ezra 3:9; Neh. 3:18; 10:9).

HENNA *See* PLANTS, PERFUMES and SPICES

HEPHER 1. A city (141-197) conquered by Joshua on the west side of the Jordan River (Josh. 12:17; 1 Kgs. 4:10).

2. A descendant of Manasseh through Gilead (Num. 26:32).

3. A descendant of Judah (1 Chron. 4:6).

4. One of David's mighty men (1 Chron. 11:36).

HEPHZIBAH Mother of Manasseh, King of Judah (2 Kgs. 21:1).

HERDS *See* BEASTS, 4

HERES An unidentified pass east of the Jordan from which Gideon turned back from his pursuit of the Midianites (Judg. 8:13).

HERESH A descendant of Levi (1 Chron. 9:15).

HERESY Mentioned only once in the NIV and that time in the plural. A philosophy or sect the opposite of orthodoxy (2 Pet. 2:1). The Greek word, however, is several times rendered sect or party with the same connotation. Twice it is referred to Christianity (Acts 5:17; 24:5, 14; 28:22).

HERMAS A Christian at Rome to whom Paul sent greetings (Rom. 16:14).

HERMES *See* DEITIES

HERMOGENES A professed Christian who deserted Paul (2 Tim. 1:15).

HERMON, MOUNT Called by the Sidonians "Sirion" and by the Amorites "Senir" (Deut. 3:9; 1 Chron. 6:23; Ezek. 27:5). The Hebrew text once calls it "Siyon" (Deut. 4:48). *See also* GEOGRAPHY OF THE HOLY LAND.

HERODIANS *See* SECTS

HERODIAS The adulterous granddaughter of Herod the Great who was instrumental in getting John the Baptist beheaded (Mk. 6:17-19).

HERODION A Christian at Rome and relative of Paul to whom he sent greetings (Rom. 16:11).

HERODS, THE Antipater of Idumea was the power behind the weak Jewish high priest, Hyrcanus II (63-40 B.C.); *see* HASMONEANS. Having assisted Julius Caesar at a crucial point in a war against Egypt, Antipater was rewarded with the official procuratorship (oversight) of Israel in 47 B.C. He appointed his sons, Phasael and Herod, as governors respectively of Jerusalem and Galilee. When Antigonus II (40-37) took Jerusalem and deposed his uncle Hyrcanus II, Phasael committed suicide but Herod escaped to Rome, where he received appointment as king over Israel.

With the backing of Rome, this man now known as Herod the Great (37-4 B.C.) recaptured Jerusalem. After the decisive battle of Actium in 31, Herod managed to win the friendship of Augustus Caesar and was confirmed in his kingship. Through suspicion and jealousy Herod had murdered his uncle Joseph and a number of other relatives. In 29 B.C. he put his wife, Mariamne, to death, and later her mother Alexandra. Herod's oldest son, Antipater, slandered Herod's two sons by Mariamne and caused the execution of both in 7 B.C., but Antipater himself was caught attempting to poison Herod and was executed in the last days of his father's reign in 4 B.C.

Herod's Idumean (Edomite) ancestry created popular Jewish opposition from the start; and this increased with his ruthless suppression of all enemies. He oppressed the people to bribe his Roman masters; he was a strong Hellenist, without biblical religion. He erected many Greek buildings, even establishing the Greek cities of Caesarea and Sebaste (Samaria). Yet he sought to pacify his Jewish subjects by reconstructing the Jerusalem temple on magnificent lines, starting in 20 B.C. (compare John 2:20, to be dated A.D. 27). Herod kept peace and order; but his increasing cruelty and suspicion were climaxed at the close of his life by his attempt to kill Christ in the slaughter of the Bethlehem innocents (Mt. 2).

Upon the death of Herod the Great in 4 B.C., the rule was divided among three of his sons (Lk. 3:1). Archelaus was appointed ethnarch (ruler of the people) of Judea (4 B.C.—A.D. 6). At the first he killed 3,000 Jews in a Passover riot; and when he went to Rome for the kingship, the people opposed him (as in Jesus' parable in Luke 19:12-27) and the title was not granted. Joseph and Mary went to Nazareth to avoid him (Mt. 2:22). He was deposed and sent to Gaul for his cruelties and in his place were appointed Roman procurators from A.D. 6-41, including Pontius Pilate (26-36).

Herod Antipas (4 B.C.—A.D. 39), the most capable of the brothers, was made tetrarch (ruler of one-fourth) of Galilee and built his capital, Tiberias, on the Sea of Galilee. He divorced a daughter of Aretas IV of Arabia to marry his niece Herodias who had deserted her husband, Herod Philip,

another of the brothers but not a tetrarch. For this he was
condemned by John the Baptist (Mt. 14:4-12), whom he
killed. He was defeated by Aretas in 36, so that he had to
appeal to Rome for help. He thought that Jesus was John
risen from the dead (Mt. 14:2). Christ called him "that fox"
(Lk. 13:31, 32), and he participated in Pilate's trial of Christ
(Lk. 23:7-12). The third brother, Philip (4 B.C.—A.D. 34),
tetrarch of Trachonitis and other areas toward Damascus, is
noted chiefly for his enlarging of Paneas, which he named
Caesarea Philippi (Mt. 16:13).

Herod Agrippa I was a grandson of Herod the Great and
Mariamne, who went to Rome, became a personal friend
of Caesar Caligula, and supported his rise to emperor. Caligula
rewarded Agrippa with the tetrarchy of Trachonitis, vacant
since Philip's death in 34, with the added title of king three
years later. Herodias in envy incited her husband Antipas
to seek kingly status too, over Galilee. But Agrippa anticipated
the rivalry, had Antipas banished to Gaul, and himself
received Galilee in A.D. 39. Being in Rome at the time of
Caligula's murder in 41, he encouraged Claudius to take the
throne and was rewarded with Judea and Samaria. He was
now king over all the land once held by Herod the Great.
Herod Agrippa I was careful to observe the law and conciliate
the Jews; but part of this policy involved his murder of
James the apostle, brother of John, and his attempted murder
of Peter (Acts 12:1-19). God smote him in A.D. 44 for
accepting divine honors (Acts 12:20-23).

His son, Herod Agrippa II, was to have been made king;
but because of his youth (age 17) the procuratorship was
reinstituted. After the death of his uncle Herod, king of Chalcis
in Lebanon, Agrippa II was given the latter's kingdom in A.D.
48. Two years later he was transferred to Trachonitis, to
which parts of Galilee were added in 55. He was made
guardian of the Jerusalem temple and, with his licentious
sister-mistress, Bernice, heard Paul's defense before the
procurator Festus (Acts 25-26). Agrippa supported the Romans
in the Jewish wars of 66-70 and maintained a corrupt life in
Rome for thirty years thereafter. (J.B.P.)

HERON *See* BIRDS, 5

HESHBON A city (226-134) of the Moabites east of the Jordan which
was taken by Sihon the Amorite king. The Israelites took it
from the Amorites and it became the tribal area of the
Reubenites (Num. 21:21-31; Josh. 13:15-17). The city and
surrounding area changed hands between Israel and the
Moabites several times. The Moabite inscription adds details
to the biblical account (Judg. 11:26; 1 Sam. 12:9, 11).

HESHMON An unidentified town in the tribal area of Judah (Josh. 15:27).

HETH Descendant of Noah, Ham and Canaan and the ancestor of the Hittites (Gen. 10:15). One of the great peoples of biblical times.

HETHLON An unidentified place in Syria on the northern boundary of the Israel described in the final vision of the prophet Ezekiel (Ezek. 47:5; 48:1).

HEZEKIAH 1. See KINGS OF JUDAH AND ISRAEL.

2. An ancestor of the prophet Zephaniah (Zeph. 1:1).

3. The ancestor of some who returned from the Babylonian captivity with Zerubbabel (Ezra 2:16).

4. A leader of the people who signed the covenant with Nehemiah (Neh. 10:17).

HEZION Grandfather of Ben-Hadad, king of Syria (1 Kgs. 15:18).

HEZIR 1. The head of one of the courses of the priests (1 Chron. 24:15).

2. One who signed the covenant with Nehemiah (Neh. 10:20).

HEZRO, HEZRAI One of David's Thirty men (2 Sam. 23:35).

HEZRON 1. An unidentified place on the southern border of Judah (Josh. 15:3).

2. A son of Reuben (Gen. 46:9).

3. A descendant of Judah (Gen. 46:12), whose name also appears in both the genealogies of Jesus (Mt. 1:3; Lk. 3:33).

HIDDAI One of David's Thirty men; also called Hurai (2 Sam. 23:30; 1 Chron. 11:32).

HIEL One from Bethel who rebuilt Jericho in the time of King Ahab and upon whom Joshua's curse fell (1 Kgs. 16:34; Josh. 6:26).

HIERAPOLIS A city in Asia in the territory of Phrygia in which Epaphras had labored, mentioned to the Colossians by Paul (Col. 4:12, 13).

HIGH PLACES Elevated places associated with the worship of pagan deities, in the Bible in particular association with Canaanite worship. The Israelites were commanded by the Lord through Moses to destroy all the high places after they entered the land west of the Jordan (Num. 33:52), and their failure to do this caused them to adopt idolatrous worship which ultimately resulted in their punishment by God and their being sent into foreign captivity. During intermittent times of revival under certain judges and kings they, as a part of their reforms, destroyed high places (1 Kgs. 12:32, 33; 2 Chron. 31:1; 33:3; 2 Kgs. 23). Prior to the building of the temple in Jerusalem the Israelites on occasion also made their sacrifices on high places, but to the Lord their God (1 Kgs. 3:2-5).

HIGH PRIEST *See* PRIESTS

HILEN *See* HOLON, 1

HILKIAH 1. The father of Eliakim who was King Hezekiah's palace administrator (2 Kgs. 18:18).

2. The high priest during the reign of King Josiah who found the Book of the Law and was sent by the king to the prophetess Huldah to inquire of the Lord. He was an ancestor of Ezra (2 Kgs. 22; Ezra 7:1).

3. An ancestor of Levi, musician in the temple (1 Chron. 6:45).

4. A grandson of Hosah who was among the capable men in David's day (1 Chron. 26:11).

5. One who stood beside Ezra as he read the law to the people (Neh. 8:4).

6. A leader of the priests who returned with Zerubbabel from the captivity in Babylon (Neh. 12:7).

7. Father of Jeremiah the prophet (Jer. 1:1).

8. Father of one of the men that King Zedekiah sent with a letter to Nebuchadnezzar in Babylon (Jer. 29:3).

HILL COUNTRY *See* GEOGRAPHY OF THE HOLY LAND

HILLEL Father of Abdon, one of the judges of Israel (Judg. 12:13).

HIN *See* WEIGHTS AND MEASURES

HIND *See* BEASTS

HINGE The Hebrew word rendered "hinges" in Proverbs 26:14 occurs only once in the Bible and hence its meaning is not certain. From its context it is assumed that it is some sort of "hinge." As we know from archaeologists, doors turned on parts that protruded from the top and bottom and fitted into sockets, but not on metal hinges as we know them today. The NIV renders other Hebrew words for "hinge" by "socket" (1 Kgs. 7:50).

HINNOM, VALLEY OF A literal translation of the text in some places would read "valley of the son of Hinnom." In the NIV it appears as Valley of Ben Hinnom (son of Hinnom on occasion, Ben being the Hebrew word for "son"). Nothing is known about this man except that he gave his name to the valley that runs south on the west side of the ridge on which is located today the ancient walled city of Jerusalem. The Hinnom runs south for about a half mile and then turns sharply east, cutting off the ridge entirely, joins the Kidron Valley, and together they run on south. This valley separated the tribal area of Judah, on the south of it, from that of Benjamin on the north (Josh. 14:8; Neh. 11:30). Here pagan cults burned their children to their gods in a part that came to be known as Topheth (Jer. 7:31; 32:35; 2 Kgs. 23:10). Even some Israelites were drawn into this pagan rite (2 Chron. 28:1-3). In the reforms of King Josiah the place was defiled by him and the burning of children was stopped (2 Kgs. 23:10).

The Hebrew words for this valley, *ge hinnom* or *ge ben hinnom*, were transliterated into Greek as Gehenna, and because of the fires that continually burned there the latter word was used to convey the concept of eternal hell fire in the teaching of Jesus. Of the twelve occurrences eleven are from the lips of Jesus. Usually rendered "the fire of hell!" which elsewhere is called eternal (Mt. 5:22; 18:9; 25:41).

HIRAH A friend of Judah who lived at Adullam (Gen. 38:1, 12).

HIRAM 1. A king of Tyre, a Phoenician, who helped David and Solomon with cedar and pine logs and laborers for the building of their palaces and the temple (2 Sam. 5:11; 1 Kgs. 5:8-12). Solomon built ships at Ezion Geber, and Hiram sent sailors who knew the sea to serve on Solomon's trading ships (2 Chron. 9:21). Solomon supplied Hiram with produce (1 Kgs. 5:10, 11) and gave him twenty cities which Hiram did not like. He is also called Huram (2 Chron. 2:3, footnote).

2. A man whose father was Phoenician and his mother Jewish who was a craftsman skilled in bronze work. King Soloman brought him to Jerusalem to work on the temple (1 Kgs. 7:13ff.). He is also called Huram (1 Kgs. 7:13ff.; 2 Chron. 4:11; 2:13).

HIRELING One hired as a laborer. The regulations concerning them were spelled out and reflected in the Bible, especially the prophets (Ex. 12:43-45; Job. 7:2; Mic. 3:5; Isa. 21:16).

HISTORY *See* ASSYRIA, BABYLONIA, CALENDAR, CHRONOLOGY, EGYPT, HASMONEANS, HERODS, JUDGES OF ISRAEL, KINGS OF JUDAH AND ISRAEL, PERSIA, ROME, ROMANS, SELEUCIDS, GEOGRAPHY OF THE HOLY LAND.

HITTITES One of the great powers of the ancient world at the time of Assyrian and Babylonian power (2 Kgs. 7:6; Josh. 1:4). During Bible times from Abraham on they were a prominent people throughout the land of Israel (Gen. 23:10; Ex. 23:23, 28; 2 Sam. 11:3-24; Neh. 9:8). Joshua overwhelmed them in his conquest of Palestine at the "waters of Merom" (Josh. 11:1-9). There was considerable intermarriage between the Israelites and the Hittites which the prophet condemned (Ezek. 16:3, 45). Some Hittites served under King David, and Solomon made them slaves (1 Sam. 26:6; 1 Kgs. 9:20, 21). Their empire ended with the fall of Carchemish to the Assyrians in 717 B.C. which is also reflected in the biblical record of King Hezekiah (2 Kgs. 19:13). Within the lifetime of modern biblical scholars the Hittites were written off by most with the words, "a people known only from the references to them in the Bible." Many even doubted their existence until the excavations of Hugo Winckler in 1906-07. Today we know more about them from extrabiblical sources than we do from the Bible, and that is quite considerable.

HIVITES A people whose identity is yet unknown. They were descended from Canaan and together with a number of other groups inhabited early Palestine (Gen. 10:17). The center of their population appears to have been in the area of Mount Hermon in Lebanon (Judg. 3:3; Josh. 11:3). King Solomon enslaved them together with the related groups (1 Kgs. 9:20, 21). Some equate the Hivites with the Horites and the Hittites. The problem is not yet resolved.

HIZKI A descendant of Benjamin (1 Chron. 8:17).

HIZKIAH A descendant of David and Solomon (1 Chron. 3:23).

HOBAB Jethro was the father-in-law of Moses (Ex. 18:1). The Numbers 10:29 passage is not sufficiently clear to let it be known whether Hobab or Reuel were other names for Jethro. One of them was called Moses' father-in-law in that text.

HOBAH An unidentified place N of Damascus to which Abraham pursued the captors of Lot (Gen. 14:15).

HOBAIAH One whose descendants could not find the family records after the return from the captivity in Babylon and so was excluded from the priesthood (Ezra 2:61, 62).

HOD A descendant of Asher (1 Chron. 7:37).

HODAVIAH 1, 2, and 3. Descendants of Manasseh, Benjamin, and David (1 Chron. 5:24; 9:7; 3:24).

4. Ancestor of some Levites who returned from the Babylonian captivity with Zerubbabel (Ezra 2:40; Neh. 7:43).

HODESH Wife of a descendant of Benjamin (1 Chron. 8:9).

HODIAH 1. A descendant of Judah (1 Chron. 4:19).

2. A Levite who helped to explain the Book of the Law of Moses as Ezra read it (Neh. 8:7).

3, 4, and 5. Three who signed the covenant with Nehemiah (Neh. 10:10, 13, 18).

HOGLAH The daughter of a descendant of Manasseh who had no sons for whom, therefore, a special inheritance law was made (Num. 26:33; 27:5-7).

HOHAM A king of Hebron, one of the five who allied themselves against Joshua and the Israelites, and lost his life because of it (Josh. 10:3, 22-26).

HOLINESS The basic concept in the words holy, holiness, hallow, sanctify, and sanctification is separation. In the Bible it is separation from sin and evil and separation unto God and his ways. Holiness is intended to be the character of the life of man who has entered into a personal relationship to God through faith. It also may refer to things separated to God for worship. From Exodus 3:5 to Revelation 22:19 the words "holy," "holiness," "sanctify" and their derivatives occur hundreds of times. God is holy as is his name and word, his Son and his Spirit (Ex. 15:11; Lev. 20:3; Jer. 23:9; Mk. 1:24; Isa. 63:10, 11). He has consecrated or hallowed his tent of meeting (the tabernacle) and temple, his altar, and the sacrifices, his city Jerusalem, and Zion (Ex. 40:6-9; 2 Chron. 29:5-7; Num. 18:17-19; Neh. 11:1, 18; Obad. 17). In the NT considerable emphasis is placed on the need for holiness in the believer (the temple of God) and on the holiness of the Church itself (1 Cor. 3:16, 17; Eph. 2:19-22). The Pauline Epistles commence with a doctrinal section which is followed with an extended section describing holy living, as Rom. 1-11 and 12-16. Christ died for the Church in order to make it holy and thus its individual members are called "saints" (holy) (Eph. 5:25-27; Rom. 1:7; Eph. 1:1; Phil. 1:1; Col. 1:2). *See also* CHRIST; WORK OF and SALVATION, APPLICATION OF.

HOLM *See* TREES

HOLON 1. An unidentified city in the hill country of Judah (Josh. 15:51; 21:15), also called Hilen (1 Chron. 6:58).

2. An unidentified site in Moab (Jer. 48:21).

HOLY OF HOLIES *See* TABERNACLE AND TEMPLE

HOLY PLACE *See* TABERNACLE AND TEMPLE

HOLY SPIRIT *See* GOD, NAMES OF, GODHEAD

HOMAM, HEMAN A grandson of Seir the Horite also called Heman (Gen. 36:22; 1 Chron. 1:39). In a footnote to the Genesis passage he is called Hemam.

HOMER *See* WEIGHTS AND MEASURES

HONEY The product of the bee, first wild and later domesticated. The word may also refer to a sort of thick syrup made from grapes, a favorite of the Arabs (Ps. 81:16; Judg. 14:8; 2 Chron. 31:5). It was an important item for both food and export (Prov. 24:13; Gen. 43:11). Honey and honeycomb figuratively refer to sweet and pleasant things (Prov. 16:24).

HONOR When referring to God, the translation of this word and the word glory is usually "majesty" or "splendor." In the OT the reference is usually to man, and the translation is "honor." It conveys the idea of respect and esteem for or from other persons. It is a gift from God and consists of physical and spiritual blessings. It may be forfeited if man sins against God. In both Testaments great emphasis is placed on the showing of honor to one's parents. It is one of the Ten Commandments (Ex. 20:12; Mt. 15:4; Eph. 6:1-3). Jesus has been crowned with honor as the result of his having suffered death to redeem mankind and in due time to him every knee will bow and every tongue confess (2 Pet. 1:16-21; 1 Tim. 1:17; 6:16; Rev. 4:9; 5:9-12; 7:12).

HOOK The English translation of many Hebrew words and one Greek word which refer to such items as: hooks that support the curtains of the tabernacle by fastening them to the pillars or cross rods; hooks put in animals or captives by which to lead them; hooks for fishing; hooks for picking up hot meat called forks (Ex. 26:31-33; Ezek. 19:9; 2 Kgs. 19:28; Amos 4:2; Job 41:1; Ex. 27:3).

HOOPOE *See* BIRDS, 5

HOPE In the Bible this word is used in the usual sense of expecting and trusting without any particular theological meaning (Ruth 1:12). It has in addition a very distinct theological connotation, closely tied with faith. In the OT God is the hope of Israel (Jer. 14:7, 8; Ps. 62:5; 65:5). The Greek word in the NT is *elpis* and carries the idea of hope, trust, and faith as may be seen from the contexts of Hebrews 10:23 and Ephesians 1:12. It is clearly expressed elsewhere (Rom. 5:2; Gal. 5:5; Eph. 1:11-14). NT hope is also the hope of eternal life (1 Cor. 15:19-26ff.). Paul presents a concept of deliverance for this physical universe as well (Rom. 8:19-25), associated with man's final redemption. The apostle also interestingly ties together the hope of the Christian with the hope of Israel (Acts 26:6-8; 28:20).

HOPHNI *See* PHINEAS

HOPHRA A Pharaoh of the time of Jeremiah whose doom he predicted (Jer. 44:30).

HOR 1. The mountain in the Negev, near the border of Edom (104-017), where Aaron died (Num. 20:22-29).

2. A mountain in Lebanon on the N border of the land given to Israel (Num. 34:7, 8).

HORAM A king of Gezer defeated by Joshua (Josh. 10:33).

HOREM An unidentified site in the tribal area of Naphtali (Josh. 19:38).

HORESH An unidentified place in the Desert of Ziph where David hid from Saul and Jonathan covenanted with David (1 Sam. 23:15-18). In the KJV the word is translated "wood."

HOR HAGGIDGAD A stop on the exodus route of the Israelites from Egypt also called Gudgodah (Num. 33:32, 33; Deut. 10:7).

HORI, HORITES 1. Founder of the Horites and a son of Seir (Gen. 36:20, 22). Horites were found at Mount Seir as early as the time of Abraham (Gen. 14:6). They were dispossessed by the Edomites, the descendants of Esau, with whom they intermarried (Deut. 2:12, 22). *See also* HIVITES.

2. The father of the Simeonite representative among the twelve spies (Num. 13:5).

HORMAH A city (146-069) in the tribal area of Judah and Simeon (Josh. 15:30; 19:4; Judg. 1:17). Earlier the Israelites tried unsuccessfully to take the area by force after God had decreed judgment upon them for the evil recommendation that the twelve spies brought back from Canaan (Num. 14:39-45).

HORN A container made from the horn of an animal for holding liquids. It is sometimes translated "writing kit" in the NIV

(Ezek. 9:2; 1 Sam. 16:1). Symbolically horns represent force (1 Kgs. 22:11; Zech. 1:18-21). *See also* ALTAR and MUSIC.

HORNET *See* BEASTS, 6

HORONAIM A place (211-055) in Moab (Isa. 15:5).

HORONITE A designation of Sanballat perhaps referring to his place of origin (Neh. 2:10, 19).

HORSE *See* BEASTS, 4

HOSAH 1. A town (perhaps 170-293), on the northern border of Asher, near Tyre (Josh. 19:29).

2. A gatekeeper before the Ark of the Covenant in David's day (1 Chron. 16:38).

HOSANNA A word which if literally translated would mean "save please" but which was and is used as an exclamation of praise (Mt. 21:9).

HOSEA One of the Minor Prophets, who was commanded to marry Gomer, and love her even though she was unfaithful. Through this experience he learned something of God's love for his people, though they too were unfaithful (Hos. 1:1, 3; 3:1).

HOSEA, BOOK OF *See* PROPHETS, MINOR

HOSHAIAH 1. One of the leaders of the dedication procession after the rebuilding of the wall of Jerusalem by Nehemiah (Neh. 12:32).

2. Father of one of the commanders who opposed Jeremiah (Jer. 42:1; 43:2ff.).

HOSHAMA A descendant of David and Solomon (1 Chron. 3:18).

HOSHEA 1. *See* KINGS OF JUDAH AND ISRAEL.

2. The name of Joshua prior to the time that Moses changed it (Num. 13:16).

3. A leader of the tribe of Ephraim in the days of David (1 Chron. 27:20).

4. One who signed the covenant with Nehemiah (Neh. 10:23).

HOTHAM 1. A descendant of Asher (1 Chron. 7:32, 35).

2. The father of two of David's mighty men (1 Chron. 11:44).

HOTHIR One of the sons of a seer of David (1 Chron. 25:4, 28).

HOUR *See* TIME

HOUSE An abode for humans from the simplest types for peasants to palaces for nobles or royalty, including temples for deities. In the hill country of Palestine the lower parts of houses were made of field or dressed stone while the upper part might be of mud or mud bricks dried in the sun. Where stone was a scarce commodity the entire structure was made of mud bricks. Wood was used for the roof support and sometimes for the superstructure as well. On the wooden support would be laid brushwood with mud plaster on top of that. Roofs were usually flat and had a multiplicity of uses. It was the duty of a good son to keep the mud roof properly plastered during the rainy season.

From the street one usually entered a courtyard off of which were the doors to the several rooms. The floors of the rooms might be of beaten earth or earth packed over a layer of rough stones. In better homes stone slab floors were used and some even were plastered with lime and earth mixtures. Wooden doors were used early, in some cases with locks and keys. Windows were treated as small doors usually high in the walls. Hearths for fire existed, but rarely was there a chimney. The smoke escaped through the doors and windows. Modern archaeologists have learned much about the floor plans and structures of houses in antiquity. Almost any archaeological report will show plans.

HOUSEHOLD GODS *See* DEITIES

HUBBAH A descendant of Asher (1 Chron. 7:34). In the KJV the name appears as Jehubbah.

HUKKOK A town (175-252) in the tribal area of Naphtali by the waters of Merom (Josh. 19:34).

HUKOK *See* HELKATH

HUL A descendant of Noah and Shem (Gen. 10:23; 1 Chron. 1:17).

HULDAH A prophetess in the days of King Josiah (2 Kgs. 22:14; 2 Chron. 34:22).

HUMTAH An unidentified site in the hill country of Judah (Josh. 15:54).

HUNDREDS The name of a military unit (Ex. 18:21; Num. 31:14).

HUNGER Literally to be physically hungry, figuratively to want eagerly (Deut. 28:48; Mt. 5:6).

HUNTING Pursuing wild animals for food or pleasure or for safety from dangerous ones. Weapons, snares, or nets, dogs and falcons were commonly used. The blood of game animals had to be poured out on the ground and covered with earth as part of the Levitical dietary laws (Lev. 17:13). Among the weapons used were the bow and arrow, the spear, the sword, or even, the club (Gen. 27:3; Mic. 7:2; 1 Sam. 17:40).

HUPHAM A descendant of Benjamin perhaps also called Huppim and even Huram (Num. 26:39; Gen. 46:21; 1 Chron. 8:5).

HUPPAH Head of one of the priestly courses (1 Chron. 24:13).

HUPPIM *See* HUPHAM

HUR 1. A man who with Aaron held up the hands of Moses during a battle with the Amalekites and later assisted Aaron in the administration of the Israelites (Ex. 17:10, 12; 24:14).

2. Grandson of Bezalel of the tribe of Judah who was both a skilled artist and craftsman in the work of the tabernacle and also gifted by God to teach others (Ex. 31:2-5; 35:30-34).

3. A descendant 'of Judah and son of Caleb, founder of Bethlehem (1 Chron. 2:19; 4:1, 4).

4. A king of Midian (Num. 31:8).

5. Father of one Rephaiah who worked on the wall of Jerusalem with Nehemiah (Neh. 3:9).

HURAI *See* HIDDAI

HURAM *See* HIRAM and HUPHAM

HURAM ABI *See* HIRAM

HURI A descendant of Gad (1 Chron. 5:14).

HUSBAND *See* MARRIAGE

HUSHAH A descendant of Judah (1 Chron. 4:4).

HUSHAI The friend of David who stayed in Jerusalem in order to counter the advice of Ahithophel when David had to flee (2 Sam. 15:32-37; 17:5-15).

HUSHAM A king of Edom who reigned there before Israel had a king (Gen. 36:34, 35; 1 Chron. 1:43, 45).

HUSHIM, HUSHITES 1. A son of Dan probably also the one called Shuham (Gen. 46:23; Num. 26:42, 43).

2. Descendants of Benjamin (1 Chron. 7:12).

3. One of the two wives of a descendant of Benjamin (1 Chron. 8:8, 11).

HYENA *See* BEASTS, 8

HYMENAEUS One who had adopted heresies for which he was excommunicated by Paul (1 Tim. 1:19, 20; 2 Tim. 2:17, 18).

HYMN *See* MUSIC

HYPOCRISY, HYPOCRITE In the NIV used only in NT. Where the KJV uses these translations in the OT the NIV usually uses "godless" or "ungodly" (Isa. 33:14; Job. 8:13). These words are transliterations into English of Greek words which meant to act a part in a play or to pretend. Hence in English these words carry the negative connotation of feigning to be what one is not. Some scholars feel that this is what is meant in NT usage while others feel strongly that the NT meaning is more like that of the OT, namely, opposition to God and thus the wickedness of the one who opposes him.

HYSSOP *See* PLANTS, PERFUMES, AND SPICES

I

IBEX *See* BEASTS, 2

IBHAR One of the sons of David, born in Jerusalem (2 Sam. 5:15).

IBIS *See* BIRDS

IBLEAM A town (177-205) in Asher which was ceded to Manasseh (Josh. 17:11).

IBNEIAH, Descendants of Benjamin (1 Chron. 9:8).
IBNIJAH

IBRI A descendant of Levi (1 Chron. 24:27).

IBSAM A grandson of Issachar (1 Chron. 7:2). In the KJV the name appears as Jibsam.

IBZAN *See* JUDGES OF ISRAEL

ICHABOD Grandson of Eli. His mother died during his birth and gave him this name when she was told that the glory of God had departed from Israel. The words *i* and *chabod* literally mean "no glory" (1 Sam. 4:19-22).

ICONIUM A city in Asia Minor visited by Paul on his missionary journeys where he endured persecutions (Acts 13:51; 14:19-21; 2 Tim. 3:11).

IDALAH An unidentified site in the tribal area of Zebulun (Josh. 19:15).

IDBASH A descendant of Judah (1 Chron. 4:3).

IDDO 1. Father of one of Solomon's twelve officers in charge of providing his food (1 Kgs. 4:14).

2. A descendant of Levi (1 Chron. 6:21).

3. An officer over part of the tribe of Manasseh in the time of David (1 Chron. 27:21).

4. A prophet who wrote some of the history of King Solomon and his son and grandson (2 Chron. 9:29; 12:15; 13:22).

5. The grandfather of the prophet Zechariah (Zech. 1:1, 7).

6. The head of some temple servants from Casiphia who sent men to help Ezra after the Babylonian captivity (Ezra 8:17).

7. Father of a priest in the days of Joiakim (Neh. 12:16).

IDOL, IDOLATRY *See also* "Images" under DEITIES. This was the worship of false gods, usually by means of images. Whenever images were involved, the Israelites were commanded to "destroy them out" of their land. They failed to do this and eventually it led them into idolatry and the punishment of foreign captivity (Ex. 23:23, 24; Deut. 7:5; 1 Kgs. 14:22-24; 16:30-33). In the NT, the OT concept is carried over and made even more stringent in that putting anything ahead of God was considered idolatry (Eph. 5:5).

IDUMEA *See* GEOGRAPHY OF THE HOLY LAND

IEZER A descendant of Manasseh (Jeezer in the KJV), also called Abiezer (Num. 26:30; Josh. 17:2).

IGAL 1. The spy that represented the tribe of Issachar (Num. 13:7).

2. One of David's mighty men, son of Nathan (2 Sam. 23:36).

3. A descendant of David (1 Chron. 3:22), spelled Igeal in the KJV.

IGDALIAH "A man of God" in Jeremiah's time (Jer. 35:4).

IGEAL *See* IGAL, 3

IIM An unidentified site in Judah (Josh. 15:29).

IJON A town (205-308) in the tribal area of Naphtali, early captured by the Syrian king Ben-Hadad and later by the king of Assyria, Tiglath-Pileser III (1 Kgs. 15:20; 2 Kgs. 15:29; 2 Chron. 16:4).

IKKESH Father of Ira, one of David's Thirty (2 Sam. 23:26).

ILAI One of David's mighty men, also called Zalmon (1 Chron. 11:29; 2 Sam. 23:28).

ILLYRICUM *See* DALMATIA

IMAGE, *See* DEITIES and IDOL, IDOLATRY
IMAGES

IMLAH The father of the prophet Micaiah who lived in the days of King Ahab (1 Kgs. 22:8-28).

IMMANUEL, The name given by Isaiah to the child whose special birth he
EMMANUEL predicted, applied to Jesus in the NT (Isa. 7:14; 8:8; Mt. 1:23), which means "God with us."

IMMER 1. Head of one of the priestly divisions in the days of David (1 Chron. 24:14).

2, 3, 4, and 5. Priests by this name are mentioned in Ezra and Nehemiah, some of whom may be descendants of the Immer above. One is noted among those who returned with Zerubbabel from Babylon, another as one who married a foreign wife in that period, another as the father of one who helped Nehemiah repair the wall of Jerusalem, and another as an ancestor of some who lived in Jerusalem after the return (Ezra 2:37; 10:20; Neh. 3:29; 11:13).

6. Father of the priest who beat Jeremiah the prophet and put him in the stocks (Jer. 20:1, 2).

7. One of the places in Babylonia where Jewish captives were kept (Ezra 2:59).

IMMORTAL, The NT concept of immortality is that of eternal life of the
IMMORTALITY whole person, spirit and body. At death the nonmaterial part of man goes either to paradise or to a place which is described as one where the inhabitant is "in agony in this flame" (Lk. 23:43; 16:24). The material part, or body, goes to the grave (Ps. 88:5). In the biblical concept there is to be a resurrection in which the bodies, restored in the nature of the case, come out of the graves, are reinhabited by their spirits, and commence the eternal form of their existence either to live or to be condemned (Dan. 12:2; Isa. 26:19; Ps. 16:9-11; Job 19:25-27; 1 Thess. 4:16; John 5:28, 29; 1 Cor. 15:12-54). The NT presents the picture of all the resurrected

gathered before God for separation. They are to be judged on the basis of what they did in life and those whose names are not found in the "book of life" will be "thrown into the lake of fire." The basis of the separation for the two aspects of eternal life is as to whether those judged are considered by Christ as "my sheep" or not, those for whom he made the atonement when he laid down his life (Jn. 10:7-11, 27-30). Eternal life for the believer is not an inactive endless existence but rather freedom from all the evils of this present world and active service of worshiping God in fellowship with his Son their Savior. *See also* DEAD, ABODE OF.

IMNA A descendant of Asher (1 Chron. 7:35).

IMNAH 1. A son of Asher (Gen. 46:17). In the KJV the name appears as JIMNAH.

2. A Levite who lived in the days of King Hezekiah (2 Chron. 31:14).

IMPERIAL REGIMENT The name of the segment of Roman soldiers whose centurion was responsible for bringing Paul to Rome (Acts 27:1).

IMRAH A descendant of Asher (1 Chron. 7:36).

IMRI 1. A descendant of Judah who returned from captivity (1 Chron. 9:4).

2. Father of one of the men who built the wall of Jerusalem with Nehemiah (Neh. 3:2).

INCARNATION *See* CHRIST, LIFE OF

INCENSE Incense which was burned to make a pleasant odor was used in either religious worship or to honor a distinguished individual. The prescription for making incense for the worship of God was regulated in the law and this type was not allowed to be used for other purposes (Ex. 30:34-38). There was an altar of incense overlaid with pure gold placed in the temple itself just in front of the veil that separated the holy place from the outer part of the temple. Here Aaron, and later the high priest in Israel, burned incense daily and on the Day of Atonement he carried incense within the veiled area itself (Ex. 30:1-9; Lev. 16:11-14ff.).

INDIA The Persian king Xerxes reigned from India to Ethiopia (Cush), the only references to India in the Bible (Esth. 1:1; 8:9).

INGATHERING, FEAST OF *See* CALENDAR and FESTIVALS

INHERITANCE Inheritance was fully and carefully regulated by law in ancient Israel. This referred to the land owned by a family as well as to items of personal property. The land had to stay within the family. The estate was divided into so many portions, being the number of the sons, plus one. The heir, the firstborn, then received two of these portions, called a double portion, and the other sons shared equally the remainder. If there were no sons then the estate could go to a daughter but it was necessary for her to marry within the tribe as the land was never allowed to leave it. If there were no daughter it still had to stay within the family or tribe and this too was under legislation (Deut. 21:17; Num. 27:8-11; 36:6-9). The heir cared for the women but if there was no heir then the next of kin on the husband's side was required to marry her and raise up seed for the deceased relative (Ruth 3:8-13). *See* "Levirate Marriage" under MARRIAGE.

The word inheritance is used in symbolic senses in the Bible. It refers to such items as the land of Canaan promised by God as an inheritance to Abraham and his seed after him; Israel as God's inheritance; Christ being God's heir; those who believe in Christ as being adopted by God and thus fellow heirs with Christ (Num. 34:2; 1 Kgs. 8:36; Gen. 17:7, 8; Deut. 32:9; Jer. 10:16; Heb. 1:2; 9:14, 15; Rom. 8:17). The inheritance of the believer is the blessing of God in this present life and the blessings of an eternal state free from evil and wickedness in the future life (Mt. 25:34; 1 Cor. 6:9-11; 1 Pet. 1:3-5).

INIQUITIES *See* SIN

INK A mixture of lamp-black or vegetable soot and gum arabic moistened with water (Jer. 36:18; 2 Jn. 12).

INN In the NIV the word is used only in the account of the birth of Jesus and the story told by Jesus of the Samaritan who cared for the injured traveler found on the Jericho road (Lk. 2:7; 10:34). References to "lodging places" are found. Inns were not like our concept of hotels or lodging places. They were more frequently than not merely an enclosure where a person could spend the night either in the open courtyard, or in a stall around its edges, or in a cave opening off of the yard. Since these lacked comfort and since the keeper often had a bad reputation it became customary for travelers to seek the hospitality of friends (2 Kgs. 4:8; Heb. 13:2).

INSECTS *See* BEASTS

INSPIRATION *See* SCRIPTURE

INTERCESSION *See* PRAYER

INTEREST *See* DEBT

INVOKE To call on someone for help or to call down a curse or a blessing upon oneself or another (2 Sam. 14:11; Mt. 26:74).

IPHDEIAH A descendant of Benjamin (1 Chron. 8:25).

IPHTAH An unidentified site in the western foothills of Judah (Josh. 15:43). In the KJV the name appears as JIPHTAH.

IPHTAH EL An unidentified valley between the tribal areas of Asher and Zebulun (Josh. 19:14, 27).

IR A descendant of Benjamin (1 Chron. 7:12).

IRA 1. A priest in the time of David (2 Sam. 20:26).
2 and 3. Two of David's Thirty (2 Sam. 23:26, 38).

IRAD A grandson of Cain (Gen. 4:18).

IRAM One of the chiefs of Edom descended from Esau (Gen. 36:43).

IRIJAH The captain of the guard who seized Jeremiah (Jer. 37:13, 14).

IR NAHASH A site (190-010) in the tribal area of Judah (1 Chron. 4:12).

IRON Iron did not come into general use until the time of the Hittites in the middle of the second millennium B.C. Prior to that some beads of meteoric iron were found in predynastic Egypt plus one mass of iron from sixth dynasty times. There is one early reference to iron in the Bible probably of the meteoric variety (Gen. 4:22). Israel had trouble driving out the Canaanites since they had iron while Israel had not (Judg. 1:19; Josh. 17:18). The Philistines controlled the ability to sharpen iron instruments (1 Sam. 13:19, 20). Later the Phoenician craftsmen taught the Israelites this art after which it spread rapidly to all sorts of uses in Israel: for instruments of war, for farming, and for building (2 Chron. 2:11-14; Job 20:24; 2 Sam. 12:31; 1 Chron. 22:14). The iron yoke was a symbol of slavery and captivity, and iron symbolized strength for both security and destruction (Ps. 107:10, 11; Jer. 28:13; Job 40:16-18; Dan. 7:7).
2. *See* YIRON.

IRPEEL An unidentified site in the tribal area of Benjamin (Josh. 18:27).

IR SHEMESH An unidentified site in the tribal area of Dan (Josh. 19:41).

IRU A son of Caleb (1 Chron. 4:15).

ISAAC The son of Abraham and Sarah, husband of Rebekah, and father of Esau and Jacob (Gen. 21:3; 22:7; 24:67; 25:21, 25, 26). In obedience to the command of God Abraham went to Moriah to offer his son as a sacrifice but God prevented it and provided a substitute instead (Gen. 22:2, 12, 13). With his herdsmen he had many of the same troubles that his father did in Gerar and Beersheba (Gen. 26). His mother conspired with Jacob and stole the ancestral blessing from Esau. Isaac died in Hebron (Gen. 27:1-10; 35:27-29).

ISAIAH One of the major writing prophets, son of Amoz, who lived and prophesied in the days of the kings of Judah, Uzziah, Jotham, Ahaz, Hezekiah, and perhaps also Manasseh (Isa. 1:1). In the OT we learn a few details of his life from his relations with King Hezekiah (2 Kgs. 19, 20; 2 Chron. 32:20-32), otherwise only from the book that bears his name. In the NT twenty of his prophecies are cited in connection with fulfillments, more than those of any other single prophet, five of them in Romans and the rest in the Gospels and Acts. In the NT besides the quotations, there is the incident of the Ethiopian eunuch who was reading Isaiah and to whom an angel of the Lord sent Philip as an expositor (Acts 8:26-35).

ISAIAH, BOOK OF The first of the Major Prophets, the Book of Isaiah, consists of sixty-six chapters, representing a prophetic ministry of nearly sixty years (c 739-683 B.C.), and covering a wide variety of themes. Because of the wealth of predictions concerning Christ, Isaiah has been called "the evangelical prophet." The unity of the authorship of the entire book is clearly attested by the NT evangelists and apostles (Mt. 3:3; 12:17, 18; Acts 8:34; Rom. 10:16, 20). (Note esp. John 12:38-41, which definitely asserts the same author for Isaiah 6:9, 10 and Isa. 53:1.) The veracity of Christ and his apostles is therefore at issue in the question of Isaiah's authorship of chapters 40-66.

Nevertheless, because of a rationalistic aversion to the possibility of supernatural revelation and fulfilled prophecy, higher criticism since Johann Doederlein (1789) has argued for a later authorship ("Deutero-Isaiah") for chapters 40-66. Since this writer foresaw the conquest of Babylon by Cyrus of Persia, he must have written shortly before the fall of Babylon in 539. Nineteenth-century higher critics have sought to prove even later authorship for chapters 56-66. The objective evidence of the text itself cannot, however, be reconciled with postexilic authorship. (1) It is inconceivable that the true name of the author of the admittedly sublimest passages in all of Hebrew prophetic literature could have been totally forgotten, when even the two-page prophecy of Obadiah still bears the author's name. (2) The eighth-century prophet Isaiah evidently knew about the coming Babylonian captivity (cf. 13:1: "An oracle concerning Babylon that son of Amoz saw"). He even knew of the restoration from exile (cf. 6:13 which states that after the complete devastation, depopulation, and exile of Judah, a remnant, a "tenth" shall return to the land, a promise which Isaiah evidently claimed when he in 7:3 named his firstborn son Shear-Jashub, which meant "a remnant shall return"). (3) Isaiah 40-66 refers to idolatry as a gross and prevalent evil in contemporary Judah (cf. 57:4-5, with its reference to infant sacrifice practiced most commonly in the reign of Manasseh). Isaiah 57:7 indicates idolatrous worship upon the high places; Isaiah 65:2-4 and 66:17 refer to the abominable pagan rites in temple gardens. All responsible modern authorities agree that no idolatry was practiced in postexilic Judah, and the testimony of Ezra, Zechariah, Nehemiah, and Malachi (which inveigh against all the current evils and abuses of this period) by their silence about idolatry conclusively confirm this. (4) The extreme degeneracy and moral breakdown deplored in chapters 58 and 59 correspond most closely with conditions known to exist in Judah under Manasseh (696-641 B.C.). (5) Stylistic resemblances are unmistakable between Isaiah I and Isaiah II (cf. 14:27 and 43:13; 35:10 and 51:11; 11:12 and 56:8; 34:8 and 61:2; 11:6-9 and 65:25; 35:6 and 41:18; 11:2 and 61:1; 1:11, 14 and 43:24; 28:5 and 63:3; and many others).

The remarkable correspondence and allusions linking together all parts of the book into an artistic unity have convinced even such liberal scholars as W. H. Brownlee that Isaiah is indeed a literary unity, although (according to him) composed in the postexilic period (because of the elements of fulfilled prophecy, explainable to him only as prophecy after the fulfillment).

The text of Isaiah may be divided into eight main sections. I. Volume of Rebuke and Promise (chaps. 1-6) admonishing the backslidden nation to turn back to the Lord (Yahweh) in repentance, lest they be visited with invasion, devastation, and exile. II. Volume of Immanuel (chaps. 7-12) predicts the coming Messiah as God Incarnate (9:6) and the downfall of Damascus and Samaria within the next few years, and ultimately Assyria as well. Messiah will be descended from David and unite Jewish and Gentile believers under his rule (ch. 11). III. Volume of Burdens upon the Nations (chaps.

13-23) Babylon, Philistia, Moab, Damascus, Samaria, Ethiopia, Egypt, Edom, Arabia, Tyre, and even Jerusalem itself. IV. General Judgment and Promise (chaps. 24-27), speaking of punishment for oppressors and the preservation of God's true believers. V. Volume of Woes upon Believers in Israel (chaps. 28-33); doom predicted for drunkards and scoffers both in Israel and in Judah, but a Foundation Stone will be laid in Zion for true believers. Confidence in God is opposed to confidence in pagan allies such as Egypt. VI. Second Volume of General Judgment and Promise (chaps. 34-35), total destruction of Gentile world power; the highway of holiness is opened up for the redeemed. VII. Volume of Hezekiah (chaps. 36-39). The deadly anger of Sennacherib's invasion is miraculously averted in response to the prayer of faith. Chapter 38 tells of Hezekiah's near-fatal illness of ten years previously, which ultimately led to his boastful display of his treasures to the Babylonian envoys. VIII. The Volume of Comfort (chaps. 40-66) is subdivided into three sections: A. The Purpose of Peace (40-48); B. The Prince of Peace (49-57); C. The Program of Peace (58-66).

Some of the sublimest passages on the transcendence and sovereignty of God are found here; and his proof of scriptural inspiration through fulfilled prophecy (41:21-26; 42:9, 23; 44:7, 8). Most notable are the passages on the Lord's (Yahweh's) Servant, a term including both spiritual Israel as God's covenant nation, and the personal, Messianic Servant, who is Christ himself; thus the clearest and most moving description of the crucifixion and its meaning are found in chapter 53 (which sets forth Christ as a vicarious substitutionary atonement for truly believing Israel, and thus precludes the notion that Israel itself could be the Servant of the Lord intended here). His gospel is clearly set forth in 61:1-4, and the ultimate triumph and glory of true Israel are proclaimed in the clearest and most encouraging terms. (G.L.A.)

ISCAH A niece of Abraham, daughter of Haran (Gen. 11:29).

ISCARIOT, JUDAS *See* APOSTLES

ISHBAH A descendant of Judah (1 Chron. 4:17).

ISHBAK A son of Abraham by Keturah (Gen. 25:2).

ISHBI-BENOB A Philistine giant who was killed while trying to kill David (2 Sam. 21:16, 17).

ISH-BOSHETH *See* ESHBAAL

ISHHOD A descendant of Manasseh (1 Chron. 7:18).

ISHI 1 and 2. Two descendants of Judah (1 Chron. 2:31; 4:20).

3. Father of the leaders of the Simeonites who defeated the Amalekites (1 Chron. 4:42).

4. A descendant of Manasseh (1 Chron. 5:24).

ISHIJAH One who married a foreign wife during the Babylonian captivity (Ezra 10:31).

ISHMA A descendant of Judah (1 Chron. 4:3).

ISHMAEL 1. The son of Abraham by Hagar and thus half-brother to Isaac. Because of the jealousy of Sarah he and his mother were driven out into the desert where he grew up as an expert hunter with the bow (Gen. 16:3, 15; 21:9, 10, 17-21). He was the ancestor of the Ishmaelites, married an Egyptian wife, and died at the age of 137 (Gen. 21:21; 25:12-18).

2. A descendant of Saul and Jonathan (1 Chron. 8:38).

3. The father of Zebadiah who was over the house of Judah in the days of King Jehoshaphat (2 Chron. 19:11).

4. A military officer who supported the priest Jehoiada and helped him bring the young Josiah to the throne (2 Chron. 23:1ff.).

5. A member of the royal family of Judah who organized and carried out the assassination of Gedaliah whom Nebuchadnezzar of Babylon had made governor of Judah after he had captured Jerusalem (2 Kgs. 25:23-25; Jer. 40:8—41:18).

6. A priest who married a foreign wife during the Babylon captivity (Ezra 10:22).

ISHMAIAH, ISMAIAH 1. A Gibeonite who joined David at Ziklag and one of David's mighty men among the Thirty (1 Chron. 12:4).

2. David's commander from the tribe of Zebulun (1 Chron. 27:19).

ISHMERAI A descendant of Benjamin (1 Chron. 8:18).

ISHPAH, ISPAH A descendant of Benjamin (1 Chron. 8:16).

ISHPAN A descendant of Benjamin (1 Chron. 8:22).

ISHUAH, ISHVAH A son of Asher (Gen. 46:17).

ISHUI, ISHVI 1. A son of Asher (Gen. 46:17).

2. A son of King Saul (1 Sam. 14:49).

ISLAND, ISLE There are a number of islands mentioned by name in the Bible. Those that are named are found only in the NT, and as the result of Paul's travels (Acts 27:16; 28:1), or John's imprisonment (Rev. 1:9). The word is used in the OT (Isa. 24:15; 41:5; Ezek. 26:10) but is translated often as "coast" (Isa. 20:6).

ISMAKIAH A Levite in the days of King Hezekiah (2 Chron. 31:13).

ISRAEL The name given by the angel to Abraham's grandson and Isaac's son Jacob, and that which the Israelites were and are called (Gen. 32:28; 35:10). At times in Israel's history the term applied to all the twelve tribes and at other times to the northern confederacy of ten tribes as distinct from Judah. For Israel's history *see* JUDGES OF ISRAEL, KINGS OF JUDAH AND ISRAEL, CALENDAR and CHRONOLOGY. For her religion see SACRIFICES AND OFFERINGS, FESTIVALS, TEMPLE.

ISSACHAR The son of Jacob who gave his name to a tribe (Gen. 30:18; 35:23).

ISSHIAH 1. A descendant of Issachar (1 Chron. 7:3).

2. One who joined David at Ziklag (1 Chron. 12:6).

3. At the end of David's reign he organized the priests for service. One of these was Isshiah (1 Chron. 23:20).

4. Another Levite of David's days (1 Chron. 24:21).

ISSUE *See* SICK, SICKNESS

ITALIAN REGIMENT *See* CORNELIUS

ITALY *See* GEOGRAPHY OF THE HOLY LAND

ITCH *See* SICK, SICKNESS

ITHAI One of David's mighty men (1 Chron. 11:31; 2 Sam. 23:29).

ITHAMAR One of the four sons of Aaron by Elisheba (Ex. 6:23). Though a priest he was on one occasion rebuked by Moses for not following the prescribed ritual (Lev. 10:16-18). From his descendants came some of the men who conducted the priestly courses (1 Chron. 24:3, 4). A descendant of his, Daniel, returned from the Babylonian captivity with Ezra (Ezra 8:2).

ITHIEL 1. One of the two to whom Proverbs 30 was addressed (Prov. 30:1).

2. A descendant of Benjamin (Neh. 11:7).

ITHLAH An unidentified site in the tribal area of Dan (Josh. 19:42). In the KJV the word appears as Jethlah.

ITHMAH One of David's mighty men, a Moabite (1 Chron. 11:46).

ITHNAN An unidentified site in the south of the tribal area of Judah (Josh. 15:23).

ITHRA *See* JETHER

ITHRAN 1. A descendant of Seir, a Horite (Gen. 36:26).

2. A descendant of Asher (1 Chron. 7:37).

ITHREAM A son of David born at Hebron (2 Sam. 3:5).

ITHRITE A clan that lived at Kiriath Jearim from which came two of David's mighty men (1 Chron. 2:53; 11:40).

ITTAI A Philistine from Gath who fought with David and became commander of one-third of David's army. In Absalom's rebellion he followed David into exile and returned with him (2 Sam. 15:18-23; 18:2).

ITURAEA *See* GEOGRAPHY OF THE HOLY LAND

IVORY Ivory was imported from India and used chiefly for inlay and decoration. Solomon's great throne was of ivory overlaid with gold (1 Kgs. 10:18). King Ahab built a palace overlaid with ivory (1 Kgs. 22:39). It was a mark of luxury and as such its abuse was denounced by the prophet Amos (Amos 3:15; 6:4).

IVVAH An unidentified site, perhaps in Syria, but captured by the armies of the Assyrian king Sennacherib (2 Kgs. 18:34).

IYE ABARIM An unidentified stopping place along the wilderness route of the Israelites in their exodus from Egypt (Num. 21:11).

IZHAR A descendant of Levi (Ex. 6:18; 1 Chron. 6:2).

IZLIAH A descendant of Benjamin (1 Chron. 8:18).

IZRAHIAH A descendant of Issachar (1 Chron. 7:3).

IZRAHITE A man belonging to an unidentified family or town called Izrah. One Izrahite was the captain of the fifth army division that served the king (1 Chron. 27:8).

IZRI A musician in David's time (1 Chron. 25:11).

IZZIAH One who married a foreign wife during the Babylonian exile (Ezra 10:25). In the KJV the name appears as Jeziah.

JAAKAN *See* AKAN

JAAKOBAH A descendant of Simeon (1 Chron. 4:36).

JAALA, JAALAH Descendant of some of Solomon's servants who returned from the exile with Zerubbabel, also called Jaalah (Neh. 7:58; Ezra 2:56).

JAAR An unidentified site mentioned in connection with Ephrathah (Ps. 132:6; see NIV footnote).

JAARE-OREGIM Since he is called Jair in the parallel account and since the word *oregim* (Hebrew for weaver) also appears in the next line it is generally felt that the name of this individual is only Jair (2 Sam. 21:19, see footnote; 1 Chron. 20:5).

JAARESHIAH A descendant of Benjamin (1 Chron. 8:27).

JAASIEL 1. One of David's mighty men (1 Chron. 11:47).

2. One who was over the Benjamites in David's day (1 Chron. 27:21).

JAASU, JAASAU One who married a foreign wife during the Babylonian captivity (Ezra 10:37).

JAAZANIAH 1. One of the leaders who called on Gedaliah after he had been made governor of Jerusalem by Nebuchadnezzar, also called Jezaniah (2 Kgs. 25:23; Jer. 40:8; see NIV footnote).

2. One of the Rechabites in the days of Jeremiah (Jer. 35:3).

3. An idolatrous elder of Israel in the days of Ezekiel (Ezek. 8:11).

4. A prince of Israel who was giving wicked counsel in the days of Ezekiel (Ezek. 11:1-4).

JAAZIAH The father of Beno and descendant of Levi in David's time (1 Chron. 24:26).

JAAZIEL A Levite and temple musician in David's time, also called Aziel (1 Chron. 15:18, 20).

JABAL A son of Lamech and descendant of Cain (Gen. 4:20).

JABBOK A principal tributary of the Jordan River on the east side about midway between the Sea of Galilee and the Salt Sea. Its banks housed many towns and settlements in antiquity. It arises near Amman and flows north for a distance before it turns westward. East of the S to N portion lived the Ammonites (Num. 21:24). The E to W part was the border between the Amorites with their king Sihon on the south and Og the king of Bashan on the north (Judg. 11:22; Josh. 12:5). Later it divided N and S Gilead where the two halves of the tribe of Gilead were settled (Josh. 12:2-6). It was at a ford on this river that Jacob wrestled with the man who changed his name from Jacob to Israel (Gen. 32:22-28).

JABESH 1. Father of the Shallum who murdered the king of Israel and reigned in his stead only one month (2 Kgs. 15:10, 13).

2. Short term for Jabesh Gilead.

JABESH GILEAD A city (214-201) a night's march east of the Jordan River also called Jabesh (1 Sam. 11:1), located in the tribal area of half the tribe of Manasseh (Num. 32:33). The people of the city except 400 virgins were killed by the rest of Israel for not coming to Mizpeh to help in the action against Benjamin, and the 400 were given to Benjamites as wives (Judg. 20:1; 21:8 and context). Saul delivered the city from the Ammonites and then was made king of all Israel. The men of Jabesh Gilead much later rescued Saul's corpse from the walls of Beth Shan (1 Sam. 11:1-15; 31:11-13).

JABEZ 1. A descendant of Judah (1 Chron. 4:9, 10).

2. An unidentified site in Judah (1 Chron. 2:55).

JABIN 1. King of Hazor in Galilee whom Joshua defeated and killed (Josh. 11:1-11).

2. Another Canaanite king of Hazor whose forces under Sisera were defeated by Deborah and Barak in the period of the Judges (Judg. 4:2, 12-16, 24).

JABNEEL 1. A town (126-141) in the tribal area of Judah on its border with Dan near Joppa, also called Jabneh (Josh. 15:11; 2 Chron. 26:6). It became the center of the Sanhedrin after the expulsion of the Jews from Jerusalem by the Romans and its history continues to the present.

2. A town (198-235) in the tribal area of Naphtali (Josh. 19:33).

JABNEH *See* JABNEEL

JACAN, JACHAN A descendant of Gad (1 Chron. 5:13).

JACHIN *See* JAKIN

JACINTH *See* PRECIOUS STONES AND METALS

JACKAL *See* BEASTS, 8

JACOB 1. The father of Joseph the husband of Mary (Mt. 1:15).

2. Also called Israel after his wrestling all night with the angel at the River Jabbok (Gen. 32:28). He was the son of Isaac and Rebekah and grandson of Abraham and Sarah, brother of Esau, husband of Leah and Rachel and father of the twelve sons who became heads of the tribes of Israel (Gen. 25:21-26; 29:31—30:24; 25:16-18, 23-26). He bought the birthright from his twin brother Esau and stole the paternal blessing by deceiving his father (Gen. 25:29-34; 27:1ff.). For these actions he had to flee from Palestine. In Paddan Aram he served Laban for his two wives, their maids, who became his concubines, and a great wealth of cattle and sheep (Gen. 28:1—31:21). After fleeing again, he was overtaken by Laban; he made a treaty with the angel, and had his name changed. He became reconciled with his brother on his return to Palestine and dwelt at Shechem (Gen. 31:22—33:20). Later he moved farther south where he continued until famine forced the entire family down to Egypt to the land of Goshen where he died. He was buried in Hebron (Gen. 35:27; 42:1-4; 46:1-7; 49:33; 50:13). His famous blessing of his sons is recorded in Genesis 49.

JADA A descendant of Judah, a Jerahmeelite (1 Chron. 2:28, 32).

JADAH A descendant of Saul also called Jehoaddah (1 Chron. 9:42; 8:36). Jarah is suggested in the footnote at 1 Chronicles 9:42.

JADDAI, JADDAU One who married a foreign wife during the time of the Babylonian captivity (Ezra 10:43).

JADDUA 1. One who signed the covenant with Nehemiah (Neh. 10:21).
2. A priest who lived into the reign of Darius the Persian (Neh. 12:11, 22).

JADON One who helped repair the wall of Jerusalem in the time of Nehemiah (Neh. 3:7).

JAEL Wife of Heber the Kenite who acquired fame in Israel for having killed Sisera the leader of the army opposing Deborah and Barak (Judg. 4:17-22; 5:24).

JAGUR An unidentified site in the southern part of the tribal area of Judah (Josh. 15:21).

JAHATH 1. A descendant of Judah (1 Chron. 4:2).
2, 3, and 4. Three Levites (1 Chron. 6:20, 43; 23:10, 11; 24:22).
5. A Levite in the time of King Josiah who was an overseer of temple repairs (2 Chron. 34:12).

JAHAZ A Levitical city (236-110) east of the Jordan in the tribal area of Reuben also later called a city of Moab (Num. 21:23; Josh. 13:15, 18; 21:36; Jer. 48:34).

JAHAZIEL 1. A Benjamite who joined David at Ziklag (1 Chron. 12:4).
2. A priest in David's time who accompanied the Ark to Jerusalem (1 Chron. 16:6).
3. A Levite appointed to service by David in his later years (1 Chron. 23:19).
4. A Levite who prophesied in the time of King Jehoshaphat of Judah (2 Chron. 20:14).
5. The father of one who came back from the Babylonian captivity with Ezra (Ezra 8:5).

JAHDAI A descendant of Judah related to Caleb (1 Chron. 2:47).

JAHDIEL A head of a family of Manasseh (1 Chron. 5:24).

JAHDO A descendant of Gad (1 Chron. 5:14).

JAHIEL *See also* JEHIEL. A man in charge of David's treasury (1 Chron. 29:8).

JAHLEEL A son of Zebulun (Gen. 46:14; Num. 26:26).

JAHMAI A grandson of Issachar (1 Chron. 7:2).

JAHZAH A Levitical town in the tribal area of Reuben (1 Chron. 6:78). Later when it had been taken by the Moabites the judgment of God fell on it (Jer. 48:21).

JAHZEIAH One of the four who opposed Ezra on his decision about mixed marriages (Ezra 10:15).

JAHZERAH A priest who was perhaps also called Azarel (1 Chron. 9:12; Neh. 11:13).

JAHZIEL, JAHZEEL A son of Naphtali (Gen. 46:24; 1 Chron. 7:13).

JAIR, JAIRITE 1. *See also* JUDGES OF ISRAEL and JAARE OREGIM.

2. A descendant of Manasseh (Num. 32:41; Deut. 3:14).

3. Father of Mordecai and grand-uncle of Queen Esther (Esth. 2:5).

4. One Ira a Jairite was a priest of David (2 Sam. 20:26).

JAIRUS A synagogue ruler whose daughter Jesus raised from the dead (Mk. 5:22; Lk. 8:41).

JAKEH The father of the Agur who wrote Proverbs 30 (Prov. 30:1).

JAKIM 1. A descendant of Benjamin (1 Chron. 8:19).

2. The head of one of the priestly divisions in the days of David (1 Chron. 24:12).

JAKIN 1. A son of Simeon also called Jarib (Gen. 46:10; 1 Chron. 4:24).

2. Leader of the twenty-first division of priests in David's days (1 Chron. 24:17).

3. A priest living in Jerusalem in the time of Nehemiah (Neh. 11:10).

4. The name of the S pillar in the porch of Solomon's temple made of cast bronze by Huram of Tyre (1 Kgs. 7:13-22).

JALAM A son of Esau (Gen. 36:5).

JALON A descendant of Judah and Caleb (1 Chron. 4:17).

JAMBRES One who together with Jannes opposed Moses; mentioned only in the NT (2 Tim. 3:8).

JAMBS Structural parts of a gate, decorative in the vision of Ezekiel 40:9; 41:3.

JAMES 1. Son of Zebedee, one of the Twelve; *see* APOSTLES.

2. Son of Alphaeus, one of the Twelve; *see* APOSTLES.

3. A brother of Jesus who was unbelieving during the life of Jesus but who saw Jesus in one of the resurrection appearances (Mt. 13:55; Jn. 7:5; 1 Cor. 15:7). He became the leader of the Jerusalem church and presided at its first council (Acts 15:6, 13; 21:17, 18; Gal. 1:19). He is most probably also the author of the book that bears this name and brother of Jude the author of another book (Jas. 1:1; Jude 1).

4. Father of one of the apostles by the name of Judas, not Iscariot (Lk. 6:16).

5. One of whom a Mary is called mother and identified by some with number 2 above (Mt. 27:56).

JAMES, EPISTLE OF One of the books of the NT and ascribed by tradition to James the brother of the Lord. *See* JAMES, 3. "The twelve tribes scattered among the nations" to whom the book was addressed, could not be the Jews of the Diaspora. The belief that the epistle was written to Jewish Christians or to Christians who considered themselves the new Israel is inconclusive. It is perhaps better to think of its having been written directly to Jewish Christians in the first instance, because of the presence of Jewish legal references (2:2; 4:2, 11; 5:12) and the absence of things against which Paul so often warns the Gentile Christians, and in the second instance to all the people of God as with the other books of the NT. The message is not a treatise upon a single theme but rather remarks on a number of miscellaneous items of significance to the Christians: trials and temptations; doing and not merely hearing the word of God; loving all without partiality towards rich or poor; control of the tongue; coveting and speaking evil of one another; enduring patiently under suffering; and others. The section 2:14-26 stresses the other side of the coin from the one which Paul emphasizes so well. Faith and works supplement one another, for saving faith (Paul) is to manifest itself in good works (James) and if the latter is not visible one may question the genuineness of the former.

JAMES, SON OF ALPHAEUS *See* APOSTLES

JAMES, SON OF ZEBEDEE *See* APOSTLES

JAMIN 1. A son of Simeon (Gen. 46:10).

2. A descendant of Judah, Caleb, and Jerahmeel (1 Chron. 2:27).

3. A Levite who helped to explain the law as Ezra read it (Neh. 8:7).

JAMLECH A descendant of Simeon (1 Chron. 4:34).

JANAI, JAANAI A descendant of Gad (1 Chron. 5:12).

JANIM, JANUM An unidentified town of Judah in the hill country (Josh. 15:53).

JANNAI, JANNA An ancestor of Joseph, husband of Mary of whom Jesus was born (Lk. 3:24).

JANNES *See* JAMBRES

JANOAH 1. A town (173-265) in the tribal area of Naphtali noted as being captured by Tiglath-Pileser of Assyria (2 Kgs. 15:29).

2. A town (184-173) on the borders of Ephraim (Josh. 16:6, 7). In the KJV it is spelled Janohah.

JAPHETH A son of Noah and according to the names of his sons the ancestor of the Indo-European peoples from the south coasts of Europe to Persia (Gen. 5:32; 10:2-5).

JAPHIA 1. A town (172-232) on the eastern border of the tribal area of Zebulun (Josh. 19:12).

2. A king of Lachish who fought against Joshua, lost and was killed (Josh. 10:3, 22, 26).

3. A son of David (2 Sam. 5:15).

JAPHLET A descendant of Asher (1 Chron. 7:32, 33).

JAPHLETITES A clan on the border of the allotment to the descendants of Joseph (Josh. 16:1-3).

JARED The father of Enoch and listed in the genealogy of Jesus (Gen. 5:18; Lk. 3:37).

JARHA An Egyptian slave who was allowed to marry the daughter of Sheshan a Jerahmeelite (1 Chron. 2:34, 35).

JARIB 1. A son of Simeon also called Jakin (1 Chron. 4:24; Gen. 46:10).

2. One who was sent by Ezra to Iddo asking that some ministers for the house of God be sent to Jerusalem (Ezra 8:16).

3. A priest who married a foreign wife during the Babylonian captivity but agreed to put her away on his return (Ezra 10:18).

JARMUTH 1. A city (147-142) in the western foothills in the tribal area of Judah (Josh. 15:35).

2. A Levitical city (199-222) in the tribal area of Issachar, also called Remeth and Ramoth (Josh. 21:29; 19:21; 1 Chron. 6:73).

JAROAH A descendant of Gad (1 Chron. 5:14).

JASHAR, BOOK OF A book not now in existence and known only from its quotations found in the Bible (Josh. 10:13; 2 Sam. 1:18). The LXX of 1 Kings 8:53 also refers to it.

JASHEN Father of some of David's mighty men; also called Hashem (2 Sam. 23:32; 1 Chron. 11:34).

JASHOBEAM One of David's mighty men also called Josheb Basshebeth (1 Chron. 11:11; 2 Sam. 23:8). He was one who joined David at Ziklag (1 Chron. 12:6).

JASHUB 1. A son of Issachar (Num. 26:24; Gen. 46:13) also called Iob in footnote of the second reference.

2. One who married a foreign wife during the captivity in Babylon (Ezra 10:29).

JASHUBI LEHEM An unidentified place in Judah (1 Chron. 4:22).

JASON Paul's host at Thessalonica who also sent greetings to the church at Rome (Acts 17:5-9; Rom. 16:21).

JASPER *See* PRECIOUS STONES AND METALS

JATHNIEL A Levite and gatekeeper in David's time (1 Chron. 26:2).

JATTIR A Levitical town (151-084) in the hill country of Judah (Josh. 15:20, 48; 1 Chron. 6:57).

JAVAN A son of Japheth and grandson of Noah whose name passed on to the Ionians (Gen. 10:2, 4, 5).

JAVELIN *See* ARMS AND ARMOR

JAZER, JAAZER A town in Gilead east of the Jordan in the tribal area of Gad which became a Levitical city (Num. 21:24-32; 32:34, 35; Josh. 21:39).

JAZIZ One who was over David's flocks (1 Chron. 27:31).

JEALOUS, JEALOUSY In the Bible both men and God show this attitude. It may be a negative jealousy or it may be zeal for, that is, jealousy of something or jealousy for something which later is often called zeal. Rachel was jealous of Leah's ability to bear children and the young man who reported to Moses was jealous for Moses (Gen. 30:1; Num. 11:26-29). Both kinds of jealousy are also well attested in the NT but rendered as "envy," or "zeal" or "desire" (Rom. 1:29; Isa. 9:7; Zech. 1:14-17; 8:2, 3).

A special case of jealousy is that of a husband who thinks that his wife has been unfaithful. The test is her reaction after drinking the "bitter water" that brings the curse (Num. 5:11-25).

JEARIM A hill on the border of the tribal area of Judah, also called Kesalon (Josh. 15:10).

JEATHERAI A descendant of Levi (1 Chron. 6:21).

JEBERECHIAH The father of one of the witnesses to what Isaiah wrote on a scroll (Isa. 8:1, 2).

JEBUS *See* JERUSALEM

JEBUSITES A clan first mentioned in Genesis 10:16 as descending from Canaan and living in the hill country before Israel conquered it (Gen. 15:17-21; Josh. 3:10). They lived on in Jebus (Jerusalem) until David finally conquered and drove them out (Judg. 19:11; 2 Sam. 5:6-9). The threshing floor of Araunah was purchased by David from a Jebusite and later became the site of Solomon's temple (2 Sam. 24:16-18).

JECHONIAH *See* "Jehoiachin" under KINGS OF JUDAH AND ISRAEL

JECOLIAH The mother of King Azariah of Judah (called Uzziah in v. 32) (2 Kgs. 15:2).

JECONIAH The name of Jehoiachin found in a number of places (1 Chron. 3:16). *See* "Jehoiachin" under KINGS OF JUDAH AND ISRAEL

JEDAIAH 1. A descendant of Simeon (1 Chron. 4:37).

2. Head of the second priestly division as arranged by David in his latter years (1 Chron. 24:7).

3. A Jerusalem priest who returned from the Babylonian exile (1 Chron. 9:10).

4. Ancestor of some priests who came back from the exile with Zerubbabel (Ezra 2:36).

5 and 6. Two other priests who returned with Zerubbabel (Neh. 12:6, 7).

7. One who worked with Nehemiah to repair the wall of Jerusalem (Neh. 3:10).

8. An exile who came back from Babylon to Jerusalem and gave silver and gold for the rebuilding of the temple (Zech. 6:10, 14).

JEDIAEL 1. A son of Benjamin (1 Chron. 7:6).

2. A mighty man of David (1 Chron. 11:45).

3. One of David's gatekeepers (1 Chron. 26:2).

JEDIDAH The mother of King Josiah (2 Kgs. 22:1).

JEDIDIAH The name given by the prophet Nathan to the baby Solomon (2 Sam. 12:25).

JEDUTHUN 1. One of the Levites that David put over the ministry of music in the temple (1 Chron. 25:1-6). One of his sons was a gatekeeper before the Ark of the Covenant (1 Chron. 16:38).

2. The name is found in the heading of a number of Psalms (39, 62, 77). *See also* PSALMS, TITLES OF.

JEGAR SAHADUTHA The stone set up as a pillar of witness between Laban and Jacob. So called by Laban in Aramaic. Jacob called it in Hebrew Galeed (Gen. 31:47).

JEHALLELEL 1. A descendant of Judah (1 Chron. 4:16).

2. Father of one of the Levites who helped King Hezekiah cleanse the temple (2 Chron. 29:12).

JEHDEIAH 1. A Levite who served in David's day (1 Chron. 24:20).

2. David's servant in charge of the donkeys (1 Chron. 27:30).

JEHEZKEL Head of the twentieth priestly division in David's time (1 Chron. 24:16).

JEHIAH A Levite doorkeeper for the Ark in David's days (1 Chron. 15:24).

JEHIEL 1. A Levite musician in David's time and also in charge of his treasure (1 Chron. 15:18, 20; 23:8).

2. A tutor for the sons of David (1 Chron. 27:32).

3. A son of King Jehoshaphat of Judah (2 Chron. 21:2).

4. A Levite appointed by King Hezekiah of Judah to help with the repair of the temple storerooms (2 Chron. 31:13).

5. A chief officer in the temple in the days of King Josiah (2 Chron. 35:8).

6. The father of one of those who returned with Ezra from the Babylonian captivity (Ezra 8:9).

7. Father of one who married a foreign wife during the captivity (Ezra 10:2).

8 and 9. Two who married foreign wives during the captivity (Ezra 10:21, 26).

JEHIELI The same as JEHIEL, 1 above (1 Chron. 26:21, 22).

JEHIZKIAH A chief of the tribe of Ephraim who stood against enslaving the men and women of Judah in the days of King Ahaz of Judah (2 Chron. 28:12, 13).

JEHOADDAH *See* JADAH

JEHOADDAN, JEHOADDIN The mother of King Amaziah of Judah (2 Chron. 25:1; 2 Kgs. 14:2). The second name is a variant of the first (see footnote at 2 Kgs. 14:2).

JEHOAHAZ *See* KINGS OF JUDAH AND ISRAEL. There are three kings by this name.

JEHOASH *See* KINGS OF JUDAH AND ISRAEL. There are two kings by this name.

JEHOHANAN 1. A Levite gatekeeper in the temple in David's day (1 Chron. 26:3, 12).

2. A military commander in the army of King Jehoshaphat (2 Chron. 17:15).

3. Father of a military commander of hundreds when Joash was made king (2 Chron. 23:1).

4. Head of a priestly family after the return from Babylon (Neh. 12:13).

5. One who married a foreign wife during the time of the Babylonian captivity (Ezra 10:10, 28).

6. Son of the Tobiah who corresponded with others in an attempt to make Nehemiah afraid to continue the work (Neh. 6:17-19).

7. A priest who was with Nehemiah at the dedication of the wall of Jerusalem (Neh. 12:42).

JEHOIACHIN *See* KINGS OF JUDAH AND ISRAEL

JEHOIADA 1. Father of one of David's valiant military commanders (2 Sam. 8:18; 23:20).

2. One of David's counselors and grandson of Jehoiada, 1 (1 Chron. 27:34).

3. The priest who helped to enthrone the only royal son that Athaliah was not able to kill. He ultimately was able to get Jehoash-Joash on the throne and have Athaliah himself killed (2 Kgs. 11:1-4, 12, 18, 20-21).

4. One who led a group to David at Hebron. Perhaps the same as number 1 above (1 Chron. 12:27).

JEHOIAKIM *See* KINGS OF JUDAH AND ISRAEL

JEHOIARIB 1. A priest who came back from the exile in Babylon also called Joiarib (1 Chron. 9:10; Neh. 11:10).

2. The head of one of the priestly divisions in the days of King David (1 Chron. 24:7).

JEHONADAB *See* JONADAB, 2

JEHONATHAN 1. A Levite sent by the king of Judah, Jehoshaphat, to teach the law to his people (2 Chron. 17:8).

2. A priest in the days of Joiakim (Neh. 12:18).

JEHORAM *See* KINGS OF JUDAH AND ISRAEL. There are two kings by this name.

JEHOSHABEATH *See* JEHOSHEBA

JEHOSHAPHAT 1. *See* KINGS OF JUDAH AND ISRAEL.

2. Father of the Jehu who became a king of Israel (2 Kgs. 9:2, 14).

3. The recorder in the time of David and Solomon (2 Sam. 8:16; 1 Kgs. 4:3).

4. Solomon's man in Issachar responsible for getting the food for the king's household (1 Kgs. 4:17).

JEHOSHAPHAT, VALLEY OF An unidentified valley into which God is to bring the nations of the world for judgment (Joel 3:2, 12). Many have identified it with the lower parts of the Kidron Valley. There seems to be no substantial reason for accepting this identification.

JEHOSHEBA The daughter of King Jehoram of Judah also called Jehoshabeath who saved the life of Jehoash-Joash and hid him until her husband was able to get him enthroned (2 Chron. 22:11; 2 Kgs. 11:2ff.).

JEHOZABAD 1. One of the assassins of King Josiah of Judah (2 Kgs. 12:19-21).

2. A Levite whom David appointed as one of the gatekeepers for the temple (1 Chron. 26:4).

3. A descendant of Benjamin who served King Jehoshaphat (2 Chron. 17:18).

JEHOZADAK One who was taken into captivity by the Babylonians. The father of the High Priest Joshua at the time of the return from the captivity (1 Chron. 6:14, 15; Ezra 3:2; Neh. 12:26; Hag. 1:1; Zech. 6:11). Spelled also Josedech, Jozadak.

JEHU 1. *See* KINGS OF JUDAH AND ISRAEL.

2. A prophet who prophesied against King Baasha of Israel and also Jehoshaphat of Judah. He wrote a set of annals (1 Kgs. 16:1; 2 Chron. 19:1-3; 20:34).

3. A descendant of Judah (1 Chron. 2:38).

4. A descendant of Simeon (1 Chron. 4:35).

5. A descendant of Benjamin who joined David at Ziklag (1 Chron. 12:3).

JEHUCAL One sent by King Zedekiah to the prophet Jeremiah requesting prayer, also called Jucal (Jer. 37:3; 38:1). He was among the princes who recommended the death of the prophet. In the footnote at 38:1 (NIV) the Hebrew text reads Jucal.

JEHUD A town (139-159) in the tribal area of Dan (Josh. 19:45).

JEHUDI An officer of King Jehoiakim, sent to Baruch to hear what was in the scroll which the prophet Jeremiah had dictated (Jer. 36:14-23).

JEIEL 1. A descendant of Reuben (1 Chron. 5:7).

2. A descendant of Benjamin and ancestor of Saul (1 Chron. 8:29). The name is not in the Hebrew text.

3, 4, and 5. One of David's mighty men, a Levitical member of a choir for bringing up the Ark and a Levitical harpist (1 Chron. 11:44; 15:18, 21).

6. Ancestor of Jahaziel who prophesied in the days of King Jehoshaphat (2 Chron. 20:14).

7. A secretary in the army of King Uzziah (2 Chron. 26:11).

8. A Levite chief who contributed to the great public Passover in the days of King Josiah (2 Chron. 35:9).

9. One who married a foreign wife during the Babylonian captivity (Ezra 10:43).

JEKABZEEL After the return from the Babylonian captivity a town (148-071) inhabited by some of the returnees (Neh. 11:25).

JEKAMEAM A descendant of Levi in the days of David (1 Chron. 23:19).

JEKAMIAH 1. A descendant of Judah via Jerahmeel (1 Chron. 2:41).

2. One of the sons of King Jehoiachin (Jeconiah) (1 Chron. 3:18).

JEKUTHIEL A descendant of Judah (1 Chron. 4:18).

JEMIMAH A daughter of Job (Job 42:14).

JEMUEL A son of Simeon also called Nemuel (Gen. 46:10; Num. 26:12).

JEPHTHAH *See* JUDGES OF ISRAEL

JEPHUNNEH 1. The father of Caleb, one of the twelve spies sent to Canaan by Moses (Num. 13:6).

2. A descendant of Asher (1 Chron. 7:38).

JERAH A descendant of Shem and son of Joktan, father of a number of eastern clans (Gen. 10:26).

JERAHMEEL 1. A descendant of Judah and brother of Caleb with whom David had contact when he was at Ziklag (1 Chron. 2:9, 25-42; 1 Sam. 27:10; 30:29).

2. A son of Caleb (1 Chron. 2:42).

3. A son of King Jehoiakim sent to arrest the prophet Jeremiah (Jer. 36:26).

JERED A descendant of Judah (1 Chron. 4:18).

JEREMAI One who married a foreign wife during the Babylonian captivity (Ezra 10:33).

JEREMIAH 1. Jeremiah of Libnah was the father of Hamutal, the mother of kings Jehoahaz and Zedekiah of Judah (2 Kgs. 23:31; 24:18).

2. A descendant of Manasseh (1 Chron. 5:24).

3, 4, and 5. A descendant of Benjamin who joined David at Ziklag and two descendants of Gad who joined David at the stronghold in the wilderness (1 Chron. 12:4, 10, 13).

6. A priest who signed the covenant with Nehemiah (Neh. 10:2).

7. A priest who returned with Zerubbabel from the Babylonian captivity, father of the head of a priestly family in the days of Joiakim (Neh. 12:1, 12).

8. Father of Jaazaniah, a Recabite whom Jeremiah took to the house of the Lord (Jer. 35:3, 4).

9. One who participated with Nehemiah in the dedication of the wall of Jerusalem (Neh. 12:34).

10. The writing prophet, son of Hilkiah, from Anathoth, who prophesied to Judah from the days of King Josiah to the very end of the Kingdom of Judah, even after their being taken into captivity to Babylon. He was then taken into Egypt (Jer. 1:1, 2; 39:1-8, 11-14; 43:5-7). His life was a tumultuous one, often in trouble with the other Israelites because of his prophecies of doom (Jer. 25:1ff.; 36:20ff.; 37:11ff.; 43:6). He was the author of two books, one bearing his own name and the other "Lamentations."

JEREMIAH, BOOK OF, AND THE LAMENTATIONS OF These two works are from the pen of Jeremiah (10 above), who lived and wrote during the declining days of the Kingdom of Judah just prior to their Babylonian captivity. The Book of Jeremiah has a logical rather than a chronological order for the presentation of its material. Through chapter 25 the prophet is primarily concerned with the sins of Jerusalem and Judah and the impending captivity as a punishment from God for their sins (Jer. 3:6-13; 7:15). In the middle section, chapters 26 through 45, the prophet becomes autobiographical and recounts his evil treatment by the king and populace for his prophecies of impending doom. He discusses the last days of Jerusalem prior to the Babylonian captivity and his being carried to Egypt. He is threatened with death (26:11), imprisoned (38:6), and under constant threat by the establishment. In this section he prophesied an end to the captivity, return from it, and that ultimately a new covenant would be established by God with them when he will have regathered them from a far greater diaspora than the one to Babylon, from a worldwide diaspora. This new covenant is tied in to the new covenant of the NT by the writer of the Book of Hebrews (30:1-3; 31:31-34; 32:37-44; Heb. 8:8-12). Israel and Judah, regathered from all the countries of the diaspora and not merely Babylon, will share in the new covenant which the Church has been enjoying for some two thousand years. The final section of the book deals with prophecies against specific cities and countries: Egypt, Moab, Edom, Damascus, Babylon among others (Jer. 46-52).

The Lamentations of Jeremiah are five elegies or lamentations wrung from the prophet at the thought of the fall of Jerusalem. Their structure deserves a note. The first four are acrostics, that is, the successive verses begin with the letters of the

Hebrew alphabet in order. There are twenty-two verses (22 letters of the alphabet) in chapters 1, 2, and 4. Chapter 3 has 66 verses and is a triple acrostic, three verses to each letter of the alphabet in order. While chapter 5 has twenty-two verses it is not an acrostic at all. This style is quite atypical as far as Hebrew poetry in general is concerned and thus is of special interest.

JEREMOTH, JERIMOTH 1 and 2. Two descendants of Benjamin (1 Chron. 7:8; 8:14).

3. A Levite assigned to the work of the house of the Lord by David, also called Jerimoth (1 Chron. 23:23; 24:30; 25:4, 22).

4. David's officer over the tribe of Naphtali (1 Chron. 27:19).

5, 6, and 7. Three who married foreign wives during the Babylonian captivity (Ezra 10:26, 27, 29).

JERIAH A descendant of Moses, also called Jerijah (1 Chron. 23:19; 26:31).

JERIBAI One of David's mighty men (1 Chron. 11:46).

JERICHO A green oasis (192-142) with an abundant water supply located where the central mountain ridge of Palestine tapers off before the desert that stretches to where the Jordan River begins. The water supply, its winter climate, its location near an important ford of the Jordan and its defense capabilities all contribute to its long history. This history goes back to prepottery neolithic times and makes it probably among the oldest post-Flood cities in the Middle East. As the Israelites were encamped opposite it in the plains of Moab the elders of Moab and Midian hired Balaam to curse them. This failed but turned into a promise of blessing (Num. 22, 23, 24). Later we read that two spies searched out the city's defenses for Joshua (Josh. 2:1). The city was taken by Israel in a spectacular manner and destroyed under the leadership of Joshua (Josh. 6), and not rebuilt for centuries, until the time of King Ahab of Israel (1 Kgs. 16:34). It then became again an important city and so remained through the time of the monarchy, the time of Ezra and Nehemiah and the time of Christ. Nearby was built what is called NT Jericho (2 Kgs. 2:18; 25:5; Ezra 2:34; Mk. 10:46).

JERICHO, PLAINS OF *See* GEOGRAPHY OF THE HOLY LAND

JERIEL A grandson of Issachar (1 Chron. 7:2).

JERIJAH *See* JERIAH

JERIMOTH 1. A grandson of Benjamin (1 Chron. 7:7).

2. Another descendant of Benjamin who joined David at Ziklag (1 Chron. 12:5).

3. *See* JEREMOTH, 3.

4. The father-in-law of King Rehoboam (2 Chron. 11:18), and a son of David.

5. A Levite in the days of King Hezekiah of Judah (2 Chron. 31:13).

JERIOTH A wife of Caleb (1 Chron. 2:18).

JEROBOAM *See* KINGS OF JUDAH AND ISRAEL. There were two kings by this name.

JEROHAM 1. Grandfather of the prophet Samuel (1 Sam. 1:1).

2 and 3. Fathers of three different Benjamites, two of whom joined David at Ziklag (Joelah and Zebadiah) and one who returned from the Babylonian captivity (1 Chron. 12:7; 9:8).

4. Father of a priest who returned with Zerubbabel from the Babylonian captivity (1 Chron. 9:12; Neh. 11:12).

5. Father of the leader of the tribe of Dan in David's day (1 Chron. 27:22).

6. Father of a commander of a hundred in the days of King Josiah, whom Jehoiada used to help enthrone this king (2 Chron. 23:1).

JERUB-BAAL Another name for Gideon. *See* JUDGES OF ISRAEL.

JERUB-BESHETH *See* JERUB-BAAL

JERUEL An unidentified area, the Desert of Jeruel, in the tribal area of Judah (2 Chron. 20:16).

JERUSALEM *Topography.* Jerusalem is located at an elevation of 750 meters above sea level in the hills of Judea. The original settlement was on a ridge above the perennial Gihon spring (the Virgin's Fountain). There is another spring to the south, En-Rogel (Job's Well), which is not in as advantageous a position as Gihon.

The ridge above Gihon was easily defended, bounded on the east by the Kidron or Jehoshaphat Valley, and on the west by the central valley called the Tyropean by Josephus. The shape of the latter is today obscured by about fifty feet of fill. The hill to the west of the Tyropean, which is today called "Mount Zion," is bounded on the west by the

Hinnom (Gehenna) Valley, which curves to the east to meet the other two valleys.

The Jebusite city captured by David was restricted to the eastern ridge and was less than ten acres in size. Solomon built the temple to the north. The extent and exact direction of later expansion under the Judean kings is uncertain. It is now known that the western hill, "Mount Zion," was not incorporated until the time of Agrippa I (A.D. 40-44), in whose time the city had expanded to a size of 310 acres.

Names. The earliest extrabiblical reference to Jerusalem is in newly discovered texts from Ebla (twenty-third century B.C.) followed by those in the execration texts of the nineteenth to eighteenth centuries B.C. from Egypt. The fourteenth century B.C. Amarna letters from Egypt mention *Urusalim*, and its king, Abdi-Heba (a Hurrian name). The name of Jerusalem, *Yeru-Shalem*, appears to mean "foundation of (the god) Shalem." The abbreviated form, Salem (Heb. *Shalem*), first occurs in Genesis 14, when Abraham offered a tithe to Melchizedek, its king. Moriah, where Abraham offered his son Isaac (Gen. 22:2), has been interpreted as Jerusalem (2 Chron. 3:1).

In the period of the Judges, the city was called Jebus, after its inhabitants the Jebusites, who are probably related to the Hurrians (Judg. 19:10). With the capture of the Jebusite stronghold by David, it is called the City of David or Zion, possibly "stronghold of water." By the time of Josephus the name "Zion" had been transferred to the western hill. The term Ophel, strictly speaking applies to the northern part of the eastern ridge toward the temple area, but is commonly used of the entire eastern ridge. A cryptic term Ariel, which may mean "hearth of God," or less probably "lion of God," is used in Isaiah 29:1, 2.

Excavations. Archaeologists have been faced with formidable problems in the excavation of Jerusalem. Since the city is still inhabited, very few areas are free for excavations. Extensive quarrying has taken place on Ophel, removing traces of early occupations. The huge Herodian temple platform has irrevocably buried any remains in that area from the OT period. Nonetheless, the efforts of a century of work have yielded important data. The first important efforts were the tunnels and shafts dug by a British army engineer, Charles Warren, in 1867-70. Most important are the excavations which have been conducted by Kathleen Kenyon primarily at Ophel from 1961-67. Excavations begun by Benjamin Mazar in 1968 south of the temple, those begun by Nahman Avigad in the Jewish Quarter in 1969, and those begun by Y. Shiloh in the Ophel area since 1978, have added immensely to our knowledge of Jerusalem, especially in the Herodian period.

The Pre-Davidic and United Monarchy Periods. Some traces of habitation from the third millennium B.C. have been found. The earliest structure on Ophel is a massive "Jebusite" wall discovered by Kenyon just above the Gihon spring. It was built about 1900 B.C. and was used until about 800 B.C. by the Israelites. Joshua defeated Adoni-Zedek, the king of Jerusalem, and his allies (Josh. 10) but Jerusalem was not liberated from the Jebusites until the time of David.

After having made Hebron, to the south of Jerusalem, his capital, David and his men moved against the Jebusites at Jerusalem (1 Chron. 11; 2 Sam. 5). It is possible that the *tsinnor* by which Joab led the attack, is a "water shaft" (2 Sam. 5:8) which led from the waters of Gihon inside the Jebusite walls discovered by Warren in 1867. David built himself a palace (2 Sam. 5:11) and having brought back the Ark of the Lord (2 Sam. 6) desired to build a temple for it. To that end he purchased the threshing floor of Araunah the Jebusite (2 Sam. 24:18-25), but the building of the temple was to be accomplished by his son Solomon and not himself. In excavations in the southern part of Ophel, Weill in 1913-14 discovered curious tunnel-like structures, which he interpreted as the tombs of David and other kings. This is very doubtful. Historically unfounded is the tradition of David's tomb venerated by pious Jews today on "Mount Zion."

David (2 Sam. 5:9) and Solomon (1 Kgs. 9:15) are both said to have repaired the "terraces" (Heb. *millo*). Kenyon interprets this to mean the massive platforms on the eastern edge of Ophel, which needed constant repair.

With the help of Phoenician craftsmen sent to him by Hiram, king of Tyre, Solomon spent thirteen years building his own palace (1 Kgs. 7:1), and seven years building the first temple (1 Kgs. 6:38). The only possible traces of a Solomonic building to be found are a Proto-Ionic column and a segment of a casemate wall found by Kenyon in the northern part of Ophel. Traces of Solomon's temple must lie buried under the temple platform built by Herod. The so-called "Stables of Solomon," however, in the southeastern part of the platform are simply the supports built by Herod, and later rebuilt by the Crusaders.

The Divided Kingdom. The present city walls of Jerusalem are largely the work of Suleiman the Magnificent (sixteenth century A.D.), resting on earlier foundations. The walls form a square, enclosing the temple area in the southeastern quarter. Both "Mount Zion" and Ophel are outside the walls to the south.

The Iron Age settlement in Jerusalem has been clarified by recent discoveries. Mazar has found near the southwest corner of the temple platform tombs (eighth century B.C.), which he suggests may represent a royal cemetery. To the west Avigad has uncovered a massive "Broad Wall" (see Neh. 3:8), which probably enclosed the *Mishneh* or "second quarter" (2 Kgs. 22:14; Zeph. 1:10). He suggests that the wall was probably built by Hezekiah.

In preparation for the siege by the forces of the Assyrian king, Sennacherib, in 701 B.C., Hezekiah built a tunnel from the Gihon spring to the site of Siloam, 1,000 feet to the southwest. The actual course of the tunnel, which may still be traversed today, by taking an S-shaped course covers about 1,800 feet. In 1880 an inscription of Hezekiah was found in the tunnel. This described in vivid terms the meeting of the teams who had worked from both ends. The Assyrian general who taunted the inhabitants of Jerusalem stood "at the aqueduct of the upper pool on the road to the Washerman's Field" (Isa. 36:2). He was probably standing on the southern end of the western ridge, facing Siloam. Assyrian records confirm the biblical account of the failure of the Assyrians to capture Jerusalem.

In 597, however, Nebuchadnezzar the king of Babylon, captured Jerusalem and in 587-86 he destroyed the temple. Mass burials with decapitated bodies found by Weill in Ophel may date to this attack. In 1975 Avigad found arrowheads which had been shot by the Scythian archers of the Babylonians.

After the capture of Babylon by the Persians in 539, the Jews were allowed by Cyrus to return to Jerusalem. After some delay the temple was rebuilt in 516. When Nehemiah visited Jerusalem in 445, however, the city walls were still unrepaired. In Nehemiah 2:14 we read that "there was not enough room for my mount to get through." The vast tumble uncovered by Kenyon illustrates this verse. The postexilic walls were constructed for the reduced size of the population. Now that we know that the circuit was only 2,600 meters (since the western ridge was not settled until later), Nehemiah's claim that the walls were repaired within fifty-two days (Neh. 6:15) is that much more credible.

The Intertestamental Period. In the late fourth century B.C. the Perisan Empire was overrun by the Macedonian army of Alexander the Great. There is a legend that Alexander visited Jerusalem. For about a century Palestine was contested by the Seleucids of Syria and the Ptolemies of Egypt. In 198 the Seleucids gained control. Antiochus IV imposed a forced policy of Hellenization upon the Jews, desecrating the temple by the sacrifice of swine in 168. He also erected a gymnasium and installed a Syrian garrison on the Akra, overlooking the temple area. The Akra is possibly to be located on the site of the Citadel. The archaeologist Johns found in the Citadel a Seleucid coin of the second century. The Maccabees rededicated the temple in 165, but succeeded in liberating the Akra only in 142. There are signs of Hasmonean construction in the Citadel area. It is possible that Josephus' first north wall which runs from the Citadel to the temple area, directly west-east, south of the present David Street, dates from this time.

Two structures dated by earlier excavators to the Jebusite period are now to be dated to the Hellenistic period. The so-called "Jebusite tower" and "Jebusite ramp" excavated by MacAlister and Duncan in 1923-25 on the brow of Ophel have been shown by Kenyon to be Hellenistic. A massive gate on the west side of Ophel, excavated by Crowfoot and Fitzgerald in 1927-28, is also thought by Kenyon to be Hellenistic. In the Kidron Valley below the southeast corner of the temple area, the so-called Tomb of the Bene Hezir and Tomb of Zechariah are Hellenistic.

Herod the Great. In 63 B.C. Pompey made Syria a Roman province. In Palestine he intervened on behalf of the high priest Hyrcanus against his brother Aristobulus. Some of the latter's followers established themselves in the temple area which Pompey forcibly seized. Entering the Holy of Holies, Pompey was surprised to find it bare.

Hyrcanus was advised by Antipater, an Idumaean. One of Antipater's sons, Phasael, was made prefect of Jerusalem, and another, Herod, prefect of Galilee. In 40 B.C. Parthians attacked Jerusalem, carrying off Phasael and later killing him. Herod fled to Rome, where he was proclaimed king of the Jews. In 37 B.C. after a five-month siege he captured Jerusalem with the aid of Roman troops.

Herod, an admirer of Hellenistic culture, provided Jerusalem with a stadium, a theatre, and a hippodrome. He built himself a sumptuous palace in the area south of the Citadel. To the north of the palace he erected three massive towers, named Phasael, Hippicus (after a friend), and Mariamne (after his wife). Phasael, the tallest, towered forty-five meters high. The base of Phasael has been incorporated in the northeast tower of the Citadel, popularly called "David's Tower."

Northwest of the temple area Herod built a fortress, named Antonia, after his friend Marc Anthony. The court of the Antonia with its huge flagstones, some inscribed with Roman names, has been uncovered in the basement of the Sisters of Zion building. This calls to mind the "pavement" of John 19:13 where Jesus was tried before Pilate. Other scholars believe that the place of judgment before Pilate was in Herod's palace.

Herod's supreme accomplishment was the rebuilding of the second temple, a project begun in 20 B.C. and not finally completed until A.D. 64, just a few years before its utter destruction. The huge platform, 2,575 feet by 985 feet, is known today as the Haram or "Sanctuary," and comprises about one-sixth of the area of the present walled city. Mazar has determined that Robinson's Arch at the southwest corner of the temple platform supported a monumental staircase rather than a bridge across the upper Tyropean Valley as in the case of Wilson's Arch further north. Herod would have used the former. The common people ascended to the temple mount through the Huldah Gates in the south, remains of which may be seen today, the Double Gate under the al-Aksa Mosque, and the Triple Gate. The so-called "Golden Gate," through which Jesus entered the temple area on Palm Sunday, was blocked by Turks to prevent Christ from reusing it. The present structure is a late reconstruction, resting, however, on earlier remains.

The large, beautifully drafted Herodian masonry may be seen at both the southeastern and the southwestern corners of the Haram. At the former point it extends sixteen meters above the surface, and (from information from Warren's shaft) twenty-four meters below the surface. In 1968 Mazar exposed Herodian pavement south of the southwestern corner. The famous Western or Wailing Wall is a portion of Herodian masonry on the west, a focal point of Jewish devotion up until 1948, and now once again since 1967.

Jesus Christ. Two of the scenes of Jesus' acts of healing have been identified with certainty. The pool of Bethesda, with its five porches (Jn. 5:2) has been excavated in the property of the Church of St. Anne, just north of the Haram. The actual site of the miracle may have been in a cave to the east. The pool of Siloam (Jn. 9:7), where Hezekiah's tunnel ends, is also well known. Other sites are not as certainly identified.

The tradition of the Coenaculum, site of the Last Supper, shown on Mount Zion, does not go back before the fourth century A.D. On the traditional site of the House of Caiaphas, M. Broshi in 1971-72 uncovered unique frescoes of birds. The Jewish Quarter of the walled city contains the remains of the Upper City where the wealthy high priests lived. Avigad found there a stone weight with the name Bar Kathros, one of the priestly families in the Talmud accused of exploiting the people. He found also, among many interesting things, extensive remains of a massive basilica from the seventh century A.D., the Nea Church.

Great controversy has surrounded the question of the Lord's crucifixion and burial. Dissatisfied by the appearance of the traditional site of the Church of the Holy Sepulchre, some Protestants have favored a rocky knoll north of the Damascus Gate. This is called Gordon's Calvary, after General Charles Gordon who popularized the site in 1883. The hill has two cavities which give it the appearance of a skull, but these cavities are probably recent. Nearby is the so-called Garden Tomb pointed out as the site of Christ's burial. The tomb, however, is not earlier than A.D. 300.

The site of Calvary was covered by the forum and temple of Venus of Hadrian's pagan city of Aelia Capitolina. Helena, the mother of Constantine, in the fourth century A.D. "rediscovered" the site and the Church of the Holy Sepulchre was rebuilt over Calvary and the supposed tomb of Christ. To be authentic the site must lie outside the second northern wall described by Josephus. Unfortunately, the description that he gives is not clear. But there is every reason to believe that the tradition for Calvary is sound. Kenyon's excavations in the Muristan area south of the Church of the Holy Sepulchre has demonstrated that this area was outside the walls until the second century A.D. Quarrying between A.D. 30-68, however, may have demolished the authentic tomb.

Acts of the Apostles. The Greek inscription of Theodotus found by Weill on Ophel may refer to the synagogue of the freedmen, mentioned in Acts 6:9. Agrippa I, grandson of Herod the Great, became king over Judea in A.D. 40, after having ruled in other areas earlier. His sudden death in A.D. 44 is recorded in Acts 12:20. It was he who killed James the son of Zebedee (Acts 12:2) and imprisoned Peter. In his short four years over Judea, Agrippa proved himself to be a vigorous builder.

Josephus says that Agrippa began the building of the third north wall, which was not completed until just before the war with Rome (see below). Kenyon's recent excavations now reveal that it was he who was responsible for the incorporation of the western hill, "Mount Zion." On the Bishop Gobat School on Mount Zion Maudslay in 1975 traced remains of towers and cisterns. Bliss and Dickie in 1894-97 uncovered a magnificent paved street in the Tyropean Valley, which Kenyon dated to Agrippa's time.

On Paul's final visit to Jerusalem a riot was precipitated because the Jews thought that Paul had taken a Gentile into the inner temple area (Acts 21). Two copies of the Greek inscription warning Gentiles not to go beyond the Court of the Gentiles upon penalty of death have been recovered.

Jewish War of 66-70. To quell the revolt which began under Nero in 66, Titus with an army of 65,000 men besieged Jerusalem in 70. Agrippa's third north wall was hastily finished by the Jewish defenders. The exact line of this wall has been one of the most controversial problems. Robinson in 1838 first noticed traces of a massive wall north of the present wall. In 1925-27 Sukenik and Mayer excavated considerable portions of this wall; in 1940 further sections were uncovered. The exposed portions form a line about 375 meters long. Sukenik claimed that this was the third wall.

Vincent, however, claimed that this wall did not fit the enthusiastic description of Josephus, and suggested that the third wall should lie under the present north wall. Excavations by Henessey at the Damascus Gate convinced him and Kenyon that Vincent's proposal was correct. These British excavators suggest that the Sukenik-Mayer wall was set up by Titus as a circumvallation wall.

In 1972 additional sections along the Sukenik-Mayer line, including two towers projecting outward, were uncovered. This new discovery supports the view that this was the third wall.

After the destruction of the third wall, Titus' troops took the Antonia in July, burned the temple in August, and finally seized the Upper City in September. Titus left the three towers of Herod as a monument, and installed the Tenth Legion in a camp to the south of the Citadel. In 1947 and in 1968 Avi-Yonah excavated remains of an installation of the Tenth Legion at Givat Ram, a western suburb of Jerusalem.

Evidences of the Roman siege of Jerusalem include thick layers of ash found by Mazar and Avigad, Roman catapult balls from below the Convent of the Sisters of Zion, and the skeletal remains of a woman from a house in the Upper City.

Bar Cochba Revolt. From the evidence of some coins it now appears that Hadrian's decision to rebuild Jerusalem as a pagan city, Aelia Capitolina, was the cause and not the result of the Bar Cochba revolt in A.D. 132-35. After the defeat of the rebels, Hadrian forbade the entrance into Jerusalem of Jews and of Christians of Jewish extraction. The famous Ecce Homo arch at the beginning of the Via Dolorosa is actually part of a triple arch set up by Hadrian. Kenyon has found remains of Aelia's southern wall just south of the Haram area. Much of the present walls probably are shaped by the walls of Aelia. The Roman sewer down the north-south depression of the walled city is still the main sewer of this area.

Professor Mazar's excavations south and east of the Haram coupled with those of Professor Avigad inside the city wall in the Jewish Quarter of the city have made herculean contributions to unraveling the history of Jerusalem. Excavations continuing in the Ophel will produce many additions. (E.M.Y.)

JERUSHA Mother of King Jotham of Judah (2 Kgs. 15:33; 2 Chron. 27:1).

JESARELAH A son of Asaph also called Asarelah (1 Chron. 25:2, 14).

JESHAIAH 1. A grandson of Zerubbabel in the royal line after the return from the Babylonian captivity (1 Chron. 3:21).

2. A musician who prophesied using the harp in David's day (1 Chron. 25:3).

3. One of those in charge of the treasuries of the house of the Lord in David's days (1 Chron. 26:25).

4. A family head who returned with Ezra from the Babylonian captivity (Ezra 8:7).

5. One sent to help Ezra from the place Casiphia (Ezra 8:17-19).

6. An ancestor of Sallu or descendant of Benjamin in the return from the captivity in Babylon (Neh. 11:7).

JESHANAH A town (174-156) in the tribal area of Ephraim taken from Israel by King Abijah of Judah (2 Chron. 13:19).

JESHEBEAB Head of the fourteenth priestly division in the time of David (1 Chron. 24:13).

JESHER A son of Caleb (1 Chron. 2:18).

JESHIMON A word which means desert and is sometimes translated that way or as wasteland (Deut. 32:10; Num. 21:20). When used as a proper noun it refers to the desert area SE of Hebron near the Salt Sea, in which latter place David hid from Saul (1 Sam. 23:19, 24).

JESHISHAI The ancestor of a family of Gadites (1 Chron. 5:14).

JESHOHAIAH An ancestor of a Simeonite (1 Chron. 4:36).

JESHUA 1. Also called Joshua, the son of Nun (Neh. 8:17; Ex. 17:9).

2. Head of a priestly division in David's time who assisted in the distribution of gifts (1 Chron. 24:11).

3. A Levite in the days of King Hezekiah (2 Chron. 31:15).

4. Ancestor of some who returned with Zerubbabel from the Babylonian captivity (Ezra 2:6).

5. The high priest in the days of Zerubbabel, also called Joshua (Ezra 3:2; Zech. 3:3, 8). He played a prominent role in postexilic days. See especially the books of Haggai and Zechariah.

6 and 7. Ancestor of some priests, and some Levites, who returned from Babylon with Zerubbabel (Ezra 2:36, 40).

8. Father of a Levite in Ezra's days (Ezra 8:33).

9. Father of one who worked on the reparation of the wall of Jerusalem with Nehemiah (Neh. 3:19).

10. A Levite who helped to explain the law as Ezra read it (Neh. 8:7).

11. A Levite who signed the covenant with Nehemiah (Neh. 10:9).

12. A town (149-076) occupied by returnees from the captivity in Babylon (Neh. 11:26).

JESHURUN A name of the land of Israel, used in poetry (Deut. 32:15; 33:5, 26; Isa. 44:2).

JESIMIEL A descendant of Simeon (1 Chron. 4:36).

JESSE A descendant of Boaz and Ruth and father of King David (Ruth 4:18, 22; 1 Sam. 17:12).

JESUS 1. *See* CHRIST, LIFE AND TEACHINGS OF and CHRIST, WORK OF.

2. Jesus who is called Justus, who sent greetings to the church of Colosse (Col. 4:11). *See also* JUSTUS, 3.

JESUS CHRIST *See* CHRIST, LIFE AND TEACHINGS OF and CHRIST, WORK OF.

JETHER 1. A son of Gideon the judge of Israel (Judg. 8:20).

2. Father of the Amasa whom Joab murdered, also called Ithra (1 Kgs. 2:5; 2 Sam. 17:25, footnote).

3. A descendant of Judah and Jerahmeel (1 Chron. 2:32).

4. Another descendant of Judah (1 Chron. 4:17).

5. A descendant of Asher, also called Ithran (1 Chron. 7:38).

JETHETH A chief of Edom descended from Esau (Gen. 36:40).

JETHLAH *See* ITHLAH

JETHRO The father-in-law of Moses who was also called Reuel (Ex. 3:1; 2:18). Hobab is the son of Jethro (Reuel), therefore an in-law of Moses (Num. 10:29). It was Jethro who advised Moses on how to set up his administration through appointed assistants (Ex. 18:13-27; 24:1).

JETUR A son of Ishmael (Gen. 25:15).

JEUEL 1. A descendant of Judah who returned from the Babylonian captivity (1 Chron. 9:6).

2. A family head who came back from Babylon with Ezra (Ezra 8:13). In the KJV his name appears as JEIEL.

JEUSH, 1. A son of Esau (Gen. 36:4).
JEHUSH
2. A descendant of Benjamin (1 Chron. 7:10).

3. Another descendant of Benjamin and of Saul (1 Chron. 8:39).

4. A Levite in the days of David (1 Chron. 23:10, 11).

5. A son of King Rehoboam of Judah (2 Chron. 11:19).

JEUZ A descendant of Benjamin (1 Chron. 8:10).

JEW The word used to refer to the men of Judah as from the times of Jeremiah. There are many instances of its use, especially in the plural, in that book, in Ezra, Nehemiah, and Esther, and, of course in the NT where the greater number of uses occur. Prior to the sixth century B.C. these people were called "men of Judah" (2 Kgs. 16:6). At first the word Jew was used of the men of Judah, but since the majority of those who returned from the captivity in Babylon belonged to this tribe or came from the former Kingdom of Judah it came to refer to any descendant of Abraham, any Israelite in the larger sense (Mt. 2:2; Esth. 2:5). In the NT the word Jew comes to be used as the opposite of Gentile in a very general sense (Acts 14:1, 2, 5; 1 Cor. 1:23; Gal. 2:14, 15).

Much persecution by the hands of Christians has come to "the Jews" since the beginning of their diaspora in A.D. 70. By some this is blamed on the Apostle John, the writer of the fourth Gospel, who again and again refers to "The Jews." Once the crucifixion of Christ became tied to "the Jews" it was easy for the Christians to find a reason for the denigration and persecution of those who refused to accept their message about Christ. Then pagans enquired of the early Christian missionaries about the concept that if Jesus is the Messiah why they had not accepted him as such. When the Christians could find no adequate answer for this, they began the use of the *ad hominem* argument against "the Jews."

The Jews were blamed for everything that went wrong. All the nasty personal accusations and corporate charges against their rituals as being demonic were easily accepted in the "dark ages" of medieval times. Unfortunately the modern enlightenment has not yet been able to throw off these charges so ingrained in world and Christian thought. The Jews are still discriminated against in most parts of the world and the Christian Church is only very slowly setting a better pattern.

It is difficult, in view of the subsequent history, to convince any member of the Jewish community that John's Gospel is not an anti-Semitic book, but rather a book which anti-Semites can easily use for their infamous purposes. People and not the book are at fault.

It is also difficult in view of all the history subsequent to the times of Emperor Constantine to convince the Christians that not all Jews were involved in the crucifixion, not the Jewish apostles, not the Jewish authors of the books of the NT, not the Jews in remote corners of the Roman Empire of those days, and certainly not the descendants who were not even born in those days. Some Jewish leaders of that time, and an aroused mob cried, "Crucify him. His blood be upon us and our children," but this could not be all "the Jews." Furthermore when the NT plainly states that only Romans could give an execution in those days, that the Romans did in fact crucify Christ, and especially when the NT is so crystal clear that Christ was crucified for all of our sins, as Gentiles, it is a travesty for us to keep harping on the line that "the Jews" are to be punished for the crucifixion of Jesus. This is especially true of any Christian who is such because he believes that Christ's death atones for the sins of mankind, his own in particular. The Roman action of their procurator is clear. Notice the constant use of "they" in referring to the Romans and their soldiers (Mt. 27:2, 11-14, 24, 37, 54, 58; Jn. 19:31, 32; 1 Cor. 15:3; Rom. 5:6-11). This truth is clear and so is the Christian theology that his death was to atone for our sins.

JEZANIAH *See* JAAZANIAH

JEZEBEL 1. Daughter of the king of Sidon, queen of King Ahab of Israel, and mother of the Athaliah, who married the king of Judah and thus introduced the pagan worship of Baal into both Israel and Judah (1 Kgs. 16:30-32; 2 Kgs. 8:16-18, 25, 26). Jezebel fed 450 prophets of Baal and 400 prophets of Asherah at her table and killed any prophet of the Lord she could find (1 Kgs. 18:4, 13, 19; 2 Kgs. 9:7). The story of her running battle with the prophet Elijah, that of the slaughter of the entire house of Ahab, and of Jezebel's own tragic death is one of the great classics of OT history. This began with her opposition to the God of Israel and was triggered in particular by her murder of Naboth in order to seize his vineyard at Jezreel (1 Kgs. 21:1—22:40; 2 Kgs. 1:17; 9:1—10:11).

2. In the NT Thyatira there was a "woman Jezebel, who calls herself a prophetess" who misled the people (Rev. 2:18-20).

JEZER A son of Naphtali (Gen. 46:24).

JEZIEL A Benjamite who joined David at Ziklag (1 Chron. 12:3).

JEZRAHIAH A leader of the temple choirs at the time of the dedication of the wall of Jerusalem rebuilt by Nehemiah (Neh. 12:42). See the same name (in Hebrew) but transliterated *Izrahiah* and referring to a different individual in 1 Chronicles 7:3.

JEZREEL 1. A descendant of Judah (1 Chron. 4:3).

2. A son of the prophet Hosea (Hos. 1:4, 5).

3. The site, unidentified, from which David got his wife Ahinoam (1 Sam. 25:43; 27:3).

4. A city (181-218) west of the base of Mount Gilboa in the tribal area of Issachar (Josh. 19:17, 18). King Ahab of Israel had a palace there (1 Kgs. 21:1). *See* JEZEBEL, 1, for the chief incidents that took place in the town. The valley below the city is known as the Valley of Jezreel and is to be distinguished from the Plain of Esdraelon (the Greek language form of the word Jezreel) which is the same as the Plain of Megiddo, the larger valley to the west of Jezreel. *See also* GEOGRAPHY OF THE HOLY LAND.

JIDLAPH Son of Nahor and nephew of Abraham (Gen. 22:22).

JIPHTAH *See* IPHTAH

JOAB 1. A descendant of Judah (1 Chron. 4:14).

2. One whose descendants came back from the Babylonian captivity with Zerubbabel (Ezra 2:6).

3. A son of David's sister Zeruiah (1 Chron. 2:15, 16) and commander-in-chief of David's armies (2 Sam. 2:18; 8:16). He led David's men against the rebellions created by descendants of Saul and by his own sons (2 Sam. 2:12ff.; 18:2, 14). He was ruthless in battle or with anyone who opposed him or the king. In the end he supported the wrong son of David for the succession and for it lost his life (1 Kgs. 1:5-7, 13; 2:19, 25, 28-34).

JOAH 1. A recorder in the days of King Hezekiah of Judah (2 Kgs. 18:18).

2. A descendant of Levi in the time of King Hezekiah (2 Chron. 29:12).

3. A Levite among the divisions of the gatekeepers in the days of King David (1 Chron. 26:4).

4. A recorder in the days of King Josiah (2 Chron. 34:8).

JOAHAZ *See* KINGS OF JUDAH AND ISRAEL

JOANAN An ancestor of Joseph, the father, so it was thought of Jesus in Luke's chronology (Lk. 3:27).

JOANNA The wife of Herod's steward Chuza who had been healed by Jesus and for whom she helped provide means (Lk. 8:1-3). She was one of the women at the tomb the morning of Jesus' resurrection (Lk. 24:10).

JOASH 1. *See* KINGS OF JUDAH AND ISRAEL. There are two of these kings, both also called Jehoash.

2. The father of Gideon, the judge of Israel (Judg. 6:11).

3. A son of King Ahab (1 Kgs. 22:26).

4. A descendant of the royal line after the exile (1 Chron. 4:22).

5. A grandson of Benjamin (1 Chron. 7:8).

6. A Benjamite who joined David at Ziklag (1 Chron. 12:3).

7. One who was over the stores of oil of King David (1 Chron. 27:28).

JOB,
JOB, BOOK OF His name is associated with one of the major wisdom literature books of the OT. His locality was "the land of Uz," but there seems to be little agreement among scholars as to his date or the location of Uz. Some feel that the book is pre-Mosaic and reflects only a patriarchal background. Others feel that such reflections can come from a backward, relatively isolated area where Canaanite contacts and customs from earlier times were still known. Such, for example, could be the area of Edom (Jer. 25:20; Lam. 4:21). Solomonic times would fit well in view of the fact that in the land of the Bible that was an era of wisdom, and wisdom literature. The book has the structure of the Code of Hammurabi (reversed) a poetic section sandwiched in between two prose sections. It is also similar to the Krt legend from Ugarit in style and structure and this epic is Canaanite from the time of the Judges of Israel.

In chapters 1-2 we are told of Job's great calamities and losses which he bemoans in chapter 3. From chapter 4 through 37 is the running debate between Job and Eliphaz, Bildad, and Zophar and finally the argument with the younger Elihu. They were trying to prove him self-righteous and he was maintaining his innocence. Then God appeared in controversy with Job (chaps. 38-42) in which God pointed out the right and the power of the Almighty to do as he feels best with his creatures to establish his own interests in their lives and through their witness. Job learned the lesson and his vision of God greatly increased. He then repented in dust and ashes for his former failure to understand (Job. 42:1-6).

JOBAB 1. A descendant of Shem (Gen. 10:29).

2. A king of Edom (Gen. 36:33).

3. A king of Madon who allied himself with Jabin of Hazor and was defeated by Joshua at the battle of the Waters of Merom (Josh. 11:1, 5, 8, 9).

JOCHEBED The descendant of Levi who married Amran and became the mother of Aaron, Moses, and Miriam (Num. 26:59; Ex. 6:20).

JODA, JUDA An ancestor of Jesus in Joseph's line (Lk. 3:26).

JOED A descendant of Benjamin (Neh. 11:7).

JOEL 1. Son of Pethuel and author of one of the Minor Prophets (Joel 1:1).

2. An ancestor of the prophet Samuel (1 Chron. 6:36), also called Shaul (1 Chron. 6:24).

3. A son of the prophet Samuel (1 Sam. 8:2; 1 Chron. 6:33).

4, 5, 6, and 7. Descendants of Simeon, Reuben, Gad, and Issachar (1 Chron. 4:35; 5:4, 12; 7:3).

8, 9, and 10. One of David's mighty men. A Levite of David's time who helped before the tent of meeting and helped with the temple treasury, and David's officer over the tribe of Manasseh (1 Chron. 11:38; 23:8; 26:22; 27:20).

11. A Levite in the time of King Hezekiah of Judah (2 Chron. 29:12).

12. One whose descendants married a foreign wife during the time of the Babylonian captivity (Ezra 10:43).

13. An overseer of Nehemiah's time, a Benjamite (Neh. 11:9).

JOEL, BOOK OF *See* PROPHETS, MINOR

JOELAH A descendant of Benjamin who joined David at Ziklag (1 Chron. 12:7).

JOEZER A descendant of Benjamin who joined David at Ziklag (1 Chron. 12:6).

JOGBEHAH A site on the route Gideon took when he defeated the two kings of Midian (Judg. 8:11).

JOGLI Father of the Benjamite Bukki of the tribe of Dan who was in charge of the division of the land under Moses (Num. 34:22).

JOHA 1. A descendant of Benjamin (1 Chron. 8:16).

2. One of David's mighty men (1 Chron. 11:45).

JOHANAN 1. A military leader of the remnant of Judah after the Babylonian captivity had begun and Gedaliah had been made the governor. Johanan rescued those taken captive by Ishmael of the royal house who rebelled against the Babylonians. Taking Jeremiah and others with him he went down to Egypt to escape Babylonian reaction (2 Kgs. 25:23; Jer. 40:15; 41:11—43:7).

2. A son of King Josiah (1 Chron. 3:15).

3. A descendant of King David in the royal line (1 Chron. 3:24).

4. A priest who served in the temple (1 Chron. 6:9, 10).

5 and 6. Two who joined David at Ziklag, one from Benjamin and one from Gad (1 Chron. 12:4, 12).

7. Father of a leader in Ephraim in the days of King Ahaz of Judah (2 Chron. 28:12).

8. One who returned from the Babylonian captivity with Ezra (Ezra 8:12).

9. *See* JEHOHANAN, 4.

JOHN 1. *See* JOHN THE BAPTIST.

2. *See* APOSTLES.

3. John Mark, *see* MARK.

4. The father of the Apostle Peter (Jn. 1:42).

5. A member of the high priestly family (Acts 4:6).

JOHN, EPISTLES OF Differences of opinion exist among scholars as to whether the Gospel of John, the three Epistles of John, and the Book of Revelation were all written by the same John, by several, by a Johanine school, or by several and edited by one. The early church considered that the Gospel and the first Epistle were both written by the apostle. The style and ideas of the second and third Epistle indicate a very strong probability that the author is also John the Apostle. All four of these documents, the Gospel and the three Epistles, have many similarities in thought, in language, and in style.

There is no recognizable plan for the five chapters of the first Epistle. In these, however, heresies are attacked and admonitions given. False teachers are called antichrists and liars. The author stated that the true doctrine is that Jesus is the Christ, the Son of God come in the flesh, and that to deny this is to be antichrist and a liar (1 Jn. 4:15; 4:2, 3; 2:22). One of the strong emphases of the first Epistle, sounded also in the others, is that the disciples are to love one another, for love is of God. One who does not love does not know God, for he is love. In the second and third Epistles the opening and closing thoughts are the same while the second was written to "the chosen lady and her children" and the third to a "Gaius." In the second Epistle the author emphasized again the thoughts of the first: be wary of false teachers especially those that deny that Jesus Christ has come in the flesh; keep the commandments but particularly the one to love one another. Half of the third Epistle is commendatory of Gaius and perhaps others for their hospitality shown to visiting brethren, and the other half is concerned with one Diotrephes whose conduct was not exemplary.

JOHN, GOSPEL OF *See* GOSPELS, THE FOUR

JOHN THE BAPTIST The son of Zechariah and Elizabeth, the forerunner and baptizer of Jesus (Lk. 1:5-25, 57-60; Mt. 3:1-3, 13-17). For rebuking Herod the Tetrarch for having married his brother Philip's wife he was beheaded (Mt. 14:3, 4). The incident has achieved fame in drama, song, and art (Mt. 14:6-11).

JOIADA 1. One who worked on the wall of Jerusalem with Nehemiah (Neh. 3:6), called also Jehoida.

2. A son of the priest Eliashib. One of his sons married the daughter of Nehemiah's opponent Sanballat the Horonite and for that Nehemiah "drove him away from me" (Neh. 12:10; 13:28).

JOIAKIM The father of the high priest Eliashib in the days of Nehemiah (Neh. 12:10, 12, 26; cf. 13:28).

JOIARIB 1. See also JEHOIARIB, 1.

2. One sent to find some Levites by Ezra when he noticed that none of the sons of Levi had volunteered for service in the temple at Jerusalem (Ezra 8:15, 16).

3. Descendants of Judah who settled in Jerusalem after the exile (Neh. 11:3-5).

4. A priest in Nehemiah's day (Neh. 11:10; 12:6).

JOKDEAM An unidentified site in the hill country of Judah (Josh. 15:56).

JOKIM A descendant of Judah (1 Chron. 4:22).

JOKMEAM A Levitical town (195-171) in the tribal area of Ephraim (1 Chron. 6:68).

JOKNEAM A Levitical town (160-230) on the S edge of the Plain of Megiddo guarding one of the major passes through the Carmel range (Josh. 12:22; 19:11; 21:34; 1 Kgs. 4:12).

JOKSHAN A son of Abraham by Keturah (Gen. 25:2).

JOKTAN A descendant of Noah and Shem (Gen. 10:22-26).

JOKTHEEL 1. An unidentified site in the western foothills of Judah (Josh. 15:33, 38).

2. The name given to the Edomite place (205-020) called by them Sela after King Amaziah of Judah conquered it (2 Kgs. 14:7).

JONADAB 1. The nephew of David who planned the rape of Absalom's sister Tamar by Amnon the son of David (2 Sam. 13:1ff.).

2. Also called Jehonadab, son of Recab. He commanded his descendants that they should not drink wine or even engage in the growing of grapes (Jer. 35:6-10; 2 Kgs. 10:15, 23).

JONAH One of the writing prophets, son of one Amittai (2 Kgs. 14:25). He was sent by God to Nineveh to prophesy but fled in a ship for Tarshish, was shipwrecked, rescued by a great fish, vomited up on the shore, and went then to Nineveh. The city "repented" but other than this statement there is no knowledge of just what happened (Jonah 1:1-7; 2:10; 3:3, 10; 4:11).

JONAH, BOOK OF *See* PROPHETS, MINOR

JONAM An ancestor of Joseph, the father, so it was thought, of Jesus (Lk. 3:30).

JONATHAN A very popular personal name in ancient Israel meaning "God has given."

1. A grandson of Moses (NIV) and priest in Dan. The Hebrew text reads "Manasseh" (Judg. 18:30).

2. A son of Saul, and perhaps the best known of the Jonathans; a very close personal friend of David, defeater of the Philistines, and yet in the end defeated and killed by them (1 Sam. 13:16; 18:1; 14:13-15; 18:3; 31:8). David's elegy on Saul and Jonathan is one of the beautiful poems of the Bible (2 Sam. 1:19, 27).

3, 4, and 5. A nephew, an uncle, and one of David's Thirty (2 Sam. 21:21; 1 Chron. 27:32; 2 Sam. 23:32).

6. A son of Abiathar, a priest descended from Eli. The son was a close ally of David (2 Sam. 15:24-30; 17:17-20).

7. A descendant of Judah and Jerahmeel (1 Chron. 2:32, 33).

8. One in charge of some of David's storehouses (1 Chron. 27:25).

9. The father of the head of one of the houses of Judah which returned from the Babylonian captivity (Ezra 8:6).

10. One who opposed Ezra's policy on mixed marriages made during the Babylonian captivity (Ezra 10:15).

11. A Levite descendant of Joshua in Nehemiah's time (Neh. 12:11).

12. A priest, head of a priestly family in the time of Nehemiah (Neh. 12:14).

13. The father of Zechariah who was a member of one of the musical groups at the dedication of the rebuilt wall of Jerusalem (Neh. 12:35).

14. A secretary whose house had been made a prison in which Jeremiah the prophet was incarcerated (Jer. 37:15, 20).

15. A number of important people in post-Old-Testament or Maccabean times.

JOPPA A very ancient and important city (126-162) on the Palestine seacoast, the port for the city of Jerusalem. It was in the tribal area of Dan but they apparently never conquered it. It was the most important city of the northern part of the Philistine Plain. Egyptians had shops here for the repair of their war chariots. From Solomon's time it was under Israelite control until Seleucid and then Roman times. The Maccabees burned it in part and the Romans destroyed it. Lumber for both the first and second temples came in through this port. It was involved in the Jonah story and in several incidents in the ministry of the Apostle Peter (Josh. 19:46; 2 Chron. 2:16; Ezra 3:7; Jonah 1:3; Acts 9:36-43; 11:5-13).

JORAH *See* HARIPH, 1

JORAI A descendant of Gad (1 Chron. 5:13).

JORAM 1 and 2. *See* KINGS OF JUDAH AND ISRAEL. There were two by this name also called Jehoram.

3. The son of Toi, king of Hamath, also called Toi in the Hebrew text, who was sent to congratulate David. Joram is also called Hadoram (2 Sam. 8:10; 1 Chron. 18:10).

4. A descendant of Levi (1 Chron. 26:25).

JORDAN, VALLEY OF, PLAINS OF, RIVER OF *See* GEOGRAPHY OF THE HOLY LAND

JORDAN OF JERICHO Possibly an early name for the Jordan River (Josh. 20:8, footnote).

JORIM An ancestor of Joseph, the father, so it was thought, of Jesus (Lk. 3:29).

JORKEAM, JORKOAM A descendant of Judah and Caleb (1 Chron. 2:44).

JOSECH An ancestor of Joseph, the father, so it was thought, of Jesus (Lk. 3:26).

JOSEDECH *See* JEHOZADAK

JOSEPH 1. The son of Jacob and Rachel. His dreams incurred the wrath of his brothers who sold him into slavery in Egypt (Gen. 30:24; 37:5-11, 19-28). In Egypt he became next to the pharaoh and was the savior of his own people who came because of the famine to live in Egypt in the land of Goshen. He died at the age of 110 and his bones were taken by Moses at the time of the exodus of the Israelites and ultimately buried in Shechem (Gen. 41:37-44; 50:26; Ex. 13:19; Josh. 24:32).

The beautiful stories of Joseph's treatment of his brothers in return for their evil treatment of him are recorded in Genesis 42-50. His rise to fame and power in Egypt are in chapters 40-41.

2. Father of Igal who was the spy representing the tribe of Issachar when Moses sent the twelve to spy out the land (Num. 13:7).

3. A son of Asaph in the time of David, a musician for the temple (1 Chron. 25:2).

4. One who married a foreign wife during the time of the Babylonian captivity (Ezra 10:42).

5. Head of a priestly family in the days of Joiakim who came up from the Babylonian captivity with Zerubbabel (Neh. 12:14).

6 and 7. Two ancestors of Joseph, the father, so it was thought, of Jesus (Lk. 3:24, 30).

8. The husband of Mary the mother of Jesus, a carpenter who lived in Nazareth of the seed of David (Mt. 1:16; 13:55; Lk. 2:4). The relationship of Mary, Joseph, and Jesus is clearly explained in Matthew 1:18-25.

9. A brother of Jesus also called Joses (Mt. 13:55; Mk. 6:3; Mt. 27:56; Mk. 15:40).

10. Joseph of Arimathea, a disciple of Jesus who buried Jesus' body in his own tomb (Mt. 27:57-60).

11. Joseph called Barsabbas the one of the two not chosen in the casting of the lot for the successor to Judas Iscariot (Acts 1:23).

12. Joseph called Barnabas by the apostles, a Levite from Cyprus who sold a field and brought the proceeds to the apostles (Acts 4:36-37).

JOSES *See* JOSEPH, 9

JOSHAH A descendant of Simeon (1 Chron. 4:34).

JOSHAPHAT 1. One of David's mighty men (1 Chron. 11:43).
2. A priest who was to blow a trumpet before the Ark when David was returning it to Jerusalem (1 Chron. 15:24). Spelled Jehoshaphat in the KJV.

JOSHAVIAH One of David's mighty men (1 Chron. 11:46).

JOSHBEKASHAH, JOSHBAKASHAH A Levite musician in the time of David (1 Chron. 25:4, 24).

JOSHEB BASSHEBETH *See* JASHOBEAM

JOSHIBAH A descendant of Simeon (1 Chron. 4:35).

JOSHUA 1. The son of Nun, successor of Moses and leader of the Israelites in their conquest of Canaan (Ex. 33:11; Num. 27:12-23; Josh. 1:1-3). He was one of the two of the twelve spies who brought back a report that the Israelites should go up and take the land and forty years later he led them in (Num. 13:8; 14:6-10; Josh. 1:1ff.). He was successful in conquering the land and then having it divided between the tribes (Josh. 7 and 14). He is also called Hoshea (Num. 13:8, 16).

2. A man in whose field in Beth Shemesh the Ark stopped on its way back from the Philistines (1 Sam. 6:14, 18).

3. The governor of Jerusalem in the days of King Josiah (2 Kgs. 23:8).

4. An ancestor of Joseph, the father, as it was thought, of Jesus (Lk. 3:19).

JOSHUA, BOOK OF The author of the book about Joshua's conquest and settlement of the land of Canaan is not known. The evidence points to a time of writing before David since he did not know of the temple (Josh. 9:27) but after the rise of the Judges of Israel since he refers to Othniel and also to the migration north of the tribe of Dan (15:17; 19:47). His references to Sidon rather than Tyre indicate a date earlier than 1200 B.C. (11:8; 13:4-6). There is considerable evidence of an author who was an actual eyewitness, living early in the fourteenth century. Chapters 1-12 describe the conquest and 13-22 the settlement of the tribes. The two final chapters contain the great leader's final addresses.

JOSIAH 1. *See* KINGS OF JUDAH AND ISRAEL.

2. A son of Zephaniah who gave gold and silver for the crown of the High Priest in postexilic times (Zech. 6:10, 11).

JOSIPHIAH Father of some who returned from the Babylonian captivity with Ezra (Ezra 8:10).

JOTBAH A Levitical city (176-248) in the tribal area of Judah also called Juttah and the home of the king of Judah's mother (2 Kgs. 21:19; Josh. 15:55).

JOTBATHAH A stop of the children of Israel on their exodus route from Egypt (Num. 33:33, 34; Deut. 10:7).

JOTHAM 1. *See* KINGS OF JUDAH AND ISRAEL.

2. The youngest son of Jerub-Baal, or Gideon (Judg. 7:1), and the only one of his sons to escape the murders of Abimelech his brother.

3. A descendant of Judah and Caleb (1 Chron. 2:47).

JOURNEY, SABBATH DAY'S The distance one could legally travel on the Sabbath. Surmises and later extrabiblical references place it somewhere between two and four thousand cubits. See footnote which reads "about ¾ of a mile" (Acts 1:12).

JOY A part of the complex called "fruit of the Spirit" and thus also a part of the character of God (Gal. 5:22, 23; Ps. 104:31). Whereas happiness and sadness do not exist at the same time, joy and sorrow can and do. Jesus endured the sorrow and pain of the cross because of the joy he had at the same time (Heb. 12:2).

JOZABAD 1, 2, and 3. Three who joined David at Ziklag, one from Benjamin and two from Manasseh (1 Chron. 12:4, 20).

4. A Levite overseer in the house of the Lord in the time of King Hezekiah of Judah (2 Chron. 31:13).

5. A leader of the Levites in the days of King Josiah (2 Chron. 35:9).

6. One of the assassins of King Jehoash (Joash) also called Zubad (2 Kgs. 12:21; 2 Chron. 24:26).

7. A Levite treasurer in the temple of Ezra (Ezra 8:33).

8 and 9. A priest and a Levite who married foreign wives during the captivity (Ezra 10:22, 23).

10. A Levite who explained the law as Ezra read it (Neh. 8:7).

11. A Levite chief in Jerusalem after the return from the Babylonian captivity (Neh. 11:16).

JOZADAK *See* JEHOZADAK

JUBAL A descendant of Noah and Cain, sons of Lamech, "the father of those who play the lyre and pipe" (Gen. 4:21).

JUBILEE The Jubilee year in ancient Israel was every fiftieth year. In it all Israelites who had come under bondage to another Israelite had to be set free, all ancestral lands had to be returned to their original owners, and the land had to have rest from agriculture (Lev. 25:10-12ff.).

JUCAL *See* JEHUCAL

JUDAH 1. A son of Jacob and Leah and head of one of the twelve tribes from which came the royal line and eventually Jesus. In the Joseph incidents he was the spokesman to his brethren, to his father and to Joseph in Egypt later. Not only does his name come to be associated with a tribe but it also is associated with the Kingdom of Judah (the two tribes in the south) and from it after the exile the term Jew came to be applied to all the descendants of Abraham by Sarah (Gen. 29:35; 43:3, 44:15ff.). *See also* JEW.

2. Ancestor of some Levites who returned from the Babylonian captivity with Zerubbabel, called in NIV Hodoviah. See the footnote which reads "Hebrew, Yehudah, probably a variant of Hodaviah" (Ezra 3:9, footnote).

3. A Levite who married a foreign wife during the captivity (Ezra 10:23).

4. An overseer in Jerusalem after the return from the captivity. A descendant of Benjamin (Neh. 11:9).

5. A Levite who returned from the captivity with Zerubbabel (Neh. 12:8).

6. A leader of Judah who was involved with Nehemiah in the dedication of the restored wall of Jerusalem (Neh. 12:34).

7. A musician who had a part in the dedication of the wall of Jerusalem (Neh. 12:36).

8. One of the ancestors of Joseph, the father of Jesus, so it was thought (Lk. 3:30).

JUDAH, JUDEA AND MOUNTAINS OF, WILDERNESS OF *See* GEOGRAPHY OF THE HOLY LAND

JUDAS A very popular name in Maccabean times and then later in the NT.

1 and 2. Two of the twelve apostles.

3. A brother of Jesus (Mt. 13:55; Mk. 6:3).

4. A Jew of Galilee who raised an insurrection in ancient Israel shortly after the birth of Jesus (Acts 5:37).

5. Paul's host in Damascus where Ananias met him (Acts 9:11).

6. Judas Barsabbas, who reported in Antioch on the Jerusalem Council (Acts 15:22ff.).

JUDAS ISCARIOT *See* APOSTLES

JUDE, EPISTLE OF The author of this Epistle is considered to have been a brother of Jesus, see JUDAS, 3 above. The principal thrust of the little letter is against false teaching in the church (v. 4). He developed elaborately his condemnation of them (5-16), and instructed his readers as to their duty in such case (17-23). It is not clear as to whether he quoted from the actual Book of Enoch or whether he is quoting from an unnamed source something that tradition ascribed to Enoch. The dating of the Book of Enoch is not clear.

JUDGE A civil magistrate. The administration of Moses was suggested by his father-in-law Jethro, and judges were set up over groups from a size of ten to a size of thousands (Ex. 18:13-26). After the establishment of the monarchy the system was continued even though the king himself also heard cases directly (1 Kgs. 3:28; 1 Chron. 23:4). These persons apparently abused their offices since the prophets found many occasions for rebuking them (Mic. 3:11; Amos 5:12). In the NT there are many references to this office but God himself is the chief judge of all (Heb. 13:4; Rev. 18:8). The Father has committed judgment to the Son (Jn. 5:22-24; Acts 10:42; 17:30, 31).

JUDGES, BOOK OF The seventh book of the OT containing the accounts of the judges of Israel from the time of the conquest of Palestine to the time of Samuel (Judg. 2:16). On the judges themselves and their chronology, and therefore the content of this book itself, see the next entry and the article CHRONOLOGY. The Book of Ruth is usually associated with the Book of Judges since it is set in the same time. In this "postscript" to Judges we have the story of Ruth and Boaz and the early ancestry of King David and hence also the early ancestry of Jesus. In neither Judges nor Ruth do we have any claim as to authorship.

It is quite generally assumed that the author of the Book of Judges wrote from existing sources in the very early days of the monarchy under Saul and that it reflects much earlier material. The period of time in which the events recorded took place is also difficult to determine since there is so much difference among scholars as to the date of the conquest of Israel, all the way from about 1380 B.C. to 1220 B.C., both dates being held by leading conservative scholars. Secular and liberal scholars quite uniformly hold the latter date.

Chapters 3-16 of Judges recount the events from Othniel to Samson. The first two chapters bridge the historical gap from Joshua and recount the partial success only of driving out the pagans. The concluding chapters recount some special events that took place in the general period: the Levite who worked privately for anyone's pay; the migration northward of the tribe of Dan; and the brutal treatment of the concubine of the Levite which resulted in the decimation of the men of Benjamin (Judg. 17-18, 19-21).

THE JUDGES OF ISRAEL The biblical "judge" was a leader of Israel, divinely appointed to deliver and lead his people. Judicial capacity was only one aspect of his activity and was often slight (but see Judg. 4:5; 1 Sam. 7:15-17).

Twelve such people are described in the Book of Judges in addition to Eli and Samuel who also judged Israel (1 Sam. 4:18; 7:15).

The chronology of the judges depends upon the following principles: (a) Their period reaches from the first oppression after the death of Joshua to the establishment of the kingdom in Israel. (b) Since the date of the death of Joshua is unknown, one must work backward from 1043 B.C., the probable date of the accession of Saul (*see* KINGS OF JUDAH AND ISRAEL). Then if the period in 1 Samuel 7:2 of "twenty years" and Israel's "lamenting after the Lord" is equated with the length of Samuel's leadership as the last judge, 1063 must mark the overthrow of the Philistine oppression that preceded Samuel (1 Sam. 7:7-14); and this, in turn, provides a basis for the tentative dating of the rest of the events of the period. (c) Certain sections of Judges record events that had only local significance and that overlap events in other areas. For example, while the Philistines were overwhelming Israel on the west, the Ammonites were simultaneously oppressing the tribes east of the Jordan (Judg. 10:7). The terms therefore of Jephthah, who fought Ammon, and of Ibzar, Elon, and Abdon, the three minor judges that followed

(10:17—12:15), must have run concurrently with the forty-year Philistine oppression. (d) A given period of oppression or deliverance may embrace more than one judge. Ehud's eighty-year peace (3:30), for example, includes the period of Shamgar ("He too saved Israel," 3:31). Similarly the twenty-three years of Tola seem to embrace the twenty-two of Jair (10:1-3), since only the former is said to have "saved Israel." Again, much of Eli's judgeship, together with all of Samson's (16:31), belong under the forty years of Philistine oppression. Samson, in reality, accomplished no deliverance at all but simply "led Israel for twenty years in the days of the Philistines" (15:20).

Tabulation therefore of the dated oppressions and subsequent saving of Israel results in the following outline:

	Years	Dates (B.C.)
Samuel's judgeship (1 Sam. 7:2), including his sons at the end (8:1)	20	1063-1043
Philistine oppression (Judg. 10:7; 13:1) (including Ammonite, etc. in the east)	40	1103-1063
Tola's deliverance (10:2, footnote), including Jair	23	1126-1103
Abimelech's misrule (9:22ff.)	3	1129-1126
Gideon, judge (8:28)	40	1169-1129
Midianite oppression (6:1)	7	1176-1169
Deborah and Barak (5:31)	40	1216-1176
Canaanite oppression by Jabin (4:3)	20	1236-1216
Ehud (3:30), including Shamgar	80	1316-1236
Moabite oppression by Eglon (3:14)	18	1334-1316
Othniel (3:11)	40	1374-1334
Mesopotamian oppression by Cushan-Rishathaim (3:8)	8	1382-1374

The total period is thus 339 years (compare the 300 years down to Jephthah in Judges 11:26-29).

During these almost three-and-a-half centuries of the judges, biblical history demonstrates a repeated cycle of sin by the Israelites, servitude to their enemies as a result, their supplication to God, and his salvation that followed. Chapter 2 of Judges serves as a summary and presents these basic propositions: God's wrath at sin (2:11, 14), God's mercy upon repentance (2:16), but man's depravity (2:19). Under the judges, when "everyone did as he saw fit" (17:6; 21:25), individual responsibility proved a failure; man on his own inevitably goes wrong. (J.B.P.)

JUDGMENT An opinion passed down by men, or as is more often the case, a sentence or an actual calamity sent by God for punishment. More notable among the latter are: the Fall, the Flood, the confounding of tongues at the Tower of Babel, the Babylonian captivity, and the subsequent worldwide diaspora, the deliverance of believers by the judgment placed on Christ, and the final judgment of those who fail to accept that deliverance worked out by Christ (Gen. 3:1ff.; 11:1-8; Deut. 28:15, 25; 28:58-68; Mt. 25:31ff.; Jn. 3:16-19; 2 Thess. 1:5-10; 2 Pet. 3:8-13).

JUDGMENT HALL *See* PRAETORIAN GUARD, PRAETORIUM

JUDITH A wife of Esau (Gen. 26:34).

JULIA A Christian lady in Rome to whom Paul sent greetings (Rom. 16:15).

JULIUS A Roman centurion in whose charge Paul was sent to Rome when he appealed to Caesar (Acts 27:1-3).

JUNIAS A Christian in Rome to whom Paul sent greetings (Rom. 16:7).

JUSHAB HESED A son of the Zerubbabel who brought Israelites back from the Babylonian captivity (1 Chron. 3:20).

JUSTIFICATION *See* CHRIST, WORK OF

JUSTUS 1. The surname of Joseph Barsabbas. *See* JOSEPH, 12.

2. A host of Paul at Corinth, Titius Justus (Acts 18:7).

3. The surname of the Jesus who was Paul's comforter in his imprisonment in Rome (Col. 4:11).

JUTTAH *See* JOTBAH

KABZEEL A city (148-071) on the border of Judah with Edom. One of David's mighty men came from there (Josh. 15:21; 2 Sam. 23:20).

KADESH, KADESH BARNEA 1. Kadesh Barnea (096-006) also called Meribah Kadesh in the Desert of Zin (Deut. 32:51; Ezek. 47:19) and earlier known as Enmishpat (Gen. 14:7). Here the children of Israel encamped after leaving Mount Sinai and from here Moses sent out the twelve to spy out the land of Canaan. After the forty years of wandering they returned here and began their final journey that was to lead them into the promised land (Deut. 2:14; 9:23; Josh. 10:41; 14:7; Num. 33:37; Judg. 11:17).

2. Kadesh on the Orontes (291-444) where the famous battle took place between the Egyptians under Pharaoh Ramses II and the Hittites in 1288 B.C. Not noted in the Bible.

KADMIEL Two postexilic Levites who returned from the Babylonian captivity with Zerubbabel and Ezra and one who signed the covenant with Nehemiah (Ezra 2:40; 3:9; Neh. 9:4; 10:9).

KADMONITES A nomadic people who lived between Syria and the Euphrates River (Gen. 15:19).

KAIN, CAIN A city (165-100) in the hill country of the tribal area of Judah (Josh. 15:57).

KAIWAN *See* DEITIES

KALLAI A priest in the days of Nehemiah (Neh. 12:20).

KAMON A town (218-221) in Gilead where the judge, Jair, was buried (Judg. 10:5).

KANAH 1. A ravine that was a part of the border between the tribal areas of Ephraim and Manasseh (Josh. 16:8; 17:9).

2. A location (178-290) on the north border of the tribal area of Asher, east of Tyre (Josh. 19:28).

3. See Cana, the NT town, not to be confused with 2 above.

KAREAH The father of JOHANAN, 1 (Jer. 40:8).

KARKA, KARKAA A place (089-007) on the southern border of the tribal area of Judah (Josh. 15:3).

KARKOR An unidentified site where Gideon destroyed the army of the Midianites under Zeba and Zalmunna (Judg. 8:7ff.).

KARNAIM, PROVINCE OF *See* GEOGRAPHY OF THE HOLY LAND

KARTAH An unidentified city in the tribal area of Zebulun (Josh. 21:34).

KARTAN An unidentified Levitical site in the tribal area of Naphtali (Josh. 21:32; 1 Chron. 6:77, footnote).

KATTATH An unidentified site in the tribal area of Zebulun (Josh. 19:15).

KATYDID *See* BEASTS, 6

KEBAR, CHEBAR A river in Mesopotamia or perhaps a large canal beside which the exiles from Palestine lived during the Babylonian captivity (Ezek. 1:1, 3).

KEDAR A son of Ishmael and grandson of Abraham, the founder of a nomadic tribe (Gen. 25:13; Ezek. 27:21).

KEDEMAH A son of Ishmael and founder of a nomadic tribe (Gen. 25:15; 1 Chron. 1:31).

KEDEMOTH A site (233-104) in the desert area east of the Jordan River in the tribal area of Reuben (Deut. 2:26; Josh. 21:37).

KEDESH 1. An unidentified site in the tribal area of Issachar (1 Chron. 6:72, 76). Mentioned in connection with Daberath (foot of Mt. Tabor).

2. An unidentified site in the tribal area of Judah (Josh. 15:23).

3. Kedesh in Naphtali (202-237) SW of the Sea of Galilee (Josh. 12:22; 19:37). The town figures in the battles of Deborah and Barak and was later captured by the Assyrians (Judg. 4:6-11; 2 Kgs. 15:29).

4. Kedesh in Galilee (199-279) usually thought to be farther north than 3 and yet in the area of that tribe, a city of refuge (Josh. 20:7; 21:32).

KEDORLAOMER, CHEDORLAOMER A king of Elam who fought with a coalition of kings at Sodom and Gomorrah (Gen. 14:1, 4, 5, 17).

KEILAH 1. A city (150-113) in the western foothills of Judah which David rescued from the Philistines but then had to abandon (Josh. 15:44; 1 Sam. 23:1-13).

2. A descendant of Judah and Caleb (1 Chron. 4:19).

KELAIAH A Levite who married a foreign wife during the Babylonian captivity, also called Kelita (Ezra 10:23).

KELAL, CHELAL A man who married a foreign woman during the time of the Babylonian captivity (Ezra 10:30).

KELITA 1. *See* KELAIAH.

2. One who explained the law as Ezra read it (Neh. 8:7).

3. One who signed the covenant with Nehemiah, perhaps the same person as 2 above (Neh. 10:10).

KELUB, CHELUB 1. A descendant of Judah (1 Chron. 4:11).

2. Father of one of David's officers (1 Chron. 27:26).

KELUBAI A descendant of Judah. In Hebrew *Kelubai* is a variant of Caleb (1 Chron. 2:9, footnote). *See also* CALEB.

KELUHI, CHELLUH One who married a foreign woman during the Babylonian captivity (Ezra 10:35).

KEMUEL 1. A nephew of Abraham (Gen. 22:21).

2. The representative of the tribe of Ephraim in the division of the land (Num. 34:24).

3. The father of the man who was over the tribe of Levi in David's day (1 Chron. 27:17).

KENAANAH,
CHENAANAH
1. A descendant of Benjamin (1 Chron. 7:10).

2. Father of the false prophet Zedekiah who prophesied in the days of Ahab (1 Kgs. 22:11, 24).

KENAN A near descendant of Adam (Gen. 5:9).

KENANI,
CHENANI
A Levite in the time of Ezra (Neh. 9:4).

KENANIAH,
CHENANIAH
1. A Levite director of singing in the time of David (1 Chron. 15:22).

2. One who with his sons were officials and judges (1 Chron. 26:29).

KENATH A city (302-241) east of the Jordan in Bashan. Its conqueror changed its name to Nobah (Num. 32:42; 1 Chron. 2:23).

KENAZ 1. A grandson of Esau. *See also* KENIZZITE (Gen. 36:11, 15).

2. Father of Othniel and nephew of Caleb (Josh. 15:17; Judg. 1:13).

3. A grandson of Caleb (1 Chron. 4:15).

KENITES A tribal group descended from Hobab were in the land by the time of Abraham and still there at the time of Joshua's conquest of it (Gen. 15:19; Judg. 4:11; Num. 24:21, 22). In Moses' time Heber the Kenite was living among the Midianites. He was the brother-in-law of Moses (Judg. 4:11). They moved with the Israelites to Canaan and maintained a close relationship with them at least through the time of King David (Judg. 4:11; 5:24; 1 Sam. 15:6; 30:26-29).

KENIZZITE A tribe or group in the land as early as Abraham (Gen. 15:19). Caleb of the tribe of Judah is called the son of a Kenizzite (Num. 32:12; Josh. 14:6, 14). It is not known from which Kenaz this group is descended.

KEPHAR
AMMONI,
CHEPHAR-
HAAMMONAI
An unidentified site in Benjamin (Josh. 18:24).

KEPHIRAH,
CHEPHIRAH
A Gibeonite city (160-137) assigned to Benjamin still occupied after the return from the Babylonian captivity (Josh. 9:17; 18:26; Ezra 2:25).

KERAN,
CHERAN
A descendant of Esau (Gen. 36:1, 26).

KEREN-HAPPUCH A daughter of Job (Job 42:14).

KERETHITES, CHERETHITES Perhaps originally from Crete, a people who lived in the south of the tribal area of Judah-Simeon (1 Sam. 30:14; 2 Sam. 8:18; Ezek. 25:16; Zeph. 2:5).

KERIOTH A city (215-105) east of the Jordan in Moab which is pictured by the prophet Jeremiah as ruined under God's judgment (Jer. 48:24; Amos 2:2).

KERIOTH HEZRON A city (161-083) in the tribal area of Judah, also called Hazor (Josh. 15:25).

KERITH, CHERITH An unidentified ravine east of the Jordan where Elijah hid from King Ahab and was fed by the ravens (1 Kgs. 17:3, 5). Some think it was in Gilead.

KEROS Ancestor of some who returned from the Babylonian captivity with Zerubbabel (Ezra 2:44).

KERUB An unidentified site in Babylonia from which some returned to Palestine after the captivity but who were unable to prove their Israelite descent (Ezra 2:59).

KESALON, CHESALON A village (154-132) on the northern border of Judah near Mount Jearim (Josh. 15:10).

KESED, CHESED A nephew of Abraham (Gen. 22:22).

KESIL, CHESIL An unidentified town in the south of Judah (Josh. 15:30).

KESULLOTH, CHESSULOTH A town (180-232) on the border between the tribal areas of Zebulun and Issachar (Josh. 19:18).

KETURAH The wife of Abraham after the death of Sarah, also called his concubine. From their sons many of the tribes of desert people originated (Gen. 25:1ff.; 1 Chron. 1:32ff.).

KEY, KEY OF THE KINGDOM Literally, a key opens or locks doors or gates. In antiquity they were usually massive in size and made of metal or of wood with metal or wooden pegs (Judg. 3:25). The symbolic use in Scripture is, however, the more important one. It represents authority, power, and control, usually delegated by God. The prophet speaks of the key of the house of David which appears again in the Revelation as the key of David, speaking of the power of David's descendant, the Messiah, to admit or exclude men from his kingdom (Isa. 22:22; Rev.

3:7). The key given to Peter and through him to the Church has the same signification. Belief in the confession Peter made, "You are the Christ, the Son of the living God" is the key to admittance to the Church and in part to eternal life as well. Believing or rejecting this message given to Peter for proclamation is the key to salvation and Peter, knowing it was the key, realized it had to be passed on to others (Matt. 16:15-19). There are keys for the Abyss and Hades (Rev. 1:18; 20:1).

KEZIAH, KEZIA A daughter of Job (Job 42:14).

KEZIB, CHEZIB An unidentified place where Judah's wife bore him a son (Gen. 38:5).

KIBROTH HATTAAVAH The stop on the wilderness journey of the Israelites where they craved for meat and God gave them quail from which many of them died (Num. 11:34, 35; 33:16, 17; Deut. 9:22).

KIBZAIM An unidentified site in the tribal area of Ephraim (Josh. 21:22).

KID *See* BEASTS

KIDNEY *See* EMOTIONS and SACRIFICES AND OFFERINGS

KIDON, CHIDON The name of the threshing floor, or of its owner, where Uzzah died for touching the Ark (1 Chron. 13:9).

KIDRON, CEDRON Called a valley and brook but literally only a wadi immediately east of the city of Jerusalem and its eastern border. Important incidents in the life of Jesus took place there on the last night before his crucifixion. These included his prayers in Gethsemane and his arrest (Jn. 18:1ff.).

KILEAB, CHILEAB The second son of David also called Daniel (2 Sam. 3:3; 1 Chron. 3:1).

KILION, CHILION A son of Naomi and brother-in-law to Ruth the Moabitess (Ruth 1:2-5).

KILMAD, CHILMAD An unidentified place that traded with the city of Tyre (Ezek. 27:23).

KIMHAM, CHIMHAM A Gileadite who went with King David on David's return after the rebellion of Absalom (2 Sam. 19:37-40; 1 Kgs. 2:7).

KINAH An unidentified site in the southern area of the tribe of Judah (Josh. 15:21, 22).

**KING,
KINGSHIP** In the extrabiblical ancient world the king was considered a divine being. In earliest time each city had its own king. The idea of empire grew up later. In the Bible, a king was merely considered to have been appointed by God and not divine in his own right. As early as the time of Abraham and before the Israelite monarchy there were many city kings and local area kings in Canaan (Gen. 14:1, 2; 20:2; 36ff.; Josh. 12:7-24). Earlier God had intimated that Israel too would have a king (Gen. 17:6; Deut. 17:14-20). The stories of the KINGS OF JUDAH AND ISRAEL begin with Saul and end with the Babylonian captivity. In the NT Jesus Christ is presented as God's King and Ruler (Rev. 1:5; 15:3; 17:14; 1 Cor. 15:24).

**KINGDOM
OF GOD,
KINGDOM
OF HEAVEN** The former would seem to be the more general of the two phrases as it appears throughout the NT while the latter is limited to Matthew. For this reason some contrast the two and state that the latter is messianic only, the establishment of the Kingdom of God on earth, while the former is universal, entered only by the new birth. According to some interpretations, the two have almost all things in common. The two phrases are considered by very many as virtually synonymous. This latter position is held also by many premillennarians and thus the distinction is not a necessary one for the maintaining of that position. God's kingdom is here now in the hearts of men and will be established literally on the earth for a time before it becomes eternal in the heavens (Mt. 12:28; Jn. 3:3, 5-7; 1 Cor. 15:24-26).

KINGS *See* KINGS OF JUDAH AND ISRAEL

**KINGS,
BOOKS OF** The Books of 1 and 2 Kings contain the history of Judah and Israel from the end of David's reign to the fall of Jerusalem to the Babylonians and the beginning of that captivity. The history of the KINGS OF JUDAH AND ISRAEL is the content of these two works by an unknown author who had before him written source material (1 Kgs. 11:41; 14:19, 29; 2 Chron. 32:32).

First and 2 Chronicles, also by an unknown author, would seem to have been written around the time of Ezra as the end of 2 Chronicles is the beginning of Ezra. Thus 2 Chronicles carries the history of Israel beyond that of 2 Kings. Furthermore, the entire emphasis of 1 and 2 Chronicles is different. First Chronicles starts with genealogies that enable Jews living in the time of Ezra to carry their ancestral records back to the beginnings (chaps. 1-9). The two books also carry fully a version of the history of David and Solomon to the building of the first temple (1 Chron. 10—2 Chron. 9) apparently for the information of those interested in building the second temple, the temple of Ezra. From chapters 10 to 35, the historical emphasis is on the southern kingdom, Judah, and in particular the reforms of King Josiah.

KING'S DALE *See* SHAVEH

KING'S GARDEN *See* SILOAM, POOL OF

KING'S HIGHWAY *See* GEOGRAPHY OF THE HOLY LAND, the biblical roads

KINGS OF JUDAH AND ISRAEL When Samuel the judge grew old and his sons proved corrupt and took bribes (1 Sam. 8:3, *see* JUDGES OF ISRAEL), the Israelites came to him requesting that he institute a kingship. Their motivation was twofold: (a) they wanted to be "like the nations" (1 Sam. 8:5), forgetting that God had chosen them to be holy and separate (Lev. 20:26); and (b) they wanted a leader in battle (1 Sam. 8:12; 12:12), forgetting that it was their own unfaithfulness, and their demands for a king, that were the cause of their defeats. Yet even in their sinful request, Israel was accomplishing God's original purpose, namely, to prepare a kingdom for his Son Jesus Christ who would some day appear and rule (Gen. 49:10; Ps. 2:6, 7; Lk. 1:32, 33). So the basic idea of the kingdom was a right one, even though Israel's particular motives in seeking it were wrong.

God therefore directed Samuel to anoint a king (1 Sam. 8:7, 22), which he did: Saul, of the tribe of Benjamin (1 Sam. 10:1, 24; 11:15). Yet this very answer to Israel's request proved in itself to be their punishment. Saul it is true won a series of victories (1 Sam. 14:47, 48), but ended up wasting his nation's resources in the fruitless pursuit of his rival David (1 Sam. 19-26), and then falling in an overwhelming defeat before the Philistines (1 Sam. 31). God then established as king the man after his own heart (1 Sam. 13:14), David, of the tribe of Judah (1 Sam. 16:13; compare Gen. 49:10), initially in Hebron over Judah alone (2 Sam. 2:4) and seven and a half years later in Jerusalem over all the twelve tribes of Israel, (2 Sam. 5:7). This was the dynasty that ruled the united kingdom of Israel during the seventy-three years until its division into Israel in the north and Judah in the south, then continued upon the throne of Judah throughout its existence, and that has now attained its imperishable goal in the kingdom of Jesus Christ (Mt. 1:6-16).

Dating for the kings of Judah and Israel is determined by their correlations with other clearly datable events of ancient history. The two earliest are the termination of Ahab's reign over Israel in 853 B.C. and the commencement of Jehu's in 841. A counting backwards and forwards from those dates then produces the following overall outline for the kings:

DIVIDED KINGDOM

ISRAEL			B.C.	JUDAH		
Jeroboam I	1 Kgs. 14:20	22 yrs.	930	Rehoboam	1 Kgs. 14:21	17 yrs.
			913	Abijah	1 Kgs. 15:1-2	3 yrs.
Nadab	1 Kgs. 15:25	2 yrs.	910	Asa	1 Kgs. 15:9	41 yrs.
Baasha	1 Kgs. 15:33	24 yrs.	909			
Elah	1 Kgs. 16:8	2 yrs.	886			
Zimri	1 Kgs. 16:15	(7 days)	885			
Omri (with Libni)	1 Kgs. 16:23	12 yrs.	885			
Ahab	1 Kgs. 16:29	22 yrs.	874			
			869	Jehoshaphat	1 Kgs. 22:42, cf. 2 Chron. 16:12 and 2 Kgs. 8:16 with 2 Kgs. 3:1	25 yrs.
Ahaziah (son of Ahab)	1 Kgs. 22:51	2 yrs.	853			
Joram (son of Ahab)	2 Kgs. 3:1	12 yrs.	852	Jehoram (coregent in 853 and full power)	2 Kgs. 17:1-17 2 Kgs. 8:16-17	8 yrs.
Jehu	2 Kgs. 10:36	28 yrs.	841	Ahaziah	2 Kgs. 8:25-26	1 yr.
			840	Athaliah	2 Kgs. 11:3	7 yrs.
			835	Joash	2 Kgs. 12:1	40 yrs.
Jehoahaz	2 Kgs. 13:1	17 yrs.	814			
Jehoash	2 Kgs. 13:10	16 yrs.	798			
			796	Amaziah	2 Kgs. 14:1-2	29 yrs.
Jeroboam II (coregencies were involved)	2 Kgs. 15:1-2 14:2, 17; 13:10	41 yrs.	793			
			767	Azariah (also called Uzziah; coregencies involved)	2 Kgs. 15:1-2	52 yrs.
Zechariah	2 Kgs. 15:8	6 mos.	753			
Shallum	2 Kgs. 15:13	1 mo.	752			
Menahem	2 Kgs. 15:17	10 yrs.	752			
Pekahiah	2 Kgs. 15:23	2 yrs.	742			
Pekah	2 Kgs. 15:25, 27, 32 (full power in 740)	20 yrs.	740			
			739	Jotham (coregent but full power only in 739)	2 Kgs. 15:5, 32-33	16 yrs.
			736	Ahaz (coregent but full power in 736)	2 Kgs. 16:1-2	16 yrs.
Hoshea	2 Kgs. 17:1	9 yrs.	732			
			726	Hezekiah (coregent but full power in 726)	2 Kgs. 18:1-2	29 yrs.
FALL OF SAMARIA			722			
			697	Manasseh	2 Kgs. 21:1	55 yrs.
			642	Amon	2 Kgs. 21:19	2 yrs.
			640	Josiah	2 Kgs. 22:1	31 yrs.
			609	Jehoahaz	2 Kgs. 23:31	3 mos.
			609	Jehoiakim	2 Kgs. 23:36	11 yrs.
			598	Jehoiachin	2 Kgs. 24:8	3 mos.
			597	Zedekiah	2 Kgs. 24:18	11 yrs.
			586	FALL OF JERUSALEM	2 Kgs. 25:8	

The united kingdom under David and Solomon, 1003-930
B.C., marked the high point in the ancient state of Israel.
David enlarged his borders on all sides (2 Sam. 8:1-14),
so that his son, Solomon, inherited an empire in which he
"ruled over all the kingdoms from the River (Euphrates) to
the land of the Philistines, as far as the border of Egypt"
and "Judah and Israel were as numerous as the sand on the
seashore" (1 Kgs. 4:20-21). This marked the fulfillment of
God's territorial promises to the founding Hebrew patriarchs
(Gen. 15:18; 22:17). David is also noted for making
Jerusalem a religious as well as a political capital. He brought
into it the sacred Ark of God's presence (2 Sam. 6),
established the Levitical singers and the services of worship
about it (1 Chron. 15-16), and he made preparations for
God's temple (1 Chron. 22, 28, 29), which Solomon was
able to construct between the years 966 and 960 B.C.
(1 Kgs. 6:1, 38). Above all, God renewed to David his
ancient covenant, specifying that out of the line of David he
would raise up his "anointed" (Hebrew, Messiah; Greek,
Christ), the Son of God, with salvation for his people
(2 Sam. 7:14; 23:5).

But Solomon in his later years lapsed into idolatry
(1 Kgs. 11:1-13) with the result that upon his death in 930
God divided the kingdom, leaving only the southern tribes
of Judah and Benjamin under the Davidic dynasty in
Jerusalem (1 Kgs. 11:31; 12:1-20, 21-24). The ten northern
tribes, however, were led away by their new king Jeroboam I
into even worse apostasy, identifying two golden calves
in their substitute sanctuaries of Dan and Bethel, as Jehovah
the God who had brought them out of the land of Egypt
(12:26-33).

The founder of the northern kingdom was henceforth
spoken of as "Jeroboam son of Nebat and his sin which he
had caused Israel to commit." His action became the
cause for the downfall both of his own dynasty and of the
entire kingdom of Israel (1 Kgs. 13:34; 2 Kgs. 17:16-23).

For over two centuries the kingdoms of Judah and Israel
lived in interaction, the south under the one line of Davidic
kings, and the north (which lacked Judah's divine sanction
upon the ruling family), through an unstable sequence of
twenty kings, representing ten different dynasties (see
Hos. 8:4). More generally, however, the relations of the
two states may be traced through a series of seven stages:

(1) Conflict, 930-865 B.C. Solomon's son, Rehoboam,
raised armies to subdue Jeroboam in Israel, but God forbad
it (1 Kgs. 12:21ff.). It was best, in preparing for the
coming of God's Son, that the more sinful north be allowed
to go its own way. Still, hostilities continued (1 Kgs.
14:30), even after Judah was humbled before God by the

invasion of Shishak in 926 (2 Chron. 12:6-8; *see* EGYPT). Abijah of Judah continued the war and won a great victory through faith (2 Chron. 13:18). Baasha, founder of the second dynasty in Israel, pressed the conflict and built up Ramah, only a few miles north of Jerusalem. Asa of Judah hired Ben-Hadad I of Damascus to divert Baasha, which gave temporary relief; but God rebuked Asa's reliance upon foreign mercenaries rather than upon himself (2 Chron. 16:7). Omri, who established Israel's fifth dynasty, proved to be a strong monarch, founding Samaria as the northern capital and making an alliance with Phoenicia through the marriage of his son Ahab to the pagan Sidonian princess Jezebel. But this produced disastrous effects, not only in the north as Jezebel sought to establish Phoenician Baalism and persecuted those who remained faithful to Israel's God Yahweh, but also in the south. For though Judah had trusted God up to this point and prospered (2 Chron. 16:9), its reforming king Jehoshaphat (see 2 Chron. 17:6-9; 20:12, 20; 17:2-5) yet weakened and introduced a new period.

(2) Alliance, 865-841 B.C. Specifically, Jehoshaphat married his son Jehoram to Athaliah, the daughter of Ahab and Jezebel in the north (datable prior to the birth of their son Ahaziah in 863) (2 Kgs. 8:26). Yet the alliance lost in war, when Ahab was killed by a stray arrow at Ramoth Gilead in 853 (1 Kgs. 22:29-35), and when Moab, Edom, and other formerly dependent territories revolted (2 Kgs. 1:1; 3:27; 8:20-22). When the prophets Elijah and Elisha, as a part of their general reform, anointed Jehu to wipe out the dynasty of Omri in the north, 841 B.C., Jehu slew Ahaziah of Judah as well (2 Kgs. 9); and the government was left in the hands of his Baal worshiping mother Athaliah. So paradoxically, at the very moment that Jehu was wiping out Baalism in Samaria, Athaliah was sponsoring it in Jerusalem. Compromise and sin had brought national failure to Judah (2 Chron. 21:10).

(3) Mutual oppression, 841-790 B.C. There followed a period of domination by the Arameans of Damascus over both of the Hebrew kingdoms (2 Kgs. 10:32-33; 12:17-18; 13:3, 7). The boy king Joash was returned to the throne of Judah in place of his grandmother Athaliah (2 Kgs. 11:12), and he was able to restore the temple through his well-known money chest (2 Kgs. 12:4-16). But later he fell into sin and slew Zechariah the priest who tried to correct him (2 Chron. 24:17-22). In 803 Adad-nirari III of Assyria subdued Damascus (2 Kgs. 13:5) and Jehoash of Israel, encouraged by Elisha, succeeded in recovering his people's losses to Aram in three great battles (2 Kgs. 13:14-25).

The mutual relations of Judah and Israel now entered their next stage:

(4) Domination of the south by the north, 790-782 B.C. Amaziah of Judah had reconquered Edom; but his successes had led him to a foolish challenge of Jehoash in the north, despite the warning fable of the latter (2 Kgs. 14:9, 10). In the ensuing battle, Amaziah was defeated, and a part of the wall of Jerusalem was broken down. The domination seems to have lasted until the death of Jehoash in 782.

(5) Mutual prosperity, 782-752 B.C. The long reigns of Jeroboam II in the north and Azariah (Uzziah) in the south were marked by mutual recognition and expansion. The former, aided by the prophet Jonah, controlled land from Hamath in the north to the Salt Sea in the south; (2 Kgs. 14:25) the latter conquered Ammon and the Arabs to the east and Philistia to the west (2 Chron. 26). But while Uzziah, except for his last days, was marked by piety, Samaria's luxuries were leading to moral and spiritual decay (see the prophecies of Hosea or Amos).

(6) Domination of the north by the south, 752-743 B.C. In the twenty years beginning with 752 Israel lapsed into chaos, marked by five different dynasties. Under such circumstances Azariah, almost upon the default of the north, took over the leadership in foreign affairs, particularly against Assyria, and came to control southward down to Elath on the Red Sea (2 Chron. 26:2). Tiglath-Pileser III, however, marched against Azariah. In 743 Hamath fell and Rezin of Damascus, Hiram II of Tyre, and Menahem of Israel were forced to pay heavy tribute (2 Kgs. 15:19). The Assyrians turned back and Azariah was left untouched. Jotham ruled well as regent during his father Azariah's leprosy (2 Kgs. 15:5).

(7) Conflict, 743-722 B.C. Suffering in the north from Assyria seems to have provoked the final stage in the relations of the two kingdoms, one of hostility in which the north attempted revenge. Pekah of Israel, with Rezin, king of Syria, attacked Judah's new, weak, and thoroughly corrupt king Ahaz (1 Kgs. 16:1-5) and took Elath (1 Kgs. 16:6). Ahaz disregarded the prophecies of Isaiah, who predicted the imminent fall of both Samaria and Damascus (Isa. 7:1ff.), submitted to Tiglath-Pileser and appealed for his help against Pekah and Rezin (2 Kgs. 16:7) in 734 B.C. The Assyrians destroyed Damascus and took part of Israel captive (2 Kgs. 15:29). Hoshea murdered Pekah to become the last king of Israel from 732 to 722 (2 Kgs. 15:30). Hezekiah assumed the regency in Judah in 728, a year or two before the deaths of both Tiglath-Pileser and Ahaz (Isa. 14:28, 29), and Shalmaneser V and Sargon

II proceeded to take captive the remaining tribes of the north in 722 (2 Kgs. 17:3-6).

For almost another century and a half Judah was able to maintain its independent existence. Some time after his first official year in 726 (cf. 2 Chron. 29:3 and 30:1-2, which could not have been in the same year), Hezekiah instituted sweeping national reforms and in 701 was able to reassert his independence from Assyria, despite serious losses (2 Kgs. 18:13-16; 19:35-36). His long-lived but generally evil son Manasseh (697-642) forfeited both the spiritual and political achievements of his father (2 Kgs. 21:1-16; *see also* ASSYRIA) and became the cause of Judah's ultimate downfall (2 Kgs. 21:11; 23:26; 24:3). Only Josiah, with his three stages of reformation in 632, 628, and 622 (the greatest of all based upon the rediscovered law book of Moses, 2 Chron. 34:3, 8, 14-21), was able to prepare God's people spiritually for the maintenance of their faith in God and the promises of his word (see 2 Kgs. 23:25) through the days of exile and temptation that would elapse until the coming of that final King, the Lord Messiah (see Isa. 7:14; 9:6-7; 11:1-5). Three of Josiah's sons occupied the throne between 609 and 597. All were evil, and with the four deportations by Nebuchadnezzar that brought to an end the kingdom of Judah (*see* BABYLONIA) the son of the eldest was warned that no ordinary human being from among his descendants could ever again sit upon the throne of David (Jer. 22:30). (J.B.P.)

KINNERETH, CHINNERETH 1. The Sea of Galilee. *See* GEOGRAPHY OF THE HOLY LAND.

2. A fortified city (200-252) in the tribal area of Naphtali on the NW of the Sea of Galilee (Josh. 19:35).

3. The region around Kinnereth which included what later came to be called the plain of Gennesaret (1 Kgs. 15:20; Mt. 14:34).

KINSMAN-REDEEMER *See* MARRIAGE

KIR 1. A place in Mesopotamia from which Arameans had emigrated to Syria (Amos 9:7), and to which the Assyrians later exiled them (Amos 1:5).

2. A city (217-066) of Moab (Isa. 15:1) also called Kir Hareseth (2 Kgs. 3:25; Isa. 16:7, 11; Jer. 48:36).

KIR HARESETH *See* KIR, 2

KIRIATHAIM, KIRJATHAIM 1. A city (220-128) in Moab given by Moses to the tribe of Reuben (Num. 32:37; Josh. 13:15-19; Jer. 48:1, 23).

2. An unidentified Levitical site in the tribal area of Naphtali (1 Chron. 6:76). *See also* KARTAN.

KIRIATH ARBA *See* HEBRON

KIRIATH ARIM See Ezra 2:25, footnote. Considered to be the same as KIRIATH JEARIM.

KIRIATH BAAL *See* BAALAH and KIRIATH JEARIM

KIRIATH HUZOTH An unidentified place in Moab in the Balaam stories (Num. 22:39).

KIRIATH JEARIM A town in the tribal area of Judah later given to Benjamin also called Baalah and Kirjath Baal (Josh. 15:9, 60; 18:14, 28). When the Philistines returned the Ark of God it was brought here by the men of Beth Shemesh before being taken twenty years later to Jerusalem by David (1 Sam. 6:21—7:2; 1 Chron. 13:5, 6).

KIRIATH SANNAH *See* DEBIR

KIRIATH SEPHER *See* DEBIR

KISH 1. The father of King Saul (1 Sam. 9:1-3).

2. A descendant of Benjamin (1 Chron. 8:30).

3. Father of some men who married the daughters of Eleazar who had no sons at his death (1 Chron. 23:21, 22).

4. A Levite in the time of King Hezekiah (2 Chron. 29:12).

5. An ancestor of the uncle of Queen Esther, Mordecai (Esth. 2:5).

KISHI The father of a Levitical musician appointed by David also called Kushaiah (1 Chron. 6:44; 15:17).

KISHION A Levitical city (187-229) in the tribal area of Issachar (Josh. 19:20; 21:28).

KISHON A river whose source is in Mt. Tabor and Mt. Gilboa and which flows westward through the Plain of Megiddo to empty into the Mediterranean. Here Deborah and Barak defeated the Canaanite coalition under Sisera and here too the false prophets of Jezebel were killed after Elijah's victory on Mt. Carmel (Judg. 4:7, 13; 5:21; Ps. 83:9; 1 Kgs. 18:40).

KISLEV *See* CALENDAR

KISLON, CHISLON The father of the representative of the tribe of Benjamin involved in the division of the land of Canaan among the tribes (Num. 34:21).

KISLOTH TABOR Probably identical with KESULLOTH.

KISS Besides the normal use of a kiss as a greeting between friends and relatives it was used in the worship of pagan deities or as a sign of homage to a king. Judas Iscariot used it as a means of identifying his Master whom he wished to betray to the authorities (1 Kgs. 19:18-20; Ps. 2:11; Mt. 26:48, 49). In early church times there was a "holy kiss," a special type of greeting (Rom. 16:16; 1 Cor. 16:20). Also called "kiss of love" (1 Pet. 5:14).

KITE *See* BIRDS, 5

KITLISH A site in Judah in the western foothills (Josh. 15:40).

KITRON An unidentified site in the tribal area of Zebulun (Judg. 1:30).

KITTIM The Hebrew name for Cyprus which was inhabited originally by people descended from Javan, Greeks (Gen. 10:4; 1 Chron. 1:7). It is translated Cyprus on a number of occasions (Isa. 23:1, footnote). The ships of Kittim (Dan. 11:30, footnote) were most probably ships of Grecian design. The NIV calls them "ships of the western coastlands."

KNEADING TROUGH These, also called kneading bowls, were used in the making of bread. On the night of the Lord's passing through at the first Passover the Israelites took their dough before the yeast was added, and carried it in kneading troughs bound in their clothing (Deut. 28:5, 17; Ex. 8:3; 12:34).

KNIFE A sharp instrument of flint (for circumcision, shaving, or making a sickle) or of metal used as a sword, a razor, for killing a sacrifice, or for normal cutting (Josh. 5:2-3; 1 Kgs. 18:28; Ezek. 5:1; Gen. 22:6, 10; Prov. 23:2).

KOA A site east of Mesopotamia listed among those whose people were about to invade Judah (Ezek. 23:23).

KOHATH, KOHATHITE A son of Levi (Gen. 46:11) and the name of his descendants (Num. 3:17-20, 27-31).

KOLAIAH 1. The father of the false prophet Ahab in the days of Jeremiah (Jer. 29:21).

2. A descendant of Benjamin after the return from the Babylonian captivity (Neh. 11:7).

KORAH, KORAHITE 1 and 2. A son and a grandson of Esau (Gen. 36:5, 14-18).

3. A descendant of Judah and Caleb (1 Chron. 2:43).

4. A Levite from whom descended the Korahite clans who were the doorkeepers and musicians of the tabernacle and the temple (Ex. 6:21, 24; Num. 26:58; 1 Chron. 26:1; 2 Chron. 20:19). The sons of Korah are named in the titles of Psalms 42, 44-49, 84-85, 87-88.

5. One who led a revolt against Moses and lost his life, and that of the others involved with him, by being swallowed up by the earth (Num. 16).

KORAZIN, CHORAZIN A site just north of the Sea of Galilee denounced by Jesus at the same time he denounced Bethsaida and Capernaum (Mt. 11:21).

KORE 1. A Korahite gatekeeper of the temple (1 Chron. 26:1).

2. A Levite over the offerings in the days of King Hezekiah (2 Chron. 31:14).

KOUM, CUMI An Aramaic word meaning "arise" used by Jesus in raising the daughter of the ruler (Mk. 5:41).

KOZ, COZ A descendant of Judah (1 Chron. 4:8).

KUKOK *See* HELKATH

KUSHAIAH *See* KISHI

LAADAH A descendant of Judah (1 Chron. 4:21).

LAADAN *See* LADAN

LABAN The brother of Rebekah and father of Jacob's two wives Leah and Rachel who covenanted with Jacob in Gilead (Gen. 24:29; 29:16, 25-30; 31:24ff.).

LACHISH At first a royal city (135-108) of the Canaanites and then a Judean border fortress guarding one of the important approaches from the western foothills into the hill country west of Hebron (Josh. 10:3, 31, 32; 15:39). Its burning in about 1230 B.C. is ascribed to the Israelite conquest by some but by others to a later Egyptian raid. King Rehoboam of Judah made it a fortified city (2 Chron. 11:9). It was taken by the Assyrian king Sennacherib as a preface to the surrender of Hezekiah of Judah (2 Chron. 32:9; 2 Kgs. 18:14, 17). It was resettled after the return from the Babylonian captivity (Neh. 11:30). Here was found the famous cache of twenty-one inscribed ostraca called "The Lachish Letters."

LADAN, LAADAN 1. An ancestor of Moses' successor Joshua (1 Chron. 7:26). 2. A Levite son of Gershom also called Libni (1 Chron. 23:7; Ex. 6:17).

LAEL The father of Eliasaph, a Levite leader of the families (Num. 3:24).

LAHAD A descendant of Judah (1 Chron. 4:2).

LAHMAN An unidentified site in the western foothills of Judah (Josh. 15:40).

LAHMI A brother of the giant Goliath (1 Chron. 20:5).

LAISH 1. A city (211-294) near the headwaters of the Jordan River which was conquered by the Danites and renamed Dan (Judg. 18:7-29); also called Leshem (Josh. 19:47). *See also* LAISHAH.

2. The father of the man to whom Saul gave his daughter Michal, David's wife (1 Sam. 25:44).

LAISHAH A site in the tribal area of Benjamin (Isa. 10:30).

LAKE OF FIRE *See* DEAD, ABODE OF

LAKKUM, An unidentified site in Naphtali (Josh. 19:33).
LAKUM

LAMA *See* ELOI, ELOI LAMA SABACHTHANI

LAMB The young of the sheep and even of the goat, a delicacy for food and milk and used as a sacrificial animal (Deut. 32:14; Gen. 22:7). Lambs were sacrificed on all the holidays in the tabernacle and temple but they were especially important at Passover. The lamb was to be totally eaten in the Passover night or else it was to be burned the next morning (Ex. 12:1-13). *See also* LAMB OF GOD.

LAMB OF GOD The name given to Jesus by John the Baptist (Jn. 1:29, 36). It signifies the redemptive character of the death of Christ and places it in the context of the Passover sacrifices of the OT which in time came to be the picture of redemption from sin (1 Cor. 5:7).

LAMECH Son of Methushael also called Methuselah (Gen. 5:26) and descendant of Cain (Gen. 4:18ff.).

LAMENTATIONS, *See* JEREMIAH, BOOK OF
BOOK OF

LAMP, A vessel for giving light and its stand, often just a niche in a
LAMPSTAND wall. While no description of a lamp is found in the Bible archaeologists have given us a full picture. A lamp consisted of a hollow saucer or bowl of clay in which the oil would

be placed. A pinch was made in the lip where the wick could be laid. So well known is their stylistic development that lamps are used as one of the criteria for the dating of archaeological strata. Lampstands are usually mentionéd in connection with the golden candlestick in the tabernacle and temple (Ex. 25:31, 37; 2 Chron. 4:19, 20). It is only natural that the lighted lamp would have symbolic meaning, speaking to man of the Light of God: his Word, his salvation, his guidance (Ps. 119:105; 2 Pet. 1:19; Isa. 62:1; Ps. 18:28).

LANCE *See* ARMS AND ARMOR

LANDMARK *See* BOUNDARY STONES

LAODICIA A city in Asia Minor and seat of an important church in post-NT times. It is mentioned a number of times by Paul in his letter to the church at Colosse and is the recipient of one of the letters of John, the writer of the Book of Revelation (Col. 2:1; 4:13-16; Rev. 1:11; 3:14).

LAPPIDOTH, LAPIDOTH The husband of the prophetess Deborah (Judg. 4:4).

LASEA A seaport town in Crete mentioned in connection with Paul's travels (Acts 27:8).

LASHA An unidentified site on the eastern side of the Canaanite clans (Gen. 10:19).

LASHARON An unidentified site taken by Joshua (Josh. 12:18).

LAST DAYS, HOUR, TIME *See* ESCHATOLOGY

LAST SUPPER The combination of words is not found in the Bible but it refers to the supper on the evening before the crucifixion of Jesus when he sat down to a Passover supper and converted it into what the church considers the first communion or eucharistic service (Mt. 26:17-29).

LATIN The language of ancient Rome and Israel and one of the three languages in which the inscription was written which was placed above the cross of Jesus (Jn. 19:20).

LATTICE A construction made by crossing laths or other material to cover an opening for privacy, ventilation, or adornment (Judg. 5:28; Prov. 7:6).

LAVER A large vessel containing water which was in the courtyard between the tent of meeting and the altar. It was used for the washing of the feet and hands of the priest who served there (Ex. 30:18-28).

LAW *See also* DECALOGUE. The term refers to commandments or laws in general and to the Ten Commandments in particular. Some laws were civil or social in character, others religious, and still others moral. The first could change as religion developed or changed. The second could be superseded if the society changed. The latter as expressing the character of God and his universe is unchangeable. All three types are a part of the system found in the Bible.

While Israel existed as a religious commonwealth, she had a civil and social system of laws for regulating the conduct of the members of the society living together (Lev. 1, 4-6, 16; Num. 15; Deut. 12).

From the perspective of history it is clear that the civil and social legal systems of ancient Israel were done away either by being ignored, abrogated, or modified through the ages after Israel ceased to be a nation in her own land (Ex. 21-22; Deut. 21:18-21; Num. 5; 35:9-28; Deut. 17:8-17). The operation of the state, the family, man to man relationships, came in for much legislation.

Examples of moral legislation are equally easy to note. Beginning with the Ten Commandments themselves: duties toward God and duties toward man are found abundantly in the Bible (Ex. 20:3-11). In the NT Jesus reemphasized the OT law that one is to love the Lord his God with all his powers first and then to love his neighbor as himself (Mt. 22:36-40; Deut. 6:5; Lev. 19:18; Rom. 13:8-10; Phil. 2:3-8).

As Israel was a theocratic society with religious practices to be kept, such as sacrificing of animals, she needed legal instruction as to the procedure to follow. God is a Spirit and requires that he be worshiped in spirit and in truth (Jn. 4:23, 24). A set of moral principles expressing God's character and person are needed for the eternal guidance of all men. This is the moral law.

Just as God's character, nature, and will cannot change, the moral principles of his revelation, the Bible, never change and are always binding on his creatures. Morality does not come from human declarations but by divine revelation.

An important emphasis in the NT is that the natural or ordinary man is impotent to keep the law blamelessly. It is too high and exacting. Therefore the "new birth," a regeneration of the heart, is necessary. "Create in me a pure heart, O God" (Ps. 51:10) is an OT prayer but an item emphasized in the NT as the most basic consideration for the ability to keep the law of God (Rom. 7:4—8:2; Gal. 2:16—5:23). It is in this sense that Christ is declared to be the goal of the law, not the end. The Greek word *telos* can be translated as "end" or "goal." As the English word "end" also means "goal" it should have been translated thus in Romans 10:4.

A common notion widely held is that the NT is opposed to the law and for this reason anti-Jewish. Two points are missed in this criticism: (1) much of the law ended or was changed by Jewish leaders themselves by adaptation to the changed circumstances in which they found themselves without a temple and out of the land when the first and second Jewish commonwealths ended; and (2) the NT picks up where the OT prophets left off with the emphasis that the attitude of the heart is basic to keeping moral law, adding only that the atonement of Christ, appropriated by faith, was a necessary prerequisite to the ability to keep moral law. The NT adds, further, that Christ, being God manifest in the flesh and thus sinless, kept all the requirements of the law and freely imputes this obedience to the believer as a part of the salvation which he gives to man who believes.

The NT consistently presents as the duty of man conformity to the moral image of God, conformity to law, and, as man's goal, more and more sanctification or separation from sin and evil and separation to God and his holiness (Mt. 5:19, 20, 22, 28, 34, 39; Eph. 1:3; 6:2; Gal. 5:13-26). If one compares Galatians 5:18 with 5:25, 26 the NT picture becomes clear, not opposed to the law per se, but requiring something much more than mere outward conformity.

LAWYER A term in the Bible that denoted a class of men especially trained to understand the OT law, to teach it to the next generation of lawyers, and to decide for those who requested it on specific questions of law (Lk. 7:30; 11:45; 14:3).

LAYING ON OF HANDS In both Testaments this act could signify the giving of a blessing, benediction or parental inheritance, or the bestowal of the gifts and rights of an office (Gen. 48:14-20; Deut. 34:9; Mt. 19:13-15; Acts 13:3). In the OT sacrificial system it also symbolized the transfer of sin from an individual or people to the sacrificial animal (Lev. 16:21). In the NT it was the external symbol of the giving of the Holy Spirit to an individual (Acts 19:6). By extension, from 1 Timothy 4:14 and 2 Timothy 1:6, it became for the church a part of the procedure for the ordination of one of its clergymen.

LAZARUS 1. The brother of Martha and Mary who was raised from the dead by Jesus (Jn. 11:5; 43ff.).

2. The poor man in the parable of the rich man and Lazarus told by Jesus (Lk. 16:19ff.).

LEAD One of the important metals in antiquity (Num. 31:22). It was used in the reduction of silver (Jer. 6:27-30). Tarshish traded with Tyre for her lead (Ezek. 27:12). It had many commercial uses: weights, sinkers for fishnets, and for plumblines.

LEAH Elder daughter of Laban and one of Jacob's wives, mother of some of the founders of the tribes of Israel (Gen. 29:16, 23, 31ff.).

LEANNOTH, MAHALATH *See* PSALMS, TITLES OF

LEBANA, LEBANAH An ancestor of some sons who were temple servants in the second temple in the days of Ezra and Nehemiah (Neh. 7:48; Ezra 2:45). There are two spellings of the name of the same man.

LEBANON *See* GEOGRAPHY OF THE HOLY LAND

LEBAOTH *See* BETH LEBAOTH

LEBONAH A town (173-164) between Shiloh and Shechem (Judg. 21:19).

LECAH A descendant of Judah (1 Chron. 4:21).

LEEKS *See* PLANTS, PERFUMES, AND SPICES

LEGION The chief and largest unit of the Roman army but never used in that sense in the Bible. There it is used only in a figurative sense, of largeness numerically (Mt. 26:53; Mk. 5:9, 13; Lk. 8:30).

LEHABITES, LEHABIM Descendants of Ham who occupied the N coast of Africa W of Egypt, thought to be the ancestors of the Libyans (Gen. 10:13; 1 Chron. 1:11). *See also* LIBYA.

LEHI An unidentified site in the tribal area of Judah where Samson killed 1,000 Philistines with a jawbone and for that reason also called Ramath Lehi (Judg. 15:14-19).

LEMUEL An unknown king whose mother taught him the proverbs (Prov. 31:1-9).

LENTILS *See* PLANTS, PERFUMES, AND SPICES

LEOPARD *See* BEASTS, 8

LEPER, LEPROSY *See* SICK, SICKNESS

LESHEM *See* DAN, DANITES and LAISH, 1.

LETUSHITES, The descendants of a grandson of Abraham by Keturah (Gen.
LETUSHIM 25:3).

LEUMMITES, The descendants of grandson of Abraham by Keturah (Gen.
LEUMMIN 25:3).

LEVI 1. A son of Jacob by Leah and founder of one of the tribes of
Israel, the one that served in Israel's religion (Gen. 29:34;
34:25ff.; Num. 3:5-9).

2 and 3. Two ancestors of Joseph, who was the husband of
Mary and the father, as it was thought, of Jesus (Lk. 3:24,
29).

4. A tax collector who became one of Jesus' disciples (Mk.
2:14; Mt. 9:9), also called Matthew.

LEVIATHAN *See* BEASTS, 9

LEVITES The descendants of Levi who by their loyalty to Moses and
to God at the time Aaron built the golden calf were set aside
for the service of God (Gen. 35:23; Ex. 32:2-7; 25-29).
These were the priests and other officers of God in the
service of the tent of meeting and later the temple, the
treasury, the music and song (Num. 3:5-13, 38; 1 Chron.
6:31, 33ff.; 2 Chron. 17:8, 9; Ezra 8:15ff.; Neh. 7:43). In the
NT it is stated that since perfection could not be brought by
man, not even by the Levitical priesthood, it was necessary
for another priest, from a different tribe and order, to come
to do the work of atonement and sanctification, namely Jesus,
a priest after the order of Melchizedek, who antedated the
Levitical system. The service priests and Levites were
divided into twenty-four groups, called courses. Each had its
own head and its own function and each served for a week
in rotation (1 Chron. 24, 25; Lk. 1:8).

LEVITICAL *See* CITY OF REFUGE
CITY

LEVITICUS, *See* PENTATEUCH
BOOK OF

LIBNAH 1. A city (138-115) in the western foothills of Judah captured
by Joshua and designated as one of the Levitical cities (Josh.
10:29-32; 21:13). It was one of the cities besieged by King
Sennacherib of Assyria (2 Kgs. 19:8). The wife of King
Josiah and mother of two of Judah's kings came from Libnah
(2 Kgs. 23:31; 24:18).

2. An unidentified stop on the Israelite exodus route from
Egypt (Num. 33:20, 21).

LIBNI 1. A descendant of Levi (1 Chron. 6:17).

2. A Levite son of Gershon also called Ladan. *See also* LADAN, 2 (Ex. 6:17).

LIBYA A part of N Africa W of Egypt. It was the country of the Lehabites. Cyrene was one of its cities (Ezek. 30:5; Dan. 11:43; Acts 2:10). *See also* LEHABITES.

LIEUTENANT *See* SATRAP

LIFE *See also* IMMORTALITY. The term life may refer either to the animate part of man or animal, physical or natural life, or it may refer to that part of man's "life" after death, spiritual or eternal life. That is, it may refer to two parts of man's existence: the period of his earthly existence, his lifetime, or to his eternal existence into which he enters through death. Both are presented as gifts of God to his creatures. Physical life was given in the acts of creation. In the case of man, his body was formed from the dust of the ground and he became animate when God breathed into his nostrils the breath of life. At this point man became a living being. All animals before him already were "living creatures" (Gen. 1:20-25; 2:7). The words rendered "living creatures" in Genesis 1:24 are the same as "living being" in 2:7. According to the NT, eternal life is also the gift of God and it is mediated through faith in the atonement made by Christ in his death and resurrection (Jn. 3:36; 5:24; Rom. 5:10; Eph. 2:1-8).

LIFE, LAMB'S BOOK OF, AND TREE OF These expressions are found only in Revelation (3:5; 13:8; 17:8; 20:12, 15; 21:27), except for the references to the latter in Revelation and in the creation narratives (Gen. 2:9; 3:22, 24; Rev. 22:2, 14, 19). The book contains a record of those who inherit eternal life. The "tree" found originally in the Garden of Eden turns up again in the account of eternal life in Revelation.

LIGHT AND DARKNESS The former is the symbol of purity and holiness while the latter is the symbol of sin and the outer darkness reserved for the devil and his angels. Light has many symbolic meanings: God is light (1 Jn. 1:5); believers dwell in light (Eph. 5:8, 9); Jesus is the light of the world (Jn. 8:12); God's written revelation is called light (Ps. 119:105); and believers or special emissaries of God are light (Phil. 2:15; Jn. 5:35).

LIGHTS, FEAST OF *See* CALENDAR and FESTIVALS

LIKHI A descendant of Manasseh (1 Chron. 7:19).

LILIES *See* PSALMS, TITLES OF, 2

LILY *See* PLANTS, PERFUMES, AND SPICES

LINEN A product of the flax plant. Its fibers were woven usually by women in an art learned in Egypt (Ex. 35:25; Prov. 31:13, 19). The plant itself was grown in the Jericho area and perhaps also in the low area around Beth Shan (Josh. 2:3, 6). It was used for all kinds of clothing and cloths for many other purposes as well. *See also* PLANTS, PERFUMES, AND SPICES.

LINUS A Christian with Paul at Rome who sent greetings to Timothy (2 Tim. 4:21).

LION *See* BEASTS, 8

LIVER *See* EMOTIONS

LIZARD *See* BEASTS, 6

LOAF *See* BREAD

LOAN *See* DEBT

LOCUST *See* BEASTS, 6

LOD The Lydda (140-151) of the NT, a town in the western foothills of Judah near Joppa (1 Chron. 8:12; Ezra 2:33; Acts 9;32, 35, 38).

LO DEBAR A town (207-219) east of the Jordan, in Gilead, the home of Mephibosheth, Saul's grandson, and of Makir, a helper of David (2 Sam. 9:4-6; 17:27).

LOG *See* WEIGHTS AND MEASURES

LOIS The grandmother of Timothy (2 Tim. 1:5).

LONELY PLACE *See* DESERT

LOOKING GLASS *See* MIRROR

LOOPS The coverings of the tabernacle were held together by the clasps which went through the loops of goat's hair or other material (Ex. 26:4-11).

LORD The English translation of a number of Hebrew and Greek words used of both God and men to express the recognition of respect or authority. As applied to God see GOD, NAMES OF. As applied to men it shows respect, as to a master, or ownership. The recognition of a noble (Gen. 23:11; 1 Kgs. 1:31; Mt. 20:25). When the reference is to a human it is spelled in lower case letters without capitals. In the OT when the reference is to God it is written Lord. In the overwhelming number of cases in the NT the reference is to Jesus and God the Father.

LORD OF HOSTS *See* GOD, NAMES OF

LORD'S DAY A day consecrated to the Lord Jesus Christ for rest and worship, the first of the week as a memorial to his resurrection which took place on that day (Rev. 1:10). It was sharply contrasted with the sixth day or the Sabbath as far as observance of the day was concerned. One could consider any day sacred since as far as salvation was concerned all days were alike (Rom. 14:5, 6). It became customary for Christians to assemble on that day and to break bread together (Acts 20:7).

LORD'S PRAYER The title given to the prayer which Jesus taught his disciples to pray (Mt. 6:9-13; Lk. 11:2-4), commonly called in many languages the "Our Father."

LORD'S SUPPER The name commonly given to the meal that Jesus ate with his disciples the night before he was crucified, the supper which started as a Passover meal but which Jesus changed as a memorial service to be kept by the Church until his return (1 Cor. 11:20; 10:16; 11:27; Mt. 26:17, 26-28; 1 Cor. 11:17-32).

LOT 1. The nephew of Abraham who emigrated with him to Canaan but left him there to go down to Sodom and Gomorrah. Here he was captured by foreign kings, rescued by Abraham, escaped the destruction of the cities and became the ancestor of the Moabites and the Ammonites (Gen. 11:27, 31; 13:8-12; 14:12ff.; 19:1-30).

2. A portion or a share of something that one receives, that is, a piece of land or a position in service (Josh. 15:1).

3. Like dice to be cast on the ground, or other devices to be drawn from a receptacle, for making decisions. This was a very common method to help make decisions in the ancient world and in the Bible (Esth. 3:7; Jonah 1:7; Mt. 27:35; Acts 1:24-26).

LOTAN The first son of Seir and founder of the Horite clan in Edom (Gen. 36:20, 22, 29; 1 Chron. 1:38, 39).

LOVE This is an inner emotion or drive which both initiates and maintains relationships as between human beings or as between men and God whether it be friendship, loyalty, kindness, or even mercy and pity. The Bible in the OT knows of love in the human society, love within the family, sexual love, the love of man for God and the electing, covenant love of God for his people (2 Sam. 1:26; Ruth 4:15; 2 Sam. 13:1, 15; Deut. 6:5; 7:6-9). In the NT while the above nuances are also found the main thrust is different. God is love by nature and man's chief end is to love God supremely and to glorify him by keeping his commandments. There is emphasis also upon the need for man to love his fellow man (1 Jn. 4:7-12, 16, 19-21). Involved in this is the keeping of the commandments of God (1 Jn. 5:2, 3; Mt. 22:36-40). God's love for men includes his redeeming them, supplying all their needs, and securing for them a place in his presence throughout eternity (Rom. 5:8; Phil. 4:19; Rom. 8:28-39; Eph. 2:4-8).

LOVE FEAST While the term is found only once in the Bible (Jude 12) the concept grew up in the early church from a communal meal apparently eaten in connection with the observance of the Lord's Supper. Abuses soon also entered and the Apostle Paul warned the church against them. The practice died out in general use (1 Cor. 11:20-29, 33, 34).

LUCIUS 1. A man from Cyrene who was a Christian in Antioch (Acts 13:1).

2. One associated with Paul who sent greetings to the Christians at Rome (Rom. 16:21).

LUD, LUDITES 1. Lud, a son of Shem (Gen. 10:22).

2. The Ludites were descended from Ham, another son of Noah who became the father of the Ludites, perhaps the ancient Lydians (Gen. 10:13). Some scholars think that the Ludites were North African people. If so they are not now identifiable.

LUHITH An unidentified town in Moab (Isa. 15:5).

LUKE The writer of the third Gospel and of the Book of Acts, apparently both a physician and a historian (Col. 4:14; Lk. 1:1-5; Acts 1:1-3). The "we" sections of the Book of Acts (16:10-17; 20:5-15; 21:1-8; 27:1—28:16) indicate that he traveled with Paul extensively. Except for two other references (Philem. 24; 2 Tim. 4:11) we know nothing more about this unusual man. There is much speculation in the form of tradition.

LUKE, GOSPEL ACCORDING TO *See* GOSPELS, THE FOUR

LUST Several Hebrew and Greek words are thus translated and they carry the ideas of delight in, desires for the things of the world, passionate desire as well as sexual desire (Ps. 68:30; Prov. 11:6; 1 Thess. 4:5; 1 Jn. 2:16, 17; Mt. 5:28; Rom. 1:24; Eph. 4:22).

LUTE *See* MUSIC

LUZ 1. A site on the N border of the tribal area of Benjamin. Here Jacob had his dream in which he saw angels ascending and descending a ladder. He changed its name to Bethel (Josh. 18:13; Gen. 28:19).

2. A city in the land of the Hittites (Judg. 1:26).

LYCAONIA A district in Asia N of the Taurus mountain range whose cities Lystra and Derbe were visited by the Christians who were escaping the persecution in Iconium (Acts 14:1, 5, 6).

LYCIA *See* GEOGRAPHY OF THE HOLY LAND

LYDDA *See* LOD

LYDIA 1. A lady from the city of Thyatira who sold purple goods in Philippi. She became a convert of Paul and groups of believers met in her house (Acts 16:14, 15, 40).

2. A site or area mentioned in a message about Egypt in association with Cush (Upper Egypt) and Put (Jer. 46:9), and also with all Arabia and Libya (Ezek. 30:5); and in lament for Tyre in connection with Persia and Put (Ezek. 27:10). *See* PUT.

LYRE *See* MUSIC

LYSANIAS The tetrarch of Abilene, a small region in Lebanon (Lk. 3:1).

LYSIAS Claudius Lysias, a Roman officer who arrested Paul and later sent him to Caesarea to be judged (Acts 21:32ff.; 23:26ff.).

LYSTRA A site in Lycaonia to which some persecuted Christians fled (Acts 14:1, 5, 6). Caesar had one of his military strongholds there. Paul healed a man whose feet were crippled from birth, with a resultant uproar in the city (Acts 14:8-18). Here too Paul was stoned and left for dead (Acts 14:19). In spite of it all a church was established which Paul visited again on a later missionary journey (Acts 16:1-2).

M

MAACAH, MAACATH, AND MAACATHITES

1. A son of Nahor and nephew of Abraham (Gen. 22:24).

2. A wife of David and the mother of Absalom (2 Sam. 3:3).

3. The father of Achish, the king of Gath (1 Kgs. 2:39, 40).

4. The wife of King Rehoboam of Judah and mother of his successor Abijah. Her grandson, King Asa, deposed her from her place of influence in the kingdom because of her idolatry (1 Kgs. 14:31; 15:2, 10, 13). The relationship between Maacah, Abijah, and Absalom (Abishalom) is not clear (see 2 Chron. 11:22; 13:2).

5. A concubine of Caleb (1 Chron. 2:48).

6. The wife of Makir, a descendant of Manasseh.

7. The wife of Jeiel the father of Gibeon (1 Chron. 8:29).

8. The father of one of David's mighty men (1 Chron. 11:43).

9. The father of the head of the Simeonites in David's service (1 Chron. 27:16).

10. A small kingdom on the western border of Bashan north of Gilead whose people the Maacathites fought with the Ammonites against David and on being defeated became his servants (Deut. 3:14; Josh. 12:5; 2 Sam. 10:6-19). The Israelites did not expel, them but dwelt among them and

some of their descendants later assisted David and others in Israel (Josh. 13:13; 2 Sam. 23:34; 2 Kgs. 25:23).

MAADAI One who married a foreign wife during the Babylonian captivity (Ezra 10:34).

MAADIAH, A family from whom came a head of a priestly family after
MOADIAH the return with Zerubbabel from the Babylonian captivity (Neh. 12:5, 17).

MAAI One who helped with musical instruments in the dedication of the rebuilt wall of Jerusalem (Neh. 12:36).

MAARATH An unidentified site in the tribal area of Judah (Josh. 15:59).

MAASAI A priest in postexilic times (1 Chron. 9:12).

MAASEIAH 1. A Levite gatekeeper in David's time (1 Chron. 15:18, 20).

2. One of the military officers who helped the priest Jehoiada to put the young Jehoash-Joash on the throne of Judah (2 Chron. 23:1ff.).

3. An officer of King Uzziah of Judah (2 Chron. 26:11).

4. A son of King Ahaz of Judah (2 Chron. 28:7).

5. The governor of Jerusalem in the days of King Josiah sent to help repair the temple (2 Chron. 34:8).

6, 7, 8, and 9. Four who married foreign wives during the Babylonian captivity (Ezra 10:18, 21, 22, 30).

10. The father of one of those who built a portion of the wall of Jerusalem in Nehemiah's time (Neh. 3:23).

11 and 12. Two who stood with Ezra as he read the law to the people in Jerusalem (Neh. 8:4, 7). One of them instructed the people in the law.

13. One who signed the covenant with Nehemiah (Neh. 10:25).

14 and 15. Descendants of Judah and of Benjamin who returned from the Babylonian captivity (Neh. 11:5, 7).

16 and 17. Two priests who were involved in the musical part of the program of dedication of the rebuilt wall of Jerusalem (Neh. 12:41, 42).

18. The father of a priest that the king sent to inquire of the prophet Jeremiah (Jer. 21:1; 29:25).

19. The father of the false prophet Zedekiah in the days of Jeremiah (Jer. 29:21).

20. Keeper of the door of the temple in the days of Jeremiah (Jer. 35:4).

MAATH   An ancestor of Joseph, the father, so it was thought, of Jesus (Luke 3:26).

MAAZ   A descendant of Judah and Jerahmeel (1 Chron. 2:27).

MAAZIAH   1. Head of the twenty-fourth priestly division in the service of the tabernacle as arranged by David (1 Chron. 24:18).

2. One who signed the covenant with Nehemiah (Neh. 10:8).

MACBANNAI, MACHBANAI   A descendant of Gad who joined David (1 Chron. 12:13).

MACBENAH, MACHBENAH   A descendant of Caleb (1 Chron. 2:49).

MACCABEES   Judas, son of the priest Mattathias, was called the Maccabee, from the Hebrew or Aramaic *maqqaba*, which means "hammer." It may have arisen from the crushing blows that Judas, as hero of Israel's revolt against Antiochus IV, inflicted upon his people's oppressors (*see* SELEUCIDS). The term Maccabean is sometimes applied to his party or, less accurately, to his family's entire dynasty (*see* HASMONEAN and the family chart there).

At his death in 167 B.C. Mattathias appointed Judas to be the continuing leader against Antiochus, his Syrian armies, and his policy of Hellenization. By strategy, courage, and the grace of God, Judas Maccabeus won four victories: over Apollonius, near Samaria (1 Macc. 3:10-12); over Seron, at Beth Horon (1 Macc. 3:23, 24); over Ptolemy, Nicanor, and Gorgias, at Emmaus, 166 B.C. (1 Macc. 4:12-22); and over the viceroy Lysias, at Bethsura, 165 (1 Macc. 4:33, 34). As Judas affirmed, "Victory in battle standeth not in the multitude of a host, but strength is from heaven. They come unto us in fulness of insolence and lawlessness, to destroy us and our wives and our children; but we fight for our lives and our laws" (1 Macc. 3:19-21). In December, 165, Judas cleansed the Jerusalem temple and reestablished the daily sacrifice. This event continued to be observed as the Feast of Dedication or "Lights" (John 10:22; *see* CALENDAR).

Judas went on to subdue the surrounding areas of Idumea, the area east of the Jordan, and Philistia (1 Macc. 5). Lysias and the young Antiochus V (164-162) defeated Judas at Bethzacharias, 163 (1 Macc. 6:31-47); but revolt in Antioch caused them to withdraw. Judas was granted religious liberty (1 Macc. 6:57-60). Demetrius I (162-150), however, appointed Alcimus, a corrupt Hellenizer, as high priest, whom Judas opposed and drove out (1 Macc. 7:15). Judas destroyed a supporting Syrian army of Nicanor at Adasa, March 161, and is supposed to have concluded a treaty with the Romans

(1 Macc. 8). But in April, at Elasa before an even larger Syrian army under Bacchides, with most of his forces having fled, Judas Maccabeus died in battle (1 Macc. 9:1-22), leaving his brothers to carry on the struggle to its ultimately successful conclusion.

The title Maccabees, 1 and 2, also identifies two of the intertestamental writings of the Apocrypha that describe the career of Judas and accompanying events. First Maccabees is a historical work of great value. It exhibits a pious spirit (as in 3:51) but makes no claim of miracles; it is patriotic and pro-Hasmonean. Second Maccabees is an inartistic abbreviation of a lost history of Jason of Cyrene (2 Macc. 2:23), emphasizing the theology of Pharisaism (2 Macc. 7:9), stressing the miraculous (2 Macc. 3:23-24), and making reference to purgatory and prayers for the dead (2 Macc. 12:44-45). It more readily grants the imperfections of the Hasmoneans (as in 2 Macc. 10:20). The following tabulation suggests something of the comparative place of 1 and 2 Maccabees among the fifteen books of the Apocrypha.

Book	Approx. Date	Orig. Lang.	Type of Lit.	Contents	Purpose
1 Esdras	200 B.C.	Aram.	Fiction	The Bible, plus	On rebuilding the temple
2 Esdras	A.D. 100	Aram.	Apocalypse	Prophecies	To encourage oppressed Jews
Tobit	175 B.C.	Aram.	Fiction	Tobias' trip	To enforce Pharisaism
Judith	150 B.C.	Hebr.	Fiction	Jerusalem saved	Nationalistic Judaism
Rest of Esther	125 B.C.	Greek	Fiction	Additions	To make Esther religious
Wisdom of Solomon	A.D. 40	Greek	Philosophy	Didactic poetry	For Pharisaism's faith
Ecclesiasticus	180 B.C.	Hebr.	Wisdom	Didactic poetry	Toward Sadduceeism
Baruch	200 - 100 B.C.	Hebr.	Legend	Letter to exile	For Jews in trouble
Jeremy	125 B.C.	Aram.	Polemic	Letter to exile	Against idolators
Song of the Three Children	150 B.C.	Aram.	Fictional add. to Daniel	Prayer and hymn	Independent praises
Susanna	150 B.C.	Aram.	Fictional add. to Daniel	Woman rescued	To teach morality
Bel	150 B.C.	Aram.	Fictional add. to Daniel	Daniel vs. idols	Against idolatry
Prayer of Manasses	50 B.C.	Hebr.	Lyric	Penitent prayer	For repentance
1 Maccabees	75 B.C.	Hebr.	History	Judah 175-135	To glorify Hasmoneans
2 Maccabees	50 B.C.	Greek	Legend	Judah 187-160	To enforce Pharisaism

(J.B.P.)

MACEDONIA *See* GEOGRAPHY OF THE HOLY LAND

MACHINE *See* ARMS AND ARMOR

MACHIR *See* MAKIR

MACHPELAH A field and cave near Hebron which Abraham bought from Ephron the Hittite for a burial ground. The patriarchs are buried here under a great Moslem mosque today (Gen. 23:9-19; 25:9; 49:30; 50:13).

MACANDEBAI, MACHANDEBAI One who married a foreign wife during the Babylonian captivity (Ezra 10:40).

MADAI A son of Japheth and grandson of Noah, ancestor of the Medes (Gen. 10:2).

MADMANNAH A town (143-086) in southern Judah founded by a descendant of Caleb (Josh. 15:21; 1 Chron. 2:49).

MADMEN A town (217-077) in Moab noted in the dirge of Jeremiah (Jer. 48:2).

MADMENAH An unidentified site in the tribal area of Benjamin (Isa. 10:31).

MADNESS *See* SICK, SICKNESS

MADON An unidentified site northwest of the city of Tiberias whose king was defeated by Joshua (Josh. 11:1; 12:19).

MAGADAN *See* DALMANUTHA

MAGBISH An unidentified site from which some came back with Zerubbabel from the Babylonian captivity (Ezra 2:30).

MAGDALENE *See* MARY

MAGDIEL A chief of the Edomites (Gen. 36:43).

MAGGOTS *See* BEASTS, 6

MAGIC, MAGICIAN *See* DIVINATION

MAGOG A son of Japheth and grandson of Noah, the land from which Gog is to come. This attack is noted in the prophets (Gen. 10:2; Ezek. 38-39; Rev. 20). Early historians identify the area as that from which the Scythians came in the sixth century B.C. The places associated with Magog in Genesis and 1 Chronicles are located in Asia Minor and not in the area of modern Russia as some students of prophecy believe. *See also* MESHECH.

MAGPIASH One who signed the covenant with Nehemiah (Neh. 10:20).

MAHALAH *See* MAHLAH

MAHALALEEL See next entry

MAHALALEL 1. A descendant of Seth and Noah, called Mahalaleel in the genealogy of Joseph, the father, so it was thought, of Jesus (Gen. 5:12; Lk. 3:37).

2. A descendant of Judah after the return from Babylon (Neh. 11:4).

MAHALATH 1. A daughter of Ishmael and wife of Esau also called Basemath (Gen. 28:9; 36:3).

2. A wife of King Rehoboam of Judah, granddaughter of David (2 Chron. 11:18).

MAHALATH LEANNOTH *See* PSALM, TITLES OF

MAHANAIM A Levitical town (214-177) and city of refuge on the border between Gad and Manasseh east of the Jordan in Gilead. It was so named by Jacob after angels met him there on his return from Paddan-aram (Josh. 13:26, 30; 21:38; Gen. 32:2). It was briefly the capital of Israel and David stayed there while waiting out the rebellion of his son Absalom (2 Sam. 2:8; 15:10; 19:32).

MAHANETHDAN An unidentified site between Beth Shemesh and Kiriath Jearim where God's spirit first began to stir in Samson; a camp of the tribe of Dan as they were enroute to take Laish (Judg. 13:25; 18:12).

MAHARAI One of David's thirty mighty men (2 Sam. 23:28; 1 Chron. 27:13).

MAHATH 1. A Levite appointed by David to serve with the temple musicians in the time of David (1 Chron. 6:35).

2. A Levite who served in the time of King Hezekiah to help purify the temple (2 Chron. 29:12).

MAHAVITE The family name of one of David's mighty men (1 Chron. 11:46).

MAHAZIOTH One assigned by David to praise God in song and music in the temple (1 Chron. 25:4, 30).

MAHER-SHALAL-HASH-BAZ Symbolic name given to a son of the prophet Isaiah. The symbolism pointed to the destruction of Syria and Ephraim (Isa. 8:1-3).

MAHLAH, MAHALAH 1. The eldest daughter of a man of Manasseh who had no son and who therefore inherited the father's land (Num. 26:33; 27:1; 36:11).

2. A descendant of Manasseh. It is not stated whether this person is a man or a woman (1 Chron. 7:18).

MAHLI 1. A descendant of Levi and son of one Merari in the time of Moses (Ex. 6:19; Num. 3:20).

2. Another descendant of Levi, son of Mushi, in the time of David (1 Chron. 6:47; 23:21).

MAHLON Ruth's first husband, son of Naomi (Ruth 1:2, 4; 4:10).

MAHOL The father of some wise men referred to in connection with the wisdom of Solomon (1 Kgs. 4:31).

MAHSEIAH, MAASEIAH Grandfather of the staff officer Seraiah to whom Jeremiah gave a message when he entered into the Babylonian captivity (Jer. 32:12; 51:59).

MAID, MAIDEN, WOMENSERVANTS, AND SLAVE GIRLS The translation of a number of words used many times in the OT but only a few in the NT. Some of these words refer to girls as the property of owners (slave girls), handmaids or maidservants (Lev. 19:20; Lk. 12:45). Another refers to a young unmarried girl who could also be a womanservant (2 Kgs. 5:2; Esth. 2:4). Yet another refers to a young girl of marriageable age, but never, as far as known context is concerned, having been married or known a man. This is the word translated "virgin" and found in the much discussed "virgin birth" prophecy of Isaiah 7:14 (Also translated "maidens"; see Gen. 24:43 and Ps. 68:25). It is the word rendered "virgin" from the Greek of the Isaiah passage in Matthew 1:23. The word translated "virgin," "virginity" in many cases in the OT, and also in the NT is the Hebrew word *bethulah* (Gen. 24:16; Lev. 21:14; Deut. 22:19; 1 Cor. 7:28). This word refers to a girl who is in most cases secluded and therefore has not known a man. However, there are in the literature references to a *bethulah* who had been married, and therefore presumably had known a man (Joel 1:8). The Aramaic incantation literature has other cases. It was for this reason that Isaiah could not use this normal word for a virgin (*bethulah*) but instead chose the one of which no case of cohabitation with a man is known.

MAKAZ An unidentified site near Beth Shemesh (1 Kgs. 4:9).

MAKHELOTH An unidentified stop on the Israelite exodus from Egypt (Num. 33:25, 26).

MAKI The father of the representative of the twelve spies from the tribe of Gad (Num. 13:15).

MAKIR, 1. A son of Manasseh and the father of Gilead after the
MACHIR conquest (Num. 26:29; 32:39, 40).

2. The protector of Saul's grandson Mephibosheth and helper of King David (2 Sam. 9:4, 5; 2 Sam. 17:27ff.).

MAKKEDAH An unidentified site in the western foothills of the tribal area of Judah conquered by Joshua (Josh. 10:10, 16; 15:41).

MALACHI, *See* PROPHETS, MINOR
BOOK OF

MALCAM, A descendant of Benjamin (1 Chron. 8:8-9).
MALCHAM

MALCHIAH *See* MALKIJAH

MALCHIRAM *See* MALKIRAM

MALCHUS The servant of the High Priest whose ear Peter cut off on the night before Christ's crucifixion (Jn. 18:10).

MALKIEL, A grandson of Asher (Gen. 46:17).
MALCHIEL

MALKIJAH, 1. A descendant of the Levite Kohath whom David put in
MALCHIJAH, charge of the service of song in the temple service (1 Chron.
MALCHIAH 6:40).

2. Head of one of David's priestly divisions (1 Chron. 24:9).

3 and 4. Two who married foreign wives during the Babylonian captivity (Ezra 10:25, 31).

5, 6, and 7. Three who worked on the repairing of the wall of Jerusalem with Nehemiah (Neh. 3:11, 14, 31).

8. One who stood with Ezra as he read the law to the people (Neh. 8:4).

9. A priest who signed the covenant with Nehemiah (Neh. 10:3).

10. A priest involved in the dedication ceremony of Nehemiah's restored wall of Jerusalem (Neh. 12:42).

11. The father of one who was sent to Jeremiah by King Zedekiah (Jer. 21:1; 38:1ff.; 1 Chron. 9:12).

12. A son of King Zedekiah who had a cistern in which Jeremiah was imprisoned (Jer. 38:6).

MALKIRAM A descendant of King Jehoiachin who was in the captivity in Babylon (1 Chron. 3:18).

MALKI-SHUA, MELCHISHUA A son of Saul (1 Sam. 14:49).

MALLOTHI, MALOTHI A musician appointed by David with others to serve in the temple (1 Chron. 25:4, 26).

MALLOW *See* PLANTS, PERFUMES, AND SPICES

MALLUCH 1. A descendant of Levi (1 Chron. 6:46).

2 and 3. Two who married foreign wives during the Babylonian captivity (Ezra 10:29, 32).

4 and 5. Two who signed the covenant with Nehemiah (Neh. 10:4, 27).

6. One from the priests and Levites who returned from the Babylonian captivity with Zerubbabel (Neh. 12:2).

MALTA An island south of Sicily where Paul was shipwrecked (Acts 28:1).

MAMRE An Amorite living in Abraham's days beside some great trees, "the great trees of Mamre" which came to identify a place where Abraham later lived (Gen. 14:13, 24; 18:1; 23:17, 19).

MANAEN A Christian of Antioch who had been brought up with Herod the tetrarch (Acts 13:1).

MANAHATH 1. A town (167-128) in Edom to which some descendants of Benjamin were deported (1 Chron. 8:6).

2. A descendant of Esau and of Seir the Horite (Gen. 36:23).

MANAHATHITES *See* MANAHATH

MANASSEH 1. A son of Joseph who became the head of one of the tribes of Israel (Gen. 41:51; 48:1).

2. *See* KINGS OF JUDAH AND ISRAEL.

MANDRAKE *See* PLANTS, PERFUMES, AND SPICES

MANGER A trough, box, or stall used for feeding cattle, and translated in the RSV also as crib or stall. Luke states that at his birth

Jesus was placed in a manger (Lk. 2:7, 12, 16; Isa. 1:3; translated "stall" 1 Kgs. 4:26).

MANNA A special food provided by God for the Israelites during their wilderness wanderings. It is called "bread," it came at night, and was white. It was like coriander seed, looked like resin, tasted like wafers made with honey and olive oil, and the people had to grind it in a handmill or crush it in a mortar, then cook it in a pot or make it into cakes. The description indicates that it was not a natural phenomenon, but rather supernatural. It stopped when the Israelites no longer had need of it for food (Ex. 16:31-35; Num. 11:6-9; Josh. 5:12; Ps. 78:24; Jn. 6:31).

MANOAH The father of Samson (Judg. 13:12, 24; 14:3).

MAN OF SIN *See* ANTICHRIST

MANSLAYER Anyone who killed another human being deliberately was a murderer and had to be put to death. The accidental killer of an individual was called a manslayer. The assembly was required to judge between the manslayer and the avenger of blood. In the meantime the manslayer was required to find asylum in a city of refuge and could stay there until the death of the high priest. He was then free to return to his own city (Num. 35:6-28; Ex. 21:14).

MAN, SON OF *See* GOD, NAMES OF, GODHEAD

MANTLE *See* DRESS

MAOCH Father of Achish king of Gath (1 Sam. 27:2).

MAON 1. A town (162-090) in the western foothills of the tribal area of Judah (Josh. 15:55). David hid from Saul in the Desert of Maon (1 Sam. 23:25). It was the home of Nabal and Abigail the latter of whom later became one of David's wives (1 Sam. 25).

2. A descendant of Caleb (1 Chron. 2:42-45).

MARA The name Naomi gave herself after the death of her husband and sons (Ruth 1:20).

MARAH An unidentified watering place for the Israelites in their desert wanderings on their exodus from Egypt. The water was bitter and Moses sweetened it (Ex. 15:23; Num. 33:8, 9).

MARALAH A border site belonging to Zebulun, north of Megiddo (Josh. 19:11).

MARDUK *See* DEITIES

MARESHAH 1 and 2. Descendants of Judah and Caleb (1 Chron. 2:42; 4:21).

3. A city (140-111) in the western foothills of the tribal area of Judah which King Rehoboam fortified and where King Asa defeated the Ethiopian (Cushite) army. It was the home of the prophet Eliezer who spoke against the alliance of Jehoshaphat of Judah with the wicked King Ahaziah of Israel (Josh. 15:44; 2 Chron. 11:5-12; 14:9-15; 20:35-37).

MARK, GOSPEL ACCORDING TO *See* GOSPELS, THE FOUR

MARK, JOHN The son of Mary of Jerusalem in whose home Christians stayed while Peter was in prison; a companion of Paul and Barnabas on the first missionary journey. Because Paul refused to take him on the second journey, he went with Barnabas to Cyprus. Later Paul speaks of him lovingly. The tradition of the very early church is that he is the author of the Gospel that bears his name and the content of his book is believed to be what he learned from Peter (Acts 12:12, 25; 15:37; 13:4; 15:39; Col. 4:10; 2 Tim. 4:11). Peter called him "son."

MARKET, MARKETPLACE In the Book of Acts (Acts 16:19; 17:17), the markets are typical Greek marketplaces, the centers of public life, the *agora*. Temples, public buildings, the courts, and judges were located there. In the OT and in the four Gospels, the marketplaces were the typical oriental streets of small shops in front of which children played, men stood around and visited or worked, and the sick were often laid for the pity of the passerby (Ps. 55:11; Prov. 7:12; Mt. 11:16). In such places many of Jesus' miracles of healing took place (Mk. 6:56).

MAROTH An unidentified site in the tribal area of Judah whose inhabitants were still expecting good when God had prophesied the opposite (Mic. 1:12).

MARRIAGE The union of a man and a woman first consummated in the Garden of Eden between Adam and Eve. This union became the pattern for all others (Gen. 2:24; Mt. 19:4-6). The father of the man made the selection of the woman and the father of the woman gave his daughter to the husband to be (Gen. 24:4; 29:23, 28; 34:8; Josh. 15:16). A purchase price, called a bride price, was paid to the father of the bride (Gen. 31:15; Ex. 22:17; 1 Sam. 18:25). The father of the bride usually gave her a gift called the "dowry" which might be property, or a maid. This was her own money and property, and from it she had to supply her husband with a concubine, sometimes her own maid, if she herself was unable to present him with a male heir. This piece of legislation known also from the Assyrian archives discovered in ancient Nuzu is reflected in the Abraham, Sarah, Hagar account (Gen. 16:1-3). Other examples of dowries are recorded (Josh. 15:18, 19; 1 Kgs. 9:16). The first step after the agreements was the betrothal or "pledge to marry" but not the same as the actual marriage itself which came later (Deut. 20:7). In the matter of adultery a betrothed woman was considered just as if married. This explains the actions of Joseph the husband of Mary the mother of Jesus (Deut. 22:23, 24, 28, 29; Mt. 1:18-20). At the time of the actual marriage a legal contract was drawn up and witnessed, as is known again particularly from the Nuzu documents but also reflected in the Bible. Other practices still seen in the Orient today were a part of the actual wedding itself: beautiful clothes, ornaments, the veil worn by the bride, the feast and procession of the bridegroom and his friends, and on occasion a bridal procession as well to the place of the ceremony (Song 3:11; Isa. 61:10; Gen. 24:65; Judg. 14:10, 11; Ps. 45:14). Music accompanied the processions and was a prelude to the wedding banquet (Jer. 7:34; Judg. 14:10, 11).

The function of a marriage was more than to enable two people to love and live together. It was to produce a progeny and to supervise the raising of the children to be an object lesson of the relation of God to his people. In this the role of the parents is particularly important and is very clear both in the OT and NT (Isa. 54:5, 6; Eph. 5:21—6:4).

Levirate marriage, or the duty of a brother-in-law, is described in Deuteronomy 25:5-10, the marriage that is required when a brother dies without a son. In such case the husband's brother is required to marry the widow and raise up a family in the name of the deceased (Ruth 2:20; 4:10). He is called the kinsman-redeemer. If the brother refuses to marry the woman, she spits in his face, slaps his face with one of his own sandals, and his line is known thereafter as the family of the unsandaled.

Polygamy in the OT resulted from lust as well as the desire for male heirs and as a part of international treaties was marriage between the two groups. In the NT it is always assumed that marriage is to be between one man and one woman only. Marriage after divorce except under certain carefully regulated circumstances is considered adultery (Mt. 19:9). *See also* DIVORCE.

MARSENA A prince of Persia and Media who had special access to the Persian king, Xerxes (Esth. 1:1, 14).

MARTHA The sister of Mary and Lazarus (Lk. 10:38, 39; Jn. 11:2, 20).

MARY 1. The virgin mother of Jesus. Her song, known today as the Magnificat, was in reaction to the announcement made to her by the angel Gabriel (Mt. 1:18, 23; Lk. 1:26ff., 46ff.). She was with her son at the performance of some of his miracles and at the crucifixion where Jesus commended her to John (Jn. 2:1; 19:25ff.; 21:24).

2. The mother of James and Joseph, and perhaps the wife of Clopas. She was present both at the crucifixion and the resurrection (Mt. 27:56; Mk. 15:40, 47; 16:1; Jn. 19:25).

3. The sister of Martha and Lazarus, the Mary who anointed the feet of Jesus (Lk. 10:38; Jn. 11:2, 20, 32; 12:3).

4. Mary Magdalene from whom seven demons had come out; one of the women who accompanied Jesus to minister to him (Lk. 8:1, 2). She too was present at the crucifixion and at the empty tomb (Mt. 27:56, 61; 28:1).

5. The mother of John Mark (Acts 12:12).

6. One to whom Paul sends greetings at Rome (Rom. 16:6).

MASHAL *See* MISHAL

MASKIL *See* PSALMS, TITLES OF

MASREKAH An unidentified royal site in Edom before Israel had a king (Gen. 36:36).

MASSA A son of Ishmael (Gen. 25:14).

MASSAH An unidentified site in Horeb where Moses drew water from a rock (Ex. 17:7; Deut. 6:16; 9:22; 33:8).

MATRED Mother of a wife of the king of Edom (Gen. 36:39; 1 Chron. 1:50).

MATRITES A family of Benjamites to which King Saul belonged (1 Sam. 10:21).

MATTAN 1. A priest of Baal in the time of wicked Queen Athaliah who was killed in Jehoiada's reform (2 Kgs. 11:18).

2. The father of one who recommended the death of Jeremiah (Jer. 38:1).

MATTANAH An unidentified stop on the Israelite exodus route (Num. 21:18, 19).

MATTANIAH 1, 2, and 3. Three Levites, one in the time of David, an ancestor of one in the time of King Jehoshaphat of Judah, and one in the time of King Hezekiah of Judah (1 Chron. 25:4; 2 Chron. 20:14; 29:13).

4, 5, 6, and 7. Four who married foreign wives during the time of the Babylonian captivity (Ezra 10:26, 27, 30, 37).

8. The original name of the last king of Judah, Zedekiah (2 Kgs. 24:17).

9, 10, and 11. Three Levites in postexilic times, one of them a musician with Zerubbabel (1 Chron. 9:15; Neh. 11:17; 12:8, 25).

12. Ancestor of a priest who shared in the dedication of the walls of Jerusalem as rebuilt in Nehemiah's time (Neh. 12:35).

13. Ancestor of one of the keepers of Nehemiah's storerooms (Neh. 13:13).

MATTATHA An ancestor of Joseph, the father, so it was thought, of Jesus (Lk. 3:31).

MATTATHIAS 1 and 2. Two of the ancestors of Joseph, the father, so it was thought, of Jesus (Lk. 3:25, 26).

3. *See* "Maccabees" under HASMONEANS.

MATTATTAH, One who married a foreign wife during the time of the **MATTATHAH** Babylonian captivity (Ezra 10:33).

MATTENAI 1 and 2. Two who married foreign wives during the time of the Babylonian captivity (Ezra 10:33, 37).

3. The head of the priestly family in the days of Joiakim and Nehemiah (Neh. 12:19).

MATTHAN An ancestor of Jesus through his mother's line (Mt. 1:15).

MATTHAT 1 and 2. Two ancestors of Joseph, the father, so it was thought, of Jesus (Lk. 3:24, 29).

MATTHEW *See* APOSTLES

MATTHEW, GOSPEL *See* GOSPELS, THE FOUR
ACCORDING TO

MATTHIAS The disciple chosen by lot to replace Judas Iscariot (Acts 1:24ff.).

MATTITHIAH 1. A Levite musician in the time of David (1 Chron. 15:18, 21).

2. A Levite chosen by David to minister before the tabernacle (1 Chron. 16:5).

3. A descendant of Levi in postexilic times who was in charge of baking the offering bread (1 Chron. 9:31).

4. One who married a foreign wife during the time of the Babylonian captivity (Ezra 10:43).

5. One who stood at the right hand of Ezra as he read the law to the people (Neh. 8:4).

MATTOCK A special type of pickaxe with a point at one end and a blade for grubbing at the other. It needed frequent sharpening, which was difficult for the Israelites since only the Philistines could do it (1 Sam. 13:20, 21).

MEAL OFFERING *See* SACRIFICES AND OFFERINGS

MEALS The words breakfast, dinner, and supper are used in Scripture. The first is found only in connection with the postresurrection appearance of Jesus at the seashore (Jn. 21:12). The references to supper except for one (Lk. 17:8) are either in connection with the Lord's Supper or an eschatological supper (Lk. 22:20; 1 Cor. 11:20, 25; Rev. 19:9, 17). There are also several references to dinner (Mt. 22:4; Jn. 12:2). These three words are not to be confused with their modern counterparts as to time or content. As is still the custom today in the more primitive parts of the orient, the first meal comes late in the morning, the men leaving for work without eating at all or just taking a piece of bread or cheese. At some time between ten and twelve in the morning a principal meal is eaten, called dinner. This meal is often eaten at work and therefore consists of things that can either be taken by the workman to his work or brought there later by wife or children. When the day's work is done, which today is between two and four in the afternoon, the supper is eaten unless that supper is to be a festive meal on the order of a banquet.

Bread, usually in the shape of a patty or modern pancake (pita), was the staple item and was usually eaten with meat gravy, sour wine, or certain seeds ground up into a paste with a little oil. Fruits and grains were usually in good supply and great variety. The meat came from sheep, goats, lambs, kids, fatted calves, and from wild game as it was available. Fish was everywhere available. Milk, and particularly a cheese made from curdled milk and kept in skins, was an integral part of the diet.

The meal was eaten while seated on the floor in earlier times. After the return from the Babylonian captivity the custom of eating the evening meal reclined on couches around a table, banquet style in those days, was known in Palestine (John 21:20). The hands, not knives, forks, and spoons, were used for eating. There was a profusion of different types of bowls and plates about which we are learning more with the progress of modern archaeology. From such stories as the Egyptian record of Sinuhe's travels in Palestine, we learn additional information about foods and family conditions in that land at that time.

MEASURE *See* WEIGHTS AND MEASURES

MEBUNNAI One of David's thirty mighty men; also called Sibbecai (2 Sam. 23:27; 1 Chron. 11:29).

MECHERATHITE *See* MEKERATHITE

MECONAH, MEKONAH An unidentified place in the western foothills of Judah inhabited by those who returned from the captivity with Zerubbabel (Neh. 11:28).

MEDAD One who prophesied in the Israelite camp in the desert in the days of Moses (Num. 11:26, 27).

MEDAN A son of Abraham by Keturah (Gen. 25:2).

MEDEBA A city (225-124) east of the Jordan in Moab, that was initially in the tribal area of Reuben. David fought there. The city is currently noted because of the ancient mosaic map of Palestine, the remains of which are to be found in the floor of the fifth century church there (Num. 21:30; Josh. 13:9; 1 Chron. 19:7ff.).

MEDES, MEDIA *See* GEOGRAPHY OF THE HOLY LAND

MEDICINE *See* SICK, SICKNESS

MEDIUM *See* DIVINATION

MEEK, MEEKNESS The word is perhaps best defined by the variety of ways the Greek and Hebrew words are translated: gentle, humble, downtrodden, oppressed. It is set forth as the proper attitude toward God, one of humble dependence, and the proper attitude toward others. It is the opposite of rich, arrogant, defiance of God, and shows complete reliance on one's own abilities, might and power (Ps. 10:17; 37:11; Isa. 29:19; Mt. 5:5; Eph. 4:2; Col. 3:12; Jas. 3:13). Moses is described as the meekest of men (Num. 12:3). In the complex of characteristics called the fruit of the Spirit, it is listed as "gentleness" (Gal. 5:22, 23).

MEGIDDO, PLAINS OF *See* GEOGRAPHY OF THE HOLY LAND

MEHETABEL 1. The wife of an Edomite king (Gen. 36:39; 1 Chron. 1:50). 2. The grandparent of one hired by Sanballat and Tobiah to discourage Nehemiah (Neh. 6:10).

MEHIDA The ancestor of some temple servants who returned from the Babylonian captivity with Zerubbabel (Ezra 2:52; Neh. 7:54).

MEHIR A descendant of Judah (1 Chron. 4:11).

MEHOLAH, MEHOLATHITE The man to whom King Saul gave one of his daughters as wife (1 Sam. 18:19) and the unidentified place from which he came.

MEHUJAEL A descendant of Adam through Cain (Gen. 4:18).

MEHUMAN One of the eunuchs of the Persian king, Xerxes (Esth. 1:10).

MEHUNIM *See* MEUNIM

ME JARKON An unidentified place in the original tribal area of Dan, perhaps near Joppa (Josh. 19:46).

MEKERATHITE, MECHERATHITE Added to the name of one of David's mighty men, perhaps a place or area, Mekerath, from which he came (1 Chron. 11:36).

MEKONAH *See* MECONAH

MELATIAH One who worked on the repair of the walls of Jerusalem with Nehemiah (Neh. 3:7).

MELCHISHUA *See* MALKI-SHUA

MELCHIZEDEK A king of Salem and priest of the Most High God. Abraham paid tithes to him and was blessed in turn by this Melchizedek. There was also a priestly order of Melchizedek which long antedated the Aaronic priesthood (Gen. 14:18-20; Ps. 110:4). It should be noted in addition, however, that this priest was also a king which was not the case with the Aaronic priesthood. All other references to this man and to his priesthood are in the book of Hebrews. Here we are told that he was a high priest and that his ancestry is shrouded in mystery since it is not known. He was king of Salem, that is, king of peace, and the translation of his name is "king of righteousness" (Heb. 7:14). Salem is usually identified as Jerusalem (Ps. 76:2). The thrust of the NT references all in the one book is that Christ is superior to all creatures and men, and specifically in this Melchizedek connection, that Christ's royal priesthood is of a kind that preceded the Aaronic and that continues after it even forever (Heb. 7:23—10:18).

MELEA An ancestor of Joseph, the father, so it was thought, of Jesus (Lk. 3:31).

MELECH A descendant of Benjamin, Saul, and Jonathan who returned from the Babylonian captivity (1 Chron. 8:34-35; 9:40, 41).

MELKI, MELCHI 1 and 2. Two ancestors of Jesus, the father, so it was thought, of Jesus (Lk. 3:24, 28).

MELITA *See* MALTA

MELON *See* PLANTS, PERFUMES, AND SPICES

MEMPHIS The first capital of united Egypt (before 3000 B.C.) often mentioned in secular sources but in the Bible only in the prophetic writings. When the Jews fled Jerusalem after the revolt at the time of Gedaliah (c. 580 B.C.) they went to Memphis (Noph in Hebrew text, see NIV footnote at 44:1; Jer. 41:16-18; 44:1). The prophet Jeremiah predicted that Memphis would become a ruin (Jer. 46:13-19). Ezekiel also predicted its difficulties (Ezek. 30:13-16). Apparently the earlier prediction of Hosea was fulfilled in this descent of Jews to Egypt (Hos. 9:6).

MEMUCAN One of the legal experts consulted by the Persian king, Xerxes (Esth. 1:14, 16, 21).

MENAHEM *See* KINGS OF JUDAH AND ISRAEL

MENAN *See* MENNA

MENE, MENE, TEKEL, AND PARSIN This expression is found only in Daniel 5:25 accompanied with an explanation (Dan. 5:26-28). Daniel noted that *Mene* meant that God had numbered the days of the kingdom of Belshazzar and brought it to an end, *Tekel* that the king was weighed on the scales and found wanting, *Peres* that his kingdom was given to the Medes and Persians. All of this took place that very night. Literally these three words refer to weights: *mene* is the Hebrew mina, *tekel* is the Hebrew shekel and *peres* is the Hebrew half-mina.

MENNA, MENAN An ancestor of Joseph, the father, so it was thought, of Jesus (Lk. 3:31).

MEONOTHAI A descendant of Judah, Caleb, and Othniel (1 Chron. 4:13, 14).

MEPHAATH A Levitical town (239-140) in the tribal area of Reuben in Moab (Josh. 13:18; 21:37).

MEPHIBOSHETH 1. A son of Saul by Aiah's daughter, Rizpah (2 Sam. 21:8, 9).

2. Son of Jonathan and grandson of Saul; also called Merib-Baal. He was only a child when his father was killed. A friend, Makir, reared him until David finally took over the provision for him (2 Sam. 4:4; 1 Chron. 8:34; 2 Sam. 9:4-7).

MERAB The daughter of King Saul promised to David but given to another (1 Sam. 14:49; 18:17-19).

MERAIAH Head of a priestly family in the days of Nehemiah (Neh. 12:12).

MERAIOTH 1. An ancestor of Ezra (Ezra 7:3).

2. Ancestor of some priests who returned from the Babylonian captivity (1 Chron. 9:11; Neh. 11:11).

MERARI A son of Levi and ancestor of the Merarites (Gen. 46:11; 1 Chron. 6:1; Josh. 21:40; Ezra 8:19).

MERATHAIM Jeremiah's symbolic name for Babylon in his oracle against that city and nation (Jer. 50:21).

MERCY *See* COMPASSION

MERCY SEAT *See* TABERNACLE

MERED A descendant of Judah (1 Chron. 4:17).

MEREMOTH 1. A priest who acted as a treasurer of the second temple who also helped Nehemiah in the rebuilding of the wall of Jerusalem (Ezra 8:33; Neh. 3:4, 21).

2. One who married a foreign wife during the days of the Babylonian captivity (Ezra 10:36).

3. One who signed the covenant with Nehemiah (Neh. 10:5).

4. The head of a priestly house in the days of Nehemiah (Neh. 12:3, 15).

MERES An expert in matters of law and justice to King Xerxes in Persia (Esth. 1:14).

MERIBAH, 1 and 2. Two different unidentified stops of the Israelites in
MERIBATH their wanderings during the exodus from Egypt. In one of
KADESH them Moses struck the rock at a place called Horeb in
Rephidim; in the other near Kadesh Barnea he was commanded
to speak to the rock but struck it instead (Ex. 17:1-7; Num.
20:1-13). For this failure to do as God told Moses, he lost his
right to enter the Promised Land (Deut. 32:51).

MERIB BAAL The son of Jonathan, also called MEPHIBOSHETH.

MERODACH *See* DEITIES

MERODACH- A king of Babylon. *See* BABYLON.
BALADAN

MEROM, Until recently thought to be the same as the marshes of the
THE WATERS OF Huleh Lake of the Sea of Galilee. Recent research, however,
places it (190-275) in the center of the mountains of Upper
Galilee near Mount Merom. A great battle of Joshua's northern
campaign was conducted here (Josh.11:5-7).

MERONOTHITE A resident of an unidentified area called Meronoth in the
tribal area of Naphtali (1 Chron. 27:30; Neh. 3:7).

MEROZ An unidentified place in Galilee whose inhabitants were cursed
because they refused to heed the call for help from Deborah
and Barak (Judg. 5:23).

MESHA 1. A descendant of Benjamin (1 Chron. 8:9).

2. A king of Moab who recorded his deeds on the famous
"Moabite Stone." He threw off the yoke of Israel in the days
of King Jehoram of Israel. The record of his sacrificing one
of his sons to his God is recorded (2 Kgs. 3:4, 5, 26, 27).

3. A place in the territory where the Joktanites lived, between
Mesha and Sephar (Gen. 10:30).

4. A son of Caleb the brother of Jerahmeel (1 Chron. 2:42).

MESHACH *See* SHADRACH

MESHECH 1. A grandson of Noah and son of Shem called Mash in the
Hebrew text of Genesis 10:23; see the footnote there
(1 Chron. 1:17).

2. A son of Japheth and grandson of Noah (Gen. 10:2).

MESHELEMIAH The father of the Zechariah who was a gatekeeper in the
time of the return from the Babylonian captivity, also called
Shelemiah and perhaps even Shallum (1 Chron. 9:21; 26:14;
9:17).

MESHEZABEL, MESHEZABEEL
1. Ancestor of one who worked with Nehemiah on the repair of the wall of Jerusalem (Neh. 3:4).

2. One who signed the covenant with Nehemiah (Neh. 10:21).

3. Father of an important official in Jerusalem after the return from the Babylonian captivity (Neh. 11:24).

MESHILLEMITH, MESHILLEMOTH
1. Ancestor of a priest in Nehemiah's day; also called Meshillemoth (1 Chron. 9:12; Neh. 11:13).

2. A descendant of Ephraim in the days of King Ahaz (2 Chron. 28:12).

MESHOBAB
A descendant of Simeon (1 Chron. 4:34).

MESHULLAM
1. The grandfather of one sent by King Josiah to the temple to inquire of the high priest (2 Kgs. 22:3).

2. A son of Zerubbabel of the royal line after the return from Babylon (1 Chron. 3:19).

3, 4, 5, and 6. A descendant of Gad and three of Benjamin (1 Chron. 5:13; 8:17; 9:7, 8).

7 and 8. Two priests, one the father of Hilkiah and the other the son of Meshillemith (1 Chron. 9:11, 12).

9. A Levite who helped in the repair of the first temple in the days of King Josiah (2 Chron. 34:12).

10. One sent by Ezra to Iddo to bring Levites from Casiphia (Ezra 8:16).

11. One who was against Ezra on his ideas of mixed marriages (Ezra 10:15).

12. One who married a foreign wife in the days of the Babylonian captivity (Ezra 10:29).

13 and 14. Two who worked on the repair of the walls and gates of Jerusalem in the days of Nehemiah (Neh. 3:4, 6).

15. One who stood with Ezra as he read the law to the people (Neh. 8:4).

16 and 17. Two who signed the covenant with Nehemiah (Neh. 10:7, 20).

18, 19 and 20. Two priests and a gatekeeper in the days of Joiakim and Nehemiah (Neh. 12:13, 16, 25).

21. One involved with Nehemiah in the dedication of the rebuilt wall of Jerusalem (Neh. 12:33). Perhaps the same as number 18.

MESHULLEMETH
The wife of King Manasseh (2 Kgs. 21:19).

MESOBAITE
See MEZUBAITE

MESOPOTAMIA *See* GEOGRAPHY OF THE HOLY LAND

MESSIAH *See* CHRIST, LIFE AND TEACHINGS OF and GOD, NAMES OF, GODHEAD

METALS *See* PRECIOUS STONES AND METALS

METHEG HAMMAH, METHEG-AMMAH An unidentified site that David took from the Philistines (2 Sam. 8:1).

METHUSELAH A descendant of Noah and Seth and father of Lamech, who is recorded as living longer than any other individual in the Bible (Gen. 5:21-27; 1 Chron. 1:3). His name is included in the genealogy of Joseph, the father, so it was thought, of Jesus (Lk. 3:37).

METHUSHAEL, METHUSAEL A descendant of Adam and Cain and father of a Lamech other than the descendant of Methuselah above (Gen. 4:18).

MEUNIM, MEHUNIM Ancestor of some temple servants who returned with Zerubbabel from the Babylonian captivity (Ezra 2:50).

ME-ZEHAB The grandfather of the wife of Hadad, king of Edom (Gen. 36:39; 1 Chron. 1:50).

MEZOBAITE, MESOBAITE The place or area from which one of David's mighty men came, Mezoab, or perhaps a title (1 Chron. 11:47).

MIAMIN *See* MIJAMIN

MIBHAR One of David's mighty men (1 Chron. 11:38).

MIBSAM 1. A son of Ishmael and grandson of Abraham (Gen. 25:13).

2. A descendant of Simeon (1 Chron. 4:25).

MIBZAR A chief of Edom descendant from Esau (Gen. 36:42).

MICA, MICAH, MICHA, MICHAIAH 1. A son of Mephibosheth and great-grandson of King Saul; also called Micah (2 Sam. 9:12; 1 Chron. 8:34).

2. A Levite active after the return from the Babylonian captivity; also called Micaiah (1 Chron. 9:15; Neh. 12:35).

3. One who signed the covenant with Nehemiah (Neh. 10:11).

MICAH 1. An Ephraimite who made an idol and then later got a priest for himself and his idol. The idol and priest were later taken by the Danites to their new town of Dan in the north (Judg. 17:1-13; 18:2-27, 30).

2. A descendant of Reuben (1 Chron. 5:5).

3. Son of Mephibosheth. *See* MICAH, 1.

4. A Levite of David's days (1 Chron. 23:20).

5. The father of one sent by King Josiah to inquire of the Lord for him, also called Michaiah (2 Chron. 34:20; 2 Kgs. 22:12).

6. One of the minor prophets. *See* PROPHETS, MINOR.

MICAH, BOOK OF *See* PROPHETS, MINOR

MICAIAH, 1. The only prophet who foretold the defeat of King Ahab at **MICHAIAH** Ramoth Gilead, an act for which he was imprisoned (1 Kgs. 22:8-28).

2. The mother of King Abijah of Judah. In the Hebrew text it is Maacah (2 Chron. 13:2; 1 Kgs. 15:2).

3. One sent by King Jehoshaphat of Judah to teach throughout the cities of Judah (2 Chron. 18:8).

4. One who was with Nehemiah when the walls of Jerusalem were dedicated (Neh. 12:41).

5. A son of Gemariah who reported the existence of Jeremiah's scroll in the days of King Jehoiakim (Jer. 36:11, 13).

6. *See* MICAH, 2, 5.

MICHA *See* MICA

MICHAEL 1. The father of one of the twelve spies in the time of Moses. The representative of the tribe of Asher (Num. 13:13).

2, 3, 4, 5, and 6. Descendants of the following: two of Gad, one of Levi, one of Issachar, and one of Benjamin (1 Chron. 5:13, 14; 6:40; 7:3; 8:16).

7. A descendant of Manasseh who defected to David at Ziklag before he was king (1 Chron. 12:20).

8. The father of one of David's officers from the tribe of Issachar (1 Chron. 27:18).

9. A son of King Jehoshaphat of Judah (2 Chron. 21:2-4).

10. The father of Zebadiah who was a leader in the return from the Babylonian captivity (Ezra 8:8).

11. The great prince in the visions of Daniel who stands for his people, Israel (Dan. 10:13, 21; 12:1), called "the archangel" in the NT (Jude 9; Rev. 12:7).

MICHAIAH *See* MICAIAH

MICHAL The daughter of Saul, whom David married. She saved David's life but was taken from him by the king and given to another. Later, she was offended by David's conduct when he was bringing the Ark up to Jerusalem (1 Sam. 14:49; 18:20; 19:11-17; 25:44; 2 Sam. 6:16-23).

MICMASH, MICHMASH A city (176-142) in the tribal area of Benjamin that guarded one of the important passes up into the hill country from Jericho. Here Jonathan started a battle that won a great victory over the Philistines (1 Sam. 13:2-23), and here too the British under General Allenby made an important breakthrough against the Turks in 1918. The Assyrians left their baggage here (Isa. 10:28). Men returned to this place from the Babylonian captivity (Ezra 2:27; Neh. 7:31; 11:31).

MICMETHATH, MICHMETHAH A place (175-176) on the border between the tribal areas of Manasseh and Ephraim (Josh. 16:6; 17:7).

MICRI, MICHRI A descendant in the tribe of Benjamin (1 Chron. 9:8).

MIDDIN A town (188-127) in the southern desert of the tribal area of Judah (Josh. 15:61).

MIDIAN, MIDIANITES The first was a son of Abraham by Keturah and the second a people descended from him who lived in a land that bore his name (Gen. 25:1-3; 37:28, 36). Their land was both east and west of the Jordan rift, the Arabah, and south of Palestine proper. Moses spent forty years here before he began to lead the exodus. His wife came from the area (Ex. 2:15—3:1). Because of later developments, God had to command the Israelites to smite the Midianites who apparently had allied themselves with the sins of Moab (Num. 25:17). Gideon, the judge, delivered the Israelites from the oppression of the Midianites (Judg. 6:1—9:17). Later references in the Bible all refer back to these times and these events.

MIGDAL EDER *See* EDER

MIGDAL EL An unidentified site in the tribal area of Naphtali (Josh. 19:38).

MIGDAL GAD A city (140-105) in the western foothills of the tribal area of Judah (Josh. 15:37).

MIGDOL 1. The Israelites encamped between Migdol and the sea just before crossing the Red Sea. Site unknown (Ex. 14:2).

2. An unidentified site in northern Egypt where the Jews settled in the days when Jeremiah was taken there (Jer. 44:1; 46:14).

3. A place, unidentified, in northern Egypt which God says he will destroy when he destroys all Egypt. Perhaps 2 and 3 are the same (Ezek. 29:10; 30:6, NIV).

MIGRON An unidentified place in the tribal area of Benjamin. King Saul was here with his troops, and the Assyrian conqueror passed that way too (1 Sam. 14:2; Isa. 10:28).

MIJAMIN, MIAMIN, MINIAMIN 1. Head of a priestly division in David's days (1 Chron. 24:9).

2. One who married a foreign wife in the days of the Babylonian captivity (Ezra 10:25).

3. One who signed the covenant with Nehemiah (Neh. 10:7).

4. A priest who returned from the Babylonian captivity with Zerubbabel (Neh. 12:5).

5. A Levite who assisted Nehemiah with music in the dedication of its rebuilt walls of Jerusalem (Neh. 12:41). *See* MINIAMIN.

MIKLOTH A descendant of Benjamin (1 Chron. 8:32).

MIKNEIAH A Levite musician in David's day (1 Chron. 15:18, 21).

MIKTAM *See* PSALMS, TITLES OF

MILALAI One who was with Nehemiah in the dedication of the rebuilt wall of Jerusalem (Neh. 12:36).

MILCAH 1. The wife of Abraham's brother Nahor and grandfather of Rebekah, wife of Isaac (Gen. 11:29; 24:15, 67).

2. One of the daughters of the Zelophehad who died without leaving a son as heir (Num. 26:33).

MILCOM *See* DEITIES

MILE *See* WEIGHTS AND MEASURES

MILETUS, MILETUM A seaport city in Asia visited by Paul on one of his missionary journeys (Acts 20:15-17; 2 Tim. 4:20).

MILL, MILLSTONE An apparatus used to grind grain into flour. It consisted of flat or slightly concave-convex upper and lower stones. The upper stone was turned by hand with a stick placed in a hole on its upper surface. Some larger stones were of a different type with the lower stone conical at the top fitting into a conversely shaped upper stone which had holes on the outside for the insertion of beams which were then pushed or pulled by men or animals for its rotation (Deut. 24:6; 2 Sam. 11:21; Mt. 18:6; Isa. 47:2).

MILLENNIUM A thousand years. *See* ESCHATOLOGY

MILLET *See* PLANTS, PERFUMES, AND SPICES

MILLO *See* BETH MILLO and TERRACES, SUPPORTING

MINA *See* WEIGHTS AND MEASURES

MIND The translation of a number of Greek and Hebrew words which involve both the reflective thinking of the brain and the emotional thinking noted together with the heart. For example, one of the words translated "mind" is the Hebrew word *leb* or "heart" (Isa. 46:8; 65:17; Jer. 3:16; 19:5). The heart was considered the center of the entire personality and as such a natural rendering would be "mind." For Paul's difference between flesh and mind and spirit, see PAUL, LIFE AND TEACHINGS OF.

MINIAMIN 1. A Levite in the days of King Hezekiah who was one of the distributors of the gifts given to the Lord (2 Chron. 31:15).

2. A priest who helped Nehemiah in the dedication of the rebuilt wall of Jerusalem (Neh. 12:41). *See* MIJAMIN.

MINISTER In both Testaments, one who serves or assists. The minister may be either free or bond but if the latter he is more than a simple bond servant. Joshua was Moses' assistant but not his servant (Josh. 1:1). Epaphroditus took care of Paul's needs but was not the servant of either the minister or his congregation (Phil. 2:25). The basic idea in the Bible is service, even though the nature of the service is not always spelled out (Ex. 30:20; Isa. 56:4-6; Mt. 25:44; 2 Tim. 1:18; Col. 4:7). The majority of uses in the OT are connected with service in the tabernacle or temple (Ex. 28:43; 2 Chron. 29:11). In the NT the word at first had a nontechnical use but even there the beginnings of the concept of ministers as minor officers in the church is clear and some of the requirements for a holder of this office are spelled out (1 Tim. 4:6; Rom. 15:16; Acts 6:4; 2 Cor. 5:18; Eph. 4:11, 12; 1 Tim. 3:12; 5:17). Those who ministered in NT times were called elders, presbyters, deacons, deaconesses, or bishops. The gradual development of these various offices into the positions they hold today in various denominations is postbiblical for the most part, a development through need, and not a development of exegesis of Scripture.

MINJAMIN, Head of a priestly family in the days of Nehemiah (Neh.
MINIAMIN 12:17).

MINNI A people and an area in the mountain region northeast of Mesopotamia, mentioned only in Jeremiah 51:27.

MINNITH An Ammonite city east of the Jordan in the tribal area of Reuben which Judge Jephthah conquered in order to free Israel from their yoke (Judg. 11:32-33).

MIRACLES, MIRACULOUS The word "miracle" is used in the OT only in Exodus 7:8, but the concept is noted in the NIV under such terms as "wonders" or "miraculous signs" (Ex. 4:21; Ps. 78:43). In the NT these words are used chiefly in connection with promises that the followers of Jesus would do supernatural things (1 Cor. 12:10; 28, 29), extraordinary events not capable of explanation by natural causes but requiring some superhuman power and coming to pass for a sign. The common rendering in the NIV for this kind of phenomenon is sign or miraculous sign (Isa. 8:18; Mt. 12:38-39; 16:1; Deut. 13:1; Ex. 7:3; Acts 2:43).

MIRIAM 1. The sister of Moses (Num. 26:59; Ex. 2:4ff.; Num. 12:1ff.; 20:1).

2. A descendant of Judah and Caleb (1 Chron. 4:17).

MIRMAH, MIRMA A descendant of Benjamin (1 Chron. 8:10).

MIRROR The early looking-glasses were of smoothed metals, primarily brass, and hence not as functional as modern ones of glass; hence Paul's reference of seeing in a mirror dimly (Job. 37:18; 1 Cor. 13:12; Jas. 1:23).

MISHAEL 1. A Levite cousin of Moses and Aaron who helped to carry the bodies of Nadab and Abihu out of the camp (Lev. 10:4, 5).

2. One who stood with Ezra as he read the law to the people (Neh. 8:4).

3. *See* SHADRACH.

MISHAL, MISHEAL A Levitical city (164-253) in the tribal area of Asher also called Mashal (Josh. 19:26; 21:30; 1 Chron. 6:74).

MISHAM A descendant of Benjamin (1 Chron. 8:12).

MISHMA 1. A son of Ishmael (Gen. 25:14).

2. A descendant of Simeon (1 Chron. 4:25, 26).

MISHMANNAH A descendant of Gad who defected to David (1 Chron. 12:10).

MISHRAITES A clan of Kiriath Jearim descended from Judah (1 Chron. 2:53).

MISPAR, MIZPAR One who returned from the Babylonian captivity with Zerubbabel, also called Mispereth (Ezra 2:2; Neh. 7:7).

MISPERETH *See* MISPAR

MISREPHOTH MAIM A region or city in Phoenicia near Sidon to which place Joshua pursued his enemies after the battle of the Waters of Merom (Josh. 11:8; 13:6).

MITHCAH One of the desert stops of the Israelites in their exodus from Egypt (Num. 33:28, 29).

MITHNITE The family name or place from which came Joshaphat one of David's mighty men (1 Chron. 11:43).

MITHREDATH 1. A Persian treasurer (Ezra 1:8).

2. A Persian officer involved in the attempt to stop the building of the walls of Jerusalem in the days of Nehemiah (Ezra 4:7, 12).

MITYLENE A seaport on the island of Lesbos, southeast of Asia Minor where Paul stopped on his third missionary journey (Acts 20:14).

MIZAR Mount Mizar would seem to be a part of the Hermon range, unidentified (Ps. 42:6).

MIZPAH 1. As a common noun *mizpeh* (Hebrew, *mitspeh*; English, *mizpah*) refers to a lookout point or a watchtower (2 Chron. 20:24; Isa. 21:8). The word is associated with at least five other place names to indicate local sites, high spots.

2. Mizpah of Benjamin (170-143) is a city of Benjamin on the border between the kingdoms of Israel and Judah, not far north of Jerusalem. It has not only been located with Tell en-Nasbeh as in the grid reference above, but also with a modern place called Nebi Samwil (Josh. 18:26). It was involved in the wars between Judah and Israel (1 Kgs. 15:22, and the account which precedes it). In the time of the prophet Samuel, it was the center of worship for all the Israelites (1 Sam. 7:5-16; 10:17ff.).

3. Mizpah of Gilead, an unidentified site east of the Jordan north of the Jabbok River where Laban and Jacob covenanted (Gen. 31:49). Under Judge Jephthah the Israelites encamped there before fighting the Ammonites (Judg. 10:17; 11:11, 29, 34).

4. Mizpah of Judah, an unidentified site in the western foothills of the tribe of Judah (Josh. 15:38).

5. Mizpah of Moab, an unidentified site in Moab where David left his parents during part of the time of his military troubles (1 Sam. 22:3).

6. The region of Mizpah or the Valley of Mizpeh, an area into which Joshua pursued the defeated enemy after the battle of the Waters of Merom (Josh. 11:3, 8).

7. Ramath Mizpah (223-169), a site in the tribal area of Gad, by some equated with 3 above (Josh. 13:26).

MIZPAR *See* MISPAR

MIZZAH An Edomite descendant of Esau (Gen. 36:13, 17).

MNASON A Cypriot resident of Jerusalem, a Christian who hosted Paul after his third missionary journey (Acts 21:16).

MOAB, PLAIN OF, DESERT OF *See* GEOGRAPHY OF THE HOLY LAND

MOADIAH *See* MAADIAH

MOLADAH A town (142-074) in the southern part of the tribal area of Judah. Since Simeon's area overlapped with that of Judah, it is also listed in the tribal area of Simeon (Josh. 15:26; 19:2; Neh. 11:26).

MOLECH *See* DEITIES

MOLID A descendant of Judah (1 Chron. 2:29).

MOLOCH *See* DEITIES

MONEY Coined money was not introduced into Palestine until the reign of Darius I, under the Persian empire. Prior to that time, payments in silver and gold (or bronze) were made in the form of bullion ingots weighed out in the scales, and calculated as gerahs (1/20 shekel), bekahs (1/2 shekel), shekels (c. 4/10 oz.), or even as manehs (a maneh varied from 50 or 60 to 100 shekels). Even the unit referred to as *kesitah* in the footnotes of Genesis 33:19, Joshua 24:32, and Job 42:11 was an uncoined measure of weight, possibly amounting to 1430 grams (judging from Arabic *qistun*). It may have borne a merchant's stamp on it, but it was not a government-guaranteed coin, stamped with an official device.

The first regularly minted money was coined in the Kingdom of Lydia in Asia Minor around 700 B.C. and consisted of gold staters (sometimes of electrum, a mixture of three parts of gold to one of silver) and (later on), silver sigloi. These bore the forepart of a lion facing the forepart of a bull; the reverse of the coin was simply a crude punch of no particular shape (as was true of the imperial Persian currency right down to the fourth century B.C.). The earliest pure silver

coinage was minted on the Greek island of Aegina south
of Attica; it bore a sea-tortoise on its obverse, and dated
from about 650 B.C. Persian gold darics (with a kneeling
figure of the robed king as an archer) and silver sigloi, more
or less identical in size and shape, appeared in large numbers
by the time of Darius I (521-485 B.C.). The *'adarkōn* of
1 Chronicles 29:7 probably refers to the gold daric (at least
as a unit of weight), and the silver drachma (a Greek
denomination) in Ezra 2:69. Silver tetradrachmas (i.e., four-
drachma pieces) from Athens, with the head of Athena on
the obverse and on owl on the reverse, have been discovered
in excavations of the fifth century level in Palestine. After
the Alexandrian conquest in 334, Macedonian and Greek
currency replaced the Persian in the entire Near and Middle
East. The silver coinage of Alexander bore the handsome
head of Heracles in lion's-mane headdress and the enthroned
Zeus on the reverse. The gold staters (weighing two gold
drachmas) had the head of Athena in Corinthian helmet, with
the goddess Nike on the reverse. After Alexander's death,
Palestine came under the rule of the Ptolemaic Dynasty
in Egypt, until the Seleucid emperor, Antiochus III, wrested
it away from them ca. 200 B.C. Thus the Seleucid and
Ptolemaic issues dominated Judean finance until the Maccabean
revolt in 168 B.C. But even under the Hasmonean Jewish
dynasty the native mintage seems to have been confined to
bronze lepta, beginning with John Hyrcanus I (135-105);
the silver shekels and subdivisions of shekel formerly attributed
to the Hasmoneans have been shown by more recent
archeology to have been from the First Revolt (A.D. 68-70).
Thus the Jews must have used Hellenistic silver issues,
despite their pagan devices. Of particular importance was the
Tyrian tetradrachma (or shekel) bearing the head of Heracles
Baal Melqart, and a strutting eagle on the reverse, probably
the predominating type of silver piece in the payment which
Judas Iscariot received as the price of betraying Christ.
With the rise of Herod the Great, the Hasmonean lepta were
replaced by Herodian, while the silver was provided by the
Hellenistic drachmas, didrachmas, and tetradrachmas (all
of which are mentioned in the NT) and by Roman denarii.
This latter coin, about the size and value of a drachma,
almost invariably bore "the image and superscription of
Caesar" (i.e., the reigning emperor, whether Augustus,
Tiberius, Claudius, or Nero) on its obverse (Mt. 22:20, 21).
The bronze coins mentioned in the NT include: the *assarion*
(translated "penny" in the NIV) or Roman *as* (Mt. 10:29;
Lk. 12:6), worth $\frac{1}{16}$ of a denarius; the *kodrantēs* or Roman
quadrans (also translated "penny" in the NIV) (Mt. 5:26; Mk.
12:42), worth $\frac{1}{4}$ *as*; and the *lepton*, or smallest bronze of all

(translated) "copper coins" in the NIV) (Mk. 12:42; Lk. 12:59). These last were usually the old Hasmonean issue, or the Herodian bronzes, or else the mintages of the various Roman procurators, such as Pontius Pilate (who issued two types: either with an augur's wand or a simpulum ladle as obverse device). If the widow whom Christ observed (Mk. 12:42) was using the most recently minted "mites," these would have been the issue she cast into the offering box. But more likely she would have used the old Hasmonean lepta, free of pagan devices. See also table of weights and measures in the NIV. (G.L.A.)

MONSTER OF THE DEEP *See* BEASTS, 9

MONTHS, NAMES OF *See* CALENDAR

MOON, NEW MOON, FEAST OF The luminary for the night, given with the sun "to mark seasons, and days, and years" (Gen. 1:14). The new moon, marking the start of a new month, was like the Sabbath in that special prayers and rituals were performed as prescribed by the law (Num. 28:11-15; 29:6; 10:10; 2 Kgs. 4:23; Ps. 81:3). It is well known that the worship of the moon was a common practice of the extrabiblical world of antiquity and may even have intruded into false worship in Israel, but there is no evidence of it as an extensive practice. *See also* CALENDAR and FESTIVALS.

MORDECAI 1. Esther's cousin who had reared her. He saved the life of King Xerxes and later thwarted the plan of Haman to exterminate the Jews of Persia (Esth. 2:7, 21ff.; 4:7ff.).

2. One who returned from the Babylonian captivity with Zerubbabel (Ezra 2:2).

MOREH 1. An unidentified hill near which the Midianites were encamped against the Israelites before Gideon defeated them. Probably somewhere near the Valley of Jezreel (Judg. 7:1).

2. An unidentified place near Shechem where Abraham camped and where he erected an altar to God (Gen. 12:6, 7; see also Deut. 11:30).

MORESHETH, MORESHETH GATH A city (141-115) in the tribal area of Judah from which the prophet Micah came (Jer. 26:18; Mic. 1:1, 14).

MORIAH, MOUNT *See* GEOGRAPHY OF THE HOLY LAND

MOSERAH, MOSEROTH An unidentified stop of the children of Israel in their wanderings during their exodus from Egypt (Deut. 10:6; Num. 33:30, 31).

MOSES The Levite son of Amram and Jochebed, rescued at his birth by the daughter of the pharaoh and reared in that court (Ex. 6:20; 2:1-10). As an adult he killed an Egyptian and fled to Midian where he met and married Zipporah the daughter of Jethro (Ex. 2:11-22). After the death of the pharaoh, forty years after Moses' flight, he returned and led the Israelites out of Egypt to the borders of the promised land of Canaan. His history of miracle working and leadership is interwoven with all the laws given by God through him for the life of the people after their entry into the land of Canaan (Exodus 20 through Deuteronomy; note especially Leviticus 18:4, 5). Before his death on Mt. Nebo at the age of 120 (Deut. 34:7) he had led his people in the conquest of the area east of the Jordan and in the settlement of some of the tribes there (Num. 21:21ff.; Deut. 2:26ff.; 3:1ff.). It is the name of Moses that has always been associated with the Law of Israel, the foundation of life and practice for Israel and the Jews to this day, and the foundation of the faith of the Church as well.

MOUNT ZION *See* JERUSALEM and GEOGRAPHY OF THE HOLY LAND

MOZA 1. A descendant of Benjamin and King Saul (1 Chron. 8:36, 37).
2. A descendant of Judah and Caleb (1 Chron. 2:46).

MOZAH An unidentified site (165-134) in the tribal area of Benjamin (Josh. 18:26).

MUPPIM A son of Benjamin (Gen. 46:21). He was also called Shephuphan and Shupham (1 Chron. 8:5; Num. 26:39) and his clans either Shuphites or Shuphamites (1 Chron. 7:12; cf. 7:7; Num. 26:39).

MURDERER *See* MANSLAYER

MUSHI, MUSHITES The first is a descendant of Levi and the second the family he founded (Ex. 6:19; Num. 3:33).

MUSIC, MUSICAL INSTRUMENTS 1. Music has one pre-Flood reference, to harp and flute, where we note that Jubal was the father of all those who play these instruments (Gen. 4:21). Nothing further is added in the Scriptures about this music in this very ancient time. In post-Flood times, music was associated with social merrymaking, with summons to battle, in battle, and with worship (Gen. 31:27; Judg. 7:20-22; 1 Sam. 13:3, 4; Josh. 6:4ff.; 1 Chron. 25:1). There is no record that music as an organized art with choirs and orchestras was in use in Israel prior to the time of the great musician, King David. David was a brilliant poet, musical instrumentalist, and organizer of musicians (2 Chron. 7:6; 1 Chron. 15:27, 28; 16:5, 6; 6:31; 16:37, 42). There are many references to psalms, songs, hymns, chants, and music (Ps. 47:7; Eph. 5:19; Ex. 15:1; Ezek. 32:16; 1 Sam. 18:6). There are many references to dances and dancing in connection with the praise of God with music, song and choirs (Ps. 150:4; Judg. 11:34). An interesting item is the "lament of the bow" (2 Sam. 1:17, NIV). It appears that men were trained in the use of shooting the bow to a cadence of the rhythm of poems. *See also* PSALMS, TITLES OF and SELAH.

2. Musical instruments may be summarized under the three headings percussion, wind instruments, and stringed instruments. (1) Percussion instruments did not have variable pitch and so were used as noisemakers and for rhythm indicators. For the most part, they were held in the hand and struck by the hand. Those mentioned include the *tambourine* used like the modern triangle or drum (Ps. 81;2; 149:3; Isa. 30:32; 2 Sam. 6:5; Gen. 31:27). The *cymbal* was in form and use much like its modern counterpart by the same name (1 Chron. 16:42; 25:1; Ps. 150). The *sistrum* is only mentioned in 2 Samuel 6:5, purely a noisemaker like a rattle or castanet; the *gong* mentioned in connection with the cymbal (1 Cor. 13:1) and *bells* mentioned only in connection with the robes of the priests and the harness of horses, apparently for the purpose of calling attention to their passing (Ex. 28:33; Zech. 14:20). Several of these instruments were not used in worship but were used by the women, for the most part to add din to the jubilation.

(2) The most frequently mentioned wind instrument is the *shofar, horn,* or *trumpet.* It was usually the horn of a ram but later included that of other animals as well. It could even be of metal. It is most frequently rendered by trumpet or rams' horns (2 Sam. 6:15; Lev. 25:9; Josh. 6:4, 8, 13). Its most common uses were in connection with battle and with special religious events and festivals (Judg. 3:27, 28; Ps. 81:3). In the NT the word is used in connection with the trumpet to be sounded by God at the end of time (1 Thess. 4:16; 1 Cor. 15:52; Rev. 8:7ff.). It was not an orchestral instrument. *Flutes* were apparently shrill in sound and often coarse. If they were used in orchestras for worship in the temple, it was apparently not a common use. They were used in joyous or ecstatic times (1 Sam. 10:5; Job. 21:12; 1 Cor. 14:7).

(3) There were several stringed instruments in the general family of the harp: the *harp* itself, the *lyre,* and the *lute.*

These were the instruments especially used in religious worship and orchestration. David was a specialist (1 Chron. 13:8; 15:16, 20, 28; Ps. 33:2; 71:22; 150:3). The major difference between these three would seem to be in the number of strings and in the shape of the part that held the strings. The *zither* is mentioned in Daniel 3:7.

MYRA A southern port of Lycia in Asia Minor where Paul stopped on his voyage to Rome as a prisoner (Acts 27:2-5).

MYRRH *See* PLANTS, PERFUMES, AND SPICES

MYRTLE *See* PLANTS, PERFUMES, AND SPICES

MYSIA A district in the northwest part of Asia Minor visited by Paul on his second missionary journey (Acts 16:7, 8).

MYSTERY The transliteration of a Greek word, *mysterion*, used frequently by Paul and otherwise found four times in Revelation (1:20; 10:7; 17:5, 7). In the Gospels it is translated by the word "secret" (Mt. 13:11; Lk. 8:10; Mk. 4:11). In Paul's writings, however, it had a very special meaning. As the word *mysterion* came into the Bible by way of Greek paganism, we must find its meaning both from that source and from its NT contexts. It is a secret passed on only to the initiated and unknown until it is revealed. In its specialized adaptation in Pauline theology it is a synonym for the gospel message, "by my gospel and the proclamation of Jesus Christ, according to the revelation of the mystery hidden for long ages past, but now revealed and made known through the prophetic writings by the command of the eternal God, so that all nations might believe and obey him" (Rom. 16:25, 26; 1 Tim. 3:16). It is the gospel message in all its ramifications: the working of sin from which deliverance must come (2 Thess. 2:7); Christ himself who is the deliverer (Col. 2:2, 3; 4:3; 1:26-28); that the Gentiles are now also heirs of God (Eph. 3:3-6, 7-12) and that this is to be made known through the Church even though it was in the eternal purpose of God from the beginning; and, eventually to unite all things in Christ (Eph. 1:9, 10). As with the Greek concept of *mysterion*, which required initiation into the group in order that the mystery could be understood, so it is with the gospel. It requires the "new birth" of the individual in order to understand the salvation which is in Christ (Jn. 3:3, 7, 16, 17).

NAAM A son of Caleb of the tribe of Judah (1 Chron. 4:15).

NAAMAH 1. The sister of Tubal-Cain (Gen. 4:22).

2. The mother of Judah's King Rehoboam, a wife of Solomon, an Ammonite (1 Kgs. 14:21, 31).

NAAMAN, NAAMITES 1, 2, and 3. A son, a grandson and a great-grandson of Benjamin (Gen. 46:21; Num. 26:40; 1 Chron. 8:7; see footnote at 8:3 on Abihud and compare with v. 7). They were called Naamites.

4. The Syrian officer cured of leprosy by the prophet Elisha after dipping seven times in the Jordan (2 Kgs. 5:1-27).

NAAMATHITE One of Job's friends, Zohar, was from this unidentified area of Naamah in NW Arabia and therefore a Naamathite (Job 2:11; 42:9).

NAARAH 1. One of the wives of Ashur, a descendant of Judah.

2. A city (190-144) near Jericho in the tribal area of Ephraim (Josh. 16:7). Perhaps also the Naaron of 1 Chron. 7:28 on the border of Benjamin and Ephraim.

NAARAI One of David's mighty men also called Paarai (1 Chron. 11:37; 2 Sam. 23:35).

NAARAN *See* NAARAH

NABAL The wealthy herder who refused David's request for help. When he realized the implications of what he had done he took sick and died. David married his widow (1 Sam. 25:2-42).

NABOTH The owner of the vineyard in Jezreel that King Ahab coveted and which Queen Jezebel procured for him by having Naboth murdered (1 Kgs. 21). *See* JEZEBEL.

NACON Owner of the threshing floor where Uzzah died for touching the Ark and where the Ark remained some time before David again tried to bring it to Jerusalem (2 Sam. 6:6ff.; 1 Chron. 13:9); also called Kidon.

NADAB 1. A son of Aaron and a priest but killed for offering strange fire before the Lord (Ex. 6:23; 28:1; Lev. 10:1, 2).

2. *See* KINGS OF JUDAH AND ISRAEL, a king of Israel.

3. A Jerahmeelite (1 Chron. 2:28).

4. A descendant of Benjamin (1 Chron. 8:30).

NAGGAI An ancestor of Joseph, the father, so it was thought, of Jesus (Lk. 3:25).

NAHALAL An unidentified site in the tribal area of Zebulun also called Nahalol (Josh. 19:15; 21:35; Judg. 1:30).

NAHALIEL An unidentified site or valley (?) where the Israelites stopped east of Jordan at the end of their exodus wanderings (Num. 21:19).

NAHALOL *See* NAHALAL

NAHAM The brother-in-law of one Hodiah and thus brought into the line of Judah (1 Chron. 4:19).

NAHAMANI One who returned from the Babylonian captivity with Zerubbabel (Neh. 7:7).

NAHARAI One of David's thirty mighty men (2 Sam. 23:37).

NAHASH 1. A king of the Ammonites from whom Saul took Jabesh Gilead and who became a supporter of David (1 Sam. 11:1ff.; 2 Sam. 10:1, 2).

2. The father of Abigail, husband of Jether (2 Sam. 17:25).

NAHATH A descendant of Esau (Gen. 36:13; 1 Chron. 1:37).

NAHBI The representative from Naphtali among the twelve spies sent out by Moses (Num. 13:14).

NAHOR 1 and 2. A grandfather and a brother of Abraham (Gen. 11:22-27).

NAHSHON A descendant of Judah who was assigned to assist Moses; a brother-in-law of Aaron, and an ancestor of David and Joseph, the father, so it was thought, of Jesus (Num. 1:7; Ex. 6:23; Ruth 4:20; Lk. 3:32).

NAHUM 1. One of the minor prophets who came from Elkosh (Nah. 1:1).

2. An ancestor of Joseph, the father, so it was thought, of Jesus (Lk. 3:25).

NAHUM, BOOK OF *See* PROPHETS, MINOR

NAIL, NAILING The translation of several Hebrew and Greek words (rendered nails, pegs, tent pegs). These were first made of stone chips, wood or bone and later of metal. The finger-nail and the tent-peg are included (Deut. 21:12; Dan. 4:33; Judg. 4:21, 22; Zech. 10:4). The nail of the general kind known today was also driven by a hammer at that time (Jer. 10:4; 1 Chron. 22:3). The one NT reference is to the nails used to fasten Jesus to the cross (Jn. 20:25). The word "nailing" is used once also by Paul where he talks of God's nailing to the cross the legal demands against man (Col. 2:14).

NAIN A village in Galilee near Mount Tabor where Jesus raised a widow's son from the dead (Lk. 7:11-17).

NAIOTH An unidentified place near Jerusalem where David stayed with Samuel on one of his flights from the jealousy of King Saul (1 Sam. 19:18—20:1).

NAKEDNESS This may mean without any clothing at all, or merely poorly clothed (Gen. 2:25; Jas. 2:15; Jn. 21:7).

NAOMI The wife of Elimelech and mother-in-law of Ruth who helped her to find Boaz that he might perform the role of the next of kin in the case of the deceased relative and husband (Ruth 1:2, 4; 2:20-22; 4:13).

NAPATH *See* DOR

NAPHISH A son of Ishmael and grandson of Abraham (Gen. 25:15).

NAPHTALI The son of Jacob and one of his concubines who gave his name to one of the twelve tribes of Israel. The tribal area was just west of the Sea of Galilee (Gen. 30:7-8; Josh. 20:7).

NAPHTUHITES A people of Egypt descended from Ham. Much conjecture exists as to their location and relationships (Gen. 10:13; 1 Chron. 1:11).

NARCISSUS Greetings were sent by Paul from Rome to those in his household (Rom. 16:11).

NARD *See* PLANTS, PERFUMES, AND SPICES

NATHAN 1. A son of David, one in the genealogy of Joseph, the father, so it was thought, of Jesus (2 Sam. 5:14; Lk. 3:31).

2. A prophet in David's time who prevented him from building the temple, who rebuked him for his murder of the Hittite and his adultery with Bathsheba, and supported Solomon for the throne. He wrote a record of the times of both David and Solomon (2 Sam. 7:4, 8-13; 12:1-14; 1 Kgs. 1:38; 1 Chron. 29:29; 2 Chron. 9:29).

3. The father of Igal, one of David's Thirty (2 Sam. 23:36).

4. One sent by Ezra to Casiphia to bring back some Levites after the end of the Babylonian captivity (Ezra 8:16-17).

5. One who married a foreign wife during the Babylonian captivity (Ezra 10:39).

6. A Jerahmeelite (1 Chron. 2:36).

NATHANAEL *See* APOSTLES

NATHAN-MELECH An official who had a room near the entrance to the house of the Lord (2 Kgs. 23:11).

NATION This is one English translation for the Hebrew *goy* and the Greek *ethnos*, both meaning nation. While Israel is also called a *goy*, one among the many nations, this word usually refers to non-Israelite nations. Another but rare translation in NIV is "pagans" (1 Cor. 12:2).

NAZARETH, NAZARENE A town in lower Galilee in the tribal area of Zebulun. It is never mentioned in the OT but because of its association with Mary and Jesus it is many times noted in the NT. A Nazarene, one from that town, was a term often applied to Jesus by himself and by others (Mt. 2:23; 21:11; Acts 22:8; 2:22; Mk. 14:67). The followers are once referred to as the sect of the Nazarene (Acts 24:5).

NAZIRITE These were people in Israel who renounced grapes and all its products, including wine; who renounced the use of the razor, and who could never come in touch with a dead body. The laws relative to them are found in Num. 6:1-23. (*See also* Judg. 13:5). John the Baptist was probably a Nazirite from birth (Lk. 1:15). Nazirite vows generally were permanent; they could also be temporal to fulfill some special need of the one taking upon himself or herself the vow (Acts 21:23-27).

NEAH An unidentified site in the tribal area of Zebulun (Josh. 19:13).

NEAPOLIS The seaport of Philippi in ancient Macedonia which was visited by Paul on his second missionary journey (Acts 16:11).

NEARIAH 1. A descendant of Judah and David in the royal line (1 Chron. 3:22-23).

2. A descendant of Simeon (1 Chron. 4:42).

NEBAI One who signed the covenant with Nehemiah (Neh. 10:19).

NEBAIOTH A son of Ishmael and grandson of Abraham (Gen. 25:13).

NEBALLAT A town (146-154) in the tribal area of Benjamin mentioned with Lod and Ono (Neh. 11:34).

NEBAT The father of Jeroboam the first king of the northern kingdom, Israel (1 Kgs. 11:26).

NEBO, MOUNT *See also* DEITIES and GEOGRAPHY OF THE HOLY LAND

NEBUCHAD-NEZZAR, NEBUCHAD-REZZAR A king of Babylon, often mentioned in the Bible, who lived in the beginning of the sixth century B.C. The latter form of the name is found in NIV only in the footnotes to Nebuchadnezzar in Jeremiah and Ezekiel. He was the son and successor of the founder of the neo-Babylonian empire and the victor over the Egyptians at Carchemish on the Euphrates (2 Chron. 35:20; Jer. 46:2). This important victory put the entire area, including Palestine, under his control (2 Kgs. 24:1). Several kings of Judah, Jehoiakim, Jehoiachin, Zedekiah and governor Gedalish were his tools and puppets. *See* BABYLON, and KINGS OF JUDAH AND ISRAEL.

NEBUSHAZBAN An officer of King Nebuchadnezzar of Babylon in the siege of Jerusalem (Jer. 39:11-14).

NEBUZARADAN A commanding officer of Nebuchadnezzar at the destruction of the temple and the city of Jerusalem who was ordered to take care of Jeremiah (2 Kgs. 25:8-10; Jer. 39:11).

NECKLACE A chain worn around the neck for ornaments or rings (Song 4:9).

NECO The Pharaoh of Egypt who assisted the Assyrians in their last days, removed Jehoahaz from Judah's throne and placed Jehoiakim upon it, killed King Josiah in battle, and then marched to Carchemish to fight the Babylonians where he was defeated by Nebuchadnezzar (2 Kgs. 23:29-35; 2 Chron. 35:20—36:4; Jer. 46:2).

NECROMANCER *See* DIVINATION

NEDABIAH A descendant of King Jehoiachin (1 Chron. 3:18).

NEEDLE, EYE OF The phrase is found only in one statement by Jesus in Matthew 19:24 and its parallels in Mark and Luke. He was teaching how impossible it is for one bound up in his riches to enter the Kingdom of God. There seems to be no support for the idea of the eye of a needle being a small gate within a larger one.

NEGEV *See* GEOGRAPHY OF THE HOLY LAND

NEHELAM, NEHELAMITE An unidentified place from which the false prophet who opposed Jeremiah came (Jer. 29:24-32).

NEHEMIAH 1. One who returned from the Babylonian captivity with Zerubbabel (Ezra 2:2).

2. One who helped in the repair of the walls of Jerusalem in the days of another Nehemiah (Neh. 3:16).

3. The cupbearer to the Persian King Artaxerxes (Neh. 1:11) who returned to Jerusalem with the blessing of the king in order to hasten the finishing of the rebuilding of the city and wall. He returned to Babylon but soon came back to Jerusalem to deal with irregularities there. Details are scattered throughout the book that bears his name.

NEHEMIAH, BOOK OF The book that records the rebuilding of Jerusalem and the reforms instituted by Nehemiah in the worship of God in the restored temple. It covers the final history of Israel to be recorded in the OT from about 445-420 B.C. In chapters 1 and 2 there is recorded his return to Jerusalem followed (3:1—7:4) by an account of the rebuilding under great difficulties caused by some who did not wish to see the city rebuilt. Genealogies of those who returned from the captivity in Babylon are recorded (7:5-73). The spiritual revival and signing of a covenant are found in three chapters (8-10). Prior to the dedication of the completed walls and final reforms some additional genealogies are recorded (11-13).

NEHUM One who returned from the Babylonian captivity with Zerubbabel (Neh. 7:7).

NEHUSHTA The wife of Judah's King Jehoiachin (2 Kgs. 24:8).

NEHUSHTAN *See* SERPENT OF BRONZE

NEIEL A town (171-255) on the border between Asher and Zebulun (Josh. 19:27).

NEKODA 1. Ancestor of some temple servants who returned from the Babylonian captivity with Zerubbabel (Ezra 2:48).

2. Ancestor of some who returned with Zerubbabel but could not prove their Israelite ancestry (Ezra 2:60).

NEMUEL 1. A son of Simeon also called Jemuel (Num. 26:12; Gen. 46:10).

2. A descendant of Reuben (Num. 26:9).

NEPHEG 1. A descendant of Levi (Ex. 6:21).

2. A son of David (2 Sam. 5:15).

NEPHILIM Although translated "giants" in the KJV the meaning of the word is not clear and hence the Hebrew word is simply transliterated in the NIV. They were not angelic fallen beings. They are called also "sons of Anak" a reference which is of little value in determining who or what they were (Gen. 6:4; Num. 13:33).

NEPHTOAH, WATERS OF A spring (168-133) on the border between Judah and Benjamin (Josh. 15:9; 18:15). The Egyptian word for water was *mer*. Thus this site in Egyptian was *mer nephtah*, the name of one of their kings.

NEPHUSSIM Ancestors of some temple servants who returned from the Babylonian captivity with Zerubbabel (Ezra 2:50; Neh. 7:52).

NER The father of Abner, the commander of Saul's army (1 Sam. 14:50, 51).

NEREUS A Christian in Rome to whom Paul sent greetings (Rom. 16:15).

NERGAL *See* DEITIES

NERGAL-SHAREZER The officer of Nebuchadnezzar who released the prophet Jeremiah from prison (Jer. 39:3, 13, 14).

NERI An ancestor of Joseph, the father, so it was thought, of Jesus (Lk. 3:27).

NERIAH Father of Baruch the scribe of Jeremiah (Jer. 32:12).

NET String or cord woven into mesh and used for the catching of birds, fish, or animals. In the NT the word is used only in the literal sense. In the OT it is used figuratively of chastisement of a people or a person, or of snares that might entrap them (Job. 19:6; Ps. 10:9).

NETAIM An unidentified site in the tribal area of Judah where some potters lived (1 Chron. 4:23).

NETHANEL 1. The representative of the tribe of Issachar chosen to assist Moses (Num. 1:8; 7:18, 23).

2. A brother of King David (1 Chron. 2:14).

3. A priest in the time of David whose duty was to blow the trumpet before the Ark (1 Chron. 15:24).

4 and 5. A Levite and a gatekeeper in David's day (1 Chron. 24:6; 26:4).

6. One sent by King Jehoshaphat to the towns to teach his people (2 Chron. 17:7).

7. A Levite in the days of King Josiah of Judah (2 Chron. 35:9).

8. A priest who married a foreign wife during the time of the Babylonian captivity (Ezra 10:22).

9. The head of a priestly family in the days of Joiakim and Nehemiah (Neh. 12:21).

10. A priest who was with Nehemiah at the dedication of the rebuilt walls of Jerusalem (Neh. 12:36).

NETHANIAH 1. The father of one by the name of Ishmael in the last days of Judah. Ishmael assassinated Gedaliah (2 Kgs. 25:23, 25).

2. A son of Asaph the seer in David's days (1 Chron. 25:2, 12).

3. One of the Levites sent out by Jehoshaphat to teach (2 Chron. 17:8).

4. The father of one sent to remonstrate with Baruch, Jeremiah's scribe (Jer. 36:14).

NETOPHAH, NETOPHATHITE Netophah was a town (171-119) in the hill country of Judah near Bethlehem (2 Sam. 23:28-29; Ezra 2:22; 1 Chron. 9:16).

NETTLE *See* PLANTS, PERFUMES, AND SPICES

NEW MOON, *See* CALENDAR and FESTIVALS
FEAST OF

NEWS, GOOD Besides its use to refer to news in general the words are used together with others, such as "good news about Jesus," "good news of the kingdom of God," "the good news is preached to the people." In these and similar cases it is the gospel news about the person and work of Christ relative to salvation that is the point of reference (Acts 8:35; Lk. 4:43; Mt. 11:5).

NEZIAH Ancestor of some temple servants who returned from the Babylonian captivity with Zerubbabel (Ezra 2:54).

NEZIB A village (151-110) in the western foothills of the tribal area of Judah (Josh. 15:43).

NIBHAZ *See* DEITIES

NIBSHAN A town (186-123) in the desert of the tribal area of Judah (Josh. 15:62).

NICANOR One of the first seven chosen to assist the Twelve in the temporal affairs of the church called deacons in the KJV (Acts 6:5).

NICODEMUS A member of the Council who came to enquire of Jesus by night with the result that Jesus gave him the most famous reference to the new birth (Jn. 3:16). The entire account appears in John 3. He also spoke for Jesus to the leaders of his day and later brought spices for the burial of Jesus and assisted Joseph of Arimathea in the entombment (Jn. 7:45-50; 19:39).

NICOLAITANS *See* SECTS

NICOLAS One of the groups of seven chosen to assist in the temporal affairs of the church, called deacons in the KJV (Acts 6:5).

NICOPOLIS A city on the west coast of Greece where Paul determined to winter on one occasion (Tit. 3:12).

NIGER A prophet or teacher in the church at Antioch. He is referred to as "Simeon called Niger" (Acts 13:1).

NIGHTHAWK *See* BIRDS

NILE The main river of Egypt, starting on the equator it flows 2,500 miles to the Mediterranean. The Hebrew text uses the word for a stream with the definite article preceding it.

The stream in Egypt is, of course, the Nile. Hence, the NIV renders "the stream" in Hebrew by "Nile" in English (Gen. 41:1; Ex. 4:9; Isa. 19:5, 6). No reference to it is found in the NT.

NIMRAH An unidentified site in Gilead assigned to the tribal area of Gad (Num. 32:3).

NIMRIM, WATERS OF An unidentified source of water in Moab which prophets say is "desolate" (Isa. 15:6; Jer. 48:34).

NIMROD A grandson of Ham and described as a mighty hunter and founder of an area called the land of Nimrod (1 Chron. 1:10; Gen. 10:9; Mic. 5:6). (See footnote at 1 Chron. 1:10.)

NIMSHI Father or perhaps grandfather of King Jehu of Israel (1 Kgs. 19:16; 2 Kgs. 9:2, 14, 20).

NINEVEH A city founded by Nimrod, the great-grandson of Noah. It was important throughout all the history of the Middle East until the fall of the Assyrian empire to Babylon in 612 B.C. It is located on the Tigris opposite modern Mosul. *See also* ASSYRIA and NIMROD.

NISAN *See* CALENDAR

NISROCH *See* DEITIES

NOADIAH 1. A Levite treasurer in the temple (Ezra 8:33).

2. A prophetess opposed to Nehemiah (Neh. 6:14).

NOAH 1. A daughter of the Zelophehad who had no sons (Num. 26:33).

2. The maker of the ark that saved people and animals in the great Flood and the father of Shem, Ham, and Japheth. The rainbow was given to him by God as a sign (Gen. 6; 9:8, 13-17).

NOB A town (173-134) in the tribal area of Benjamin. The incident with Doeg the Edomite against the priests because they had helped David took place here (1 Sam. 21:1; 22:9-19; Isa. 10:32).

NOBAH 1. A descendant of Manasseh who conquered the town of Kenath (302-241) and named it after himself (Num. 32:42).

2. An unidentified site near which Judge Gideon defeated the Midianites (Judg. 8:11).

NOD An unidentified district east of Eden to which Cain went (Gen. 4:16).

NODAB An unidentified site east of Judah against which Israel made war (1 Chron. 5:19).

NOGAH A son of David (1 Chron. 3:7; 14:6).

NOHAH A son of Benjamin (1 Chron. 8:2).

NOSE, NOSTRILS, NOSE RING The nose is the normal organ of breathing but as the nostrils quiver when one is angry, one word serves in Hebrew both for the organ itself and for the emotion "anger" (Gen. 27:45; Ex. 4:14; 11:8). For the Hebrew word "nose" the translators used "organ" and "face" as well as "nose" (Gen. 19:1). Psalm 10:4 in Hebrew reads literally "the height of his nose." It is translated "in his pride." The phrase "slow to anger" is an interesting case in point (Ex. 34:6; Neh. 9:17), literally, slow of nostrils. Rings for adornment were sometimes placed in the nose as also was the ring or hook of captivity (Gen. 24:47; Isa. 37:29).

NUMBERED (CENSUS) *See* CENSUS

NUMBERS, BOOK OF *See* PENTATEUCH

NUMBERS, SIGNIFICANCE OF From early times the Hebrews used the decimal system in counting as is clear from the emphasis on the tens and hundreds. The numbers were first spelled out as words, then the letters of the alphabet in sequence stood for the numbers, *aleph* for one, *beth* for two, *gimel* for three, et cetera. There was also a system of strokes but of its origin and development not too much is yet known. This came in some time after the return from Babylon. Numbers were also used symbolically throughout the ancient world and in the Bible as well. Considerable caution must be exercised in interpreting numbers symbolically since much subjectivity is involved. Each number stands for many things, and thus there is not, nor can be, complete agreement as to just exactly what a given number symbolized. For an example, the number three may be taken by some to be the symbol of the Trinity. Obviously it does not mean that in the interpretation of Jews. To some, three means emphasis, or even completeness (but so does seven). There were to be three festivals per year, daily prayers were to be three times in the day, there was a three-year taboo on the fruit of a tree for its first three years, ritual baths were to be on the third as well as the seventh day

(Ex. 23:14; Dan. 6:10; Lev. 19:23; Num. 19:11, 12). Some numbers seem to have been used, in some cases at least, as round numbers. Such is forty for a generation and seventy for the number of sons a famous man is supposed to have. Nor is it always possible to be certain that a small number does not merely represent "a few" and not an exact number. This would be an idiomatic and not a symbolic use (Jer. 36:23; Isa. 17:6). A further idiomatic use would be the fairly numerous use in poetry of the three-four or four-five motif (Prov. 30:15, 18, 29; 6:16). Of even the number seven, by all considered to be the most symbolic, one may only state that its symbolic uses are so many and varied that it is virtually impossible to summarize them briefly. Among the more common would be completeness, finality or consummation, and perfection. Seven days make a full week and seven years a cycle. Caution is thus advised.

NUN The father of Joshua (Ex. 33:11).

NURSE The word has three usages in the Bible, none corresponding to the concept of nurse in modern medical terms. One is the maid; another the wet-nurse who supplied milk for a baby when the mother for any reason was not able; third is the man or woman who cared for the small children in a family (Gen. 24:59; Ex. 2:7; 2 Kgs. 11:2; 2 Sam. 4:4). The word nurse is also used in a figurative sense (Isa. 49:23; Num. 11:12).

NUTS *See* PLANTS, PERFUMES, AND SPICES

NYMPHA The Christian lady of Colosse in whose home the early church of Colosse met (Col. 4:15).

435 ■

OAK *See* TREES

OATH This was an appeal to God to be a witness of the truth of some statement or of the binding character of some promise or agreement (Gen. 21:24; 42:51-53; 2 Chron. 15:12-14). In addition to swearing by God "as surely as the Lord lives" swearing was done by the name of the other person, by one's own head, by the life of the king, by the temple, by Jerusalem, but never by a strange god (1 Sam. 14:39; 1:26; Mt. 23:16; 1 Sam. 17:55; Josh. 23:7). Jesus forbade swearing by heaven, by earth, or by Jerusalem, and gives his reasons (Mt. 5:34-36). This indicates that others used those terms in oaths.

OBADIAH 1. A descendant of Gad who defeated David's forces (1 Chron. 12:9).

2. The father of the representative of the tribe of Zebulun in David's administration (1 Chron. 27:19).

3. The steward of King Ahab who feared God and hid his prophets from Jezebel who determined their death (1 Kgs. 18:3ff.).

4. One of the men whom King Jehoshaphat sent to teach his people (2 Chron. 17:7).

5. A Levite overseer in the days of the reforms of King Josiah of Judah (2 Chron. 34:12).

6. A descendant of David who lived after the return from the Babylonian captivity (1 Chron. 3:21).

7. A descendant of Issachar (1 Chron. 7:3).

8. A descendant of King Saul (1 Chron. 8:38).

9. A Levite of postexilic times also called Abda (1 Chron. 9:16; Neh. 11:17).

10. The head of a family who returned from the Babylonian captivity with Ezra (Ezra 8:9).

11. One who signed the covenant with Nehemiah (Neh. 10:5).

12. A gatekeeper in the days of Joiakim and Nehemiah (Neh. 12:25).

13. One of the minor prophets known only by his book, one chapter in length. *See* PROPHETS, MINOR.

OBADIAH, BOOK OF *See* PROPHETS, MINOR

OBAL *See* EBAL, 2

OBED 1. An ancestor of Joseph, the father, so it was thought, of Jesus, and the son of Boaz and Ruth (Lk. 3:32; Ruth 4:17-21).

2. A descendant of Judah and Jerahmeel (1 Chron. 2:37).

3. One of David's mighty men (1 Chron. 11:47).

4. A gatekeeper of the tabernacle in David's day (1 Chron. 26:7).

5. Father of one who helped Jehoiada put the youthful Joash on the throne (2 Chron. 23:1).

OBED-EDOM 1. The name of the man in whose house David left the Ark after the death of Uzzah who died because he touched it (2 Sam. 6:10, 11).

2. A gatekeeper before the Ark in David's time (1 Chron. 15:18; 16:38).

3. A keeper of the temple gold, silver and vessels in the days of King Amaziah (2 Chron. 25:24).

OBEDIENCE, OBEY In both Testaments the words for obey carry also the idea of hearing. The two concepts are inseparable. The Hebrew *shama'* means both to hearken to and to obey, as does also the Greek word *hupakouo*. The biblical concept is, then, of a hearing that takes place under the need to comply with what is heard. The child hears and obeys his parents, the pupil his teachers, the employee his employer, all mankind hears God and is expected to obey (Col. 3:20, 22; Ex. 19:5, in both cases the Greek and Hebrew is the usual word for "to hear"). Obedience to God's laws and statutes was the expected way of living for the Israelite (Lev. 18:4, 5). Disobedience would bring severe punishment even *diaspora* (Deut. 28:58, 59, 64). Obedience is the supreme test of faith in God, or as the NT puts it "faith without works is dead" (1 Sam. 15:22-24; Jas. 2:14-26). Thus obedience and faith are always very closely linked in the Bible. The most illuminating illustration to be found is in the treatment of the incidents in the life of Abraham in the NT (Rom. 4:1-3; Jas. 2:21-26).

Another Hebrew word is also translated in the NIV as "obey." Its basic meaning is "to guard." Thus the language of the OT has the two: obey equals "hear" and obey equals "guard" (Ps. 119:8, 17, 34; Ex. 34:11).

OBEY *See* OBEDIENCE

OBIL An Ishmaelite who was in charge of the camels of David (1 Chron. 27:30).

OBLATION *See* SACRIFICES AND OFFERINGS

OBOTH An unidentified stopping place on the Israelites' journey to Moab during their desert wanderings (Num. 21:10, 11; 33:43, 44).

OBSERVE *See* OBEDIENCE

OCRAN The father of the man from the tribe of Asher who assisted Moses in the taking of the census (Num. 1:13).

ODED 1. The father of the prophet who spoke for God to King Asa (2 Chron. 15:1ff.).

2. A prophet who opposed the attempts of King Pekah of Israel to enslave men and women from the tribe of Judah (2 Chron. 28:9ff.).

ODOR *See* AROMA

OFFERING *See* SACRIFICES AND OFFERINGS

OG The king of Bashan who was defeated by the Israelites under Moses and his territory given to the tribe of Manasseh. He was a man of gigantic proportions needing an oversized bed (Num. 21:33ff.; Josh. 13:29, 30; Deut. 3:11).

OHAD A son of Simeon (Gen. 46:10).

OHEL A son of Zerubbabel in the royal line after the exile (1 Chron. 3:20).

OHOLAH In the parable concerning Judah and Israel in Ezekiel 23 she is called a prostitute. Her sister, symbolizing the Kingdom of Judah, is called Oholibah. With the first he predicts the Assyrian captivity and with the second the Babylonian.

OHOLIAB An assistant of Bezalel the craftsman who assisted in the detail work of the tent of meeting (the tabernacle), the Ark of the testimony and the other furnishings (Ex. 31:6; 35:34).

OHOLIBAH *See* OHOLAH

OHOLIBAMAH 1. A wife of Esau (Gen. 36:2).
2. A chief of Edom descended from Esau (Gen. 36:41).

OIL In the Bible almost without exception the oil of the olive which was used for food, cooking, a medicament, and illumination, in addition to its use in ceremonial anointing (Ex. 29:2; 25:6; 29:7; Lk. 10:34).

OINTMENT *See* PLANTS, PERFUMES, AND SPICES

OLIVE *See* TREES

OLIVES, MOUNT OF, OLIVET *See* GEOGRAPHY OF THE HOLY LAND

OLYMPAS A Roman Christian to whom Paul sent greetings (Rom. 16:15).

OMAR An Edomite, a grandson of Esau (Gen. 36:11, 15).

OMEGA *See* GOD, NAMES OF, GODHEAD

OMEN *See* DIVINATION

OMER *See* WEIGHTS AND MEASURES

OMRI 1. *See* KINGS OF JUDAH AND ISRAEL
2 and 3. Descendants of Judah and Benjamin (1 Chron. 7:8; 9:4).
4. David's officer over the tribe of Issachar (1 Chron. 27:18).

ON 1. A descendant of Reuben (Num. 16:1).
2. *See also* HELIOPOLIS.

ONAM 1. A grandson of Seir, a Horite, and descendant of Esau (Gen. 36:23).

2. A descendant of Judah, a Jerahmeelite (1 Chron. 2:26, 28).

ONAN A son of Judah who refused to do his duty as a brother-in-law for which God put him to death (Gen. 38:4, 10). *See* MARRIAGE.

ONESIMUS The slave of Philemon who ran away from his master. He became a Christian, and Paul sent him back to his master with the request that he be freed (Philem. 1:8ff.).

ONESIPHORUS One whose household was commended by Paul because its head had often been kind to Paul during his imprisonment in Rome (2 Tim. 4:19; 1:16-18).

ONION *See* PLANTS, PERFUMES, AND SPICES

ONO A town (137-159) in the coastal plain in the tribal area of Benjamin (1 Chron. 8:12). After the return from the Babylonian captivity many settled there (Ezra 2:33; Neh. 6:2; 7:37; 11:35).

ONYCHA *See* PLANTS, PERFUMES, AND SPICES

ONYX *See* PRECIOUS STONES AND METALS

OPHEL *See* JERUSALEM

OPHIR 1. A descendant of Shem (Gen. 10:29).

2. The unidentified land occupied by the descendants of Ophir, 1. It was an area where there was much gold. It required sailing to get there (1 Kgs. 9:28; 10:11; 2 Chron. 9:10). Much was brought to Israel by Solomon and Hiram of Tyre.

OPHNI An unidentified site in the tribal area of Benjamin (Josh. 18:24).

OPHRAH 1. A descendant of Judah annd Othniel (1 Chron. 4:14).

2. A town (178-151) in the tribal area of Benjamin, modern Taiyibeh (Josh. 18:23).

3. A town (177-223) in the tribal area of Manasseh that belonged to the Abiezrites where the angel of the Lord commissioned Gideon as Judge of Israel (Judg. 6:11, 15, 24; 8:27, 32).

ORACLE The word is used of the introductory formula to a message usually given by God directly to a prophet but may also be of human origin (Isa. 15:1; 17:1; 19:1; 21:1, 11; Num. 24:22-24; Prov. 30:1; 31:1). The word itself is not used in the NIV but "words of God" replace it. The reference is to God's revelation, the Bible itself.

ORCHESTRA *See* MUSIC, MUSICAL INSTRUMENTS

ORDAIN In the OT the English translation of a number of Greek and Hebrew words which carry the ideas of instituting; how to do something in the prescribed manner; establishing; and setting apart for a special duty or office with or without a ceremony (1 Kgs. 12:33; 1 Chron. 15:13; Ex. 29:9, 29, 33-35). In the NT hands were laid on officers of the church for certain work even though there is no instruction that it be done or perpetuated (1 Tim. 4:14; 2 Tim. 1:6). The practice was extended in post-NT times.

OREB A leader of Midian captured and killed in Gideon's victory over Midian (Judg. 7:25; 8:3).

OREN A Jerahmeelite descendant of Judah (1 Chron. 2:25).

ORION A heavenly constellation mentioned in connection with others, namely the Bear and Pleiades (Job. 9:9; 38:31, 32; Amos 5:8).

ORNAMENTS Objects of adornment whether on man or beast (Judg. 8:26; Prov. 25:12; Gen. 24:53; Isa. 3:16-23; Jer. 2:32). These were also worn by men (Ex. 33:4-6).

ORPAH The daughter-in-law of Naomi who did not go with Naomi and Ruth when they returned from Moab to Naomi's country, Israel (Ruth 1:3, 4, 14).

ORPHAN The fatherless. The Bible expresses great concern for them and often enjoins God's people to care for them (Ex. 22:22; Mal. 3:5; Jas. 1:27; Ps. 10:14).

OSPREY *See* BIRDS, 5

OSTRICH *See* BIRDS, 6

OTHNI A Levitical gatekeeper in the days of David (1 Chron. 26:7).

OTHNIEL *See* JUDGES OF ISRAEL

OVEN The oven for baking in antiquity did not differ greatly from the oven used in modern times by the Bedouin or other primitive peoples of the Middle East. Many are noted in modern excavations. They were, and are, cylindrical structures of clay two or three feet in diameter and two or three feet high. They are usually built on the floor and often inside the house. A quick hot fire was built inside the oven and then the ashes were removed and the moist flat cakes of dough were stuck on the hot insides of the oven. When dry the dough would fall from the wall and the "bread" would be removed from the oven. Ovens were also made with stone. Grass, thorns, shrubs, and even dung or a mixture were used as fuel (Lev. 2:4). In the NT translated as "the fire" in the NIV (Mk. 6:30).

OVERSEER A word used for an office in the NT church. Overseers were frequently referred to as bishops (1 Tim. 3:1, 2; Tit. 1:7; Phil. 1:1; Acts 20:28). The hierarchical distinction we know today did not begin until after the first century A.D. In 1 Peter 2:25 Jesus is called "Overseer."

OWL *See* BIRDS, 5 and Isaiah 34:15

OX *See* BEASTS, 4

OZEM 1. A brother of David (1 Chron. 2:15).

2. A Jerahmeelite and descendant of Caleb (1 Chron. 2:25).

OZNI A descendant of Gad, also called Ezbon (Num. 26:16; Gen. 46:16).

PAÁRAI *See* NAARAI

PADAN, *See* ARAM
PADAN-ARAM

PADON Ancestor of some temple servants who came back from the Babylonian captivity with Zerubbabel (Ezra 2:44).

PAGAN *See* NATION

PAGIEL The representative of the tribe of Asher both when the census was taken in the days of the desert wanderings and later (Num. 1:13; 2:27; 7:72, 77).

PAHATH-MOAB 1. The ancestor of some who returned from the Babylonian captivity with Zerubbabel (Ezra 2:6; 8:4; 10:30).

2. Father of one who worked on the rebuilding of the wall of Jerusalem in the days of Nehemiah (Neh. 3:11).

3. One who signed the covenant with Nehemiah (Neh. 10:14).

PAI *See* PAU

PAINT, PAINTING Paint was used both for persons and things. In the former case it might be eye-paint or other cosmetics and in the latter it was liquid color applied to walls, buildings, pottery, carvings, and, in the nonbiblical world, idols. Colors used were blue, green, red, yellow, black, white, and those produced by mixing certain of these. The words themselves are used only a few times in the Bible and half are in connection with the eyes. The hands, feet, nails, and hair were often stained with henna and produced the characteristic orange-red color. The color, but not its use, is noted twice in the Bible (Song 1:14; 4:13). For eye-paint the special colors were the green copper ore malachite and the dark gray ore of lead galena which were made into a paste and then drawn around the eye to produce an oblong shape, added to the eyebrow to extend it and sometimes placed under the eye as well (Jer. 4:30; 2 Kgs. 9:30; Ezek. 23:40). The son of King Josiah painted his palace with red produced from hematite or iron ore, a color mentioned again only in connection with the idolatrous drawings of the Assyrians (Jer. 22:14; Ezek. 23:14). Much of the painted pottery being found by the archaeologists was also decorated with red hematite which when baked took on more of a reddish-brown color.

PALACE The residence of a king or a high dignitary such as the high priest (Mt. 26:3). The first to be noted in the Bible is in the time of David and Solomon (1 Kgs. 4:6; 1 Chron. 28:2). The palace of Ahab follows (1 Kgs. 22:39; 2 Kgs. 10:5; 2 Sam. 5:11). Palaces (sometimes fortresses) of the kings of Babylon, Egypt, Ben-Hadad of Syria (called "fortresses" in the NIV; Jer. 49:27), the multiple palaces of Jerusalem and that of Pilate the Roman procurator are mentioned (Dan. 4:29; Jer. 43:9; Esth. 2:8; Jer. 17:27; Mk. 15:16). The house of Solomon ("fortress") contained both stone locally cut and much wood supplied by his friend Hiram king of Tyre (2 Chron. 2:1-3, 8-9). Ahab's, on the other hand, was called a house of ivory and contained much decorative ivory and white marble. Perhaps even entire walls were faced with ivory (1 Kgs. 22:39). While the archaeologists have discovered the locations of many palaces, for the most part they have only the floor plans. It should be remembered that the ravages of time or wrecking by the ancient conquerors have left nothing but these except for a few notable exceptions, the palace of Nebuchadnezzar of Babylon being one. Some of the literary sources, however, such as those of Josephus, supply valuable descriptions.

PALAL One who worked on the repair of the walls of Jerusalem in the days of Nehemiah (Neh. 3:25).

PALESTINE *See* PHILISTIA

PALLU A son of Reuben (Gen. 46:9; Num. 26:5).

PALM TREE *See* TREES

PALSY *See* SICK, SICKNESS

PALTI The representative of the tribe of Benjamin among the twelve spies sent into Canaan by Moses (Num. 13:9).

PALTIEL 1. The representative of the tribe of Issachar in the dividing of the land among the tribes (Num. 34:26).

2. The man to whom Saul gave his daughter Michal, David's wife, after he had taken her away from David, also called Palti (1 Sam. 25:44 and footnote, 2 Sam. 3:15).

PAMPHYLIA *See* GEOGRAPHY OF THE HOLY LAND

PAPER *See* PAPYRUS

PAPHOS A city on the island of Cyprus visited by Paul on his first missionary journey where the blinding of the false prophet at the word of Paul led to the conversion of the Roman proconsul Sergius Paulus (Acts 13:6-14).

PAPYRUS A reedlike plant growing to heights of over ten feet in aquatic areas, particularly in ancient Egypt, but to some extent in Palestine also. The ancients wove it into mats, used it thus for tents, made baskets and even boats from it. Paper (our word comes from "papyrus") was made by drying together thin strips of the inner pith to a material of the consistency of modern heavy wrapping paper. It soon becomes brittle and decays easily in damp climates and for these reasons many of the early manuscripts did not preserve at all or at best only in a fragmentary condition (Job 8:11; Isa. 18:2; 2 Jn. 12).

PARABLE Used infrequently in the OT (Ps. 78:2; Prov. 26:7, 9; Ezek. 17:2; 24:3; Hos. 12:10). It is a brief narrative intended to illustrate a single idea. The parable is different from the fable or myth, from the allegory and from the proverb in that it does not mix the natural and the symbolic. It is a story with a point. But for the few cases noted all the other occurrences are those used by Jesus in his teaching ministry. He stated that it was an effective method for revealing truth to the spiritually illuminated while keeping it hid from others (Mt. 13:10-16). A list of the better known parables would include: those of the sower and the seed; the workers in the vineyard; the ten virgins; the talents; the good Samaritan; the prodigal son; and the Pharisee and the tax collector; (Mt. 13:1-23; 20:1-16; 25:1-13; 25:14-30; Lk. 10:30-37; 15:11-32; 18:9-14).

PARADISE *See* DEAD, ABODE OF

PARAH An unidentified site in the tribal area of Benjamin (Josh. 18:23).

PARAN, MOUNT PARAN, DESERT OF PARAN SW of Elath (Egion Gebod). Paran is a site in the Sinai. *See* DESERT and GEOGRAPHY OF THE HOLY LAND.

PARAPET A protective wall, elevation, or barrier required in the law to be constructed at the edge of a roof (Deut. 22:8).

PARCHED, PARCHED GRAIN In general the word indicates something dried up (Jer. 17:6; 48:18; Hos. 13:15). With respect to grain it means roasted. In the KJV it is called parched "corn," an archaic word referring to a grain. In the NIV what is called "parched corn" in the KJV is called "roasted grain" in some references and "roasted corn" in others (Lev. 23:14; Ruth 2:14). Corn as known today was unknown in antiquity. What is translated "corn" was some kind of grain. It was parched by roasting in a pan or even by holding some stalks near the coals of a fire. A food staple used as one of the most common items of the diet of all the people (Lev. 2:14; 23:14; Josh. 5:11).

PARCHMENT One of the ancient writing materials, made from the skins of animals and thus more durable than papyrus. It is different from leather in that it is not tanned. The form called vellum is a better quality, made from the skins of calves or kids (2 Tim. 4:13). *See also* PAPYRUS.

PARENTS *See* MARRIAGE

PARMASHTA One of the ten sons of Haman all of whom lost their lives in the abortive attempt to destroy the Jews of Susa in the days of Esther (Esth. 9:9).

PARMENAS One of the seven chosen by the early Christians to minister to the temporal needs of the church, called deacons in the KJV (Acts 6:5).

PARNACH The father of the representative of the tribe of Zebulun in the dividing of the land among the tribes (Num. 34:25).

PAROSH 1. Ancestor of some who returned from the Babylonian captivity with Zerubbabel and Ezra (Ezra 2:3; 8:3; 10:25).

2. The father or ancestor of one who worked on the repair of the walls of Jerusalem in the days of Nehemiah, perhaps the same as 1 above (Neh. 3:25).

3. One who signed the covenant with Nehemiah (Neh. 10:14).

PARSHANDATHA One of the sons of Haman (Esth. 9:7). *See* PARMASHTA.

PARSIN *See* MENE, MENE, TEKEL, AND PARSIN

PARTHIANS Noted in the Bible only in Acts 2:9 where Jews from this area were in Jerusalem in the time of the first Christian Pentecost. Parthia was a small country NW of the old Persia, within the area of modern Iran.

PARTRIDGE *See* BIRDS, 4

PARTY *See* HERESY

PARUAH The father of one of King Solomon's chief food gathering officers, from the tribe of Issachar (1 Kgs. 4:17).

PARVAIM An unidentified place from which Solomon received a certain type of gold (2 Chron. 3:6).

PASACH A descendant of Asher (1 Chron. 7:33).

PASCHAL Refers to Passover celebration. *See* CALENDAR and FESTIVALS.

PAS DAMMIM *See* EPHES DAMMIM

PASEAH 1. A descendant of Judah (1 Chron. 4:12).

2. The ancestor of some who returned with Zerubbabel from the Babylonian captivity (Ezra 2:49).

3. The father of Joiada in the days of Nehemiah (Neh. 3:6).

PASHHUR, 1. A priest who beat and then put the prophet Jeremiah in
PASHUR stocks (Jer. 20:1-6).

2. The father of Gedaliah the governor of Jerusalem after the last king had been deported (Jer. 38:1).

3. One who urged Judah's last king to imprison Jeremiah and execute him for making the people afraid (Jer. 38:1-4).

4. The ancestor of some priests who returned from the Babylonian captivity with Zerubbabel (Ezra 2:38; 10:22).

5. One who signed the covenant with Nehemiah (Neh. 10:3).

PASSOVER *See* CALENDAR and FESTIVALS

PASTORAL *See* PAULINE EPISTLES
EPISTLES

PASTORS The pastor is the religious shepherd or leader of a people. The word is used in the NIV only in Ephesians 4:11 but found frequently in the Hebrew and Greek texts, and usually translated here as "shepherd." Christ is the "good Shepherd" (Jn. 10:11-14; Heb. 13:20; 1 Pet. 2:25; 5:4; Mk. 6:34). Quite naturally the word is used of those who herd sheep (Lk. 2:8). Israel's leaders were called shepherds of Israel (Jer. 3:15; 17:16; 23:1-2; Ezek. 34:1-16).

PASTURE LANDS OF SHARON *See* GEOGRAPHY OF THE HOLY LAND

PATARA An important port of Lycia located in SW Asia Minor where Paul stopped on his final journey to Jerusalem (Acts 21:1).

PATHROS The name of a land in Upper Egypt, southern Egypt, mentioned in the Bible only in the prophets in some most interesting references. God is to destroy it and then return the Egyptians to it after forty years (Ezek. 30;14; 29:14). Many Jews were there after the fall of Jerusalem to the Babylonians (Jer. 44:1, 15; Isa. 11:11), and it is one of the places from which God is to return the Jews to Palestine in one of the eschatalogical descriptions.

PATHRUSIM The people from the area of Pathros in Upper Egypt (Gen. 10:14).

PATIENCE The translation of two Greek words, one of which signifies endurance under affliction or trials, rendered sometimes by "steadfastness" in the RSV, and the other "long-suffering" (Jas. 5:10; 1:3-4; Rom. 12:12; Eph. 4:2; 2 Tim. 4:2). It is listed as one of the ingredients in the "fruit of the Spirit" (Gal. 5:22). It is used only six times in the RSV (Prov. 14:17; 25:15; Ps. 37:7; 40:1; Job 6:11; Eccles. 7:8) but it is related to the Hebrew word "long" and is found in combination with other words, the combination of which indicates the concept of patience (Prov. 14:29; 19:11), slow to anger, for an example.

PATMOS A small island of some twenty-five square miles with a rocky coastline, one of those used by the Romans for the banishment of prisoners. It was located in the Aegean Sea S and W of Asia Minor. John found himself imprisoned here because of his religious testimony (Rev. 1:9).

PATRIARCH While this English word is found in the RSV only six times, the idea behind it is common, "father, fathers of old, forefathers" and refers to the founders of the Hebrew people and their religion, specifically to Abraham, Jacob, and his twelve sons, and to David (Heb. 7:4; Acts 7:8, 9; 2:29).

PATROBAS A Christian at Rome to whom Paul sent greetings (Rom. 16:14).

PAU, PAI The unidentified capital city of King Hadar of Edom, called by both names (Gen. 36:39; 1 Chron. 1:50).

PAUL, LIFE AND TEACHINGS OF "A Hebrew born of Hebrews," Saul, who is also called Paul, was raised from earliest youth in the strict traditions of Pharisaism, first in his home at Tarsus, and then at Jerusalem under the instruction of Gamaliel I (Phil. 3:5; 2 Cor. 11:22; Acts 22:3). As one zealous for the law and eager to keep Israel united in its commitment in days of approaching Messianic blessing, Saul early directed his efforts against Jewish believers in Jesus of Nazareth; for, as he saw it, their leader had been discredited by crucifixion and their schismatic preaching could only further delay Israel's promised Messianic age. Thus we first read of Saul as officiating at the martyrdom of Stephen, imprisoning Christians in Jerusalem, and taking the initiative in returning believers who had fled for safety to areas outside of Palestine (Acts 7:58—8:3; 9:1-2; Phil. 3:6; 1 Cor. 15:9). But, though undoubtedly earnest and motivated by a desire to do God's will as he understood it, he was actually, as he later came to realize, opposing God "ignorantly in unbelief" (1 Tim. 1:13).

While traveling to Damascus to extradite Christians, Saul was confronted by the risen and glorified Christ who asked: "Saul, Saul, why do you persecute me?" (Acts 9:22, 26). It was then that the young rabbi came to see that Jesus was and is Israel's long awaited Messiah whose person and work have been vindicated by God. And in commitment to this risen Lord, Saul found (1) the ancient tension of his people, that of divine promise and awaited fulfillment, brought to consummation; (2) true righteousness and intimate fellowship with God; and (3) the understanding that redemption in Jesus has universal significance, being intended for Gentiles as well as Jews. It was this encounter on the road to Damascus that transformed Saul's thought and life; though, of course, the implications of this meeting and of his commitment were later more fully explicated via the ministry of Ananias in Damascus, a three-year period of meditation in Arabia, and certain situations providentially controlled during his succeeding ministry.

The preaching of the converted young Pharisee began almost immediately in Damascus, where he proclaimed Jesus, whom he had persecuted, as indeed "the Christ (Messiah)" and "the Son of God" Acts 9:19-22, KJV). Then after three years in Arabia, he took up the ministry among Hellenistic Jews in Jerusalem that had lain dormant since Stephen's death; but he faced the same opposition which once he himself had led, and was forced to leave for Caesarea and from there to Tarsus (Acts 9:26-30; Gal. 1:18-24). Probably he continued to witness in Tarsus, his hometown, where he resided for an additional ten years; though we hear nothing of his work during these years from either Luke in Acts or Paul in his letters, unless the recollection of his many afflictions in 2 Corinthians 11:23-27 included experiences from this time. It was Barnabas who sought him out in Tarsus and involved him in the ministry at Antioch of Syria, where he ministered for at least a year preaching Christ to many and taking a leading part in the collection for famine-stricken believers in Jerusalem (Acts 11:25-30).

While at Antioch, the Holy Spirit called Paul, together with Barnabas, to minister more widely in the Roman empire; and the Book of Acts records three journeys undertaken in carrying out this mandate. The first was with Barnabas, accompanied by John Mark, to cities of Cyprus and southern Asia Minor (Acts 13-14). On this journey God led Paul to testify directly to Gentiles, apart from any necessary relation to the synagogue or to Judaism. It is at this point in the record where he begins to be called by his Roman name, Paul, rather than his Jewish name, Saul (Acts 13:9). Here was a new and somewhat revolutionary aspect in the Christian mission, about which many Jewish Christians were uncertain. But matters were clarified at the Jerusalem Council, where the Jerusalem apostles concluded that, while they could hardly join in a direct ministry to Gentiles themselves, they could not stand in opposition to God's evident working through Paul in such an enterprise (Acts 15). The second and third missionary journeys were with Silas, a prominent Jerusalemite Christian, with Timothy from Lystra serving as their principal aide. After revisiting believers in Asia Minor, Paul pushed on by divine direction to evangelize Macedonia and Achaia (Greece) on the second journey (Acts 15:36—18:22). And on the third, together with strengthening churches in areas traversed before, the apostle centered his activities at Ephesus (Acts 18:23—20:38). Following his recorded ministry in the eastern part of the empire, the apostle went to Jerusalem with representatives from the major centers of Gentile Christianity to present a gift of money to the impoverished believers there. While in Jerusalem, he was accused of attacking the Jewish religion and disturbing the peace of Rome; and as a result, was confined to prison at Caesarea for two years. On appeal to Caesar, he was transferred to Rome and there imprisoned for another two years (Acts 21-28). From references and allusions in the Prison and Pastoral Epistles, it may be inferred that Paul was released from this first Roman imprisonment and carried on a further ministry in lands surrounding the Aegean Sea. Clement of Rome, writing in A.D. 95, speaks of the apostle preaching as far west as Spain and tells of his martyrdom at Rome (1 Clem. 5:6), probably in A.D. 67 under Emperor Nero and sometime during the later sixties or early seventies of his life.

The message of Paul is briefly stated in such passages as Romans 3:21-31, Galatians 4:4-5, 2 Corinthians 5:17-21, Philippians 2:6-11, and Colossians 1:15-23; and may be summarized in five points: (1) The law and the prophets were meant to witness to the righteousness of God and to prepare men for the coming of the Messiah, not to be an end in and of themselves. (2) Jesus of Nazareth is God's Messiah, come at the appropriate time in history, who in his person and work has made redemption available for all men. (3) Man needs to respond to Jesus by faith, apart from any thought of human merit, in order to experience forgiveness and reconciliation with God. (4) This message of gratuitous salvation must be preached to Gentile and Jew alike, and on the same basis, for there is ultimately no distinction before God. (5) On the basis of new life "in Christ," the Christian is called upon to live a new life in this world, a life that reflects Christ's attitudes, imitates Christ's actions, and proclaims Christ's redemptive message. For Paul, in fact, both religion and life are encompassed and controlled by the relationship of being "in Christ." (R.N.L.)

PAULINE EPISTLES, THE The letters of Paul can appropriately be grouped according to the missionary journeys or imprisonments of the apostle. Probably the earliest is the Letter to the Galatians, written about A.D. 49, just prior to the Jerusalem Council of Acts 15, to converts of southern Galatia won to Christ during Paul's first missionary journey and from Antioch in Syria (or on the way from Antioch to Jerusalem); though others, stressing the affinities between Galatians and Romans, view it as composed during the third missionary journey, from Ephesus or the region of Macedonia, sometime between A.D. 53 and 57, and addressed to converts of northern Galatia won on the second journey. The Judaizers who followed Paul into Asia Minor taught fidelity to the Mosaic Law as a precondition to full acceptance by God, and argued against the legitimacy of a direct approach to Gentiles in the Christian mission. Evidently they also depreciated Paul's apostolic qualifications and represented themselves as bringing a truer form of the gospel. Paul's response to such a threat was this emotionally laden letter, alternately stern and tender, in defense of the liberty of the Christian. Galatians has been aptly called "the charter

of Christian liberty," and throughout the whole epistle the
note of grace reverberates. The letter may be outlined
as follows: (1) Salutation and occasion for writing, 1:1-9;
(2) Paul's apostolic authority and the authenticity of his
message, 1:10—2:20; (3) Exposition on liberty in Christ,
3:1—4:31; (4) Exhortations to liberty in Christ, 5:1—6:10;
and (5) Postscript on sacrificial living, 6:11-18.

Written from Corinth on the second missionary journey,
probably about A.D. 50-51, are the two letters addressed to
the Thessalonians. The church at Thessalonica had been
founded by Paul on his second journey (Acts 17). Arriving in
Athens, the apostle sent Timothy back to Thessalonica
(1 Thess. 3:1-3). Timothy later returned to Paul, reporting
on conditions at Thessalonica. First Thessalonians is in
response to that report. In it are interwoven (1) commendation
for growth, zeal, and fidelity; (2) encouragement in face of
local persecution; (3) defense of the apostle's motives against
pagan attack; (4) teaching regarding holiness of life;
(5) instruction regarding the coming of the Lord; and
(6) exhortation to steadfastness and patience. Evidently the
Thessalonian believers misunderstood this first letter, for the
apostle had to write 2 Thessalonians a few months later to
correct their false notions regarding the return of Christ and
the ethical disorders resulting therefrom. While the Christian
lives in eager expectation of his Lord's return, Paul had to
insist that imminency must not be construed to mean
immediacy; rather, it is the basis for steadfastness and dogged
persistence. Few today doubt the Pauline authorship of
1 Thessalonians. The authenticity of 2 Thessalonians, however,
has been suspicioned in many quarters, chiefly because the
eschatological section of 2:1-12 is either too crassly Jewish or
too different from 1 Thessalonians to be by Paul. But with
the realization that though early Christians found fulfillment in
Jesus they still shared with Judaism expectations regarding
the future, much of the objection to the Jewish character
of Paul's eschatology disappears; and though the two letters
differ in tone and temper, this is largely a reflection of the
situation addressed.

On his third missionary journey, Paul wrote 1 and
2 Corinthians and Romans. First Corinthians was composed
during the apostle's extended ministry at Ephesus
(1 Corinthians 16:8, 19), probably about A.D. 55 or 56, in
response to disquieting reports brought to his attention
concerning the church at Corinth. Paul had written the
Corinthians earlier (5:9, 10), but that letter was misinterpreted.
In the meantime, some in the church wrote him seeking his
guidance on certain matters. In his reply, Paul included:
(1) Salutation, 1:1-9; (2) Disorders reported by the family of
Chloe (divisions and strife), 1:10—4:21; (3) Disorders widely

rumored (immorality, pride, lawsuits), 5:1—6:20; (4) Matters concerning which the church wrote (marriage, food offered to idols, decorum of women in worship, observance of the Lord's Supper, spiritual gifts), 7:1—14:40; (5) The resurrection, 15:1-58; and (6) The collection and conclusion, 16:1-24. On all these matters Paul wrote in strong pastoral tones; and while he instructed as to specific situations, he also gave principles which can be applied to similar circumstances today. In A.D. 95, Clement of Rome wrote in a similar vein to the church at Corinth, citing Paul's admonitions in 1 Corinthians in support. That attestation is the earliest for any of Paul's letters, and, coupled with internal evidence, has silenced any doubts regarding the authenticity of the first epistle. Written from Macedonia (Philippi?), probably between A.D. 55 and 57, 2 Corinthians is the apostle's earnest response to the triumphs and continuing difficulties in the Corinthian church. Its content may be outlined as follows: (1) Salutation and thanksgiving, 1:1-11; (2) Paul's answer to his critics, 1:12—7:16; (3) The collection for the poor of Jerusalem, 8:1—9:15; (4) Paul's vindication of his apostolic authority, 10:1—13:10; and (5) Conclusion, 13:11-14. Stylistically, the letter is noted for its breaks and changes of tone. Two self-contained units have often been identified: (1) Chapters 1-9, ending with a brief doxology and expressing a conciliatory tone, and (2) Chapters 10-13, ending with another doxology and speaking in tones of severity and warning. Many also consider 6:14—7:1 a unit detached from its context, suggestion that perhaps it is part of the "lost" letter of 1 Corinthians 5:9. Various answers have been proposed to explain these divisions and arrangements, but in none of them is Pauline authorship denied. *See also* ROMANS, THE LETTER TO THE.

The letters to the Colossians, Philemon, the Ephesians, and the Philippians were written during Paul's two-year imprisonment in Rome, probably during A.D. 61-63. In Colossians the apostle was countering a syncretistic and dualistic type of religious philosophy which taught that since the world of matter is defiled and intrinsically opposed to God, man must seek true knowledge and union with deity in some higher sphere of the nonmaterial. On such a view, the incarnation of our Lord and his work on the cross are either rejected or considered an inferior first step toward reconciliation with God.

Paul, in his answer, did not minimize the humanity and sacrifice of Christ; rather, he gloried in the incarnation and the cross, for by them God effected man's redemption (Col. 1:20-22). To the specific objections of the heresy confronted, however, the apostle proclaimed the cosmic Christ in whom all fullness dwells and in whom the believer finds complete fulfillment (1:15ff.; 2:9ff.).

The Letter to Philemon was addressed to one of Paul's converts living in Colosse, whose slave Onesimus had robbed his master and fled to Rome. Brought to Christ by Paul, Onesimus had proven helpful to the apostle while in prison. Now Paul wrote on his behalf, urging Philemon to receive him back as a "beloved brother in the Lord." From the references to Tychicus and Onesimus in Colossians 4:7-9, and the greetings of Colossians 4:10-17 and Philemon 23-24, it can be deduced that the two letters were written and sent at the same time, probably about A.D. 61 or 62.

Ephesians reflects no specific local situation and its tone, together with the omission of "to the Ephesians" in the leading ancient manuscripts, has led many to view it as something of a circular letter sent widely to churches in Asia Minor. Prominent doctrines include the Church as the Body of Christ, the foundational nature of the apostles and prophets, predestination, the believer's relation "in Christ," and the demolishing of the distinction between Jew and Gentile. It also was delivered by Tychicus (Eph. 6:21), very likely written shortly after Colossians.

In Philippians Paul wrote to thank believers for their financial aid (Phil. 4:10-19) and to commend Epaphroditus, their messenger to him in prison, against any possible criticism that he had not completed his task (2:25-30). He also took the occasion to explain regarding his present circumstances, to exhort to steadfastness, unity, and humility, and to warn regarding the Judaizers. In that Paul alluded to an approaching trial (1:20ff.) and expressed his hope to visit Philippi shortly (2:24), the letter may be taken to have been written toward the end of his first Roman imprisonment, about A.D. 63.

Assuming a release at his first trial, a further ministry in lands surrounding the Aegean, and a second trial at which capital punishment was imposed, Paul wrote 1 Timothy and Titus during the period of release in A.D. 64-66 and 2 Timothy just prior to his death in A.D. 67. In his first letter to Timothy, the apostle sought to encourage his young colleague in his pastoral responsibilities at Ephesus. He exhorted Timothy to deal decisively with certain false teachers and gave instruction regarding the qualifications for leaders and the treatment of various members in the church. In his letter to Titus, the minister of the church at Crete, Paul again admonished as to pastoral duties, dealing with (1) qualifications for leaders in the church, (2) the need to oppose false doctrine, (3) treatment of various classes of members in the church, and (4) proper attitudes for believers in a pagan society.

Second Timothy is chronologically later than the other Pastoral Epistles, and breathes a different atmosphere. Whereas in 1 Timothy and Titus the apostle was free to make plans and move about at will, in 2 Timothy he was a prisoner and the end was rapidly approaching. Apparently written from Rome while awaiting execution, Paul was anxious for Timothy to come to him before winter. But more than this, he was concerned that Timothy be exemplary in his life and faithful to the ministry to which he had been called. This final letter of the great apostle is rich and varied. Interwoven are touching appeals, ringing charges, and the note of triumph in face of imminent decapitation. It is, in fact, the great apostle's last will and testament; which, after many years of service for Christ, he closed with repeated shouts of victory (2 Tim. 4:6-8, 16-18). (R.N.L.)

PAULUS *See* SERGIUS PAULUS

PAVEMENT *See* GABBATHA

PEACE Used in the Bible as in modern times, both as a greeting and to indicate calm as between men, or as between men and God, or of a man within himself (2 Kgs. 9:17-31; Mk. 4:39; Lk. 10:5; Josh. 9:15; Job 22:21; Isa. 57:21; Num. 6:26). Paul indicated that our peace with God is made through Jesus Christ (Rom. 5:1; Col. 1:19-20). Peace in the world is predicted for eschatological days (Isa. 9:6-7; 11:6-9; Mic. 4:1-4).

PEACE OFFERING *See* SACRIFICES AND OFFERINGS

PEACOCK *See* BIRDS, 7

PEARL *See* PRECIOUS STONES AND METALS

PEDAHEL The representative of the tribe of Naphtali in the division of the land among the tribes of Israel (Num. 34:28).

PEDAHZUR The father of Gamaliel who represented the tribe of Manasseh in the census taking of Moses (Num. 1:10).

PEDAIAH 1. The father of King Jehoiakim's mother (2 Kgs. 23:36).

2. A son of King Jehoiachin and either the father or nephew of the Zerubbabel who brought back some of the captives from the Babylonian captivity (1 Chron. 3:18, 19).

3. The father of one of David's officers (1 Chron. 27:20).

4. One who helped to repair the walls of Jerusalem in the days of Nehemiah (Neh. 3:25).

5. One who stood with Ezra as he read the law to the people (Neh. 8:4).

6. A descendant of Benjamin (Neh. 11:7).

7. A Levite appointed as treasurer by Nehemiah (Neh. 13:13).

PEKAH *See* KINGS OF JUDAH AND ISRAEL

PEKAHIAH *See* KINGS OF JUDAH AND ISRAEL

PEKOD A small Aramean tribe living on the Lower Tigris River in the days of Jeremiah and Ezekiel (Jer. 50:21; Ezek. 23:23).

PELAIAH 1. A descendant of King Solomon (1 Chron. 3:24).

2. One who helped to explain the law after Ezra read it to the people (Neh. 8:7).

3. One who signed the covenant with Nehemiah (Neh. 10:10).

PELALIAH A priest who served in the days of Nehemiah (Neh. 11:12).

PELATIAH 1. A descendant of Zerubbabel (1 Chron. 3:21).

2. A descendant of Simeon (1 Chron. 4:42).

3. One who signed the covenant with Nehemiah (Neh. 10:22).

4. A son of Benaiah and prince of the people against which Ezekiel gave one of his oracles (Ezek. 1:1-13).

PELEG A descendant of Shem in whose days "the earth was divided." A possible reference to the confounding of the languages of the peoples (Gen. 10:25; 11:16-19).

PELET 1. A descendant of Judah and Caleb (1 Chron. 2:47).

2. A descendant of Benjamin who joined David at Ziklag (1 Chron. 12:3).

PELETH 1. A descendant of Reuben who was a part of the rebellion against the leadership of Moses (Num. 16:1).

2. A descendant of Judah and Jerahmeel (1 Chron. 2:33).

PELETHITES An unidentified group who along with the Cherethites comprised the bodyguard of King David (2 Sam. 8:18; 15:18; 1 Kgs. 1:38, 44).

PELONITE An unidentified title or place from which two of David's mighty men came (1 Chron. 11:27, 36; 27:10).

PELUSIUM An Egyptian fortress town on their NE frontier called "the stronghold of Egypt" (Ezek. 30:15, 16).

PEN An iron stylus or a reed pen for writing (Job 19:24; Ps. 45:1; 3 Jn. 13).

PENIEL, PENUEL A place (215-176) east of the Jordan River where Jacob wrestled all night with the man who subsequently blessed him (Gen. 24:22-31). Gideon destroyed the town and Jeroboam I of Israel later rebuilt it (Judg. 8:8-17; 1 Kgs. 12:25).

PENINNAH One of the wives of Elkanah, the father of Samuel (1 Sam. 1:2-4).

PENNY *See* MONEY

PENTATEUCH This term (lit. "five volumes") refers to the first five books of the OT, commonly called "The Five Books of Moses." Exodus 17:14 and 24:4 affirm that Moses personally wrote down God's words, and Exodus 24:7 that he read these words to the Israelite people. Deuteronomy 31:9 states that Moses had a complete written copy of the Law delivered to the priests. Joshua was bidden by God (Josh. 1:8) to study faithfully the written Pentateuch daily; King David referred to this written Law when he bade Solomon to study and obey it (1 Kgs. 2:3). Jesus referred to Moses as the personal author of Deuteronomy 24:1 (Mt. 19:8), and of the Messianic prophecies in the Torah (Jn. 15:46, 47). Paul quoted Moses as author of Deuteronomy 18:15 (Acts 3:22), and also of Leviticus 18:5 (Rom. 10:5). There is no reason to doubt that Christ and the apostles regarded Moses as the author of the Pentateuch. This is confirmed by the internal evidence of the text. Its author must have been originally a resident of Egypt, for he referred to Egyptian seasons and weather conditions rather than to Palestinian (Ex. 9:31-32), and employed a larger number of Egyptian names and loan-words than in any other part of the OT. He compared the lush verdure of the Jordan plain to a locality in Egypt (Gen. 13:10) which would be meaningful only to a reading public familiar with Egypt but unfamiliar with Palestine. Likewise he dated the founding of Kirjath-arba (the ancient name of Hebron) by reference to the building of Zoan in Egypt (Num. 13:22), and he described Shalem in Canaan as "a city of Shechem which is in the land of Canaan" (Gen. 33:18). He referred to Jerusalem only once, as "Shalem" (Gen. 14:18), which would be an unthinkable omission if at the time of composition of the Pentateuch Jerusalem had been the royal capital for several centuries (as many OT scholars allege). Among all the detailed injunctions concerning worship in Exodus and Leviticus there is not the slightest mention of a guild of Levitical singers or of the use of musical instruments, even though these became very prominent elements in Israelite worship from 1000 B.C. onward. The predominant type of legislation in Exodus, Leviticus, and Numbers is nomadic or agricultural; even in Deuteronomy there is very little special reference to urban conditions or the problems of a mercantile society, such as obtained from the time of David onward. Thus it is fair to say that the objective data bearing upon the Pentateuch point to its composition prior to the Hebrew conquest of Canaan. Moses was raised as an adopted son of the royal house in Egypt, enjoying the finest opportunities of education among a highly literate people, at a time when even Semitic slaves at the Egyptian mines at Serabit el-Khadim (Sinai Peninsula) were writing their records in alphabetic letters; hence the former arguments based upon Moses' alleged illiteracy must be totally abandoned. Moses had every incentive to commit to writing the constitution of the new theocracy to be set up in the land of Canaan, and he had forty years in which to finish it. Since the numerous references to God's covenant with the patriarchs in Exodus through Deuteronomy point to a prior record of the establishment of this covenant, a book like Genesis, which contained this record, was absolutely indispensable to make Exodus through Deuteronomy intelligible. This confirms the NT indications that Moses was the author of Genesis also, as well as of the other four.

Genesis, then, sets forth the beginnings of the human race and the preservation of a godly remnant through the time of the Flood (chapters 1-11). Next it relates the career of Abraham (chapters 12-25) and then the life of Isaac and his family (25-26). The career of Jacob and the birth of his twelve sons (27-36) is followed by the adventures of Joseph (37-50), who prepared the way for his family to increase to a great nation during the 430 years of their residence in Egypt.

Exodus resumes the narrative with the birth of Moses at a time when Israel has become a nation of oppressed slaves. His training for leadership and his call to lead Israel out of bondage are set forth in chapters 1-4. The contest with Pharaoh, the ten plagues, and the Red Sea crossing are covered by 5-18. The confrontation between the nation and Yahweh at Sinai and the giving of the law (beginning with the Ten Commandments) are dealt with in 19-23. Provisions for priesthood, worship, and sacrifice are given in chapters 24-31. Chapters 32-33 relate the apostasy connected with the worship of the golden calf. Chapters 34-40 resume instruction concerning worship, with warnings against idolatry and provisions for claiming God's forgiveness and grace; it closes with the solemn dedication of the tabernacle to God's service.

Leviticus contains a manual of special instruction for the priests and Levites in their spiritual service to the nation.

Regulations concerning the various types of sacrifice (1-7) are followed by a record of the consecration of Aaron and his sons to the priesthood (8-10). Laws of purification and separation from defilement (unclean foods, leprosy, etc.) come next (11-15), followed by the ordinances of the Day of Atonement (Yom Kippur) in chapter 16, and the sanctity of the altar and the atoning blood (17). Laws against unchastity, uncleanness, and idolatry (18-20) lead to a discussion of priestly holiness and priestly duties (21-22). The religious calendar with all the seven feasts (23) leads to the symbols of consecration and the penalties for desecration (24) followed by the laws concerning the sabbatical year and the year of jubilee (25). Chapter 26 outlines the blessings of obedience and the curses upon disobedience (with such remarkable foreknowledge of the future exile and restoration of Israel as to compel the antisupernaturalist to resort to some theory of postexilic authorship to explain it away). The payment of tithes and vows is discussed in the final chapter.

Numbers resumes the narrative of Israel's journey through the wilderness. After a census of the troops of the twelve tribes (1-4), laws aimed at excluding defilement from the camp (5) lead up to the establishment of the Nazirite order, closing with the Aaronic benediction (6). The twelve tribes dedicate treasures to the tabernacle (7) and witness the installation of the priests in their service of the tabernacle (8). The first annual Passover and the rules concerning the following of the pillar of cloud take up chapter 9. The journey from Sinai to Kadesh Barnea (10-14) is marked by rebellions against Moses' authority, culminating in Israel's refusal at Kadesh Barnea to trust God for conquest of Canaan. For this they are condemned to die off in the wilderness during the next forty years. Chapter 15 gives rules concerning certain types of sacrifice and the punishment for blasphemy. The abortive rebellion of Korah leads to renewed confirmation of Aaronic priesthood (16-17) and an explanation of the service role of Levites toward the priests (18). After a second smiting of the rock at Kadesh and a repulse by the Edomites, the Israelites arrive at Moab and crush Sihon and Og of Transjordan (20-21). After the encounter with King Balak and the prophet Balaam, (22-25) arrangements are drawn up for the coming conquest of Canaan, the apportionment of its territories, and the crushing of the Midianites (26-36).

Deuteronomy contains a final restatement of the Law delivered by the aged Moses as his parting charge to Israel to remain a holy commonwealth, walking in love toward God, obedience to his will, and abhorrence toward all the idolatries of Canaan. Chapters 1-4 contain a historical review of God's gracious dealings with his covenant people (the insertion of this type of historical survey characterized second millennium suzerainty treaties, but not those of the first millennium). Chapters 5-26 contain the stipulations in God's "treaty" with Israel, the laws by which the holy commonwealth is to live. Basic commandments (5-11), statutes of worship, and of a holy life (12-16) and judgments concerning specific offenses, relationships, and duties (17-26) make up this section. Chapter 17 has rules to govern future kings; chapter 18 concerns future prophets and the Messianic Prophet; 27-33 contain warning and prediction (some of which point to the fall of Jerusalem to Titus in A.D. 70), and set before every Israelite the alternatives of blessing and of curse. The Song of Moses sets forth the nation's responsibility to keep God's covenant with an earnest warning against apostasy. Chapter 33 contains a prediction and blessing for each of the twelve tribes, and chapter 34 presents an obituary notice and eulogy, doubtless added soon after Moses' death. (G.L.A.)

PENTECOST *See* CALENDAR and FEASTIVALS

PENUEL 1. A descendant of Judah (1 Chron. 4:4).

2. A descendant of Benjamin (1 Chron. 8:25).

PEOPLE OF GOD A phrase which indicates the relationship between the God of Israel and Israel in the OT and in the NT either that same relationship or that between God and the Church (Num. 11:29; Judg. 5:11; 1 Sam. 2:24; Mal. 3:16-17; Rom. 11:1-2; 2 Cor. 6:14-18; 1 Pet. 2:9-10).

PEOR 1. A place(163-119) put in the tribal area of Judah in the LXX of Josh. 15:59).

2. The name of a high mountain peak in Moab from which Balaam was supposed to curse Israel (Num. 23:28).

3. A short form of Baal-peor. *See* DEITIES.

PERAZIM *See* BAAL PERAZIM

PERDITION In Revelation 17:8, 11 the reference is to the final state of the wicked, the common meaning of the word in our day. King David in his twice recorded poem spoke of the torrents of perdition engulfing him but went on to note how God saved him from them (2 Sam. 22:5; Ps. 18:4). The only other references are by Jesus of Judas Iscariot and by Paul of "the man of lawlessness (marg. man of sin)," the Antichrist, who is called son of perdition (Jn. 17:12; 2 Thess. 2:3).

PERES *See* MENE, MENE, TEKEL, AND PARSIN

PERESH A descendant of Manasseh (1 Chron. 7:16).

PEREZ A son of Judah by Tamar, one in the genealogy of Jesus (Gen. 38:29; Ruth 4:12, 18; Lk. 3:33).

PEREZ UZZAH The name given by David to the place where God killed Uzzah for putting out his hand to touch the Ark, even though he thought he was doing it to protect the Ark from falling (2 Sam. 6:8; 1 Chron. 13:11).

PERFECT, PERFECTION The rendering of two Hebrew and one Greek word meaning "end," "finished," "completed." The words do not mean final and or ultimate completion and perfection but a completed state as of a given time. Job was twice declared by God to be perfect (the Hebrew word is translated "blameless" in the RSV), yet he had much to learn so that in the end he was more "perfect" (Job 1:8; 2:3). The man of God is being completed but his final completion awaits his resurrection (Jas. 3:2; Phil. 3:12). The term is a relative one, showing relationship between time and the absolute state of completeness, perfection.

PERFUMES *See* PLANTS, PERFUMES, AND SPICES

PERGA The chief city of ancient Pamphylia in SE Asia Minor visited by Paul on his first missionary journey (Acts 13:13-25).

PERGAMUM A city in Mysia in W Asia Minor to which one of the seven letters found in the Revelation was written (Rev. 1:11; 2:12).

PERIDA Ancestor of some of Solomon's servants who returned with Zerubbabel from the Babylonian captivity (Neh. 7:57; Ezra 2:55), also called Peruda.

PERISH To be lost or destroyed in either the physical or spiritual sense (Gen. 41:36; Deut. 8:20; Jn. 3:16; 2 Pet. 3:9).

PERIZZITES An ethnic group in the land of Palestine when Abraham, and later the Israelites after the years in Egypt, dwelt there. They are mentioned along with groups whose identity is known today—Canaanites, Hittites, Horites—and with others whose identity, like their own, is not currently known (Gen. 13:7; 15:20; Ex. 3:8; Josh. 3:10; Neh. 9:8).

PERSIA One of the sons of Japheth was Madai (Gen. 10:2), the ancestor of the Medes and of a related, Indo-European speaking people, the Persians. Both settled in the mountains east of Mesopotamia. In about 650 B.C. the ancient Persian dynasty was founded by Achaimenes. The fourth of his line married a daughter of Astyages the Mede; and from this union came Cyrus II (the Great), who reigned from 558 to

529. Cyrus overcame Astyages in 550 and incorporated
the Median empire into his own, fulfilling Daniel's prediction
of a dual empire: the bear that was higher on one side
(Persia over Media, Dan. 7:5; compare 2:32, 39), and the
ram with two horns, of which the latter was the higher (8:3,
4, 20). By 546 Cyrus had defeated the Lydians in the west
and by 539 the Bactrians of Afghanistan, so that he held from
the Aegean to the borders of India. In October of 539 the
Babylonians under Belshazzar were defeated by his general
Gobryas, perhaps to be equated with "Darius the Mede" who
received the kingdom of Babylon (5:31), though only for a
short period (compare 9:1 and 11:1). Cyrus himself then
assumed control over the former Babylonian empire, including
Judah in the west.

Under his general policy of conciliating conquered peoples,
Cyrus issued an edict to the Jews in 538, authorizing their
return from exile and reinstitution of temple worship in
Jerusalem (2 Chron. 36:22-23; Ezra 1:1-4), as had been
specifically predicted by Isaiah over a century and a half
before (Isa. 44:28; 45:1). Samaritan opposition was able to
stop the temple's reconstruction (Ezra 4:1-5, 24) until after
the death of Cyrus' son and successor Cambyses (529-522),
possibly because of the latter's wish to avoid trouble near
the border of Egypt, which he conquered in 525.

Darius I (522-485) succeeded to the throne of Persia only
after lengthy conflicts with rivals and insubordinate governors.
He accordingly reorganized the empire into twenty-one
satrapies, in a system that combined local autonomy, central
power, and an efficient system of checks and balances. His
reasonableness is illustrated by his handling of the report
of Tattenal, satrap of the fifth (Syrian) province (Ezra 6:1-
12), which accomplished the final rebuilding of the temple
between 520 and 515 (verse 15). By 512 he had conquered
the Punjab in India and Thrace in Europe, though Athens
escaped at Marathon in 490 B.C.

His son Xerxes I (485-465) was weak and thoroughly
corrupt, as indicated all too clearly by the events in the Book
of Esther in 483 B.C. (Esth. 1:3) and 479-474 (2:16; 3:7).
Between these two periods Xerxes (Ahasuerus) was engaged
in mounting a massive attack on Greece (as predicted in
Dan. 11:2). His forces, however, were routed at Salamis
harbor, Sept. 20, 480; and European culture was saved.
Harem intrigues then controlled Persia until his murder and
replacement by Artaxerxes I (465-424). Under Artaxerxes
Judah prospered. In 458 he granted Ezra the authority by
which he led back a second return of the Jews from Babylon
(Ezra 7-8) and instituted reforms (9-10), while only a renewed
Samaritan opposition stopped the rebuilding of the city walls

of Jerusalem (4:7-23; 9:9). Even this was achieved in 444 when Artaxerxes granted special authority as governor to his Jewish cupbearer, Nehemiah (Neh. 2:5-8; 6:15).

The Old Testament comes to a close, chronologically, with the Book of Nehemiah, the last ruler that he mentioned being Darius II, the Persian (423-404) (Neh. 12:22; compare 13:6, 7). Among Persia's later monarchs, Artaxerxes II suffered an invasion in 401 by Greek mercenaries; but it was Darius III in 331 who finally fell before the Greek troops of Alexander the Great, as predicted by Daniel long before (Dan. 8:5-7, 21; 11:13). (J.B.P.)

PERSIS A Christian at Rome to whom Paul sent greetings (Rom. 16:12).

PERUDA *See* PERIDA

PESTILENCE *See* SICK, SICKNESS

PESTLE The wooden or stone instrument held in the hand with which to grind or crush the material in a mortar (Prov. 27:22).

PETER, EPISTLES OF Internal evidence reflects clearly in the first Epistle the mind and life of the Apostle Peter. This with the unanimous testimony of the early fathers going back to about A.D. 125 gives us the assurance of Petrine authorship. The second Epistle purports to have been written by Peter (2 Pet. 1:1) but has the least external attestation of any NT book. All that exists comes from a very late period, mid-third century. Internal evidence and tradition (late) make it feasible to accept a Petrine authorship, however. While some date the first Epistle around A.D. 100 and the second even later, a good case can be made for dates between A.D. 65 and 70. In the first Epistle the author is concerned to make clear the Christian message of salvation (1 Pet. 1:3-12) and the moral and ethical obligations for the Christian resulting from that salvation. As he led up to a discussion of proper conduct under suffering (4:12—5:11) it is assumed that those to whom he wrote were in need of encouragement to help them to endure their then present lot. In the second Epistle the author was concerned to point out the presence, nature, and perils of turning away from the truth of the gospel and the written word of God (2 Pet. 2:1-22). He urged patient endurance and conformity to the truth in view of the coming Day of the Lord with all that that will mean in judgment for the wicked and blessing for the believer (2 Pet. 3:8-18).

PETER, SIMON *See* APOSTLES

PETHAHIAH 1. The head of a priestly division in David's time (1 Chron. 24:16).

2. A priest who married a foreign wife during the time of the Babylonian captivity (Ezra 10:23).

3. A Levite in the time of Ezra (Neh. 9:5).

4. A Levite overseer in the time of Nehemiah (Neh. 11:24).

PETHOR A place in Mesopotamia, the home of Balaam who was called in by Balak to curse Israel (Num. 22:5; Deut. 23:4).

PETHUEL The father of the prophet Joel (Joel 1:1).

PEULLETHAI A Levite gatekeeper of the tabernacle in David's days (1 Chron. 26:5).

PHANUEL The father of the prophetess Anna when Christ was born (Lk. 2:36).

PHARAOH A title meaning "the great house," or a title used as a name for a king of Egypt. The great majority of the occurrences of this word are in the Pentateuch and secondly elsewhere in the OT. There are only five occurrences in the NT (Acts 7:10-21; Rom. 9:17; Heb. 11:24). From before 3000 B.C. to the time of the Persian conquest (525 B.C.) there were some twenty-six dynasties, perhaps more in view of the silent Hyksos period. Abraham had contact with a Pharaoh (Gen. 12:15ff.). So too did Joseph, his brothers, and his father Jacob (Gen. 39-50). This latter period was concluded with the conflict of Moses and Aaron with the Pharaoh that led to the exodus of the Israelites (Ex. 1-14). There were important contacts between King Solomon and the Pharaohs, Solomon marrying one of the daughters of a Pharaoh (1 Kgs. 3:1; 9:16). Among the others that are mentioned, but very occasionally, is Pharaoh Neco who defeated and killed King Josiah of Judah (2 Kgs. 23:29-35).

PHARAOH-HOPHRA *See* HOPHRA

PHARISEES *See* SECTS

PHARPAR *See* DAMASCUS

PHICOL Captain of the armies of King Abimelech of Gerar in the days of Abraham (Gen. 21:22, 32; 26:26).

PHILADELPHIA A city in W Asia Minor in the province of Lydia which was one of the early strongholds of Christianity. The city suffered from many severe earthquakes as of A.D. 17 (Rev. 1:11; 3:7).

PHILEMON The owner of a slave by the name of Onesimus. Paul pleaded with the owner to take the runaway back and to treat him as a brother. *See also* PAULINE EPISTLES.

PHILEMON, BOOK OF *See* PAULINE EPISTLES

PHILETUS One of the false teachers condemned by Paul (2 Tim. 2:17).

PHILIP 1. *See* APOSTLES

2. One of the first deacons of the church, called also an evangelist (Acts 6:5). He was God's messenger at the conversion of the Ethiopian eunuch and Paul's host in Caesarea (Acts 8:26ff.; 21:8, 9). He had four unmarried daughters who prophesied.

3 and 4. Two of the Herods bore this name. *See* HEROD.

PHILIPPI A city in E Macedonia about ten miles up river from the Aegean Sea, not to be confused with Caesarea Philippi. *See* CAESAREA PHILIPPI. Paul visited it on his second missionary journey and later wrote an epistle to them. It was the first city of Europe to hear his message. Here he met Lydia the seller of purple dye and established a church in her home, and here he was jailed by owners of a slave out of whom he drove an evil spirit (Acts 16:12-40; 20:6; Phil. 1:1; 1 Thess. 2:2).

PHILIPPIANS, BOOK OF *See* PAULINE EPISTLES

PHILISTIA Another word for Palestine. Palatine is found four times in the KJV; in the RSV it is rendered Philistia, appearing the same four times and five others (Ex. 15:14; Isa. 14:29, 31; Joel 3:4; Ps. 60:8; Zech. 9:6). The reference is to the coastal strip south of Joppa and west of the Shephelah, an area inhabited by the Philistines from whom the area derived its name. *See* PHILISTINE CITIES and GEOGRAPHY OF THE HOLY LAND.

PHILISTINE CITIES *See also* WAY OF THE PHILISTINES and GEOGRAPHY OF THE HOLY LAND.

PHILOLOGUS A Christian lady in Rome to whom Paul sent greetings (Rom. 16:15).

PHINEAS, PHINEHAS 1. A son of Eli and brother of Hophni. *See* HOPHNI.

2. Father of a priest in the time of Ezra (Ezra 8:33).

3. A grandson of Aaron who settled at Gibeah after the conquest and ministered at Bethel (Ex. 6:25; Num. 25:7ff.; Josh. 24:33; Judg. 20:9).

PHLEGON A Christian at Rome to whom Paul sent greetings (Rom. 16:14).

PHOEBE A deaconess of the church at Cenchrea who was commended to the Christians at Rome by Paul (Rom. 16:1).

PHOENICIA *See* GEOGRAPHY OF THE HOLY LAND

PHOENIX A harbor on the south side of the island of Crete which Paul hoped to reach on his journey to Rome. The wind drove them past it (Acts 27:12).

PHRYGIA *See* GEOGRAPHY OF THE HOLY LAND

PHYGELUS One who deserted Paul (2 Tim. 1:15).

PHYLACTERY Mentioned only in Mt. 23:5, a small receptacle which contained some verses from the Bible that were bound on the arm and forehead by long leather thongs during prayer. These were: Ex. 13:1-10; 11-16; Deut. 6:4-9; 11:13-21.

PHYSICIAN Originally one who rendered first-aid to the wounded, a healer in that sense (Jer. 8:22; 2 Chron. 16:12; Lk. 5:31). *See* SICK, SICKNESS. Luke, the writer of Acts and the third Gospel, was a physician and these persons in ancient Egypt also embalmed the dead (Col. 4:14; Gen. 50:2).

PI BESETH A city in the delta region of Egypt occupied over a long period of time but mentioned in the Bible only in connection with Ezekiel's prophecy against Egypt (see Ezek. 30:17 footnote).

PICK A sharp instrument of iron mentioned only in connection with saws and iron axes with which the Ammonites were either tortured or made to work by King David (2 Sam. 12:31; 1 Chron. 20:3).

PIG *See* BEASTS, 10

PIGEON *See* BIRDS, 4

PI HAHIROTH An unidentified town or place in N Egypt where the Israelites last encamped before crossing the Red Sea (Ex. 14:2, 9; Num. 33:7).

PILATE The procurator or Roman governmental representative in Palestine at the time of the crucifixion of Christ. Pontius was his family name (Lk. 3:1; Mt. 27; Mk. 15; Lk. 23; Jn. 18:29—19:38). Pilate delivered Jesus, after the trial before him, to be crucified and saw that the execution was carried out. His name has been found on an inscription in the excavations at Caesarea.

PILDASH A son of Nahor and therefore nephew to Abraham (Gen. 22:22).

PILHA One who signed the covenant with Nehemiah (Neh. 10:24).

PILLAR A stone monument set up as a memorial or an object of worship, called a *massebah* in Hebrew (more literally *matstsebah*) (Gen. 35:20; Ex. 23:24; 24:4). There were other stone memorials as well as the *masseboth* (Josh. 4:19-24). Stone pillars or columns were also used in buildings both for structural reasons and for beauty. Stone pillars have been found standing alone in excavations for which no satisfactory explanation exists (1 Kgs. 7:6; 15:22).

PILTAI A priest in the days of Nehemiah and the high priest Joiakim (Neh. 12:17).

PIM A weight equal to about two-thirds of a shekel which the Philistines charged the Israelites for sharpening a plowshare or mattock. Found only in 1 Samuel 13:21.

PINE TREE *See* TREES

PINON An Edomite chief and descendant of Seir (Gen. 36:41).

PINT *See* WEIGHTS AND MEASURES

PIPE *See* MUSIC, MUSICAL INSTRUMENTS

PIRAM The king of the city of Jarmuth who joined an alliance against Joshua, was defeated and killed (Josh. 10:3ff.).

PIRATHON A town (165-177) in the hill country of Ephraim from which one of the minor judges and one of David's mighty men came (Judg. 12:13-15; 2 Sam. 23:30).

PISGAH A mountain peak in Transjordan just NW of Mount Nebo from which one could look down on the Israelite encampment and from which Balak tried to get Balaam to curse Israel (Num. 21:20; 23:14). From this altitude God showed Moses the promised land into which he would not be allowed to go (Deut. 3:27; 34:1).

PISHON An unidentified river that flowed out of the Garden of Eden (Gen. 2:11).

PISIDIA *See* GEOGRAPHY OF THE HOLY LAND

PISPAH A descendant of Asher (1 Chron. 7:38).

PISTACHIO *See* PLANTS, PERFUMES, AND SPICES

PIT *See* DEAD, ABODE OF

PITCH An inflammable (Isa. 34:9) viscous or semiliquid mineral substance found in the area of the Dead Sea and in Mesopotamia. The ark of Noah and the basket of bulrushes of the baby Moses were caulked with it (Gen. 6:14; Ex. 2:3). It is rendered by "pitch" (Gen. 6:14; Ex. 2:3). It was used in lieu of cement in building with bricks in Mesopotamia (Gen. 11:3).

PITCHER An earthenware jar fired in a kiln and used for storing grain or other material (Eccles. 12:6; Jer. 35:5). Much is known about these as the result of modern archaeological work.

PITHOM An as yet unidentified city in Egypt which along with Rameses was built for the Pharaoh of the time of the Israelite exodus by the captive Israelites (Ex. 1:11).

PITHON A descendant of Saul (1 Chron. 8:35).

PITY *See* COMPASSION

PLAGUE *See* SICK, SICKNESS

PLAGUES OF EGYPT These were the evil happenings to the Egyptians which God used to induce the Pharaoh to let the Israelites leave Egypt. Some endeavoring to circumvent miracles try to find naturalistic explanations for all of these. This is not very satisfactory, especially when the timing of the events is taken into consideration. The water of Egypt became blood, frogs covered the land as did lice and flies, and a plague of some sort hit all the livestock. This plague was followed by boils on man and beast. Then there came hail which destroyed crops and animals in the open to be followed by a plague of locusts. Darkness came suddenly on the land and finally the firstborn of man and animal where the angel did not see the atoning blood died suddenly in one night. Throughout biblical history these incidents are used as warnings for God's people (Ex. 7:14—12:36).

PLAINS *See* GEOGRAPHY OF THE HOLY LAND

PLANTS, PERFUMES, AND SPICES

Some seventy items are discussed in this article and another two dozen under trees. (*See* TREES.) Due to the fact that the references to many of these items in the Bible are so few a measure of uncertainty exists in every effort to define them in modern terms. These more difficult areas are noted below. Scientific names are left, with but a few exceptions, for more exhaustive treatments which may be found in the multi-volume encyclopedias.

PLANTS FOR FOOD

1. Wheat, Barley, Spelt, and *Millet* were the ancient and common staples, annual grasses sown with the early winter rains and reaped in May-June. The first two in their modern varieties are well known generally. Spelt is a form of *Triticum* (wheat) (Ex. 9:32; Isa. 28:25; Ezek. 4:9). Millet, used in Ezekiel 4:9, may be either *Panicum miliaceum* or one of the sorghums. "Roasted grain," "new grain," and "roasted corn" usually refer to wheat (Deut. 8:8; 1 Sam. 25:18; Lev. 2:14; Ex. 9:31; Num. 5:15).

2. Beans and *Lentils* are well known staple items of the ancient diet. The former is the common broad bean and the latter, identified through its modern Arabic name, is *Lens esculenta* commonly used in pottage (Gen. 25:34; 2 Sam. 17:28; 23:11; Ezek. 4:9).

3. Onions, Garlic, and *Leeks* are three bulbous members of the *Allium* (lily) family of which some seventy or more varieties are known. The first two are well known even today in the occidental world. The third looks like an elongated onion, is usually eaten raw, and quite evidently was an item of Israelite diet beloved by them while enslaved in Egypt (Num. 11:5). All were well-known staples in the ancient diet. It should be noted that the Hebrew word rendered leeks in the passage above is many times translated "grass" elsewhere in all the versions.

4. Cucumbers and *Melons* (Num. 11:5; Isa. 1:8; Jer. 10:5). The second is a variety of our commonly known watermelon, red inside. The first is much more likely to have been a muskmelon, known in the Middle East from earliest times, a sweet melon and not our modern cucumber.

5. Grapes and *Raisins,* the latter a dried form of the former (1 Sam. 25:18). The former for wine and its leaves as a vegetable are so well known as to need no special description. The fruit of the vine is as much a staple in Palestine of antiquity as wheat, milk, or honey. The number of references to grapes, milk, and honey are about equal and those to bread only slightly outnumber wine.

6. Nuts were of the pistachio and almond variety and perhaps also the walnut. There is only one reference to the pistachio

(Gen. 43:11), but there are many references to the almond nut, tree and flower taken together (Gen. 43:11; Eccles. 12:5; Ex. 25:33). See also below. There is also a reference to "a grove of nut trees" (Song 6:4).

FLOWERING PLANTS (including trees) As noted in the general introduction above nearly 100 flora species are mentioned in the Bible but only a few are noted in connection with their flowers and the identification of some of these is not certain. (A question mark after a flower indicates the uncertainty of the identification of the Hebrew word involved.)

1. *Almond.* Its flower is mentioned in connection with Aaron's rod which put forth buds and blossoms. And on the golden lampstand of the tabernacle were patterned almond flowers (Num. 17:8; Ex. 25:33; 37:19).

2. The *Chabatstselet* is rendered: *Rose* (of Sharon) (?), *Crocus* (?), and it may even have been a narcissus (Song 2:1; Isa. 35:1).

3. The *Flax* and *Henna* were flowering and noted as such in the Bible. The first was grown for fiber and seeds, the second for a reddish-brown dye (Ex. 9:31; Song 1:14; 4:13).

4. The *Lily* and *Lotus* are both mentioned in connection with flowers but the exact identity of neither is sure (1 Kgs. 7:26; Job 40:21-22).

5. The *Reed* or *Papyrus* (*see also* below) and *Vine* are noted as bearing flowers (Job 8:12; Song 2:13; Isa. 18:5).

6. Among the trees, all of which have a flower of course, the *Olive* and the *Pomegranate* are specifically mentioned with their flowers (Song 2:13; Job 15:33; Song 6:11).

7. The *Grass* of the field is noted with its flower more often than any other single plant, and especially in connection with teaching the transitory character of life (Isa. 40:6-8; 1 Pet. 1:24).

SPINY PLANTS There are some 100 plants in this category in Palestine and some fourteen Hebrew words refer to the spiny shrubs of one or more of the 100 kinds. The identification or equation of these words with an exact English botanical equivalent is virtually impossible. They include: *bramble(s)*, *briar(s)* (also spelled brier[s]), *nettles, thistle(s), thorn(s), thorn-bush* (also written thornbush) (Judg. 9:14-15; Lk. 6:44; Isa. 55:13; 5:6; Isa. 34:13; Hos. 9:6; 2 Kgs. 14:9; Hos. 10:8; Mk. 15:17; Isa. 7:19).

PLANTS FOR SEASONING Eight are noted in the NIV: *Caraway, Coriander, Cummin, Dill, Mint, Mustard, Rue, Saffron.* Dill is sometimes rendered anise in the KJV (Mt. 23:23) even though a true anise is not grown in Palestine. Dill is used in pickling and an oil from the seed is medicinal as well (Isa. 28:25-27). *Coriander sativum* is a known annual from whose seed a medicine and a condiment are made (Ex. 16:31; Num. 11:7). The manna was like coriander seed and looked like resin (Num. 11:7). Cummin is an aromatic seed somewhat like caraway (Isa. 28:27) and not used greatly in modern times (Isa. 28:25-27; Mt. 23:23). Three species of the aromatic leaf and flower, mint, grow in Palestine and are used for their aroma and flavor (Mt. 23:23; Lk. 11:42). Mustard is a common weed in modern Palestine growing to tree height. Oil from its small seeds was used as a condiment, *Brassica nigra* (Mt. 13:31). In the NT its small seed was used as an illustration for faith. Rue, one of the *Rutas,* was used as a medicine and condiment. It is used only in Luke 11:42 where the parallel is dill. Saffron is the pollen of a crocus used both to dye food and in medicine. Used only in Song of Solomon 4:14.

PERFUMES, SCENTS, OINTMENTS, DRUGS Here again we deal with a number of names used but rarely in the text of the Bible, some well known because of the continuity of their use and some not easy to identify. Except in Numbers 24:6 and Song of Solomon 4:14 where *aloes* seems to be a tree (perhaps incorrectly translated for "oak") it refers to a plant somewhat like a century plant. As used in the Bible, however, it would seem more probable that the reference is to some aromatic wood (Ps. 45:8; Jn. 19:39). From *balm* which appears to be a tree a medicinal substance was secured. The identity is not known perhaps because of the paucity of the references (Gen. 37:25). It was a spice, however. *Henna* is a shrub from whose dried leaves a reddish dye is secured that is used as a cosmetic and a hair coloring today. It is not clear how extensively it was used as such in biblical times (Song 1:14). *Cane, sweet cane, calamus,* and *sweet calamus*, are grasses that yield sweet volatile oils such as citronella, for an example (Ex. 30:23; Isa. 43:24; Jer. 6:20). *Cinnamon* was an import into Palestine and not a native plant (Ex. 30:23; Song 4:14; Rev. 18:13). *Cassia* is a translation of two Hebrew words whose meaning is not clear. One might be a tree of the cinnamon type and the other an aromatic shrub. Both would be imports to Palestine (Ex. 30:24; Ps. 45:8). *Myrrh* is a resin or gum exuded from a tree from which both a drug and a perfume were made. It was used in embalming and, like cassia, cinnamon, aloes, and others, in making the holy oil of the temple used for anointing (Prov. 7:17; Jn. 19:39). *Nard* is a perennial herb with a strongly aromatic root and was an import to Palestine (Song 4:14; Jn. 12:3). *Frankincense* was made from a gum-resin of several trees of the genus *Boswellia* and was an import to Palestine (Ex. 30:34ff.). *Galbanum* is both an incense and a medicine derived from a plant of the same family as the carrot. It was used in the tabernacle incense (Ex. 30:34). Another ingredient of perfumes was *onycha,* found in the Bible only in Exodus 30:34. Its origin is not clear. *Myrtle* is a many-branched shrub used in perfumery and one of the "four kinds" required in the Feast of Booths, *Myrtus communis* (Neh. 8:15; Isa. 41:19; Zech. 1:8-11).

MISCELLANEOUS PLANTS
1. Bitter herbs. An unidentified herb used in the Passover meal (Ex. 12:8; Num. 9:11).

2. Broom tree, a shrub that can grow high enough to make shade for animals under it, *Retama raetam.* Its roots were used for food (Job 30:4; 1 Kgs. 19:4-5).

3. Papyrus, a reed that grows near water from which baskets and boats were made. From its pith, paper (papyrus) was made (Ex. 2:3; Job 8:11; Isa. 18:2).

4. Linen, a well-known modern plant, but noted only twice in the Bible (Esth. 1:6; Isa. 19:9).

5. Flax was used in the textile industry. Linen was made from its fibres and its seeds were used both for food and paint oil (Ex. 9:31).

6. Gourd. Several varieties existed. One was poisonous but used for medicinal purposes (2 Kgs. 4:39-41). It was also called the vine of Sodom (Deut. 32:32).

7. Hyssop. It was used for the sprinkling of the sacrificial blood and Jesus was offered vinegar on it (Ex. 12:22; Lev. 14:4; Jn. 19:29). Its buds and seed pods are used to make capers.

8. Mandrake found only in Gen. 30:14-16 and Song 7:13 refers to the druglike fruit of the plant but is not an aphrodisiac as legend would have it.

9. Nard, called a "very expensive perfume," was used by Mary when she poured perfume on Jesus' head and feet (Jn. 12:3; Mk. 14:3; Song 4:13, 14). Described as an aromatic Himalayan and East Indian plant.

Many of these plants are only rarely mentioned in the Bible and not enough information is given for identifications that are sure.

PLASTER Used only in three contexts in the NIV, all in connection with plastering of walls (Lev. 14:41-48; Deut. 27:2-4; Dan. 5:5). The plaster might be a mixture of clay and straw, of gypsum and ashes, or slaked lime and sand.

PLEDGE *See* DEBT

PLEIADES A grouping of stars known by the same name today (Job 9:9; 38:31; Amos 5:8).

PLUNDER When an enemy was defeated the victor took his goods as plunder or booty, his property and persons as the prize of war. In some cases in ancient Israel the enemy and the property were called "condemned things" (Deut. 13:17) and "devoted" to the Lord (Josh. 6:17-19). The goods went to the temple treasurer and the persons were killed.

POETRY In the NT the easily recognized poems are all to be found in the Gospels connected with the birth narratives of John and Jesus. We know them today as the Magnificat of Mary, the prophecy of Zacharias, the Gloria in Excelsis of the angels and the Nunc Dimittis of Simeon (Mt. 1:46ff.; 1:68ff.; 2:14; 2:29ff.). These are in the Hebrew poetic style recited by Jews originally. Elsewhere in the NT it is a matter of elevated, lyrical language or eloquence that creates the feeling of poetry, not a certain form, in spite of the fact that the language is Greek. Classical Greek poetry secured its poetic form by careful attention to a form built around syllabic feet and vowel length. This poetry is totally unknown in the OT and since the writers of the NT were Jews of the OT tradition it only peeks through the elevated passages of the NT (Eph. 5:14; 1 Tim. 3:16; 6:16; Rom. 11:33—12:2; 1 Cor. 13). The Hebraic style comes through very clearly in the longer quotations of poetic portions of the OT (Rom. 10:18-20; 11:9, 10; 3:10-18).

As we have noted, Greek poetry secured its poetic style by a rhythm of syllabic feet and vowel length. Our English poetry traditionally secured its rhythm by a rhythm of accents. The poetry of the OT used neither method. Its rhythm is one of thoughts and ideas repeated, contrasted or advanced in parallel or successive lines of the poem. Illustrations will help the reader to understand. The synonymous or repeated style in its simplest form develops its thought in alternate lines with the in-between lines being the ones that repeat the thoughts.

"The earth is the Lord's, and the fulness thereof;
   the world, and they that dwell therein;
For he hath founded it upon the seas,
   and established it upon the floods.
Who shall ascend into the hill of the Lord?
   or who shall stand in his holy place?" (Ps. 24:1-3, KJV).

The contrasted or antithetic style is found abundantly, but especially in the Proverbs. The thought of the second line is in contrast with that of the first:

"A wise son maketh a glad father,
    but a foolish son is the heaviness of his mother.
Treasures of wickedness profit nothing,
    but righteousness delivereth from death.
The Lord will not suffer the soul of the righteous to famish,
    but he casteth away the substance of the wicked" (Prov. 10:1-3, KJV).

The advanced style is usually referred to as synthetic parallelism. While it is not parallelism in the strictest sense of that word, the technique is used so frequently that there is agreement among all scholars that this was a deliberate poetic device. The second line advances the thought of the first.

"He is like a tree planted by streams of water,
    which yields its fruit in season, and whose leaf does not wither. . . .

Not so, the wicked!
    They are chaff that the wind blows away" (Ps. 1:3, 4).

In all three basic types there are interesting variations and minor stylistic features. There is no poem altogether made up of one form of parallelism. Extra lines are here and there thrown in also. No extended portion resembles Greek or English poetic style with syllabic or accentual rhythm. Strophes and epistrophes and acrostics do appear but are very rare, certainly only incidental features. The poetic rhythm comes from the repetition of ideas with the various forms intermingled quite casually within any given poem.

It is estimated that about one third of the OT is poetry. It is easily identified. Whenever one or more of the three parallelisms or repetitions noted above appear, there is poetry.

POISON This came either from reptiles or certain plants. An evil tongue of a human is referred to as full of poison (Job 20:16; Ps. 140:3; Hos. 10:4; Deut. 29:18; Jas. 3:8).

POKERETH-HAZZEBAIM, POCHERETH OF ZEBAIM The ancestor of some who returned with Zerubbabel from the Babylonian captivity (Ezra 2:57).

POMEGRANATE *See* TREES

PONTIUS PILATE *See* PILATE

PONTUS *See* GEOGRAPHY OF THE HOLY LAND

POOL, POOLS Natural or artificial reservoirs for holding water. In a country totally devoid of rainfall for seven to nine months of every year, these become very important for survival. Among the interesting ones noted in the Bible for some special event that took place beside the pool are those at Gibeon, Hebron, Samaria, Hezekiah's, the upper, lower, and old pools (2 Sam. 2:13ff.; 4:12; 1 Kgs. 22:38; 2 Kgs. 18:17; 20:20; Isa. 22:9, 11).

POOR The translation of several Hebrew and Greek words meaning poor in a material sense, weak, unfortunate, or afflicted. The Mosaic Law was very specific on the subject of care for the poor and gave considerable space to the subject. Because Israel became careless in this matter the prophets took up the theme in extended passages (Ex. 22:25; 23:3-11; Lev. 19:9-15; 25:25-30, 39-54; Deut. 24:10-22; Isa. 10:1, 2; Amos 2:6; 5:7; Mal. 3:5). Jesus associated himself with the poor and showed great concern for them although his major emphasis was on the spiritually poor. The NT gives considerable evidence of concern among the members of the early church for the poor in their midst, even to the appointing of special officers, deacons, for their care (Lk. 6:20-26; 2 Cor. 6:10; Jas. 2:3-6; Acts 6:1-6; Gal. 2:10).

POPLAR *See* TREES

PORATHA One of the sons of Haman, the opponent of the Jews in the Persian court in the time of Esther (Esth. 9:8).

PORCH The entrance room of a building or courtyard, frequently roofed. The RSV usually renders it "vestibule." Important buildings such as King Solomon's palace and the temple (NIV "portico") had elaborate vestibules while even relatively simple buildings had such entry ways. The latter is now well known from the excavations (1 Kgs. 7:6ff.; 6:3; Mt. 26:71; Jn. 5:2; Ezek. 40:7ff.).

PORCIUS *See* FESTUS

PORPHYRY *See* PRECIOUS STONES AND METALS

PORTENT *See* MIRACLES

PORTICO *See* PORCH

POSSESSION Besides the usual meaning of this word in the sense of ownership, it is used to refer to possession of an individual by a demon. *See* DEMON, DEMONIAC.

POST These refer to doorposts or gateposts. One of the words used is rendered in the RSV as threshold (Ex. 12:7; Ezek. 45:19; 2 Chron. 3:7). The word is also used in the sense of a place of duty. The priests stood at their posts (2 Chron. 7:6).

POT The English translation for more than a dozen Hebrew and Greek words for ceramic and metal vessels. *See* POTTERY.

POTIPHAR The officer of Pharaoh to whom Joseph was sold (Gen. 37:36; 39:1ff.).

POTIPHERA The priest of On in Egypt and the father-in-law of Joseph (Gen. 41:45).

POTSHERD A piece of broken pottery also called sherd. Job used them to scrape himself and he describes the underparts of leviathan as like potsherds with their rough edges (Job 2:8; 41:30). One of the gates of the city of Jerusalem was called the "Potsherd Gate," presumably near the quarter of the potters and where they dumped their broken material (Jer. 19:2).

POTTAGE A thick vegetable soup or stew with meat added occasionally (Gen. 25:29-34; 2 Kgs. 4:38-40).

POTTER, POTTERY Pottery was the ancient ceramic, used for many things besides dishes and other vessels. Clay was worked and then baked at high temperatures in an oven with a resulting product of a stonelike character. In the latter end of the neolithic times, after about 5000 B.C., man discovered the art of pottery making. At first it was very crudely done. Later the wheel came into use and vessels of finer shape and greater variety resulted. Painting was known from very early times and much of it was from iron ore and thus reddish or reddish brown in color. Simple geometric designs and later more ornate drawings of birds and animals were used. Burnishing to a high gloss was also known from at least 2500 B.C. The potter's wheel at first was a very simple and small affair consisting of two stones. The lower had a hole in its flat upper surface and the upper stone had the nipple in its flat undersurface to fit that hole. This stone, flat also on the upper surface, was turned while the potter made his vessel upon it. Some of these were only inches in diameter. Bowls, platters, jugs, juglets, storage jars of massive proportions, strainer jars, lamps, cooking pots, and other vessels were made. The styles of all of these vessels varied through the centuries and that development is well known to all archaeologists so much so that it is by the style of the pottery that they date the various strata of their excavations.

In various periods there were beautiful imports, for example, the Mycenaean ware of the Late Bronze period (Isa. 41:25; 45:9; Jer. 18:2-6).

POTTER'S FIELD The piece of ground bought by the priests for the burial of strangers with the money with which Judas betrayed Jesus. The place is called "Akeldama" which translated means "field of blood" (Mt. 27:7, 10). *See also* AKELDAMA.

POUND *See* MONEY and WEIGHTS AND MEASURES

PRAETORIUM, PRAETORIAN GUARD The praetorium was originally the name of the tent of a Roman general. Later it came to be the name of the palace or residence of an important Roman official or even any important house or villa. The praetorian guard, used in the RSV only in Philippians 1:13, might refer to a bodyguard or to the military or imperial court in a praetorium. In the NT the praetorium was the judgment hall (Mt. 27:27; Mk. 15:16; Jn. 18:28, 33; Acts 23:35).

PRAISE The giving of thanks, blessing or glory to living or inanimate things, and especially to men or God (Gen. 29:35; 1 Chron. 16:4; Ps. 146:1; Lk. 19:37; Eph. 1:6-14). Praises often take the form of poems or songs (1 Chron. 16:9; 2 Chron. 29:30). A prominent theme of the NT is the praise of God for spiritual redemption (Eph. 1:5-7).

PRAYER In its most simple form prayer is conversation and intercession with God. One may address a prayer, a request or petition, to a man or men, but here we are concerned with prayers to deity. These may be the recitation or reading of liturgical prayers or they may be spontaneous creations of the heart and mind. Prayer can include petition and intercession, thanks and praise, adoration, and meditation. The Bible does not lay down laws relative to the time and place for prayer nor does it require any particular attitude or position to be assumed by the one who is praying. The word "pray" and its related forms are used well over 400 times in the RSV. This does not include cognate words such as "ask," or "petition."

PREACH, PREACHER, PREACHING This is to herald or forthtell a message committed to one by another. The prophet was a preacher. He passed on the messages given to him by God. In the RSV these words are found only fourteen times in the OT but scores of times in the NT where the role of the OT prophet no longer existed. Modern preaching consists of disseminating the message of the Bible, the Word of God, in any of several different ways.

PRECIOUS STONES AND METALS In the case of the precious stones it is often difficult to make accurate and specific identifications in terms of stones known today. This is frequently true in view of the fact that the paucity of the number of references to them in the Bible does not give enough data for positive identification. Of the precious stones twelve were found in the breastplate of the high priest, starting with Aaron (Ex. 28:19) and in the walls of the New Jerusalem (Rev. 21:19, 20). Some are in both.

PRECIOUS STONES

1. Agate, Carnelian, Chalcedony, Chrysoprase, Jasper, Onyx, Sardonyx, Ruby are varying forms of quartz or chalcedony, a kind of colored quartz with the lustre of wax. Carnelian is red. Chalcedony is often milky or grayish. Chrysoprase is apple-green. The ruby is also red and may be the same as the carnelian or sardius. The sardonyx is a form of onyx and is used only in Revelation 21:10 (Ex. 25:7; 28:17, 19; 39:10; Ezek. 28:13; Gen. 2:12; Rev. 21:19, 20). Some of these are found as only onyx in the Bible and no one of them more than twelve times.

2. Alabaster, Marble. Marble is a recrystalized limestone, a form of calcite or calcium carbonate. Alabaster is another of this group much used in making perfume jars or bottles. There are only three occurrences of the first and five of the second noted in the NIV (Song 5:15; Mt. 26:7; 1 Chron. 29:2).

3. Amethyst, a purple quartz, one that adorned the high priest's breastplate (Ex. 28:19; 39:12; Rev. 21:20).

4. Basalt, not really a precious stone but one of great importance since because of its hardness it was used in grinding. Vessels of various types were made from it. It is a black volcanic rock common in Palestine even if not mentioned in the Bible.

5. Beryl, Emerald, Turquoise. The emerald is a green precious stone of some kind, green beryl, feldspar, or turquoise. Beryl is perhaps a "poor man's" emerald, a green feldspar (Ex. 28:17, 20; Rev. 21:19, 20). The carbuncle may be a green beryl (Ex. 28:17; 39:10; Ezek. 28:13).

6. Chrysolite in modern times is a golden-yellow topaz, one of the high priest's stones in the breastplate (Ex. 28:20; Ezek. 1:16; 28:13; Rev. 21:20).

7. Coral is the hard calcerous skeleton of certain types of marine animals, pinkish or red in color (Job 28:18; Ezek. 27:16).

8. Flint is an impure form of quartz, a very hard stone. From it were made some of man's first implements (Ex. 4:25; Josh. 5:2; Isa. 17:1).

9. Jacinth, one of the stones in the high priest's breastplate and in the walls of the New Jerusalem. It's identity is not certain (Ex. 28:19; Rev. 21:20).

10. Pearl, not a stone but usually listed with them because it was and is an important jewel (Mt. 7:6; 13:45; Rev. 21:21).

11. Sapphire, some consider it a fine form of corundum while others think that in antiquity the Hebrew word behind it referred to lapis lazuli.

12. Lapis lazuli. See footnote at Ex. 24:10. It was blue in color (Ex. 24:10; Rev. 21:19).

13. Topaz was probably a form of quartz. There were various varieties as far as color is concerned but the yellow was the most prized (Ex. 28:17; 39:10; Rev. 21:20).

METALS *1. Copper* and *Bronze* are translations of the one Hebrew word *nechosheth.* The first is a pure metal. Bronze is an alloy of copper and tin while brass (not used in the NIV) is the alloy of copper. Copper was gold and metallic iron and the earliest metal used by man. From the middle of the fourth millennium B.C. (with the exception of the unexplained reference in Genesis 4:22 to Tubal-Cain who worked with both copper and iron prior to the time of the Flood of Noah's days) man began to use copper tools and implements of many types to replace those of stone he had been using (Deut. 8:9; Job 28:2; Lk. 21:2). Copper was usually hammered, while bronze was cast.

2. Bronze, Iron, Lead, Silver, and *Tin* are mentioned in connection with being melted in a furnace or forged (Isa. 44:12; Ezek. 22:18-20). Bellows are noted in Jer. 6:29. These had to be refined or even extracted by heat from ores which contained them in combination with other chemicals. What some refer to as "mercury or quicksilver" is the dross resulting from this refining. Dross was used as a slip on pottery or other objects and in a figurative sense of wicked people (Ps. 119:119; Prov. 25:4; Isa. 1:22, 25; Ezek. 22:18, 19).

3. Gold was one of the earliest natural minerals or metals used in ornaments and for decorating (Gen. 2:11, 12, and many others). Goldsmiths, images covered with gold, cloth woven with gold are noted (Isa. 40:19; 30:22; Ps. 45:13).

4. Iron was smelted from an oxide and carbonate. The ore, hematite, was early used as a paint for pottery (Gen. 4:22; Num. 31:22 and many others). There is one reference to a blacksmith (Isa. 44:12). Its use in the Bible before the Flood is interesting from the point of view of the archaeologist who puts the "iron age" not before 1202 B.C. Perhaps the Genesis reference is to meteoric iron.

5. *Lead* is extracted from galena, lead sulphide. Metallic lead is very rare. See above (Num. 31:22; Ezek. 22:18, 20).

6. *Silver* in earliest times was more costly than gold. This changed only as late as the middle of the first millennium B.C. when the quantity of available refined silver had greatly increased. Silver was used for jewelry, for vessels in palace, tabernacle and temple (Gen. 13:2; Num. 7:13). References to a silversmith and silver overlay are found (Judg. 17:4; Acts 19:24; Isa. 30:22).

7. *Tin* was extracted from an ore, found at first in streambeds, and mined in Roman times (Num. 31:22; Ezek. 22:18, 20; 27:12).

PREDESTINED The word is defined in Acts 4:28, what God predetermined in his plan. In Romans 8:28, 29 Paul made the point that God works for the good of those who love him: he calls according to his purpose those whom he predetermined would be conformed to the image of his Son. God predestines both events and persons, both individuals and groups. This is otherwise called his election and those thus affected are called the elect. *See also* ELECTION.

PREDICT To foretell or prophesy. "The new moons predict what shall befall" (Isa. 47:13). The prophets of the OT frequently spoke about future events. They predicted or foretold what God had revealed to them was to come to pass later (Rom. 9:29; 1 Pet. 1:11). The apostles of the NT also foretold future events but much more rarely (Jude 17). *See also* PROPHET, PROPHECY.

PREFECT Used only in Daniel of some appointed to a position of authority (Dan. 2:48; 3:2, 3, 27; 6:7).

PREPARATION DAY Friday, the day of preparation for the Sabbath or Passover (Mt. 27:62; Mk. 15:42; Lk. 23:54; Jn. 19:14, 31, 42).

PRESIDENTS Like "prefect" above a word appearing only in Daniel (Dan. 6:2-7), referring to top administrators in the realm of the Persian king Darius. There were three, of which Daniel was one.

PRIESTS, PRIESTHOOD The priest is a minister of religion whether pagan, Jewish, or Christian (Gen. 41:45; 31:10; 1 Pet. 2:4, 5). During the time of the wilderness wanderings after the exodus from Egypt, God gave to the Israelites the instructions concerning the founding and procedure for the priestly order in Israel.

There too he chose the tribe of Levi to be the priestly tribe (Ex. 28-29; Lev. 8; Num. 3).

Numbers 8:14-19 is a key section in respect to the call and role of the Levites in the service of God and his people. In ancient Israel there was a high priest (or chief priest), Levites who were priests, and Levites who were not priests but served God and his people in other capacities. That is, all priests were Levites, but not all Levites were priests. On the pre-Mosaic priest *see* MELCHIZEDEK. On Christ as priest *see* CHRIST, WORK OF. The Book of Hebrews treats this latter subject at considerable length (Heb. 6:10—7:17; 1:3; 2:9; 8:5; 7:27; 9:26). There is also in the NT in particular, but not exclusively, a priesthood of believers (Ex. 19:5, 6; 1 Pet. 2:5-9). As the believer takes the message of God to men he executes the function of a priest (Rev. 1:5, 6).

PRINCE, PRINCESS While the princess is the wife or daughter of a king or a chief, the prince may be any person of prominence who has authority. There were princes of nations, princes of cities, and even important merchants were called princes (Gen. 34:2; 2 Kgs. 20:5; Ezek. 28:2; Isa. 23:8). Messiah is called prince, and so are important demons as well as their leaders (Dan. 9:25); Isa. 9:6; Lk. 11:15). The NIV frequently translates it "ruler" (Mt. 2:6; Rev. 1:5).

PRINCIPALITIES These are powerful angels or demons as organized against God and his people (Col. 2:15; Eph. 3:10; 6:12).

PRISCA *See* PRISCILLA

PRISCILLA The wife of Aquila, also called Prisca, who with her husband left Rome and joined Paul after the persecutions in Rome (Acts 18:2; Rom. 16:3).

PRISON A place of incarceration, be it under custody or guard only or in a place of confinement, even a dungeon (Lev. 24:12; 1 Kgs. 22:27; Jer. 37:16). Two special cases of imprisonment are noted, that of former disobedient spirits now, and that of Satan to come (1 Pet. 3:19, 20; Rev. 20:7).

PROCHORUS One of the seven first deacons of the church (Acts 6:5).

PROCONSUL A Roman official of high rank in both the military and civil spheres. Paul converted one and was tried before another (Acts 13:7-12; 18:12).

PROCURATORS *See* PILATE

PROFANE To defile or desecrate by doing the forbidden at a holy place or with the holy things. In the NT to be godless was to be profane (Ex. 20:25; Lev. 18:21; 19:29; Num. 18:32; 1 Tim. 1:8-11).

PROMISE This word and those related to it occur nearly 100 times in the OT of the NIV even while there is no Hebrew word that specifically means "to promise." When God is the subject of the verbs that normally mean to say, to speak, or to swear, and when his people are the recipients of the message, the translators rendered these three words "to promise." "And I promise [I say] that I will bring you up out of the affliction of Egypt" (Ex. 3:17, RSV). And also, "so that the Lord may bring to Abraham what he has promised [spoken] him" (Gen. 18:19, RSV). As God does not change, his word is his promise. Great OT promises were made to or about individuals: to those in the Garden of Eden which included the proto-evangelium, the first promise of redemption from sin (Gen. 3:14-19); to Abraham, reaffirmed to his son and grandson and later to Moses at the time of the constitution of the theocracy, that God would make of him and his seed a great nation through whom all the families of the earth would be blessed, a promise that included both the coming of Messiah for spiritual blessing and redemption and the promise that the land of "Palestine" would perpetually be Israel's (Gen. 18:19; 26:1-5; 17:6-8; 15:18; Jn. 8:56; Gal. 3:16); to King David that his throne would be established forever, never lacking one to sit upon it, a promise Christians see fulfilled in the Messiah Jesus (2 Sam. 7:16; Ps. 89:20, 29-37; Lk. 1:31-33; Acts 2:29-32); and to all Israel that they would be gathered from any part of the world into which they might be driven and brought back to the land of their forefathers and there be made again into a great nation prior to the great Day of the Lord in the end of days (Jer. 23:5-8; Ezek. 11:17; 28:25, 26; 36:24-28; 37:24-28). In the opinion of the Jewish Christians in post NT times this promise to Israel had not at that time been fulfilled. It was, in their opinion, not to come to pass until after the time known as the time when God will have "visited the Gentiles, to take out of them a people for his name" (Acts 15:14-16).

In the NT three words related in form convey the idea of promise. Here too it is God in relation to his people. Foremost among NT promises is the one in which God shows his intention to visit his people in the person of his Son to redeem them from sin. Paul indicates that all God's promises are focused in this particular promise (2 Cor. 1:19, 20; Eph. 3:4-6) and that the promise to Abraham included both the circumcision (Israel according to the flesh) and those who have the faith of Abraham (Gentiles who become related to God through Christ) (Rom. 4:11, 13, 16; Gal. 3:6-9, 13, 14).

Important NT promises include the coming again of Christ and eternal life for the believer (2 Pet. 3:9; Heb. 6:15; Jas. 1:12).

PROPHET,
PROPHETESS,
PROPHECY

Two basic concepts underlie these three words: forthtelling and foretelling. The first is the more basic and frequent. It means that one person becomes the "mouthpiece" for another. This is the Hebrew word *nabi'*. Aaron played this role for his brother Moses (Ex. 7:1). Prior to the time of Samuel a prophet was called a "seer" in Israel, *ro'eh* (1 Sam. 9:9). Later there were schools of prophets and those in them were "sons of the prophets" (2 Kgs. 4:38; 2:3-15). In earliest times there were many prophets who spoke only: Gad, Nathan, Ahijah, Jehu, Elijah, and Elisha being but some of them (1 Sam. 22:5; 1 Kgs. 1:23; 14:2; 16:7; 18:36; 2 Kgs. 9:1). We do not know the names of the authors of the biblical books of Joshua, Judges, Kings, and Samuel but they are commonly known as the former prophets. Their message is one of forthtelling primarily. The writing prophets, in which there is also much foretelling or predictive material in addition to the parts which are delivering other messages from God (forthtelling), are Isaiah, Jeremiah, Ezekiel, and those called the twelve minor prophets, Hosea to Malachi in the common English texts. In all the rest of the OT, and in fact in all the rest of the Bible as well, everything is forthtelling and in that sense prophetic. Scattered through all these other parts predictive material, foretelling, is also to be found. It should not be thought that because a given book is found in the third section of the Hebrew canon it is not prophetic. All of these books meet the requirement of forthtelling and many of them contain sections of foretelling as well. One in each Testament is even put in the apocalyptic class where the foretelling is by way of visions and strange symbolisms, Daniel and Revelation.

The message of the prophets, whether nonwriting or writing, is very generally the same. The first part is rebuke from God for sin and for departure from God's ways. The second part is that because of this sin, God's judgment is to come upon the person or people under condemnation. The third part, and this is true in general only in the cases of rebuke on the people as a whole, is that because of God's love for his people he will bring great blessing upon them after they have learned their lessons in the chastisement and have turned back to God. Such a cycle may be seen in Deuteronomy 28-30.

The prophetess may be only the wife of a prophet or she may be an actual female prophet (Isa. 8:3; Ex. 15:20; 2 Kgs. 22:14; Lk. 2:36).

For examples of predictive prophecy *see* PROMISE. *See also*
DIVINATION.

PROPHETS, BOOKS OF THE MINOR The dating of the writing of these twelve books is uncertain
in some cases and much debated in that of others. There is a
tendency on the part of some scholars to lower the dates to
exilic or even postexilic times. After six of the twelve it is
quite generally agreed that a question mark should be placed:
Joel, Obadiah, Nahum, Habakkuk, Zephaniah, and Malachi.
These do not state in their introductions the name(s) of the
kings of their days, nor are there sufficient historical allusions
in the text of the books to be of much value in dating them.
Traditionally they are all called prophets to the southern
kingdom, to Judah, and with question marks in respect of
their dates are put at about 800, 650, 640, 630, 550 and 430
B.C. respectively. Micah dated himself in the reigns of Jotham,
Ahaz, and Hezekiah, a prophet to Judah. This would be from
about 740 to 700 (Mic. 1:1). Zechariah and Haggai are exactly
datable to the second year of Darius, 520 B.C. They prophesied
to Judah after the exile (Hag. 1:1; Zech. 1:1). The prophets
to the northern kingdom, Israel, were Jonah, Amos, and
Hosea. The first is variously dated between about 750 and
the beginning of the sixth century B.C. Amos stated that
he saw the vision in the days of Uzziah of Judah and Jeroboam
of Israel, two years before an earthquake. The reigns of
these two kings overlapped between about 780 and 740 B.C.
(Amos 1:1). Hosea noted that the word of the Lord came
to him in the days of Uzziah, Jotham, Ahaz, and Hezekiah of
Judah and Jeroboam of Israel. This would give a date of about
the same as Amos (Hos. 1:1).

Some notes on content should be appended. These are in
order of the books themselves in the Bible.

Hosea. The book begins with the account of the prophet's
marriage, which was an illustration of God's dealing with his
people, both the married wife, Israel, and the "bride," the
Church (Hos. 1-3; Rom. 9:25, 26). The rest of the book
is concerned with noting the sin of God's people, impending
judgment, exhortations to repentance, and God's love, the
last in chapter 11.

Joel. A plague of locusts is discussed and used as the basis
for urging the people to repent and to give a promise of
blessing if they will. In the second cycle we are told about
God's judging the nations and of judgment being followed by
the blessing of deliverance for Israel.

Amos. After a discussion of God's judgments on nations
around Judah and Israel and upon these two themselves, the
prophet launched into a description of God's coming judgments

and the blessings that will follow them for his OT people. The famous passage 9:11-15 is used in part by James in Acts 15:16, 17 to settle the discussion at that Jerusalem Council, and to show that God had a future for Israel, for Jews, at the conclusion of the "church age."

Obadiah was a prophecy on Edom's judgment by God and subsequent blessing.

Jonah contains the famous incidents connected with this prophet's running away from God, his return and trip to Nineveh to deliver God's message there.

Micah predicted God's judgment on Samaria and Jerusalem, the return from the captivity, and God's ultimate blessings on his people in the end of days. One of the well-known predictions on the birth of Christ is found in 5:2.

Nahum predicted the destruction of Nineveh.

Habakkuk concerned himself in the beginning with the righteousness of God in punishing people, follows it with a message of doom on the Chaldeans, and ends with the beautiful prayer of chapter 3.

Zephaniah concerned himself with God's judgment on a number of peoples and God's promise to send great deliverance through the messianic age later.

Haggai urged the people on in their rebuilding of the postexilic temple.

Zechariah commenced with six chapters of visions, some of them highly symbolical. Chapters 7 and 8 are concerned with the keeping of the fasts now that the people are back in Jerusalem and the fact that the fasts will become feasts and all nations will receive the blessing (8:20-23). The final six chapters are concerned with God's judging the nations but his having mercy on his people when the Prince of Peace will come.

Malachi described God's love for his people but complained about the negligence of people and priests and called them back to the Law. The book ends with a prophecy that Elijah is to return before the Day of the Lord.

PROPITIATION *See* CHRIST, WORK OF

PROSELYTE The concept is much earlier than the only occurrences of the word in the NT would indicate (Mt. 23:15; Acts 2:10; 6:5). In these cases the reference is to Gentile proselytes to Judaism in pre-Christian times. The Greek word used in these three cases is the word the LXX uses with which to translate the Hebrew word *ger* which literally means "sojourner," one for some reason taking refuge with a foreign people. At some time before the rise of the NT the word changed in meaning from immigrant sojourner to convert.

PROSTITUTE Several Hebrew and Greek words are thus rendered in the NIV. Religious prostitution was practiced at pagan shrines by male and female prostitutes and this is noted in the Bible (Deut. 23:17; 1 Kgs. 14:24). The law of Israel forbade parents to force their daughters into this practice, its priests to marry them, or their wages to be brought into the house of God (Lev. 19:29; 21:7; Deut. 23:18). Prostitutes could be punished by being burned or stoned to death. Promiscuity was forbidden both men and women. The penalty was death (Deut. 22:20-29; Lev. 21:9). The word "dog" is used of male prostitutes and sodomites in other passages as well. *See also* ADULTERY and FORNICATION.

PROVERB A saying, often very short but not necessarily so, pithy and colorful, expressing a commonly observed fact or piece of wisdom. Doubtless as long as man has lived, wisdom was passed on in this way, but samples in writing become numerous only with the beginning of the second millennium B.C. In the Bible such sayings are widely scattered but an important collection is, of course, the Book of Proverbs. S. H. Blank in *Interpreter's Dictionary of the Bible* (Abingdon, 1976) has used a pointed and delightful description, "capsulated wisdom."

PROVERBS, BOOK OF In Proverbs 1:1, 10:1, and 25:1 the words appear "the proverbs of Solomon." In the third of the references there is added, "copied by the men of Hezekiah king of Judah." At the head of chapter 30 we find "the sayings of Agur" and at the head of chapter 31 "the sayings of King Lemuel." At 22:17 and 24:23 we find "the sayings of the wise," which are believed to cover some eighty-two verses, or a little less than two and one-half chapters out of the book of thirty-one chapters. It is suggested that these seven headings indicate that the Book of Proverbs is a collection of various sets of proverbs, collections attributed or ascribed to the various persons mentioned, and that these persons are not themselves the authors. Those who take this point of view usually suggest that the compiling into the present form of the collection took place at the earliest not long before 685 B.C. even though some of the individual proverbs may have been collected or even composed by Solomon himself after 950 B.C. The more traditional view is that while we do not know who Agur or Lemuel were, and even "the wise," yet "the proverbs of Solomon" do indicate authorship and that there is not sufficient objective evidence to deny it. There was, obviously, later collecting and perhaps even editing, but the basic work is the collecting or composing or some of both by King Solomon who prayed for and was given by God a wise and discerning mind (1 Kgs. 3:9-12).

In the first nine chapters there are found longer and shorter treatments of the theme which contrasts sin and righteousness. Here in an extended passage wisdom is personified as a righteous woman and sin as a harlot. The section from 10:1 to 22:16 is a collection of one verse proverbs. Here in addition to synonymous parallelism as the poetic style we find an abundance of antithetic parallelism. *See* POETRY. In 22:17 to the end of chapter 29 there are again proverbs of varying lengths but the basic message is the same. It is in this part that we find the proverbs so much like those in Egyptian writing. Finally we find the chapters with the words of Agur and Lemuel, in some respects like what precedes as far as content is concerned, but with an interesting stylistic form scattered through the first and extolling of a good wife in the second (Prov. 30:18, 19, 21-23; 31:10-31).

PROVIDENCE The Westminster Assembly defined God's works of providence as his "most holy, wise, and powerful preserving and governing all his creatures and all their actions." In post-OT times the term "the divine providence" was a common term for God (Dan. 4:34, 35; Ps. 37:23, 24; Heb. 1:3).

PROVINCE A word appearing almost exclusively in the postexilic books of Ezra, Nehemiah, Esther, and Daniel to refer to Babylonian or Persian administrative districts. It is found in the NT in the same sense of district (Acts 23:34; 25:1). In the NT the word district is used in the normal broad English sense of area.

PRUNING HOOK A blade of iron attached to a handle and used for cutting off unwanted branches or shoots from a vine (Lev. 25:3, 4; Isa. 2:4; Joel 3:10).

PSALMS, BOOK OF On poetic style *see* POETRY. On the titles see next entry, and SONGS OF ASCENT. In the titles of many of the psalms names of individuals are found. Traditionally these have been considered the authors of those psalms and the Hebrew particle *le* in front of the names has been called the *lamed* of authorship. The name of David appears at the head of seventy-three. Two which do not have that name, or any other, at their head are ascribed to David in the NT (Ps. 2; Acts 4:25; Ps. 95; Heb. 4:7). Four that do carry his name in the title are authenticated as Davidic in the NT (Ps. 16; 32; 69; 110; Acts 2:25; Rom. 4:6; Acts 1:16; Rom. 11:9; Lk. 20:42;

Acts 2:34). Furthermore no psalm bearing any other name in the title or containing any late historical allusion is ascribed to David or associated with him in the NT. These several lines of evidence, together with our knowledge of the man himself as a musician and poet, point to Davidic authorship for these particular psalms. Other names appearing in the titles are: Asaph (50, 73-83); Solomon (72, 127); Heman (88); Ethan (89); Moses (90); the sons of Korah (42-49, 84, 85, 87).

The collection of 150 psalms is divided into five books, each separated from the other by a short doxology at the end, "Blessed be the Lord, the God of Israel, from everlasting to everlasting! Amen and Amen!" being one of the forms (Ps. 1-41; 42-72; 73-89; 90-106; 107-150). Book I consists of personal and individual prayers all but the first of which are ascribed to David by either the heading, the NT or the LXX. Books II and III are largely national prayers of which only 66, 67, and 71 are anonymous. The last two books are largely liturgical psalms. While some of these are ascribed to David the majority are anonymous.

Numerous attempts to classify the psalms as to content and use have been made. These will be found by comparing the various encyclopedias and commentaries. In brief summary here we may note among the various types the following: (1) prayers for blessing, protection or actual help in various types of adversity, and for the needs of others (102, 86, 88, 21, 67); (2) penitential prayers, requesting forgiveness (not confessions as such) and psalms of praise for blessings received (6, 32, 145, 104); (3) psalms in which the author confesses his beliefs in various items of doctrine including God's sovereignty, or those in which he expresses his worship (97, 136, 147, 145); (4) a special class called imprecatory in which the writer calls on God to punish his enemies (109, 59); (5) psalms extolling God's revelation, his Word, his Law (1, 19, 119); (6) psalms of the wisdom literature type (37, 49, 78). One special category should be mentioned in addition, the Messianic. The NT declares David to be a prophet and that not only in the sense of forthtelling as in all of his psalms (Ps. 16, 110; Acts 2:29-31, 34, 35). That others of his psalms are also predictive is evidenced by the use of excerpts from them in the NT where the predictive meaning is pointed out (Ps. 2 cf. Acts 4:24-30; Ps. 22 cf. Jn. 19:23, 24).

PSALMS, TITLES OF In the titles of the psalms there are some seventeen words whose exact meaning is debated or unclear. Twelve of these are transliterated because of the uncertainty as to just what they do signify. Three can be translated but teach us nothing that is helpful with any degree of certainty. Two cannot be translated.

1. Choirmaster, Hebrew *menatstseah,* is found at the head of fifty-five psalms (Ps. 4, 5, 6, 39). Some suggest these belong to a "Director's collection." Others think the word refers to the character of these psalms: God's blessing or victory is indicated by them; or they are triumph songs. Perhaps it is most probable that the word refers to the head of the musicians or to the master of the religious ceremonies where they were used. This last is inferred from Psalm 39:1 where Jeduthun may be the name of one such.

2. Lilies.

3. Do not destroy. See number 10 below.

4. Doe of the morning.

5. Dove on Far-off Terebinths. See number 10 below.

6. Jeduthun. See last sentence of number 1 above. Some suggest another alternative, namely that the word is a reference to some expression of confession or penitence (Ps. 39).

7. Maskil. It is suggested that psalms so indicated are either meditations or teaching psalms (Ps. 74-79).

8. Miktam. Some suggest "meaning unknown." Others note that they all seem to be laments and suggest they were connected with atonement rituals (Ps. 16, 56-60).

9. Shiggaion. Some suggest that the reference is to a religious or cultic practice the nature of which is unknown. Others suggest a choral song of a wild, vehement character, usually irregular in form (Ps. 7).

10. "Cue Words." With the three exceptions noted above in numbers 3-5 all these are transliterated only from the Hebrew. One theory is that they are names of ancient melodies to which the particular psalm might be sung. Others think they are musical instructions of some unknown kind. In some cases below a third alternative is suggested.

(1) *Alamoth.* The third alternative suggested is that the music is to be rendered "flutingly" or perhaps with a high tone (Ps. 5).
(2) *Do not destroy,* number 3 above (Ps. 57-59, 75).
(3) *Dove on Far-off Terebinths,* number 5 above. One suggests also the possibility of some connection with the dove sacrifices (Ps. 56).
(4) *Eduth.*
(5) *Gittith* (Ps. 8, 81).
(6) *Doe of the Morning,* number 4 above. Also possibly connected with some sacrifice (Ps. 22).

PTOLEMAIS *See* ACCO

PUAH   1. A Hebrew midwife in Egypt at the time of the birth of Moses (Ex. 1:15).

2. A son of Issachar also called Puvah (1 Chron. 7:1; Gen. 46:13).

3. One of the minor judges of Israel (Judg. 10:1).

PUBLIUS   A Roman official in Malta in Paul's visit there (Acts 28:7ff.).

PUDENS   A Christian who sent greetings to Timothy by Paul's letter (2 Tim. 4:21).

PUL   An alternate name for Tiglath-Pileser king of Assyria (2 Kgs. 15:19).

PUNISHMENT   Several types of punishment are noted in the Bible. The most frequently mentioned is death for: idolatry, adultery, blasphemy, witchcraft, kidnapping, reviling a parent, and other offenses. This could be by stoning, burning, by the sword, or by being sawn asunder. As additional disgrace or curse the dead body could be hung until the setting of the sun on the day of the execution (Lev. 20:2, 10, 14; 24:16; Ex. 22:18; 21:15-17; 32:25-28; Deut. 22:23, 24; Heb. 11:37). Other forms of punishment short of death included: stripes or lashes, being cut with metal, being punished in kind by fine or by restitution (Deut. 22:18, 19; 25:2, 4; 2 Cor. 11:24; 2 Sam. 12:31; Ex. 21:23-25, 30). Punishment was usually meted out by the courts and their appointees or by the avenger of blood after the courts had declared the person guilty. God frequently meted out punishment directly (Gen. 4:9-16).

Eternal fire, destruction, punishment are noted in the NT for those who reject God's love in Christ (Mt. 25:31-46; Jn. 3:16-19). *See* ABODE OF THE DEAD.

PUNITES   Descendants of the tribe of Issachar (Num. 26:23).

PUNON   A stopping place (197-004) in the Israelites' wilderness wandering after their leaving Sinai (Num. 33:42, 43).

PUR   A foreign word meaning "lot." Lots were cast in order to obtain oracles. This was done in Persia to determine the most propitious time for the murder of the Jews there by Haman in the days of Queen Esther (Esth. 3:7; 9:24-26). Today Purim (the plural in the Hebrew form) is the Jewish festival each spring to commemorate the deliverance through the work of Mordecai and Esther.

PURAH   A servant of Judge Gideon (Judg. 7:10, 11).

PURIFICATION The law of Moses required ceremonial purification after contact with the dead, after childbirth, and after having had certain diseases (Num. 19:11-19; Lev. 12:1-8, 13, 14). Mark 7:3, 4 gives a good picture of the attitude of the time. The NT also emphasizes the need for purity but gives a greater emphasis upon inner purity, purity of thought and motive (Mt. 5:27ff.; 1 Cor. 5:9-13; 6:18-20). Ritual washing, bathing, or baptizing were considered important. *See* BAPTISM and CLEAN AND UNCLEAN.

PURIM *See* PUR, CALENDAR, FEASTIVALS

PURITY *See* CLEAN AND UNCLEAN and PURIFICATION

PURPLE *See* COLORS

PURSE Baglike containers of leather or woven material drawn together at the neck by a cord or a leather thong and used for a receptacle for money or its equivalent (Prov. 1:14; Isa. 46:6; Lk. 22:35, 36).

PURSLANE *See* PLANTS, PERFUMES, AND SPICES

PUT 1. The third son of Ham (Gen. 10:6).
2. A geographical area thought to be in Libya (Nah. 3:9; Jer. 46:9).

PUTEOLI The Italian seaport near Naples where Paul landed on his imprisonment journey to Rome (Acts 28:13).

PUTHITES A family descended from Judah (1 Chron. 2:53).

PUTIEL The father-in-law of Eleazar, son of Aaron (Ex. 6:25).

PUVAH *See* PUAH

PYRRHUS A man of Berea whose son accompanied Paul as he left Greece (Acts 20:4).

QUAIL *See* BIRDS, 4

QUART *See* WEIGHTS AND MEASURES

QUARTUS A Christian who sent greetings by Paul's letter to the church in Rome (Rom. 16:23).

QUEEN Three types are of note in the Bible: the wife of a king, the mother of a king, and one who rules in her own person. In the latter category are the well known Queen of Sheba in Solomon's day, the Queen of the Ethiopians in early Christian times, and Athaliah who ruled Judah after the death of her husband (1 Kgs. 10:1, 4, 10-13; Acts 8:27; 2 Kgs. 11:1, 3). Among the better known wives of kings are Vashti and Esther of Persia (Esth. 1:9; 2:22). Since the mother of the king is mentioned so frequently in the Bible we cannot but conclude that this person extended great influence over the reigning monarchs (1 Kgs. 2:19; 14:21; 15:2).

QUEEN OF HEAVEN A female deity and object of worship mentioned as one to whom the Hebrew women of the time of Jeremiah made offerings. Some identify her with Ashtoreth, Ishtar and Venus, goddesses of love and fertility in Canaan, Babylon, and Rome (Jer. 7:18; 13:18; 29:2; 44:17-25).

QUIRINIUS The governor of Syria at the time of the birth of Jesus (Lk. 2:2).

QUIVER *See* ARMS AND ARMOR

R

RAAMA, RAAMAH The grandson of Ham (Gen. 10:7; 1 Chron. 1:9; Ezek. 27:22).

RAAMIAH One who returned from the Babylonian captivity with Zerubbabel, also called Reelaiah (Neh. 7:7; Ezra 2:2).

RAAMSES *See* EGYPT

RABBAH 1. A city (238-151) of the Ammonites, modern Amman in Jordan, and before that Philadelphia. The iron bedstead of King Og of Bashan, measuring thirteen and a half feet long by six feet wide, was kept there (Deut. 3:11). David conquered it and later the prophets have much to say about it (1 Chron. 20:1; Jer. 49:2, 3; Ezek. 25:5; Amos 1:14).

2. Rabbah in Judah is the Rubute of the Amarna Letters which was formerly thought to be another name for Beth Shemesh but now is identified with a tell between Gezer and the entrance to the valley ("the corridor") leading to Jerusalem (Josh. 15:60).

RABBAT AMMON *See* GEOGRAPHY OF THE HOLY LAND

RABBI, RABBONI In OT times these were names for teachers, particularly teachers of the law. In the NT they were used as titles of honor in addition. Translated they mean "my master" (Mt. 23:7-8; Jn. 1:38; 9:2; 20:16).

RABBIT *See* BEASTS, 5

RABBITH An unidentified town in the tribal area of Issachar thought by some to be the same as DABERATH (Josh. 19:20).

RABSARIS The title of an unidentified type of Assyrian official but thought by some to be a designation for eunuchs at the court (2 Kgs. 18:17; Jer. 39:3, 13).

RABSHAKEH The title for a type of administrative court official in the Assyrian and Babylonian court (2 Kgs. 18:17—19:8; Isa. 36:2—37:8).

RACAL An unidentified city in the tribal area of Judah to which David sent captured Amalekite booty (1 Sam. 30:29).

RACHEL The younger sister of Leah and second wife of Jacob for whom Jacob served a total of fourteen years and mother of Joseph and Benjamin (Gen. 29; 30:23ff.; 35:16ff.). She died in childbirth and was buried near Bethlehem (Gen. 35:19, 20). As a mother in Israel she is pictured as rising from the dead to weep for her children going into captivity. It is this that the NT considers prophetic of the slaughter of the children in Bethlehem by Herod at the time of the birth of Jesus (Jer. 31:15; Mt. 2:18).

RADDAI A brother of David (1 Chron. 2:14).

RAHAB 1. A harlot of Jericho who protected the two Israelite spies in the days of Joshua (Josh. 2:1ff.; 6:17ff.).

2. The mother of Boaz and mentioned in the genealogy of Jesus (Mt. 1:5).

3. *See also* BEASTS, 9 and DEITIES

RAHAM A descendant of Caleb (1 Chron. 2:44).

RAIN This varies from thirty plus inches per year in the hill country of Palestine-Syria to zero to four inches in the southern part of Palestine, the modern Negeb, the Sinai peninsula and Egypt, and in the desert area to the east of the Jordan Rift and south of Syria. The heavy rains come in late November through early March. Before and after this period come the usually lighter early and latter rains respectively, the former coming in October-November and the latter in March-April. The early rains soften the sunbaked hard ground and prepare it for plowing while the lighter latter rains bring the crop to maturity (Joel 2:23; Jer. 5:24; Deut. 11:14). The absence of rain produced famine in a country so completely dependent upon it and its withholding by God was a terrible punishment (Deut. 28:22-24). God used drought in the punishment of Ahab, Jezebel and the false prophets (1 Kgs. 17:1; Jas. 5:17-18).

RAINBOW God used the rainbow after Noah, his family and the animals came out of the ark as a sign that he would never again destroy the whole earth with a flood (Gen. 9:8-17). Ezekiel likens the glory of God to the beauty of a rainbow and John on Patmos saw God's throne encircled by one (Ezek. 1:28; Rev. 4:3).

RAISINS *See* PLANTS, PERFUMES, AND SPICES

RAKEM A descendant of Manasseh (1 Chron. 7:16).

RAKKATH A city (199-245) in the tribal area of Naphtali probably under or near modern Tiberias (Josh. 19:35).

RAKKON An unidentified town in the tribal area of Dan (Josh. 19:46).

RAM 1. An ancestor of David and Jesus (Ruth 4:19; Mt. 1:3, 4; Lk. 3:33).

2. The son of Jerahmeel of Judah and nephew of number 1 above (1 Chron. 2:9, 25, 27).

3. The name of the family from which Elihu, one of Job's friends, came (Job 32:2).

4. The male of the sheep, a sacrificial animal (Lev. 5:15; 6:6).

5. On battering ram *see* ARMS AND ARMOR.

RAMAH 1. An unidentified town in the tribal area of Asher (Josh. 19:29).

2. A town (172-140) in the tribal area of Benjamin just north of Jerusalem, frequently mentioned in the accounts of Samuel, David, Saul, Asa and postexilic groups (1 Sam. 15:34; 19:18; 2 Chron. 16:1ff.; Neh. 7:30). Rachel's weeping for her children lost in the captivity was heard in Ramah (Jer. 31:15; Mt. 2:18). *See* RAMATHAIM ZUPHIM.

3. A fortified city (187-259) in the tribal area of Naphtali in the hills of lower Galilee (Josh. 19:36).

4. An unidentified town of Simeon in the tribal area of Judah; also called Ramoth (Josh. 19:8; 1 Sam. 30:27).

RAMATHAIM ZUPHIM, RAMATHAIM-ZOPHIM A place in the hill country of Ephraim where Samuel the prophet was born (1 Sam. 1:1). In all other references to Samuel in the NIV his city is called Ramah. In 1:1 his parents leave their home in Ramathaim Zuphim but return to their home in Ramah in 1:19. *See* RAMAH, 2.

RAMATH LEHI *See* LEHI

RAMATH MIZPAH *See* MIZPAH

RAMESES *See* EGYPT

RAMIAH One who married a foreign wife during the exilic times (Ezra 10:25).

RAMOTH A Levitical town (199-222) in the tribal area of Issachar also called Jarmuth and Remeth (1 Chron. 6:73; Josh. 21:29; 19:21). The Crusaders Belvoir was built here; called today Kokab el-Hawa and Kokhav-Hayarden; recently excavated.

RAMOTH GILEAD A fortified town (244-210) in Gilead in Transjordan, a city of refuge for the Israelites (1 Kgs. 4:13; 22:3; 2 Kgs. 8:28).

RANSOM The price for the redemption of a slave or reparation for damages (Ex. 21:30; Lev. 19:20; 1 Sam. 14:45). In the NT the word is connected with the work of Christ in his life and death by which he redeemed his people and gave them salvation (Mt. 20:28; 1 Tim. 2:6; Rev. 5:9).

RAPHA A son of Benjamin (1 Chron. 8:2).

RAPHAH A descendant of Saul also called Rephaiah (1 Chron. 8:37; 9:43).

RAPHU The father of the representative from Benjamin among the twelve spies (Num. 13:9).

RAT *See* BEASTS, 5

RAVEN *See* BIRDS, 8

RAZOR A shaving instrument, first made of flint, then of bronze and finally of iron. A Nazirite as long as his vow was on him was not allowed to let a razor come on him and the priests could not shave the corners of their beards (Num. 6:5; Lev. 21:5). The word is also used symbolically: of the tongue as a sharp razor, and of punishment by a foreign power (Ps. 52:2; Isa. 7:20).

REAIAH 1. A descendant of Judah also called Haroeh (1 Chron. 4:2; 2:52).

2. A descendant of Reuben (1 Chron. 5:5).

3. The ancestor of some temple servants who came back from the Babylonian captivity with Zerubbabel (Ezra 2:47).

REBA A king of Midian who was killed by the Israelites in Moses' time (Num. 31:8; Josh. 13:21).

REBEKAH, REBECCA The wife of Isaac and mother of Esau and Jacob (Gen. 22:23; 24:15-30ff.; Rom. 9:10-12).

RECAB *See* RECHAB

RECAH An unidentified place in the tribal area of Judah (1 Chron. 4:12).

RECHAB, RECAB 1. One of the two murderers of Ishbosheth (2 Sam. 4:2, 5, 9).

2. The founder of the order known as Rechabites (2 Kgs. 10:15; Jer. 35:6ff.).

RECONCILIATION *See* CHRIST, WORK OF

RECORDER A high ranking official in the royal courts of Israel, more than just a royal scribe (2 Sam. 8:16; 2 Kgs. 18:18; Isa. 36:22).

REDEEMER, REDEMPTION *See* CHRIST, WORK OF

RED HEIFER The ashes of a red heifer were used in the ceremonial cleansing of one defiled by contact with the dead (Num. 19:2, 9, 20, 21).

RED SEA Literally, "sea of reeds," *yam suph.* The word "red" in the words "red sea" came by way of the Greek translation and the Latin, but where they got it is unknown. Originally it would seem to have applied to the Egyptian "Papyrus Lake" near Baal-zephon but later apparently spread to include the entire Persian Gulf and even the Indian Ocean (Ex. 13:18; 15:22; Ps. 136:13-15). God miraculously took the Israelites through it but the army of Egypt was drowned in it. Elath, where Solomon built his trading fleet and Ezion Geber were on the "Red Sea" (1 Kgs. 9:26). But this was obviously a different place from that crossed earlier by the Israelites in their exodus from Egypt.

REED 1. *See* PLANTS, PERFUMES, AND SPICES

2. The stalk of a reed was used as a measuring rod, and was six cubits in length (Ezek. 42:16-19).

REELAIAH One who returned from the Babylonian captivity with Zerubbabel; also called Raamiah (Ezra 2:2; Neh. 7:7).

REFINING Refers to two different processes in the Bible. One is the filtering or straining of liquids, such as wine, and the other is the process of liquifying a metal and removing the sludge or dross (Isa. 25:6; Ps. 12:6). It is also used of the purifying of people (Mal. 3:3).

REFRESHING, TIMES OF Noted only in Acts 3:19 and referring to a spiritual time of blessing coming from the Lord when people turn to the Messiah.

REFUGE, CITIES OF Three cities on either side of the Jordan River which were set aside as places to which the accidental killer of a human being could flee for refuge from the avenger of blood until his case could be heard by the courts. These were: Bezer, Ramoth Gilead, and Golan in the East and Kedesh, Shechem, and Hebron in the West (Josh. 20:7-8).

REGEM A descendant of Caleb (1 Chron. 2:47).

REGEM-MELECH One of those sent by the people of Bethel to inquire of the Lord about keeping the fasts (Zech. 7:2).

REGENERATION *See* CHRIST, WORK OF

REHABIAH A grandson of Moses, a Levite (1 Chron. 23:17).

REHOB 1. A town (177-280) in Galilee, the northernmost place to which the twelve spies penetrated, near Dan, the same as Beth Rehob (Num. 13:21; 2 Sam. 10:6-8).

2. A town (166-256) in the tribal area of Asher (Josh. 19:28-30).

3. The father of a king of Zobah (2 Sam. 8:3, 12).

4. One who signed the covenant with Nehemiah (Neh. 10:11).

REHOBOAM *See* KINGS OF JUDAH AND ISRAEL

REHOBOTH 1. An unidentified city in Edom and the home of one of their kings by the name of Saul (Gen. 36:37; 1 Chron. 1:48).

2. An unidentified place near Beersheba where Isaac dug a well after he left Abimelech of Gerar (Gen. 26:7-22).

REHOBOTH IR A city in Assyria (Gen. 10:11).

REHUM 1. One who came back from the Babylonian captivity with Zerubbabel, also called Nehum (Ezra 2:2; Neh. 7:7).

2. A commander in Jerusalem in the time of Ezra who wrote a letter against Jerusalem to the Persian king Artaxerxes (Ezra 8:4, 5).

3. One who helped to repair the walls of Jerusalem in the days of Nehemiah (Neh. 3:17).

4. One who signed the covenant with Nehemiah (Neh. 10:25).

5. A priest who returned from the Babylonian captivity with Zerubbabel (Neh. 12:3).

REI One who backed Solomon for the throne against Adonijah (1 Kgs. 1:8).

REKEM 1. A city (192-971) in Edom.

2. A king of Midian killed by the Israelites in the time of Moses (Num. 31:8).

3. A descendant of Caleb (1 Chron. 2:43, 44).

4. An unidentified city in the tribal area of Benjamin (Josh. 18:27).

RELEASE, YEAR OF This was the Year of Jubilee, the year when they proclaimed liberty throughout the land to all the inhabitants. It recurred every fifty years (Lev. 25:10; Ezek. 46:17). In this year a Jew held as a slave by another Jew or property held temporarily by a Jew who was not the original owner was set free or returned. Some, apparently based on an early erroneous translation, consider the seventh or sabbatical year as a year of release also. That was merely a year of remission of debts (Deut. 15:1-3).

REMALIAH The father of King Pekah of Israel (2 Kgs. 15:25, 27, 30).

REMEMBRANCE, BOOK OF Books to contain reminders, records, were kept in antiquity, especially at the royal courts (Ex. 17:14; Esth. 3:1) and there was a set of officers called "recorders." But one case is of special importance, God's book of remembrance noted in Malachi 3:16. In this book were recorded the names of those who feared (believed) the Lord and thought on his name. Some think this is a roster of believers analogous to the book of life of the NT. *See also* RECORDERS.

REMETH *See* RAMOTH and YARMUTH

REMNANT Something that is left over. In the Bible it frequently refers to the remnant of a community of people, the remainder upon whom the hope of future rebuilding and growth depend (Gen. 45:7; 2 Kgs. 19:29-31; Isa. 10:20-22). One of the major eschatological themes of the OT is that God will regather his remnant from all countries where they have been scattered and bring them back to the land of their fathers and there again make them into a great nation which will be his spiritual people and witness to the world (Mic. 2:12; Zech. 8:11-13; Isa. 11:11). *See also* PROPHET, PROPHETESS, PROPHECY. Paul referred to Christian converts from Judaism in his day as a "remnant, chosen by grace" (Rom. 11:5).

REND, OF CLOTHES This was a sign of mourning, sorrow, or repentance practiced to this day by members of the Jewish community (2 Sam. 3:31; Jer. 36:24). Under certain circumstances priests were not allowed to show this sign of mourning (Lev. 10:6; 21:10). The prophet invited the people to return to God by rending their hearts and not their clothes (Joel 2:13).

REPENTANCE *See* CHRIST, WORK OF

REPHAEL A Levite gatekeeper in the days of David (1 Chron. 26:7).

REPHAH A descendant of Ephraim (1 Chron. 7:25).

REPHAIAH 1, 2, and 3. Descendants of Judah, Simeon, and Issachar, respectively (1 Chron. 3:31; 4:42; 7:2).

4. *See* RAPHAH.

5. One who helped to repair the wall of Jerusalem in the days of Nehemiah (Neh. 3:9).

REPHAIM, VALLEY OF REPHAIM 1. A Hebrew word sometimes translated "the dead" or "shades." With the exception of the reference in Isaiah 26:19 their case would seem to be a hopeless one (Ps. 88:10; Prov. 9:18; Isa. 14:9; 26:14).

2. An ethnic term referring to the pre-Israelite inhabitants of Palestine and sometimes in both the RSV and the KJV translated "giants" (1 Chron. 20:4-8; Deut. 2:11).

3. The Valley of the Rephaim (sometimes called the Valley of the Giants) is a fine agricultural area near Jerusalem on the SW side. The Philistines frequently tried to take it from Israel (Josh. 15:8; 18:16; 2 Sam. 5:18-22; Isa. 17:5).

REPHAN *See* DEITIES

REPHIDIM A stopping place for the Israelites on their exodus route from Egypt, not identified with certainty. Here Moses struck the rock and secured water, the Israelites defeated the Amalekites, and possibly it is also here that Jethro met and counseled Moses (Ex. 17:1, 8; 18:5).

REPTILE *See* BEASTS, 1

REQUITE Positively to repay for a service and negatively to repay for a wrong (Deut. 32:41; 2 Sam. 3:39; Ps. 62:12). An interesting case of requiting good for evil is the Messianic reference in Psalm 41:10 compared with John 3:18.

RESEN An unidentified city in Assyria (Gen. 10:12).

RESHEPH A descendant of Ephraim (1 Chron. 7:25).

REST A word with many references in the Bible: God rested from his work of creating; the seventh day was to be a day of rest; the land was to have rest from farming every seventh year; the Israelites were promised rest in the land of Canaan; Christ promised a spiritual rest of soul for those who believe in him; and Christ has a rest for the people of God yet future (Gen. 2:2; Ex. 16:23; Lev. 25:4; Deut. 12:9; Mt. 11:28; Heb. 4:1-11).

RESURRECTION In this article we speak only of rising from the dead. In the biblical concept man in a disembodied state is incomplete. The departed soul is waiting for the redemption of the body. At the resurrection of the body the two are joined again for eternity (Rom. 8:23; 2 Cor. 5:3ff.). The only clear reference to resurrection in the OT is in Daniel 12:2: "Multitudes who sleep in the dust of the earth will awake: some to everlasting life, others to shame and everlasting contempt." There are a few other OT passages which point in this direction but on the whole the OT is silent on this particular subject (Ps. 16:10ff.; cf. Acts 2:25ff.; Ps. 49:14ff.; Job 19:25-27). The resurrection of Christ is the capstone of all his ministry and his teaching. It is by that fact that he is declared to be the Son of God with power (Rom. 1:4). His resurrection was the necessary complement to his atoning death (Rom. 4:24, 25). *See* CHRIST, LIFE OF; CHRIST, WORK OF; and PAUL, LIFE AND TEACHINGS OF.

In the NT one of the simplest statements is "there will be a resurrection of both the righteous and the wicked" (Acts 24:15). In fact, these two resurrections are described separated in time by 1000 years (Rev. 20:4-15; 1 Thess. 4:16; 1 Cor. 15:23, 24). The certainty of resurrection and the nature of it are described by Paul at great length in 1 Corinthians 15:12-54. Our resurrection bodies will be like our Lord's after resurrection (1 Jn. 3:2; Phil. 3:20, 21).

RETURN, FROM *See* CHRONOLOGY; PERSIA; EZRA, BOOK OF; and NEHEMIAH,
EXILE AND BOOK OF
CAPTIVITY

REU A descendant of Shem (Gen. 11:18-21; Lk. 3:35), one in the genealogy of Jesus.

REUBEN The eldest son of Jacob (Gen. 29:32). He saved Joseph when some of his other brothers wished to kill him and later offered his own sons as security that he would bring Benjamin safely back from Egypt (Gen. 37:19-22; 42:37). The tribe settled in Transjordan after the exodus from Egypt (Num. 32:1-5, 33).

REUEL 1. A son of Esau (Gen. 36:4.)

2. The father-in-law of Moses. *See* JETHRO and HOBAB (Ex. 2:18).

3. The father of the leader of the people of Gad during the wilderness wanderings (Num. 2:14).

4. A descendant of Benjamin (1 Chron 9:8).

REUMAH The concubine of Nahor the brother of Abraham (Gen. 22:24).

REVEAL, The making known of truth. God makes himself known to
REVELATION man by and in the person and work of his Son, Jesus Christ, in nature, and by his Spirit speaking to holy men of old who recorded what was revealed to them in a historical document that became known as the Scriptures or the Bible (2 Cor. 5:19; 1 Tim. 3:16; Col. 1:15; Jn. 14:8-9; Heb. 1:1, 2; Ps. 19:1ff.; 2 Pet. 1:20, 21; 2 Tim. 3:16; 2 Pet. 3:15, 16; 1 Tim. 5:18). *See also* SCRIPTURE.

REVELATION, The last book of the Bible. Indications in the book itself and
BOOK OF in early Christian tradition show that it was written by the Apostle John on the island of Patmos on the coast of Asia Minor after the fall of Jerusalem in A.D. 70. The book records a series of visions which Jesus Christ gave to John through an angel. The book is both a revelation *from* Jesus Christ and a revelation *of* Jesus Christ. The major divisions and ideas of the book are:

Chapter 1. Heading of the book; John's greeting to the seven churches of Asia; the initial vision of the majestic coming again of Jesus Christ.

Chapters 2 and 3. Seven letters from Christ to the churches of Asia. These were churches established during Paul's ministry about the years 50-56 when all Asia heard the gospel (Acts 19:10). Paul's work, followed by John's ministry after the fall of Jerusalem, established these strong churches and helps us to understand the church history of the following centuries. The early church councils took place in Asia Minor and some of the best recorded events of early church history are linked to people and places of Asia Minor: Papias of Hierapolis, Ignatius of Antioch, and Polycarp of Smyrna appear in the first age following the apostles.

Chapters 4 and 5. John had a vision of the throne of God in heaven, with Jesus crucified, yet living and standing before the throne, about to receive an important document.

Chapters 6 and 7. The seals of the document Jesus received are opened by him. The events which follow the breaking of the seven seals are probably meant to portray the history of the church in the centuries between the close of the apostolic age and the time of the end when Christ comes again.

Chapters 8-11. John saw the events which follow as seven successive trumpets were sounded. This period is probably three and one-half years, the time of the work of the two witnesses of chapter 11. This period ends with the seventh trumpet which is the time of the resurrection of dead believers of all time and the instant transformation of those still living.

Chapters 12-14. John introduced a series of pictorial events which probably coincide with events already narrated, or which are to follow in chapters 15-19. They would serve as illustrative and confirmatory material. Among the most significant of these is the famous picture of the birth of a male child (chapter 12). This is often taken to portray Christ, but on reflection this is seen to be very unlikely. Christ was not caught up to heaven as soon as he was born, nor can we imagine him being about to be devoured by Satan. The same Greek word is used ("caught up") as is used of the resurrection of believers in 1 Thessalonians 4. A more likely interpretation is that the resurrection of believers is intended and that the figure of a male child who is to rule shows the reign of the resurrected and glorified believers with Christ over a world which has been delivered from the bondage of corruption and brought into the glorious liberty of the sons of God as Romans 8 indicates.

Chapters 15-19. The events of this section are portrayed by another series of seven: The seven bowls of wrath. Since a central part of prophecy of the last times is the seventieth *seven* of Daniel, and this seven is seven years long, it is obvious that John is orienting his book to Daniel's prophecy. The seven trumpets concern the first three and a half years, culminating in the resurrection of the church; the last half of the *seven* is concerned with the dreadful judgments God will bring on earth, culminating in the destruction of a great complex of religious and political evil called Babylon. Chapters

17 and 18 show in detail the cosmic importance and dreadfulness of the destruction of a society in rebellion against its Creator and Redeemer.

In the vision of *Chapter 20,* John saw the result of the coming of Christ from heaven with his glorified believers. Satan is bound for a thousand years. Believers who came to life three and a half years before serve as priests and reign as kings under Christ for the thousand years of blessedness. This is in a world where the will of Christ is done and the nations have beaten their swords into plowshares and their spears into pruning hooks, and are not learning war any more. At the conclusion of the period Satan is released, deceives the nations, and then is cast with the wicked into eternal punishment, the lake of fire.

Chapters 21 and 22. This section begins with the complete dissolution of the present universe and the introduction of a new creation, a new heaven and earth, the eternal habitation of glorified believers. The beauty and perfection of their state is described in terms of a community in which Christ dwells in radiance and splendor. Evil is forever banished; Christ's people serve him and behold his face.

The book concludes with a series of communications parallel to the opening paragraphs of the book. The angel messenger of the beginning appears again (22:8-11); Christ speaks directly again (v. 12-20) words of encouragement and warning. John echoes the longing of believers of all ages: "Amen. Come, Lord Jesus!"

The value of the book arises from the relevance of predictive prophecy to the progress of the work of redemption. Redemptive deed and redemptive word are both necessary. In the case of future events, both the deeds and explanation are given in advance. The ultimate value of the book arises from a serious commitment to its truth as a genuine divine revelation, relating to actual historical events. If really true, men may find encouragement or warning and act accordingly. (W.B.W.)

REZEPH An important town in Assyria on one of the caravan routes between Assyria and Palestine (2 Kgs. 19:12; Isa. 37:12).

REZIN 1. A king of Damascus and an ally of Pekah, king of Israel, against Ahaz of Judah (2 Kgs. 15:37, 38).

2. Ancestor of some temple servants who returned from the Babylonian captivity with Zerubbabel (Ezra 2:48).

REZON A Syrian leader who opposed himself to Solomon (1 Kgs. 11:23).

RHEGIUM A town in southern Italy where Paul stopped on his journey to Rome, modern Reggio (Acts 28:13).

RHESA The son of Zerubbabel and an ancestor of Jesus (Lk. 3:27).

RHODA A maid in the house of Mary, the mother of John Mark (Acts 12:13).

RHODES A large island between Crete and the mainland of Asia Minor to the NE where Paul stopped on his journey from Troas to Caesarea to Jerusalem for the last time (Acts 21:1).

RIBAI A Benjaminite and father of one of David's thirty mighty men (2 Sam. 23:29).

RIBLAH An ancient Syrian town near the head waters of the River Orontes situated at the meeting point of the Egyptian and Mesopotamian military highways. King Jehoahaz of Judah was put in bonds there by Pharaoh Neco, and later King Zedekiah was captured by the Babylonians and brought there where he saw his sons killed before his own eyes were put out. Other captive Judeans were also killed there at the same time (2 Kgs. 23:33; 25:6, 7, 20, 21).

RIDDLE A puzzling saying or question whose hidden meaning takes imagination or ingenuity to discover. The best example in the OT is found in the story of Samson (Judg. 14:12-19). The queen of Sheba tested the wisdom of Solomon with her hard questions (riddles) (1 Kgs. 10:1). They are also found in the poetic, especially the wisdom literature (Ps. 49:1-4; Prov. 1:5, 6; Ezek. 17:2). They are even found in the prophets who also used them on occasion.

RIGHTEOUSNESS The basic concept in the word is rightness or justness in respect of the norm indicated in the particular context whether in matters of weights and measures, or in matters of judges, rulers, and kings and their attention to law and government, or rightness in speech or ethics (Deut. 25:15; Lev. 19:15; Deut. 1:16; Isa. 58:2; Prov. 8:8; 1:3; 2:9). Man in and of himself or through his own efforts is incapable of making himself righteous in God's sight and that is why the NT presents the concept of righteousness coming through the atoning work of Christ imputed to the believer. *See* CHRIST, WORK OF and PAUL, HIS LIFE AND TEACHING (Rom. 3:19, 20, 21-26).

RIMMON 1. The father of the men who killed Ishbosheth, Saul's son (2 Sam. 4:2-9).

2. A Syrian god worshiped in Damascus (2 Kgs. 5:18).

3. A city (179-243) in the tribal area of Zebulun, a Levitical city (Josh. 19:13; 1 Chron. 6:77) also called Rimmono.

4. An unidentified town in the tribal area of Judah-Simeon in the S., perhaps more properly called En Rimmon. It was resettled after the return from the Babylonian captivity (Josh. 15:32; Neh. 11:29; 1 Chron. 4:32).

5. The Rock of Rimmon was near Gibeah and the place to which the Benjaminites fled when being attacked by the rest of Israel in punishment for their treatment of the Levite and his concubine (Judg. 20:45-47; 21:13).

RIMMONO *See* DIMNAH and RIMMON

RIMMON PEREZ An unidentified stopping place of the Israelites on their exodus journey from Egypt (Num. 33:19, 20).

RING The English translation of a number of Hebrew and Greek words referring to signet or seal rings, nose rings, and earrings, rings for the staves and curtains of the tabernacle and temple and their vessels when needing transportation. They were symbols of wealth, dignity and authority (Gen. 41:42; 24:30, 47; Esth. 8:2-10; Lk. 15:22; Gen. 35:4; Ex. 25:12-27; Jas. 2:2).

RINNAH A descendant of Judah (1 Chron. 4:20).

RIPHATH A descendant of Noah through Jephath (Gen. 10:3; 1 Chron. 1:6).

RISSAH An unidentified stop on the route of the Israelite exodus from Egypt (Num. 33:21, 22).

RITHMAH An unidentified stop of the Israelites on their exodus route from Egypt (Num. 33:18-19).

RIVER In the OT the common words for river are two, the *nahar* (Greek *Potamos*) and the *nahal*. The first is the word for river as that word is usually understood in our western terminology. Those mentioned in the Bible include: Tigris, Euphrates, Jordan, Abanah, Pharpar, Chebar, Gozan, Kishon, River of Egypt (Wadi el-Arish), Jabbok. The Nile, and once the Tigris, is called a *ye'or*. The *nahal* on the other hand usually refers to a torrent that appears only after a rain. The rest of the time the river bed is dry. This is commonly called in the Middle East a wadi and in the English translations because of the normal dryness of the bed a "valley," a "brook," or a "ravine" (1 Kgs. 17:4-7; 1 Sam. 17:40; Deut. 21:4-6; Job 30:6).

RIVER OF EGYPT *See* EGYPT, RIVER OF and RIVER above

RIZIA A descendant of Asher (1 Chron. 7:39).

RIZPAH A concubine of Saul whose two sons along with the five sons of Merab-Michal were killed by the Gibeonites with David's consent. Because of her mourning David gave Saul and Jonathan and the seven sons of Saul proper burial (2 Sam. 3:7ff.; 21:1-14).

ROADS, BIBLICAL *See* GEOGRAPHY OF THE HOLY LAND

ROBE *See* DRESS

ROCK The translation of two Hebrew words, *sela* and *tsur* and, of course, of the Greek word *petra*. The most important usages in the Bible are the symbolic. God is Israel's rock and fortress, *sela* (2 Sam. 22:2) and *tsur* (Ps. 31:3). As these words are synonyms their translations are not consistent, they are interchangeable. In the NT the figurative meaning is noted when believers in Christ are called living stones in a spiritual house, and when Christ calls Simon, his disciple, *petros* because of the basic truth in Peter's confession, the foundation stone of truth on which his church was to be built, "You are the Christ, the Son of the living God" (1 Pet. 2:5; Mt. 16:13-18).

ROCK BADGER *See* BEASTS, 5

ROD *See* WEIGHTS AND MEASURES

ROD, ROD OF AARON, ROD OF MOSES A stick cut from the branch of a tree or a rod made from iron and used for various purposes which would include beating an individual or individuals in punishment, or merely as a cane or staff (Gen. 32:10; Isa. 30:31; Prov. 22:15; 23:13, 14; Rev. 12:2; 19:15). Aaron's rod was his staff with which God performed some of the miracles in the incidents that led up to Pharaoh's letting the Israelites leave Egypt. It was often referred to as Aaron's rod that budded and was later placed in the Ark (Ex. 7:8-20; 8:16-17; Heb. 9:4). Moses' rod was also used in many miracles connected with the exodus and the wilderness wanderings (Ex. 4:17-20; Num. 20:8-11; Ex. 9:23; 14:16; 17:5-7).

ROD, WEAVERS *See* BEAM

RODANIM 1. One of the grandsons of Japheth, son of Noah (Gen. 10:4; 1 Chron. 1:7).

2. A tribe descended from Javan, the Rhodians from the island of Rhodes. Perhaps the word Dodanim refers to the same people.

ROE DEER *See* BEASTS, 2

ROGELIM A city (223-215) in Gilead and the home of Barzillai who was a friend of David (2 Sam. 17:27; 19:31).

ROHGAH A descendant of Asher (1 Chron. 7:34).

ROMAMTI-EZER A Levitical musician in the time of King David (1 Chron. 25:4, 31).

ROMAN *See* ROME, CITIZEN OF ROME, ROMAN

ROMANS, LETTER TO THE The Pauline authorship of the Letter to the Romans is so well attested by external and internal evidence that few have challenged it. Written from Corinth at the close of the apostle's recorded missionary journeys and before his final trip to Jerusalem (Rom. 15:17-33), the letter can be dated about A.D. 57 or 58. The Greek world in the eastern part of the Roman empire had been evangelized (15:19, 23). The flame had been kindled and the fire was spreading, and Paul desired to transfer his ministry to the Latin world, going as far west as Spain (15:24). Evidently he expected to use Rome as his base of operations, much as Antioch of Syria had served previously. He earlier had hoped to go directly to Rome from Achaia, but his presence was essential at Jerusalem in the presentation of the Gentile contribution to impoverished Jewish Christians there (15:22ff.). Therefore, in place of a visit, in preparation for his future coming to them, and to declare the righteousness of God, Paul sent this formal letter to the Christians of Rome.

The longest and most systematic of Paul's writings, Romans is more a comprehensive exposition of the gospel than a letter as such. Some have suggested, in fact, that the body of the work may have been composed by the apostle early in his ministry and was circulated among his Gentile churches as something of a missionary tractate giving a resume of the apostle's message; and when directed to Rome, received its personal elements of chapters 15 and 16. Such a view would go far toward explaining the uncertainties within the early church as to the relation of chapters 15 and 16 to the rest of the writing, the absence of "in Rome" at 1:7 and 1:15, in some minor manuscripts, and the presence of two doxologies at 15:33 and 16:27.

Romans may be divided into five sections: (1) Introduction, 1:1-17; (2) Doctrinal exposition, 1:18—8:39; (3) Israel and the Church, 9:1—11:36; (4) Practical exhortations, 12:1—15:13; and (5) Conclusion, 15:14—16:27. In the "doctrinal exposition" (1:18—8:39), Paul asserts the equality of Jew and Gentile before God and that true righteousness is based only upon the justifying work of Jesus Christ, to which and to whom man responds by faith. While recognizing certain advantages given to Israel by God historically, the apostle insisted that ultimately both Jew and Gentile stand equally before God in condemnation and equally in need of the righteousness which only God can impart. And in contrast to the human desire to gain acceptance before God by works, the apostle insisted that God's one requirement is faith: a loving and thankful response, as exemplified by Abraham and as needs to characterize the Christian life continually. In his discussion of the relation of "Israel and the Church" (9:1—11:36), Paul made the distinction between spiritual and national Israel, spoke of Christians as in continuity with spiritual Israel, yet declared God's future restoration of the nation. In his "practical exhortations" (12:1—15:13), he urged that these theological truths be expressed as living realities in his addressees' corporate and individual lives; and in the process, his words often echoed teachings of Jesus.

The church at Rome was of mixed racial background. Evidently at first Jewish Christians were in the majority; but after the Edict of the Emperor Claudius in A.D. 49, temporarily banishing Jews from Rome, Gentile Christians were predominant. The Letter to the Romans spoke to both elements. It speaks to both today. (R.N.L.)

ROME, CITIZEN OF ROME, ROMAN The city-state of Rome was founded, traditionally, in 753 B.C., when certain villages on the Tiber River, composed of Latin and Oscan peoples, united on the "seven hills" (Rev. 17:9) for protection against the Etruscans. Republican government replaced kings in 509. During the next two centuries the common citizens, or plebeians, gained increasing rights against the patrician nobility; and Roman domination came to extend over the surrounding lands. By 265 B.C. Rome had conquered the Greeks of southern Italy and gained control of the peninsula. Conquered territories were amalgamated into Rome by implanted colonies and allowing local self-government. Roman citizenship spread, which, together with the Roman location, discipline, and faithfulness to treaties, contributed to the city's success.

Rome's foreign expansion began as a result of the Punic Wars: in 241 Rome took Sicily from Carthage, and later Spain. Empire appeared when Sicily was not brought into alliance but was assigned an imperial governor. Roman expansion into the east had been predicted long before by Balaam (Num. 24:24) and by the prophet Daniel (Dan. 11:30) under the phrase "ships of Kittim" (Cyprus); for Rome did indeed enter the Near East from the Mediterranean. Soon after 200 B.C. Rome began to move against the kingdoms of the Macedonian generals who had succeeded Alexander the Great. Antiochus III of Syria was checked at Magnesia in what is now Turkey in 190, as predicted by Daniel (11:18); and his son Antiochus IV, in Egypt in 168 (v. 30; *see* SELEUCIDS). Simon, the brother of Judas Maccabaeus, was confirmed as an independent ruler in Judah in 143 (1 Macc. 14:16-19, 24; compare 8:17 and 12:1), under the Roman policy of keeping their rivals weak through a balance of power.

Up to this point Rome's approach to the east had been one of preventing aggression, not of effecting it. But imperialism arose in the second century B.C. Rome's last colony was founded in 184 and assimilation slowed down. Treaty obligations were increasingly neglected; and mistreatment arose as Greek greed, self-expression, and love of luxury infected Rome. During the Mithradatic War of 74-63 B.C., the Roman senate gave its general Pompey extraordinary powers over the Near East. He converted Syria into a Roman province in 64 and the following year intervened in the politics of the Jews, capturing Jerusalem, and ending the kingdom of the Hasmoneans. After a period of Persian invasions, Palestine was converted into a client kingdom of Rome under Herod the Idumean (37-4 B.C.); and Herod was able to maintain his position when Augustus Caesar in 30 B.C. became Rome's emperor, in fact if not in name.

While Augustus chose to govern his frontier provinces directly, pacified provinces were generally under the senate with annually appointed procounsuls as governors (as in Acts 13:7). A standing army maintained the *pax Romana* (Roman peace); emperor worship arose in the provinces. Palestine came under the general supervision of the Syrian legate. Quirinius conducted the census for taxation which took Joseph and Mary to Bethlehem (Lk. 2:1, 2) in about 5 B.C. Juda of Galilee led a revolt against such a census in A.D. 6-8 (Acts 5:37). Upon the death of Herod in 4 B.C., his son Archelaus went to Rome seeking the kingship, but he was opposed by a delegation of the Jews (compare Lk. 19:12-27) and his kingship was not granted. Instead Augustus divided the area among Herod's sons as tetrarchs (see Lk. 3:1); and Joseph and Mary, with the child Jesus, deliberately avoided the Judean territory of Archelaus (Mt. 2:22). In A.D. 6 he was deposed for cruelty, and in his place were appointed Roman procurators. It was under the fifth of these, Pontius Pilate (26-36) that Christ was crucified; see Acts 24:27 on the later governors Felix and Festus.

Rome is described in Daniel as "the legs of iron" in the image that represented the world's successive empires (Dan. 2:33), and the powerful beast with the great iron teeth (7:7), "forasmuch as iron breaketh in pieces and subdueth all things" (2:40, KJV). Yet the *pax Romana* permitted travel and communication in ways better than ever before or for 1500 years after (see Acts 27; Rev. 18:11-19), making possible the rapid spread of Christianity. Roman law was rough, but generally effective in protecting the Christians from their first enemies, the Jews. An enterprising man could become a "Roman" by effort or by purchase (Acts 22:25-28); and Paul's Roman citizenship saved him more than once, as it restrained lawlessness (compare 2 Thess. 2:6).

Jews from Rome were among the first converts to Christ at Pentecost (Acts 2:10), and a Gentile church developed at Rome before any apostle arrived. Paul wrote his Epistle to these Romans in about A.D. 52 and was brought as a prisoner to Rome in 60, when he could speak even of "saints in Caesar's household" (Phil. 4:22). Though released in 62, Paul seems subsequently to have lost his life in Rome, as did also Peter (see 2 Tim. 4:6, 16; 2 Pet. 1:14). Because of their refusal to worship the emperor the church suffered persecution that reached an initial peak under Nero, who died in A.D. 68.

The Book of Revelation describes Rome in its ruthlessness as a harlot, "drunken with the blood of the martyrs of Jesus" (Rev. 17:1-7, 18). Yet it served, indeed, to punish the Jews for their rejection of Christ (Mt. 21:41; 23:39; compare 27:25); general Titus destroyed Jerusalem in A.D. 70 (just as Jesus and the prophets had predicted (Lk. 21:20-24, compare Zech. 11:15-16). But Rome itself was then destined to be consumed by others (Zech. 11:17; Rev. 14:9-11; 17:16; 18:2-8), fulfilled historically in the fall of Rome in A.D. 476 in the west, and of Constantinople in 1453, capital of the Roman empire in the east. (J.B.P.)

ROOF In biblical times the roof was flat and made of or covered with mud. In the dry hot weather this mud baked in the sun. In the rainy season it had to be continually watched and patched with additional mud plaster. One mark of a good son at Ras Shamra-Ugarit was that he plastered his father's roof in rain. The family spent much time on this roof-patio and often slept there in hot weather (1 Sam. 9:25, 26; Eccles. 10:18; Lk. 5:19; Acts 10:9).

ROOT OF DAVID, JESSE The word root is usually used in a figurative sense as we use the phrase "root of the matter," or in the sense of source or place of origin (Job 19:28; Deut. 29:18; Jer. 12:2). The Root of David and the Root of Jesse are taken as references to Christ the Messiah (Isa. 11:1, 10; compare Rom. 15:12; Rev. 5:5; 22:16).

ROSE *See* PLANTS, PERFUMES, AND SPICES

ROSE OF SHARON *See* PLANTS, PERFUMES, AND SPICES

ROSH Mentioned only in Genesis 46:21 as a son of Benjamin. He is not mentioned in either of the other two places the sons of Benjamin are mentioned (Num. 26:38, 39; 1 Chron. 8:1-5). The RSV translates it "chief prince" in Ezek. 38:2, 3; 39:1.

ROYAL LAW These two words are used together only in James 2:8 and refer to the Law: "You shall love your neighbor as yourself."

RUBY *See* PRECIOUS STONES AND METALS

RUE *See* PLANTS, PERFUMES, AND SPICES

RUFUS 1. The father of the man from Cyrene who carried the cross of Jesus (Mk. 15:21).

2. A Christian to whom Paul sent greetings in his letter to Rome. He is thought by some to be the same as number 1 above (Rom. 16:13).

RULER The translation of several Hebrew and Greek words which are also translated in a number of other ways. A ruler may refer to a king, overseer, leader, deputy, magistrate, head of a synagogue (Mk. 5:38), mayor of a city (Acts 17:6-8), and even to "the world rulers of this present darkness, the spiritual hosts of wickedness in the heavenly places" (Eph. 6:12, RSV).

RUMAH The home (177-243) of the mother of King Jehoiakim (2 Kgs. 23:36).

RUNNELS Watering troughs for flocks (Gen. 30:38-41).

RUSH, RUSHES A reedlike plant usually found in marshes or near rivers. *See* PLANTS, PERFUMES, AND SPICES.

RUTH The Moabitess wife of one of the sons of Naomi who left her native Moab and went with her mother-in-law as she went back to Bethlehem after the death of Naomi's two sons and husband. She married Boaz and became an ancestress of David and Jesus (Ruth 1:2; 4:10-22; Mt. 1:15).

RUTH, BOOK OF *See* JUDGES, BOOK OF

SABACHTHANI *See* ELOI, ELOI, LAMA SABACHTHANI

SABBATH The last day of a seven-day week. Following the precedent found in the creation story where God finished all his work in six days and then rested on the seventh, the seventh day has become the weekly day of rest and prayer and worship for the Jews (Gen. 2:1-3; Ex. 16:23-29; 20:8-11). The prophets frequently reminded the people of their obligation to keep the Sabbath and in fact to break it was punishable by death (Num. 15:32-36; Isa. 56:2-5; Jer. 18:21-27). The codification of things prohibited on the Sabbath was made during the years between the end of the writing of the OT and the beginning of the Common Era. While it was Jesus' custom to go into the synagogue on the Sabbath Day his attitude of opposition to the rigidity of that codification was clear. He taught that their observance of the Sabbath was more rigid than God intended, for God made the Sabbath for man's benefit and not vice versa (Mk. 2:27). It was not wrong to do good or to heal or even to pluck grain from the ears of the plants if one needed food on that day (Jn. 15:1-18; Mk. 2:23-28). At first the Christians, all being Jews, continued the Sabbath as a day of rest, study, and prayer while at the same time they began their worship also on the first day of the week as that was the day of commemoration of the Resurrection of Jesus (Acts 2:1; 1 Cor. 16:1, 2).

SABBATH DAY'S JOURNEY   *See* WEIGHTS AND MEASURES, "Measures of Length"

SABBATICAL YEAR   *See also* CALENDAR and FEASTIVALS. This was the final year in the cycle of seven. In it the land was to lie fallow (Lev. 25:2-5).

SABEANS   (The Hebrew spelling is *sheba*). A Semitic people resident in the SW part of the Arabian Peninsula who were well known as traders (Job 1:15; Isa. 45:14; Joel 3:8). They lived in the fertile area known as the Yemen and carried on extensive trade to the N and W, having colonies even in N Africa (Gen. 10:7, 28; 25:3; Ezek. 38:13). One of their queens visited King Solomon to test his wisdom with hard questions, and probably in the interests of trade in their gold, precious stones and spices (Ps. 72:15; Isa. 60:6; Ezek. 27:22). The spelling Sabeans is found in the NIV only four times (Job 1:15; Isa. 45:14; Ezek. 23:42; Joel 3:8).

SABTAH, SABTA   The third son of Cush who in turn was the grandson of Noah. This name was applied to a tribe descended from him which most scholars locate in an unidentified area in SW Arabia (Gen. 10:7; 1 Chron. 1:9).

SABTECA   A son of Cush and like the word above the name of an unidentified locality probably in Arabia (Gen. 10:7; 1 Chron. 1:9).

SACAR   1. The father of one of David's mighty men also called Sharar (1 Chron. 11:35; 2 Sam. 23:33).

2. A Levite gatekeeper in the days of David (1 Chron. 26:4).

SACKCLOTH   A rough garment of cloth made from goat's or camel's hair. There is some difference of opinion as to whether it was a full garment or a smaller one like a loincloth, but there is no evidence that it was used primarily because of its qualities of physical discomfort since it was the ordinary garment of the shepherd and the poor. It had a well-known symbolic meaning from very early times. It was a symbol of mourning, and it was also used by entire groups in time of national emergencies (2 Sam. 3:31; Neh. 9:1; 2 Kgs. 6:30; 19:1, 2).

SACRED   A translation of a word that is more frequently rendered by "holy" or "sanctified." The basic idea is separation from profane to divine use (Ex. 30:25; Josh. 6:19; Zeph. 3:4).

SACRIFICE, CHRIST'S   *See* CHRIST, WORK OF

SACRIFICES AND OFFERINGS   Though there are prescriptions and formulas regarding sacrifices and offerings of the Mosaic system scattered through the last three books of the Pentateuch, the basic materials are in chapters 1 to 7 of Leviticus. All were to be presented at the national sanctuary (tabernacle, temple) in connection with the rituals at the brazen altar. So after prescribing the details of construction of the building and its furnishings and their dedication, the narrative continues with detailed instructions concerning the five types of sacrifices to be presented at the altar (Lev. 1-7). This is followed by narrative of the investiture of the priests and of the first rituals enacted (Lev. 8-10). The instruction came to Moses from the Lord who "spoke to him from the tent of meeting."

Both priests and sacrifices existed from primeval times. The first sacrifices are mentioned in connection with the immediate offspring of our first parents (Gen. 4) and Hebrew priests are mentioned among the nation before the giving of the Law (Ex. 19:22, 24). Sacrifices were a part of the culture. In the laws of the Pentateuch (note the manner of their introduction at Leviticus 1:1-2, "When any of you brings an offering to the Lord" etc.), they were appropriated and regulated by the Lord and for him, rather than invented by Moses.

There were five distinct kinds of Mosaic sacrifices (see below), each with its own special ritual. The immediate purpose of the offerings was religious symbolism. We do not learn much of that symbolism from the Pentateuch, but the rest of the OT, especially the Prophets, tells us much concerning its immediate meaning in OT times. The NT, specifically relating it (as type to antitype) to the redemptive work of Jesus (*see* CHRIST, WORK OF) finds the many facets of Christian salvation foreshadowed in it. This is in addition to complex social significance as part of the calendar of feasts and festivals (*see* FESTIVALS). One (burnt offering) symbolized self-dedication. The meal- and peace-offerings were eucharistic, in that they were expressions of love and devotion to God and visible "means of grace" whereby communion at "the Lord's table" was enacted. The sin- and trespass-offerings were expiatory, that is, for sins' atonement.

We must remember that the OT followers of Mosaic religion did not have at hand the Books of Galatians and Romans to tell them that the Law (of Moses) was a "pedagogue" to lead them to Christ (Gal. 3:24, KJV), to give knowledge of sin (Rom. 3:10), nor the Book of Hebrews to tell them the sacrificial rituals were types (predictive symbols) of Christ's sacrifice (Heb. 9:6-10). Yet, they did

know that sacrifice was the divinely appointed means for
them to receive forgiveness of sin (Lev. 4:31, 33-35; Num.
15:26, 28). "Without the shedding of blood there is no
forgiveness" was primarily an OT revelation (Lev. 17:11; cf.
Heb. 9:18-22). Yet the reason *why* shed blood effected
forgiveness is a NT revelation, even though some OT saints
might have connected it with the Messiah's death on the
basis of Isaiah 53. Essentially their faith rested in the verity
of God's word, not on their understanding of *how* God was
going to make the system work.

It is instructive in this connection to observe something of
the *order* of the offerings. In the description of Leviticus
1-7 they are in the order of burnt offering, grain offering,
fellowship offering, sin offering, and guilt offering. This appears
to be because the primeval offerings were the first two and
possibly the third. Atonement for sin is a less conspicuous
element in these. But in actual observance, the sin offering,
having to do primarily with atonement for sin, was always
first. The sacrifices of devotion, being acts performed by
forgiven sinners, appropriately followed those which provided
the appointed bases for forgiveness. The sacrifices for
forgiveness of sins had two aspects. On the one hand they
secured atonement for fractures of the national law, whenever
the offense was one of human frailty through ignorance,
error, or neglect (Num. 15). There was no remission of
temporal punishments in cases of obstinate willful lawbreaking
(Num. 15:27-31; cf. Heb. 10:26ff.). On the other hand, the
prophetic writings show there was a distinct spiritual
significance, as a means of expressing repentance and receiving
forgiveness, which could have belonged to it only as a type
of the Great Atonement (i.e., Christ's sacrifice).

Any treatment of the sacrifices which stops short of the
typical significance of them—so far as it can be determined
by NT study and by principles derived by comparison of
all Scripture—is less than Christian interpretation. Reserve
and humility must be observed in stating the specific typical
significance apart from specific NT statements, but those
statements are clear that the typology is more extensive than
the NT authors specifically delineate. Thus reverent research
and preaching on typology of a sort presently not popular,
is biblically justified and will inevitably recur in the churches.

The comprehensive Hebrew word for all offerings of every
sort was *Qorban,* derived from a verb which in the causative
stem means to bring near. This word was understood in
NT times to mean presented, given, dedicated (Mk. 7:11,
12). So, it indicated simply that the "offerings" (KJV, RSV) or
"oblations" (RV, ASV) were simply things dedicated to God for
his use and disposal. This word is used for all offerings
collectively (Lev. 1:2; 7:37, 38), of the burnt offering (1:3),

grain offering (2:1), fellowship offering (3:1), sin offering (Lev. 4:23), and of the guilt offering (Num. 5:5-10). It is also used of Aaron's consecration offering (Lev. 6:20), the Nazirite consecration offering (Num. 6:14, 21), the Passover sacrifice (Num. 9:7, 13), oxen and wagons dedicated for the Levites to use (Num. 7:3, 4), gifts at the dedication of the tabernacle, booty given to God (Num. 31:50), and even wood for the altar fires, a related word (Neh. 10:35; 13:31). So anything dedicated by men for official use or consumption in the tabernacle ceremonies, whether slain sacrifice or not, was *Qorban*. The word does not seem to have been used in the case of dedicated persons.

In addition, while all offerings were *holy*, those either wholly burned or eaten officially by priests were *most holy* (Lev. 2:3). And those, such as the fellowship offering, which were expressions of devotion, were called "sweet savour" (KJV) or "pleasing odor" offerings.

The animal sacrifices were all of domesticated varieties (including birds) such as were also according to dietary laws, clean for food (Lev. 1:2, 14). The probable reason was that as life-sustaining (food) animals they were fit symbols and when cooked could be masticated as the rituals required. Also, as having cost the offerers something they were true "sacrifices." The fact that edible game was not admitted supported this supposition.

THE BURNT OFFERING (Lev. 1:1-17; 6:8-13)

Name. The Hebrew *olah* means simply "an ascent" (Ezek. 40:26). The idea of burning is not inherent in the word. The idea emphasized was that the entire carcass *ascended* to God (in the smoke and vapors). *"Holocaust"* (all-burned) is less used but preferable.

Varieties. A male of the herd (oxen) (Lev. 1:3); of the flock, a male sheep or goat (1:10); fowl, dove, or pigeon (1:14). The specimen was to be without visible blemish. Ritual was the same in each case except for fowl which were allowed only in cases of extreme poverty of offerers (cf. Lk. 2:22-24; 2 Cor. 8:9).

Ritual. The (a) unblemished animal was led to the door of the "tent" of meeting, where (b) the offerer laid his hand upon the animal's head and then (c) killed it. Thereupon the officiating priest (d) caught some of the blood, made an act of presentation to God, sprinkled some about the altar and perhaps poured out the excess into some channel which carried it away. The priest next (e) flayed the animal and cut it in pieces. Then (f) a fire of wood was ignited on the altar and (g) the parts of the animal, including head and fat, washed legs, and entrails were placed on the fire where they were completely consumed.

Subsequent to the ceremony the ashes were carried away to a clean place "outside the camp." The skin of the animal became the property of the officiating priest and was his "fee" (Lev. 7:8), a very valuable item in that day.

There were complementary offerings of meal (see meal-offerings) and wine (Lev. 23:18) with the burnt offering (Ezra 7:17; Num. 28, 29; Judg. 13:19). Though not special "offerings," both salt (Lev. 2:13; cf. Mk. 9:49) and oil (Num. 28:11) might be added at some point in the ritual.

THE GRAIN (MEAL) OFFERING (Lev. 2; 6:14-18)

Name. Derived from the fact that grain, usually ground to flour, was the basic element. The Hebrew word *minhah* really means "gift, present, tribute."

Varieties. It might be uncooked fine flour, cakes baked in an oven or in a pan, or it might be fried in a pan. It could even be parched green ears of grain. Probably only wheat was used.

Added Materials. Both oil and frankincense were added as well as salt.

Excluded Materials. Honey, very sweet and leaven, very sour (2:11).

Ritual. It was much more simple than that of the burnt offering since no slaughter of an animal was involved. The cereal was (a) presented to the Lord by bringing it to the priest at the door of the tabernacle, after the offerer himself first anointed it with oil. From the mixture (b) the officiating priest took a handful and (c) put on it frankincense, brought to the altar by the offerer as part of his "gift." Then (d) the priest put the portion, thus treated, on the altar where it would be burnt with one of the animal sacrifices. (e) Evidently as part of the sacrifice and not merely to help the priest with his personal maintenance, the priest ate the rest of the meal-offering in the tabernacle precincts (cf. 6:16).

The meal-offering was always (apparently) accompanied with a portion of wine as a drink-offering (libation). (See Ex. 29:40; Lev. 23:13; Num. 15:5, 10.) The Law gives no regulations for disposal of it.

The grain offering seems never to have been offered apart from the burnt offering or fellowship offering (Num. 15:1-13; Ex. 29:38-40).

THE FELLOWSHIP (PEACE) OFFERING (Lev. 3:7:11-21; 28-34)

Name. The word is always in plural in this connection, indicating superlative degree: lit. "slaughtered sacrifice of peaces," to be interpreted loosely as "a slain animal sacrifice celebrating fullness of welfare, blessedness" etc. (In the Septuagint "sacrifice of salvation" is accurate.)

Varieties. Male or female specimens (unblemished) of oxen or sheep or goats.

Occasion. This is bound up with the significance of it. It was brought as an (a) expression of thanks to God (Lev. 7:11-15) in which case both leavened and unleavened bread were brought with it; (b) for fulfillment of a vow, as a votive offering (Lev. 7:16-18); (c) as a free-will expression of devotion (Lev. 7:16-18). (d) On the basis of texts such as Judges 20:26; 21:4; 1 Samuel 13:9; 2 Samuel 24:25 it is held that it might also accompany special prayer.

Ritual. The first four stages are the same as for burnt offering, but after the ritual with the blood, the ceremony continued with opening of the carcass, removal of all the abdominal fat, including that of kidneys and entrails. This together with the "caul" of the liver and the two kidneys were burned on the altar (in the case of the sheep also the fat tail). Then the carcass was divided. The breast (brisket) was given to the priests officiating at the temple for a "wave offering" (i.e. presented to God by moving it right and left) who then cooked and ate it (Lev. 7:15-17). The right shoulder was given to the individual priest officiating. Before he and his family ate it, it was "heaved," i.e., moved up and down (heave offering), before the Lord (Lev. 7:32, 33). The rest of the carcass was returned to the offerer to be used for festive purposes. For regulations regarding eating it see Leviticus 7:13-21; 22:29, 30 and Deuteronomy 12:5-12.

THE SIN OFFERING (Lev. 4; 5:1-13; 6:24-30) There is a problem of interpretation, too technical for discussion in this limited space, over whether 5:1-13 applies to sin offering or trespass-offering. We follow several leading authorities in applying it to the sin offering.

Name. The word *Hatta'th* may be rendered sin (as in 4:3) or sin offering as well as punishment for sin (Lam. 4:22). It is derived from the verb to fail, miss, or as in the moral realm, to sin. It is so named because its occasion was specific acts of sin against God's law.

Varieties. About the same varieties of animals as the *shelem* or peace-offering. In addition, the red heifer of Numbers 19 and the two goats of the Great Day of Atonement were sin offerings.

Occasions. Reading of the sections of Leviticus indicated and Numbers 15:22-31 will show that when one personally committed some breach of the Law of God (through ignorance, weakness, or rashness), and it came to his attention and weighed on his conscience, this offering was appointed as the means of forgiveness. Likewise national sin offerings were prescribed.

Ritual. In general it was the same as for burnt- and peace-offerings down to disposal of the carcass. Following that it was different from either. In certain cases the blood was sprinkled seven times before the veil of the sanctuary (Lev. 4:6, 7); sometimes blood was placed on the horns of the altar of incense (4:7, 18) and usually also on the horns of the brazen altar. The same inner parts as in the case of the peace-offering were burnt on the altar. In the case of an offering for the sin of a priest or the whole congregation the carcass, together with entrails, legs, dung, and skin, was burnt outside the camp (4:12, 21). In other cases it was officially eaten by the priests (6:24-26).

THE GUILT (TRESPASS) OFFERING (Lev. 5:14—6:7; 7:1-5) The word "trespass-offering" is rendered in the NIV very accurately as "guilt offering."

The ritual of this offering was in almost all respects the same as that of the sin offering, with two exceptions. It usually consisted of a ram to which was added a fifth of the value of the ram (according to the priest's evaluation) in money and presented to the priest. This indicates that the "guilt offering" was an offering for sin in which the offense given admitted of some sort of human estimation and recompense, so that in addition to the atonement required there might also be the payment of a restitution.

An examination of the passages (Lev. 5:14—6:7; 7:1-7; Num. 5:5-8) shows that the sins in view in the trespass-offering were those in which the offender had made a false oath in some dealing with other men. The breaking of an oath made the act not only a wrong against man but a sin against God as well. Thus a part of the ritual was restitution of the value of loss involved to man plus a fifth part and this was necessary before the offering could be accepted at God's altar. It is blessed to read in the prophecy of Isaiah 53:10 that Christ became our Guilt-offering. (R.D.C.)

SACRILEGE Making the sacred unclean or profaning it. In the LXX this Greek word is used to translate the Hebrew word which the NIV renders "abomination" there (Dan. 9:27; 11:31; 12:11).

SADDUCEES *See* SECTS

SAFFRON *See* PLANTS, PERFUMES, AND SPICES

SAINT(S) A translation of words which basically mean "holy," "sanctified" or "set apart" from the profane to the sacred. In the OT the reference is usually to those consecrated to God's service or to Israel as God's people (Ps. 89:5; 132:9; Deut. 7:6; Ps. 50:5). In the NT, while the word would have the usages just noted, it came to have a more frequent reference to those who were "in Christ," to Christians (Phil. 1:1; Eph. 1:1; 3:8, 18; 1 Tim. 5:10).

SAKIA A descendant of Benjamin (1 Chron. 8:10).

SAKKUTH *See* DEITIES

SALA An ancestor of Jesus, also called Salmon and Salma (Lk. 3:32; Ruth 4:20, 21; Mt. 1:4, 5; 1 Chron. 2:11).

SALAH *See* SHELAH, 1

SALAMIS One of the main cities of Cyprus, visited by Paul on his first missionary journey (Acts 13:5).

SALATHIEL *See* SHEALTIEL

SALECAH A city (311-212) in the eastern part of Bashan assigned to the tribal area of Gad. In KJV and elsewhere also spelled Salcah, Salchah (Deut. 3:10; Josh. 13:11; 1 Chron. 5:11).

SALEM A city or area over which Melchizedek was king and because of Psalm 76:2 identified with Jerusalem (Gen. 14:18; Heb. 7:1, 2). *See also* JERUSALEM.

SALIM While the exact location is not known most agree that it is to be found in the area some seven to eight miles S of Bethshan in the Jordan Valley. John baptized at Aenon near Salim (Jn. 3:23).

SALLAI 1. A descendant of Benjamin in Nehemiah's days (Neh. 11:8).

2. A priest in the days of Nehemiah also called Sallu (Neh. 12:7, 20).

SALLU 1. A descendant of Benjamin who lived in Jerusalem after the return from the Babylonian captivity (1 Chron. 9:7; Neh. 11:7).

2. *See* SALLAI, 2.

SALMA 1. The father of Boaz, the husband of Ruth, also called Salmon and Sala (1 Chron. 2:11; Ruth 4:20, 21; Mt. 1:4, 5; Lk. 3:32).

2. A Calebite founder of Bethlehem (1 Chron. 2:51-54).

SALMON *See* SALMA, 1

SALMONE One of the points or capes of the island of Crete which figures in the "shipwreck" voyage of Paul (Acts 27:7).

SALOME 1. The daughter of Herodias who danced before Herod. At her mother's request she asked for the beheading of John the

Baptist. Her name does not appear in the Bible but she is referred to in Matthew 14:6ff. and in Mark 6:22ff.

2. A woman present at both the crucifixion and the empty tomb of Jesus (Mk. 15:40; 16:1).

SALT Israelite salt came either from the Phoenicians in the N or from the region at the SW of the Dead Sea where there is a hill or mountain of rock salt (Zeph. 2:9). This Dead Sea salt was of a poor quality and the outer part of the salt cakes or chunks soon lost its salty flavor. Jesus used this in his teaching that his disciples were the "salt" of the earth (Mt. 5:13; Mk. 9:50). In the OT newborn babies were rubbed with salt and salt was required to be used with certain sacrifices (Ezek. 16:4; Lev. 2:13; Ex. 30:35). The reference to the "covenant of salt" (Num. 18:19) meaning a permanent covenant probably arose from the preservative quality of salt. Salt was also a symbol of desolation, as when Abimelech having destroyed Shechem sowed it with salt (Judg. 9:45).

SALT, CITY OF A Judean city N of Engedi and probably to be identified with Qumran where an Iron Age city was discovered below the Hellenistic one (Josh. 15:62).

SALT SEA A salt lake at the southern exit of the Jordan River sometimes called "Eastern Sea" or "Sea of the Arabah" (Deut. 3:17; Zech. 14:8). It lies between the Judean hills and mountains of Moab, from map grid 130 north to 50 south and 185 west to 203 east. Often called the lowest spot on earth, its surface is nearly 1300 feet below sea level and its depth runs from a few feet to about 1300. Its area is approximately 390 square miles in a geological rift that runs from the Caucasus mountains in the north to the heart of Africa in the south. Because of its high salinity (averaging 30%) no life is found in it. It is exceedingly rich in minerals which are being mined currently. A fertile valley in Abraham's day, it became a waste shortly thereafter (Gen. 13:10). Oases made livable areas around its shores, the one at En Gedi (187-097) has a long history and was often frequented by King David (1 Sam. 24:1). One at En Feshka (192-126) supplied water to the Qumran or Dead Sea Scroll community. The prophet predicts a freshening of the waters of the Salt Sea with the production of rich life (Ezek. 47:8-10). Two of Herod's "impregnable" fortresses were located in this desolate area, at Masada and Machaerus, the former becoming the place of the last stand of the Jewish Zealots in A.D. 70. *See also* GEOGRAPHY OF THE HOLY LAND.

SALT, VALLEY OF An unidentified valley, some place it in the tribal area of Judah while others put it in Edom, where the Israelites and the Edomites fought periodically (2 Sam. 8:13-14; 2 Kgs. 14:7).

SALU The father of the Israelite who was killed for bringing a Midianite woman into the camp of Israel (Num. 25:14).

SALUTATIONS In biblical usage to salute meant to greet. It could be the simple greetings between people meeting on the street, formal greetings between ordinary people and rulers or the greetings expressed at the beginnings or ends of letters (1 Sam. 25:6; Lk. 10:5; Dan. 2:4, 5; 1 Cor. 1:1-3; Eph. 6:23, 24).

SALVATION, APPLICATION OF The first interpretation of the person and redemptive work of Jesus Christ in the NT was given by an angel to Joseph, the husband of the virgin: "Thou shalt call his name Jesus: for he shall save his people from their sins" (Mt. 1:21, KJV). Thus is introduced to the NT the concept of save, salvation, Savior. The OT word for salvation is embodied in the name Jesus, a rendering into the Greek of the Hebrew name Joshua, "Jehovah saves." The word "to save" (Hebrew *yashau*) meant to be wide and roomy and came to mean "prosperous and free; by extension to save, help, rescue, be in good health."

An understanding of the biblical doctrine of salvation presupposes an understanding of what man is—fallen, lost, and under condemnation. Salvation is the renewal and restoration of man from all he lost in the fall. It is not only escape from the wrath of God, but deliverance from all the effects of sin, including also the spiritual blessings which come in Christ.

It is thus both a positive and a negative idea. Two texts will show the two sides. First Thessalonians 5:9 says, "God did not appoint us to suffer wrath, but to receive salvation through our Lord Jesus Christ." This is the negative side— escape from wrath. Second Peter 1:3 states that, "His divine power has given us everything we need for life and godliness," which is the positive side.

This salvation is comprehensive as to time. For it is not only a past act (2 Tim. 1:9) and a future goal (Rom. 13:11), but also a present process (1 Cor. 1:18). It is, however, very frequently ideally presented as completely finished, the present possession of all who believe in Christ (Rom. 8:29, 30) and absolutely certain as to its final issue (1 Thess. 5:24).

The Bible states plainly that the Triune God is in every respect the sole author of salvation (Jas. 1:17; 1 Jn. 4:4; Mt. 1:21; Tit. 3:4-6). Jesus Christ, the second Person of the Godhead, is the special mediator of this salvation and apart from him there is no salvation (Acts 4:12; Jn. 14:6).

Two problems have arisen among those who accept the foregoing statements. This is to say simply that Christians have differed on these two questions. The first may be put in this manner: Granting that God only is the author of salvation, how is it conveyed to man? That is, how, specifically, does God bring this benefit to an individual man? There have been those who said it comes through mystical experience, imparted directly through the Holy Spirit, quite apart from any means whatsoever. At the opposite extreme there have been those who said it is conveyed through divinely appointed church ordinances varying from two in most Protestant systems (baptism and the Lord's Supper) to five (matrimony and ordination among the so-called sacraments do not directly relate to salvation) in Catholic systems. Evangelical Christianity affirms that while there is a proper place for mystical experience and the observance of sacraments (ordinances), neither is a usual, invariable, or necessary means of bringing salvation to men. Rather, salvation is conveyed simply through the instrumentality of a message. The NT name for this message is "Good News" or "gospel." This message is from God regarding his Son and his redemptive work; the message is recorded in Scripture, preached by various messengers and applied by the Holy Spirit. The Bible itself speaks very plainly on this point. Paul declares, "It pleased God through the folly of what we preach to save . . ." (1 Cor. 1:21); "Thou hast known the Holy Scriptures which are able to make thee wise unto salvation" (2 Tim. 3:15, KJV). In another place Paul stated that the gospel is the power of God to salvation (Rom. 1:16). The Scriptures declare that there is a "message" ("words," KJV) that has power to save (Acts 11:14) and that it is the implanted Word which produces new birth (1 Pet. 1:23) without which no one can enter God's heavenly kingdom (Jn. 3:1-16).

The second question relates to the method by which men receive salvation. John 1:12 and 13 raises the question and settles it. It is not by some biological inheritance ("not of blood"); nor is it by self-determination, that is, legalistic works ("nor of the will of the flesh"); nor by the efforts of others for us ("nor of the will of man"). The same text states, "to all who received him [Christ], to those who believed in his name, he gave the right to become children of God." Thus we learn that faith is the means by which men receive salvation. Innumerable texts amplify this statement. They are the very texts that changed the lives of the Protestant reformers of the sixteenth century—Luther, Zwingli, Calvin, and others—and gave the world that breath of spiritual revival called the Reformation. Appropriately these men called themselves "evangelical," that is, believers in and preachers of the gospel. To quote all these texts of Scripture and comment on them would be to turn this article into an evangelistic tract. Among the most striking are: Ephesians 2:8-10; Acts 16:30, 31; John 3:16; 5:24; and Romans 10:9, 10.

Any preaching of this divine truth inevitably calls forth a large number of biblical and theological terms. Some of these terms have self-evident meanings, but most require biblical explanation. An arrangement of them frequently used by the author of this article follows:

Election	God's act for man	Previous to man's decision
Calling	God's work for man	
Repentance	Man's act	At the time of man's decision
Faith	Man's act	
Conversion	Man's act	
Justification	God's act for man	
Regeneration	God's work for man	
Adoption	God's act for man	
Sanctification	God's work in man	Subsequent to man's decision in this life
Perseverance	God's work in man	
Glorification	God's work in man	Subsequent to man's decision, subsequent to this life, at the coming of Christ

The above outline indicates that all of salvation, from election and calling to final glorification, are by God's grace and in union with Jesus Christ. It is beyond the scope of this article fully to demonstrate this statement. A reading of the following texts will be convincing, to the persevering reader who looks them up, as regarding the comprehensive basis of all aspects of salvation in divine grace: Acts 18:27; 20:24; Romans 5:2, 15, 20, 21; 11:5; 1 Corinthians 15:10; 2 Corinthians 12:8, 9; Galatians 1:15; Ephesians 1:7; 2:8; 1 Thessalonians 2:16; 2 Timothy 2:1; Titus 3:5; Hebrews 12:28; and 1 Peter 3:18. Among the passages which support the statement that all of Christian salvation takes place in union with Jesus Christ are: Romans 6:1-11; 7:4; 8:1; 1 Corinthians 1:4, 5; 10:16-18; Ephesians 1:4-7; 2:5, 6, 10, 13; Colossians 2:12; 2 Timothy 1:9. The above outline also distinguishes three things as to the character of each of the eleven events or processes involved in Christian salvation. Some are God's act *for* man while others are God's work *in* man. An act is here distinguished from a work. We think of such an event as a divine appointment or thought, such as is involved in the forgiveness of sin as an act. A work on the other hand is an event which produces objective effects—as for example, God's call by which he reaches the heart of man and draws him to himself. Three of them are designated as man's act. Faith, for example, is something man himself does. God does not and cannot do it for him, though he may enable him to do it. It is not called a work for works are meritorious. To assign merit to any of these acts of man would be to deny grace (Rom. 4:1-5; 11:6). Hence, these three distinctions are very important to an accurate understanding of a Christian's salvation.

Grace is the favor of God extended toward sinful men, unmerited by them, and in spite of their demerit. Every aspect of salvation, including even those aspects which involve man's acts—repentance, faith, and conversion—are by God's grace. The first Jerusalem church acknowledged this in saying, "God has even granted the Gentiles repentance unto life" (Acts 11:18). Paul declared it true of faith (as all aspects of salvation): "For it is by grace you have been saved, through faith— and this not from yourselves, it is the gift of God" (Eph. 2:8). See below on conversion.

Union with Christ is the vital spiritual connection with the Godhead, through the second Person by virtue of which life is imparted to all believers which begins in eternity with our election: "He chose us in him before the creation of the world" (Eph. 1:4), continues through all stages of salvation and is consummated by our final glorification (Rom. 8:11, 18-25). This union is symbolized in the ordinances of baptism (Rom. 6:1ff.), and the Lord's Supper (1 Cor. 11:23-26). It is the theme of many of Jesus' discourses (Jn. 6-15) and of many other passages in the NT (Eph. 1; Rom. 6).

Election is the name the Bible gives to God's choice of all who believe unto salvation and effectuation of the same. In spite of all the problems and objections to this doctrine, the Bible everywhere boldly traces all the initiative in salvation to God; none at all to man. Whether we can explain it or not (and it is not inexplicable, for God has explained why it is necessary in the doctrine of sin), it is man's duty to believe it. Some clear texts are Ephesians 1:1, 4, 5, 11; and Acts 13:48). This last text reads, ". . . and all who were appointed for eternal life believed."

Calling is of two sorts. God genuinely invites all men to accept his gospel, receive his Son and thus be saved (Jn. 3:16-18; Rom. 10:13). But if God did no more than simply sound forth the message none would be saved, for because of sin and the fall "the preaching of the cross is to them that perish foolishness" (1 Cor. 1:18, KJV) and "the natural man receiveth not the things of the Spirit of God: for they are foolishness unto him: neither can he know them, because they are spiritually discerned" (1 Cor. 2:14, KJV). This is to say, man is "depraved," without power to turn to God without God's enabling. Thus, though faith is wholly man's act, God enlightens his soul invariably enabling the elect to believe (1 Cor. 12:3; cf. Jn. 6:27, 44, 65). The going forth of a divine power in enablement, working in the heart a desire for things of God is denominated "special calling." It is a work of God in man by which he brings man to Christ. Reference to this effective or special call is made at 1 Corinthians 1:24 and Romans 8:30. In the latter passage the connection between election and calling appears.

Repentance and *faith* are two aspects of one act of man which together are called *conversion*. To turn from sin is repentance; to turn toward God is faith; viewed together they are conversion. In the Bible saving faith is that act of the whole man (Rom. 10:9, 10) whereby, giving up the whole project of pleasing God by his own effort the sinner throws himself on the mercy of God, trusting God's grace working through redemption (*see* CHRIST, WORK OF) to save him from death, the wages of sin, and to give him without charge the gift of eternal life. "For the wages of sin is death, but the free gift of God is eternal life in Christ Jesus our Lord" (Rom. 6:23, RSV). "Now to one who works, his wages are not reckoned as a gift but as his due. And to one who does not work but trusts him who justifies the ungodly, his faith is reckoned as righteousness" (Rom. 4:4, 5, RSV); "And without faith it is impossible to please him [God]. For whoever would draw near to God must believe that he exists and that he rewards [Gr. becomes a rewarder of] those who seek him" (Heb. 11:6, RSV). See also John 6:27-29; Romans 3:21-26 and Philippians 3:4-9. Such a trust in God will always be accompanied (and preceded) by that regret for sin, disgust with it, and turning from it that the Bible calls repentance (Acts 2:37, 38; 17:30-34). Whole-souled faith is represented in Scripture as invariably leading to obedience. Hence many texts use the words almost interchangeably (Heb. 11:8). It should be added that biblical faith is a far more rugged product than mere quiet expectation that somehow everything will "come out right." Indeed repentance takes place only as it is acknowledged that all will *not* come out right unless a change is made. Nor does saving faith occur without evidence (Rom. 10:19). It does not base itself on sight; rather on the testimony of God concerning his Son given in the Scriptures. *Conversion* is seldom found by that name in Scripture. More often terms such as "turn" and "return" are used. These are indistinguishable from repentance in most texts, especially in the OT where the words appear hundreds of times, especially in the Prophets.

Justification is the act of God whereby he declares the sinner righteous and treats him as righteous. This he does for the sake of Christ and on the basis of his redemptive work. As used in connection with salvation, justification is always of undeserving persons. That is to say, the only subjects of this justification (exoneration, acquittal) are denominated "ungodly" (Rom. 4:5) and "sinners" (Rom. 3:19-24). The entire doctrine of justification is summarized in Romans 3:24, 25 (RSV): "They [i.e., sinners] are justified by his grace as a gift, through the redemption which is in Christ Jesus . . . to be received by faith." (1) The *subjects* are sinful men—"they," referring to the preceding verse, "All have sinned." There is no other kind of man. If God justifies any man whatsoever that man will be a sinner. There is no other kind of man on earth. (2) The *fact* is that man is "being justified." It is important to remember that this does not mean to make righteous but to declare righteous and to treat as righteous. It is a forensic act which, while changing a sinner's status before God the judge of all, leaves the sinner's character as sinner unaffected. Change of character is related to regeneration and sanctification (see below). (3) The *method* is "by . . . grace." In the law courts, from which the term justify comes, justification is supposed to be only of the truly innocent; the offenders are properly convicted, or declared guilty. The glory of divine grace is to justify those who deserve condemnation. (4) The *manner* is "as a gift." The more usual translation is "freely" meaning without payment of any price whatsoever (Isa. 55:1). Salvation of man must be in this manner, for nothing an unbeliever does pleases God (Heb. 11:6; Jn. 6:28, 29). How can a man in open rejection of the Son please the Father with tithes, donations, pilgrimages, or acts of devotion? (5) The *basis* is "through the redemption which is in Christ Jesus." For God to declare a sinner righteous as an act of omnipotence would be a misuse of power. No human judge would be approved for such a lawless act toward a lawbreaker. For God to do so would bring God under the condemnation of his own rules and bring him under the woe he has denounced upon others (Isa. 5:20). That basis is called "redemption" in Romans 3:24 (KJV) and is in the next verse represented as a "propitiation" of God's wrath. The RSV goes far astray at this point in rendering this word *hilasterion* as "expiation." The Greek word has the invariable sense of appeasement or propitiation of wrath throughout ancient Greek literature. It is hence arbitrary and wholly unjustified to give it a different sense in the NT. *Expiation* (which is indeed treated in other contexts) has

reference to sins; *propitiation* has reference to the wrath
(penalty) involved in broken laws and offended persons. See
CHRIST, WORK OF; see also "faith" above.

Regeneration is generally understood today as that work of
God in man whereby his heart (his moral and spiritual
faculties) is renewed by the very presence of the Holy Spirit
in the believing sinner's own body. He is given a love of
God and of his Word. He receives spiritual discernment to
know and respond to spiritual things whereas before he was
"dead in . . . transgressions and sins" (Eph. 2:1; cf. 4:17-
19). Paul connected this with the believer's union with Christ:
"Therefore, if anyone is in Christ, he is a new creation; the
old has gone, the new has come" (2 Cor. 5:17). It is also
described as a "washing of rebirth and renewal by the Holy
Spirit" (Tit. 3:5). Jesus declared it to be indispensable for
salvation (Jn. 3:1-10).

Adoption is not a work of God external to himself, but
rather an act of God's reckoning, as is also justification. Those
in whom God works regeneration (i.e., another birth) are
counted by God as having all rights and privileges as members
of God's family. This doctrine is peculiar to the portions of
the NT written by Paul (see Gal. 3:23—4:7). Paul uses the
word "adoption" in connection with the believers' future
resurrection as well (Rom. 8:23).

Sanctification is a work of God in believers whereby their
moral character is refined so that it truly corresponds with
and equals their official standing before God as justified and
adopted. If God is going to justify ungodly sinners such a
work is necessary. The important thing to see, and this is
basically what the Protestant Reformation was all about,
is that God justifies us, while we are still sinners, in response
to our faith. Then he begins to purify us inwardly. He gives
us eternal life when we do not deserve it, when we could not
possibly merit it. Then he finishes his work progressively by
purifying our lives through his Spirit and Word, both working
through Providence, consummating this work ultimately
when our bodies are raised from the dead, though certainly
purifying the soul completely when at death we go to be with
him in "the Glory." Some passages on which this doctrine
rests are 1 Thessalonians 3:11-13; 5:23-24; Romans 6;
Ephesians 5:25-27; 1 John 3:1-3; and Hebrews 12:1-17. The
Bible also makes mention (chiefly several times in the book
of Hebrews) of a positional holiness or sanctification. This
is the act of God in setting us aside for himself and is related
to the idea of the holiness of consecrated things used only
for God's service, as the OT tabernacle, its vessels and
furniture. It is by virtue of this sanctification that all Christians

are called saints, holy, sanctified men (Eph. 1:1; Phil. 1:1; Col. 1:2; Rom. 1:7; 1 Cor. 1:2).

Perseverance is closely related to *sanctification.* It is, from the standpoint of the believer's own experience, a name given to the permanence of the believing sinner's striving toward perfection throughout life, in spite of slips, falls, and failures. From the point of view of God's work in us, perseverance is the perfection of God's work of saving us. He whom God effectually calls, who believes on Christ truly and sincerely, will persevere in faith until the end of life on earth. There may be lapses, but there will also be renewals. Judas, the traitor, who apostatized and never returned and who was a "son of perdition" right along (Jn. 17:12) is cited frequently as an example of a professed believer who did not persevere because he was a hypocrite all the time. Peter who denied the Lord, but shortly wept bitter tears of genuine repentance and died after a life of faithful service to Christ, is an example of a genuine believer who, though he slipped for a brief time, did not fall forever (Lk. 22:31-32). Passages frequently cited in support of this doctrine are: Romans 11:28, 29; 8:28, 29; Philippians 1:6; 2 Thessalonians 3:3; 2 Timothy 1:12; and 1 Peter 1:5. The strongest text is probably the following: "My sheep hear my voice, and I know them, and they follow me; and I give them eternal life, and they shall never perish, and no one shall snatch them out of my hand. My Father, who has given them to me, is greater than all, and no one is able to snatch them out of the Father's hand" (Jn. 10:27-29, RSV).

Glorification is that future event when all the saved shall be raised from the dead (or translated if still alive on earth) in glorified bodies, like Christ's body, free from sin and all its effects, prepared to dwell forever in the presence of the risen glorified Christ, of all the holy angels, and of one another forever. It is the consummation of sanctification and perseverance. Some of the passages which speak of this are Romans 5:2; 8:19, 30; Philippians 3:20, 21; 1 Corinthians 15:43; and Colossians 1:27. (R.D.C.)

SALVE An unidentified compound of medicinal value for the eyes (Rev. 3:18).

SAMARIA *See* GEOGRAPHY OF THE HOLY LAND

SAMARITANS One tradition has it that when the leaders of Samaria and its environs were deported by the Assyrians the leaders of other communities were brought in to replace them. The intermarriage of these peoples produced the Samaritans. Because of this intermarriage the Samaritans came to be disliked by the Jews. The Samaritans themselves, however, hold that not all of them were deported, that those who went into exile returned, and that they are the true descendants of the original Israelites. The matter of the double deportations is a matter of history (2 Kgs. 17:24). There is, however, no evidence of Assyrian or other foreign elements in the practice of these people or in their religion, a fact that militates against the concept of assimilation. The word itself is found in the OT only in 2 Kings 17:29, but appears much more frequently in the NT and in the extrabiblical literature of that later period (Jn. 4:9; Acts 8:25). The Samaritans have a long tradition going back to the early times of the kings of Judah and Israel. They rejected all of the OT except the five books of Moses, and believed that Mount Gerizim, not Jerusalem, was where God intended he be served.

SAMGAR-NEBO An officer, or a title of an officer, of the Babylonian king Nebuchadnezzar who was present and involved in the taking of Jerusalem (Jer. 39:3).

SAMLAH A king of Edom (Gen. 36:36, 37).

SAMOS An island in the Aegean. Paul sailed past it at the end of his third missionary journey (Acts 20:15).

SAMOTHRACE, SAMOTHRACIA An island in the Aegean on the route of Paul's second missionary journey (Acts 16:11).

SAMSON *See* JUDGES OF ISRAEL

SAMUEL A judge, a priest, and a prophet in eleventh to tenth century B.C. Israel (1 Sam. 7:6, 9; 9:9; Acts 13:20). He was born in answer to his mother's special prayers and given to God for his service at the tabernacle at Shiloh (1 Sam. 1:19-20; 1:11; 2:11). He was God's messenger to anoint both Saul and later David as kings (1 Sam. 10:1; 16:13). One of the better known stories about him is the attempt by Saul to consult him through the necromancer (witch) at Endor (1 Sam. 28:8-19).

SAMUEL, BOOKS OF The biblical tradition as to the authorship of the books of 1 and 2 Samuel comes from 1 Chronicles 29:29 where the Chronicles of Samuel, Nathan, and Gad are mentioned, together with the statement of 1 Samuel 10:25 where Samuel is said to have written in a book the rights and duties of kingship. It is therefore most probable that several authors were involved, Samuel providing the material or the copy for the part that involved his own life. The story of the birth of Samuel, his call to the priesthood, the stealing of the Ark by the Philistines and its return are told in chapters 1-6.

Chapter 7 contains the prophet's challenge to Israel and the defeat of the Philistines. The relations of Saul and Samuel are found in chapters 8-15, and of David and Samuel in chapters 16-25. The account of the life of David continues to the end of the book and through all of 2 Samuel.

SANBALLAT The governor of Samaria and Nehemiah's most bitter opponent who, in a time of Nehemiah's absence from Jerusalem, got his daughter married to the son of the high priest. Nehemiah ejected him from the temple upon his return (Neh. 2:10, 19; 4:1-8; 6:1-14; 13:28).

SANCTIFY, SANCTIFICATION *See* CHRIST, WORK OF, HOLINESS and SALVATION

SANCTUARY *See* TABERNACLE AND TEMPLE

SANDAL *See* DRESS

SANDAL-THONG *See* DRESS

SANHEDRIN This council, called *synedrion* is Greek from which it came into Hebrew as a loan word *sanhedrin,* was the supreme tribunal of the Jews after the return from the Babylonian captivity through NT times. It is also found in reference to lesser councils as well. In Roman times (after 63 B.C.) the council was given important powers over Jews in the area, powers that were recognized even by Jews living abroad (Acts 22:5, cf. 26:12). But these began to wane in A.D. 70 and the organization itself is lost to history by the fourth century A.D. Even during the period 70 to 400 its real powers were taken over by the Beth Din (court) which met in various places from Javneh to Tiberias.

SANNAH *See* DEBIR

SANSANNAH A town (140-083) in the tribal area of Judah near Ziklag (Josh. 15:31).

SAPH A Philistine descendant of the giants also called Sippai who was killed at Gob (2 Sam. 21:18; 1 Chron. 20:4).

SAPHIR *See* SHAPHIR

SAPPHIRA The wife of Ananias and member of the early church in Jerusalem. They lost their lives for lying to the Lord (Acts 5:1-10).

SAPPHIRE *See* PRECIOUS STONES AND METALS

SARAH, SARAI The wife of Abraham, also called Sarai at the first (Gen. 11:29; 17:15). She was the mother of Isaac, died at the age of 127, and was buried in the cave of the Hittite Machpelah in Hebron (Gen. 21:1-7; 23:1, 2, 19). Before the birth of Isaac, Sarah gave her handmaid to Abraham as a concubine and the resultant son was called Ishmael, who with his mother was driven out into the wilderness (Gen. 21:8ff.).

SARAI The earlier name of Sarah above.

SARAPH A descendant of Judah (1 Chron. 4:22).

SARDIS One of the cities in Asia Minor to which a letter was directed by the author of the Book of Revelation (Rev. 1:11; 3:1-4).

SARDONYX *See* PRECIOUS STONES AND METALS

SARGON The Assyrian king who finally took Samaria (his father had begun the siege) and who is named as the attacker of Ashdod (2 Kgs. 17:3 ff.; Isa. 20:1). *See* ASSYRIA.

SARID A town (172-229) in the tribal area of Zebulun (Josh. 19:10-12).

SARSEKIM The name or the title of one of the princes of Babylon involved in the final taking of Jerusalem (Jer. 39:3).

SASHES A part of the dress bound around the waist translated "headband" in the KJV (Isa. 3:20, NIV).

SATAN *See* DEVIL

SATRAP Viceroys or governors of provinces having considerable power. In the KJV they are called lieutenants or princes. Darius of Persia organized his empire into twenty satrapies (Ezra 8:36; Esth. 9:3; Dan. 6:1-7).

SATYR A demon whose character and appearance are not defined exactly. The root meaning of the Hebrew word as "hairy one." Sacrifices were made to them and they are mentioned as dancing on the ruins of Babylon (Isa. 34:14; Lev. 17:7; Isa. 13:21).

SAUL 1. *See* KINGS OF JUDAH AND ISRAEL.

2. *See* SHAUL, 1.

SAVED *See* CHRIST, WORK OF

SAVIOR *See* CHRIST, WORK OF

SAW A knife with a notched blade used for cutting wood, stone, or even in the torture of humans (Isa. 10:15; 1 Kgs. 7:9; 2 Sam. 12:31; Heb. 11:37).

SCAB *See* SICK, SICKNESS

SCALES 1. An instrument or a part of an instrument used in weighing, sometimes called a balance (Isa. 40:12; Prov. 16:11).

2. The scales of a fish. Only fish having both scales and fins were considered ceremonially clean (Lev. 11:9-12). Something like scales fell off of Paul's eyes when his sight was restored to him, doubtless a symbolic or figurative use (Acts 9:18).

SCARLET A red color dye for fabrics and leather obtained from the bodies of certain insects. This thread and cloth made from it was highly prized in ancient Israel (Ex. 25:4; 28:5; 38:23; Lev. 14:49; Mt. 27:28).

SCENT *See* PLANTS, PERFUMES, AND SPICES

SCEPTER The staff or baton of a king (sometimes held by a lesser poser) which symbolized his power and authority (Gen. 49:10; Esth. 5:2; Isa. 14:5).

SCEVA A Jewish high priest whose sons in Ephesus were trying to exorcise evil spirits in the name of Jesus (Acts 19:13-16).

SCORPION *See* BEASTS, 6

SCORPION PASS A pass south of the Salt Sea (Dead Sea) on the southeastern border of Judah, between Judah and the Amorites (Num. 34:4; Josh. 15:3).

SCOURGE, SCOURGING, STRIPES Beating with a rod or a hide whip for the purposes of discipline for slaves, children, and fools. Forty strokes or stripes was the maximum allowed under biblical law and thirty-nine were usually given to allow for an error in counting (Prov. 13:24; 26:3; 1 Kgs. 12:11; Deut. 25:1-3). Scourging was done in the synagogues and came to be applied for infraction of many of the laws for whose breaking no particular penalty was laid down in the Bible (Mt. 23:34). Pilate had Jesus scourged, but Paul being a Roman citizen could not be scourged (Jn. 19:1; Acts 22:24-29). There is one reference to the tongue as a scourge (Job. 5:21). This word may also be used in a much broader sense, that of an evil or a plague happening to an individual (Josh. 23:13; Ps. 91:10).

SCREECH OWL *See* BIRDS

SCREEN Three screens or veils are mentioned in connection with the tabernacle. One was at the gate of the outer court, one at the entrance to the tabernacle itself, and the third separated the innermost part of the tabernacle, which contained the Ark, from the rest of the tabernacle. This screen was called the "veil of the screen," two words for the same thing being used (Ex. 38:18; 39:38; 40:21). These are not specifically mentioned in connection with the temple, but it may be assumed that they existed as the latter was patterned after the former, and in the account of the day of Christ's crucifixion it is recorded that the "curtain" of the temple was torn in two (Mt. 27:51).

SCRIBE At first the scribe was a sort of secretary, an official in charge of documents, but the term took on a special meaning to refer to a professional student and teacher of the law (Ezra 4:8; 7:6, 12; 2 Kgs. 22:3-8; Mt. 2:4). Since Jesus' view of additions to the written law, whether by interpretative manipulation or by extensions, differed from that of the scribes of his day the NT has many references to this class of professions (Mt. 15:1; 12:28-38).

SCRIPT Many scripts (methods of writing) were known throughout the period of history covered by the Bible but this word is used in the NIV in connection with the story of Esther where we read that the king sent letters to all the provinces in the script of each particular province (Esth. 1:22; 3:12; 8:9).

SCRIPTURE The name "Bible" does not appear in the book referred to by that name. The most comprehensive name, employed by the book itself in a comprehensive way, is "Scripture" with the variations "the Scripture," "the Scriptures," and "holy Scriptures" (2 Tim. 3:16; cf. 15; James 4:5; Mt. 26:54). It is a book of two main parts, an OT of thirty-nine books composed before the birth of Jesus and a NT of twenty-seven books composed in the first decades after the death of Jesus. Information in the OT itself, coupled with modern knowledge of ancient chronology indicates that the first portions of the OT were written by Moses about 1400 B.C. and the last portions about 400 B.C. The NT books came into existence between about the years A.D. 45 and possibly as late as A.D. 95.

The confidence that Christian people have always placed in this book they call "the Bible" is indicated in the attitude of Jesus himself, and that circle of first followers called apostles. These men had the books of the OT already and were themselves soon to be engaged in the production of the NT. Jesus said, "Scripture cannot be broken" (Jn. 10:35); he rebuked the Jews of his time saying they were wrong in their opinions because of ignorance of the Scriptures (Mt. 22:29). On one occasion he went so far as to say that even a resurrected saint's message could have no higher authority than that of Moses and the OT prophets (Lk. 16:29-31). Paul, author of over a dozen NT books, declared in one of them that even an angel of heaven could have no authority to correct or modify the message of his (Paul's) book (Gal. 1:8) and in other writings the same Apostle Paul cited the OT writings as the highest possible divine authority (Rom. 4:3; cf. 9:17; 10:10, 11; 11:2). His characteristic answer to questions of belief is, "What does the Scripture say?" (Rom. 4:3). Similar expressions are to be found in all parts of the NT.

This confidence was characteristic of the official creeds of the Church even in ages when ignorance and overemphasis on forms and ceremonies caused the Bible to fall into disuse. Denial of the inspiration and authority of the Bible has been a heresy in all periods of Church history, except among so-called "liberal" churches in very recent times.

When the Reformation of the sixteenth century took place, the leaders, who thought of themselves as the restorers of original Apostolic Christianity, took as their basic principle that the Scriptures of the OT and NT are the only source of Christian doctrines, entirely sufficient in themselves as a guide to salvation and the good life. (See Lutheran, Reformed, Presbyterian, Anglican, Congregational, Baptist, and Methodist statements, Philip Schaff, *The Creeds of Christendom* Vol. III, pp. 93-97, 832, 362, 381-389, 489-492, 600-606, 742, 935).

The evangelical sons and daughters of the Reformation have these same opinions regarding the Bible. They find the Bible making claim to divine authority and ultimate truth; their reading of it does not convince them that the Bible fails to support its claims in its statements about reality, in whatever realm it speaks. Of course, the Bible does not speak on many questions. There is for example no specific deliverance in the Bible on calculus or quantum physics. Where the matters in which technical science is interested are mentioned in the Bible it is not in a technical manner, but in a "phenomenal" manner, that is, in language of appearance, as people of all ages have done. Thus the universe is not described in the creation narrative of Genesis 1 in scientific language, but rather as it appears to men, as "the heaven and earth." The heaven is further analyzed as sun, moon, and stars. Upon further analysis the teachings of the Bible about itself may systematically be arranged as follows:

God of the Bible. The Bible never defines God or attempts to prove him. But this book which starts with "In the beginning

God" soon provides sufficient *data* about God that readers know. He is "that infinite and eternal Spirit in whom all things have their source, support, and end." The reader soon realizes that the God of the Bible, through providence (government of the world), is in general charge of things, that nothing ever happens, from the fall of a raindrop to the fall of an empire, which is outside his control. Convinced that God is not only big but infinitely so, not only wise and powerful, but infinitely so, he has no difficulty in accepting a book as written by special divine power and guidance.

The preparation of men who wrote the Bible. We know the names of many of the authors; for example, Paul wrote the Epistle to the Romans, and Jeremiah wrote the first fifty-one of the fifty-two chapters of the large book which bears his name. Some Scriptures are anonymous, for example the latter parts of Proverbs, many Psalms and the Books of Kings and Chronicles. It is not important who they were. It is important that they were prepared by God for their task as authors of Scripture. One of them says God "set me apart before I was born and . . . called me by his grace" (Gal. 1:15), for his special work as revealer of God. Another says about the same in language which suggests preparation both by heredity and experience (Jer. 1:4ff.). Though each, in a sense, was prepared to speak to his own generation (Acts 13:36) there was also a timelessness about their work, for being in touch with true reality they could speak enduring timeless truth (Jn. 10:35; Mt. 5:17-20).

The authority of the human authors to speak and write for God. One thinks of Nabal's words, "Many servants are breaking away from their masters these days" (1 Sam. 25:10). So there are and were many seemingly nice people who claim to speak for God yet are either self-deceived or liars. Out of the clamor of claims and counterclaims in religion how can one know what is right?

The answer to this question is crucial. If the people of Bible times had no basis other than popularity, education, or glamor upon which to judge a prophet's truth claim, then it is hard to accept their judgments as correct. Why were certain authors and their books rejected and others received? To answer this scripturally is to provide the principle of *canonicity*, as it is called.

The biblical teaching is that God fully certified each of these men to his own generation as a man with authority to speak (or write) for God. The best place to begin is with certain words of Moses in Deuteronomy chapters 13 and 18. After forty years as their leader, Moses, the aged man of God knew his death was near and that divine guidance for his people in Canaan was indispensable. First, he strictly proscribed any intercourse whatsoever with Canaanite religious institutions and practices, especially those connected with attempts to forecast the future. His exact words, containing a remarkable list of pagan practices, some still observed in civilized modern dress, are to be found in Deuteronomy. At the same time Moses announced the establishment of the office of prophet, to furnish a continuing line of accredited divine messengers. Their authority to speak for God was to be no less than that of Moses, himself, and they were to be believed and obeyed (Deut. 18:15-19).

At this juncture the basis for infallible recognition of the authentic messenger or detection of the imposter was announced. That basis was fivefold: (1) The messenger must be a Hebrew, "from among you, from your brethren," not a foreigner but an indigenous minister. This principle is confirmed in the NT (Rom. 3:1, 2). (2) The messenger would always speak in the name of Jehovah, the Hebrew proper name of the one true God of all the earth. Thus monotheism was insured (Deut. 18:15, 18, 22; cf. 13:1-18). (3) Special supernatural verification was to be furnished by ability to accurately predict the near future (Deut. 18:21, 22; cf. Gen. 15:14-16; 18:10-14; 21:1, 2; Ex. 3:11, 12; cf. 19:1ff.; 4:14; cf. 4:27, 28). Many chapters of the OT and NT furnish examples of this test in operation. A very striking one is Jeremiah 28. (4) Ability to perform miracles was a fourth sign (Deut. 13:1ff.; cf. Acts 2:33; Heb. 2:1-5). Moses and Aaron had used this extensively in connection with the Exodus from Egypt. There was finally (5) the requirement that the messenger in each case would present a message consistent with that of Moses and other previous prophets. He would in no case inaugurate a new religion (Deut. 13).

A very striking case wherein all these five marks are seen in impressive display is the case of Elijah (1 Kgs. 17, 18). Another is that of Jesus himself. (See also Jeremiah 28.)

It is important to see that no church meeting or conclave of ecclesiastics conferred authority, that is, "canonized" any biblical book. The books carried from their human authors the marks of authentic messages from God. The people received them as such long before churchmen got around to discussing or listing them.

By applying these tests, when the OT period came to an end, the Jewish people knew exactly which books belonged to the canon of Scripture. Josephus, a first century Jewish historian, is very emphatic on this point (*Against Apion*, Book II, section 8). The evidence of the NT and the Masoretic text (official Hebrew biblical text) is to the same effect. These books are the thirty-nine of the Hebrew Bible and of Protestant affirmation.

There are other books of religious interest, some emanating from pre-Christian times, others from post-Christian times, often called *pseudepigrapha*, that were anciently read by Christians or Jews. Books so called are generally regarded by no religious body as inspired Scriptures. Certain others, mainly composed originally in Greek, usually by English speaking Protestants, called the *Apocrypha*, are received by the Roman Catholic Church as Scripture; though considered by many theologians as of lesser authority than the books of the Hebrew canon, they are sometimes called deuterocanonical.

The books, usually referred to as the Apocrypha, are fourteen in number as published under Protestant auspices. (1) *I Esdras*. This book of nine fairly long chapters goes over the history of the canonical books of Ezra and Nehemiah (also called III Esdras). (2) *II Esdras*. This book of sixteen chapters relates mainly to alleged visions and revelations received by Salatiel during the Babylonian captivity. It is highly fanciful and falls far short of credibility. (3) *Tobit*. An unhistorical tale of fourteen chapters teaching Jewish piety. (4) *Judith*. A fictitious patriotic tale of sixteen chapters with "Judith," a beautiful Jewish widow as heroine, and Halofernes, a general of "Nabuchodonosor" as villian. (5) *Additions to Esther*, sixteen chapters. (6) *Wisdom of Solomon*. Nineteen chapters in imitation of the biblical Proverbs. (7) *Ecclesiasticus* (also called Wisdom of Sirach). Fifty-one chapters, much of religious value in the style of the biblical books of wisdom. (8) *Baruch* with the *Epistle of Jeremy*. Supposed supplement to the canonical book of Jeremiah by the prophet's amanuensis and a letter of Jeremiah. (9) *The Song of the Three Holy Children*. An attempt to supplement the story of the "fiery furnace" incident; inserted after Daniel 3:23, sixty-eight verses. (10) *History of Susanna*. Sixty-four verses of pious detective story about protection of a young wife's virtue, partly through the wisdom of Daniel. (11) *Bel and the Dragon*. A marvelous story of idolatry and a dragon in the days of Daniel and King Cyrus, forty-two verses. (12) *The Prayer of Manasses*. An attempt to report the penitential prayer of evil King Manasseh mentioned at 2 Chronicles 33:13, only a few lines in length. (13) *1 Maccabees*. This book of sixteen chapters gives a generally trustworthy report of events in Palestine from about 175 to 135 B.C. (14) *2 Maccabees*. Enlarges on certain details of 1 Maccabees. Not generally regarded as so reliable a history as 1 Maccabees.

Though St. Jerome, official translator of the Roman Latin Vulgate Bible, rejected all fourteen books of the Apocrypha, the Council of Trent (1546) and the First Vatican Council (1870) declared all except *I* and *II Esdras* and *The Prayers of Manasses* "sacred and canonical."

Although Protestants have always regarded the fourteen books as noncanonical they have been many times published with the Bible as useful and conducive to piety. Luther's German Bible (1534) printed the Apocrypha as an appendix and all editions of the Authorized Version of the English Bible (KJV) carried them up to 1827. They are now published separately.

A pair of verses in the NT will summarize the fact that the content of the biblical books has God as its ultimate source, that is, *it is divine revelation:* "In many and various ways God spoke of old to our fathers by the prophets; but in these last days he has spoken to us by a Son" (Heb. 1:1, 2, RSV).

These verses tell us that actual information was conveyed from God to man, facts and data that could be formed into propositions and organized into a creed or catechism, plus, of course, much of ineffable personal experience (Ex. 3:1ff.; Isa. 6:1ff.; 2 Cor. 12:1-4). The idea of "revelation" is neither pure factual datum nor pure experience or "event." It is both and more besides.

We understand that the "many and various ways" by which God spoke to prophets in OT times include such revelations as the visions of Isaiah, the dreams of Daniel, Moses' tablets of stone inscribed by supernatural means, the inner voice of the Spirit when David sang psalms, the researches of Kings and Chronicles under the power of God's Spirit, or the personal experiences of Matthew in his Gospel. All were methods of revelation in the meaning of Hebrews 1:1. The NT revelation came not from a mere human prophet but from "a Son" of God, the second person of the Godhead supernaturally incarnate as Jesus of Nazareth. All the NT is directly or indirectly from him. Shortly before his death he announced that his apostles would complete the revelation he was leaving unfinished (Jn. 14-16), but it would be *his* revelation nonetheless.

Thus, while acting freely as individuals (Paul, for example was never more fully Paul than when writing 2 Corinthians, an intensely personal letter), what these men wrote was divine revelation as to its matter.

The word "inspired" is the misleading word used for *the result of the work of such men, inspired writings.* What is the meaning of this word? Essentially it means the same as the expression "Word of God." If the president or prime minister sends a letter, makes a speech, signs his name to a note typed by his secretary or even confirms a telephone message of his wife, it is his word. He stands behind it. It bears the force of his authority. When Paul preached in Thessalonica on his second great missionary journey he preached the message he distinctly said was given him "through a revelation" (Gal. 1:11, 12). So later Paul could write to the Thessalonians (1 Thess. 2:13), "When you received the word of God, which you heard from us, you accepted it not as the word of men, but as it actually is, the word of God." When Paul said, "All Scripture is inspired by God" (2 Tim. 3:16, RSV) he did not mean anything less than that it was produced by God, created by him. A better translation than *in*spired would be *out*spired. Just as the breath of the wind makes a cloud of dust, so the breath of God creates Scripture, mediately, of course, by human writers. A common biblical figure is being employed. The breath of God is an anthropomorphism for his creativity: "By the word of the Lord were the heavens made, their starry host by the breath of his mouth" (Ps. 33:6; cf. Gen. 1:3, 6, 9, 14, 20, 24, 26; Heb. 11:1).

Holding as they do such a high view of their Holy Scriptures, it is not surprising that Christians attach a great deal of importance to understanding the meaning of the Bible. They believe that understanding sufficient for salvation is not attained except by the illumination of the soul of man by the God who inspired the Bible. Man as he exists apart from the special saving power of God is "dead in trespasses and sins" (Eph. 2:1); "the natural man receiveth not the things of the Spirit of God, for they are foolishness unto him" (1 Cor. 2:14, KJV), and of his rational faculties it is written that they have "the understanding darkened, being alienated from the life of God through the ignorance that is in them" (Eph. 4:18, KJV). Hence the Spirit of God is active in leading sinners, through the Scriptures, to see that Christ is Lord (1 Cor. 12:1-3) and growth in spiritual understanding of the Bible will come only in response to humble prayerful search. (R.D.C.)

SCROLL A papyrus or parchment (leather) roll, usually with writing on it. This was the "book" of biblical times (Jer. 36:2-32; Rev. 5:1-9).

SCROLLS, DEAD SEA The name given to the manuscripts found in caves W of the Dead Sea in 1947 and in subsequent years. These consist of biblical manuscripts (at least portions of all OT books except Esther are included); LXX, Targumis, and Apocryphal fragments, and secular documents which contain valuable information about the beliefs and practices and hopes of the sect itself. The Qumranic documents come from the time of the last few centuries B.C. to the first century A.D. South of Qumran there were found many fragments from the time of Bar-kokhba, A.D. 132-135, mostly dealing with business matters. The secular documents are of extreme importance as they throw much light on a period of history for which not too much written material exists. The biblical manuscripts take us 1000 years nearer to the original documents than any previously existing manuscripts of the OT books. Thus for textual criticism they are a most valuable tool.

SCYTHIANS Horse-riding fighters, nomads, who came into the world of the fertile crescent in the late eighth century from W Siberia. The word is used in the Bible only in Colossians 3:11. Some think that the Ashkenaz were Scythians. *See* ASHKENAZ.

SEA COW *See* BEASTS, 5

SEA, DEAD *See* DEAD SEA and GEOGRAPHY OF THE HOLY LAND

SEA, EASTERN *See* DEAD SEA

SEA, THE GREAT *See* GEOGRAPHY OF THE HOLY LAND

SEA, THE SALT *See* DEAD SEA

SEA, THE WAY OF *See* GEOGRAPHY OF THE HOLY LAND

SEA, MOLTON Called the brazen or bronze sea in the KJV, this was a very large vessel of bronze cast by Hiram, King of Tyre, and placed somewhere in the temple precincts. It stood five cubits high and had a diameter of ten cubits. It was broken up when Jerusalem fell and taken in pieces as booty to Babylon (1 Kgs. 7:23-26; 1 Chron. 18:8; 2 Kgs. 25:13, 16).

SEA OF ARABAH *See* SALT SEA

SEA OF EGYPT A term for the Sea of Reeds (Red Sea) which the Israelites crossed when they left Egypt. Used only in Isaiah 11:15.

SEA OF GALILEE *See* GEOGRAPHY OF THE HOLY LAND

SEA OF GLASS John in his Revelation twice refers to "what looked like a sea of glass, clear as crystal" being before the throne of God. No additional detail is known (Rev. 4:6; 15:2).

SEA, RED *See* GEOGRAPHY OF THE HOLY LAND

SEAH *See* WEIGHTS AND MEASURES

SEAL An engraved stamp, ring, or cylinder for making an impression which would be proof of authenticity, either the substitute for or the authenticating of a signature. Stamp seals were first used in the fourth millennium B.C. and the engraved cylinder came a little later. These were either impressed on or rolled on soft clay in earliest times and in later times on wax. The Egyptian scarab was such a seal. From the

Palestinian excavations have come many stamped jar handles, indicating not content but ownership. In both Testaments the word is used literally and figuratively or metaphorically as well. In the OT God seals up the sins of men (Deut. 32:34; Job 14:17; 33:16). In the NT Paul's converts are God's seal on Paul's ministry (1 Cor. 9:2), and believers are said to be sealed with the promised Holy Spirit and sealed for the day of redemption (Eph. 1:13; 4:30). The NT sealing of the believer is called the *arrabon* in Greek, a word transliterated from the Hebrew *'errabon* and used in clear OT contexts which show its meaning to be "a pledge." See the story in Genesis 38:12-26. The gift of the Spirit is the pledge, token, seal, earnest, that the one engifted will ultimately be fully redeemed.

SEASON *See* TIME

SEAT, JUDGMENT Mentioned with the final judgment of mankind by God (Rom. 14:10; 2 Cor. 5:10).

SEAT, MERCY A seat built on top of the Ark of the Covenant where God met with his people (Ex. 25:17; Lev. 16:2-15; Heb. 9:5).

SEAT, MOSES' In Matthew 23:2, the only reference in the Bible, Jesus said that the scribes and Pharisees sit on Moses' seat. In later tradition we learn that this was a seat allegedly made for Moses to sit upon as the giver of the Law, or a place where the Law itself was placed on occasion. One was found in the excavation of Chorazin.

SEBA The son of Cush who gave his name to the Sabeans (Gen. 10:7).

SEBAM *See* SIBMAH

SECACAH A town (187-125) in the tribal area of Judah (Josh. 15:61).

SECOND DEATH *See* DEATH

SECRETARY *See* SCRIBE

SECT *See* HERESY

SECTS The religious and political groups or sects noted in the NT are placed in three groups: those more particularly Greek in origin or approach; those distinctly Jewish; and, a few of lesser significance or of which little is really known.

GREEK *Epicureans,* mentioned in the Bible only in Acts 17:18, were Greeks who held a philosophy that happiness could be achieved by serenity and detachment. They had no fear of divine intervention in this life or of punishment after death or of resurrection. The concept of the pursuit of pleasure to bring happiness is a later doctrine of this group.

Stoics, also mentioned only in Acts 17:18 in the Bible, were other Greeks whom Paul met in Athens. One seeks salvation in aligning himself with the will of the universe, takes and accepts things as they are.

Gnostics are not mentioned in the Bible by name. They were a heretical sect of the first two Christian centuries. Some of the statements of the NT reflect a conscious opposition to their teachings. Their views diminished the importance of the historicity of the facts about Jesus' life, death, resurrection, and ascension, teachings which brought opposition from the NT writers. The dualistic views of Gnosticism and their concept of man's salvation being merely the release of the soul of man from its imprisonment in the body and its ultimate absorption into its source ran into heavy opposition in the church.

JEWISH Of these the Scribes, Sadducees, and Pharisees are the most frequently mentioned in the NT. The words are not found in the OT since their origins are in post-OT times. One Zealot is mentioned in the NT, and the Essenes not at all.

Scribes. See also SCRIBE. These were they who preserved the law and the manuscripts, were the "doctors" (intense scholars) of the law, the teachers of the law, and those who were prepared and able to act like "lawyers" with respect to this law. Their clashes with Jesus usually came because of his teaching with authority, an authority which did not in their opinion always conform to the law as they saw it. In spite of this the NT tells us that some of them believed in him (Mt. 7:29; Mk. 12:38; Mt. 8:19). Some of them sided with Paul on the doctrine of the resurrection as against the Sadducees (Acts 23:9).

Sadducees. Their origin is not clear and is much debated. They had little following among the common people but were generally from the most wealthy and powerful families. In Herodian and Roman times their influence was at its height in the powerful Sanhedrin but this died out after the fall of Jerusalem in A.D. 70. As against the Pharisees they accepted only the written law, rejected the idea of the immortality of the soul and that of bodily resurrection (Mt. 16:1-12; 22:23; Acts 23:6-8).

Pharisees. Called *Hasidim*, this movement arose during the early second century B.C. in reaction to secularization trends when the military leaders also took on the role of high priest.

Unlike the Sadducees they believed in the immortality of the soul, in life after death, in resurrection, in a future judgment day, in the coming of Messiah. Also, unlike the Sadducees, they did not believe in a rigidly fixed law but rather that it could be adapted to changing conditions after careful study. A majority vote would make the decision binding on all. In other words, they felt that the oral law was a vital factor as well as the Scriptures, the written law. Some were deeply involved in temple and state affairs trying to have the law applied in these spheres, even to working with the Romans if need be. Others, a minority of them, withdrew from such contacts to pursue a more specifically religious way of life. As they were very rigorous and strict interpreters and appliers of the law, it was only inevitable that hypocrites would arise among them and the Talmud referred to seven types. Because of their strict interpretations of the law it was also inevitable that they would clash with Jesus and that Jesus would take the position that one's righteousness had to exceed that of theirs if he would enter the kingdom of heaven (Mt. 5:20). (The reason for this latter position was that entrance to the kingdom of heaven was not by works, or legal obedience, but by faith in God's promises of deliverance through a Messiah and through atonement based on shed blood, in Jesus' teaching.) Since the majority of the NT references to this group are concerned with law keeping and righteousness, the majority of the references found there are therefore negative. This has created a picture of Pharisees in the churches that is not fully in conformity with the facts relative to their beliefs, zeal, and points of agreement with Jesus and Paul.

Zealots. The Zealots formed a political party in late Hellenistic times, the end of the first century B.C. They were strongly opposed to the Roman rule over Israel and to all those who accepted it. Their activity was greatest in post-NT times virtually ending with their mass suicide on Masada in A.D. 73 rather than their being forced to bow to Rome and her paganism. The word is found only twice in the Bible and both of these refer to one of Jesus' disciples, Simon the Zealot (Lk. 6:15; Acts 1:13).

Essenes. A religious sect among the Jews in the last century B.C., much like the Pharisees in faith, but with their own distinctive view as well. They did not, for example, believe in physical resurrection. They rejected the concept of private property and led a communal life, mostly on farms scattered widely in the Palestine world of their day. If the Qumran community was an Essene one then we have much more information about them than existed formerly, but this equation is debated still. They are not mentioned by name in the Bible.

MISCELLANEOUS About the *Nicolaitans* little is known. Were they followers of the Nicolaus of Acts 6:5? Was it their purpose to introduce certain pagan practices into the church to make it easier to get proselytes? They are noted only negatively (Acts 2:6, 15).

The *Herodians* are noted only in the NT and there as opponents of Jesus (Mt. 22:16; Mk. 3:6; 12:13). Little is known of them. Were they propagandists for the hated Herod?

The *Hellenists* and the *Hebrews* are two mutually exclusive groups in NT times. They are referred to in only a very limited number of passages. The latter were apparently Jews who were not influenced by the Hellenization tendencies of their day. Paul was one of them (Acts 6:1; Phil. 3:5; 2 Cor. 11:22). The Hellenists or Grecians were the Greek speaking persons of any race, the opposite of "barbarians" or illiterate ones. They included Jews (Rom. 1:14; Acts 6:1; 9:29; 11:20). A Hellene, on the other hand, was a non-Jew, a Greek, and the term was virtually a synonym for Gentile (Rom. 1:16).

SECU, SECHU An unidentified site in the tribal area of Benjamin (1 Sam. 19:22).

SECUNDUS A traveling companion of Paul whose home was in Thessalonica (Acts 20:4).

SEER *See* DIVINATION and PROPHETS

SEGUB 1. A descendant of Judah (1 Chron. 2:21, 22).

2. The son of the Hiel who lost his life when Jericho was rebuilt as Joshua had predicted many years earlier (1 Kgs. 16:34).

SEIR, *See* GEOGRAPHY OF THE HOLY LAND
MOUNT, WAY OF

SEIRAH, Either a city or an area in Ephraim to which Ehud, the judge,
SEIRATH escaped after killing the king of Moab (Judg. 3:26).

SELA 1. A place (205-020) in Edom which was conquered by King Ahaziah of Judah often called Petra today.

2. An unidentified place on the border between Judah and the Amorites (Judg. 1:36).

3. An unidentified place in Moab (Isa. 16:1).

SELAH A term of unknown meaning used three times in Hab. and seventy-one times in Ps. Some suggest it was a direction for the conductor, others that it had some liturgical function (Hab. 3:3; Ps. 3:4, 8; 4:2, 4).

2. A former name of Juktheel (2 Kgs. 14:7). *See* JOKTHEEL.

SELED A descendant of Judah and Jerahmeel (1 Chron. 2:30).

SELEUCIA *See* GEOGRAPHY OF THE HOLY LAND

SELEUCIDS Upon the death of Alexander the Great in 323 B.C. his empire passed, not to his young son but, as Daniel had long before predicted, to his leading commanders, the Diadochi, or "successors" (Dan. 11:4; compare 8:8, 22). Ptolemy took over Egypt; but his chief general was Seleucus, who became an independent king in Babylon in 311 and had conquered to the Indus by 302. He took Syria, where he established Antioch as the capital of what became the Seleucid dynasty (11:5). Its earlier members were forecasted in Daniel's prophecies, while the later Seleucids played a major part in the histories of the Macabbees and Hasmoneans.

The son of Seleucus, Antiochus I, and his grandson Antiochus II fought with Ptolemy II in 275-271 and 261-252 respectively; but a truce was sealed by the marriage of Ptolemy's daughter Berenice to Antiochus II, who put away his wife Laodice. The latter, however, took revenge by murdering both Berenice and Antiochus (Dan. 11:6). Ptolemy III avenged the death of his sister and took Antioch (vv. 7, 8). Laodice's son Seleucus II later attempted to invade Egypt but was defeated (v. 9).

Of the two sons of Seleucus II (v. 10), the elder, Seleucus III, had only a brief reign; but the younger, Antiochus III, the Great, pressed the war with Egypt. He conquered as far as Transjordan and Gaza; but Ptolemy IV met and defeated him at Raphia, 217, though he failed to follow up his advantage (vv. 11-12). Antiochus III spent 212-204 conquering to the Caspian Sea and India. He resumed the attack upon Egypt in 202; the general of young Ptolemy V was ultimately defeated at Paneas in northern Palestine; and in 198 B.C. Jerusalem welcomed Antiochus and Syrian rule (vv. 13, 16). A Seleucid princess was later married to Ptolemy (v. 17). Antiochus lost out, however, to the Romans at Magnesia in what is now Turkey, in 190 B.C. (v. 18) and died three years later (v. 19). Seleucus IV represented a loss of power and attempted to rob the Jerusalem temple (v. 20).

Upon the death of Seleucus, his brother Antiochus IV usurped the throne (v. 21). He had two wars with Ptolemy VII, winning the first (vv. 25-28), in 170-169, but being repulsed from Egypt by Rome in the second (vv. 29, 30), in

168. He determined to unify his empire under Hellenistic culture (v. 30; 1 Macc. 1:41ff.). When he was opposed by the Jews, he worked destruction in Jerusalem, slaughtered the pious, and set up the "abomination of desolation," an altar of Zeus, in the temple (Dan. 11:31; 12:11), in December 168. He prohibited all Jewish customs. Some of the Jews submitted, others fled, but many resisted (1 Macc. 1:62-64; 2 Macc. 7), and finally retook and cleansed the temple in December 165 (*see* MACCABEES). Antiochus IV died in 164, about three and a half years after the abomination had been set up (Dan. 12:11).

After two years Demetrius I murdered his young cousin Antiochus V, but he could not break Jonathan, the brother of Judas Maccabeus, in Judah (1 Macc. 9:58-73; 2 Macc. 13:1-8). Alexander I, Balas, who was held to be another son of Antiochus IV, defeated and killed Demetrius I in 150; but the latter's son Demetrius II appeared in 147 and two years later killed Alexander I. To gain the favor of Jonathan, Demetrius II granted him certain districts in Samaria (1 Macc. 11:28-37). The infant son of Alexander, Antiochus VI, was now brought forward by a general, Trypho, who later took the crown for himself and put Antiochus to death. In his struggles with Trypho, Demetrius II granted Simon, the last of the brothers of Judas, in 143 B.C. the political independence for which the Jews had so long fought (13:36-43).

After the capture of Demetrius II by the Parthians (Persians), his brother Antiochus VII overcame Trypho; but when Antiochus attempted to reimpose the Seleucid yoke on the Jews, Simon's troops defeated him decisively (16:8-10). Antiochus was able to subdue Simon's son, John Hyrcanus I; but after the death of Antiochus VII in 129 and the reassumption of the Syrian throne by his brother Demetrius II, who had been released by the Parthians, the latter found himself too occupied with attacks by Alexander II, Zabinas, said to be the son of Alexander I, Balas, to pursue further aggression against the Jews. In 109 Hyrcanus fought off Antiochus IX, a nephew of Demetrius, and took Jezreel. The sons of Hyrcanus, Aristobulus I (105-104) and Alexander Jannaeus (104-78) continued to enlarge Israel while Antiochus IX fought with his resurgent cousin, Antiochus VIII. Of the latter's sons, Demetrius III sought to stir up civil revolt against Alexander Jannaeus in 88, but Antiochus XII was defeated by the rising nation of the Nabatean Arabs in 85, who extended their power to Damascus. The last of the Seleucids was a grandson of Antiochus IX, Antiochus XIII; he was deposed after a five year reign when the general Pompey converted Syria into a province of Rome in 64 B.C. (J.B.P.)

SEMACHIAH A gatekeeper in David's day (1 Chron. 26:7).

SEMEIN, SEMEI An ancestor of Jesus (Lk. 3:26).

SENAAH The ancestor of some who returned from the Babylonian captivity with Zerubbabel (Ezra 2:35).

SENATE Mentioned only in Acts 5:21 and probably the same as the Sanhedrin. *See* SANHEDRIN.

SENEH The southern of two peaks at the pass of Micmash. The other was Bozez (1 Sam. 14:4).

SENIR, SHENIR The Amorite name of Mount Hermon (Deut. 3:9).

SENNACHERIB A king of Assyria in the time of Hezekiah of Judah. *See* ASSYRIA.

SEORIM The head of one of the priestly divisions as David set them up (1 Chron. 24:8).

SEPARATE *See* HOLINESS

SEPHAR The eastern limits of the settlement of the sons of Joktan (Gen. 10:30).

SEPHARAD Mentioned only in Obadiah 20, an unidentified place to which some of the people of Jerusalem were taken captive.

SEPHARVAIM An unidentified place in Syria or Mesopotamia from which the Assyrians brought captives to be settled in Samaria (2 Kgs. 17:24-31; 18:34).

SEPULCHRE *See* BURIAL

SERAH A daughter of Asher (Gen. 46:17).

SERAIAH 1. David's scribe or secretary; also called Shavsha, Sheva, and perhaps Shisha (2 Sam. 8:17; 1 Chron. 18:16; 2 Sam. 20:25; 1 Kgs. 4:3).

2. The chief priest executed by Nebuchadnezzar at the time of the fall of Jerusalem, also an ancestor of Ezra (2 Kgs. 25:18-21; Jer. 52:24-27; Ezra 7:1).

3. One who joined Gedaliah the governor of Judah at Mizpah after the fall of Jerusalem (2 Kgs. 25:23).

4 and 5. Descendants of Judah and Simeon (1 Chron. 4:13, 14, 35).

6. One who returned from the Babylonian captivity with Zerubbabel (Ezra 2:2).

7. One who signed the covenant with Nehemiah (Neh. 10:2).

8. A priest in the days of Nehemiah (Neh. 11:11).

9. One sent by King Jehoiakim to arrest Jeremiah (Jer. 36:26).

10. The quartermaster of King Zedekiah to whom Jeremiah gave a message for the king as he was being taken into captivity (Jer. 51:59).

SERAPHIM Mentioned only in Isaiah 6:2, 6. They were heavenly beings with human forms but each with six wings. All we know about their persons and roles is to be found in these two verses. Some think they were winged serpents.

SERED A son of Zebulun (Gen. 46:14).

SERGIUS PAULUS The proconsul of Cyprus who became a Christian through the ministry of Paul (Acts 13:7, 12).

SERMON ON THE MOUNT The teaching of Jesus recorded in Matthew 5-7. Some place the site where these teachings were given in the hills above Capernaum and others place it near the Horns of Hattin between Nazareth and the southern end of the Sea of Galilee. In this section of the teaching of Jesus there are to be found: the Beatitudes (5:3-10); some details Jesus adds to older and well known laws (5:17-48); and miscellaneous teachings about proper living and conduct (6:1—7:29).

SERPENT *See* DEITIES, DEVIL, and BEASTS, 1

SERPENT OF BRONZE *See* SERPENTS, FIERY

SERPENTS, FIERY God sent these among the Israelites in the wilderness as a punishment. Their poison was fatal and acted quickly which may be an explanation of the word "fiery." God told Moses to set up Nehushtan, a bronze figure of a serpent on a pole, and instructed those bitten by the fiery serpents to look at this bronze replica and that then he would heal them. This is the imagery behind the account found in John 3:14-16 (Num. 21:4-9; 2 Kgs. 18:4).

SERUG A descendant of Shem (1 Chron. 1:26).

SERVANT One, male or female, under the service of another. These might be domestic, governmental, or even free ministers or officials of God or a king (Ex. 12:45; 2 Kgs. 19:6; Ex. 14:31).

SERVANT OF THE LORD A term applied many times to Moses (Josh. 13:8; 22:2-5; 1 Chron. 6:49; 2 Chron. 24:6, 9; Neh. 1:7, 8; Mal. 4:4). While Moses is the servant *par excellence* a number of other persons are occasionally also called God's servants: Abraham, Caleb, David, Israel (Gen. 26:24; Num. 14:24; 2 Sam. 3:18; Lk.1:54). In the NT several who serve Christ are called servants of God: Paul, James, Jude, Peter, John (Tit. 1:1; Jas. 1:1; Jude 1; Rev. 1:1). Moses predicted that God would raise up later a prophet like himself (Deut. 18:15). Peter decided that this prophet was Christ (Acts 3:22, 23). In the Book of Isaiah two servants are noted. One is God's witnessing servant (Isa. 43:10-13, 22; 44:1, 2; 41:8-10) and the other is the one to bring light to the Gentiles (Isa. 42:1-4; Mt. 12:15-21; 49:5, 6; Lk. 2:26-32; Acts 26:22, 23). The latter servant, the one whose work is described in detail in Isaiah 52:13—53:12 has always been considered by Christians to be Christ himself.

SETH One of the sons of Adam (Gen. 4:25, 26). He is listed in the genealogy of Jesus (Lk. 3:38).

SETHUR The representative of the tribe of Asher in the twelve spies sent to spy out Canaan by Moses (Num. 13:13).

SEVEN, SEVENTY *See* NUMBERS, SIGNIFICANCE OF

SHAALBIM A city (148-141) in the tribal area of Dan also called Shaalabbin (Josh. 19:42).At the first it was occupied by Amorites but the Israelites finally subjugated them (Judg. 1:35; 1 Kgs. 4:9).

SHAALBON The home town of one of David's mighty men (2 Sam. 23:32).

SHAALIM, SHALIM An unidentified area through which Saul went looking for his father's asses (1 Sam. 9:4).

SHAAPH Two descendants of Caleb (1 Chron. 2:47, 49).

SHAARAIM 1. An unidentified city in the tribal area of Judah (Josh. 15:36; 1 Sam. 17:52).

2. A city in the tribal area of Simeon called Sharuhen in the parallel list and therefore located at (100-076) (1 Chron. 4:31; Josh. 19:6). Sharuhen is a well-known city of the Egyptian records and times of the Hyksos.

SHAASHGAZ A eunuch in charge of King Ahasuerus' concubines (Esth. 2:14).

SHABBETHAI Levites in the days of Ezra and Nehemiah (Ezra 10:15; Neh. 11:16).

SHADES The name of the dead in Sheol, ghosts. They are lifeless, therefore, and are not able to do anything, whether good or bad. The word is used in the plural only (Job. 26:5; Ps. 88:10; Isa. 14:9; 26:14-19; KJV, footnotes).

SHADOW The sun dial was a device for measuring time and is noted in the Bible only in connection with King Ahaz (2 Kgs. 20:9-11; Isa. 38:8). In this case some think that the "dial" was a stairway whose steps (literal rendering of the Hebrew *ma'alot* here translated "shadow") marked the time of day as the shadow passed over them.

SHADRACH One of the three companions of Daniel, along with Meshach and Abednego. These were the names given to Hananiah, Mishael, and Azariah by the eunuch of the king of Babylon. They were cast into the fiery furnace for refusing to bow to the image of the Babylonian king (Dan. 1:7; 3:20ff.).

SHAGEE, SHAGE The father of one of David's mighty men (1 Chron. 11:34).

SHAHARAIM A descendant of Benjamin (1 Chron. 8:8).

SHAHAZUMAH, SHAHAZIMAH An unidentified town in the tribal area of Issachar (Josh. 19:22).

SHALIM *See* SHAALIM

SHALISHA An unidentified area through which Saul passed while looking for his father's lost asses (1 Sam. 9:4).

SHALLEKETH, SHALLECHETH A gate in the W part of the enclosure of the temple (1 Chron. 26:16).

SHALLUM 1. The assassin of King Zechariah of Israel. *See* KINGS OF JUDAH AND ISRAEL.

2. One of the alternate names of King Jehoahaz of Judah. *See* KINGS OF JUDAH AND ISRAEL.

3. The husband of the prophetess Huldah (2 Kgs. 22:14).

4. A descendant of Jerahmeel (1 Chron. 2:40, 41).

5. A descendant of Simeon (1 Chron. 4:25).

6. A priest and one of the ancestors of Ezra (1 Chron. 6:12, 13; Ezra 7:2).

7. A son of Naphtali also called Shillem (1 Chron. 7:13; Gen. 46:24).

8. One who returned from the Babylonian captivity with Zerubbabel; a gatekeeper (Ezra 2:42).

9. A descendant of Levi, a gatekeeper after the return from exile (1 Chron. 9:17).

10. Father of one who refused to let the men of Israel bring captives of the Judeans into Ephraim (2 Chron. 28:12).

11 and 12. Two who married foreign wives during the time of the Babylonian captivity (Ezra 10:24, 42).

13 and 14. Two who worked with Nehemiah on the repair of the walls of Jerusalem (Neh. 3:12, 15).

15. An uncle of the prophet Jeremiah (Jer. 32:7).

16. The father of the keeper of the threshold in the days of Jeremiah (Jer. 35:4).

SHALMAI The ancestor of some temple servants who returned from the Babylonian captivity with Zerubbabel (Neh. 7:48; Ezra 2:46) also called Shamlai.

SHALMAN An unidentified foreign king noted only in Hosea 10:14.

SHALMANESER *See* ASSYRIA

SHAMA One of David's mighty men (1 Chron. 11:44).

SHAMED *See* SHEMED

SHAMER *See* SHEMER

SHAMGAR *See* JUDGES OF ISRAEL

SHAMHUTH One of David's mighty men, the same as Shammoth (?) (1 Chron. 27:8; 11:27).

SHAMIR A Levite in David's day (1 Chron. 24:24).

SHAMLAI *See* SHALMAI

SHAMMA A descendant of Asher (1 Chron. 7:37).

SHAMMAH 1. An Edomite descendant of Esau (Gen. 36:13).

2. A brother of King David also called Shimeah, Shimea, Shimma and Shimei (1 Sam. 16:9; 2 Sam. 13:3; 1 Chron. 2:13; 2 Sam. 21:21).

3. One of David's mighty men (2 Sam. 23:11, 12).

4. Another of David's mighty men also called Shammoth and Shamhuth (2 Sam. 23:25; 1 Chron. 11:27; 27:8).

SHAMMAI 1, 2, and 3. Three descendants of Judah (1 Chron. 2:28, 44, 45).

SHAMMOTH *See* SHAMMAH, 4

SHAMMUA, 1. The representative of the tribe of Reuben among the
SHAMMUAH twelve spies sent to Canaan by Moses (Num. 13:4).

2. A son of David also called Shimea (2 Sam. 5:14; 1 Chron. 3:5).

3 and 4. A Levite and a priest in Nehemiah's day (Neh. 11:17; 12:18).

SHAMSHERAI A descendant of Benjamin (1 Chron. 8:26).

SHAPHAM A descendant of Gad (1 Chron. 5:12).

SHAPHAN 1. A secretary of King Josiah (2 Kgs. 22:3ff.).

2. The father of one of the idolatrous elders of the house of Israel (Ezek. 8:11).

SHAPHAT 1. The representative of the tribe of Simeon among the twelve spies sent by Moses to spy out the land of Canaan (Num. 13:5).

2. The father of the prophet Elisha (1 Kgs. 19:16).

3 and 4. A descendant of David and a descendant of Gad (1 Chron. 3:22; 5:12).

5. One of David's herdsmen (1 Chron. 27:29).

SHAPHER *See* SHEPHER

SHAPHIR, An unidentified place mentioned only in Micah 1:11.
SAPHIR

SHARAI One of those who married a foreign wife during the Babylonian captivity (Ezra 10:40).

SHARAR *See* SACHAR, 1

SHAREZER 1. A son of Sennacherib (2 Kgs. 19:37). *See* ASSYRIA.

2. One who came from Bethel to inquire of the Lord in the days of King Darius (Zech. 7:2).

SHARON, The maritime or coastal plain from Joppa north to the Plain of
PLAINS OF Dor, south of Mt. Carmel. *See* GEOGRAPHY OF THE HOLY LAND.

SHARUHEN *See* SHAARAIM, 2

SHASHAI One who married a foreign wife during the Babylonian captivity (Ezra 10:40).

SHASHAK A descendant of Benjamin (1 Chron. 8:14, 25).

SHAUL, SAUL 1. An Edomite king descended from Esau (Gen. 36:37, 38).

2. A descendant of Simeon (Gen. 46:10).

3. An ancestor of Samuel the prophet (1 Chron. 6:24).

4. *See also* JOEL, 2.

SHAVEH KIRIATHAIM An unidentified place in Transjordan where the Emim were defeated (Gen. 14:5).

SHAVEH, VALLEY OF The valley where Abraham met Melchizedek; also called the King's Valley (Gen. 14:17; 2 Sam. 18:18). It is suggested that this is another name for the Kidron Valley in Jerusalem, or a part of the Hinnom Valley.

SHAVSHA *See* SERAIAH, 1

SHEAL One who married a foreign wife during the time of the Babylonian captivity (Ezra 10:29).

SHEALTIEL, SALATHIEL The father of Zerubbabel (Ezra 3:2; Mt. 1:12; Lk. 3:27) and listed in both of the genealogies of Christ in the NT.

SHEARIAH A descendant of King Saul (1 Chron. 8:38; 9:44).

SHEAR-JASHUB The symbolic name given by Isaiah to one of his sons (Isa. 7:3).

SHEBA 1. *See* SABEANS.

2. One who rebelled against David and was later beheaded for it (2 Sam. 20:1ff.).

3. A descendant of Gad (1 Chron. 5:13).

4. A son of Joktan in the line of Seth (Gen. 10:28).

5. A place from which a queen came to visit Solomon, the Queen of Sheba. *See* SABEANS.

SHEBAH *See* SHIBAH

SHEBANIAH 1. A priest in the days of David (1 Chron. 15:24).

2. A Levite who stood with Ezra at the reading of the law (Neh. 9:4, 5).

3, 4, and 5. A priest and two Levites who signed the covenant with Nehemiah (Neh. 10:4, 10, 12).

SHEBARIM An unidentified place between Ai and Jericho to which the men of Ai chased the Israelites (Josh. 7:5).

SHEBAT *See* CALENDAR

SHEBER A descendant of Caleb (1 Chron. 2:48).

SHEBNA, A steward and secretary of King Hezekiah. Isaiah denounced
SHEBNAH him (Isa. 22:15ff.; 2 Kgs. 18:18, 26, 37).

SHEBUEL 1. One of the division chiefs in David's administration also called Shubael (1 Chron. 23:16; 24:20; 26:24).

2. A Levitical musician in David's day, also called Shubael (1 Chron. 25:4, 20).

SHECANIAH, 1. A descendant of Zerubbabel (1 Chron. 3:21, 22).
SHECHANIAH 2. The head of one of the priestly divisions in David's day (1 Chron. 24:11).

3. A priest in the days of King Hezekiah (2 Chron. 31:15).

4. One who returned from the Babylonian captivity with Ezra (Ezra 8:5).

5. The father-in-law of the Tobiah who opposed Nehemiah (Neh. 6:18).

6. One who married a foreign wife during the Babylonian captivity (Ezra 10:2).

7. A priest who returned from the Babylonian captivity with Zerubbabel (Neh. 12:3).

SHECHEM 1. The son of Hamor, the man from whom Jacob bought land on which to erect his tent (Gen. 33:19; Judg. 9:28).

2. The man who violated Dinah, Jacob's daughter, and brought about the slaughter of all of Hamor's sons (Gen. 34).

3. One from the tribe of Manasseh listed in the census after the plague (Num. 26:31; Josh. 17:2).

4. A Canaanite city (176-179) in the hill country of Ephraim which became important as an Israelite political and religious center (Josh. 20:7; 24;1; 9:1-7; 1 Kgs. 12:1; Acts 7:16).

SHEDEUR The father of the representative of the tribe of Reuben in the census that Moses took (Num. 1:5; 2:10).

SHEEP *See* BEASTS, 2

SHEEP GATE *See* JERUSALEM

SHEERAH, The daughter of Ephraim who built Upper and Lower Beth
SHERAH Horon (1 Chron. 7:24).

SHEHARIAH A descendant of Benjamin (1 Chron. 8:26).

SHEKEL *See* MONEY and WEIGHTS AND MEASURES

SHEKINAH *See* GLORY OF THE LORD

SHELAH, 1. A descendant of Shem, son of Noah (Gen. 10:24).
SALAH
2. A son of Judah (Gen. 38:5, 11).

3. *See also* MESHELEMIAH.

SHELEMIAH 1. One of the gatekeepers in David's administration also called Meshelemiah and perhaps even Shallum (1 Chron. 9:21, 31; 26:1, 2, 9-14).

2 and 3. Two who married foreign wives during the Babylonian captivity (Ezra 10:39, 41).

4. The father of one who worked on the wall of Jerusalem with Nehemiah (Neh. 3:30).

5. A priest whom Nehemiah made treasurer (Neh. 13:13).

6. The ancestor of one sent by the princes to fetch Baruch to read his scroll (Jer. 36:14).

7. The father of one sent by King Zedekiah to Jeremiah requesting prayer (Jer. 37:3).

8. The father of one sent to arrest Jeremiah (Jer. 37:13).

SHELEPH A son of Joktan and descendant of Shem (Gen. 10:26).

SHELESH A descendant of Asher (1 Chron. 7:35).

SHELOMI The father of the representative of the tribe of Asher in the division of the land of Canaan between the tribes (Num. 34:27).

SHELOMITH 1. The mother of one who was stoned for blaspheming (Lev. 24:11).

2. A daughter of Zerubbabel (1 Chron. 3:19).

3. A Levite also called Shelomoth (1 Chron. 23:18; 24:22).

4. A son of King Rehoboam of Judah (2 Chron. 11:20).

5. One who returned from the Babylonian captivity with Ezra (Ezra 8:10).

SHELOMOTH 1. A Levite of the time of David (1 Chron. 23:9).

2. Another Levite of David's time, also called Shelomith (1 Chron. 23:18; 24:22).

3. A descendant of Moses who lived in David's time (1 Chron. 26:25, 26, 28).

SHELUMIEL The representative of the tribe of Simeon in the census Moses took in the wilderness (Num. 1:6).

SHEM One of the sons of Noah (Gen. 5:32; 9:23; Lk. 3:36) also listed in the genealogy of Jesus.

SHEMA 1 and 2. Descendants of Caleb and Reuben (1 Chron. 2:43, 44; 5:8).

3. A descendant of Benjamin also called Shimei (1 Chron. 8:13, 21).

4. One who stood with Ezra when he read the law to the people (Neh. 8:4).

SHEMAAH A descendant of Benjamin (1 Chron. 12:3).

SHEMAIAH 1, 2, and 3. Descendants of Zerubbabel, Simeon, and Reuben respectively (1 Chron. 3:22; 4:37; 5:4).

4. A prophet to King Rehoboam and a scribe of his time (2 Chron. 11:2ff.; 12:15).

5 and 6. A Levite and father of another one in postexilic times (1 Chron. 9:14, 16).

7, 8, and 9. Three Levites in David's day: one helped to bring the Ark up, one was a scribe, and the third a gatekeeper (1 Chron. 15:8, 11; 24:6; 26:4).

10. One who helped King Jehoshaphat in the teaching of the law (2 Chron. 17:8).

11 and 12. Two Levites in the time of King Hezekiah (2 Chron. 29:14; 31:15).

13. A Levite in the time of King Josiah of Judah (2 Chron. 35:9).

14 and 15. Two who assisted Ezra: one came back from the captivity in Babylon with him; the other also returned but Ezra sent him to Casiphia to bring back some Levites (Ezra 8:13, 16).

16 and 17. Two who married foreign wives during the time of the Babylonian captivity (Ezra 10:21, 31).

18. One who helped Nehemiah with the repair of the wall of the city of Jerusalem (Neh. 3:29).

19. A prophet hired by Sanballat the Horonite to frighten Nehemiah and to try to get him to stop the repairs of Jerusalem (Neh. 6:10).

20. A priest who signed the covenant with Nehemiah (Neh. 10:8).

21. A priest who returned from the Babylonian captivity with Zerubbabel (Neh. 12:6).

22. A prince of Judah who was present at the dedication of the rebuilt wall of Jerusalem (Neh. 12:34).

23 and 24. Two musicians who were present at the dedication of the rebuilt wall of Jerusalem (Neh. 12:36, 42).

25. The father of a prophet in the days of King Jehoiakim (Jer. 26:20).

26. A prophet already in the captivity in Babylon who was opposing Jeremiah (Jer. 29:24).

27. The father of a prince in Judah who commanded Baruch to read to them the content of his scroll (Jer. 36:12).

SHEMARIAH 1. A descendant of Benjamin who joined David at Ziklag (1 Chron. 12:5).

2. A son of King Rehoboam of Judah (2 Chron. 11:19).

3 and 4. Two who married foreign women during the time of the Babylonian captivity (Ezra 10:32, 41).

SHEMEBER The king of Zeboiim defeated in the battle with Kedorlaomer and his coalition of kings (Gen. 14:2ff.).

SHEMED, SHAMED A descendant of Benjamin (1 Chron. 8:12).

SHEMER, SHAMER 1. The man who owned the hill of Samaria (1 Kgs. 16:24).

2. A descendant of Levi (1 Chron. 6:46).

3. A descendant of Asher also called Shomer (1 Chron. 7:32, 34).

SHEMIDA, SHEMIDAH A descendant of Manasseh (Num. 26:32).

SHEMINITH *See* PSALMS, TITLES OF

SHEMIRAMOTH 1. A Levite musician in the time of King David (1 Chron. 15:18).

2. A Levite who taught the law in the revival in the days of King Jehoshaphat of Judah (2 Chron. 17:8).

SHEMUEL 1. The representative of the tribe of Simeon in the division of the land of Canaan among the tribes (Num. 34:20).

2. A descendant of Issachar (1 Chron. 7:2).

SHENAZZAR A son of King Jehoiachin of Judah (1 Chron. 3:18).

SHEOL *See* DEAD, ABODE OF

SHEPHAM An unidentified place on the Upper Orontes River (Num. 34:10, 11).

SHEPHATIAH 1. A son of King David (2 Sam. 3:4).

2, 3, and 4. Two descendants of Benjamin and one of Simeon (1 Chron. 9:8; 12:5; 21:16).

5. A son of King Jehoshaphat of Judah (2 Chron. 21:2).

6 and 7. The ancestor of two groups who came back from the Babylonian captivity with Zerubbabel (Ezra 2:4; 2:57; 8:8).

8. A descendant of Judah in the days of Nehemiah (Neh. 11:4).

9. One who encouraged King Zedekiah to kill Jeremiah the prophet (Jer. 38:1ff.).

SHEPHELAH *See* "Ancient Routes and Major Towns" under GEOGRAPHY OF THE HOLY LAND

SHEPHER, SHAPHER An unidentified stopping place on the wilderness route of the Israelites (Num. 33:23, 24).

SHEPHERD *See also* PASTOR. Literally, of course, the tender of sheep. Figuratively, one divine or human, who cares for human beings. God is called the Shepherd of Israel (Gen. 49:24; Ps. 80:1; Jer. 31:10). Both Moses and Cyrus the king of Persia are called God's shepherds (Isa. 63:11; 44:28). In the NT Christ is called Shepherd (Heb. 13:20; 1 Pet. 2:25; 5:4). Jesus' discourse on the shepherd is found in John 10. The leaders of the people of God in both Testaments are also called shepherds.

SHEPHI, SHEPHO A Horite, son of Seir (1 Chron. 1:40; Gen. 36:23).

SHEPHUPHAM, SHEPHUPHAN *See* MUPPIM

SHERAH *See* SHEERAH

SHERD *See* POTSHERD

SHEREBIAH 1. A Levite in the days of Ezra who was one of the twelve to whom Ezra entrusted the offerings for the rebuilding of the temple. He also was one of the instructors in the law (Ezra 8:18-25; Neh. 8:7; 9:4, 5).

2. One who signed the covenant with Nehemiah (Neh. 10:12).

3 and 4. Two Levites in Nehemiah's days, one of whom returned from the Babylonian captivity with Zerubbabel (Neh. 12:8, 24).

SHERESH A descendant of Manasseh (1 Chron. 7:16).

SHEREZER *See* SHAREZER, 2

SHESHAI One of the descendants of the Anakim driven out of Hebron by Caleb (Num. 13:22; Josh. 15:14; Judg. 1:10).

SHESHAN A descendant of Judah and Jerahmeel (1 Chron. 2:31-35).

SHESHBAZZAR The prince of Judah who was made governor of the Jerusalem area and given the sacred vessels to take back from Babylon (Ezra 1:8-11; 5:14). He laid the foundation for the second temple (Ezra 5:16).

SHETH A name unknown except for its single use in the prophecy of Balaam in connection with the name Moab (Num. 24:17).

SHETHAR A prince of Media and Persia who served with King Ahasuerus (Esth. 1:14).

SHETHAR-BOZENAI, SHETHAR-BOZNAI One of the opponents of Ezra in his attempt to rebuild the temple (Ezra 5:3, 6; 6:13).

SHEVA 1. A descendant of Judah and Caleb (1 Chron. 2:49).

2. The secretary of King David. *See* SERAIAH, 1.

SHEWBREAD *See* SHOWBREAD

SHIBAH, SHEBAH The name of one of the wells dug by the servants of Isaac in the Beersheba area (Gen. 26:33).

SHIBBOLETH, SIBBOLETH Two ways of pronouncing the same Hebrew word meaning "an ear of grain," a dialectal difference in pronunciation. By it Judge Jephthah was able to tell whether the speaker was an Ephraimite or not (Judg. 12:6).

SHICRON *See* SHIKKERON

SHIELD *See* ARMS AND ARMOR

SHIGGAION *See* PSALMS, TITLES OF

SHIHOR, SIHOR An unidentified body of water in NE Egypt (Josh. 13:3; 1 Chron. 13:5; Isa. 23:3).

SHIHOR LIBNATH An unidentified place or river in the tribal area of Asher (Josh. 19:26).

SHIKKERON, SHICRON An unidentified town in the tribal area of Judah (Josh. 15:11).

SHILHI The father-in-law of Asa, the king of Judah (1 Kgs. 22:42).

SHILHIM An unidentified town in the S of the tribal area of Judah (Josh. 15:32).

SHILLEM *See* SHALLUM, 7

SHILOAH *See* SILOAM

SHILOH The tabernacle was first set up in Shiloh (177-162) after the conquest of the land by Joshua (Josh. 18:1, 8-10). During the time of the Judges and the time of Samuel it was the sanctuary of Israel (Judg. 18:31; 21:12-21; 1 Kgs. 14:3). In one passage the house of the Lord there was even called a temple (1 Sam. 1:9).

SHILONITE A man from the town of Shiloh above (1 Kgs. 11:29; Neh. 11:5).

SHILSHAH A descendant of Asher (1 Chron. 7:37).

SHIMEA, SHIMEAH 1. A brother of King David also called Shammah, Shimeah, Shimma and Shimei (1 Chron. 2:13; 20:7).

2. A son of King David also called Shammua (1 Chron. 3:5).

3 and 4. Two descendants of Levi (1 Chron. 6:30, 39).

5. A descendant of Benjamin, also called Shimeam (1 Chron. 8:32; 9:38).

SHIMEAM *See* SHIMEA, 5

SHIMEATH The father of one of the murderers of King Joash of Israel (2 Kgs. 12:21). *See* SHIMRITH.

SHIMEI, SHEMI, SHIMEAH, SHIMHI 1. A grandson of Levi (Ex. 6:17).

2. A descendant of Benjamin, related to King Saul, who cursed David as he was fleeing from the rebellion under Absalom. David forgave him but later suggested that Solomon should execute him (2 Sam. 16:5ff.; 19:22, 23; 1 Kgs. 2:6-36).

3. A brother of King David (2 Sam. 21:21).

4. King Solomon's officer in the tribal area of Benjamin (1 Kgs. 4:18; 1:8).

5. A brother of Zerubbabel (1 Chron. 3:19).

6, 7, and 8. Descendants of Simeon, Reuben, and Levi respectively (1 Chron. 4:26, 27; 5:4; 6:29).

9. A great-grandson of Levi (1 Chron. 6:42).

10. A descendant of Benjamin who routed the Gittites, also called Shema (1 Chron. 8:21).

11. The head of one of the divisions of the Levites in David's day (1 Chron. 25:17).

12. The keeper of King David's vineyards (1 Chron. 27:27).

13. A Levite in the time of King Hezekiah (2 Chron. 29:14).

14, 15, and 16. Three who married foreign women during the time of the Babylonian captivity (Ezra 10:23, 33, 38).

17. An ancestor of Queen Esther's cousin, Mordecai (Esth. 2:15).

SHIMEON One who married a foreign wife during the time of the Babylonian captivity (Ezra 10:31).

SHIMI *See* SHIMEI

SHIMON A descendant of Judah (1 Chron. 4:20).

SHIMRATH A descendant of Benjamin (1 Chron. 8:21).

SHIMRI 1. A descendant of Simeon (1 Chron. 4:37).

2. The father of one of David's mighty men (1 Chron. 11:45).

3. A Levite gatekeeper in David's day (1 Chron. 26:10).

4. A Levite in the time of King Hezekiah of Judah (2 Chron. 29:13).

SHIMRITH, SHIMEATH The mother of one of the murderers of King Joash of Judah, also called Shomer (2 Chron. 24:26; 2 Kgs. 12:21).

SHIMRON 1. A son of Issachar (Gen. 46:13).

2. A town (170-234) whose king fought against Joshua and was later in the tribal area of Zebulun (Josh. 11:1; 19:15).

SHIMRON MERON An unidentified Canaanite town defeated by Joshua (Josh. 12:20).

SHIMSHAI The scribe who wrote to Artaxerxes against Zerubbabel and Ezra (Ezra 4:8, 9, 17, 23).

SHINAB The king of Admah defeated by Kedorlaomer (Gen. 14:2ff.).

SHINAR A name for Babylonia (Gen. 10:10; 14:1, 9; Isa. 11:11; Zech. 5:11).

SHION, SHIHON An unidentified town in the tribal area of Issachar (Josh. 19:19).

SHIP Before the times of the kings of Judah and Israel there are only four references (Gen. 49:13; Num. 24:24; Deut. 28:68; Judg. 5:17). In antiquity the peoples who lived on rivers and oceans developed the idea of floats and ships. Inasmuch as the Hebrews were nomadic and agrarian, we do not find many references to ships and sailing prior to the days of the empire when Solomon started vast trading with many parts of the world. Even in his day the help of the Phoenician expert Hiram, king of Tyre, was needed both for the floating of the timber for the temple and palace, from Phoenicia to Jaffa, and the building of his fleet of "Ships of Tarshish" at Ezion Geber on the Red Sea (1 Kgs. 5:9; 9:26-28). Debates exist as to the meaning of the term "ships of Tarshish." Perhaps it originally referred to ships trading with Tarsus and then came to be used for all ships of that type. Some early Phoenician boats or ships had but one sail and one bank of oars. They had high poops and sterns but were in reality low overall. They may have had a crow's nest for a lookout (Ezek. 27:6, 7; Prov. 23:34). A later king, Jehoshaphat, also tried to build a trading fleet on the Red Sea but a storm destroyed the vessels before they could put to sea (1 Kgs. 22:48). Two of the best descriptions of seagoing in the OT are to be found in Ezekiel 27 and the Book of Jonah, while in the NT one is found in Acts 27-28. Sailing on the Sea of Galilee is prominent in the NT. These boats had a single sail and were equipped with oars also (Lk. 8:23; cf. Jn. 6:19). Through archaeological sources we are beginning to learn something of the great size possible for some of the early ships and of their Atlantic and around the cape of Africa seagoing possibilities.

SHIPHI A descendant of Simeon (1 Chron. 4:37).

SHIPHRAH One of the Hebrew midwives in Egypt when Moses was born (Ex. 1:15).

SHIPHTAN The father of the representative of the tribe of Ephraim in the dividing of the land of Canaan among the tribes (Num. 34:24).

SHISHA *See* SERAIAH, 1

SHISHAK The Egyptian Pharaoh who gave assylum to Jeroboam the son of Nebat. He attacked Jerusalem in the days of King Rehoboam (1 Kgs. 11:40; 2 Chron. 12:2ff.).

SHITRAI One of King David's herdsmen (1 Chron. 27:29).

SHITTIM 1. *See also* ABEL SHITTIM. The latter is the full name and the former an abbreviation of the place in Moab where the Israelites encamped before they crossed into Canaan (Num. 33:49; 25:1; Josh. 3:1; Mic. 6:5).

2. The wood from the Shittah tree, *see* TREES.

SHIZA The father of one of David's mighty men (1 Chron. 11:42).

SHOA An unidentified people mentioned only in Ezekiel 23:23.

SHOBAB 1 and 2. A son of David and a son of Caleb (2 Sam. 5:14; 1 Chron. 2:18).

SHOBACH The commander of the Syrian King Hadadezer who lost his life in a battle with the Israelites under David, also called Shophach (2 Sam. 10:16-18; 1 Chron. 19:16, 18).

SHOBAI The ancestor of some of the gatekeepers who returned from the Babylonian captivity with Zerubbabel (Ezra 2:42).

SHOBAL 1. A son of Seir the Horite (Gen. 36:20).

2. A descendant of Caleb (1 Chron. 2:50).

SHOBEK One who signed the covenant with Nehemiah (Neh. 10:24).

SHOBI One who assisted David when he was fleeing from the rebellion instigated by his son, Absalom (2 Sam. 17:27ff.; 1 Chron. 19:1, 2).

SHOE *See* DRESS

SHOHAM A descendant of Levi who lived in the time of David (1 Chron. 24:27).

SHOMER 1. *See* SHIMRITH.

2. A descendant of Asher also called Shemer (1 Chron. 7:32, 34).

SHOPHACH *See* SHOBACH

SHOWBREAD, SHEWBREAD The Hebrew literally translated means "bread of the face," that is, the bread which was put before God in the tabernacle and temple. It is also found in the NIV as "bread of the Presence." This bread consisted of twelve pancakelike bread cakes which had to be replaced each Sabbath day with new bread. The old bread was eaten by the priests. It was this which one of them gave to David when he was hungry (Ex. 25:30; 1 Chron. 9:32; 23:29; 2 Chron. 29:18; Lev. 24:5-9; 1 Sam. 21:1-6).

SHROUD A sheet of linen in which the dead were wrapped (Mk. 15:46).

SHUA 1. The father of the Canaanite woman who became Judah's wife, also called Bathshua (Gen. 38:2; 1 Chron. 2:3).

2. A woman descended from the tribe of Asher (1 Chron. 7:32).

SHUAH A son of Abraham by Keturah (Gen. 25:2). *See* SHUHAH.

SHUAL A descendant of Asher (1 Chron. 7:36).

SHUBAEL 1. A grandson of Levi (1 Chron. 24:20).

2. A Levite musician in David's day also called Shebuel (1 Chron. 25:4, 20).

SHUHAH, SHUAH A descendant of Judah (1 Chron. 4:11).

SHUHAM *See* HUSHIM

SHUHITE One of a group of people descended from Shuah. Bildad the friend of Job was one (Job 8:1; 18:1; 42:9).

SHULAMMITE The title, meaning or person unknown, applied to a young woman in Song of Solomon 6:13.

SHUMATHITES A family descended from Caleb (1 Chron. 2:53).

SHUNEM, SHUNAMMITE A place (181-223) in the tribal area of Issachar and one of a group of people from that place (Josh. 19:18; 2 Kgs. 4:8, 12-36; 1 Kgs. 2:17-22.)

SHUNI A son of Gad (Gen. 46:16).

SHUPHAM A son of Benjamin and founder of the group called Shuphamites. *See also* MUPPIM (Num. 26:39).

SHUPPIM *See* MUPPIM

SHUR, WAY OF, WILDERNESS OF *See* GEOGRAPHY OF THE HOLY LAND

SHUSHAN *See* SUSA

SHUSHAN EDUTH *See* PSALMS, TITLES OF

SHUTHELAH 1 and 2. Both a son of Ephraim and a descendant of Ephraim (Num. 26:35, 36; 1 Chron. 7:20, 21).

SIA, SIAHA Two names of the same person, an ancestor of some temple servants who came back from the Babylonian captivity with Zerubbabel (Neh. 7:47; Ezra 2:44).

SIBBECAI, SIBBECHAI One of David's mighty men also called Mebunnai (2 Sam. 21:18; 23:27).

SIBBOLETH *See* SHIBBOLETH

SIBMAH The name of a special variety of grape that came from Sebam, Sibmah (Isa. 16:8, 9; Jer. 48:32; Num. 32:38) and the name of the place itself in Transjordan.

SIBRAIM An unidentified place on the N border of Canaan (Ezek. 47:16).

SICK, SICKNESS The equating of diseases mentioned in the Bible with a modern variety is not easy because of the very limited contexts in which some of them are described there.

I. Various types of *skin diseases* were mentioned fairly frequently: *Boil, Itch, Leprosy, Scab, Tetter, Ulcer.* The *tetter* mentioned only in Leviticus 13:39 is unknown. The *scab* is noted only three times and would appear to be on the order of a ringworm (Isa. 3:17; Lev. 21:20; 22:22). The *ulcer,* another skin disease rather than in the digestive tract, is found only in *Deuteronomy 28:27.* The *itch* was a "leprosy" or a form of ringworm of the head and neck. It is found in the chapter which refers most frequently to the disease of leprosy (Leviticus 13:30-37). The *boil* is found in the same chapter, Leviticus 13:18-23 as well as elsewhere. It was one of the plagues of Egypt (Ezek. 9:9-11). A cure suggested was to lay a fig poultice on it (Isa. 38:21). *Leprosy* was apparently not what we know today as Hansen's disease but a skin disease of some other sort. Extended passages discuss it (Lev. 13:8-52; 14:7, 44-57). Miriam, Uzziah, and Simon had it (Num. 12:10; 2 Chron. 26:21; Mk. 14:3).

II. *Dropsy, Epilepsy, Palsy, Dysentery* are noted in specific cases only once each (Lk. 14:2; Mt. 17:15; Ezek. 7:27; Acts 28:8).

III. *Pestilence* and *Plague* may refer to more than one disease each. The former is noted in connection with military sieges and thus may have something to do with cholera or a fever while the latter is generally thought to be a bubonic outbreak (Lev. 26:25; Deut. 28:21, 22; Ex. 9:3; 11:1). The *tumors* of 1 Samuel 5:6-12 and 6:4-17 are considered to be a form of bubonic plague.

IV. The *Fever* may be one of several types: undulant, malarial, or that which might accompany a number of other diseases (Lk. 26:16; Mt. 8:14, 15; Acts 28:8).

V. *Madness* is used more often in a general sense of anger rather than that of insanity. The latter meaning is found, however (Deut. 28:28).

VI. *Medicine* is found three times and *physician* eleven. "A cheerful heart is good medicine" and they "used many medicines in vain" (Prov. 17:22; Jer. 46:11). One of the functions of the physician in Egypt was that of embalming (Gen. 50:2; Col. 4:14) and the writer of two of the books of the NT was a physician, Luke.

SICKLE An instrument for cutting standing grain made at first from pieces of flint set in a curved horn or piece of wood. Later they were made of metal (Deut. 16:9; Joel 3:13; Mk. 4:29).

SIDDIM, VALLEY OF A valley in the vicinity of the S of the Dead Sea where the five kings of the area fought with Kedorlaomer and his allies (Gen. 14:3-10).

SIDON *See* GEOGRAPHY OF THE HOLY LAND

SIEGE A means by which all communication in and out of a city was cut off by an enemy in an attempt to conquer it. Then large earthen mounds were built against the city wall so that the siege machines could be rolled up to the wall to batter it down or for bowmen or infantry attacks over it. On occasion tunnels were dug under the walls or other methods were used to break into the city (Josh. 10:31; Isa. 23:13; 37:33; Ezek. 4:2; 21:22).

SIEGEWORKS A barrier constructed for defense, used both literally and figuratively (Jer. 50:15; Isa. 26:1); sometimes translated "ramparts" (Ps. 48:13).

SIGNET *See* SEAL

SIHON The Amorite king of Heshbon, NE of the Dead Sea, who had many contacts with the Israelites through the time of the Judges (Num. 21:21-34; Deut. 2:24-32; Josh. 13:10-27; Judg. 11:19-21).

SIHOR *See* SHIHOR

SILAS, SILVANUS A Roman citizen and an active member of the young church in Jerusalem. With Paul and Barnabas he carried the message of the Jerusalem Council to Antioch (Acts 16:37; 15:22, 23, 32). He was with Paul on parts of his missionary journeys as may be inferred from the references in the Epistles of Paul (Acts 18:5; 1 and 2 Thess. 1:1; 2 Cor. 1:19).

SILK Silk from the silkworm was known in the Far East from very early times and in the Near East by the first millennium B.C. (Ezek. 16:10-13; Rev. 18:12).

SILLA An unidentified part of the city of Jerusalem (2 Kgs. 12:20).

SILOAM, POOL OF A pool in Jerusalem near the confluence of the Kidron, Tyropeon, and Hinnom Valleys. The water from the Gihon Spring was brought to it through the conduit built by King Hezekiah (Lk. 13:4; John 9:7-11). The King's Garden was found in this area (Neh. 3:15).

SILVANUS *See* SILAS

SILVER *See* PRECIOUS STONES AND METALS

SIMEON 1. One of the sons of Jacob who gave his name to one of the tribes of Israel (Gen. 29:33).

2. The devout man who blessed the baby Jesus as he was presented in the temple (Lk. 2:25ff.).

3. An ancestor of Jesus (Lk. 3:30).

4. *See* SYMEON.

SIMON 1. Simon Peter, one of the twelve apostles. *See* APOSTLES.

2. Simon the Zealot, another of Jesus' apostles.

3. A brother of Jesus (Mt. 13:55; Mk. 6:3).

4. A leper and the host of Jesus at Bethany (Mt. 26:6; Mk. 14:3).

5. A Pharisee who hosted Jesus (Lk. 7:37-40).

6. The father of Judas Iscariot (Jn. 13:2; 6:71; 13:26).

7. The man from Cyrene who carried Jesus' cross (Mt. 27:32; Mk. 15:21).

8. Simon Magus who tried to buy the power to confer the Holy Spirit but was rebuked by Peter (Acts 8:9ff.).

9. A tanner at Joppa and host of Peter (Acts 9:43).

SIMON PETER *See* APOSTLES

SIMON THE CANANAEAN, THE ZEALOT *See* APOSTLES

SIN Scripture does not reveal the origin of evil, although it is clear that God is not the author. When God made all things he pronounced them "good" (Gen. 1:31). There are two kinds of evil—physical or natural evil which we find in the

world in general, and moral evil, or sin, which exists in
all men's hearts. Although evil did not exist in the world at
the beginning, it soon made its presence felt when man
rebelled against God. The essence of sin is willful disobedience
to the declared will of God. When sin entered the world it
brought in its train sorrow, suffering, and death. Sin became
and still remains the great curse of human life. It describes
the evil course which man has deliberately chosen to follow
and which carries untold misery with it. The term "total
depravity" is sometimes used to describe the state of fallen
man. This does not mean that every man is as bad as he
possibly could be or that he has entirely lost every trace of
the divine image which was originally his. It does mean,
however, that sin has affected man's whole being, his will, his
thoughts, his emotions, his appetites. Because of sin, man's
will is perverted, his understanding darkened, his conscience
defiled, and his affections depraved (Eph. 4:18).

Adam's defiance of God's will not only meant that he
himself thereby forfeited his original intimate relationship with
God and became alienated from him, but the whole human
race was also affected. Man is therefore a "fallen creature,"
born with a bias toward sin which is sometimes referred
to as "the law of sin." (Rom. 5:12-15; 1 Cor. 15:22; Ps.
51:5; Rom. 7:23).

"Sin" basically means failure to meet the divine requirements.
The Bible gives a number of words which highlight different
aspects of sin. Sin in general is regarded as "missing the
mark"—failing to measure up to God's standards. It may also
be defined as "transgression"—a deliberate act of rebellion,
the crossing of a boundary which God has set. Paul distinguished
transgression, such as the sin of Adam, from sin which is
the wider term (Rom. 5:14).

Sin is essentially a moral evil, and the words used to
designate it take this into account. The word "iniquity"
conveys the idea of perversion of heart. Three different
words are used in Psalm 32:1, 2—transgression (rebellion),
sin (missing the mark) and iniquity (perversion of heart).

The words *err* and *error* convey the notion of straying
away from the right path (1 Tim. 6:10, 21). Thus false teaching
is described as error, but so also is departure from right
conduct (2 Tim. 2:18; Num. 15:22). Error, while serious, is
not so grievous as heresy which represents a more deliberate
departure from the true faith coupled with the propagation of
false teaching (Jude 11).

The Bible gives us many more words which illustrate ways
in which man's sinful disposition expresses itself. We could
sum up the situation by stating that sin is a coming short
of God's standard through an act of will which leads on to an
attitude of mind and heart which deliberately chooses to

disobey and displease God. John uses the word "lawlessness" to describe this innate human desire to be independent of God (1 John 3:4).

The word *wicked* (*wickedness*) is used in the English Bible to translate a dozen or more Hebrew words and several Greek words. The wicked are contrasted with the righteous (Ps. 73). Wickedness is pictured as an active, destructive principle at work in the world (Prov. 21:10; 29:16).

The Apostle Paul portrayed sin as something external and objective, a sort of king ruling as a tyrant over men (Rom. 7). Sin for him was an alien power attacking men from without, bringing all men under its dominion (Rom. 3:23; 5:12; 11:32).

A distinction is often drawn between sin and sins. Sin, the principle of lawlessness, is found in all men, but sins vary considerably according to heredity, environment, disposition, and circumstances. Sin might be described as the tree, whereas sins are the fruit. Sin is in our very nature and it expresses itself in various ways. Sin is a matter not only of the act but of the attitude. Such sins as pride, jealousy, greed, impurity, and self-will may be hidden within a man's heart and only occasionally reveal themselves in outward acts (Mk. 7:21-23).

Sin is consistently represented as something which God hates (Jer. 44:4), against which his holy nature must revolt (Hab. 1:13). It leads inevitably to spiritual death (Rom. 6:23; Jas. 1:15). Since man is a moral being, when he sins he is guilty in the sight of God, and this guilt incurs the divine wrath. Since men are guilty of having sinned, all stand condemned (Rom. 3:19; Ps. 14:1-3; Isa. 53:6; Rom. 3:22, 23). Although a distinction is drawn between "sins of ignorance" and "sins of presumption," and the extent of guilt is related to the degree of light given, even so sin as such is inexcusable and must always be regarded as an affront to God (Num. 15; Ps. 51:4). Any deviation from God's moral law must be punished since the claims of that law must be vindicated. The glory of the Christian gospel is that, while taking full account of the seriousness of sin, it points to One who has grappled with the problem on man's behalf and in man's stead. The simplest expression of that gospel is found in the words, "Christ died for our sins" (1 Cor. 15:3). (G.W.K.)

SIN, WILDERNESS OF *See* GEOGRAPHY OF THE HOLY LAND

SINAI, MOUNT, WILDERNESS OF *See* GEOGRAPHY OF THE HOLY LAND

SINITES An unidentified group of Canaanites (Gen. 10:17; 1 Chron. 1:15).

SIN OFFERING *See* SACRIFICES AND OFFERINGS

SIPHMOTH An unidentified village in the tribal area of Judah (1 Sam. 30:28).

SIPPAI *See* SAPH

SIRAH A cistern in an unidentified place involved in the account of the murder of Abner by Joab (2 Sam. 3:26).

SIRION *See* HERMON, MOUNT

SISERA 1. The leader of the Canaanite kings against whom Deborah and Barak were victorious. He was killed by Jael who drove a tent peg through his head while he slept (Judg. 4:2ff.; 5:24ff.).

2. The ancestor of some temple servants who came back from the Babylonian captivity with Zerubbabel (Ezra 2:53).

SISMAI, SISAMAI A Jerahmeelite descendant of Judah (1 Chron. 2:40).

SISTRUM *See* MUSIC, MUSICAL INSTRUMENTS

SITHRI, ZITHRI A Levite in the days of Moses (Ex. 6:22).

SITNAH The name of a well dug by the servants of Isaac near Gerar (Gen. 26:21).

SIVAN *See* CALENDAR

SKINK *See* BEASTS, 6

SKIRT *See* DRESS

SLANDER Untrue talk designed to harm the one against whom it is directed. If it is against God, it is called blasphemy. The Ninth Commandment concerns the bearing of a false witness (Ex. 20:16; 2 Sam. 19:24-30; Lev. 19:16; Mt. 15:19). It is many times condemned in the NT by the apostles (2 Cor. 12:20; Eph. 4:31; 1 Pet. 2:1; Rom. 1:30).

SLAVE A human being who is owned by another. Their treatment in Israel was more humane than in the neighboring countries for two reasons: the divine laws given about them, and the fact that the Hebrew and Greek words in so many cases refer to servants and not slaves in the modern sense. The latter is seen in the KJV renderings where the word "slave" is found only twice and the word "slavery" not at all. Slaves or servants could be acquired as booty in war or by abduction, by purchase, or default on debts, by birth or by one's voluntarily selling himself (Judg. 5:30; 2 Kgs. 5:2, 3; Deut. 24:7; Lev. 25:44-46; Gen. 15:3). Hebrew slaves could gain their freedom and could not be permanently enslaved (Ex. 21:2ff.; Lev. 25:25ff.; Deut. 15:12ff.). In NT times slavery is known also. Paul sent the slave of Philemon back to him (Philem. 1:16). In Christ there is neither bond nor free (Gal. 3:28; 1 Cor. 7:12). All Christians are to consider themselves servants or slaves to their Lord, to Christ himself (Rom. 6:16-22). In the passages concerning proper human relations in the family, the relationships of slaves and masters is also included (Eph. 6:5ff.; Col. 3:22ff.).

SLING *See* ARMS AND ARMOR

SLOPES *See* GEOGRAPHY OF THE HOLY LAND

SLUG *See* BEASTS, 6

SMITH Before Noah the Bible refers to one Tubal-Cain who was a worker in both bronze and iron (Gen. 4:22). This is considered by some as a historical impossibility but others think that the reference is to the cold forging of native copper and meteoric iron. The matter is not clear. Until recently it was felt that at Tell el-Kheleifeh (Ezion Geber) there was an example of an early smelting furnace and the literature has extensive descriptions. More recently however it has been determined that this is not the case but that the installation there is merely a typical example of an Iron Age fort. In Iron I (1200-900 B.C.) smelting was done in the hills to the W and N of Elath-Ezion Geber where we find that the ore was burned in open pits. In the days of the prophet Samuel there was no smith in Israel but by the times of the Kings the situation had changed (1 Sam. 13:19; 2 Kgs. 24:14-16).

SMYRNA A city on the Aegean coast of Asia Minor; a church to which one of the seven epistles in the Book of Revelation was addressed (Rev. 1:11; 2:8).

SNARES Literally snares were used in the hunting of both birds and animals (Ps. 124:7; Hos. 9:8). Figuratively a number of things are called snares: riches, false gods or prophets, a slanderer (1 Tim. 6:9; Deut. 7:16; Hos. 9:8; 1 Tim. 3:7). The child of God is warned against the wiles and snares set by the devil for his entrapment (2 Tim. 2:26).

SNOW While snow is relatively rare in Palestine, and when it does come it very rarely outlasts the heat of one sunny day, it is noted in the Bible. It is particularly used as a symbol of whiteness or purity (Ex. 4:6; Num. 12:10; Ps. 51:7; Isa. 1:18). It is used figuratively in connection with the vision of God in Daniel 7:9 and Revelation 1:14 and of the angel who stood by the empty tomb on the first resurrection morning (Mt. 28:3).

SNUFFERS Golden or bronze implements used in tending the lights of tabernacle and temple. Based on the derivation of the Hebrew word it is felt that these were not tongs but rather on the order of scissors for trimming the wicks (2 Kgs. 25:14, 15; 12:13).

SOAP This is mentioned only in Malachi 3:2 and Jeremiah 2:22 in the Bible and not too frequently even in other literature. The inference would seem to be that other materials were used for cleansing the body. The connection with the word "lye" would seem to point to the direction that the "soap" referred to was some potash dissolved in water or oil.

SOCOH 1. A town (153-194) on the E edge of the Sharon Plain N and W of Samaria, (1 Kgs. 4:10) at modern Shuweikeh.

2. A town (147-121) on the E side of the Shephelah between Adullam and Azekah near the Vale of Elah (Josh. 15:35; 1 Sam. 17:1).

3. A town (150-090) in the hill country of Judah near Debir, S of Hebron (Josh. 15:48).

SODI The father of the representative of the tribe of Zebulun in the twelve spies which Moses sent to spy out the land (Num. 13:10).

SODOM Along with Gomorrah a city held up as an example of wickedness which had to be destroyed by God. It was located in some unidentified location around the southern end of the Dead Sea, perhaps now under its waters. Its destruction is frequently pointed out in Scripture as a warning of judgment against sin (Gen. 19:24-28; Isa. 13:19; Jer. 50:40; Lk. 10:12; 17:29; Jude 7). Jerusalem is once called Sodom (Rev. 11:8).

SODOMITE *See* "Dog" under BEASTS, and DOG

SOJOURNER *See* STRANGER

SOLOMON *See* KINGS OF JUDAH AND ISRAEL

SOLOMON'S PORTICO *See* PORCH

SOLOMON'S SERVANTS The Bible gives a list of Solomon's servants, that is his princes and officers, in 1 Kings 4:1-19. Besides these Solomon made extensive use of the corvee or forced draft of the remnants of the conquered people such as the Amorites and Hittites, who were still to be found in Canaan (1 Kgs. 9:15-22). There is no doubt but that he also thus drafted the Israelites as well which may be inferred from the reaction of the people to Rehoboam after the death of the father, Solomon (1 Kgs. 12:1-11). The sons of Solomon's servants are noted among those who returned from the Babylonian captivity with Ezra and Zerubbabel (Ezra 2:55-58; Neh. 7:57-60).

SON, SONSHIP In OT usage, unlike English usage, a son may be the direct heir or any subsequent descendant. Jesus is called the son of David, the son of Abraham (Mt. 1:1). It is translated in the NIV as "children" reflecting the known usage that would cover both sexes (Gen. 3:16). Both Testaments recognize the fact that believers are called "sons of God" (Deut. 14:1; Rom. 8:14; Gal. 3:26). Sonship means membership in a group as is clear in 2 Kings 2:3-5. Thus reference may be made to the divine sonship of Christ, one with the Father and the Holy Spirit, and the sonship of all believers as being members of the family of God (Rom. 8:15; 9:4).

SON OF GOD *See* GOD, NAMES OF, GODHEAD

SON OF MAN *See* GOD, NAMES OF, GODHEAD

SONG *See* MUSIC

SONG OF SOLOMON, BOOK OF The author has been held to be Solomon because of the references to him by name in the book (1:5; 3:7, 9, 11; 8:11) as well as to many allusions that fit him well found there. Some put the book much later and some speak of later redactions of the text because of the Aramaisms and Greek words found in it. In general these differences stem from varying views held as to the origin of the Bible as a whole. Tradition puts it in Solomonic times. There is a great amount of variation in the interpretation of the book and the personages in it: a literal story of Solomon, a literal story of some in Solomon's times, an allegory only, or typical meaning. While there may be such differences of opinion the basic message is clear, namely that love is sacred and an emotion to be cherished, not played with. "Do not arouse or awaken love until it so desires" (2:7; 3:5; 8:4). Its counterpart in the NT would be the family passages in Ephesians and Colossians (Eph. 5:21—6:4; Col. 3:17-21).

SONGS OF ASCENT The translation of the titles of Psalms 120-134. It is believed that these songs were sung on the steps (degrees) going up from the women's to the men's court in the temple. Others believe that they were songs sung by pilgrims on their ascent to the temple.

SONS OF GOD *See* SON, SONSHIP

SONS OF THE *See* PROPHETS, PROPHECY
PROPHETS

SOOTHSAYER *See* DIVINATION

SOPATER A man from Berea who went with Paul on his final trip to Jerusalem (Acts 20:4).

SOPHERETH *See* HASSOPHERETH

SORCERY, *See* DIVINATION
SORCERER

SOREK, A valley near and W of Beth Shemesh occupied by the
VALLEY OF Philistines where Samson's mistress Delilah lived (Judg. 16:4).

SOSIPATER One who sent greetings to the church at Rome (Rom. 16:21).

SOSTHENES 1. A ruler of the synagogue at Corinth in Paul's day. He was beaten by the Corinthians (Acts 18:17).

2. An associate of Paul at the time of his writing the first Epistle to Corinth (1 Cor. 1:1).

SOTAI The ancestor of some of Solomon's servants who returned from the Babylonian captivity with Zerubbabel (Ezra 2:55).

SOUL, SPIRIT In both Testaments these words are used interchangeably and are synonyms even while each has its own special emphasis. Two Hebrew (*nephesh* and *ruach*) and two Greek (*psuche* and *pneuma*) words are involved. Soul is commonly used to refer to the nonmaterial part of man in ordinary relation to physical things. When the reference is to nonearthly connections, to the relationship to God in particular, it is the word spirit that is commonly used for the non-material part of man. This distinction can be seen in a comparison of Revelation 6:9 with Hebrews 12:23 in both of which the reference is to the dead. In the first reference the thought is of their former earthly connection while this is absent in the second. Man and animal alike have "soul," the difference between them is that man is created in the image of God, while the beast is not (Eccles. 3:21; Gen. 1:20). In nontheological contexts these words also mean "wind" or "breath."

SOUTH, THE *See* GEOGRAPHY OF THE HOLY LAND

SOWER, SOWING *See* FARMING

SPAIN A country in SW Europe. It is mentioned in the Bible only in Romans 15:24, 28, in connection with a hope of Paul that he might be able to visit it.

SPAN *See* WEIGHTS AND MEASURES

SPARROW *See* BIRDS, 9

SPEAR *See* ARMS AND ARMOR

SPICE, SPICES *See* PLANTS, PERFUMES, AND SPICES

SPIDER *See* BEASTS, 6

SPINNING *See* WEAVING

SPIRIT *See* SOUL

SPIRIT OF GOD, HOLY SPIRIT *See* GOD, NAMES OF, GODHEAD

SPIRITS 1. Distinguishing between spirits. Paul lists this as one of the spiritual gifts (1 Cor. 12:10). Since many false prophets were in the world it was necessary to use judgment to see which speaker, prophet, or message was of God (1 Jn. 4:1). The test was conformity to the revelation of God, his law and testimony (Isa. 8:20, NIV), the Scripture.

2. Spirits in prison (1 Pet. 3:18-20). The gospel was preached to those of old, before they died, so that they might be judged as men now living are to be judged. There is no doctrine of a second chance or a second preaching of the gospel for salvation indicated in the NT.

SPIRITUAL GIFTS As used in the NT, these words refer to certain extraordinary gifts given to Christians by the Holy Spirit to equip them for ministry, whether preaching or other service. Several lists of them are given (Rom. 12:6-8; 1 Cor. 12:1-11, 28-30; Eph. 4:7-12). The chief gift to be desired was to be able to prophesy, that is, to forthtell or preach the Word of the living God effectively (1 Cor. 14:1).

SPRING *See* FOUNTAIN

SPRINKLE As a part of the ceremony of hallowing or cleansing persons or things the priest was required to dip hyssop or his finger (Ex. 12:22; Lev. 16:14) in the blood of a sacrificial animal, in oil, or in pure water, and sprinkle the blood, the oil, or water on that which was to be hallowed to God or cleansed. If the finger of the priest was used the symbolic liquid was either sprinkled or directly applied (Ex. 29:21; Lev. 14:15-18; Num. 8:6ff.; 19:14-22). In the NT Christ is the sacrifice for man's sin and reference is made to the sprinkling of his blood in symbol on man for his cleansing (Heb. 12:24; 10:19-22; 1 Pet. 1:2). In the prophetic description of the sacrifice of the Servant of God (Isa. 52:14, 15), Christ in Christian interpretation, Isaiah noted that the "marring of the servant" will result in the "sprinkling" and thus the cleansing from sin of many. The OT symbolism is thus carried through in this passage. The RSV renders "startle" and says of the Hebrew word in a note: "The meaning of the Hebrew word is uncertain." This would seem to be for theological and not philological reasons. It might have been better to have said "the meaning of the Hebrew word at this point is uncertain for us" for they render the word, even in the very same form, in other contexts as "sprinkle" (compare Num. 19:21; Lev. 16:14).

SQUADS Quaternion. The squad consisted of a group of four soldiers. One of these served in each of the four night watches (Acts 12:4).

STACHYS A Roman Christian to whom Paul sent greetings (Rom. 16:9).

STADIA *See* WEIGHTS AND MEASURES

STALL *See* MANGER

STAR, STARS *See also* DAYSTAR. As used in the Bible these words refer to any luminous nonterrestrial body other than the sun and moon. Scientific "astronomy" was not a concern of the Bible but certain identifiable constellations are mentioned: Arcturus (the Bear), Orion, Pleiades (Job. 9:9; 38:31, 32). A number of explanations have been offered for the "star of Bethlehem" (Mt. 2:2), none of which are particularly satisfactory.

STAR-GOD *See* DEITIES

STEADFAST LOVE Steadfastness conveys the ideas of constancy, fidelity, and patient enduring. The two words "steadfast love" as used in the RSV are the translation of the Hebrew word *hesed* (Gen. 24:12; Ps. 36:5-10 and many others). On the exact meaning of this Hebrew word there is a very great body of literature. The KJV usually renders it "mercy" but in a limited number of cases by "kindness." The lexicographers suggest kindness, loving kindness, and mercy. In the NT it is related to the concept of grace.

STEPHANAS A Christian of Corinth, the members of whose house were the first converts of Achaia (1 Cor. 16:15-18).

STEPHEN One of the seven first deacons of the early church in Jerusalem. His speeches angered the religious authorities and they stoned him, making him the first Christian martyr (Acts 6:5-12).

STEPPE The more frequent translation of the Hebrew is "desert" or "wilderness" (1 Chron. 6:78; Job 39:6).

STEWARD The word ordinarily applied to a servant who oversees the affairs of his master's household (Gen. 43:16; Dan. 1:16). In the NT it has the same usage (Lk. 16:1-8) but there a religious stewardship becomes prominent. Bishops are God's stewards as are, in a sense, all Christians. Christians are expected to use their time, abilities, and possessions in God's service (Tit. 1:7; 1 Cor. 4:1, 2; 1 Pet. 4:10; Eph. 3:2).

STOCKS An instrument of punishment. The hands and feet were locked in a frame which was capable of being used also to stretch the legs of the prisoner painfully. As used in the Bible the word also is a substitute for "prison" (2 Chron. 16:10; Job 13:27; Acts 16:24).

STOICS *See* SECTS

STONE *See also* PRECIOUS STONES AND METALS. Palestine is a very stony country with bedrock being just under the surface in most places and often outcropping over large areas. Thus stone was a common item for instruments, building, weapons, and monuments. A common use was as a landmark (2 Sam. 20:8; Josh. 4:1-9; Deut. 27:2). Another use was in the construction of altars from unhewn stones (Deut. 27:5-8). Among the figurative uses is the "stony heart" which God will replace with a "heart of flesh," namely a heart of faith and trust, a new spirit (Ezek. 11:19-21). God is "Israel's Rock" (Gen. 49:24). Simon the disciple is given the name Peter (little stone) and Christ is presented as the cornerstone of a building of God, a temple made from living stones (believers) (Eph. 2:20-22; 1 Pet. 2:5-8).

STONING Certain offenses against the law of God were punishable by death by stoning. These included blasphemy, idolatry, adultery, involvement in human sacrifice, Sabbath desecration (Lev. 24:16; Deut. 13:6-10; Lev. 20:2; Num. 15:32ff.).

STOOL As used in the NIV the reference is only to God's making the enemies of Christ a stool (footstool) for his feet (Lk. 20:43; Acts 2:35; Heb. 1:13; 10:13). The delivery stool (Ex. 1:16) was a special stool on which women sat during labor. The Hebrew word *kise'* is usually rendered in the RSV and NIV by "chair" (2 Kgs. 4:10).

STORK *See* BIRDS, 5

STRANGER The translation of a Hebrew word which would be better translated as "sojourner" (Ex. 12:48, 49). In Leviticus 19:33-34 it conveys clearly the concept of "foreigner."

STRAW The stalk of wheat or barley, but unlike the western use of the whole stalk the reference is to the chopped stalk after the threshing process has taken place. It was used for food as well as for bedding (Isa. 11:7; Gen. 24:32). In Egypt it was mixed with clay in brick making. An enzyme resulting from straw in water made the working of the clay more easy (Ex. 5:7-18).

STREET In addition to the normal use of this word it could refer to a piazza-like opening in a road or street or even to the bazaar held in a street (Josh. 2:19; Jer. 37:21; Prov. 7:12).

STRIPES *See* SCOURGE, SCOURGING

STRONG DRINK *See* DRINK

SUAH A descendant of Asher (1 Chron. 7:36).

SUCATHITES A family of scribes in Judah (1 Chron. 2:55).

SUCCOTH 1. A city (208-178) in the tribal area of Gad in Transjordan (Josh. 13:27). Jacob stopped there on his return from Haran and later Gideon punished its inhabitants for not assisting his effort to expel the Midianites (Gen. 33:17; Judg. 8:5-16).

2. An unidentified stop of the Israelites on their journey after leaving Rameses (Ex. 12:37; Num. 33:5).

SUCCOTH-BENOTH *See* DEITIES

SUKKIIM A contingent in the troops of Pharaoh Shishak in his campaign against Jerusalem in the days of Rehoboam (2 Chron. 12:3).

SUN The sun divides night and day and its rising indicates the E as its setting indicates the W (Gen. 1:14; Isa. 45:6; Ps. 50:1). It is used in Scripture as a symbol of faithfulness and constancy (Jer. 31:35, 36).

SUPH An unidentified place in Transjordan where Moses delivered an address to Israel (Deut. 1:1).

SUPHAH An unidentified place, perhaps in Moab (Num. 21:14).

SUPPER *See* MEALS and LORD'S SUPPER

SURETY One who assumes responsibility for a debt or the fulfillment of an engagement by another. Judah became surety to his father for the safety of Benjamin (Gen. 43:9; 44:32). Jesus is the surety of the New Covenant (Heb. 7:22). The word carries the idea of certainty and guaranty (Gen. 15:13; Acts 12:11). An interesting idea is behind the translation in Proverbs 6:1, 2 and 17:18, namely, "to strike the hands."

SUR GATE One of the gates of Jerusalem in the times of the kings of Judah. In the parallel passage the reading is "Gate of the Foundation" (2 Kgs. 11:6; 2 Chron. 23:5).

SUSA, SHUSHAN The capital of Elam in SW Iran, ancient Persia (Esth. 1:2-5; Dan. 8:2; Neh. 1:1).

SUSANNA One of the women who served Jesus (Lk. 8:3).

SUSI A descendant of Manasseh (Num. 13:12).

SWALLOW *See* BIRDS, 10

SWEARING *See* OATH

SWIFT *See* BIRDS, 4

SWINE *See* BEASTS, 10

SWORD *See* ARMS AND ARMOR

SYCAMINE TREE *See* TREES

SYCAMORES *See* TREES

SYCHAR A village of Samaria located somewhere near Jacob's well. Jesus met the Samaritan woman there (Jn. 4:5).

SYENE A village in Egypt called Assuan today (Isa. 49:12; Ezek. 30:6). A strange prophecy of the destruction of Egypt from

Assuan to the sea is found in Ezekiel 29:10. Syene to Migdol express the totality of the land of Egypt in the same way Dan to Beersheba do for Israel.

SYMEON, SIMON
1. A Christian from Antioch also called Niger (Acts 13:1).
2. The name of the Apostle Peter in Acts 15:14.

SYNAGOGUE A word found some sixty-five times in the NT of the RSV. In the RSV it is absent in the OT. In the KJV, however, it is used once in the OT also (Ps. 74:8), where the RSV renders it "meeting places." The ancient Greek translation of the OT known as the Septuagint frequently uses the Greek word *synagoge* in reference to the assembly of Israel. The basic concept is that of a gathering of people and from this it came to be transferred to the place where they met (Lk. 12:11; 21:12; Jn. 16:2; 18:20). After the destruction of the first temple in 586 B.C. and thus during the time of the Babylonian captivity and the restoration after it the synagogue arose as a group of people meeting together for biblical instruction, study, and prayer. From that time to this day the synagogue has been the center of the religious life of the Jews. The early post-NT literature has descriptions of the buildings and the activities conducted in them. Archaeology is finding in Israel the ruins of synagogues that go back to the first and second centuries A.D.—Masada, Korazin, Capernaum, and others.

SYNOPTIC GOSPELS *See* GOSPELS, THE FOUR

SYNTYCHE A Christian woman of the city of Philippi whom Paul exhorted to be reconciled to Euodia there (Phil. 4:2, 3).

SYRACUSE A city on the E coast of the island of Sicily. Paul's ship stayed there several days on his imprisonment journey to Rome (Acts 28:12).

SYRIA *See* GEOGRAPHY OF THE HOLY LAND

SYROPHOENICIAN One who lived in the area between Tyre and Sidon. In the NT there is recorded the incident of a Greek woman of the area who won from Jesus the healing of her daughter. So important is this example of persistent asking, persistent prayer, that it finds a place in Scripture (Mk. 7:26).

SYRTIS The name of two sandbars on the N coast of Africa where it was easy for ships to run aground and thus they were feared by the ancient sailors (Acts 27:17).

TAANACH An important Canaanite city (171-214) near one of the major passes through the Carmel range, not conquered by Israel at the first but in the tribal area of Manasseh, near Megiddo. An important town in the days of David and Solomon. Recently excavated (Josh. 12:21; 17:11; 1 Kgs. 4:12).

TAANATH SHILOH A town (185-175) in N. Ephraim (Josh. 16:6).

TABBAOTH A family of temple servants who returned from the Babylonian captivity with Zerubbabel (Ezra 2:43).

TABBATH An unidentified place mentioned only in the route by which the Midianites were chased by Gideon (Judg. 7:22).

TABEEL 1. An officer of King Artaxerxes of Persia (Ezra 4:7).

2. The father of a man that Rezin king of Syria and Pekah king of Israel wanted to make king of Judah (Isa. 7:6).

TABERAH An unidentified place in the route of the exodus from Egypt where the fire of God consumed some of the people as punishment (Num. 11:3; Deut. 9:22).

TABERNACLE *Tabernaculum* is the Latin word for "tent" which was used to translate the Hebrew *ōhel* ("tent"); usually the fuller form 'ōhel mo'ēd ("the tent of meeting") is used in the Pentateuch, or else 'ōhel hā'ēdut ("the tent of the testimony"). Another common designation was hammi'kān ("the dwelling-place"). This was the portable shrine provided for the worship of God during the period of wandering in the wilderness, while the Israelites of the Exodus were making their way to Canaan. It also served their needs after the conquest until the time of King David; it was replaced in the reign of Solomon by his splendid temple around 960 B.C.

The tabernacle consisted of a large tent measuring thirty cubits by ten cubits, surrounded by a court 100 cubits by fifty. (The cubit measured between eighteen and twenty inches.) The court was enclosed by large curtains or drapes hanging from poles supported by twenty pillars on each long side and ten on each short side. At the east end was a separate hanging at the entrance. Between the entrance gate and the entrance at the east end of the tabernacle itself was: (a) a large altar for blood sacrifice, measuring five cubits by five and three cubits high; it consisted of a hollow box of acacia wood overlaid with bronze; (b) a large basin or laver (kiyyór) of bronze, containing water for washing the hands and feet of priests who were about to enter the tent itself. Inside the tent was the "Holy Place" (qōdeś), measuring twenty cubits by ten cubits and containing: (c) on the north side a gold-overlaid "table of shewbread" (śulhān welehem pānim, "table and bread of the Presence"), two cubits by one cubit, one and a half cubits tall, it was intended to hold twelve loaves made from fine flour, representing the twelve tribes; (d) on the south side a seven-branched lampstand (menórah) of beaten gold, holding seven lamps, which were to be daily trimmed and cared for by the priests; (e) right in front of the curtain leading into the inner sanctum a small golden altar for incense, one cubit square and two cubits tall; it consisted of an acacia box overlaid with gold. The separating curtain in front of it was so constructed as to permit the smoke of incense to enter and pervade the inner sanctum. This sanctum was called "the Holy of Holies" (qōdeś qedāsím), or the "oracle" (debír—"rear room"), measuring ten cubits square, and containing only the Ark of the covenant (arón berít) or "Ark of the testimony" (arón hā'ēdút), so called because it contained the two tablets of the Law (the Decalogue). It consisted of a chest made of acacia, heavily overlaid with gold, and covered with a solid gold lid called "the propitiary" (hakkappōret, AV "mercy seat"), fashioned into two facing cherubim with outstretched wings touching each other. Upon this the high priest was to sprinkle the atoning blood each yearly Day of Atonement (yóm kippúr). After being skillfully constructed under Spirit-empowered master-craftsmen, Bezalel and Oholiab (Ex. 35:30, 34), it was solemnly dedicated to

God's service on the first month of the second year after the Exodus (Ex. 40:17) and sanctified by the presence of his Shekinah glory. *See* TABERNACLES, FEAST OF, CALENDAR, and FESTIVALS. (G.L.A.)

TABITHA Also called Dorcas, a Christian woman of Joppa whom Peter raised from the dead (Acts 9:36-40).

TABLE The translation of many different Hebrew and Greek words, tables for eating, writing, moneychangers and for ritual vessels being among them. Two special tables should be noted: the tables of the Law and the table of the Lord. The former were the two stone tablets upon which the Ten Commandments were written and the latter refers to both the altar of burnt offering and the Christian communion table (Mal. 1:7, 12; 1 Cor. 10:21).

TABOR 1. On Mt. Tabor and the plain of Tabor *see* GEOGRAPHY OF THE HOLY LAND.

2. An unidentified Levitical town in the tribal area of Zebulun (1 Chron. 6:77). Perhaps to be identified with DABERATH.

TABRIMMON The father of Ben-Hadad, king of Syria (1 Kgs. 15:18).

TADMOR An important spot on one of the main trade routes between Egypt, Palestine and Mesopotamia, NE of Damascus in the desert. As such it would have great antiquity, but it came into prominence when Solomon built it up and later when the Romans made a great city, Palmyra, there (1 Kgs. 9:18; 2 Chron. 8:4).

TAHAN 1. A son of Ephraim and the founder of the Tahanites (Num. 26:35).

2. A later descendant of Ephraim (1 Chron. 7:25).

TAHASH A son of Nahor and thus nephew of Abraham (Gen. 22:24).

TAHATH 1, 2, and 3. A Levite and two descendants of Ephraim (1 Chron. 6:24; 7:20).

TAHKEMONITE, TAHCHEMONITE The family of the chief of David's three mighty men (2 Sam. 23:8).

TAHPANHES A city of ancient Egypt by an important road between Egypt and Palestine in the NE part of the Delta (Jer. 2:16; 43:7-9; 46:14).

TAHPENES The queen of Egypt whose sister married the Edomite prince Hadad (1 Kgs. 11:19-20).

TAHREA A descendant of Saul through Mephibosheth also called Tarea (1 Chron. 8:35; 9:41).

TALENT *See* MONEY and WEIGHTS AND MEASURES

TALITHA CUMI Aramaic words which Jesus spoke when he raised Jairus' daughter, "Little girl, I say to you, get up" (Mk. 5:41).

TALMAI 1. A descendant of Anak at Hebron whom Caleb drove out (Num. 13:22; Josh. 15:14).

2. The king of Geshur whose daughter was one of David's wives (2 Sam. 3:3; 1 Chron. 3:2).

TALMON A family of temple gatekeepers some of whom returned from the Babylonian captivity and resumed the same occupation in the time of Nehemiah (Ezra 2:42; Neh. 11:19).

TAMAR 1. A Canaanite woman who married Er, then Onan, and then bore Perez and Zerah to her father-in-law Judah. These were in the ancestry of Jesus (Gen. 38:6-9, 12ff.; Ruth 4:12; Mt. 1:3).

2 and 3. A sister and a daughter of Absalom (2 Sam. 13:1ff.; 14:27).

4. A city (173-024) in the SE part of Judah in the Arabah south of the Dead Sea (Ezek. 47:18, 19; 48:28).

TAMARISK *See* TREES

TAMBOURINE *See* MUSIC

TAMMUZ *See* CALENDAR and DEITIES

TANHUMETH The father of one who joined Governor Gedaliah (2 Kgs. 25:23; Jer. 40:8).

TANNER One who prepared skins by treating them with lime, the bark or leaves of certain trees, or the juice of certain plants (Ex. 25:5; 35:7, 23; Acts 10:6).

TAPHATH A daughter of King Solomon (1 Kgs. 4:11).

TAPPUAH 1. An unidentified city in the Shephelah of Judah (Josh. 15:34).

2. A city (172-168) on the border between Ephraim and Manasseh conquered by Joshua. Its spring was called En-tappuah (Josh. 12:17; 16:8; 17:7, 8).

3. A son or descendant of Hebron and Caleb (1 Chron. 2:43).

TARALAH An unidentified town in the tribal area of Benjamin (Josh. 18:27).

TAREA *See* TAHREA

TARSHISH, SHIPS OF TARSHISH 1. A descendant of Noah (Gen. 10:4), associated with others related to Javan, the probable ancestor of the Greeks in the Aegean area.

2. An unidentified port perhaps somewhere in the western Mediterranean with which important trade was conducted. It may have been as far away as western Spain. Jonah took a ship for there in his running from the Lord (Jonah 1:3). At first the trade was with this place and then later the ships which plied that route came to be called "ships of Tarshish." This type of ship then even put out from Ezion Geber in the Red Sea (1 Kgs. 10:22; Isa. 23:14).

3. A descendant of Benjamin (1 Chron. 7:10).

4. One of the seven eunuchs of the Persian king Ahasuerus (Esth. 1:14).

TARSUS A city in Cilicia in Asia Minor, the home town of the Apostle Paul (Acts 9:11; 11:25; 22:3).

TARTAK *See* DEITIES

TARTAN Not a proper name but rather a title of a top military officer in the Assyrian army (2 Kgs. 18:17).

TASSEL *See* FRINGES

TATTENAI The Persian governor west of the Jordan River who was ordered by the Persian king to help the Jews in their rebuilding of the temple in the days of Ezra, after he had tried to stop it (Ezra 5:3-6; 6:6-13).

TAVERNS, THREE The place where the Christians of Rome met Paul to accompany him to Rome, just over thirty miles SE of Rome (Acts 28:15).

TAXES, TAXING In earliest times gifts were given to rulers and other governing persons in return for protection and other favors. Later forced labor and money were required. The tribute charged by conquering monarchs was forced tax (Ex. 30:13; Josh. 16:10; 2 Kgs. 17:3; Mk. 2:14; Lk. 19:2).

TEACHER A word frequently interchanged with master in the translations and many times applied to Jesus in the NT (Mt. 8:19; Lk. 9:38). A leader in the church must be able to teach and teaching is one of the gifts of the Spirit (Eph. 4:11; 1 Tim. 3:2; 2 Tim. 2:24).

TEBAH 1. A Syrian city from which David took much spoil (2 Sam. 8:8).

2. A son of Nahor and nephew of Abraham (Gen. 22:24).

TEBALIAH A gatekeeper of the temple in David's days (1 Chron. 26:11).

TEBETH *See* CALENDAR

TEHAPHNEHES An alternate form of Tahpanhes (Ezek. 30:18 KJV, RSV).

TEHINNAH A descendant of Judah (1 Chron. 4:12).

TEKEL *See* MENE, MENE, TEKEL, AND PARSIN

TEKOA A city (170-115) of Judah S. of Jerusalem. It was one of the towns that Rehoboam fortified and the hometown of the prophet Amos (2 Sam. 14:2-9; 2 Chron. 11:6; Amos 1:1).

TELAH A descendant of Ephraim (1 Chron. 7:25).

TELAIM An unidentified place, probably in Judah, where Saul mustered his army to go against the Amalekites (1 Sam. 15:4).

TEL ASSAR An unidentified place whose gods, according to the Rabshakeh of Assyria, were not able to deliver their people from the Assyrians (2 Kgs. 19:12; Isa. 37:12).

TEL AVIV, TEL-ABIB A place in Babylonia where Ezekiel visited Jewish exiles in the days of the Babylonian captivity (Ezek. 3:15).

TELEM 1. An unidentified city of Judah (Josh. 15:24).

2. One who married a foreign wife during the Babylonian captivity (Ezra 10:24).

TEL HARSHA An unidentified place in Babylonia from which some captives returned to Israel with Zerubbabel (Ezra 2:59; Neh. 7:61).

TELL A mound in which are buried the ruins of ancient cities, one upon the other. Such cities were usually walled and in this way distinguished from other ancient town or city ruins, called Khirbets. The Hebrew word *tel* is sometimes translated "mound of ruins" (Deut. 13:16; Jer. 49:2; 30:18).

TEL MELAH, TEL-MELAH A city in the same category as Tel Harsha above (Ezra 2:59; Neh. 7:61).

TEMA One of the twelve sons of Ishmael and founder of a tribe who lived in the area of the Arabian Desert by that name (Gen. 25:12-16; Job 6:19; Jer. 25:23).

TEMAH The ancestor of some temple servants who returned from the Babylonian captivity with Zerubbabel (Ezra 2:53).

TEMAN 1. A city (197-971) in Edom where the Temanites lived. One of the most mentioned is Job's friend Eliphaz (Jer. 49:7; Job 2:11; 4:1).

2. A grandson of Esau and an Edomite chief, probably the one who gave the name to the area noted above (Gen. 36:11, 15).

TEMENI A descendant of Judah (1 Chron. 4:6).

TEMPLE, THE In the fourth year of Solomon's reign (ca.965) construction was begun on the national temple of Israel in Jerusalem (1 Kgs. 6:1). Its dimensions were double those of the tabernacle: sixty cubits by twenty cubits (the cubit being eighteen to twenty inches long); and it was thirty cubits in height. These would appear to have been the inside measurements, not including the chambers, arranged in three stories, which flanked the north and south walls, and were intended for storage purposes and living quarters for officiating priests. In front of the entrance porch at the eastern end stood two pillars of cast bronze named Jachin and Boaz (possibly pet names for *"yākín* Yahweh" ("Jehovah will establish") and *"bố'az hammelek"* ("In him the king is strong"). These were each eighteen cubits high and twelve cubits in circumference (1 Kgs. 7:15), surmounted by lily-shaped capitals five cubits in height. The temple walls were constructed of hewn stone, paneled with cedar overlaid with gold, and adorned with carved cherubim, palms, garlands, and flowers (1 Kgs. 6:18). The ceiling was flat, consisting of cedar beams with gold overlay, and roofed over with marble. The inner sanctum measured twenty cubits by twenty cubits and contained the Mosaic Ark of the covenant, set between two standing cherubim ten cubits tall, with outstretched wings five cubits wide, touching the wingtip of each other with one wing, and the wall of the sanctum with the other. The entrance to the sanctum consisted of a door with hinges (1 Kgs. 7:50) rather than the veil or curtain of the tabernacle and of Herod's temple (Mt. 27:51). Inside the "Holy Place," measuring forty cubits by twenty were placed: (a) a golden altar of incense with a cedar frame, presumably larger than that of the tabernacle (possibly two cubits square and four cubits tall); (b) ten golden lampstands of seven branches each, five on the north side and five on the south; (c) ten gold-overlaid tables of shewbread, likewise five on each side. The entrance to the Holy Place or "house" had a gold-plated door like that into the sanctum sanctorum.

In the court of the Solomonic temple was a huge round basin of bronze, ten cubits in diameter (1 Kgs. 7:23), mounted upon twelve bronze oxen who stood back to back facing toward the four compass directions. There were also ten smaller basins four cubits in diameter, each mounted upon four wheels, presumably for ceremonial cleansing of the priests, but possibly also for washing portions of sacrifices to be burnt on the altar. The altar of burnt offering was twenty cubits square and ten cubits high (2 Chron. 4:1), which must have required some sort of ramp or platform to be usable by the officiating priests. Apparently the blood of the sacrifices was carried off by a large pipe bored through a hole in the celebrated rock which is now surmounted by the Dome of the Rock (*qubbatu 'ssahrah*); the drain system carried the flow out to a spout emptying into the Kidron Valley.

The inner court of the temple was of unspecified dimensions, but built upon a higher level than the outer court (Jer. 36:10) and surrounded by a wall composed of three layers of stone surmounted by cedar beams. The "great court" (2 Chron. 4:9) was intended for the lay public, and was probably enclosed by another wall. This entire temple precinct was situated on Mt. Moriah, along with various palaces and audience halls erected on the northern sector for governmental purposes.

The second temple, erected by Zerubbabel and finally completed about 516 B.C. after two decades of frustration and delay, was apparently erected on the foundations of Solomon's temple, and was therefore of the same dimensions, although of far less expensive materials and workmanship. It seems to have contained no Ark of the covenant, since the original Ark was lost during the exile. It may have had only one lampstand in the Holy Place, since Antiochus Epiphanes found only one to carry off as spoil in 168 B.C. In December 165 the desecrated temple was cleansed and rededicated by Judas Maccabaeus. In 19 B.C. (ca.) Herod the Great undertook a major renovation and enlargement which was not finally completed until A.D. 64. He built a new porch 100 cubits wide and 100 cubits high, and a gate measuring twenty cubits by forty. An empty room above the holy place raised it another sixty cubits to a total height of 100 cubits. The size of the courts was greatly enlarged; the foundations of two of the south gates have been found under the present El-Aqsa Mosque. The entire structure was leveled to the ground by the Romans under Titus in A.D. 70 and it has never been rebuilt since that time. (G.L.A.)

TEMPTATION An attempt to entice to do evil. It may be the exact opposite of testing, which, if surmounted, brings spiritual strength and good. One is inspired by Satan, the other by God (Eph. 6:11; Job 23:10; 1 Pet. 1:7; Deut. 8:16). The record of the attempts of Satan to tempt Christ is found in Matthew 4:1-11. Christ the second Adam was victorious in his temptation while the first Adam failed in his (Gen. 3:1-7).

TEN COMMANDMENTS *See* LAW

TENS In addition to its meaning as a number, a "ten" was a military unit of troops (Ex. 18:21; Deut. 1:15).

TENT *See* TABERNACLE

TENT OF MEETING, TENT OF THE CONGREGATION *See* TABERNACLE

TERAH The father of Abraham (Gen. 11:24-28, 31-32). He is mentioned in the genealogy of Jesus (Lk. 3:34).

TERAPHIM *See* DEITIES, DIVINATION

TEREBINTH *See* TREES

TEREBINTH, DOVE OF FAR-OFF *See* PSALMS, TITLES OF

TERESH A eunuch of the Persian king Ahasuerus (Esth. 2:21).

TERTIUS Paul's amanuensis in the writing of the Book of Romans who added his own greeting at the end (Rom. 16:22).

TERTULLUS One of those who brought accusation against Paul before Felix (Acts 24:1ff.).

TESTAMENT A written document by which a person disposes of his estate after his death, usually known today as a "will." The word testament is not found in the NIV where the Greek word *diatheke* is rather rendered by "covenant" (1 Cor. 11:25; Heb. 9:15-20).

TESTIMONIES, TESTIMONY A synonym of commandments, statutes, and ordinances, the laws God gave his people by which he intended them to live and conduct themselves (Deut. 4:45; Ps. 99:7; 119:24). The word in the singular often refers to that which was placed in the Ark of the Covenant, also called the Ark of the Testimony (Ex. 40:3), the Ten Commandments, and other testimonial items which were to remind the people of their deliverance from Egypt and their preservation in the wilderness wanderings (Ex. 25:16; 31:18). In the NT God bears witness, testimony, to his Son and this is that testimony that God gave us eternal life and this life is in the Son (1 Jn. 5:9-12).

TETRARCH The title of a petty ruler in the Roman empire even though such a ruler was sometimes called a king (Mt. 14:1; Lk. 3:1; Acts 13:1; Mk. 6:14, 26). It seems probable that the three titles, king, ethnarch, and tetrarch were somewhat interchangeable. Their roles are not exactly definable.

TETTER *See* SICK, SICKNESS

THADDAEUS *See* APOSTLES

THANK OFFERING *See* SACRIFICES AND OFFERINGS

THEATER A structure which apparently did not exist in OT times but came into use in Greece in the middle of the first millennium B.C. and which is mentioned twice in the NT (Acts 19:29, 31). The ancients made use of semicircular seating arrangements in natural hollows in hillsides condusive for an audience to watch a dramatic presentation or hear a lecture.

THEBES The capital of Egypt during the eighteenth dynasty, now known as Karnak and Luxor where the ancient ruins are still standing after more than 3,000 years. God pronounced judgment upon Thebes by the prophets (Jer. 46:25; Ezek. 30:14-16).

THEBEZ A town in the tribal area of Ephraim NE of Shechem. Gideon's son took it but was also killed there when a woman dropped a millstone on his head (Judg. 9:50; 2 Sam. 11:21).

THEOPHILUS Luke addressed both of his books to a person by this name (Lk. 1:3; Acts 1:1).

THESSALONIANS, BOOKS OF *See* PAULINE EPISTLES

THESSALONICA A city in Macedonia visited by Paul on his missionary journeys (Acts 17:1, 11, 13; Phil. 4:16).

THEUDAS A Jewish leader who raised a political uprising at some time before the ministry of Christ began to which Gamaliel referred (Acts 5:36).

THISTLE *See* PLANTS, PERFUMES, AND SPICES

THOMAS *See* APOSTLES

THORNS *See* PLANTS, PERFUMES, AND SPICES

THOUSANDS The designation of a military unit in addition to its literal numerical value (Num. 31:14, 52, 54; 2 Chron. 25:5).

THRESHING, THRESHING FLOOR The latter is a flat place on very hard soil or better on rock where grain was threshed in one of several ways: by beating with a flail or by oxen who drew wooden sleds with notched bottoms over the grain. When the kernels were loosened from the stalks, wooden shovels or forks were used to toss the grain and chaff so that a strong wind would blow the chaff away and the kernels would fall below and be collected (Isa. 28:27; Deut. 25:4; Isa. 30:24).

THRONE A symbol of majesty and authority on which kings, governors, judges, and high priests would sit (Gen. 41:40; Ps. 9:7). God is pictured as seated on a throne (Isa. 6:1-3; Dan. 7:9; Rev. 4:2-11). In the end of days the Messiah and the twelve apostles will be seated on thrones (Mt. 25:31).

THUNDER Thunder and lightning are not everyday occurrences in Palestine. In fact they are rather rare and usually limited to short periods in either the spring or fall. In the Bible they are interpreted frequently as a manifestation of divine power and are a part of the imagery with which the throne of God in heaven is described (Deut. 32:41; Ezek. 1:24; Rev. 4:5; Job 26:14; 28:26). It is interesting to note the references to these storms coming from the east, as they do frequently (Judg. 5:4, 5; Mt. 24:27).

THYATIRA An important commercial center in the province of Asia in Paul's day. When Paul was in Philippi he met a seller of purple goods from Thyatira by the name of Lydia (Acts 16:12-15). One of the letters to the seven churches of Asia Minor found in the Book of Revelation was written to the church at Thyatira (Rev. 1:11; 2:18, 24).

TIBERIAS A city on the west side of the Sea of Galilee founded by Herod Antipas between A.D. 20-25 and named in honor of Tiberius Caesar who reigned in Rome from A.D. 14-37. Even as early as NT times the Sea of Galilee was also called by that name (Jn. 6:1, 23), and the city itself is once mentioned.

TIBERIUS The reigning Roman emperor at the time of the crucifixion of Christ. The baptism of Jesus took place in his fifteenth year. He reigned from A.D. 14-37 (Lk. 3:1).

TIBHATH A city in Syria which David captured and whose riches he took to Jerusalem (1 Chron. 18:8).

TIBNI *See* KINGS OF JUDAH AND ISRAEL

TIDAL The king of Golim (KJV "Nations"), one of those aligned against the confederacy at the southern end of the Dead Sea in Abraham's time (Gen. 14:1, 9).

TIGLATH-PILESER, A famous name among Assyrian kings. *See* ASSYRIA.
TILGATH-PILNESER

TIGRIS *See* HIDDEKEL

TIKVAH 1. The father-in-law of the prophetess Huldah, also called Tokhath (2 Kgs. 22:14; 2 Chron. 34:22).

2. The father of one who opposed the plan for dealing with those who had taken foreign wives during the Babylonian captivity (Ezra 10:15).

TILES A word found only in Luke 5:19 in the account of the lowering of the paralytic through the roof in order to get him into the presence of Jesus. Tiles were not a common roof material in NT times. Mark refers to "removing the roof." Some suggest that Luke is using the expression "through the tiles" in an idiomatic sense.

TILON A descendant of Judah (1 Chron. 4:20).

TIMAEUS The father of the blind Bartimaeus at Jericho whose sight was restored by Jesus (Mk. 10:46).

TIMBREL *See* MUSIC

TIME On the division of time into periods see CALENDAR. Time in the sense of knowing that a king reigned so and so many years, or that it was 480 years from the exodus to the building of the temple was known and used in ancient Israel, of course. But time is something abstract. The idea of the abstract continuity of time is foreign to biblical concept. Time in the Bible is rather the concept of a particular moment of history. They referred to events such as the exodus, the Babylonian Captivity, the earthquake (Amos 1:1), and not to time as a continuum when they used the words we render into English as "time." The Bible lays the emphasis on "times" as points at which God himself does certain things on the earth and in his universe. When we read, "My times are in your hands [God's]," the picture is not that of the x number of years that my life will run but rather of the events that will be happening to me (Ps. 31:15). When we read of "eternity" or "for ever," the concept is not the continuity of the time but rather the events of that particular period.

The Hebrew has no clear word for eternity. The words *ad* and *olam* usually translated as "eternity" refer to periods of time of which the coming end is not known or determined. Samuel was to be left at the tabernacle "for ever" (KJV), that is for the full duration of his life, for an example (1 Sam. 1:22).

TIMNA 1. A concubine of the son of Esau (Gen. 36:12).

2. A grandson of Esau (1 Chron. 1:36).

3. A daughter of Seir and Horite (Gen. 36:22).

4. A chief of Esau, that is Edom (Gen. 36:40).

TIMNAH 1. A town (141-132) near Beth Shemesh that is perhaps best known from the Samson incidents. It was in the tribal area of Dan. Uzziah took it from the Philistines and Sennacherib conquered it later (Judg. 14:5; Josh. 15:10; 19:43).

2. An unidentified town in the hill country of Judah (Josh. 15:57).

TIMNATH HERES, TIMNATH SERAH Joshua's inheritance (160-157) in the tribal area of Ephraim where he was also buried (Judg. 2:9; Josh. 19:50; 24:30). There are a number of suggestions, none of them altogether satisfactory, as to the reason for the two forms of the name.

TIMON One of the seven early deacons of the church (Acts 6:5).

TIMOTHY A young man who came to know Christ through Paul and then went on to be his close friend and traveling companion (1 Tim. 1:2; Phil. 2:19-22). He had a devout Jewish mother from whom he learned the Scriptures from infancy (2 Tim. 1:5; 3:15), factors which made him the man he was.

TIMOTHY, BOOKS OF *See* PAULINE EPISTLES

TIN *See* PRECIOUS STONES AND METALS

TIPHSAH 1. A town on the trade route between Palestine and Mesopotamia on the Euphrates River, the northernmost point of Solomon's realm (1 Kgs. 4:24).

2. An unidentified town in the tribal area of Ephraim or Manasseh, N of Jerusalem (2 Kgs. 15:16).

TIRAS One of the sons of Japheth (Gen. 10:2).

TIRATHITES A family of scribes that lived at Jabez (1 Chron. 2:55).

TIRHAKAH A king of Ethiopia, about 689 B.C., who became the king of

Egypt also, in the twenty-fifth Dynasty (2 Kgs. 19:9; Isa. 37:9).

TIRHANAH A son of Caleb (1 Chron. 2:48).

TIRIA A descendant of Judah (1 Chron. 4:16).

TIRZAH 1. The youngest daughter of Zelophehad who had no sons and so requested that his daughters be given land in the division under Joshua (Num. 26:33; 27:1; Josh. 17:3).

2. The capital (182-188) of the northern tribes for forty years until Omri built Samaria, known today as Tell el-Far'ah (Josh. 12:24; 1 Kgs. 14:17; 15:21; 16:6-23).

TISHBE, TISHBITE An unidentified city in Gilead, the home of the prophet Elijah (1 Kgs. 17:1; 21:17; 2 Kgs. 1:3, 8; 9:36).

TITHE, TITHES The principle of a ten percent tax is ancient and not limited to the Bible. Abraham was accustomed to it at the beginning of the second millennium B.C. (Heb. 7:5-9). Jacob promised it to God (Gen. 28:22). The tithe of everything (Gen. 14:18-20) was the Lord's and he gave it as an inheritance to the Levites (Lev. 27:30-32; Num. 18:21-26). The laws of tithing were spelled out in Deuteronomy 12:6-17 and 14:22-28. The economy in Roman times made tithing a difficulty but it was still observed by the faithful (Mt. 23:23; Lk. 18:12). While tithing is not required as such in the NT, proportionate giving is (1 Cor. 16:2). The proportionate giving these people were used to was the tithe.

TITIUS *See* JUSTUS

TITUS A Gentile convert to Christianity and helper of Paul. A significant event in his life was Paul's refusing to allow his circumcision in Jerusalem on the grounds that he was a Gentile and that circumcision was not necessary to salvation or membership in the church (Gal. 2:3). He served Paul in both Corinth and Crete (2 Cor. 2:13; 7:6-14; 8:6-23; 12:18). Paul wrote one of his Epistles to him.

TITUS, BOOK OF *See* PAULINE EPISTLES

TIZITE A designation of one of David's mighty men and perhaps the name of a town or place now unknown (1 Chron. 11:45).

TOAH A descendant of Levi (1 Chron. 6:34).

TOB A city and the surrounding area in Transjordan, et-Taiyibeh but not the one in modern Israel, of course. Jephtha, the judge of Israel, fled to Tob and was later called back to deliver Israel from the Ammonites (Judg. 11:3-5). Joab defeated men of Tob in his day (2 Sam. 10:6-8).

TOB-ADONIJAH A Levite who taught the law in the revival in the days of Jehoshaphat (2 Chron. 17:8).

TOBIAH 1. The ancestor of some who returned from the Babylonian captivity but could not prove their Israelite descent (Ezra 2:60).

2. An Ammonite who opposed Nehemiah in his rebuilding of Jerusalem. Nehemiah ejected him from the place he was occupying in the temple (Neh. 2:10, 19; 4:3, 7; 6:1-19; 13:4-8).

TOBIJAH 1. A Levite who taught the law in the days of revival under Jehoshaphat of Judah (2 Chron. 17:8).

2. One who brought gifts for the second temple (Acts 6:10, 14).

TOCHEN An unidentified town in the tribal area of Simeon (1 Chron. 4:32).

TOGARMAH, BETH TOGARMAH An unidentified place somewhere north of Palestine. Some put it between the Euphrates River and the Antitaurus mountains, but others feel it should be farther from Palestine. Togarmah was a descendant of Japheth (Gen. 10:3; Ezek. 27:14; 38:6).

TOHU A descendant of Ephraim and ancestor of Samuel (1 Sam. 1:1).

TOI The king of Hamath who congratulated David on his Syrian victory (2 Sam. 8:9, 10; 1 Chron. 18:9, 10); also called Tou.

TOLA *See* JUDGES OF ISRAEL

TOLAD An unidentified city in the tribal area of Simeon (1 Chron. 4:29).

TOMB *See* BURIAL

TONGUE A word used in many senses in the Bible: an organ of the body and of speech; a language (literally tongue), dialect or a people with a common language; and in a figurative sense teaching a number of things (Deut. 28:49; Judg. 7:5; Isa. 66:18; Mk. 7:35). Figuratively the tongue can be a sharp sword, a smiting instrument, or even soft (gentle) (Ps. 57:4; Jer. 18:18; Prov. 25:15).

TONGUES AS OF FIRE The phenomenon that took place on the Day of Pentecost when small flames of fire like tongues rested on the heads of the believers as they were all filled with the Holy Spirit and began to speak in tongues foreign to them (Acts 2:3, 4).

TONGUES, CONFUSION OF The confusion of the languages of men which took place in the days after Noah (Gen. 11:1ff.).

TONGUES, GIFT OF A spiritual gift mentioned in several places in the NT (Acts 2:1-13; 10:44-46; 19:6; 1 Cor. 12, 14). *See* TONGUES AS OF FIRE above. The phenomenon of glossolalia in some churches today is the modern extension of the NT phenomenon. In the NT incidents the phenomenon occurred as a miraculous sign and evidence of divine approval and acceptance of the believers involved. This was especially true of the acceptance of the Gentile believers, a matter that was very important to the understanding of the early Christians who were all from Jewish backgrounds. This attestation was a turning point in their thinking as we know from the use of the fact by Peter at the Jerusalem Council (Acts 15:7-11). The question about glossolalia, however, is not about the phenomenon in NT times but about its continued use in the churches after the close of NT times. For this all our instructions are found in the letters of Paul, particularly in his letter to the church at Corinth. He observes that this is one of the gifts of the Holy Spirit along with all the others (1 Cor. 12:8-10, 28-30). This particular one is put at the bottom of the lists which would seem to indicate some rebuke of the overemphasis made by the Corinthians. It may also be that the Spirit is laying down by that means guidance for the future of the church as well. For an example, no one was to speak unless an interpreter was present (14:27, 28). This indicates that the phenomenon was not an uncontrollable one. It had to be controlled and exercised when an interpreter was present thus making it different from the frenzy marked by heathen rites when men lost control of reason and will.

TOPAZ *See* PRECIOUS STONES AND METALS

TOPHEL An unidentified place in the wilderness wanderings of the Israelites after their exodus from Egypt. It was in the area where Moses gave his first address recorded in the book of Deuteronomy (Deut. 1:1).

TOPHETH *See* HINNOM, VALLEY OF

TOU *See* TOI

TOWER Connected with a city gate in antiquity, these were for defense. Some were large enough to be used as citadels or fortresses in time of attack. At strategic points around a city wall, especially at points where the wall turned, towers were erected for observation by the defending forces. In the vineyards and fields smaller ones were built for watching the ripening crops even as they are to this day (2 Chron. 26:9, 10; Isa. 23:13; Zeph. 1:16; 2 Chron. 27:4; Mt. 21:33). Towers were made of stone blocks or rough field stone, or even of sun dried mud bricks at varying times in the history of fortifications.

TOWER OF BABEL *See* BABEL, TOWER OF

TOWN *See* CITY

TOWN CLERK Only in Acts 19:35 in the NIV is the Greek word thus translated, elsewhere in the NT the reference is to a Jewish scribe. In the Greek world, as at Ephesus, this man was an important official, even the ruler of the city, as well as the keeper of the records.

TRACHONITIS *See* GEOGRAPHY OF THE HOLY LAND

TRADE Our knowledge of trade in the ancient world comes from literary sources for the most part, but also to some extent from ancient art and artifacts. The literary sources are the Bible, ancient contracts, mostly in cuneiform tablets and sometimes as at Nuzu and Mari in massive archives. From the excavations of the ancient cities evidence of trade is found in the artifacts of one area being found in the cities of another. A case of the latter would be the Cypriote or the Mycenaean ware, excellent potteries made abroad and imported into the area of Palestine. Ancient trade routes were well established and widely known and used. Among these were the "Way of the Sea," the "King's Highway" and the later Nabatean routes across the Negeb of Palestine. *See* GEOGRAPHY OF THE HOLY LAND. Along these routes great cities grew up for defense and for services to the traders. While the concept is clear, and abundant evidence of its taking place is clear in the Bible, the word itself is found only infrequently. Abraham was a trader at Gerar, called a "sojourner," but the first use of the word "trade" in the NIV is not until Jacob's return from Haran (Gen. 34:10, 21; 42:34). Trading is mentioned in the Prophets, fourteen times in Ezekiel alone (Ezek. 27:13-24; 28:5-18), and in a number of passages in the NT. Jesus accused the people of making

God's house a house of trade when it should have been a
house of prayer and worship (Jn. 2:16). The word was also
used in the sense of an occupation. Paul and Aquila were
tentmakers by trade (Acts 18:3).

TRANSFIGURATION The event in the life of Christ when his appearance was
transformed so that his face shone like the sun and his clothes
became dazzling white. This came from within and was not a
reflection of some light from without. For a few moments
his body was transformed into the likeness of what his
resurrection body was to become in the glorified state.
All three of the synoptic Gospels carry the story (Mt. 17:2;
Mk. 9:2; Lk. 9:28ff.).

TRANSGRESSION *See* SIN

TREE OF Like the tree of life a miraculous tree in Eden, real but
KNOWLEDGE OF unidentifiable. Sin came not from tasting this fruit but from
GOOD AND EVIL disobeying God who told Adam and Eve not to eat of it.
Theologians speculate as to the meaning of knowing good and
evil.

TREE OF LIFE A special, miraculous, and therefore unidentifiable tree that
appears only in the Garden of Eden and in Revelation 22:2
(Gen. 2:9). Adam and Eve were driven from Eden to prevent
their eating of the fruit of this tree and thus acquiring
immortality. Just what is literally meant behind the symbolism
is not clear.

TREES These were of two kinds, fruit trees and those not producing
food. In biblical times some twenty-five different types of
trees were known and the area of Palestine was much more
wooded than at present. As late as Crusader times they
hunted game in the Sharon Forest. In Turkish times the
situation was changed and Palestine lost its forests. Only
since the arrival of the Jews in the area has the situation
begun to change with the planting of millions of evergreen
trees on the hills and the growing of many citrus and other
fruit trees.

FRUIT TREES *Almond, Pistachio, Nut.* While the third is surmised only
from the one reference to "nut trees" in Song of Solomon
6:11 the other two are specifically noted by name and their
identity is sure (Gen. 30:37; 43:11).

The *Fig, Olive,* and *Palm* produced some of the important
food crops. While the palm is mentioned a number of times
the word "date" in connection with it does not appear. It
is certain, however, from extrabiblical sources that dates
were produced and eaten in the area (Num. 13:23; Mt. 7:16;

Gen. 8:11; Jer. 11:16; Song 7:7; Deut. 34:3; Joel 1:12).

The *Pomegranate* and *Apple* are both well attested food trees of biblical times (Num. 20:5; Deut. 8:8; Song 2:3; Joel 1:12).

Sycamore and *Balsam.* The sycamore was a type of fig tree and important to the economy of Palestine as judged by the fact that David had an officer in charge of them (1 Chron. 27:28). Various suggestions including the mulberry, poplar, or even that it is not a tree at all have been given about the balsam (2 Sam. 5:23, 24; 1 Chron. 14:14, 15).

OTHER TREES The *Acacia* is well known and attested. It was abundant in the Sinai and in the Jordan Valley. The Ark of the Covenant was made of this hard, durable wood (Ex. 25:10-28; Deut. 10:3).

The *Cedar,* so well known in Lebanon, *Cedrus libani* is perhaps the most frequently mentioned specific tree in the Bible. Large amounts of cedar wood were brought to Palestine by David and Solomon for the building of their palaces and the temple (1 Kgs. 5, 6, 7).

The *Cypress* is not specifically identified. It is sometimes translated as "pine logs" (Isa. 41:19; 44:14; 60:13). It is noted in reference with the cedar on a number of occasions (1 Kgs. 5:8-10).

The Hebrew words translated *"fir"* are not yet identifiable. It may refer to one of the Juniper species. There are only a few uses in the Bible (Isa. 60:13).

The *Plane* is noted in Genesis 30:37 and elsewhere, *Platanus orientalis* (Isa. 41:19).

The *Pine.* It is literally translated from the Hebrew "oil tree," not known unless it be one of the pines and so rendered in the NIV (Isa. 60:13).

The *Oak* and the *Terebinth* are very much alike in the Hebrew but are distinct trees as is clear from Isa. 6:13 and Hos. 4:13. The former is the tree *Quercus* of which two species are known in Palestine. The latter is *Pistacia palaestina.*

The *Poplar* (Gen. 30:37; Hos. 4:13) would better be translated Storax as judged from the type of area in which it grows (*Styrax*).

The *Tamarisk* is definitely identifiable. It is a fast-growing tree in the desert areas of Palestine as well as on river banks (*Tamarix*) (Gen. 21:33; 1 Sam. 22:6; 31:13).

The *Willow* is of two types, the *Salix acmophylla* of the Jordan River area of Palestine and the *Populus euphratica* of

Babylonia, rendered Poplar in the NIV (Lev. 23:40; Ps. 137:2).

Algum or almug are not able to be identified. In each use the footnote gives the other translation. Commonly called "costly woods" (1 Kgs. 10:11, 12; 2 Chron. 2:8; 9:10, 11).

Ebony noted in Ezekiel 27:15 was an import from Rhodes (Dedan in the Hebrew text).

TRESPASS *See* SIN

TRESPASS OFFERING *See* SACRIFICES AND OFFERINGS

TRIAL The word is used in the Bible in the same two senses in which we use it today, a test, and a court trial (Jas. 1:12; Acts 26:6). The most famous of the latter is the trial of Jesus. *See* CHRIST, LIFE OF. The word "trial" is not used in connection with the court cases in which Jesus' case was heard.

TRIBES A word used many times in the Bible and in the overwhelming number of cases of the twelve tribes of Israel or of one or several of them. Occasionally, as in Revelation 14:6, the reference is to all people in general. The twelve sons of Jacob were: Reuben, Simeon, Levi, Judah, Zebulun, Issachar, Dan, Gad, Asher, Naphtali, Joseph, and Benjamin. God withdrew Levi from the list of tribes for he wished to use them in the transport and care of the tabernacle and its service (Num. 1:47-53). Why Joseph was dropped from the tribal list we are not told, but his two sons, Ephraim and Manasseh, were selected to make up the number of twelve. Some suggest it was an expression of the double portion of inheritance to a firstborn son, showing that Joseph's dream was in fact true.

Before and after the conquest of the Promised Land the tribes of Reuben, Gad and one-half of Manasseh were settled in Transjordan (Num. 32:33). The settlement of the nine and one-half tribes west of the Jordan is recorded in Joshua 15-19. In the case of Benjamin and Zebulun the borders are pretty thoroughly defined. In the case of the other tribes many of the cities, but not the borders, are noted. Benjamin, Judah and Simeon were in the S, as was Dan at the first before moving to the north. Ephraim and one-half of Manasseh were located in the hill country N of Benjamin which in turn was N of Judah. The other four were north of the Jezreel Valley with Asher on the coast and Naphtali by the Sea of Galilee.

The tribes were one kingdom through the reign of Solomon, in spite of several attempts to disrupt them. After Solomon the permanent division came with ten tribes headquartered in Tirzah and then Samaria, and the two other with their capital at Jerusalem.

TRIBULATION In both Testaments the word refers to trouble of a general sort, but sometimes as a punishment from God. The NT refers in a few cases to a great tribulation (Mt. 24:21, 29; Mk. 13:19, 24; Rev. 2:22; 7:14). It is a period of unparalleled suffering in the end of days.

TRIBUNE A Roman military officer over a Cohort (Acts 21:13-37; 22:24-29).

TRIBUTE A compulsory contribution taken from an inferior by a superior, whether by a state or by a powerful individual (Esth. 1:1; Lk. 20:22; Deut. 16:10).

TRIGON *See* MUSIC

TROAS The name of a city and a region located in NW Asia Minor visited by Paul on his missionary journeys. He left a cloak, books and parchments there and asked Timothy to bring them to him (Acts 16:8-11; 20:5, 6; 2 Tim. 4:13).

TROPHIMUS A Christian from Ephesus who went with Paul to Jerusalem on his final journey to that city. Misunderstanding about him led to a riot which in turn led to Paul's arrest. Trophimus was later ill at Miletus (Acts 20:4; 21:29ff.; 2 Tim. 4:20).

TRUMPET *See* MUSIC, MUSIC INSTRUMENTS

TRUMPETS, FEAST OF *See* CALENDAR and FESTIVALS

TRUST *See* FAITH

TRUTH As used this word may refer either to facts themselves, or to the relation of a statement to the reality. The first refers to the real state of affairs in itself. The second is relational. Christ is *the truth*, in himself as a fact (Jn. 14:6). "Knowing the truth will make a person free" is an illustration of the second usage (Jn. 8:32). It is assumed in this last statement that the relationship between the two parts of the sentence is in fact true, correct, dependable, right.

TRYPHENA A Christian at Rome to whom Paul sent greetings in his Epistle to that church (Rom. 16:12).

TRYPHOSA Another Roman Christian, a woman, to whom Paul sent greetings (Rom. 16:12).

TUBAL A son of Japheth and grandson of Noah (Gen. 10:2).

TUBAL-CAIN A descendant of Cain and then Adam who was a forger of bronze and iron (Gen. 4:22).

TUMORS *See* SICK, SICKNESS

TUNIC *See* DRESS

TURBAN *See* DRESS

TURTLEDOVE *See* BIRDS, 4

TWIN, THE *See* APOSTLES

TWIN BROTHER *See* DEITIES

TYCHICUS An Asian who went with Paul to Jerusalem on his last visit to that city. Paul refers to him as a beloved brother and helper. He is mentioned in connection with carrying two of Paul's Epistles (Acts 20:4; Eph. 6:21, 22; Col. 4:7, 8; 2 Tim. 4:12).

TYRANNUS The owner of a hall in which Paul argued daily at Ephesus (Acts 19:9).

TYRE *See also* GEOGRAPHY OF THE HOLY LAND. A Phoenician coastal city (168-297) and the people of a city mentioned seventy times in the Bible. The first mention in the Bible of this already much older city is Joshua's assigning it to the tribal area of Asher (Josh. 19:29). It became a great trading center and one of its kings, Hiram, a great friend of David and Solomon, supplied them with lumber and skilled craftsmen for the building of their palaces and the temple and also Solomon's fleet (1 Kgs. 7:13, 14; 9:11, 12; 2 Chron. 2:3, 11). Oracles on Tyre are found in Isaiah 23 and Ezekiel 26-28. Jesus visited the area and he referred to it in his rebuke of Korazin and Bethsaida (Lk. 6:17; 10:13, 14). On his final journey to Jerusalem Paul's ship landed at Tyre (Acts 21:3-7).

UCAL One of the two to whom Agur's words were addressed (Prov. 30:1).

UEL One of those who married a foreign wife during the Babylonian captivity (Ezra 10:34).

ULAI A river or canal in Elam that flowed through Susa the capital (Dan. 8:2, 16).

ULCERS *See* SICK, SICKNESS

ULLA A descendant of Asher (1 Chron. 7:39).

UMMAH *See* ACCO

UNCLEAN *See* CLEAN AND UNCLEAN

UNLEAVENED BREAD When used literally this refers to bread made without any fermented dough. It was required to be used during Passover (Ex. 12:8-30). When used in a figurative sense the thought is "unmixed" (1 Cor. 5:7, 8).

UNLEAVENED BREAD, FEAST OF *See* CALENDAR and FESTIVALS

UNNI A Levite musician in the time of David (1 Chron. 15:18-20).

UNNO A Levite who returned from the Babylonian captivity with Zerubbabel (Neh. 12:9).

UPHAZ An unidentified place from which gold was procured (Jer. 10:9; Dan. 10:5).

UPPER ROOM The place of the last meal of Jesus with his disciples. Tradition puts it somewhere on the western ridge of ancient Jerusalem (Mk. 14:15; Lk. 22:12). Here Jesus started with a Passover meal and converted it into the first "Lord's Supper" for the church.

UPRIGHT *See* RIGHTEOUSNESS

UR The father of one of David's mighty men (1 Chron. 11:35).

URBANUS A Christian at Rome to whom Paul sent his greetings (Rom. 16:9).

URI 1. The father of the artist and artisan Bezalel who did the work on the tabernacle (Ex. 31:2ff.).
2. The father of the officer of Solomon in the land of Gilead (1 Kgs. 4:19).
3. A gatekeeper in the days of Ezra who married a foreign wife during the Babylonian captivity (Ezra 10:24).

URIEL 1. A descendant of Levi (1 Chron. 6:24).
2. The father of King Abijah's mother (2 Chron. 13:2).

UR OF THE CHALDEES The original home of Abraham in southern Mesopotamia from which God called him to go to Palestine. The city has been extensively excavated (Gen. 11:28-31; 15:7; Neh. 9:7).

UTHAI 1. A descendant of Judah (1 Chron. 9:4).
2. One who came back from the Babylonian captivity with Ezra (Ezra 8:14).

UZ 1. A grandson of Shem (Gen. 10:22, 23).
2. A son of Nahor and nephew of Abraham (Gen. 22:21).
3. A Horite descendant of Seir (Gen. 36:28).
4. A land in which Job lived. Incidents in Job's book and elsewhere indicate it to have been a good pasture land, there

was an important city there (Job sat in the gate), one of his friends came from Teman, and Chaldeans attacked it. These may indicate a place E of Petra. Others think it was in the land of Bashan E of the Sea of Galilee (Job 1:1, 15, 17; Jer. 25:20).

UZAI Father of Palal who worked on Nehemiah's wall (Neh. 3:25).

UZAL A descendant of Shem, the son of Noah (Gen. 10:27).

UZZA 1. The owner of the garden in which King Manasseh of Judah was buried (2 Kgs. 21:18, 26).

2 and 3. Descendants of Levi and Benjamin (1 Chron. 6:29; 8:7).

4. Ancestor of some temple servants who returned from the Babylonian captivity with Zerubbabel (Ezra 2:49).

UZZAH One of the sons of Abinadab who assisted in bringing up the Ark but died because he touched it (2 Sam. 6:3ff.).

UZZEN SHEERAH One of the towns built by a lady Sheerah, daughter of Ephraim (1 Chron. 7:24).

UZZI 1, 2, 3, and 4. A descendant of Aaron, grandsons of Issachar and Benjamin and another descendant of Benjamin (1 Chron. 6:5, 6; 7:2, 3; 7:7; 9:8).

5. A Levite overseer in the days of Nehemiah (Neh. 11:22).

6. A priest in the high priesthood of Joiakim (Neh. 12:19).

UZZIA One of David's mighty men (1 Chron. 11:44).

UZZIAH 1. One of the kings of Judah also called Azariah. *See* KINGS OF JUDAH AND ISRAEL.

2. A descendant of Levi also called Azariah (1 Chron. 6:24, 36).

3. Father of one of David's treasurers (1 Chron. 27:25).

4. A priest who married a foreign wife during the Babylonian captivity (Ezra 10:21).

5. A descendant of Judah who lived in Jerusalem after the return from the Babylonian captivity (Neh. 11:4).

UZZIEL 1. A son of Kohath and grandson of Levi (Ex. 6:18).

2. A descendant of Simeon (1 Chron. 4:42).

3. A grandson of Benjamin (1 Chron. 7:7).

4. A musician in the days of King David (1 Chron. 25:4, 18), also called Azarel.

5. A Levite in the days of Hezekiah, king of Judah (2 Chron. 29:14).

6. One who worked with Nehemiah on the repair of the walls of Jerusalem (Neh. 3:8).

VAIN The translation of a number of Hebrew and Greek words all carrying the general idea of transient and unreliable, something light and vaporous. Even taking the name of God in vain is to treat it lightly like vapor (Ex. 20:7; Ps. 2:1; 33:17; Isa. 49:4; Rom. 13:4; Gal. 4:11).

VAIZATHA One of the sons of the Haman who tried to kill the Jews but was killed himself instead (Esth. 9:9).

VALE, VALLEY *See* RIVER

VANIAH One who married a foreign wife during the Babylonian captivity (Ezra 10:36).

VASHTI A queen of King Ahasuerus of Persia just before Esther (Esth. 1:9ff.).

VEIL *See* DRESS, TABERNACLE, TEMPLE

VENGEANCE Retributive punishment, for correction but not for revenge. In the NT it is reserved for God (Rom. 12:19). In the OT also the reference is frequently to God's coming day of punishment on the wicked for their own sins (Jer. 46:10; Ezek. 25:12-17).

VERMILION *See* COLORS

VESTIBULE *See* PORCH

VILLAGES Smaller settlements, mostly for farming, grouped around a central town which was the economic and defense center for the area (Num. 21:25; Josh. 15:32; 19:39; Neh. 11:25).

VINE, VINEYARD The grape is one of the very common plants of the biblical record. It is mentioned in connection with an immediate post-Flood event (Gen. 9:20, 21) where drunkenness is also noted. Grapes were a major item of the diet in antiquity, their source of sugar, raisins and preserved as pressed into raisin cakes. A sweet juice drink (wine is mentioned as a food along with milk) and a fermented one also; and, soured, the juice was used both as vinegar, a condiment, or diluted with water it was a popular drink (Deut. 23:24; 2 Sam. 16:1; Hos. 3:1; Isa. 55:1; Eph. 5:18; Ruth 2:14; Ps. 69:21). The Bible speaks of the culture, pruning and harvesting of the grape and of its preparation for the foods above (Jer. 31:5; Song 2:15; Isa. 5:1, 2, 10; Mt. 20:1-16; Num. 22:24; Ps. 80:8-13). Winepresses and collection vats and the storage of the wine in skins are noted (Mt. 21:33-41; Isa. 16:10; Mt. 9:17). The gleanings were to be left for the poor and in the seventh year the fruit was not to be picked (Lev. 19:10; 25:3). Pruning of the vine is also noted and the pruned branches were gathered and burned (Jn. 15:16). One of the important usages of the words vine and vineyard is symbolic. Israel was God's vine brought from Egypt and planted in the Promised Land; but she turned out to be a wild vine and for this must be punished, cut off. However, then she will grow again and produce fruit fit for the vinedresser (Ps. 80:8, 9; Jer. 2:21; Isa. 5:1-7; Hos. 2:12, 14-16; Isa. 65:8, 9). In the NT Jesus calls himself the "true vine" and God his Father the "vinedresser" and his followers the "branches" which must abide in this vine to be fruitful (Jn. 15:1-11).

VINEGAR *See* VINE, VINEYARD

VINE OF SIBMAH A special grape from the town of Sibmah. *See* SIBMAH.

VINE OF SODOM A vine with clusters of poisonous grapes to which Moses compared Israel (Deut. 32:32).

VIPER *See* BEASTS, 1

VIRGIN, *See* MAID. While the words "virgin birth" are not found in the
VIRGINITY Bible the concept of virgin birth is so much a part of Christian
doctrine that it needs treatment at some point. *See* CHRIST,
LIFE OF.

VISIONS These are means by which God transfers to men information
which otherwise would not be available to them. Sometimes
the vision is described and then its interpretation given. In
most cases there is only the simple statement "the vision
that" so and so had. Then only the message itself is given
(Acts 10:9-16, 17-23; Dan. 7:2; Isa. 1:1; Obad. 1:1).

VOPHSI The father of the representative of the tribe of Naphtali in
the twelve sent by Moses to spy out the land of Canaan
(Num. 13:14).

VOW(S) Voluntary promises to God to do certain things, usually but
not exclusively in return for some desired favor. Illustrations
of both are clear (Gen. 28:20-22; Ps. 132:1-5). In the Mosaic
legislation are found sections which regulate the making and
implementing of vows, sometimes called dedications (Lev.
27; 22:17-25; Num. 15:1-10). Numbers 6 is related to the
special Nazirite vow.

VULTURE *See* BIRDS, 5

WAFERS The bread, often beaten thin before baking. The ordinary variety was baked with honey or oil (Ex. 16:31; Num. 11:8). Usually the wafer appears in the text of Scripture in connection with one of the offerings (Ex. 29:2; Lev. 7:12).

WAGES Basically this is pay for services rendered. The words are sometimes translated by "hire" or "reward." In early times paid laborers were not as common as today in view of the fact that each worked his own farm or worked for another for his keep and some extra reward in kind (Gen. 29:15; 31:7). There were not fixed wage scales. This matter was settled between the parties. The law did, however, have in it some protection for the hired one (Deut. 24:14, 15; Lev. 19:13).

WAGON *See* CART

WAHEB Noted only in Numbers 21:14. If it is a proper noun it would be an unidentified place in Moab and it would also be the only proper noun commencing with the letter "w" in the Bible.

WAISTCLOTH *See* DRESS

WALL Fields and vineyards, houses and cities had walls made of sun-dried mud bricks or of stone. In ordinary buildings the stone would be unhewn field stone. City walls often had partly-hewn stone while the more ornate palaces had well cut and finished stones. Mud was used for mortar or else nothing was used and the upper tiers, especially in certain periods or situations, were of the mud brick variety. City walls were often massive and carefully built since protection from attack was one of their chief functions.

WAR Peace was a scarce commodity in OT times. Nations, peoples, and tribes were constantly at war with one another over land or booty. During the period of Israel's judges there were oppressions by foreign powers, wars of liberation, and then a new cycle of the same. Israel's kings David and Solomon extended Israel's borders by war. After the divided monarchy, Israel was attacked again and again by some foreign power until finally both of her kingdoms were taken into captivity. Jesus predicted that there would be wars and rumors of wars to the end of days, and in the last book of the Bible we read of terrible ones connected with the last days themselves (Judg. 5:8; 11:4; 2 Kgs. 8:28; Mt. 24:6; Rev. 13:7; 17:14). Priests accompanied the troops not as modern chaplains but to give oracles (Deut. 20:1-4; 1 Sam. 14:1-3). The Christian life is called a warfare and the Christian's armor is spelled out (1 Tim. 1:18; 2 Tim. 2:3; Eph. 6:10-20).

WATCH 1. In OT times the night was divided into three watches of four hours each. In NT times the Roman order was apparently followed, four watches each of three hours (Judg. 7:19; Mk. 6:48).

2. What the KJV calls a watch the NIV calls a guard, a group of soldiers, or others who do guard duty (Mt. 27:65, 66).

WATCHER An unidentified type of heavenly being used frequently in post-OT literature but only three times in the Bible (Dan. 4:13, 17, 23).

WATCHMEN, WATCHTOWER These towers were for two purposes: to guard the cattle or produce in the field, or to guard entrance to cities or key spots around a city wall. Archaeologists have discovered remaining foundations of numerous such towers at city entrances and around their walls (Isa. 5:2; 2 Kgs. 18:8). The watchmen were those who manned such towers, or simply guards used for other purposes (Isa. 62:6; 2 Sam. 18:24-27; Hos. 9:8).

WATER, BITTER WATER, WATER OF CLEANSING In a climate such as that in Palestine where there is no rain whatsoever from late March to late November water becomes a crucially important commodity. Extensive use is made of cisterns which are filled during the rainy season. These are not sufficient, however, and so a determining factor in the planting of an ancient city was the presence of a perennial spring, or well. This has additional importance in Palestine where there are so few permanently running streams. Water was used not only for drinking and cooking but played an important role in various types of ceremonial washings. Symbolically this speaks of purification from sin (Lev. 11:32; 16:4; Ezek. 36:25; Eph. 10:22).

The water of bitterness, the water that brings the curse, was water mixed with dust from the tabernacle floor which a woman suspected of adultery was required to drink. It was a kind of trial by ordeal (Num. 5:12-31).

The water of cleansing (KJV "separation") is the water for the removal of impurity, the removal of sin (Num. 19:9; 31:23). This water was usually sprinkled on the person or thing to be cleansed (Num. 19:21).

WAVE OFFERING *See* SACRIFICES AND OFFERINGS

WAY OF THE SEA *See* "Ancient Routes and Major Towns" under GEOGRAPHY OF THE HOLY LAND

WEALTH In Bible times this meant an abundance of property which in turn consisted of land and buildings, slaves, farm stock, and commodities, and metals (Josh. 22:8). It was God who controlled this, whether to give, to withhold, or even to take away (Deut. 8:17; Job 1:9-12). The possession of wealth brings with it special dangers, either to forget God or to covet, which are sinful (Deut. 8:17, 18; Ex. 20:17). He who has it is expected to be generous, and its wise use brings God's blessings (1 Tim. 6:9, 10; 2 Cor. 8:1-5; 9:10-15).

WEAPONS *See* ARMS AND ARMOR

WEASEL *See* BEASTS, 8

WEAVING AND SPINNING The latter is the making of thread from small fibers of flax (linen), cotton, or the hair of sheep, goats, or camels. The spindle and distaff are both noted in the Bible (Prov. 31:19; Lev. 13:47; Ex. 35-36; Mt. 3:4). It was forbidden the Israelites to weave from mixed yarns (Lev. 19:19). The finished thread of yarn was woven, usually but not exclusively by women, into cloth. The Bible mentions both warp and woof the two series of threads which were at right angles to each other (Ex. 35:25, 35). There are also mentioned the weaver's beam, the shuttle, the loom, the pin, and the web (1 Sam. 17:7; Job 7:6; Judg. 16:14).

WEDDING *See* MARRIAGE

WEEK A period of time usually seven days long. It is also used in the sense of a hapted which in Daniel 9:24-27, for an example, is a seven or hapted of years. *See also* CALENDAR.

WEEKS, FEAST OF *See* CALENDAR and FESTIVALS

WEEKS OF YEARS *See* WEEK

WEIGHTS AND MEASURES It is generally agreed that weights and measures in biblical times were not sufficiently fixed and established to enable us to give the exact metrical equivalents of today. Furthermore the standards between the various ancient countries were not fixed and it was also true that within any one country two standards might prevail, for example, royal or common, light or heavy, short or long, common or of the sanctuary. From the existing evidence it is possible, nevertheless, to make rather good approximations. The description below endeavors to show relationships within the weights or measures themselves, not to discuss in detail the modern equivalents. The NIV footnotes in each case endeavor to give its modern equivalent.

LIQUID MEASURES *Log.* Mentioned only in Leviticus 14:10, 12ff., equal to one-quarter of a *kab* (two-thirds of a pint).

Hin. One-sixth of a bath and so about one gallon (Ex. 30:24; Num. 28:14).

Bath. A liquid measure equal to the ephah, about five and one-half gallons (Ezek. 45:11, 14).

Cor. Equals ten baths and equal to a homer (Ezek. 45:14; 1 Kgs. 5:11).

DRY MEASURES *Cab.* Only in 2 Kings 6:25, one-eighteenth of an ephah (?)

Omer. One-tenth of an ephah or about two quarts (Ex. 16:13-26).

Seah. Supposedly is one-third of an ephah (Gen. 18:6; 1 Kgs. 18:32).

Ephah. A dry measure equal to the bath (Ezek. 45:11, 14), about one-half of a bushel and one-tenth of a homer (Ezek. 45:11).

Homer. Equals ten ephahs and is the same as a cor (Ezek. 45:14; 1 Kgs. 4:22; 5:11).

MEASURES OF LENGTH *Finger.* Mentioned only in Jeremiah 52:21 is one-quarter of a handbreadth.

Handbreadth. The width of the hand at the base of the fingers and thus equal to four fingers, or one-third of a span (Ex. 25:25; Ezek. 40:5).

Span. The distance between the extended thumb and little finger and equal to one-half of a cubit (Ezek. 43:13).

Cubit. The length of the forearm from elbow to finger tips. These vary with individuals, of course. If one follows the lead of the Siloam inscription in Hezekiah's tunnel one could estimate the cubit as about seventeen and a half inches.

Rod. The measuring rod of Ezekiel 40:5ff. was given as six cubits.

MEASURES OF WEIGHTS

Gerah. One-twentieth of a shekel (Ex. 30:13; Ezek. 45:12).

Beka. One-half of a shekel (Ex. 38:26).

Shekel. A weight that varied considerably from time to time and in different areas as well. There were royal shekels (known only in Babylonia apparently), common shekels and temple shekels (2 Sam. 14:26; 1 Sam. 17:5; Ex. 30:13). These varied from ten grams to thirteen grams.

Mina. Equal to fifty shekels, the common mina is in some cases sixty (Ezek. 45:12; Ezra 2:69). In the NT the unit of money used in Jesus' parable of the ten minas (talents in KJV).

Talent. 3,000 shekels; also, generic term indicating a large sum.

MISCELLANEOUS MEASURES

Day's Journey. Its length is variously estimated (Gen. 30:36; Ex. 3:18). Regarding a Sabbath day's journey, there also is difference of opinion. Some put it at 2,000 cubits (Acts 1:12).

Furlong. Not used in the NT version where the Greek word is rendered as "a considerable distance," equal to about 220 yards. This is a translation of the Greek *stadion* found in the NIV as "stadia" (Rev. 14:20; 21:16), in footnotes to Luke 24:13, and John 6:19, where the meaning is also stadia. In both of these references the NIV translates it as *"miles"* (making first the adjustment of the numbers).

Pint. Mary anointed Jesus at Bethany with a pint of nard (Jn. 12:3; 19:39).

Pound. Used in the NT, a weight of twelve ounces.

WELL Wells and springs are of vital importance in the dry Palestine climate. *See* WATER. The most common Hebrew word for a well is *be'er* and is found in many place names, such as Beersheba, Beerelim, Beeroth.

WHALE *See* BEASTS

WHEAT *See* PLANTS

WHEEL At first probably just a thin section of a round log, but by about 2000 B.C. the spoked wheel was well-known. With the coming of the chariot the rumbling of wheels meant the coming of an enemy (Jer. 47:3). *See also* POTTER, POTTERY on the potter's wheel.

WHIRLWIND Any violent wind but not particularly, if at all, a tornado or whirling wind of that type. It was a strong wind that would bring destruction. The Hebrew word is often translated by "tempest" or just by "storm" (Job 27:20; Isa. 29:6; Nah. 1:3).

WICKEDNESS *See* SIN

WIDOW Concern for the lot of the widow in the OT is very marked. Along with the orphan and the stranger God requires that they be well cared for (Ex. 22:21-24; Deut. 24:19-21). *See also* MARRIAGE and there Levirate marriage. In the NT the early church also gave them special consideration (1 Tim. 5:3-16; Jas. 1:27; Acts 6:1).

WIFE *See* MARRIAGE

WILDERNESS *See* DESERT and GEOGRAPHY OF THE HOLY LAND

WILL *See* TESTAMENT

WILLOW *See* TREES

WIND God creates them and controls them for his purposes. They come from the four corners of the earth. The N wind brings cold. The S wind and the E wind bring the dry hot desert air that sometimes kills. The W wind brings the rain and the moderate breezes. This, of course, is a general characterization only. Gales come from the NW and the NE winds drive rain away (Amos 4:13; Ezek. 37:9; Hos. 13:15; 1 Kgs. 18:44, 45). The moving of the Spirit of God is likened to the movements of the wind (Jn. 3:8).

WINDOW In biblical times a rectangular opening in the wall of a house. Some had lattice-work in them and some were recessed (1 Kgs. 7:4; 6:4). One of the references is to the windows of heaven, a way of speaking of the place from which rain came (Gen. 7:11; 8:2; Isa. 24:18).

WINE *See also* VINE, VINEYARD. This has always been one of the chief products of Palestine, a food when not fermented and even when fermented. It was used as a libation offering, dangerous if intoxicating; when it sours to vinegar it is a condiment, mixed with water a favorite drink, and mixed with a drug it was given as a sedative potion to those being executed (Gen. 14:18; 27:28; Isa. 55:1; Lev. 23:13; Prov. 31:4, 5; Mk. 15:23). Priests while serving were forbidden to drink wine, and Nazirites were not even allowed to touch grapes while their vows were on them (Lev. 10:9; Num. 6:1-4). Grapes were pressed by being trodden under feet in a press usually made of stone. The juice would run out through a hole near one end into a collecting vat. The juice was put in large jars or sacks made from the skins of animals.

WINEPRESS, *See* WINE
WINE VAT

WINNOWING A process in which the chopped stalks and heads of the grain were tossed into the air so that the wind could blow the chaff away and allow the kernels of grain to fall back on to the threshing floor. At first a wooden fork, like a hay fork, is used and then later a shovel (Isa. 41:16; 30:24; Mt. 3:12).

WISDOM An attribute of God and a quality of mind of man which makes him wise and skilled (Rom. 11:33-36; Deut. 34:9; Jer. 10:9). The fear of the Lord is declared to be the beginning of wisdom (Ps. 111:10; Job 28:28; Prov. 9:10). In an extended passage wisdom is personified (Prov. 8:2ff.). The Bible contains three books in the class of "wisdom literature," what the wise men taught and wrote, and it also includes a number of the Psalms (Ps. 19, 37, 104). The books are Proverbs, Ecclesiastes, and Job. In the NT Christ is called the wisdom of God and the source of our wisdom (1 Cor. 1:24, 30). This wisdom he passes on to men through his Spirit taking his Word (the Bible) and making it clear and meaningful to men (Col. 3:16, cf. Eph. 6:18).

WISE MEN *See also* DIVINATION. The word is most frequently used to refer to men and women of understanding or those with special skills (Prov. 1:2-6; Deut. 1:13; Ex. 31:2-5).

WITCH, *See* DIVINATION
WITCHCRAFT

WITNESS One who is called upon to bear witness or to testify concerning what he knows firsthand concerning a fact or an event. It is not used in the Bible in the sense of watching something. Things may also be a witness or a testimony to an event: a heap of stone, an altar, the Ten Commandments, the Law. A single witness is not enough. The Law requires at least three (Gen. 21:30; 31:44-48; Isa. 19:19, 20; Deut. 31:26; Ex. 25:22). "To the law and to the testimony: if they speak not according to this word, it is because there is no light in them" (Isa. 8:20, KJV). The KJV rendering here fits the context better and indicates that the Bible is itself a witness to the truth that God reveals. The one who bears a false witness is to be punished as for the crime in the case in which he bears the false witness (Deut. 19:16-21). In the NT the witness may be one who bears testimony to truths about God or one who tells what he knows, saw or heard about Jesus (Jn. 3:11, 32-34; Acts 1:8; 10:41).

WIZARD *See* DIVINATION

WOLF *See* BEASTS, 8

WOMAN Eve was especially created as a "helper fit for" Adam; as a pair they were given dominion over all the creatures, and it was intended by God that they would live together "as one flesh" (Gen. 2:18-25). As a wife she had the particular role of looking after her husband's needs and being a partner with him in procreation. As a mother she becomes responsible for the care and development of the children (Gen. 24:11; 27:9; Tit. 2:4, 5). Respect for mother was mandatory and disrespect was punishable (Deut. 27:16). As a member of the total society she was deeply involved in the socioeconomic and religious life of the community. She was even involved in the political and military life of the group as we know from the involvement of the queens and queen mothers, female judges, and deliverers: Miriam, Deborah, Athaliah, Jezebel (Jer. 9:17; Prov. 31:16, 24; Acts 16:14; 18:2, 3; Judg. 4:4, 5; 1 Kgs. 19:1ff., Deut. 16:13, 14; 2 Kgs. 22:14). Consistent with the above was the often recounted equality between the men and the women. In cases of adultery both are to be killed; both parents are to be revered by the children (Lev. 20:10; Deut. 5:16). In spite of this, however, there were areas in which she had an inferior status (Lev. 27:1-7). In the NT women also played leading roles: Elizabeth, Mary, Anna, Martha, and the several Marys. After the crucifixion and ascension of Jesus, the disciples met in Mary's home. There was an early church in Lydia's home. Phoebe was a deaconess. (Acts 12:12; 16:13-15; Rom. 16:1). In the beautiful picture of the family in Ephesians 5:21-33 the role of the woman is likened to the Bride of Christ, a phrase referring to the Church.

WOMAN, YOUNG *See* MAID

WONDERS *See* MIRACLES

WOOL The fleece of sheep or goats, an important product of Palestine. The law forbad wearing garments of mixed linen and wool, and, in a country where snow is relatively rare, wool became a symbol of whiteness and so of purity (Deut. 22:11; Isa. 1:18).

WORD OF GOD *See* SCRIPTURE

WORD, THE *See* GOD, NAMES OF, GODHEAD

WORLD A word with many denotations: the inhabited universe (Lk. 21:26), the universe as a whole (Acts 4:24), the planet earth (Acts 17:24), the world of people (Jn. 16:20), the world that is at enmity with God, having different ideas than those of God (Jas. 1:27; 4:4), the place where God's revelation was given and his redemption worked out (Jn. 3:16; 2 Cor. 5:19). Concerning the origin of this world there is no distinct *ex nihilo* statement to be found in the Bible in just those terms but the concept is clear and theologically required in such a statement as: "All things were made through him [the Word, Christ], and without him was not anything made that was made" (Jn. 1:1-3, RSV). As it had a beginning so too its end is pictured. First there is to be removed from it the curse that came on it with man's sin. This takes place at the same time as the revealing of the sons of God, their receiving resurrection bodies (Rom. 8:18-23). After this the Scripture speaks of the passing away in fire of the heavens that now are and the establishment of a new heavens and a new earth (2 Pet. 3:10-13). There is not sufficient evidence to be able to describe fully just what is meant.

WORM *See* BEASTS, 6

WORMWOOD A plant with a bitter taste used metaphorically of sorrow and bitterness (Prov. 5:4; Lam. 3:15, 19). In Revelation 8:11, a star by the name of Wormwood is seen falling from heaven and turning a third of the waters on earth to wormwood so that men die from drinking it.

WORSHIP In the OT the two words most frequently used would be literally translated "work/service" and "prostrate oneself." These give the twin idea in worship, service and homage. These can be rendered to man or God, but here we are concerned with divine worship. In the earliest biblical period, that of Abraham, worship was an individual or family affair. Where there was a theophany, an altar was erected, sacrifices made, and gifts given (Gen. 22:5; 24:26, 48). When the Israelites left Egypt and during their wanderings in the wilderness, God gave the pattern of the tabernacle and the full system of worship through personal and group sacrificing. After the conquest of Palestine the tabernacle was set up at

Shiloh and institutional worship was begun. This was later replaced with the grander temple and developed ritual that included orchestras and choirs. There were added harvest festivals and, with all of them, sacrifices and offerings (Ex. 23:14-19). With the fall of Jerusalem and the destruction of the temple new systems of worship were developed in Judaism and with the rise of Christianity worship took a new route. Private worship takes on new importance and the Church developed its own liturgies that commemorate the great events in the life of Christ, particularly his atoning death and resurrection. The Lord's Supper was the most important of these (1 Cor. 11:23-26).

WRATH, WRATH OF GOD There are illustrations of the anger and fury of man in the biblical narratives but they are few (Gen. 49:7; Ps. 76:10; Prov. 15:1; 20:2; Eph. 4:31; Col. 3:8) as compared to the references to the wrath of God. His justice can not permit some to obey and others to disobey without an expression of displeasure. His holiness cannot accept sin and evil in his subjects without a reaction of negation and an attempt to correct thereby. As justice and holiness are among the infinite, eternal, and unchangeable part of his being so must, therefore, be his wrath. God's reaction to man's sin is expressed in the Westminster Shorter Catechism thus: "All mankind, by their fall, lost communion with God, are under his wrath and curse, and so made liable to all the miseries of this life, to death itself, and to the pains of hell for ever." This is of necessity and by revelation one attribute of the God of the Bible. The other, and perhaps the one that mankind is more ready to accept, is that "God . . . from all eternity . . . elected . . . to deliver them out of the estate of sin and misery, and to bring them into an estate of salvation by a Redeemer." That Redeemer, being God himself, the Son, became man by taking to himself a true body in his birth by the virgin Mary, and in that body he satisfied all the requirements of justice and holiness so that wrath could justly be removed and holiness no longer offended (Rom. 1:18-32; Eph. 2:3; Rom. 4:15; 5:9).

WRITING *See also* PAPYRUS and PARCHMENT. Besides these two, people wrote on a wide variety of other writing materials: stone, metal, clay which was usually baked for preservation. Broken pieces of pots and dishes called sherds (the result is called an ostracon), wood and linen cloth were used. On some the writing had to be with a reed stylus and ink, on some by a stylus which could make dents in the clay while it was still soft, and on others by incising in rock. The art of writing began with picture writing in Mesopotamia around 3200 B.C. The picture of an object soon came to stand also for related ideas so that the picture of a bird could also mean "flying." Pictographic writing thus developed to logographic and from that to phonetic and finally to full alphabetic writing. In Mesopotamia the pictures became highly stylized with the transfer from simple line drawing to impressing on clay with a triangular headed stylus, so much so that it is virtually impossible to recognize the original item being depicted. That writing is called "cuneiform."

In Egypt the picture writing did not change appreciably during the several millennia in which it was used. Egyptians had many uniconsonantal signs and so they were able to spell out words and an alphabetic system was easily developed. A cursive and simplified script developed in parallel with the retained picture writing. The Hittites of Asia Minor at some time after 2000 B.C. adapted the Semitic cuneiform system to write their Indo-European language. It was in Palestine, the crossroads of the world, that the first true alphabetic writing originated. At Ras Shamra (ancient Ugarit) in N Syria there was discovered in 1929 a large collection of clay tablets with a writing in cuneiform symbols on them. This turned out to be a genuine alphabet. Another, linear and not cuneiform, which was developed in the Sinai peninsula, is thought by some to be the first true alphabetic writing. From this there developed in Phoenicia the script that has come to be known as Phoenician. By a gradual process of development this produced the forms of Hebrew writing known today, the Greek and Roman writing, and through them our English alphabet as well.

Long before the events of biblical history took place in Mesopotamia, Egypt, and Palestine, well over a thousand years before these events, man knew how to read and write and to record the events of his days for posterity. In the Palestine of Moses' day many different scripts were used and the scribes of the day recorded the historic occurrences of their times. While many feel that the early books of the Bible are compilations made much later from these sources and from oral tradition (see for an example PENTATEUCH), there is no reason as far as the knowledge and use of writing is concerned not to believe that they were written at the time they indicate and by the people ascribed to them as authors (Ex. 17:14; 24:4; 34:27; Deut. 28:58; 31:9, 24; Josh. 8:32; Mk. 12:19, 26; Lk. 20:28; Rom. 10:5).

WRONGDOING *See* SIN

XERXES A king of Persia whose Greek name was Xerxes who ruled Persia from 486 to 465 B.C. He was the husband of Esther, a Jewess, and was known as a cruel despot (Esth. 1:2; 2:16, 17 and Ezra 4:6). *See also* AHASUERUS and PERSIA.

YAHWEH *See* GOD, NAMES OF, GODHEAD

YARKON RIVER *See* GEOGRAPHY OF THE HOLY LAND

YARMUK RIVER *See* GEOGRAPHY OF THE HOLY LAND

YEAR *See* CALENDAR

YEAST In the RSV the word is used only in Galatians 5:9. The Greek word is elsewhere translated "leaven," a substance added to bread dough or liquids to produce fermentation. The yeast used in ancient bread making was a piece of a former batch of dough with this element in it.

YIRON, IRON A town (189-276) in the tribal area of Naphtali (Josh. 19:38).

YOKE A wooden frame placed on or over the necks of draft animals to which would be attached by various means the vehicle to be drawn (1 Sam. 6:7; Deut. 21:3). In Scripture the word is much more frequently used of being put in a yoke to be tied to other individuals when being taken into captivity, the yoke of slavery. This then is used figuratively for subjection and servitude whether to a foreign power or even to God (Gen. 27:40; 1 Kgs. 12:4-14; Jer. 27:8-12; Mt. 11:29, 30; Gal. 5:1).

YOUNG WOMAN *See* MAID

Z

ZAANAN An unidentified place, probably in Judah, mentioned only in Micah 1:11.

ZAANANNIM An unidentified site in the tribal area of Naphtali (Josh. 19:33; Judg. 4:11).

ZAAVAN A descendant of Seir, a Horite (Gen. 36:27).

ZABAD 1 and 2. A Jerahmeelite and an Ephraimite (1 Chron. 2:36, 37; 7:21).

3. One of David's mighty men (1 Chron. 11:41).

4. One of the assassins of King Jehoash of Judah (2 Chron. 24:26).

5, 6, and 7. Three who married foreign wives during the time of the Babylonian captivity (Ezra 10:27, 33, 43).

ZABBAI 1. One who married a foreign wife during the Babylonian captivity (Ezra 10:28).

2. The father of one of the men who worked on the repair of the walls of Jerusalem in Nehemiah's day (Neh. 3:20).

ZABDI 1. The father of Achan who took some of the things at Ai that were supposed to have been destroyed (Josh. 7:1, 17, 18).

2. A descendant of Benjamin (1 Chron. 8:19).

3. One of David's officers who was over the vineyards (1 Chron. 27:27).

4. A Levite in the days of Nehemiah; also called Zicri (Neh. 11:17; 1 Chron. 9:15).

ZABDIEL 1. The father of David's man who was in charge of his affairs for the first month of each year (1 Chron. 27:2).

2. A priest in the time of Nehemiah (Neh. 11:14).

ZABUD The father of Solomon's officer over the officers (1 Kgs. 4:5).

ZACCAI The ancestor of some who returned from the Babylonian captivity with Zerubbabel (Ezra 2:9).

ZACCHAEUS A tax collector who was one of Jesus' hosts (Lk. 19:2-8).

ZACCUR, ZAKKUR 1. The father of the representative of the tribe of Reuben among the twelve spies (Num. 13:4).

2. A descendant of Simeon (1 Chron. 4:26).

3 and 4. A Merarite and an Asaphite in religious service in David's day (1 Chron. 24:27; 25:2).

5. The ancestor of some who returned from the Babylonian captivity with Ezra (Ezra 8:14).

6. One who helped Nehemiah repair the wall of Jerusalem (Neh. 3:2).

7. One who signed the covenant with Nehemiah (Neh. 10:12).

8. Father of one of Nehemiah's treasurers (Neh. 13:13).

ZADOK 1. A priest and descendant of Aaron through Eleazar (2 Sam. 8:17; 1 Chron. 6:8ff.). He was a close associate of David as was his son after him and in Solomon's day he became the head of the priesthood in Jerusalem (2 Sam. 15:24ff.; 1 Kgs. 2:26ff.).

2. The father of Jerusha the mother of King Jotham (2 Kgs. 15:33).

3. A priest and descendant of Zadok, 1 (1 Chron. 6:12).

4. A military man of valor who joined David at Hebron (1 Chron. 12:28).

5 and 6. Two who helped in the repair of the wall of Jerusalem in the time of Nehemiah (Neh. 3:4, 29).

7. One who signed the covenant with Nehemiah (Neh. 10:21).

8. One appointed treasurer by Nehemiah (Neh. 13:13).

9. An ancestor of Jesus (Mt. 1:14).

ZAHAM A son of King Rehoboam (2 Chron. 11:19).

ZAIR An unidentified city where King Jehoram of Judah fought the Edomites (2 Kgs. 8:21).

ZALAPH The father of one who helped repair the walls of Jerusalem in the days of Nehemiah (Neh. 3:30).

ZALMON 1. One of David's mighty men (2 Sam. 23:28).

2. A mountain in the area of Shechem (Judg. 9:48).

3. A region or mountain in Bashan mentioned only once and then in connection with a snowfall (Ps. 68:14).

ZALMONAH The first stop (188-021) of the Israelites after they left Mount Hor (Num. 33:41, 42).

ZALMUNNA A Midianite king killed by Gideon (Judg. 8:5-21).

ZAMZUMMIMS, ZAMZUMMITES A race of "giants" who lived east of the Jordan whose land was taken over by the Ammonites (Deut. 2:20, 21).

ZANOAH 1. A town (150-125) of Judah in the Shephelah (low country) (Josh. 15:34).

2. An unidentified town in the hill country of Judah (Josh. 15:56).

3. Either a personal name or the way of referring to the founder of the town of Zanoah (1 Chron. 4:18).

ZAPHENATH-PANEAH The Egyptian name given to Joseph by the Pharaoh (Gen. 41:45).

ZAPHON A city (204-186) in the tribal area of Gad (Josh. 13:27; Judg. 12:1).

ZAREPHATH A seacoast town (176-316) between Tyre and Sidon to which Elijah was sent (1 Kgs. 17:9, 10; Lk. 4:26).

ZARETHAN A place (205-172) mentioned in connection with the Israelite crossing of the Jordan River under Joshua (Josh. 3:16; 1 Kgs. 4:12).

ZATTU 1. The ancestor of some who returned from the Babylonian captivity with Zerubbabel and Ezra. Some of them had married foreign wives (Ezra 2:8; 8:5; 10:27).

2. One who signed the covenant with Nehemiah (Neh. 10:14).

ZAZA A Jerahmeelite (1 Chron. 2:33).

ZEALOT, *See* APOSTLES
SIMON THE

ZEALOTS *See* SECTS

ZEBADIAH 1 and 2. Two descendants of Benjamin (1 Chron. 8:15, 17).

3. One who joined David at Ziklag (1 Chron. 12:7).

4. A Levite gatekeeper in David's days (1 Chron. 26:2).

5. One of the monthly officers of King David (1 Chron. 27:7).

6. One of the Levites sent by King Jehoshaphat of Judah to teach the law (2 Chron. 17:8).

7. The governor of the house of Judah in the days of King Jehoshaphat (2 Chron. 19:11).

8. One who returned from the Babylonian captivity with Ezra (Ezra 8:8).

9. A priest who married a foreign wife during the Babylonian captivity (Ezra 10:20).

ZEBAH One of the Midianite kings killed by Gideon (Judg. 8:5ff.).

ZEBEDEE The father of the Apostles James and John (Mt. 4:21).

ZEBUDAH The mother of King Jehoiakim of Judah (2 Kgs. 23:36).

ZEBINA One who married a foreign wife during the days of the Babylonian captivity (Ezra 10:43).

ZEBOIIM One of the cities of the Arabah destroyed along with Sodom and Gomorrah (Gen. 10:19; 14:2, 8; Deut. 29:23).

ZEBOIM 1. An unidentified town occupied by Benjaminites after the Babylonian captivity (Neh. 11:34).

2. A valley in the tribal area of Benjamin (1 Sam. 13:18).

ZEBUL The governor of the city of Shechem under Judge Abimelech (Judg. 9:30).

ZEBULUN One of the twelve sons of Jacob (Gen. 30:20), the founder of one of the tribes of Israel.

ZECHARIAH Perhaps the most popular personal name in the Bible, at least a name given to more individuals than any other.

1. One of the kings of Israel. *See* KINGS OF JUDAH AND ISRAEL (2 Kgs. 14:29; 15:10).

2. The grandfather on the maternal side of King Hezekiah of Judah (2 Kgs. 18:2).

3. A descendant of Reuben (1 Chron. 5:7).

4. A great-uncle of King Saul also called Zecher (1 Chron. 9:37).

5. A Levite musician in David's day (1 Chron. 15:18).

6. A priest who took part with David in bringing the Ark up to Jerusalem (1 Chron. 15:24).

7 and 8. Two Levites in the time of David (1 Chron. 24:25; 26:11).

9. The father of Iddo who was over the tribe of Manasseh in David's service (1 Chron. 27:21).

10. One of the men sent by King Jehoshaphat to teach the law to the people (2 Chron. 17:7).

11. The father of one who prophesied to King Jehoshaphat of Judah (2 Chron. 20:14).

12. One of the sons of King Jehoshaphat (2 Chron. 21:2).

13. The son of the priest Jehoiada who prophesied in the days of King Joash of Judah and was ordered by the king to be stoned for it (2 Chron. 24:20ff.).

14. One of King Uzziah's spiritual instructors (2 Chron. 26:5).

15. One of the Levites who helped to cleanse the temple in the days of the revival under King Hezekiah (2 Chron. 29:13).

16. One who helped to repair the temple in the days of King Josiah of Judah (2 Chron. 34:12).

17. A chief officer of the temple in the days of King Josiah (2 Chron. 35:8).

18. One of the two witnesses that Isaiah the prophet used (Isa. 8:2).

19. A gatekeeper who came back from the Babylonian captivity (1 Chron. 9:21).

20 and 21. Two who returned from the Babylonian captivity with Ezra (Ezra 8:3, 11).

22. One of those sent by Ezra to Casiphia to bring some Levites back to Jerusalem (Ezra 8:16).

23. One who married a foreign wife during the time of the Babylonian captivity (Ezra 10:26).

24. One who stood with Ezra while he read the law to the people (Neh. 8:4).

25 and 26. Two descendants of Judah who came back from the Babylonian captivity (Neh. 11:4, 5).

27. A priest in the days of Nehemiah (Neh. 11:12).

28. A priest when Joiakim was the high priest in the days of Nehemiah (Neh. 12:16).

29 and 30. A priest and a Levite who were present at the dedication of the wall of Jerusalem in the days of Nehemiah (Neh. 12:35, 41).

31. One of the twelve minor prophets who by his writing tried to encourage the people in Ezra's days to finish the building of the temple (Ezra 5:1; 6:14, 15).

32. The father of John the Baptist (Lk. 1:5ff.).

33. A martyr mentioned by Jesus (Mt. 23:35; Lk. 11:51).

ZECHARIAH, BOOK OF *See* PROPHETS, BOOKS OF THE MINOR

ZECHER *See* ZECHARIAH, 4

ZEDAD A city on the N border of Palestine (Num. 34:8; Ezek. 47:15).

ZEDEKIAH 1. *See* KINGS OF JUDAH AND ISRAEL, Judah's last king.

2. A prophet of God in the days of King Ahab of Israel (1 Kgs. 22:11ff.).

3. One who signed the covenant with Nehemiah (Neh. 10:1).

4. A false prophet in the days of Jeremiah (Jer. 29:21ff.).

5. One of the princes of King Zedekiah who listened as Baruch read Jeremiah's scroll (Jer. 36:12).

ZEEB A prince of Midian killed by Gideon's men (Judg. 7:25; 8:3).

ZELAH, ZELA An unidentified town in the tribal area of Benjamin where David reburied the remains of King Saul and his son Jonathan (Josh. 18:28; 2 Sam. 21:14).

ZELEK One of David's mighty men (2 Sam. 23:37).

ZELOPHEHAD A Manassite who died without a male heir and whose daughters, therefore, were given inheritances in the division of the land in the days of Joshua (Num. 26:33; 27:1, 7; Josh. 17:3).

ZELZAH An unidentified town near Rachel's tomb on the border of Judah (1 Sam. 10:2).

ZEMARAIM 1. A city (170-147) near the N border of Benjamin (Josh. 18:22).

2. A mountain in the hill country of Ephraim N of Jerusalem (2 Chron. 13:4).

ZEMARITES A Canaanite group that lived N of Lebanon (Gen. 10:18; 1 Chron. 1:16).

ZEMER The unidentified place where the Zemarites lived. *See* ZEMARITES.

ZEMIRAH A descendant of Benjamin (1 Chron. 7:8).

ZENAN An unidentified village in the low country of Judah (Josh. 15:37).

ZENAS A lawyer whom Paul asked Titus to send to him from Crete (Tit. 3:13).

ZEPHANIAH 1. A descendant of Levi (1 Chron. 6:36).

2. A priest in the days of King Zedekiah, taken in one of the captivities and killed (Jer. 21:1; 37:3; 52:24ff.).

3. One of the minor prophets. *See* PROPHETS, BOOKS OF THE MINOR.

4. The father of a Josiah from whom they took gold and silver to make a crown for the high priest (Zech. 6:10, 14).

ZEPHANIAH, BOOK OF *See* PROPHETS, BOOKS OF THE MINOR

ZEPHATH An unidentified town in the tribal area of Judah (Judg. 1:17).

ZEPHATHAH An unidentified valley SW of Jerusalem where the Ethiopians were defeated by King Asa (2 Chron. 14:10).

ZEPHI, ZEPHO A grandson of Esau (1 Chron. 1:36; Gen. 36:11).

ZEPHON A descendant of Gad also called Ziphion (Num. 26:15; Gen. 46:16).

ZER An unidentified town in the tribal area of Naphtali (Josh. 19:35).

ZERAH 1 and 2. Two descendants of Esau (Gen. 36:13, 33).

3. A son of Judah by Tamar and the twin brother of Perez (Gen. 38:30).

4. A descendant of Simeon (Num. 26:13).

5. A descendant of Levi (1 Chron. 6:21).

6. An Ethiopian (Cushite) who invaded Judah but was repulsed by King Asa (2 Chron. 14:9ff.).

ZERAHIAH 1. An ancestor of Ezra (Ezra 7:4).

2. The father of one who returned with Ezra from the Babylonian captivity (Ezra 8:4).

ZERED, VALLEY OF, BROOK OF A valley and a brook that divided Edom and Moab and whose waters run into the Dead Sea. The Israelites encamped there before crossing into Canaan (Num. 21:12; Deut. 2:13, 14).

ZEREDAH The birthplace (159-161) of the Jeroboam who became the first king of Israel in distinction to Judah (1 Kgs. 11:26; 2 Chron. 4:17).

ZERERAH An unidentified place in the direction in which Gideon's army pursued the Midianites after their defeat (Judg. 7:22).

ZERESH The wife of the Haman in the Persian court who wished to destroy the Jews (Esth. 5:10ff.).

ZERETH A descendant of Judah (1 Chron. 4:7).

ZERETH SHAHAR A city (203-111) in Moab assigned to the tribe of Reuben (Josh. 13:19).

ZERI A Levitical musician in David's day (1 Chron. 25:3).

ZEROR An ancestor of King Saul (1 Sam. 9:1).

ZERUAH The mother of Jeroboam I, son of Nebat, the first king of Israel after the final schism (1 Kgs. 11:26).

ZERUBBABEL The grandson of King Jehoiachin who brought a group of captives back to Palestine at the end of the Babylonian captivity (1 Chron. 3:19; Ezra 2:2; Hag. 1:1) and then became governor of Jerusalem.

ZERUIAH A sister of David and the mother of three of David's important military people: Joab, Abishai, and Asahel (2 Sam. 2:18; 1 Chron. 2:16).

ZETHAM A descendant of Levi, living in David's day (1 Chron. 23:8).

ZETHAN A descendant of Benjamin (1 Chron. 7:10).

ZETHAR One of the eunuchs of the Persian King Ahasuerus (Esth. 1:10).

ZEUS *See* DEITIES

ZIA A descendant of Gad (1 Chron. 5:13).

ZIBA A servant of King Saul who was given the role of looking after his lame son (2 Sam. 9:1ff.; 16:1ff.; 19:26ff.).

ZIBEON A descendant of Seir, a Horite (Gen. 36:2).

ZIBIA A descendant of Benjamin (1 Chron. 8:9).

ZIBIAH The mother of Jehoash, King of Judah (2 Kgs. 12:1).

ZICRI 1. A descendant of Levi (Ex. 6:21).

2, 3, and 4. Three descendants of Benjamin (1 Chron. 8:19, 23, 27).

5 and 6. Two descendants of Levi (1 Chron. 8:27; 9:15).

7. A descendant of Reuben (1 Chron. 27:16).

8. A descendant of Judah (2 Chron. 17:16).

9. The father of one of the military officers who helped to put the young Joash on the throne of Judah (2 Chron. 23:1).

10. One of King Pekah's men involved in the coup that put Pekah on the throne of Israel (2 Chron. 28:7).

11. A descendant of Benjamin in the days of Nehemiah (Neh. 11:9).

12. A priest when Joiakim was High Priest in Nehemiah's day (Neh. 12:17).

ZIDDIM An unidentified town in the tribal area of Naphtali (Josh. 19:35).

ZIHA The ancestor of some temple servants who returned from the Babylonian captivity with Zerubbabel (Ezra 2:43).

ZIKLAG A city (119-088) first in the tribal area of Simeon and then in that of Judah which was taken and held by the Philistines until the time of David when Achish the Philistine king of Gath gave it to him (Josh. 19:5; 15:31; 1 Sam. 27:6; 30:1-26; 2 Sam. 1:1; 4:10). After the return from the Babylonian captivity it was again occupied by Jews (Neh. 11:28).

ZILLAH One of the wives of Lamech (Gen. 4:19, 20).

ZILLETHAI 1. A descendant of Benjamin (1 Chron. 8:20).

2. A descendant of Manasseh who joined David at Ziklag (1 Chron. 12:20).

ZILPAH Leah's slave and Jacob's concubine, the mother of Gad and Asher (Gen. 29:24; 30:9ff.).

ZIMMAH 1 and 2. Two descendants of Levi (1 Chron. 6:20, 42).

ZIMRAN A son of Abraham by Keturah (Gen. 25:2).

ZIMRI 1. A king of Israel for seven days who murdered his predecessor and then killed himself (1 Kgs. 16:8ff.).

2. A descendant of Simeon killed by Aaron's grandson for bringing a Midianite woman into the camp of Israel (Num. 25:6ff.).

3. A descendant of Benjamin (1 Chron. 8:36).

4. An ancestor of the Achan who brought trouble on Israel at Ai (Josh. 7:1, 17, 18; 1 Chron. 2:6).

5. *See also* KINGS OF JUDAH AND ISRAEL.

ZIN *See* GEOGRAPHY OF THE HOLY LAND

ZINA A descendant of Levi also called Ziza (1 Chron. 23:10, 11).

ZION *See* JERUSALEM

ZIOR An unidentified city in Judah (Josh. 15:24).

ZIPH 1. A descendant of Caleb (1 Chron. 2:42).

2. A descendant of Judah (1 Chron. 4:16).

ZIPHAH A descendant of Judah and brother of Ziph, 2 (1 Chron. 4:16).

ZIPHION *See* ZEPHON

ZIPHRON A place on the N border of Canaan (Num. 34:9).

ZIPPOR The father of the Balak who brought Balaam to curse Israel (Num. 22:2, 4, 10).

ZIPPORAH The wife of Moses (Ex. 2:21, 22; 4:24ff.).

ZITHRI *See* SITHRI

ZIV *See* CALENDAR

ZIZ A mountain pass in SE Judah near En Gedi (2 Chron. 20:16).

ZIZA 1. A descendant of Simeon (1 Chron. 4:37).

2. A son of Judah's king Rehoboam (2 Chron. 11:20).

3. *See* Zina.

ZOAN A city in NE Egypt also called Avaris. It was the Hyksos capital. Later it was called Per-Ramses and even later Tanis, from which the Hebrew name Zoan is derived (Num. 13:22; Ps. 78:12, 43; Isa. 19:11, 13; Ezek. 30:14).

ZOAR A city (194-049) connected with Sodom and Gomorrah in the attack of the kings and in the overthrow of the area by God (Gen. 13:10; 14:2-8; 19:22-30).

ZOBAH A town (162-132) and kingdom N of Palestine. Saul and David fought against it (1 Sam. 14:47; 2 Sam. 8:3-12; 10:6-8; 1 Chron. 18:3-5).

ZOBEBAH A descendant of Judah (1 Chron. 4:8).

ZOHAR 1. The father of the Hittite from whom Abraham bought the burial cave for his wife and family (Gen. 23:8; 25:9).

2. A son of Simeon (Gen. 46:10), also called Zerah.

ZOHETH A descendant of Judah (1 Chron. 4:20).

ZOPHAH A descendant of Asher (1 Chron. 7:35, 36).

ZOPHAI An ancestor of Samuel also called Zuph (1 Chron. 6:26; 1 Sam. 1:1).

ZOPHAR One of the three friends of Job (Job 2:11; 11:1; 20:1; 42:9).

ZOPHIM An unidentified height to which Balak took Balaam when he wanted him to curse Israel (Num. 23:14).

ZORAH A city (148-131) that first belonged to Dan and then went to Judah (Josh. 19:41; 15:33). The city is found in the Samson accounts (Judg. 13:2, 25; 16:31). The Danites sent their spies up north from this city (Judg. 18:11).

ZUAR The father of Nethanel, the representative of the tribe of Issachar in the census of Moses (Num. 1:8).

ZUPH *See* ZOPHAR

ZUR 1. The daughter of the Midianite chief who was killed, along with her father, by Aaron's son when she was brought into the camp of Israel (Num. 25:15; 31:8).

2. A descendant of Benjamin (1 Chron. 8:30; 9:36).

ZURIEL A descendant of Levi (Num. 3:35).

ZURISHADDAI The father of the representative of the tribe of Simeon in the census taken by Moses (Num. 1:6).

ZUZIM, ZUZITES The name of a people, not identified, who lived in the days of Abraham in an unidentified place called Ham (Gen. 14:5).